PARENTING AND CHILDREN'S INTERNALIZATION OF VALUES

PARENTING AND CHILDREN'S INTERNALIZATION OF VALUES

A Handbook of Contemporary Theory

Edited by

Joan E. Grusec

Leon Kuczynski

John Wiley & Sons, Inc.

New York • Chichester • Weinheim • Brisbane • Singapore • Toronto

Library of Congress Cataloging-in-Publication Data:

Parenting and children's internalization of values : a handbook of
    contemporary theory / edited by Joan E. Grusec, Leon Kuczynski.
        p.   cm.
    Includes bibliographical references and index.
    ISBN 0-471-12383-8 (cloth alk. paper)
    1. Moral development.   2. Socialization.   3. Parent and child.
4. Child rearing.   5. Parents—Attitudes.   6. Social values.
I. Grusec, Joan E.   II. Kuczynski, Leon, 1950–
BF723.M54P37   1997
649′.7—dc21   97-1325

Printed in the United States of America

10 9 8 7 6 5 4 3 2 1

Contributor List

Frank Barry
Family Life Development Center
Cornell University

Angela U. Branco
Institute of Psychology
University of Brasilia

Inge Bretherton
Department of Child and Family Studies
University of Wisconsin—Madison

Eunyoung Cho
Department of Child and Family Studies
University of Wisconsin—Madison

W. Andrew Collins
Institute of Child Development
University of Minnesota

Claudia Melo Dantas
Institute of Psychology
University of Brasilia

Edward L. Deci
Human Motivation Program
Department of Psychology
University of Rochester

James Garbarino
Family Life Development Center
Cornell University

Tracy Gleason
Institute of Child Development
University of Minnesota

Barbara Golby
Department of Child & Family Studies
University of Wisconsin—Madison

Jacqueline J. Goodnow
Department of Behavioural Sciences
Macquarie University
Sydney, Australia

Wendy S. Grolnick
Frances L. Hiatt School of Psychology
Clark University

Joan E. Grusec
Department of Psychology
University of Toronto

Neil Hildebrandt
Department of Psychology
University of Guelph

Grazyna Kochanska
Department of Psychology
University of Iowa

Kathleen Kostelny
Erikson Institute for Advanced Study
Chicago, IL

Leon Kuczynski
Department of Family Studies
University of Guelph

Kevin MacDonald
Department of Psychology
California State University—Long Beach

Sheila Marshall
School of Family and Nutritional
    Sciences
University of British Columbia

Tanya Martini
Department of Psychology
University of Toronto

Gerald R. Patterson
Oregon Social Learning Center
Eugene, OR

Duane Rudy
Department of Psychology
University of Toronto

Richard M. Ryan
Human Motivation Program
Department of Psychology
University of Rochester

Kathleen Schell
Department of Family Studies
University of Guelph

Arturo Sesma, Jr.
Institute of Child Development
University of Minnesota

Judith G. Smetana
Warner Graduate School of Education
    and Human Development
University of Rochester

Ross A. Thompson
Department of Psychology
University of Nebraska

Jaan Valsiner
Francis L. Hiatt School of Psychology
Clark University

Contents

Introduction and Overview

JOAN E. GRUSEC and LEON KUCZYNSKI

Bugental and Goodnow (1997) note that the study of socialization is currently experiencing a new burst of growth, in part because the content has been expanded from a single-minded focus on the acquisition of correct or moral behaviors to a concern with how people develop the skills for meeting all the demands of group life. They add that the socialization process has also come to be seen as involving many people, not just parents, who for many years were the prime focus of researcher attention. Bugental and Goodnow's observation is entirely correct. Why, then, is there need for a book that deals with children's acquisition of values and the role of parents in that acquisition?

Although it is true that researchers have moved beyond a concern with how children acquire values, this is not because the question has been adequately answered. In Emde's (1994) presidential address to the Society for Research in Child Development, he argued compellingly that value acquisition is one of the most needed as well as most neglected areas of research for developmental psychology. In a world filled with inequity, conflict, and lack of respect and caring for others, the study of how values are inculcated in childhood demands attention. Nor has the role of parents in instilling values been fully explored. Certainly, peers, extended families, the school, and the media have an impact on socialization (see, e.g., Harris, 1995; Smetana, this volume). Some (e.g., Scarr, 1992; Scarr & McCartney, 1983) have even argued that parents have little effect on the development of their children unless their behavior is outside a normal developmental range. Nevertheless, an excellent case can be made for the singular importance of parents in the development of children's values (see, e.g., Baumrind, 1993; Hoffman, 1991). There is still a strong belief as well as considerable evidence that primary caregivers, whose position in the lives of their children is unique, play a special and central role in the socialization of their children.

This book provides a comprehensive and updated presentation of what is known about the acquisition of values and about the role of parents in this acquisition. Investigators from a diversity of theoretical backgrounds have been addressing these or related issues. But areas of overlap and/or contradiction tend to be ignored when people work in isolation from other conceptual domains. By bringing the work together in one place, the similarities as well as differences in emphasis and interpretation are easier to see, and integration can begin. The final chapter starts that task. This introduction provides an overview of the book's organization and content.

The book is divided into five parts, in addition to the Introduction and the concluding chapter, which is entitled "Future Directions for a Theory of Parental Socialization."

HISTORICAL OVERVIEW OF PARENTAL INFLUENCE AND BIDIRECTIONALITY

Part I is an historical survey of theory and research concerned with parenting strategies and children's internalization of values (Chapter 1), as well as research addressed to the question of direction of effect in that process (Chapter 2).

In Chapter 1, Grusec begins with a brief discussion of the Freudian position that children internalize or take over as their own the values of their parents. This position has been the primary source of the idea that values are transmitted from parent to child rather than being constructed by the child from experience, a debate that has played a prominent role in theories of moral development and that continues to be addressed by a number of contributors to this book. Grusec then describes the historical development of two separate lines of research, one focusing on the importance of discipline techniques employed by parents during conflict and disagreement with their children, the second on styles of parenting employed during conflict. Recent reanalyses of these classic positions demonstrate that there are major similarities and overlap in what the two approaches suggest about socialization processes.

The chapter turns to parenting strategies employed in settings where conflict is not an issue, describing the role of three relationship variables in internalization of values: warmth, security, and mutual compliance. Conceptual distinctions among these three variables are emphasized. Next, imitation and modeling are discussed. Finally, Grusec notes limitations in traditional socialization theory—the assumption that the content of values is irrelevant, a cursory interest in developmental issues, a focus on a small number of parenting strategies, lack of concern with interactions between parental strategies and the larger social context, and a middle-class and Anglo-European emphasis.

In Chapter 2, Kuczynski, Marshall, and Schell present a conceptual and historical analysis of the issue of direction of effect. They contrast unidirectional with bidirectional views of development and argue that the construction of differences between parent and child is as important a question for socialization theory as is the transmission of similarity.

Thinking about the child-to-parent direction of influence goes against the grain of culturally established patterns of thought. A shift from a unidirectional to bidirectional viewpoint, then, involves a change in thinking about the basic nature of parent-child relationships. In a bidirectional perspective, children are seen as taking an active stance toward parental ideas, interpreting them, evaluating them, selecting from them, and negotiating outcomes. Power in the parent-child relationship follows different dynamics than in other relationships: Children experience more power in their relationships with their parents than with any other adult. In a bidirectional perspective, children transcend experiences with their parents so that dissimilarities between children and parents do not indicate failures of socialization (or failures of socialization science) but may be desirable developmental outcomes.

The second section of the chapter describes a general model of socialization that incorporates bidirectional assumptions. Internalization in this perspective is a recursive process by which parents and children construct personal working models of values, with both sets of beliefs continuously under development and continuously open to challenge and rethinking. Children are presented with values in the surrounding culture that are discrepant from those of their parents as well as values that change over time, and even within the family there are discrepancies in values among family members, both in reality and as perceived by the child. Value change receives further impetus because the examination and exploration of values is a healthy activity for adaptive psychological functioning. Through conflict, cooperation, mutual shaping, and observational learning, children negotiate, transform, co-construct, and select from the information parents present to them. Thus the expert versus learner dynamic is only a part of the process of acquiring values. The parent-child relationship is characterized by interdependence of needs and goals, which means that both members respond to the wishes and demands of the other. They do not, however, passively take in information from each other. They select, forget, and reject ideas as they process them, with resultant modifications in and transformations of working models.

Next, Kuczynski et al. address the implications of bidirectionality for new directions in research by outlining a number of phenomena that need to be investigated. When and how do parents change their values? How do children take the reworked material they receive from their parents and change it further? What are the conditions under which they attempt to influence their parents and so change their parents' values even further? Kuczynski et al. conclude their discussion with the observation that one way parents deal with the ecological context in which their children function is to attempt to manage it. They warn their children in advance of possible negative influences, select good schools, and find good neighborhoods in which to raise their children. A bidirectional perspective, however, reminds us that children determine how much management they will allow their parents to accomplish. They evade parental attempts to regulate their television intake; they refuse to have their whereabouts monitored. All these considerations, then, must lead researchers to ask not how it is that parents transmit values to their children but, rather, what are successful outcomes other than transmission of values, what are the conditions that foster difference, and what are those that foster similarity?

DEVELOPMENTAL CONTEXT OF PARENTING STRATEGIES AND VALUE INTERNALIZATION

Part II consists of two chapters that focus specifically on age-related concerns. Kochanska and Thompson (Chapter 3) consider the origins of conscience in the toddler and early childhood years, whereas Collins, Gleason, and Sesma (Chapter 4) write about issues related to adolescence.

Kochanska and Thompson first discuss the early development of four components of conscience: emotion, self-control capacities, motivational processes, and cognitive awareness and understanding of behavioral standards. They then move to a consideration of processes that anticipate conscience. Self-understanding allows children to view themselves as objects of evaluation and as causal agents in behavior that is appraised as right or wrong. Associated with this development of self-understanding is that of empathy as well as of emotions such as guilt, shame, pride, and embarrassment. Social referencing is another developing ability that allows the child to learn to differentiate between acceptable and unacceptable behaviors. As young children's cognitive and representational capacities increase, they acquire prototypical structures or scripts that incorporate simple rules and behavioral standards and that allow them to predict the outcomes of different actions. In the second half of the second year, children also develop sensitivity to standards and to their violations, which manifests itself in emotional responses that mark an early sense of right and wrong and an emerging system of internal standards.

Successful internalization of standards involves the practice of restraint and two temperamental inhibitory systems seem highly relevant to this practice. One is a passive inhibition system that involves anxiety and fearfulness, whereas the other is active and involves inhibitory or effortful control. Kochanska and Thompson review evidence suggesting that both these systems are implicated in children's conscience development.

In the next part of the chapter, Kochanska and Thompson consider the importance of relationships in conscience development and note the work of early researchers on parental warmth as an important precursor of successful internalization. They then turn to attachment theory with its focus on sensitive and responsive parenting as an antecedent of harmonious parent-child interaction, which in turn enhances opportunities for observational learning, reinforcement of behavioral standards, and the transmission of norms and expectations. Next, they consider mutually responsive relationships as an underpinning for child compliance. In these relationships parent and child each feel invested in and responsible for the welfare of the other and also expect a similar concern from the other. Empirical support for the hypothesis that children have an internally felt obligation to reciprocate the cooperative behavior of their parents is reviewed and the argument is made that this "committed compliance" has a self-regulated, internalized quality that links it to conscience. Kochanska and Thompson deal with another feature of the parent-child relationship that is also a contributor to early morality—shared conversations about the child's experiences.

Kochanska and Thompson's analysis makes it clear that two processes are implicated in early conscience development: positive feelings that exist between parent and child and negative feelings, such as fear and anxiety, that are associated with discipline. In the final section of the chapter, they review empirical evidence indicating that negative feelings associated with (inductive) discipline are instrumental in the conscience development of temperamentally fearful children and that positive feelings between parent and child promote conscience development in temperamentally fearless children. This work nicely demonstrates the interrelations between biological predispositions and experience in the internalization of values.

Collins et al., in Chapter 4, highlight processes involved in the development of values during adolescence and the challenge these processes provide to traditional theoretical and methodological approaches to internalization. They consider autonomy not as a means of distancing and separating the self from others but rather as arising in interdependent social interactions. Adolescence sees an increase in behavioral, emotional, and cognitive autonomy from others, an increase in sense of identity or personal coherence, and an increase in a sense of morality and responsibility. At the same time, social relationships are changing. Feelings of satisfaction with family life reach a low point in early and middle adolescence and then increase. Concurrently, adolescents are developing more relationships with nonfamily members. Nevertheless, continuities in emotional bonds make it possible for parents to continue to influence adolescents although they spend less time together. Parental influence also continues to be salient because relationships with parents are closed-field: They are constrained by kinship and involve long interaction histories and routinized interactional scripts that work against autonomy and in favor of internalization of parental values. On the other hand, relationships with others are open-field: They can be dissolved and therefore are more conducive to autonomous behavior.

Collins et al. go on to elaborate relationship processes in internalization. They argue that behavioral regulation is relational rather than intraindividual, citing considerable evidence that the quality of parent-child relationships is a major determinant of prosocial behavior. Caring parental child-rearing behaviors provide a model of socially responsible behavior, sensitive parenting promotes effective skills for autonomous responsible behavior, and positive relationships make the values of parents more attractive and salient. Similarly, peer relationships marked by closeness and positive emotional expression are also facilitators of socially responsible behavior. Behavioral regulation is additionally evident in the bilateral nature of parent-child relationships, with adolescence a time of increased exchange as children become more competent and more capable of making contributions to decision making about acceptable standards of behavior. Collins et al. highlight recent work on relations among relationships: how parent and peer processes support the regulation of behavior interdependently. As an example, children who have developed antisocial traits because of negative parenting experiences are more inclined to experience peer rejection and therefore to have their pool of friends limited to other antisocial children who support their behavior.

The final section of the chapter provides a framework for future thinking about self-direction and self-regulation in adolescence. Notions of internalization must be extended to include the skills needed to participate in relationships that contribute to behavioral regulation. They must take into account that autonomy is not a salient goal in all cultures. Developmental changes in skills for behavioral regulation that occur in adolescence must be examined. Finally, research must recognize that the contrasting of parental versus peer contributions to internalization is simplistic because these two sources provide interrelated and complementary contributions.

PARENTING STRATEGIES AND CHILD OUTCOMES: THEORETICAL FORMULATIONS

Part III includes four chapters describing approaches to socialization developed within a specific theoretical context. These are attachment theory, self-determination theory, social domain theory, and social interaction theory. The attachment and social domain perspectives have been less developed with respect to parenting and socialization, and so the authors have been presented with a special challenge in the form of extending the basic assumptions of the theory to a relatively new area of discourse. The final chapter in Part III (Chapter 9) presents a model of conformity and resistance in socialization that attempts to reconcile some of the diverse assumptions presented in various theoretical approaches.

Bretherton, Golby, and Cho (Chapter 5) discuss attachment theory and its implications for parenting and the internalization of values. Bowlby touched only lightly on issues of self-regulation and socialization, but in a very different way from Freud, suggesting that cooperation with parental demands occurs because the parent is valued rather than because the parent is feared. Bretherton et al. contrast the notion of internalization in attachment theory with that in socialization theory. For attachment theory, internalization refers to the internal working model of the self and the attachment figure in relationship. Thus all children have internalized models of relationships be they either positive or negative in nature. For socialization theorists, on the other hand, internalization occurs only when the child has taken over the positive values of society. According to attachment theory, the child who misbehaves in the parent's absence has internalized a nonresponsive and rejecting relationship in which cooperation is not willingly given. From the point of view of socialization theory, however, this child has not internalized anything. Finally, values considered important in attachment theory are those that underlie a secure attachment rather than societal values in general, with these latter the focus of socialization theory.

Bretherton et al. continue with a discussion of research linking quality of attachment and children's cooperative and compliant behavior. They underline emotionally open communication as a potentially important factor in facilitating cooperative relations with attachment figures and positive social exchanges with others. Secure attachment fosters the trust, self-confidence, and skills required to develop friendly relationships with others. In this way, then, secure attachment promotes openness to socialization outside the context of the family.

In the final part of the chapter, Bretherton et al. present an attachment perspective on authority. They note Bowlby's emphasis on the attachment figure as "stronger and/or wiser": Although greater wisdom and strength may be less salient in comforting a distressed child, they become more so in situations of real danger where the caregiver must also warn or command or retrieve the child from danger. Parallels between Baumrind's authoritarian and authoritative parents and the parents of insecurely and securely attached children are described. Finally, the question of what kinds of parental control or guidance are compatible with the notions of secure attachment is addressed. Empirical work suggests these are flexibility, sensitivity in communication about feelings, and a sense of effectiveness, aspects of control that are compatible with the values underlying attachment (empathy, role-taking, sensitivity to signals, and a sense of being in charge).

In concluding their chapter, the authors note that in secure attachment relationships the scaffolding component of authority may be more striking than the control component, that the authority of sensitive parents may have greater legitimacy in the eyes of children, that relational variables are more important than quality of firmness, that authoritarianism and rejection are equivalent, that rejection leads to hostility that motivates noncompliance, and that parenting strategies such as explanation must be nested in an atmosphere of mutual trust and caring.

In Chapter 6, Grolnick, Deci, and Ryan describe the efforts of self-determination theorists to show how children voluntarily act in accord with societal values, that is, come to "own" them. The assumption is of a natural motivational tendency to do so, with agents of socialization (parents and teachers) frequently interfering with this natural tendency by using harmful strategies, rather than by finding the best way to mobilize and support it. The theory distinguishes two types of motivation: intrinsic motivation underlying behaviors that are carried out spontaneously and that do not require internalization, and extrinsic motivation underlying behaviors performed to achieve outcomes that are separate from the activity itself. These outcomes can be external demands, proferred rewards, or internal events such as the maintenance of fragile self-esteem or a belief that an act is important for health or well-being. Internalization is required in the case of extrinsically motivated acts if the associated value is to have an enduring quality.

Grolnick et al. describe a continuum of internalization from regulation driven by external contingencies, to introjected regulation whereby imposed acts are "taken in" but maintained in original form and therefore subject to tension, to identification that is accompanied by personal valuing of the goal and, finally, to integrated regulation where a value is assimilated to a unified and coherent system that already exists in the self. Individuals can be at different points on the continuum depending on the value domain, although a degree of general personality integration with respect to values is identifiable.

For self-determination theorists, value content is a relevant variable. Aspirations for wealth, image, and fame (extrinsic aspirations) do not constitute basic psychological satisfactions in their own right but are means of obtaining other outcomes such as the maintenance of fragile self-worth. Thus they are detrimental to psychological functioning. Valuing of intrinsic aspirations such as self-acceptance, affiliation, community, and health, on the other hand, is associated with positive psychological adjustment.

Intrinsically motivated behaviors are maintained and enhanced under conditions of autonomy support, structure, and knowledge about and involvement in the child's life. Performance of an inherently interesting activity in the presence of controlling events such as rewards, threats, surveillance, or pressuring language lessens intrinsic motivation, whereas performance in an autonomy-enhancing context increases it. If the social context promotes competence and a backdrop of relational support, intrinsic motivation is also supported. In the case of extrinsically motivated behavior, the importance of social context increases. Structure, or information about relations between behavior and outcomes, must be provided within the context of a positive relationship. Structure can be provided in a manner that either supports autonomy (e.g., conveying information in a reasoned and empathic way) or is controlling (e.g., close surveillance). Unresponsive parenting creates insecurity that promotes an emphasis on exterior signs of worth.

In the final section of the chapter, Grolnick et al. consider other work on parenting in the context of self-determination theory, using the comparison to highlight unique features of the theory and to discuss methodological issues. Self-determination theory and attribution theory are similar in their emphasis on the detrimental effects of control on externalization. However, attribution theory fails to distinguish between introjected and integrated types of internalization. Nor does it specify the opposite side of control. Self-determination theory also makes it clear that techniques of discipline must be considered in the context of their use, with different techniques having positive consequences when used in autonomy-supportive ways. Parental locution and acknowledgment of the child's feelings, for example, are more important than the technique itself. With respect to methodological issues, the use of behavior as the only outcome measure in studies of internalization is problematic because of the need to distinguish between introjection and integration. Outcome measures need to be expanded to include reasons for behavior as well as the feelings accompanying that behavior.

In Chapter 7, the structural developmental perspective is represented in Smetana's analysis of the social domain approach. Historically, the hierarchical nature of parent-child relationships has been seen by cognitive developmental theorists as a constraint on moral development, leading children to focus instead on the formative role of peers. The social domain perspective underscores the importance of both parents and peers in children's active construction of adult values. Children's social judgments are critically affected by experiences in different situations and so cognition remains a central feature of the approach.

The primary proposal of the perspective is that the social world of the child is not unitary and that differentiated social interactions lead to the construction of different systems of social knowledge. The four systems are the moral, which pertains to the rights and welfare of others; the social conventional, which refers to the facilitation of actions that promote smooth social interaction; the prudential, which includes issues surrounding safety and health of the self; and the personal, which involves aspects of behavior where only individuals themselves have a right to make decisions about what is or is

not appropriate. This latter system emerges from a fundamental human need to differentiate the self from others. Differential thinking in these four domains is constructed
on the basis of different interactions and experiences within the child's social environment, interactions that include but are not limited to parental teaching.

Smetana reviews a large body of evidence relevant to understanding the origins of
social knowledge. Several themes emerge from this evidence, including that peers play
a large part in experiences with moral transgressions, that children are active in negotiation and resolution with respect to moral disputes even when parents are present, that
parents play a larger although not exclusive role in the conventional area, and that negotiation is a more frequent feature of parental behavior in the personal domain. Affect
is also an important feature of children's construction of notions of right and wrong,
with its presence or absence a marker of the distinction between moral and social conventional events although not a defining one.

Next, Smetana turns to the implications of the social domain approach for the
parental role. Of central importance is the argument that parental intervention must be
appropriate to the domain in which it is used: Reasoning would be expected to be effective only when coordinated with the act with which it is associated. Although power
assertion may be detrimental to the child's developing understanding of the social world
because it lacks information value, it may be acceptable in certain domains such as the
prudential. Warmth affects the willingness of children to listen to parental messages
and therefore to construct domain-differentiated understandings. Smetana also notes
the failure of authoritarian parents to draw boundaries between different domains and
suggests that this lack of differentiation makes them less effective in the socialization
process.

In Chapter 8, Patterson presents his work in what he describes as a "snapshot of an
in-progress strategy." The social interaction perspective, which emerged from Roger
Barker's emphasis on the observation of children in their natural context and from
Skinner's functional analysis of behavior, operates at two levels. At the macrolevel, it
assesses correlations between parenting behavior and child outcomes. At the microlevel,
it involves observations of interactions that yield information about how members of a
group change each other's behavior over time. Patterson assumes that determinants of
behavior are found in reactions provided by the social environment, albeit in the context of an active child who selects and shapes his or her environment.

The macrotheory entails the construction of performance models of parenting and
evaluation of their success in accounting for indicators of child adjustment. In this work,
information is gathered from several sources to avoid problems of shared method variance,
multiple measures of variables are obtained, across-sample and across-site replications are
carried out, and the causal status of key variables is evaluated through experimental manipulations. Results point to discipline, family problem-solving, and parental monitoring
as central aspects of successful parenting. Parents who natter, hit, are inconsistent, and
fail to follow through in the discipline situation; who have difficulty in solving family
problems with their children; and who are unaware of the activities of their children and
of the identity of their friends are more likely to have problem children. Contextual events
such as stress, divorce, and social disadvantage have an indirect impact on child outcomes
through their disruption of discipline practices.

The work began with an assessment of behavior because this was the variable most
easily measured. It has moved to include emotion and cognition as researchers developed
techniques for measuring these variables. Recent studies of emotion point to relations

between emotional variables and disrupted parenting. Angry families are less adept at problem-solving, and angry adolescents are more difficult to monitor. Low parental warmth leads to poor parental discipline. In addition, however, the child's deviant behavior augments parental coldness and rejection. Evidence that emotion has its impact on parenting behavior leads Patterson to conclude that effective parenting training must include not only training in parenting practices but training in the control of negative emotions as well. Parents' cognitions also contribute to poor parenting. Thus parents of problem children are overly inclusive in what they classify as deviant behavior as well as perceiving themselves to be more irritable. Parenting practices are seen as mediators between cognitions and child outcomes, just as they are seen as mediators between emotion and child outcomes.

Patterson turns his attention next to child cognitions such as attitudes, delay of gratification, and security of attachment. Again, he argues that they are not direct causes of child outcomes. Instead, they are by-products of the ineffective parenting that is directly responsible for negative child outcomes. Low verbal IQ, for example, is not a cause of delinquent behavior as has been argued by some but, rather, a product of delinquent behavior.

Macrotheories cannot explain how parenting practices bring about changes in the child, why children maintain behaviors across time and settings, nor how their behavior changes in form. These are questions addressed from a microtheoretical viewpoint. Reinforcement contingencies shape children's behavior. In distressed families, only coercive behaviors are effective in ending conflict, whereas in nondistressed families prosocial behaviors are also effective. Behavior is stable because the child is an active contributor to the socialization process. Antisocial boys, for example, avoid playground activities that are under the surveillance of adults. They also select friends who are similar to themselves and who therefore reinforce their antisocial behavior. Change in the behavior of aggressive boys comes about as they learn new patterns of behavior in the course of successful attempts at terminating aversive family behaviors and as they are exposed to new forms of deviant behavior in the peer group.

In the final section of the chapter, Patterson deals with general issues surrounding cognition and the concept of internalization. He argues that reinforcement contingencies controlling coercive behaviors are not actively processed and that, for this reason, neither children nor adults are very accurate perceivers of their own experiences. Their attitudes and performance do not correspond because attitudes must be accompanied by the learning of skills necessary to comply with those attitudes. For example, although parents of antisocial boys may want their children to go to college, they do not teach them the necessary academic skills. The theme of cognitions as mediators between learning experiences and outcomes is argued once again.

In the last chapter in Part III, Kuczynski and Hildebrandt consider models of conformity and resistance in socialization theory. Theirs is an attempt to reconcile some of the divergent points of view represented in various approaches to socialization theory. They outline four theoretical perspectives, discussing each in terms of general assumptions about socialization, its model of children's conformity and nonconformity or resistance to parental demands, its model of effective parenting, and its notion about the nature of the parent-child relationship.

The first perspective is that of external control, represented by two approaches, behavioral theory (e.g., Patterson, this volume) and what Kuczynski and Hildebrandt label as "traditional authoritarianism," a parenting ideology that emphasizes firm discipline in the home and school, parental authority and rights, and the use of corporal punishment. Behavior theory lacks a concept of internalization, emphasizing instead the powerful structure of external supports and sanctions that govern behavior. The aim of socialization is to gain compliance from the child, with a reliance on punitive interventions (although physical punishment is to be avoided) and avoidance of psychological strategies such as reasoning, which are seen as ineffectual in gaining immediate compliance. Similarly, traditional authoritarianism focuses on immediate compliance, with the added dimension of unquestioning obedience and the suppression of assertiveness and expressions of autonomy. Physical punishment is an accepted strategy for obtaining compliance, along with other forms of external punishment and contingent parental affection. The theories differ in their assumptions about the origins of noncompliance, with behavioral theorists seeing it in parental mismanagement of reinforcement contingencies and traditional authoritarian advocates in an innately sinful predisposition. The two approaches are similar in their treatment of relationships, seeing good ones as a consequence of positive child management rather than an antecedent.

The internal control perspective represents the more traditional approaches to socialization, including cognitive developmental theories and motivational approaches (e.g., the theories described in Chapter 1; see also Grolnick et al., this volume). Here the argument is that internal control emerges from external control and is a more developmentally advanced or superior mode of functioning. Compliance is an early precursor of internal control, with internal control motivated by variables such guilt, empathic distress, and self-determination. Internally motivated compliance is assessed by behavior in the absence of surveillance and is signaled by the presence of guilt, higher levels of moral reasoning, enthusiasm, and so on. Techniques such as reasoning, minimal use of power, choice, and autonomy-enhancing strategies are advocated. Although positive relationships facilitate the effectiveness of parenting strategies, they are emphasized less than strategies: Indeed, in the cognitive developmental approach, they are associated with a relatively immature stage of moral development.

Relational perspectives (e.g., Bretherton et al. and Kochanska & Thompson, this volume) move the parent-child relationship into the forefront. Rather than rely on a concept of internalization, the relational perspective emphasizes coregulation in the parent-child dyad, with mutual and reciprocal regulation the goals of socialization, rather than self-accepted autonomous motives. Children are inherently motivated to comply with societal regulations, to adopt social goals similar to those of their parents, and to react well to sensitive, responsive parenting. Child behavior, however, is also characterized by accommodation and negotiation rather than strict compliance. Parent practices revolve around the management of relationships, encouragement of the child's sense of control within the parent-child relationship, the provision of support for mutual coregulation of complex actions, and the teaching of more sophisticated skills for expressing resistance and negotiation.

Kuczynski and Hildebrandt draw together these three perspectives in a fourth approach that they label contextual. The three perspectives, they argue, can be considered as complementary rather than competing conceptualizations. Socialization and self-regulation occur within specific contexts that have different requirements. Social competence means adjusting one's behavior to meet the requirements of a particular situation. In the presence of an angry parent, compliance that reflects external control may be appropriate. In the case of socially valued behavior, or cultural or religious values, forms of internal control involving guilt and remorse may be called for, while reciprocal accommodation and negotiation might characterize close interpersonal interactions. Effective parents adjust their strategies to the demands of the situation. The overlap between the contextual perspective and the social domain approach to socialization presented by Smetana (this volume) is evident.

In the final section, Kuczynski and Hildebrandt stress the importance of historical context in the generation of socialization theories. Although changes in views are a reflection of an increasing knowledge base, they also mirror to some extent changes in the cultural and historical context in which the data are gathered. As values for social conformity and strict obedience have given way to those emphasizing independence and tolerance, so too have theories moved from a concern with compliance and conformity to a concern with negotiation and relatedness.

PARENTING COGNITIONS: IMPLICATIONS FOR PARENTAL INFLUENCE AND BIDIRECTIONALITY

The realization that children have an impact on their parents raises the issue of the variables determining parenting behavior. Parenting strategies are not always selected in a rational and conscious way. Part IV diverges from the main theme of the book to consider what determines parenting strategies. The study of parent cognitions and beliefs as determinants of parenting strategies is crucial for understanding parent-child interaction in a comprehensive way. This focus is provided in the chapters by Grusec, Rudy, and Martini and by Valsiner, Branco, and Dantas, with the latter emphasizing once again the bidirectional nature of the parent-child relationship, this time with particular focus on evolving parental belief systems.

In Chapter 10, Grusec, Rudy, and Martini offer an overview of parenting cognitions. They begin with a description of how parents' attributions for children's behavior, and associated affect, have an impact on parenting strategies. Parents who see behavior as intentional and blameworthy, for example, are more authoritarian or power assertive in their reactions. Perceptions of the self in relationships to others also have an impact on parenting: Low self-efficacy, or less perceived power relative to the child, results in power-assertive parenting along with reduced attentional capacity and the transmission of confusing messages to the child. Grusec et al. stress the importance of agreement between parent and child, as well as the parent's knowledge of the child's thoughts and feelings, as central for successful child rearing. Agreement reduces conflict, and knowledge of the child's position on matters allows parents to tailor their own behavior to be more persuasive in their attempts at socialization. Finally, they note that parents differ in their goals for child rearing, with internalization of values only one of several possible outcomes they attempt to achieve.

Grusec et al., in the second section of the chapter, turn to the implications of cross-cultural research on parenting cognitions for an understanding of parenting strategies and the socialization process. They note there are cultures where authoritarian parenting is practiced without the apparent negative outcomes it produces in Anglo-European cultures. The lack of detrimental outcomes they attribute to authoritarian parenting being linked to positive, rather than negative, cognitions. The argument is then made that maladaptive child outcomes may be the result, not of authoritarian parenting itself, but rather of associated negative cognitions and affect. The argument is also made that authoritative parenting may not be universally positive in its outcomes, depending instead on the particular goals that cultures wish to achieve. In Western society, autonomy is the goal and a strategy that encourages independence is therefore required. In collectivist societies, however, where interdependence is the more frequent aim, authoritative parenting becomes less important.

In the final section of the chapter, Grusec et al. address the issue of transmission versus construction of values, calling on material from the literature on parenting cognitions. Their conclusion is that some values are transmitted and others are constructed, with the outcome depending on the degree to which a particular value is seen as negotiable by the parent.

In Chapter 11, Valsiner et al. focus on bidirectionality, particularly from the parenting perspective and the co-constructionist perspective. They describe the concept of bounded indeterminacy, which maintains that development is bounded by constraints that are constantly being renegotiated. Adult-child roles are complementary, a position contained in the ideas of internalization and externalization. In internalization, the values of others are brought into the psychological domain of the self where they are modified to fit with existing thinking. Externalization is the process whereby these new sets of meanings are moved into novel contexts within the self as well as in the environment. Valsiner et al. introduce the concept of "filiating," a term that reflects the child's active counterregulation of parenting that serves to buffer him or her against possibly excessive acts of parenting. Filiating has an opposite meaning, however, when it refers to the child's maintenance of the basic parent-child relationship. Once again, then, as in the earlier chapter by Kuczynski et al., the reciprocal nature of the parent-child interaction in the acquisition of values is underlined.

The latter part of Valsiner et al.'s chapter focuses on parental belief orientations. Beliefs exist in incomplete form and become clearer or dissipate through interactions with others. Hence Valsiner et al. reject the term "belief," given the impossibility that constantly (co-constructed) ideas can ever be accorded some static status. They talk instead about belief-orientation systems that are locally constructed, constantly novel, fluid, and contradictory. Their consequences for child outcomes represent negotiated solutions. Moreover, an important point for researchers is that the very process of development means that there will always be discrepancy between action and reflection, and the implication for specific research methods is that they must be designed to illuminate change as parents and children move together through the developmental process. Thus Valsiner et al. provide yet another set of supporting arguments, this time from the perspective of parenting cognitions, for Kuczynski et al.'s thesis: The study of socialization is just as much a study of how differences between parents and children emerge as it is of how similarities develop.

PARENTAL INFLUENCE IN SOCIAL AND BIOLOGICAL CONTEXT

In Part V, socialization is considered in its broader context. Three chapters address the fact that an understanding of the acquisition of values must move beyond the confines of the family and its role in socialization. Although socialization occurs within the family, this unit is located in a larger context from which it is not immune. Nowhere is this better demonstrated than in the high-risk neighborhood described by Garbarino, Kostelny, and Barry. Consideration of cultural context by Goodnow and evolutionary issues by MacDonald further underlines the point.

Garbarino et al. provide an ecological perspective on the acquisition of values. They note that values come not only from the family but from outside sources. They also note that the community can either reinforce parental positive values or, under conditions of minimal communication, it not only can fail to reinforce values of parents but can also fail to promote prosocial values when the family is inadequate to the task. The first section of the chapter is an overview of the ecological approach with its emphasis on the interplay of systems in the child's social environment. The strength of the systems approach is that it helps to uncover connections between what might be seen as unrelated events as well as to alert one that apparently obvious solutions can make problems worse. It highlights situations in which the actions of people have significant impact even though those people have no direct contact.

The chapter moves to a discussion of social toxicity as a characteristic of high-risk environments. Phenomena such as violence, poverty, disruption of relationships, depression, and alienation—the elements of social toxicity—become poisonous to the development of children's values. Neighborhoods at greatest risk for social toxicity appear to be ones in which working- and middle-income groups have moved away, leaving an underclass with few mainstream models of traditional values. In high-risk neighborhoods, there is chronic violence. Besides providing models of negative behavior, this violence also means that parents are unable to protect their children from danger, a violation of the fundamental contract between parents and children. Nor can teachers compensate: They too are demoralized by the environment in which they find themselves. Dysfunctional behaviors such as social withdrawal, authoritarian parenting, or aggression may be encouraged because they are adaptive in the short term even if maladaptive in the long run.

Not all children are so negatively affected by the social toxicity of the high-risk neighborhood, and Garbarino et al. describe those conditions that promote resilience. They are a warm and affectionate relationship with a caring adult, an environment that includes high expectations for children and faith in their abilities, and, finally, opportunities for the child to participate in the life and work of the surrounding community.

Ultimately, however, it is the neighborhood that must be changed, and intervention becomes the focus of the last part of this chapter. Adults must have jobs, they must feel safe, and they must be involved in the community. The benefits of economic and physical security are obvious. The benefit of participation is that it provides a network of social support and develops social skills and leadership capabilities. Communities can be repaired by utilizing members who have specific characteristics including a sense of civic duty and political efficacy, a belief that some existing problems can be resolved at a local level, a real sense of community, and a high level of self-esteem. These members are in short supply as social toxicity increases. Schools have a unique ability to become involved in the revitalization of neighborhoods.

Goodnow, in Chapter 13, expands this look at neighborhood to a different context, drawing on material from the social sciences. By context, she means any collection of individuals that goes beyond the family unit, including not only ethnic or national groups, but any group with a definable membership that is held together by adherence to some set of values or practices. Goodnow demonstrates how a discussion of meanings (shared representations of events) and practices (shared activities or ways of doing things) in other settings can be used to draw implications that are relevant for the study of within-family functioning.

The social-cultural perspective alerts researchers to where values can be found. Often their source is in what seem to be matters of fact or necessity or in everyday ways of acting, thinking, and feeling. The implication for within-family analyses is that prime areas for analysis of values may be where these values have become invisible because they are so embedded in how people behave. The further implication for parenting is that values may be promulgated in less obvious or deliberate ways, such as storytelling or implicit assumptions. Goodnow next turns attention to internalization. Rather than think of it in terms of a transfer from the outer world to the inner one, the social-cultural perspective asks why a concept such as internalization is needed, splitting it into two aspects of commitment or internal direction versus asking how similarities and differences between generations come about. The relevance for within-family analyses is whether similarity across generations is created by adherence to similar behaviors without the same degree of commitment or, alternatively, commitment to a general principle that manifests itself in different behavioral outcomes. It is also possible that difference between generations is a positive outcome, and that society benefits not only from "reproduction" but from "production."

In a final section, Goodnow takes up the issue of transmission. Although the social-cultural perspective deals with specific strategies that might be employed in transmission, the stronger emphasis is on general qualities of experience. Children and other newcomers to a group find that values are expressed in many ways, and often somewhat ambiguously (e.g., through arrangements of space, forms of talk, and routine cultural practices); that frequently many expressed values are in competition; and that the group signals the extent to which a value is central and unchangeable or can be negotiated. For within-family analyses, Goodnow suggests that researchers examine the uses and consequences of ambiguity versus explicit statements of values, look for the presence of competing messages, and ask about the strategies that parents use to cope with the presence of values different from their own and the conditions under which they use them. These strategies may involve either protecting the child from exposure to these different values or prearming them so they will dismiss alternative viewpoints. Investigators should look also for the areas in which leeway is tolerated and ask about the extent to which there is agreement between parents and children in what is negotiable.

Evolution provides the broader context for MacDonald's chapter. In Bretherton et al.'s chapter, one evolutionary perspective on the development of values is offered in their exposition of the role of attachment in children's internalization of standards of behavior. Thus the need for security and protection, which has evolved in the human species and other ground-living organisms, provides an underpinning for receptivity to parental values. MacDonald extends this evolutionary perspective substantially, placing it in the context of current evolutionary psychology. He argues for the coherence of development, that is, that a large number of variables including internalization of parental values are highly interrelated: Thus variables such as parental investment in rearing, age of first reproduction, play, developmental plasticity, and intelligence have evolved as part of a coordinated response to the environment. Variation in internalization of values is therefore difficult to separate from influences of genetic variation as well as environmental correlates of adaptive functioning such as socioeconomic status, intelligence, and disciplinary style. MacDonald discusses adolescent sexual behavior as a particular example of a value that is enmeshed in other features of behavior. He also points out the importance of external cultural supports for adaptive behavior in situations characterized by low-investment parenting, where there is less likelihood of an internalized motivational system to keep children's behavior on track.

In the next section of this chapter, MacDonald argues that variations in parental investment and internalization are not the result of evolved responses to changes in the availability of resources but are, instead, influenced mainly by genetic variation in viable reproductive strategies. Finally, he focuses on warmth as a central motivational component of internalization of standards. He distinguishes between warmth and security, maintaining that the attachment system is highly malleable and unrelated to high-investment parenting and children's internalization of values. Warmth, on the other hand, is depicted as a reward system that has evolved to make family members bond together because close relationships are pleasurable. Because of this system, children are motivated to pay attention to parental values and to behave in accord with them to obtain parental approval.

CONCLUSION

The final chapter in this book is an attempt by the editors to suggest future directions for the development of a theory of socialization in the family, using themes and material that emerged from the various contributors. Five themes are identified: parental contributions to socialization, child contributions to socialization, outcomes of socialization, how similarities and differences between parents and children develop, and, finally, parenting strategies needing to be studied.

Kuczynski and Grusec argue that parents are the most crucial influence on children's acquisition of values for several reasons: From the perspective of evolutionary theory, it can be argued that there is a biological predisposition for the centrality of the parenting system; society has deeded formal responsibility to parents for child rearing and therefore supports their primary role; parents are in the strongest position to develop positive relationships with their children that facilitate the acquisition of standards and values; and, finally, parents are better able to monitor and understand their children's behavior than anyone else because of their long and sustained exposure to them.

From this focus on the parent, the chapter turns to a focus on the child. The argument is made that the child as an active contributor to socialization is a position that has long been promoted by socialization theorists, with the source of activity in the child's biology. Differences in the treatment of bidirectional influence are noted and suggestions for resolution of these differences made. Kuczynski and Grusec then address the various outcomes of socialization. They begin with self-regulation and conformity, pointing out that some contributors consider compliance as the foundation of cooperative living. Thus some form of receptivity to influence by others, including respect for authority, can be considered a fundamental value in itself. The quality of conformity is important, of course. Compliance that is motivated by external pressures is not adaptive. That which emerges as a function of willing cooperation is adaptive, often calling on mutual or coregulated activity that emerges in close social relationships. A second outcome of socialization is the content of a culture's values. Although historically, there has been little attempt to distinguish among different values, the contributors to this book make clear this must be an issue. First of all, values change over time, and so adaptability to change and periodic reexamination of values in response to new realities is a hallmark of adaptive functioning. Different forms of parenting produce different values, some of which are more conducive than others to the child's well-being. Finally, children do distinguish between different forms of social knowledge; their thinking about values is affected by the domain of those values. A final outcome of socialization involves collateral or unintended effects, including strategies for interpersonal interactions and impacts on self-esteem and peer relationships.

The issue of how differences as well as similarities arise between children and their parents in values must be central to a theory of socialization and Kuczynski and Grusec speculate on what conditions might promote this. They conclude that parents, to a considerable extent, determine degree of similarity by how strongly they feel about a value, being willing to tolerate differences in values about which they feel less strongly. Most stretching of values is likely to occur with nonmoral issues (i.e., issues that do not involve psychological or physical harm to others).

In the concluding section, attention is turned to an extension of the study of parenting strategies. Traditionally, researchers have addressed such parenting techniques as modeling, structuring of the environment, reciprocal compliance, warmth, reasoning, and power assertion. Elaborations of these strategies include acknowledgment that an active child is operating in a bidirectional context as well as in a larger socialization context. In addition to these elaborations, however, Kuczynski and Grusec note new strategies that have been proposed by contributors: shared discourse, everyday routines, cocooning or prearming children so they are protected from conflicting values, management of the parent-child relationship, appropriate flexibility, validation of the child's negative feelings, consistency of messages, and knowledge of the child's environment as well as the child's thoughts and feelings.

REFERENCES

Baumrind, D. (1993). The average expectable environment is not enough: A response to Scarr. *Child Development, 64,* 1299–1317.

Bugental, D. B., & Goodnow, J. J. (1997). Socialization processes. In W. Damon (Ed.), *Handbook of child psychology* (5th ed.). New York: Wiley.

Emde, R. N. (1994). Individuality, context, and the search for meaning. *Child Development, 65,* 719–737.

Harris, J. R. (1995). Where is the child's environment? A group socialization theory of development. *Psychological Review, 102,* 458–489.

Hoffman, L. (1991). The influence of the family environment on personality: Accounting for sibling differences. *Psychological Bulletin, 110,* 187–203.

Scarr, S. (1992). Developmental theories for the 1990s: Development and individual differences. *Child Development, 63,* 1–19.

Scarr, S., & McCartney, K. (1983). How people make their own environments: A theory of genotype→environment effects. *Child Development, 54,* 424–435.

PART I

Historical Overview of Parental Influence and Bidirectionality

CHAPTER 1

A History of Research on Parenting Strategies and Children's Internalization of Values

JOAN E. GRUSEC

This chapter presents a historical overview of socialization theory, including an analysis of the concerns of researchers who have addressed questions about parenting and children's internalization of values. It provides a background for the remaining chapters of the book, which describe expansions of basic concepts of socialization that have been developed in recent years. The chapter begins with a brief consideration of the major philosophical perspectives on child rearing, indicating how each manifests itself in current theoretical stances. It then turns to a discussion of major research perspectives on socialization, specifically, types of discipline, parenting styles, the quality of the parent-child relationship, and modeling of prosocial behavior. It leaves the question of direction of effect, that is, the child's impact on the parent, to Chapter 2, which is focused specifically on that question.

PHILOSOPHICAL AND HISTORICAL PERSPECTIVES

From the beginning of recorded history, there has been a substantial interest in how societal values are transmitted from one generation to the next. Writers from both Western and Eastern philosophical traditions have speculated about the process (see Holden, 1997), no doubt because this crucial aspect of life forces itself into the consciousness of any thoughtful member of society. A cursory overview of recent Western approaches is offered here, in part because of space limitations, but also because it forms the intellectual tradition within which researchers currently work. And it is this intellectual tradition that substantially influences scientific conceptions of the subject matter.

Speculation about how morality and values develop inevitably leads to the starting point of this development, with the question phrased in terms of the basic nature of children: Are they innately sinful, innately good, or are they neither? Human nature as inherently depraved is the traditional view of Judeo-Christian theology. When Hobbes (1651) described the life of man as "nasty, brutish, and short" he was making a formal philosophical statement of the position of innate depravity. The implications of the position for parenting strategies is evident in the writings of the Puritans who advocated strong punishment as the only antidote to the basic willfulness of children. Thus Susanna Wesley writes to her son, "Break their wills betimes; begin this great work before they can run alone, before they can speak plain, or perhaps speak at all. . . . Let a child, from a year old, be taught to fear the rod and to cry softly" (Wesley, 1872, taken from

Newson & Newson, 1974, p. 56). A less extreme version of the idea of innate depravity was formalized in psychoanalytic theory which viewed the young child as dominated by the id, possessing instinctual desires that demand immediate gratification and therefore must be controlled. As will be discussed later, this view has had considerable influence on the thinking of socialization theorists who have focused on discipline strategies and other techniques for instilling prosocial values in the child and inhibiting antisocial ones. Interestingly, the idea of innate sinfulness is surfacing in current Protestant fundamentalist ideology (see, e.g., *U.S. News & World Report,* June 3, 1996) with the argument that punishment is needed to instill respect and obedience and that spanking and physical coercion are necessary for teaching moral values.

In contrast to the position that children are inherently depraved is the position that they are inherently virtuous. The origins of this position are in Rousseau's depiction of the child as innately good, contaminated only by the clumsy intervention of society: "Everything is well when it leaves the Creator's hands, everything degenerates in the hands of man" (1762/1974). Its modern manifestation is in two major approaches: Piagetian theory and attachment theory. For Piagetians, the child develops morally in a supportive environment that fosters equality and perspective-taking. For attachment theorists (e.g., Stayton, Hogan, & Ainsworth, 1971), the human species has evolved to be compliant with the norms of society. Nonresponsive and intrusive parenting work against this biologically driven propensity, producing antisocial and noncompliant individuals who fail to internalize the values of society. From these two stances, recent childrearing advice has generally advocated gentler child-rearing interventions. "Yes, You Can!", a pamphlet published in 1995 by the Canadian magazine, *Today's Parent,* is based in this more benign tradition. In accord with contemporary advice based on scientific evidence, it advocates that when children are hungry, tired, bored, or stressed they cannot control themselves and so the best discipline is no discipline; that children should be allowed to make choices; and that, as they grow older, they should be allowed to negotiate with their parents. Thus, although the extreme permissiveness of a totally laissez-faire approach is avoided, admonishments to avoid strictness and punitiveness and to cater to the child's needs to a substantial degree are much in evidence.

Finally, there is the view that children are neither good nor evil; the child's mind is a blank slate or *tabula rasa,* on which experience leaves its mark (Locke, 1693/1884). In the context of this conceptualization of the child, Locke provided considerable child-rearing advice with a contemporary ring, including encouragement of mature behavior, the use of reasoning rather than punishment, and reliance on authority and warmth. The modern version of Locke's focus on the child's basic neutrality is most clearly seen in the behaviorist/environmentalist approach, which depicts the child as a product of learning experiences. John B. Watson, for example, spelled out a specific set of principles for child rearing that he believed derived from a conditioning perspective. He advocated that children be taught strict and regular habits and that parents avoid expressions of warmth and sentimentality (a position that Jones, 1974, notes he later regretted having espoused). Watson's approach eventually developed into the behavior modification movement that was dominant during the 1960s and that used a wide range of learning principles to address child-rearing problems. Current views most closely allied with the learning approach are those of Patterson and Bandura. Although both these researchers have considerably enlarged the basic tenets of learning theory, they both still point to the central role of experience and learning mechanisms in the child-rearing process.

SCIENTIFIC PERSPECTIVES

The history of scientific perspectives on child-rearing practices and internalization of values makes up the remainder of this chapter. The development of two of the most influential ways of viewing parenting strategies and children's internalization of values is described. One concerns effective discipline practices and the other effective parenting styles. Both focus on parental reactions in situations of conflict and both focus primarily on the influence of the parent on the child. Although both are similar in the kinds of child-rearing recommendations they promote, they differ in their theoretical antecedents. The discussion then moves to a concern with processes that are less tied to the discipline situation: features of the parent-child relationship and modeling.

The philosophical roots of theory and research on discipline practices, parenting styles, and modeling are most closely linked both to the idea that children are inherently inclined to antisocial behavior and to the notion of children as blank slates. This is because of the grounding of traditional socialization theory in both psychoanalytic and learning theory. Concern with features of the parent-child relationship, particularly in recent years, has been primed by the growth of attachment and other relationship-oriented theoretical approaches. For this reason, this work can be seen as having its philosophical base in the more positive perspective of Rousseau.

A feature of this historical survey of socialization theory with respect to parenting and children's internalization of values is its relative neglect of two of the major intellectual traditions of developmental psychology. The first is Piagetian theory and the second is behavior modification. Both appear to be highly relevant to issues concerning values and parenting strategies. The Piagetian or cognitive developmental position has a long history of concern with children's developing sense of morality and the behavior modification tradition with the ways in which children can be trained to behave in a socially acceptable manner. Why, then, have they not been central in the study of socialization? In the case of cognitive developmental theory, the answer lies in its deemphasis of the role of the parent and, in the case of behavior modification, its deemphasis of internalized motives for the control of behavior.

Piaget (1932) argued that the authoritarian relationship between parent and child is a deterrent to the child's moral development because adults, who primarily impose sanctions, foster a morality of constraint. Only when children shift to interaction with peers can they develop a more autonomous morality of cooperation or reciprocity. This is because, during peer interactions, they engage in mutual decision making where cooperation and reciprocity are fostered. As well, peer interaction offers role-taking experience that enables children to understand that there are other perspectives than their own as well as to understand the consequences of their actions for others. Had the child-rearing practices in Geneva during the 1920s and 1930s not been so authoritarian, the history of socialization theory might have been very different. In fact, Piaget believed that parental child-rearing practices could play a role in moral development if only parents would modify their generally authoritarian approach to a more egalitarian one in which mutual obligations were stressed, demands the child could not understand were avoided, and proactive techniques were practiced that would minimize punishment experiences (Hoffman, 1970). This observation suggests that, had it developed in today's world of more egalitarian child rearing, cognitive developmental theory would have a great deal to say about the importance of parenting.

And what of the absence from this history of a lengthy discussion of the principles of behavior modification? The explanation here has to do with the absence of a concept of internalization in the behavior modification literature (Walters & Grusec, 1977). Thus, whereas reasoning has been seen by socialization theorists to play an essential role in the internalization of values, its main function for behavior modifiers has been the clarification of behavioral contingencies. Because of the strong focus in the behavior modification literature on external stimulus control as well as the lack of any mechanism having to do with the internalization or incorporation of values, it has seemed to overlap little with mainstream socialization theory.

What Is the Most Effective Way to Discipline a Child?

Roots in Psychoanalytic Theory

Freud provided the first formal theoretical analysis of discipline and internalization of values. According to psychoanalytic theory, parents' imposition of values on children leads inevitably to feelings of hostility and resentment. Because children fear that expressing this hostility will elicit punishment in the form of abandonment or loss of love, however, they repress it. By adopting parental rules and prohibitions and by introjecting or internalizing the parent, children are able to maintain the repression as well as elicit the approval of their parents. One of the outcomes of introjection of the parental figure is incorporation of parental punishment for transgression, which is now transformed into self-punishment or guilt after deviation, an emotion that resembles anxiety about punishment and fear of abandonment. Thus guilt avoidance is the mechanism that underlies children's internalization of societal standards and that leads to these standards being maintained independent of external events. In this way, pschoanalytic theory, in contrast to later theories of internalization offered by social learning theorists, found the source of internalization of values in the idea of identification with the aggressor. It also laid the groundwork for the suggestion that parental values are taken over with no modification, that is, they are transmitted in their totality rather than being modified or constructed by the child.

Social Learning Theory

Psychoanalytic theory offered a rich conceptualization of human behavior. It lacked the scientific rigor, however, that characterized academic psychology. The solution was to meld the two approaches to produce a theory that addressed the complexities of human nature in a way that could be tested scientifically. The theory that was chosen from academic psychology was Hullian stimulus-response learning theory and its linkage with psychoanalytic theory marked the beginning of a movement to construct a unified theory of human behavior.

One way in which this new approach dealt with internalization of values or conscience development was through a theory of fear conditioning. Mowrer (1960) proposed that, because of repeated punishment for a deviant act, the kinesthetic cues produced by that act produce conditioned fear or anxiety. The only way in which the child can terminate this fear or anxiety is to suppress the deviant act by resisting temptation, an important feature of conscience or internalized values. Mowrer also proposed that timing of punishment was the mechanism that distinguished between the development of resistance to temptation and guilt, the latter the marker of conscience particularly emphasized by psychoanalytic theory. He suggested that punishment administered at the beginning of transgression leads to anxiety when that same transgression is initiated at later times, and that the child thereby ceases the transgression or resists temptation. Punishment administered during the course of or at the end of transgression, on the other hand, results in anxiety only after the child has transgressed, with the resultant negative emotion of guilt. Solomon, Turner, and Lessac (1968) demonstrated these effects of timing with dogs, and the paradigm of early versus late punishment became a favored one of researchers who wished to study internalization in the laboratory (e.g., Aronfreed, 1963; Parke & Walters, 1967). This particular approach, however, could not really account for the essence of internalization—relatively permanent changes in behavior that continue after pairings of behavior and punishment are discontinued.

This was the problem to which another pioneer in the social learning movement, Robert Sears, turned his attention. He began with the Freudian concept of identification as the mechanism underlying values acquisition and translated it into the concept of secondary or learned drives. In this effort to explain why a child would want to become like the parent, Sears began with dependency—the young child's wish for proximity to the mother. Because aspects of the mother such as her appearance and voice are associated with the reduction of primary drives like hunger, thirst, and physical discomfort, Sears proposed that the mother assumes secondary reward value (Sears, Whiting, Nowlis, & Sears, 1953). Being near her and being held by her, therefore, become secondarily rewarding events for the child. Behaviors designed to elicit nearness such as clinging and reaching out—behaviors categorized as "dependent"—are thereby reinforced by maternal attention.

The next problem Sears faced in this theoretical development was explaining how dependency turns into a drive that the young child displays even when all primary drives have been satisfied and, therefore, when a conditioned reinforcer such as the mother should have lost its reward value. Sears attempted to solve the problem by suggesting that dependent behaviors are sometimes reinforced and sometimes punished and that incompatible expectancies set up in this manner provide drive strength to energize dependent behaviors. From here, Sears went on to propose a theory of identification. He argued that young children cannot discriminate between their mothers and themselves and, therefore, can provide reinforcement for themselves by behaving like the mother. Because reproduction of her actions is reinforcing, a habit of responding imitatively grows up, accompanied by a secondary motivational system for which behaving like the mother is the goal response. In this way, then, Sears arrived at a theory of identification paralleling Freud's theory of anaclitic identification. It was in this form of identification, rather than one involving incorporation of the values of an aggressor as Freud had suggested, that Sears found the roots of children's internalization of values.

Accompanying the elaboration of this theory was empirical work to test it. In 1957, Sears, Maccoby, and Levin published *Patterns of Child Rearing,* the report of findings based on interviews of 379 mothers about their child-rearing practices. They assessed mothers' permissiveness and strictness in areas such as aggression, dependency, and sex. They also questioned them about their discipline usage and categorized discipline techniques into two kinds. The first they labeled "love-oriented" discipline, which included praise, social isolation, withdrawal of affection and reasoning (the latter included because it tended to covary with the first three). The second discipline category was labeled "object-oriented" and included techniques such as the use of tangible rewards, deprivation of material objects or privileges, and physical punishment. Sears et al. reported a significant relation between the use of withdrawal of love by warm mothers and their children's conscience development, that is, the extent to which they seemed to have taken maternal values and made them their own. They explained this relation by suggesting that the absence of attention associated with the discipline technique of withdrawal of love motivates the child to take on characteristics of the parent that are particularly salient at the time of discipline. These include criticism, punishment, and control as well as moral values. There is a greater desire to take on the characteristics of a warm and therefore secondarily reinforcing mother than of one who is less rewarding. In the case of object-oriented discipline, children are merely motivated to find ways of avoiding punishment and hiding from the parent, a condition hardly conducive to taking on their values. Sears et al. also found that conscience development was related to the amount of affectionate warmth the child received from the mother independent of discipline technique as well as the severity of the demands she imposed. Their explanation for the link between severity of demands and conscience development was that the more demanding a mother is the more necessary it is for her child to reproduce behavior him- or herself, rather than receiving help from the parent.

Hoffman's Analysis of Parental Discipline

In 1970, Martin Hoffman wrote an influential chapter for *Carmichael's Manual of Child Psychology*. He reviewed the existing research and theory on children's internalization of values and the role of parental discipline techniques, making a greater differentiation among discipline techniques than most previous investigators who had considered only the dichotomy between power-assertive (punishment) and non-power-assertive techniques. Hoffman distinguished between power assertion—physical punishment, deprivation of material objects or privileges, direct application of force, or the threat of any of these; love-withdrawal—direct but nonphysical expression of anger or disapproval; and induction—the giving of explanations and the use of appeals to the child's pride and desire to be mature. In the latter category, he singled out a particular type of induction—techniques containing references to the implications of the child's behavior for another individual—which he termed "other-oriented" induction. Hoffman also noted the potential importance of parental affection or warmth, which he cited as important because it provides a child with emotional security and a feeling of trust in the world's basic goodness as well as makes the parent a valued object whom the child wishes to please. On the child outcome side, Hoffman identified four aspects of internalization or moral development: resistance to temptation, guilt after deviation, moral judgment depicting an internal as opposed to external orientation, and confession and acceptance of responsibility for misdeeds.

The data from a large number of relevant studies (see Hoffman, 1970, Table 3) indicated a reasonable tendency in the case of mothers (although one that is far from overwhelming, as Hoffman indeed acknowledged) for power assertion to be negatively related to internalization (10 instances of a negative relation, 10 of no relation), induction to be positively related (9 positive instances, 2 negative instances, and 10 instances of no relation), and for there to be no clear relation for withdrawal of love (8 instances of no relation, 3 of a positive relation, and 2 of a negative relation). As well, maternal affection was somewhat related (6 positive instances, 2 negative, and 7 of no relation), although Hoffman suggested the relation was not as strong as that for induction. Although other-oriented induction was represented in some of the studies, its effects were not uniformly positive, nor was it possible to compare it with other forms of reasoning.

The picture for fathers was clearly not in accord with the prediction that induction is more effective than power assertion.

Hoffman went on to propose mechanisms underlying the differential impact of these different techniques of parental discipline. He suggested that power-assertive techniques produce anger in the child because they directly challenge the child's autonomy, they provide a model for antisocial discharge of anger, they focus the child's attention on the self rather than the harmed object, they lead to high levels of arousal that reduce the child's ability to utilize cues in the surrounding situation, and, unlike other-oriented induction, they do not take advantage of the child's empathic ability. Hoffman then offered the following conclusion:

> . . . all discipline techniques have power assertive, love withdrawal, and inductive components. The primary function of the first two is motive arousal and of the last, providing a morally relevant cognitive structure. When degree of arousal is optimal, the child attends to and is subject to maximum influence by the cognitive material. That is, focusing his attention on the harm done others as the salient aspect of his transgression helps integrate his capacity for empathy with the knowledge of the human consequences of his own behavior. This, we suggest, may be the essential contribution of the discipline encounter to the child's moral development. (p. 332)

Hoffman's overall conclusion, then, is a tempered one, although it is probably fair to say that the message has lost its subtlety over time and that emphasis has been on the superiority of reasoning over power assertion. Moreover, Hoffman's stress on other-oriented induction has not been maintained, presumably in the absence of empirical attempts to compare other-oriented with alternative kinds of reasoning. Certainly there is abundant evidence at least from naturalistic, correlational studies that power-assertive techniques in isolation are detrimental to child socialization (see Grusec & Lytton, 1988; Maccoby & Martin, 1983), and this strong conclusion from the literature has tended to obscure that power assertion in combination with other techniques, particularly reasoning or induction, might be a more optimal parenting strategy than reasoning alone. The findings of laboratory and behavior modification studies, however, that punishment by itself can be effective (e.g., Larzelere, 1996; Walters & Grusec, 1977) does raise questions about the blanket condemnation of punishment or power assertion. An obvious answer to apparently contradictory empirical evidence lies in the observation that correlational studies of parent socialization have focused on internalization or behavioral compliance in the absence of surveillance while laboratory and behavior modification studies have been more focused on immediate suppression of undesirable behavior (Grusec & Lytton, 1988). Thus it is presumably safe to conclude that the imposition of authority in the form of punishment or threat of punishment used in isolation will not be conducive to value internalization.

Alternative Explanations

Hoffman (1970), as noted, offered several explanations for the positive effects of reasoning and the negative effects of power assertion on moral development. Other explanations have been proposed over the years, although many require that reasoning be used in conjunction with some degree of power assertion. Hoffman (1983), for example, argues that reasoning contains the parent's message but that power assertion captures the child's attention so that the message can be heard. Baumrind (1983) suggests that power assertion when added to reasoning motivates the child to initiate self-controlling or self-regulatory mechanisms to avoid negative outcomes, and that these mechanisms lead to reliable habits of prosocial behavior. According to Higgins (1989), the children of parents who reason acquire relatively clear knowledge about the relation between their behavior and parental reaction to that behavior and, as a result, they have strong self-guides or a clear picture of attributes the self ought to possess. In a similar vein, Cheyne and Walters (1970) argue that rationales enhance the effects of punishment by making contingencies clearer to the child.

Constructivist approaches to the effects of disciplinary methods focus primarily on the function of reasoning. In Applegate, Burke, Burleson, Delia, and Kline's (1985) analysis, power assertion is seen to discourage the child's reflection on moral issues. In contrast, explanation and discussion allow the child to elaborate schemas for differentiating the psychological experience of others, thereby developing respect for their rights. Mancuso and Handin (1985) propose that parents' use of reasoning indicates their recognition that the child's construction of an event may differ from theirs, and consequent use of reasoning takes this difference into account as they attempt to modify that construction to be more in accord with their own.

A number of developmental researchers have used the basic notions of attribution theory to account for the differential efficacy of parenting strategies. Dienstbier, Hillman, Lehnhoff, Hillman, and Valkenaar (1975) produced a first attempt when they suggested that causal attributions made about the negative states associated with punishment determine subsequent behavior. If the perceived reason for feelings of anxiety after deviation is fear of being found out and punished, then antisocial behavior should not be suppressed when detection is not likely as in the absence of surveillance. If anxiety is attributed to some general rule about good behavior, however, then one would expect suppression even in the absence of possible detection. Walters and Grusec (1977), beginning with the notions of insufficient and overly sufficient justification (Nisbett & Valins, 1971) argued in a similar vein, suggesting that children who behave in a prosocial manner will be less likely to undergo a change in their basic value systems if they believe they have acted in response to strong external pressure than if they see less pressure in the surrounding environment. And reasoning minimizes the intrusiveness of external pressure.

An attributional analysis of parenting strategies and internalization of values was formalized in a paper by Lepper (1983). He used the minimal sufficiency principle to explain why children who are mildly punished for playing with particular toys are more likely to refrain from playing with those toys at a later time when they are not under surveillance than are children who are severely punished for the same action (Freedman, 1965). Thus he argued, as had attitude change researchers, that optimal internalization (enduring conformity) occurs under conditions where pressure is just sufficient to promote compliance. When pressure is stronger than needed, or when it is not strong enough, then internalization will not occur. In the first case, the child attributes prosocial behavior to salient external demands and, in the second case, explanations for compliance are unnecessary because there is no compliance to explain.

A New Model for Understanding Discipline Effectiveness

Emphasis on finding possible explanations for the superiority of reasoning over power assertion has distracted investigators from a closer analysis of existing data. Thus Grusec and Goodnow (1994) called for a reexamination of the data and a more fine-grained analysis of factors that have an impact on discipline effectiveness. They argued that the evidence for the superiority of reasoning over power assertion is not compelling, with the effects of different discipline techniques dependent on the sex of the parent; socioeconomic class; and age, sex, and temperament of the child. They noted the wide variety of procedures included under the labels of reasoning (e.g., other-oriented induction; statements of norms, expectations, and practical consequences; unconvincing arguments) and punishment (e.g., physical punishment, withdrawal of privileges, social isolation, displays of anger, commands, disapproval, humiliation) and suggested that these supposed different manifestations of the same strategy may, in fact, have quite different impacts on child behavior. They also pointed to evidence that parents use many techniques that are dependent on the nature of the misdeed to which they are responding: Thus attempts to characterize parents as predominantly users of a particular approach to discipline are quite misleading.

In an attempt to draw together the factors that have been shown at one time or another to influence the effectiveness of different forms of discipline, Grusec and Goodnow (1994) proposed a two-step explanation of how similarity or dissimilarity in values is achieved across generations. The first involves accurate or inaccurate perception of the parent's message, the second the child's acceptance or rejection of the perceived message. Thus a child may be responsive to complying or accommodating to parental preferences but not appear to have internalized parental values because the parent's position was poorly understood. Contrarily, the parent's message may be very accurately perceived, but the desire or motivation to act in accord with it is lacking. A useful analysis of value internalization, then, involves an understanding of what factors promote accurate perception and what promote acceptance.

With respect to accurate perception, the important features of parenting behavior would be the extent to which messages or values are clearly expressed, the frequency with which they are expressed, and the consistency of their expression. In addition, messages need to be fitted to the child's existing level of cognitive development so that they can be understood (e.g., the child should be able to take the perspective of another to understand the impact of his or her behavior on the other). Power-assertive interventions, if not too arousing, draw the child's attention to the parent's message as well as underline the importance of the message to the parent; and implicit rather than explicit messages (e.g., "this is a house, not a stable") require decoding and therefore force attention. Also, assistance in seeing the wider implications of a rule or a general principle fosters the acquisition of a general moral system. Finally comes another set of understandings, having to do with the child's perception of the parent's intention: When the parent's motives are accurately seen as being in the child's interests, the stage is set for the next stage of internalization, acceptance of the parental message.

Acceptance, according to Grusec and Goodnow (1994), rests with three sets of variables. The first has to do with the child's evaluation of the acceptability of the parent's message. Parent actions must be seen as appropriate to the nature of the misdeed, arguments must be believable, due process must be seen to be served, and the intervention must be appropriate for the particular disciplinary agent (e.g., evidence indicates that power assertion by fathers is more acceptable than power assertion by mothers; power assertion is seen in some cultural contexts to be a more usual and approved mode of intervention than in other cultural contexts). As well, an intervention must be well-intentioned and must be matched appropriately to the child's temperament, mood state, and developmental status. The second set of variables concerns the child's motivation to accept the parental message. Facilitating this motivation are high degrees of empathic arousal;

threats to feelings of security; the extent to which the value is perceived to be important to the parent; parental warmth, which increases the desire to please; a script of mutual compliance, which promotes the commonality of goals; and minimal threats to autonomy (aided by low levels of power assertion, humor, and indirect messages). The final set of variables includes conditions that lead the child to feel a value has been self-generated: These involve minimal feelings of pressure and the need to decode subtle messages.

Although reasoning and power assertion are implicated differentially in these various aspects of internalization, their roles also interweave. Reasoning and explanation are important in perceiving messages accurately, but power assertion also has a role to play when it elicits attention and imparts information. Reasoning also helps determine how acceptable a message is to the child. In addition, the analysis should consider parenting strategies other than explanation and power assertion. These include such things as implicit, subtle, and humorous messages; drama; good intentions; and sensitivity to such characteristics of the child as developmental status, temperament, and mood.

What Is the Most Effective Parenting Style?

The second major approach to discipline involves the description of parenting styles or constellations of attitudes to the child that create an emotional climate in which the transmission of values takes place. Usually these constellations of attitudes have been identified through factor analysis of parenting behaviors reflecting such variables as punitiveness, strictness, expressions of affection, and rejection. The dimensions identified by different investigators have been similar: love/hostility and autonomy/control (Schaefer, 1965); warmth and permissiveness/restrictiveness (Sears et al., 1957); warmth/hostility and restrictiveness/permissiveness (Becker, 1964); and emotional warmth/hostility and detachment/involvement (Baldwin, 1955). The best socialized children—those who were cooperative, friendly, emotionally stable, and happy—had parents who were warm, who established guidelines for behavior while allowing the child some degree of autonomy, and who clearly communicated expectations and gave reasons for them. An immediately apparent difference between these outcomes and those of investigators interested in discipline techniques, is that the outcomes appear more diverse, having moved from a focus on resistance to temptation, guilt, reparation after deviation, and moral thinking, which are associated with the internalization of values, to behaviors that might include values (e.g., cooperativeness) but that go beyond to include indices of psychosocial adjustment.

Some investigators, rather than identifying dimensions, have described categories of parenting style, thereby providing a qualitative rather than quantitative analysis of effective socialization. The most influential of these qualitative analyses has been Diana Baumrind's classification of parents as authoritarian, authoritative, and permissive.

Maccoby (1992) has presented a historical account of Baumrind's work, locating its origins in social psychology and the work of Kurt Lewin on group atmospheres. Lewin and his colleagues, distressed by the growth of totalitarianism and anti-Semitism in pre-World War II Europe, had wanted to find out how people respond to autocratic direction. They did so by constructing different kinds of experimental conditions intended to approximate different political ideologies. Young boys met in recreational and crafts groups once a week for 21 weeks, with each boy exposed to three different kinds of leadership style. In the democratically organized group, members decided themselves what they would do, with the adult's function that of actively encouraging group decision processes, offering suggestions if requested, and providing feedback on the group's functioning. The leader was rational and dispassionate to avoid strong emotional attachments with group members, which Lewin argued undermined autonomy and independent thinking. Boys in this group had cooperative relationships with their leader and worked well and competently in his absence, an indication to Lewin that even democracies can be efficient. In the authoritarian group, leaders decided what the group would do and who would do it. They praised and blamed without giving clear criteria, and they remained aloof. The outcome was that, despite privately expressed dislike, boys competed for the leader's attention and praise. When left alone, however, they stopped working and their behavior erupted into wild horseplay, a presumed manifestation of suppressed tension. Finally, in the laissez-faire group, leaders remained friendly and explained what materials and activities were available but did nothing else except give information if asked. The boys in this group, not surprisingly, were disorganized and ineffective because they lacked information about how to proceed. From a present-day perspective, one can see how authoritarian leadership orients the child to external influences, undermining intrinsic interest and leading to suppressed anger and hostility. The importance of some degree of guidance, however, is clear from the ineffectiveness of laissez-faire approaches.

The significance of Lewin's work for socialization was first grasped by Alfred Baldwin, who was a graduate student at Harvard when he encountered Lewin. Baldwin began his own research career by observing parent-child interactions in the home. He identified democratic parents who behaved as did Lewin's democratic leaders, including avoiding intense emotional involvement with their children: Those parents who did have such an emotional involvement were labeled as overprotective, overindulgent, and possessive or, to use today's terminology, they were "enmeshed" (Maccoby, 1992). Although Baldwin could not find laissez-faire parents, he did identify parents who were somewhat uninterested in their children and who, although responding to their children's demands, interacted with them as little as possible. Another group of parents exhibited this latter constellation of characteristics but also imposed strict controls. As expected, the children of democratic parents displayed the most positive outcomes, although they also tended to be dominating and aggressive to their peers. It was this drawback to democratic rearing, Maccoby suggests, that led Diana Baumrind to further refinement of what constituted a truly effective parenting style. (The direct link between Baumrind and Lewin was Hubert Coffey, an active participant in the sensitivity training movement inspired by Lewin's work, and one of Baumrind's mentors when she was a graduate student at Berkeley.)

Noting the limitations of democratic parenting (and possibly also influenced by the increasing restrictiveness of parenting practices that characterized the 1960s), Baumrind developed the tripartite division of parenting styles that has remained so influential since her work was first published in the late 1960s (Baumrind, 1967; Baumrind & Black, 1967). Baumrind contrasted authoritarian parenting with authoritative—the latter an approach that added the imposition of high standards and firm rules to the democratic style. Her permissive parenting most closely resembled Baldwin's democratic parenting in which children had few demands made on their behavior. Authoritative parents imposed rules and demanded mature behavior, but they also reasoned and negotiated with their children, taking into account their point of view and encouraging their autonomy. They exerted a form of control different from that exerted by authoritarian parents (i.e., behavioral as opposed to restrictive or psychological control). The outcome of the authoritative approach was generally positive, with the children of authoritative parents displaying greater social responsibility (achievement, peer competence, cooperativeness toward adults) and independence (social dominance, nonconformity, and purposiveness) than those of authoritarian or permissive parents. Although the results were not always totally consistent with the generalizations (for example, Baumrind, 1971, reports that sons of authoritative parents were not independent, although they were socially responsible), Baumrind's categorization remains strongly influential to this day, and her generalizations continue to be applicable at least in Anglo-European and middle-class samples (Darling & Steinberg, 1993).

The mechanisms proposed to account for the positive outcomes of authoritative parenting have not been as varied as those proposed for the superiority of reasoning over power assertion. Baumrind argued that the firm but not restrictive control evident in authoritative families helps children balance rule-following tendencies and consideration for others with autonomous and independent thinking. Lewis (1981) has offered an alternative interpretation of the data. Questioning why the strong external control imposed by authoritative parents would lead to internalization of values when attribution theory indicates that it should undermine such internalization, she has suggested that it was not firm control that led to greater independence and social competence, but the reciprocal communication that characterizes authoritative families and the success children have in modifying parental demands. Whatever the mechanisms, however, it is informative to see the overlap in conceptualizations of discipline and parenting styles. Both Baumrind and Hoffman seem to be arguing that modest amounts of power assertion (behavioral as opposed to psychological control) combined with egalitarianism (reasoning and accommodation to the child's points of view, although the latter is less emphasized by Hoffman) will facilitate children's acquisition of values.

A New Model for Understanding Parenting Styles

As was the case with types of discipline, the data have not always been consistent in the study of the impact of different parenting styles, particularly in the case of investigations carried out in different cultural contexts. These discrepancies have prompted a reconsideration of the concept of parenting styles by Darling and Steinberg (1993), who observed that parenting typologies capture a configuration of parenting practices, making it difficult to identify specific patterns of relations between an aspect of parenting and child outcomes. They offered an integrative model of parenting styles that addresses the issue of what aspects of particular parenting styles are impacting on what outcomes. They began with the observation that authoritative parenting does not have beneficial outcomes in all cultures. While authoritarian parenting is associated with timid and anxious behavior among Anglo-European children, it is associated with assertive behavior among African American girls. And, although authoritative parenting is associated with academic achievement in Anglo-European adolescents, there is no such association for Asian and African American adolescents. This discrepancy led Darling and Steinberg to the need to distinguish between content (parenting practices) and context (parenting style). Parenting practices, they suggested, comprise specific content and socialization goals. They operate in circumscribed socialization domains and involve behaviors such as spanking, showing an interest in children's activities, or requiring children to do their homework. Parenting style, on the other hand, involves behaviors that are independent of the content of socialization. It is the general emotional climate expressed by parental behaviors such as tone of voice, body language, inattention, and bursts of temper. Style conveys to the child how the parent feels about the child rather than how the parent feels about the child's behavior. Thus the authoritative parent, for example, communicates comfort with the assertion of influence, recognition of the child's separateness, and respect for the child's wishes. According to Darling and Steinberg, parent practices are the mechanisms through which parents directly help children to achieve their socialization goals; whereas parenting style affects value internalization indirectly by making children more open to socialization attempts as well as teaching them socially competent forms of interaction.

Discipline Techniques and Parenting Style

Darling and Steinberg's analysis of parenting styles and Grusec and Goodnow's (1994) analysis of techniques of discipline have much in common, indicating a degree of overlap between the two approaches to parenting on which each has specifically focused. Both reconceptualizations of existing positions have attempted to disentangle what is transmitted from how it is transmitted. With respect to what is transmitted, Darling and Steinberg refer to parenting practices that are behaviors defined by specific content (including discipline technique and message) and socialization goals. Goodnow and Grusec refer to the parental message, focusing on the degree to which that message is clearly communicated. In the case of transmission, the argument from Darling and Steinberg is in terms of attitudes toward the child that are communicated to the child and that create an emotional climate in which goals are expressed. For Grusec and Goodnow, the question is phrased in terms of conditions that make the child willing to comply with and/or accept the parent's goal. Indeed, the notion of acceptance is captured in Darling and Steinberg's suggestion that a positive emotional climate makes the child more willing to take over the parental goal. Darling and Steinberg offer an important addition to this phase of the internalization process with the suggestion that parental style also affords opportunities for children to acquire skills that come from the parent's use of explanations, encouragement of discussion, and acknowledgment of the child's perspective.

Warmth, Attachment, Shared Goals, and the Internalization of Values

So far, the focus has been on situations in which parents and children are in conflict; the parent desires one thing and the child another. The study of discipline techniques and parenting styles indicates how these issues of conflict can be resolved. Consideration of relationship variables, however, opens up another avenue to internalization of values. Here different aspects of the parent-child relationship can make the child more amenable to accepting parental values and therefore less likely to create a situation of disagreement. Rather than promoting autonomy, however, which is an outcome that flourishes under conditions of disagreement and negotiation, these variables function by facilitating relatedness with others or a community of interests.

   The three relationship variables of particular interest to researchers are parental warmth, parental protection, and mutual compliance. Each functions in its own way, a distinctiveness that has not always been maintained in discussions of the socialization process. Each will be considered in turn here, with an eye to differentiating its characteristics as well as the way in which it functions in the internalization of values.

Warmth

Warmth, that is, noncontingent physical and social reinforcement, has played a role in most formulations of values acquisition. Sears et al. (1957) found that withdrawal of love was effective only when administered by warm mothers who, presumably, set the conditions for more satisfying or reinforcing reproduction of behavior than did cold ones. Similarly, Hoffman (1970) found a role for warmth in its provision of the child with emotional security as well as its making the child more desirous of pleasing the parent. Warmth, also noted earlier, has been a ubiquitous dimension for those who have theorized about parenting style. The evidence continues to suggest that parental warmth has a role to play in the internalization of values (see Grusec & Lytton, 1988, for a review), primarily by making a child more willing to accept parental values in order to please the parent and maintain a pleasurable relationship.

Protection

The second relationship variable has a slightly shorter history of interest for those concerned with children's internalization of values, and the mechanism through which it works is somewhat less clear. But the substantial theoretical and empirical interest generated during the past 25 years by the phenomenon of attachment has inevitably led to questions about its role in the internalization of values. Effective socialization must surely be determined by the extent to which parents set the conditions for secure attachment. These conditions are different from the provision of noncontingent physical and social reinforcement, that is, warmth. Rather, they are parental sensitivity and responsivity to the child's emotional and physical distress. It is the manner in which parents serve their protective function that underlies the formation of secure or insecure attachments.

Before the function of attachment in internalization is addressed, it is useful to distinguish it further from warmth. MacDonald (1992; this volume) has identified several reasons for differentiating parental warmth and parental protectiveness. He argues that there are two independent biological systems serving positive and negative affect respectively. Thus the biological systems underlying warmth and intimacy are different from those underlying protection. Developmentalists tend to lose sight of this because there is such a strong relation in our own culture between parental responsivity to distress and warmth. There are cultures, however, where the two are quite independent. MacDonald offers several additional reasons for separating warmth and protectiveness. He notes that parental protection appears in a wide range of primates, other mammals, and birds although intimacy or warmth appears relatively rarely in these same species; that children become attached even in the absence of warmth and even in the presence of maltreatment; that there are sex differences in attraction to intimate relationships but not in security of attachment; and, finally, that attachment is a central issue for infant development but less so for the reciprocated positive social interactions that characterize later intimate relationships.

What then, is the specific role played by quality of attachment in children's internalization of values? Some of the theoretical issues underlying this question are comprehensively addressed by Bretherton, Golby, and Cho, (this volume) and by Kochanska and Thompson (this volume). Certainly there are indications in the literature that secure attachment might be related to successful acquisition of values. Crittenden and DiLalla (1988), for example, have suggested that children who are avoidantly attached may become what they term compulsively compliant as a way of gaining parental responsiveness. Presumably, however, this is superficial compliance only, and one would expect that the underlying anger engendered by parental rejection produces an environment that is hostile to genuine acceptance of parental wishes. Anxious resistantly attached children, on the other hand, learn that visible displays of anger and persistence are necessary to gain attention from the caregiving figure, even if that behavior includes noncompliance. The expectation, then, would be that the two types of insecurely attached children, for two different sets of reasons, show less internalization of values than securely attached children. Belsky and Cassidy (in press) note that both Bowlby and Tizard have implicated early maternal deprivation with behavior problems including "affectionless psychopathy," attention-seeking, restlessnes, and disobedience. As well, they cite studies indicating that insecurely attached children are less compliant and less able to control their impulses. They note conflicting evidence, however, and suggest that additional research is needed to establish whether attachment security is a causal agent or whether it simply correlates with other factors causally implicated in the development of behavior problems.

Mutual Compliance

The third relationship variable, initially proposed by Maccoby and Martin (1983), has attracted considerable attention (see, e.g., Kochanska & Thompson, this volume). Maccoby and Martin developed the concept of "receptive compliance," which stems from a generalized willingness to cooperate (or to "exchange compliances with") a parent, that is, to share the parent's goals. This they distinguish from situational compliance, which they see as stemming from external pressures. The former is more akin to or a more likely antecedent of an internalized moral system than is the latter. Maccoby and Martin note that children who are securely attached at 18 months are more likely to comply with their mothers' requests at 24 months (Matas, Arend, & Sroufe, 1978) but ask whether maternal characteristics associated with secure attachment, such as sensitivity, cooperation, accessibility, and acceptance, may lead directly to compliance without relying on quality of attachment as the intermediary. They note a direct relation between compliance at 12 months and maternal sensitivity, cooperation, and acceptance (Stayton et al., 1971) and build on this relation to develop their idea of receptive compliance. They argue that frequent playful interchanges between caregiver and very young child during which the caregiver complies with the child's directions and demands foster an atmosphere in which the child is receptively compliant. Under these conditions, mutual scripts develop that make cooperative activity possible, with both caregiver and child more likely to comply with the other's requests.

Maccoby and Martin (1983) note that mutual goals and shared compliance produce an atmosphere that is relatively conflict-free because both members of the dyad have the same agenda. The focus is on factors that lead to an atmosphere of mutual cooperation between caregiver and child that facilitates the internalization of values. Instead of leading to the study of how competing interests are fought over and negotiated, the concept of shared compliance promotes the study of how children and parents come to feel that they are engaged in cooperative efforts to achieve identical goals or how mutual identification develops where each partner invests his or her ego in that of the other. As well, Maccoby and Martin suggest, partners may be motivated to please each other even if their goals are not entirely mutual: They make the effort to postpone their own gratification to gratify the other member of the dyad.

How do mutual goals develop? It depends on the amount of conflict and the way it has been resolved at a very early point in the child's socialization. Maccoby and Martin (1983) liken early parental responsivity and dialogues with the child to "money in the bank" (p. 72) that can be spent as the child's increasing maturity necessitates greater imposition of controls and more refusals of demands.

Modeling and Values Acquisition

Identification was an important feature of theoretical accounts of socialization by Freud and Sears. In both their analyses, it was closely linked with the discipline situation. Children identify with or become like their parents even in the absence of conflict, however. Albert Bandura has been particularly active in demonstrating the important role that parental example in general plays in the development of children's values.

Bandura began his work within the social learning tradition developed by Sears and his colleagues (e.g., Bandura & Walters, 1959). However, the logical difficulties Sears was encountering in attempts to explain why children would develop a motive to act like the mother, as well as the work of Skinner, influenced Bandura and his colleague Richard Walters to set aside the drive notions of Hullian and psychoanalytic theory. Their new approach was labeled "sociobehavioristic" and it focused in particular on the problem of how novel responses are acquired. Sears had not had great success in explaining the phenomenon. Nor had learning theorists in general. Skinner's notion of the process of successive approximation was not particularly convincing in understanding how human beings acquire complex sets of behaviors. Nor did Miller and Dollard's (1941) treatment of imitation as a special case of instrumental conditioning, where social cues serve as discriminative stimuli and behavior matches to those cues are reinforced, account at all adequately for the empirical evidence that children model behavior in the absence of any kind of reinforcement.

Bandura and Walters (1963) gave up the Freudian term of identification. They also rejected drive concepts and the idea that imitative responses have to be reinforced. They promoted imitation to a central position among learning mechanisms, suggesting that it is much more efficient as a behavior change technique than direct learning. Over the years, Bandura continued to refine the position, drawing on concepts of information processing that were becoming increasingly dominant in North American psychology.

Bandura (e.g., 1977) has addressed the central problem of values acquisition, namely, how control over behavior shifts from the external environment to the self. His analysis relies heavily on the role of observational learning. The mechanism he proposes is self-regulation. People continuously judge their own actions in terms of the extent to which they live up to internal standards whose origins are in observation of the standards others set for themselves as well as through reinforcement by agents of socialization for adherence to particular standards. Bandura (e.g., 1986), in response to a long-standing criticism addressed to traditional socialization theories by researchers working within the Piagetian or related traditions of moral development (e.g., Turiel, 1983), has also specifically addressed the issue of whether standards or values are transmitted or constructed. He notes that standards of behavior are not passively absorbed but that children select from the standards of the plethora of individuals with whom they come in contact as well as the variety of standards set by the same individual in different situations. Children's selection of standards depends on such factors as the degree of similarity in competence they see between the model and themselves, their valuation of a specific activity, and the degree to which they see themselves as controlling their own behavior.

The impact of both live and symbolic models on children's acquisition of standards for behavior has been the subject of many studies (see, e.g., Bandura, 1986, for a summary of this work). However, it appears that field research, in fact, has produced little evidence that identification plays an important role in real life in conscience development (Grusec & Lytton, 1988; Hoffman, 1970). There is strong evidence that exposure to prosocial models who help, share, or show concern for others increases concern for others over a long period of time (Grusec & Lytton, 1988). However, it may be that, whereas identification with parents is helpful in establishing prosocial behavior, the evidence is less convincing for the suppression of antisocial responding because children probably have much less opportunity to observe their parents resisting temptation or experiencing guilt than to observe them showing consideration for others.

CONCLUSION

This chapter has provided a background for the chapters that follow. It has placed particular emphasis on parenting strategies that historically have been the center of attention for socialization theorists: discipline, style, relationship variables, and modeling. Many of the remaining chapters in the book emerge from theoretical perspectives that have focused less exclusively on parenting approaches and the internalization of values, and their authors will in turn provide a historical background for their own perspective on the topic of this book. Chapter 2, as noted, deals with bidirectionality, an important concern raised early and frequently within the context of traditional socialization theory (e.g., Bell, 1968). Any discussion of bidirectionality must also address the effects of genetic influences on the acquisition of values and how biologically determined features of the child interact with parenting strategies. This issue is addressed particularly in Chapter 3 (Kochanska & Thompson) as well as the chapter on evolutionary perspectives (Chapter 14).

The theoretical tradition described in this introduction has some limitations that will be noted here and discussed in detail in subsequent chapters. The first is that the traditional socialization approach is curiously content-free. The assumption has been that the same principles hold for the development of any value, regardless of its content. Thus inhibition of aggression, sharing, academic achievement, social responsibility, respect for authority, forms of address, social manners, and accepting responsibility for household work have all been treated as equivalent. In Chapter 7, Smetana addresses this issue arguing that domain-appropriate strategies are an essential part of successful socialization.

The second limitation has to do with somewhat curtailed attention to developmental issues, including early precursors of conscience in the developing sense of self and increasing ability to engage in self-control and self-regulation, as well as increasing cognitive and social competencies that alter the impact of a given parenting strategy. Developmental issues are specifically addressed by Kochanska and Thompson (Chapter 3) and by Collins, Gleason, and Sesma (Chapter 4). Smetana's chapter also takes up the theme, as one would expect from an analysis that emerges from cognitive-developmental theory.

A third feature has been a focus on a narrow set of parenting strategies, primarily reasoning and punishment and—in the context of style—on warmth, negotiation, and sensitivity to the child's needs. Some minimal attention has been paid to the use of proactive techniques or structuring of the environment to minimize temptations to misbehave (e.g., Holden, 1983), on attributions of prosocial behavior to the personality of the child (e.g., Grusec, Kuczynski, Rushton, & Simutis, 1979), and on participation in and discussion of prosocial actions (e.g., Staub, 1979). But these and other practices have not been greatly elaborated. Some suggestions for expansions on practices appear throughout the book.

Next is a relative lack of concern with the importance of the larger context as it interacts with parenting strategies. This larger context includes peers, school, and the media. The recognition that parenting does not occur in a vacuum is presented in a particularly striking fashion in Chapter 12; this discussion of the social ecological approach underlines how particularly vulnerable parenting strategies are in the wider context of a high-risk neighborhood.

Finally, traditional approaches to the internalization of values have taken a middle-class Anglo-European perspective, that devotes little attention to social class or cultural differences or the implications of differences in designing a comprehensive theoretical treatment. In Chapter 10 by Grusec et al., Chapter 12 by Garbarino et al., and Chapter 13 by Goodnow, some of these necessary expansions are begun.

REFERENCES

Applegate, J. L., Burke, J. A., Burleson, B. R., Delia, J. G., & Kline, S. L. (1985). Reflection-enhancing parental communication. In I. E. Sigel (Ed.), *Parental belief systems* (pp. 107–142). Hillsdale, NJ: Erlbaum.

Aronfreed, J. (1963). The effect of experimental socialization paradigms upon two moral responses to transgression. *Journal of Abnormal and Social Psychology, 66,* 437–448.

Baldwin, A. (1955). *Behavior and development in childhood.* New York: Dryden Press.

Bandura, A. (1977). Self-efficacy: Toward a unifying theory of behavior change. *Psychological Review, 84,* 191–215.

Bandura, A. (1986). *Social foundations of thought and action: A social cognitive theory.* Englewood Cliffs, NJ: Prentice-Hall.

Bandura, A., & Walters, R. H. (1959). *Adolescent aggression.* New York: Ronald Press.

Bandura, A., & Walters, R. H. (1963). *Social learning and personality development.* New York: Holt, Rinehart and Winston.

Baumrind, D. (1967). Child care practices anteceding three patterns of preschool behavior. *Genetic Psychology Monographs, 75,* 43–88.

Baumrind, D. (1971). Current patterns of parental authority. *Developmental Psychology Monographs, 4*(1, Pt. 2).

Baumrind, D. (1983). Rejoinder to Lewis' reinterpretation of parental firm control: Are authoritative families really harmonious? *Psychological Bulletin, 94,* 132–142.

Baumrind, D., & Black, A. E. (1967). Socialization practices associated with dimensions of competence in preschool boys and girls. *Child Development, 38,* 291–327.

Becker, W. C. (1964). Consequences of different kinds of parental discipline. In M. L. Hoffman & L. W. Hoffman (Eds.), *Review of child development research* (Vol. 1, pp. 169–208). New York: Russell-Sage Foundation.

Bell, R. Q. (1968). A reinterpretation of the direction of effects in studies of socialization. *Psychological Review, 75,* 81–85.

Belsky, J., & Cassidy, J. (in press). Attachment: Theory and evidence. In M. Rutter, D. Hay, & S. Baron-Cohen (Eds.), *Developmental principles and clinical issues in psychology and psychiatry*. Oxford, England: Blackwell.

Cheyne, J. A., & Walters, R. H. (1970). Punishment and prohibition: Some origins of self-control. In T. M. Newcomb (Ed.), *New directions in psychology* (Vol. 4, pp. 281–366). New York: Holt, Rinehart and Winston.

Crittenden, P. M., & DiLalla, D. (1988). Compulsive compliance: The development of an inhibitory coping strategy in infancy. *Journal of Abnormal Child Psychology, 16,* 585–599.

Darling, N., & Steinberg, L. (1993). Parenting style as context: An integrative model. *Psychological Bulletin, 113,* 487–496.

Dienstbier, R. A., Hillman, D., Lehnhoff, J., Hillman, J., & Valkenaar, M. C. (1975). An emotion-attribution approach to moral behavior. Interfacing cognitive and avoidance theories of moral development. *Psychological Review, 82,* 299–315.

Freedman, J. L. (1965). Long-term behavioral effects of cognitive dissonance. *Journal of Experimental Social Psychology, 1,* 145–155.

Grusec, J. E., & Goodnow, J. J. (1994). The impact of parental discipline methods on the child's internalization of values: A reconceptualization of current points of view. *Developmental Psychology, 30,* 4–19.

Grusec, J. E., Kuczynski, L., Rushton, J. P., & Simutis, Z. M. (1979). Modeling, direct instruction, and attributions: Effects on altruism. *Developmental Psychology, 14,* 51–57.

Grusec, J. E., & Lytton, H. (1988). *Social development: History, theory, and research*. New York: Springer-Verlag.

Grusec, J. E., & Redler, E. (1980). Attribution, reinforcement, and altruism: A developmental analysis. *Developmental Psychology, 16,* 525–534.

Higgins, E. T. (1989). Continuities and discontinuities in self-regulatory and self-evaluative processes: A developmental theory relating self and affect. *Journal of Personality, 57,* 407–444.

Hobbes, T. (1885). *Leviathan*. London: George Routledge & Sons. (Original work published 1651)

Hoffman, M. L. (1970). Moral development. In P. H. Mussen (Ed.), *Carmichael's manual of child psychology* (Vol. 2, pp. 261–360). New York: Wiley.

Hoffman, M. L. (1983). Affective and cognitive processes in moral internalization. In E. T. Higgins, D. Ruble, & W. Hartup (Eds.), *Social cognition and social development: A sociocultural perspective* (pp. 236–274). Cambridge, England: Cambridge University Press.

Holden, G. W. (1983). Avoiding conflict: Mothers as tacticians in the supermarket. *Child Development, 54,* 233–240.

Holden, G. W. (1997). *Parents and the dynamics of child rearing*. Boulder, CO: Westview Press.

Jones, M. C. (1974). Albert, Peter and John B. Watson. *American Psychologist, 29,* 581–583.

Larzelere, R. E. (1996). A review of the outcomes of parental use of nonabusive or customary physical punishment. *Pediatrics, 98,* 824–828.

Lepper, M. (1983). Social control processes, attributions of motivation, and the internalization of social values. In E. T. Higgins, D. N. Ruble, & W. W. Hartup (Eds.), *Social cognition and social development: A sociocultural perspective* (pp. 294–330). New York: Cambridge University Press.

Lewis, C. C. (1981). The effects of parental firm control: Reinterpretation of findings. *Psychological Bulletin, 90,* 547–563.

Locke, J. (1884). *Some thoughts concerning education*. London: C. J. Clay & Sons. (Original work published 1693)

Maccoby, E. E. (1992). Trends in the study of socialization: Is there a Lewinian heritage? *Journal of Social Issues, 48,* 171–185.

Maccoby, E. E., & Martin, J. A. (1983). Socialization in the context of the family: Parent-child interaction. In E. M. Hetherington (Ed.), *Handbook of child psychology: Vol. 4. Socialization, personality and social development* (pp. 1–102). New York: Wiley.

MacDonald, K. B. (1992). Warmth as a developmental construct: An evolutionary analysis. *Child Development, 63,* 753–773.

Mancuso, J. C., & Handin, K. H. (1985). Reprimanding: Acting on one's implicit theory of behavior change. In I. E. Sigel (Ed.), *Parental belief systems* (pp. 143–176). Hillsdale, NJ: Erlbaum.

Matas, L., Arend, R. A., & Sroufe, L. A. (1978). Continuity and adaptation in the second year: The relationship between quality of attachment and later competence. *Child Development, 49,* 547–556.

Miller, N. E., & Dollard, J. (1941). *Social learning and imitation.* New Haven, CT: Yale University Press.

Mowrer, O. H. (1960). *Learning theory and the symbolic processes.* New York: Wiley.

Newson, J., & Newson, E. (1974). Cultural aspects of childrearing in the English-speaking world. In M. P. M. Richards (Ed.), *The integration of a child into a social world* (pp. 53–82). London: Cambridge University Press.

Nisbett, R. E., & Valins, S. (1971). *Perceiving the causes of one's own behavior.* Morristown, NJ: General Learning Press.

Parke, R. D., & Walters, R. H. (1967). Some factors determining the efficacy of punishment for inducing response inhibition. *Monographs of the Society for Research in Child Development, 32,*(Serial No. 109).

Piaget, J. (1932). *The moral judgment of the child.* New York: Harcourt, Brace.

Rousseau, J. J. (1974). *Emile, or on education.* London: J. M. Dent & Sons. (Original work published 1762)

Schaefer, E. S. (1965). A configurational analysis of children's reports of parent behavior. *Journal of Consulting Psychology, 29,* 552–557.

Sears, R. R., Maccoby, E. E., & Levin, H. (1957). *Patterns of child-rearing.* New York: Row-Peterson.

Sears, R. R., Whiting, J. W. M., Nowlis, V., & Sears, P. S. (1953). Some child-rearing antecedents of aggression and dependency in young children. *Genetic Psychology Monographs, 47,* 135–234.

Solomon, R. L., Turner, L. H., & Lessac, M. S. (1968). Some effects of delay of punishment on resistance to temptation in dogs. *Journal of Personality and Social Psychology, 8,* 233–238.

Spock, B. (1957). *Baby and child care.* New York: Pocket Books.

Staub, E. (1979). *Positive prosocial behavior and morality.* New York: Academic Press.

Stayton, D. J., Hogan, R., & Ainsworth, M. D. S. (1971). Infant obedience and maternal behavior: The origins of socialization reconsidered. *Child Development, 42,* 1057–1069.

Turiel, E. (1983). Interaction and development in social cognition. In E. T. Higgins, D. Ruble, & W. Hartup (Eds.), *Social cognition and social development: A socio-cultural perspective* (pp. 333–355). Cambridge, England: Cambridge University Press.

Walters, G. C., & Grusec, J. E. (1977). *Punishment.* San Francisco: Freeman.

Wolfenstein, M. (1955). Fun morality: An analysis of recent American child-rearing literature. In M. Mead & M. Wolfenstein (Eds.), *Childhood in contemporary cultures* (pp. 168–178). Chicago: University of Chicago Press.

CHAPTER 2

Value Socialization in a Bidirectional Context

LEON KUCZYNSKI, SHEILA MARSHALL, and KATHLEEN SCHELL

Most conceptions of socialization in the context of the family are unidirectional. Children are assumed to enter a world that contains preexisting meanings, rules, and expectations held by their parents and other representatives of the encompassing culture. By interacting with their social environment, children are assumed to acquire this material so that ideas and knowledge initially outside the child are gradually transferred to inside the child. Although it is often acknowledged that children have some influence on their socialization experiences and that peers, schools, and many other influences external to the family contribute to this internalization, the dominant metaphor for the process is a unidirectional one. Socialization fundamentally involves the transmission of values, attitudes, roles, and other cultural products from the older generation to the younger generation and parents play a direct and primary role in this process.

Despite its intuitive appeal, the inadequacies of the unidirectional conception of socialization have long been apparent to social scientists. Sociologists have for several decades critiqued social mold or structural functionalist conceptions of socialization that emphasize such ideas as conformity to social norms and roles and stable transmission of values between generations. Wrong (1961), for example, suggested that such ideas assumed that society is much more integrated than it really is and that human nature is much more conforming and socialized than it really is. Feminist scholars (Ferree, 1990; Lopata & Thorne, 1978) critiqued specific conceptualizations of the products of socialization such as "sex roles" because they reified gender-linked behaviors as a stable trait, self-accepted early in life, thus obscuring that such "internalized" roles are maintained by both overt and hidden pressures for conformity and can be changed by an individual during life.

According to Kohn (1983) empirical evidence for the transmission of similarity between parents and children is modest and tends to concern "mainly political orientations, religious beliefs, and 'life styles,' not values as such or even general orientations to social reality" (Kohn, 1983, p. 1). Moreover, sociologists note that factors other than direct parent-to-child transmission contribute to the intergenerational similarities in attitudes that have been found (Glass, Bengston, & Dunham, 1986). Thus, young adult children and their parents may have similar attitudes and values because children have inherited their parents' social status (e.g., religious affiliation, race, class) or because children socialized their parents into accepting their own attitudes.

More recently, behavioral geneticists (Plomin & Daniels, 1987; Rowe, 1994; Scarr, 1993) cited the absence of empirical evidence for environmental transmission of parental characteristics to children in their critiques of socialization research. Their work emphasizes the role of biological inheritance and children's peer group experiences outside the family (Harris, 1995) in social development and socialization.

Developmental psychologists have led the search for alternative ways of thinking about parenting and socialization. In an influential review of the moral development literature, Hoffman (1970) acknowledged critiques of internalization theory and shifted attention from the transmission of content to the development of internalized motivational systems in children. "Once we discard the simplistic notion that moral standards internalized from parents persist unchanged throughout life, and accept the vulnerability of internalized standards to extreme counter pressures from without, the concept that remains—the acquisition of internal motive force by moral standards which were at first external to the individual—is still an important one" (Hoffman, 1970, p. 262).

Unidirectional perspectives on socialization were further undermined when developmental research began to adopt bidirectional models of causality to understand children's transactions with the environment. Major steps in this development included learning to perceive children's activity in knowledge construction and in social interactions with adults, the development of plausible bidirectional and systemic alternatives to parent-effect models of influence (Bell, 1968; Bronfenbrenner, 1989; Lytton, 1990; Patterson, 1982; Sameroff, 1975), and the emergence of a large body of data on parent-child interactions in natural contexts.

As a consequence, bidirectionality has become a central assumption of developmental perspectives on socialization. In their classic review of the literature on parent-child interaction, Maccoby and Martin (1983) argued that the behaviors of mothers and children are linked, one giving rise to the other in cycles of recursive causality. Their review also indicated that models of competent parental behavior need to be rethought if they are to adequately reflect the bidirectional context of socialization. "The emphasis on interaction has led us away from viewing parental behavior as something that is done *to* children or *for* children towards the view that it is done *with* children" (Maccoby & Martin, 1983, p. 78). Subsequent theoretical articles have presented reformulations of basic concepts such as "compliance," "internalization," "relationship," and the parents' role in the socialization process in a way that accommodates bidirectionality (Grusec & Goodnow, 1994; Kuczynski & Kochanska, 1990; Lawrence & Valsiner, 1993; Lewis & Feinman, 1992; Maccoby, 1992). Each of the chapters in this book incorporates one or more assumptions of bidirectionality into the author(s) own treatment of internalization and parental influence.

The purpose of this chapter is to examine the implications of bidirectionality for theories of socialization and internalization. The first section will outline major changes in the understanding of parent-child relations that have been facilitated by the shift from a unidirectional to a bidirectional perspective on parent-child relations. Bidirectionality incorporates multiple assumptions that, taken together, have profound implications for conceptualizing socialization and parents' role in the process. The second section presents a general model of socialization within the parent-child relationship that incorporates the bidirectional assumptions in a comprehensive way. The model focuses on "the big picture" of socialization and will attempt to organize contemporary developmental and sociological research on parent-child relations under the umbrella of bidirectionality. The approach to the literature is integrative and will concentrate on broad points of consensus. The final section will highlight the new research directions suggested by the model.

In a bidirectional perspective, socialization is considered to be an ongoing process where both intergenerational differences and intergenerational similarities are constructed. Further, parental attempts to pass on values to children involve not only dyadic transactions with children but also transactions with the surrounding culture and with the parents' own changing ideas about what to pass on to their children.

CHANGES IN FOUNDATIONAL ASSUMPTIONS

An intuitively accepted bidirectional conception of socialization has been slow to develop because the assumptions implicit in the unidirectional conception prevent effective thinking about the influence of the child and of the parent. Kohn (1983) noted the unexamined nature of the research problem in socialization. He suggested, "The object of research has generally been, not to demonstrate a similarity in parents' and children' values, but to explain a similarity that was assumed to exist" (p. 1). The idea that it is parents who socialize children is embedded in culture and constrains the way causality is perceived and reported in everyday life. Both parents and children have difficulty answering questions about how children influence parents despite obvious objective evidence that such influence has occurred (Ambert, 1992; Russell & Russell, 1988). Thinking about the child-to-parent direction of influence may go against the grain of culturally established patterns of thought (Ambert, 1992).

Kuczynski and Lollis (in press) characterize the unidirectional model as a web of mutually reinforcing assumptions concerning not just direction of effect but also the relative agency and power of parents and children and the essential nature of socialization and internalization. A schematic depiction of the unidirectional idea of internalization is presented in Figure 2.1 to illustrate some of the unstated assumptions of the model. The figure contains a box with the parent's beliefs, values, skills, attitudes, and motives; these presumably, are the products of the parent's earlier internalization. This is connected by a one-way arrow to a box containing the child's beliefs, values, skills, and attitudes, which are the products of his or her internalization.

Direction of Influence

In the unidirectional model, the direction of influence was from parent to child. Parents did the socializing and children did the internalizing. Key concepts of socialization such as "transmission," "internalization," and "compliance" are based on one-way metaphors of process. The very idea of socialization made it difficult to think that causality could substantially flow from child to parent. However, new causal concepts such as "interaction," "transaction," "circular causality," "dialectic," "fit," and "system" (Kuczynski & Lollis, in press; Lewis, 1990) have been developed to facilitate thinking about bidirectional influence. Moreover, bidirectionality involves not only reactions to immediate behaviors but also anticipations of the others' future behavior on the basis of past

Figure 2.1   Unidirectional Transmission Model

experiences (Lewis & Painter, 1974). These new ways of thinking about causality facilitate the assumption that influence between the parent and child is inherently bidirectional.

Agency

Implicit in the idea of one-way causality was another assumption about the roles of parents and children. Parents were perceived as active agents, the ones with the goals, the parenting styles, and the strategies. Children were considered to be passive recipients or objects of parental intentions and behaviors. Moreover, early challenges to the unidirectional model considered children's influence in terms of global characteristics such as sex, birth order, attractiveness, and temperament. A focus on such indirect influences made it easy to dismiss the child's agency and the intentionality of the child's behavior. Assumptions about agency were also embedded in key measures of child behavior. For example, the concept of children's "compliance" to parental commands considered submission to be a form of competence, whereas the concept of noncompliance considered children's attempts to display agency to be a form of deviance (Kuczynski & Kochanska, 1990).

The agency of the child has been documented in research on children's social strategies such as commands and requests directed at parents (Eisenberg, 1992; Kochanska & Kuczynski, 1991; Leonard, 1993), children's negotiation of parent-child conflict (Kuczynski & Kochanska, 1990), and children's perceptions and evaluations of parental actions (Siegel & Barclay, 1985; Siegel & Cohen, 1984). These new categories of children's behavior make it easier to perceive children as actively resisting, selecting, and negotiating parental ideas and constructing ideas of their own. This enhanced awareness of the child's activity is also facilitating a shift from an agent-object to an agent-agent perspective on parent-child socialization.

Power

The concept of parental power has been a stumbling block for bidirectionality. The central argument has been that, child effects notwithstanding, socialization fundamentally must be a process of parents influencing children because parents have more power than children, (Hoffman, 1975). Because of its links with other assumptions of the unidirectional model, the concept of assymetrical power in parent-child relations has helped to perpetuate ideas of one-way causality and of the child as passive object.

Kuczynski (1997) quesitoned the use of parental power as an argument for reinstating parent-to child interpretations of causality in socialization. The idea of power as a fixed imbalance in resources and the assumption that greater power can fuel greater causality are based on a mechanistic conception of power. Parental power may be irrelevant to many child outcomes that, for example, have a biological component. For other child outcomes the relationship between power and causality is a complex one.

A construct of "interdependent asymmetry" provides a better fit for power-dynamics in parent-child relationships (Kuczynski, 1997). Power in parent child relationships derives from a transaction of resources from three domains: culture, individual organismic development, and the parent-child relationship. Culture is a source of rights, constraints, and entitlements for both children and parents. Individual development is a source of capacities and resources that creates change in power relations throughout development. The 7-year-old has much more power than the infant and the adolescent has more power than the 7-year-old. However, even the infant has considerable capacities both to influence the parent and to blunt the parent's impact.

Most importantly, power needs to be examined in the distinctive context of the parent-child relationship. Power between parents and children follows different dynamics than power between unrelated adults and children. Parents and children interact in an interdependent, intimate relationship where each is both vulnerable and powerful with regard to the other. Their relationship has some of the characteristics of a friendship and some of the characteristics of an authority relationship. It represents what Laursen and Collins (1994) have called a "mixed relationship"—a mixture of horizontal and vertical power arrangements.

Mayall (1994) found that children experienced different power arrangements in interactions with adults in the relationship context of the family compared with the nonintimate relationship context of the school. Socialization was experienced as negotiation in the family but as prescription in the school. Adult authority was interpreted in the context of relationships in the family but in the context of institutional norms in the school. Children were more often construed as agents and subjects in the family but as projects and objects in the school. The relationship context alters children's experience of power and authority. It is likely that children experience more power in their relationships with parents than in any other adult-child relationship.

Thus, although in some abstract sense, parents can be considered more powerful than children, particularly early in a child's development, the implications of that "fact" are not straightforward in the context of the parent-child relationship. Far from resolving the question of directionality, power in the context of the parent-child relationship may act to magnify bidirectional processes in socialization.

Products

The unidirectional model had implicit assumptions about the products of internalization. Strauss (1992) described the traditional perspective as a "fax" model because it implied that parents directly transmitted a copy of their own values and other characteristics to their children.

The transmission model provides a constrained and static conception of socialization outcomes suggesting that parents take their values (presumably the products of their own childhood internalization) and then try to transmit the whole collection, without change, to their children. The focus on transmission of similarity leads one to regard dissimilarities between parents and their children as failures of socialization. Weak evidence for similarities between parents and children that can be attributed to experience has regarded by some as indicating the failure of "socialization science" itself (Rowe, 1994; Scarr, 1993). Moreover, the model focuses attention on static products but neglects process. The parents' role with regard to their own products of internalization was relatively passive. Parental agency was confined to devising strategies for passing on the burden of their own socialization but did not extend to examining or transcending their childhood acquisitions. Similarly, the model suggested that the child's cultural, personality, and moral development was somehow complete once the fax was transmitted. The unidirectional model did not encourage thoughts of the parent or the child as undergoing a continuing process of change and development (Schaffer, 1984). In contrast, as described in the following section, a bidirectional perspective highlights both process and change in internalization.

The unidirectional model placed powerful constraints on thinking about socialization and internalization. Moreover, a comprehensive shift to a bidirectional perspective encompasses a shift in a large number of starting assumptions. In the next section, a model of socialization in the context of the family will be presented to illustrate the implications of bidirectional assumptions for this conceptualization.

BIDIRECTIONAL MODEL OF SOCIALIZATION

The model presented in Figure 2.2 attempts to incorporate current assumptions about parents and children as interdependent, active agents in a process of mutual influence. The top half of Figure 2.2, (discussed in the following section) depicts the parent's working model of internalization, the child's working model, and other working models in the ecological context. These components of the model reflect assumptions about internalization and about the bidirectional processes that connect a parent, a child, and their ecological and cultural contexts. The bottom half of the model (discussed in a later section) depicts internal cognitive processes (externalization and internalization) and external social interactional processes of a specific parent-child dyad. These components of the model reflect assumptions about bidirectional processes that operate within the parent-child relationship.

Socialization in the Context of Competing Working Models

Internalization in a bidirectional perspective is considered to be a *recursive process* by which parents and children construct *personal working models* of the beliefs, attitudes, and values necessary for adaptation in family and culture. The label "working models" of internalization highlights an important difference from the unidirectional conception of internalization as a static product. In the bidirectional perspective, internalization is considered to be a lifelong process in which each person's beliefs, values, skills, attitudes, and motives are continuously under development and open to challenge and reconstruction.

This conception is similar to the idea of internalization described by Lawrence and Valsiner (1993, p. 152): "The person's intramental reconstruction of the world is a highly dynamic structure. It is never finished, but continues as a sufficient support for the person's new encounters with the world." Thus, at any point in development, the outcome under consideration is the person's current, in-process model of internalization.

It is important that the diagrams representing the working models of the parent, the child, and also other working models in the ecological context are of different shapes. It is apparent from many perspectives that it is not realistic to conceptualize the end products of socialization as the current generation's acquisition of the previous generation's characteristics. In this section, it will be shown that important sources for the development of individual differences in values can be found in the cultural and ecological context, the family context, and the context of the individual. Thus, intergenerational difference as well as intergenerational similarity are normative outcomes of the internalization process. Further, extreme levels of conformity to the values of the older generation often may not represent a desirable developmental or social outcome.

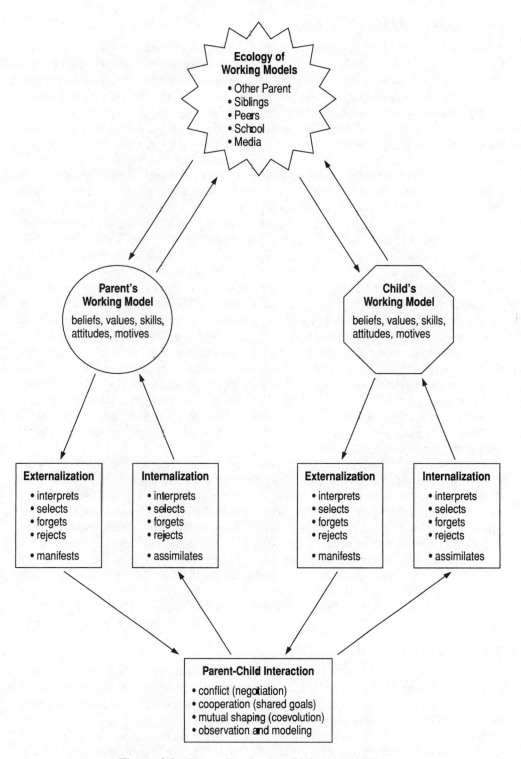

Figure 2.2   Internalization in a Bidirectional Model

The Ecological and Cultural Context

A historical examination of values suggests that social values change from one generation to another (Alwin, 1990). It has been possible to observe continual and rapid social changes in areas such as attitudes toward authority, the environment, feminism, civil rights, and sexuality during the past generation. Social change, whether it comes about by immigration, economic changes, war, or new technology routinely invalidates the experience of the older generation (Skolnick, 1988). The nonstable nature of social values means that the values parents had when their children were young may well have changed by the time their children are a few years older (Kohn, 1983). Parents experiencing the different circumstances of their children's environments may want to raise their children differently from the way they had been reared themselves to prepare their children for social life as it exists in the present (Alwin, 1988, 1990; Inkeles, 1955).

Other working models existing in the culture provide a dynamic context for parent and child socialization. Influences within the family (the other spouse, siblings, relatives) and outside the family (peers, teachers, coaches, electronic and print media) confront the child and the parent with alternative perspectives on appropriate values, attitudes, and skills that must be assimilated, managed, or ignored in the internalization process.

Baumeister (1991) suggests that the weakening of religious institutions as well as rapid economic and technical changes have resulted in a value gap or "shortage of firm bases for distinguishing right from wrong, for justifying and legitimizing actions, and for guiding individual moral choices" (p. 365). He argues that Western culture has responded to the value gap by relying on personal judgments and choices rather than allowing external institutions and community consensus to guide the selection of values. In the absence of strong consensual value bases, it has become common for people to entertain multiple perspectives, multiple values, and multiple roles (Gergen, 1991). The multiplicity of other perspectives contributes to the instability of working models created within the parent-child relationship.

The presence of other working models is not entirely a negative force in children's development. Interactions with peers and friends provide sources of knowledge, values, and skills that are different from those provided by parents (Hartup, 1996). Despite the notorious reputations of peers for being negative socialization influences during adolescence, peers also have unique positive roles in social development. Peers help each other to construct new stable and cohesive identities after the childhood identities developed in the context of early parent-child interactions no longer accommodate the physical, social, and emotional changes that occur during adolescence (Seltzer, 1982). Moreover, peers socialize each other into forms of resolving conflict not typically found in the parent-peer relationship (Laursen, 1993). Even preschoolers socialize each other into the skills of cooperative play (Corsaro & Eder, 1990) and self-disclosure (Rotenberg & Mann, 1986).

Working Models within the Family

Conceptions of the family once emphasized monolithic family environments or assumed a consistent parental alliance. More recent perspectives suggest that experiences, values, and perceptions within the family are much less shared than was once presumed. Bernard (1972) argued that in every marital union there are two marriages, hers and his. Women and men do not experience their marriage in the same way and they report their experiences differently. Similarly, Kohn (1983) noted that socialization theory failed to recognize that the mother's values do not always correspond to the father's values.

Moreover, steep increases in divorce rates during recent decades indicate that parenthood has become much more heterogeneous in its physical composition. Thus, for many children, the adults who are presently engaged in the role of parent and socializer are not the same ones who occupied these roles earlier in their development (Tesson, 1987). What is missing from the literature is an account of whose values prevail in the socialization process.

From the child's point of view, the family also does not provide a stable picture of values. Behavioral geneticists (Dunn & Plomin, 1990; Plomin & Daniels, 1987) suggest that children reared in the same home by the same parents do not have similar personalities or other characteristics unless they share genes. In this perspective, the essential nature of environments created by parents is that they are nonshared. Each sibling both objectively and subjectively experiences unique microenvironments within the same family. L. W. Hoffman's (1991) critique of the nonshared environment concept did not dispute the general conclusion that siblings in the same environment will be unlike each other. Instead, she added that the home environment is currently conceptualized as dynamic and multifaceted. Many family variables such as birth order, sex, temperament, health and appearance of the child, idiosyncratic experiences, and individual ways of perceiving the world all help explain how difference rather than similarity is a likely outcome of socialization and development in the family.

Individual Processing of Working Models

Psychological processes at the level of the individual also suggest that the active construction of difference in addition to potential similarity is a normative outcome of internalization. Research on toddler "negativism" (Wenar, 1982) and children's noncompliance to parental demands suggests that opposition may have a normative function of defending autonomy from parental encroachments (Crockenberg & Litman, 1990; Kuczynski, Kochanska, Radke-Yarrow, & Girnius-Brown, 1987).

According to Marcia's (1966) identity status paradigm, identity development in adolescence and young adulthood is facilitated by the critical exploration of and selective commitment to values, beliefs, and life directions within the social environment. Marcia proposed that Erikson's stage of Identity versus Identity-diffusion can be measured by two crucial processes—commitment and exploration. Commitment is characterized by individuals' decisions to select and act on their choices in areas that are personally important to them such as political ideologies, religious values, and career and relationship choices. Exploration is characterized by the extent to which individuals genuinely look at and experiment with various life directions, beliefs, and values beyond those held by their parents. A review of research on the identity status paradigm indicates that those who engaged in exploration and commitment are generally more adaptive to their context than individuals who have not explored (Marcia, 1994). The developmental disorder of anorexia nervosa has been found to be associated with an overly compliant, overly foreclosed, overly socialized, or "false" sense of self (Bruch, 1978; McLaughlin, Karp, & Herzog, 1985). An important parental task in this perspective is to facilitate the adolescent's exploration of ideas and values rather than fostering rigid conformity to parental values. Existing empirical evidence suggests that, within a nurturing environment, parents who tolerate disagreements with their offspring and encourage independent exploration of ideas, are more likely to have adolescents who achieve an adaptive identity status (e.g., Adams & Jones, 1983; Grotevant & Cooper, 1985).

According to co-constructionist (Lawrence & Valsiner, 1993) and interpretive perspectives (Gaskins, Miller, & Corsaro, 1992) the child's cognitive processing of parental messages ensures that what the child internalizes will be an innovative interpretation rather than a direct copy of the parent's message. Similarly, narrative perspectives on socialization (Epston, White, & Murray, 1992; Stone, 1988) suggest individuals' experiences are structured by stories such as family stories about the family identity or how family members behave. Such stories are rarely a mechanism for direct transmission because they are themselves interpretations of events whose objective truth value is not essential. With daily interactions and experiences individuals interpret and reinterpret family stories and creatively fill in gaps in the narratives (Epston et al., 1992). In this "reauthoring" of their past lives and relationships, individuals internalize something different from the values of their parents.

The idea that a degree of difference between the generations is a necessary outcome of socialization helps to redefine the research problem posed by socialization. In a bidirectional perspective, the construction of difference between the parent and child is as much an important question for socialization as is the transmission of similarity.

Socialization in the Context of a Parent-Child Relationship

The lower portion of Figure 2.2 depicts the bidirectional processes of socialization that operate in the context of a parent-child relationship. The relationship context, which is assumed to moderate internalization processes, will be discussed first. Next to be considered is a set of internal cognitive processes labeled *internalization* and *externalization* that operate for each member of the dyad. Finally, several dyadic processes that govern parent-child social interactions will be described. It will be argued that opportunities for the transformation of values exist at both the internal, individual and external, social levels of processing within the parent-child relationship.

The Relationship Context

It is significant that Figure 2.2 depicts socialization and internalization from the perspective of a single parent-child relationship. Parents and children are considered to engage simultaneously in multiple relationships throughout life. The relationship quality and history and, therefore, the strength of the various directions of influence would differ if the relationship with the other parent, a sibling, or someone outside the family was being considered.

Advances in theory on relationships suggest that social interactions and development need to be considered in the context of specific relationships (Dunn, 1993; Hartup, 1996; Hinde, 1979; Laursen & Collins, 1994; Miller & Steinberg, 1975). Earlier socialization theories tended to focus on parental strategies and child responses as if the parents and children were separate individuals reacting solely to the immediate contingencies of each other's behavior. The new developments in theory make it possible to consider that parent-child interactions are bounded by an enduring, close relationship in which both participants have an investment (Kuczynski & Lollis, in press).

The relationship context provides a framework for addressing distinctive motivational and bidirectional dynamics that pervade internalization processes in the family. Expectations based on the past history of the relationship, anticipations of the future relationship, and a sense of "ownness" or entitlement are among the factors that influence the dynamics of interactions within relationships. Two recent studies explored how control interactions between related parents and children are distinctive from interactions between unrelated women and children. Dawber and Kuczynski (1996) asked mothers how they would respond to the same transgression with their own child versus familiar and unfamiliar unrelated children. They found that mothers were more invested emotionally, had more long-term goals, used more effortful strategies, and idiosyncratic strategies with their own child than with unrelated children. In a parallel study (Hildebrandt & Kuczynski, 1996), 6- to 9-year-old children were asked about their ability to influence their own mother, their friend's mother, or an unfamiliar mother in various situations. Children reported that they expected their own mothers to be more susceptible to their influence strategies than unrelated women. Children's explanations of their power to influence their mothers revolved around the distinctive relationship context. In contrast to their strategies with unrelated mothers, children could base their approaches and expectations on an intimate knowledge of their mothers' personality, on knowledge of their mothers' reactions in similar situations in the past, and on various motivational resources stemming from the relationship.

Moreover, the parent-child relationship context is characterized by a mutual interdependence of needs and goals. Children depend on their parents for many needs including security and pleasure. Similarly, parents depend on their children for fulfilling needs for affiliation, generativity, and other gratifications (L. W. Hoffman, 1988). Parents are also sometimes passionately invested in specific long-term outcomes of socialization. Such relationship dynamics provide a basis for understanding the motivational issues underlying mutual receptivity, resistance, and negotiation during socialization. As discussed earlier, the relationship context also is crucial for understanding bidirectionality in socialization. Both the parent-to-child and the child-to-parent directions of influence are enhanced within close relationships.

Cognitive Processes

Internalization and externalization represent the individual's internal processing of values, beliefs, and other cultural products. Parents and children do not passively upload or download information from each other. Rather they act on their interactions and communications and interpret, select, forget, and reject ideas as they process or manifest the content of their working models. A distinction between internalization and externalization was originally proposed by Valsiner to describe the active and transformational nature of internalization (Lawrence & Valsiner, 1993; Valsiner, 1988). In Valsiner's conception, internalization refers to the cognitive processing that takes place as individuals assimilate experiences with the social environment into their knowledge structures. Externalization refers to the further processing that takes place as they manifest or act on what they know. "The latter relation takes the form of *externalization* of one's 'personal culture'—organization of one's environment and external appearance in ways that fit the person's internalized psychological 'needs.' The externalization of the person's (previously) internalized psychological processes reintroduces the products of internalization into the sphere of social transaction" (p. 288). Thus, cultural values and standards may undergo one process of transformation as they are internalized and another process of transformation as they are externalized.

Our conception of these cognitive processes (Figure 2.2) is somewhat broader than that of Valsiner in that it includes processes such as selecting, forgetting, and rejecting ideas in order to incorporate motivational dimensions as well as information processing within the constructs of internalization and externalization. Thus cognitive processing of cultural products transmitted during social interaction involves factors governing not only the accurate perception of cultural messages but also their acceptance (Grusec & Goodnow, 1994).

Parent-Child Interaction

Internalization does not just occur within the separate minds of parents and children. It also involves transactions in the external social environment. To affect children's behavior, parental cognitions must be mediated by their behavior during social interaction (see also Patterson, this volume). Similarly, children's cognitions must be mediated by children's social behaviors before they can have an impact on parents.

The context of social interaction should not be interpreted merely as an unequal arena where parents communicate their better understanding of the world to the children. Such has been the focus of traditional socialization research as well as Vygotskian perspectives that consider parents to be expert tutors who guide or scaffold their student apprentices in their mastery of culture (Rogoff, 1990). Parental attempts to communicate some of their greater knowledge to children provide an important aspect of socialization, especially early in children's development. However, the expert versus learner dynamic is not the only one involved in the socialization of values and it is progressively less important after middle childhood. Most beliefs, values, attitudes, and skills that parents might want to propagate are social and cultural constructions whose "truth" value is debatable. There can be many opinions about which values are appropriate at any point in time, including the opinions that children present as a result of their exposure to alternative working models. Moreover, as will be discussed subsequently, children sometimes argue from a position of greater expertise or higher moral ground than their parents. Thus, social interactions provide opportunities for both parents and children to take back important lessons into their working models.

The parent-child interaction literature will be summarized in terms of four broad categories of process: conflict, cooperation, mutual shaping, and observational learning. These categories highlight that many different processes in parent-child interactions: conscious and unconscious, cooperative and conflictual. It is not feasible to build a theory of socialization based on just one idea of social interaction.

Parent-child social interaction also provides an additional arena for the transformation of cultural ideas and values during socialization. Parents manifest their working models during socialization interactions with their children and children do likewise with their parents. This is where the beliefs, values, goals, and intentions that are the products of each person's internal processing meet the pragmatic constraints of interaction in the context of a close relationship. Children do not passively submit to parental wisdom, and parents may not be receptive to the alternative perspectives of values that children construct in their personal working models.

Prior to the 1980s, most of the literature on parent-child interaction focused on interactions involving *conflict,* with a particular emphasis on parental discipline and control of children's behavior (Maccoby & Martin, 1983; Schaffer, 1984). A prevalent assumption was that parent-child conflict provided a relatively unambiguous context for observing the parents' greater power to compel compliance and to exert a unidirectional influence on the child (Hoffman, 1975). Increasingly, however, conflict is being viewed as a bidirectional context for perspective taking (Shantz, 1987), mutual negotiation and compromise (Kuczynski & Kochanska, 1990), and the communication of acceptable intergenerational disagreement (Eisenberg, 1992; Goodnow, 1994). Thus, conflict is an important arena where parental demands and messages frequently are resisted, negotiated, and transformed.

There are also processes of *cooperation* where there is a mutual receptivity and harmonious merging of parent and child goals (Maccoby & Martin, 1983; Rheingold, Cook, & Kolowitz, 1987; Schaffer, 1984). In one view, children's dispositions to cooperate with parental requests may emerge from habits of mutual cooperation laid down early in the parent-child relationship (Maccoby & Martin, 1983; Parpal & Maccoby, 1985). From the standpoint of internalization theory, these cooperative processes are deeply bidirectional and do not merely identify a new technique for achieving children's compliance with parental wishes. Thus, children's cooperation and receptivity to parents' ideas may originate in parents' reciprocal cooperation and receptivity to the ideas of their children. Moreover, research on cooperative interactions involved in the teaching of language and cognitive tasks (Rogoff, 1990) characterizes the products of these interactions as mutual transformation or co-construction rather than the unaltered transmission of one person's ideas to another.

Another important process in parent-child interaction is *mutual shaping* (Patterson, Reid, & Dishion, 1992). In frequently occurring interactions, parents and children appear to react automatically to the immediate stimulus qualities of each other's behaviors. In so doing, parents and children gradually shape each other in ways that reflect their temperaments or socialized characteristics. This vein of research highlights automatic, unconscious, and nonoptimal processes in parent-child interaction. Research with at-risk populations (Bugental, 1992; Patterson, 1982; Vasta, 1982) suggests that parents may adopt coercive and emotionally reactive modes of interaction. In Patterson's (1982) coercive process model, family members use coercion as a form of immediate pain control rather than as thoughtful strategies to secure long-term goals. Automatic patterns of interaction have also been proposed to explain the everyday interactions of normal families. Bell's (Bell & Harper, 1977) control process model suggests that many family interactions operate according to the principle of a thermostat where each member acts to keep the other's behavior within a comfortable region of intensity. Although these models of interaction invoke relatively shortsighted goals, they do have long-term consequences. Over time, the feedback provided by children's reactions to parents and parents' reactions to children gradually and imperceptibly shapes the behavior of both partners in ways that are not forecast by the working models of either.

Early perspectives on *observational learning* emphasized the parent's modeling of appropriate behaviors as a route for the transmission of parental characteristics (Bandura, 1969). However, more recent socialization perspectives suggest that observational learning is not merely a process of children imitating parental models. Bandura's (1977) cognitive reformulation of observational learning placed greater emphasis on the child's active role in selecting, organizing and rehearsing, and enacting the modeled behavior. Contemporary studies emphasize children's active role in selecting whom and what to imitate from the ongoing stream of behavior of persons in the child's social environment (Kuczynski, Zahn-Waxler, & Radke-Yarrow, 1987; Perry & Bussey, 1979). It is also apparent that observational learning plays a role not only in transmission but also in the undermining and transformation of parental values during social interaction. For example, children may learn social skills, in part, by observing their parents' discipline and control practices (Kuczynski, Kochanska, et al., 1987). The possibility that children may attend to the parents' style of interacting and not only the content of their messages suggests that there may be a discrepancy between what the parents intend to transmit and the lessons that children learn from socialization interactions.

The processes of parent-child interaction have important implications for internalization because they provide a context for communicating and negotiating the externalized working models of the parent and the child. Moreover, it is in social transactions that parental goals and intentions may undergo another layer of transformation.

NEW RESEARCH DIRECTIONS

This section will use the paths illustrated in Figure 2.2 as a framework for exploring research literature on socialization and internalization. The review will consider the directions from parental externalization to child internalization, from child externalization to parental internalization and also connections between parent and child socialization with the context of other working models. It is acknowledged that it is particularly the traditional parent-to-child paths that have been substantially explored by research. However, the literature provides sufficient indications that the child-to-parent paths outlined in the model can also be profitably followed. These less explored paths will be emphasized in this review to highlight the new questions raised by a bidirectional perspective.

Parents' Externalization

Parental externalization highlights two kinds of activities relevant to socialization and internalization. These are processes concerned with parents manifesting their internalized working models in socialization interactions with their children and processes concerned with parents' processing of their own working models to make them more adaptive for their own well-being and for the well-being of their children. During the past decade, considerable research on parental cognition (Goodnow & Collins, 1990; Grusec, Rudy, & Martini, this volume; Sigel, McGillicuddy-DeLisi, & Goodnow, 1992) has explored the externalization processes involved in parental manifestation of their beliefs and values during social interaction. Here, we will outline some of the issues that arise from considering parental processing of their own working models of internalization.

The externalization process was neglected in the older socialization literature where the parent was depicted as an unquestioning conduit in the transmission process. There is evidence, however, that well-functioning parents do not merely download, without change, the contents of their working models into the working models of their children. Parents may actively confront and evaluate their attitudes and values. They interpret, forget, or reject aspects of their own socialized acquisitions and, essentially, choose which of their own internalized products they will attempt to pass on.

The process of reworking the beliefs and values that individuals take into their own phase of parenting has been conceptualized in various ways. Much of the field of psychotherapy is based on the premise that clients attempt to revise the working models of internalization constructed during their childhood socialization. As noted earlier, individuals may consciously reauthor their lives in daily interactions and experiences (Epston et al., 1992) as a way of breaking with older maladaptive narratives. Psychoanalytic theory suggests that parents who were neglected or abused as children may form pathological identifications with their parents and be at risk for similarly mistreating their own children. However, reworking the parental image by such processes as remembering and reexamining their own childhood experiences may enable individuals to avoid repeating negative interactions in their own parenting (Fraiberg, Adelson, & Shapiro, 1975). Alternatively, attachment theory suggests that parenting behaviors and attitudes concerning relationship are represented in working models of the self and of the parent in interaction (Bowlby, 1980). However, to remain adaptive and accurate, such working models of attachment figures must be periodically revised or updated (Main, Kaplan, & Cassidy, 1985).

An exploratory study by Chornesky (1991) suggests that a process of reworking the parental image may alter the influence of earlier working models of relationships. A nonclinical sample of fathers completed the Parental Awareness Interview (Newberger, 1977) that measured the parents' maturity of understanding of the child as a unique individual interacting with a complex changing environment. Men who had secure and "reworked secure" relationships with their fathers had higher levels of parental awareness than sons who had enmeshed or avoidant relationships with their fathers.

The parents' need to construct new knowledge and values is especially evident during the transition to parenthood. New parents reflect on their own experiences as children and may reconstitute or reject the values they experienced. Research using an adult attachment interview (Bretherton, Biringen, & Ridgeway, 1991) found that many mothers rejected aspects of their own child-rearing history and endeavored to rear their children according to methods and values different from the ones favored by their own parents. Other research indicated that parents of young children did not want to replicate the sex education they had received and were concerned about developing better ways to communicate with their children about sexuality (Geasler, Dannison, & Edlund, 1995).

Parents also consider the working models prevailing in the surrounding culture during externalization. Youniss (1994) suggested that parents are sensitive to the society around them and attempt to support their children's future social adaptation. Parents appear to be strategic in their adoption of rearing practices, striving to retain certain desirable values while rejecting or reevaluating others. As an example, Youniss cited research on parents who immigrated from one culture to another. Immigrant parents alter some behaviors to help their children adapt to social, economic, and educational context of the host society while retaining practices that balance the extent to which they want their children to retain their ethnic identity. Immigrant parents encourage their children to identify with the ethnic group to varying degrees by maintaining or discarding religious, cultural, and language practices. Similarly, Cooper (1994) found that immigrant parents change their behaviors in certain domains as they attempt to assist their children in adapting to the host society. Some Mexican American parents have aspirations for their children to attain a higher occupational status than themselves. The parents report using themselves as negative examples, rejecting their own vocations, to promote their child's interest in achievement at school. Alternatively, these parents perceive themselves as positive role models in issues of personal maturity and moral values such as respect for others.

The externalization process suggests that parents may evaluate and confront the adequacy of their own working models with reference to their adaptiveness in their own lives, the future of their children, and their fit with the surrounding culture. As a result, they may decide to promote values similar to those residing in their own working models. Sometimes, however, the decision will be to pass on values different from their own. Thus, the internalized goals and values of parents may be transformed before they even begin to attempt to influence their children in the sphere of social interaction.

Child Internalization

The process of child internalization refers to children's internal activities as they interpret, select, forget, reject, and otherwise assimilate the messages that manage to be communicated during social interaction. Grusec and Goodnow (1994) described a model of internalization that emphasizes the active nature of the child in interpreting, evaluating, and accepting or rejecting not only the parental message but also the appropriateness with which it was communicated. These investigators viewed internalization from the perspective of parents trying to communicate their values to their children; however, the listing of hurdles faced by parents also does an excellent job of illustrating how their communications become transformed during internalization. Despite the parents' best efforts, their message may once again be changed as children assimilate into their own knowledge and motivational structures the compromised and negotiated remnant of the parents' intentions.

Child Externalization

A comprehensive bidirectional model must also fully consider the child-to-parent direction of socialization. Children, like parents, have active processes of externalization where they confront their parent-fostered values with alternate viewpoints offered by peers, media, schools, and their own self-examination. As with parent externalization, two aspects of child externalization will be examined: children's reworking of their own working models, and children's manifestation of their working models in interactions with parents.

The reworking of children's working models has been described within various developmental theories. Psychoanalytic theory suggests that parental images, or internal working models are reworked at different stages of development. For example, Blos (1982) suggests that the preoedipal child idealizes the father, developing an infantile ego ideal that is relinquished in adolescence when the individual emotionally disengages from the father. Three paths of development can occur at that time: achievement of a balanced and realistic appraisal of the father, a defensive idealization of the father, and a defensive devaluation and rejection of the father. Cognitive developmental perspectives provide an alternate approach to understanding children's reworking of their own working models. Piaget (1932/1965) argued that a child moves from moral heteronomy, a blind obedience to rules imposed by adults, to moral autonomy, which is the consideration of rules as human devices constructed by equals for the sake of cooperation. With increasing experience of egalitarian peer relations, children learn that others have different viewpoints and that rules are relative to situations. These changes in working models during development suggest that the young child's values constructed in interactions with parents are altered when the values of other working models, such as peers, become salient dimensions of their social context.

Children's updating of their working models in the light of new experiences suggests that children may frequently need to reconcile or otherwise deal with conflicting sources of cultural information. The child's own working model is challenged by the parents' demands and assertions in everyday interactions. An important part of the externalization process concerns the choices that children make in resolving such confrontations between working models. Children must decide whether to accept or to challenge their parents' interpretations of situations. Such decisions may be associated with children's perceptions of the domains over which parents have authority. Smetana (Smetana & Asquith, 1994) reports that parental authority over children changes over time and across issues. For example, parents and their adolescents agree that parents have the authority to regulate moral, social conventional, and safety issues. However, with increasing age, adolescents question their parents' authority over personal issues such as regulation of activities and hairstyles. Although parents believe that adolescents should gradually gain authority over their own lives, adolescents believe they should have more authority than parents grant them.

Children may also decide to change or resocialize their parents in the light of their own values and knowledge. This dimension of the parent-child relationship is greatly in need of exploration. It is likely that children's early efforts to change their parents' minds may be shortsighted and related to their own needs. However, as parents of young children may attest, not all of children's demands are self-serving or instrumental. Schoolchildren bring into the home strong messages about long-term values as understood from their interpretations of the curriculum. For example, a child now in the school system might bring home values concerning alcohol and drug abuse, gender issues, tolerance for diversity, and care for the environment. Parents may sometimes be confronted by their children as well as exasperated with the inflexible moral authority with which children express their views.

There is evidence that adolescents take a deliberate role both as active interpreters of the peer culture and in confronting the values and beliefs of their parents. In one study (Baranowski, 1978), adolescents reported that they attempted to influence their parent's behavior in such domains as leisure activities (hobbies, sports, TV viewing, vacation sites), product purchases (house, car, appliances, personal use items), household routines (decorating, energy conservation habits, food), and personal and social life (appearance, friends, attitudes toward minorities, occupation). Mothers were more often the target of these socialization attempts than were fathers. However, adolescents said they did not try to change parents' religious and political beliefs.

Another choice children make in the externalization process is the pragmatic step of hiding their true beliefs and giving up attempts to influence their parents' development. Adolescents may increasingly engage in such withdrawal from the influence process when they are faced by evidence of inflexibility and general untrainability of their parents. Children may also decide to thwart unwelcome parental incursions into their own perspectives by refusing to cooperate with parental monitoring of their beliefs, thoughts, and behaviors. Adolescents sometimes don't tell parents the identity of their same- or opposite-sex friends, thus preventing parents from becoming overly involved in their personal lives (Feiring & Lewis, 1993).

In addition to hiding their views from parents, children select the source of input on certain issues. The source of information may or may not be the parent. Adolescents recognize that parents possess a historical perspective on events and a lived sense of outcomes. Parents are sought for input about job and career decisions, academic concerns, religious and political values and beliefs, and for deeper nurturance (Hunter, 1984; Youniss & Smollar, 1985). Alternatively, adolescents turn to peers for discussion of important immediate concerns such as dating, opposite-sex relationships, and advice on sexuality. Rawlings (1989) states what many parents of adolescents already know: that when it comes to current social issues such as dating and sex, adolescents often do not appreciate or desire " . . . the existential distance and measured perspective of their parents" (p. 144).

Like parents, children do not passively download their working models into the sphere of social interaction. In the process of externalization, children think about and evaluate what they have internalized and decide how to act on what they believe. In so doing, they further transform their working models.

Parents' Internalization

Parents too, have their own processes of internalization that operate throughout life and call for periodic reassessment of what they believe or value in the light of interacting with their children and their own changing environment. Theoretical treatments of changes in working models during adulthood have been considered under the rubric of adult resocialization (Daly, 1992). Thus after the primary socialization during childhood in the family context, individuals undergo secondary resocialization outside the family context. A bidirectional perspective suggests that children may play an important role as agents of their parents' resocialization.

Existing studies on children in the role of socializing agents suggest that children have a significant influence on the socialization and development of parents. Ambert's (1992) review of the child effects literature suggested 11 areas where children have important positive and negative impacts on their parents' lives: (a) parental health; (b) the physical location and social position that parents occupy in society, as well as the structure of their daily lives; (c) parental employment, especially that of the mother; (d) how much money they have at their disposal; (e) the quality of marital and family relations; (f) the parents' repertoire of interactional and emotional experiences; (g) the parents' participation in the community; (h) the parents' mood and personality; (i) the parents' attitudes, values and beliefs; (j) the parents' future life plans; (k) the parents' feelings of control over their own lives. Such a list indicates that children's influence on their parents' lives and circumstances is large and comprehensive.

The idea that parents may be influenced inadvertently by children may be socially acceptable. However, as suggested earlier, the notion that parents actually internalize long-term lessons from their children runs against the grain of cultural expectations. Therefore, in terms of the present model, it is useful to consider why parents might wish to "interpret" and "select" rather than "forget" and "reject" the messages emanating from their children.

One answer is that children provide a critical, changing, and inescapable environmental context for parental development. Frankel (1991) found opportunities for the psychological development of parents at every stage of their children's lives: transition to parenthood, infancy, childhood, adolescence, and adulthood. Early childhood provides regular crises and sacrifices, conflicts and dependence, the tasks of caregiving and nurturance, the induction into the world of play and toys. Each of these may disrupt the parents' established identity and challenge the parent to adapt to new roles and new patterns of living and thinking. During later stages of childhood and adolescence, additional opportunities for parents to examine their identity, beliefs, values, and sex role standards come regularly from the experience of guiding children through their own socialization experiences or from direct confrontations from their children. Finally, learning to separate from children and to accept their children's autonomy provides further hard lessons in the parents' individuation. Thus, child rearing provides decades of specific interactions and experiences that may not fit the working models that parents initially bring to the task. In adapting to the problems of child rearing, parents may undergo continual development in the content of their working models of internalization.

Another approach to understanding parental internalization considers the child's potential role in mediating parents' adaptation during rapid periods of social change. The case of immigrants adapting to a completely new culture is useful to illustrate the potential role of children in the periodic resocialization of their parents. Ambert (1992) suggested that the predicament of new immigrant parents in North America is especially interesting for the study of child effects on parents. Through schooling and immersion in the culture of the host country, children of immigrants become rapidly more proficient than parents in the language and the behavioral repertoires, values, and attitudes, and other skills needed for success. Thus, immigrant parents may be at a disadvantage in the socialization process and may have diminished ability to influence their children. Ambert speculated that, under these conditions, children are uniquely placed to have either a negative or a positive impact on the parents' adaptation to the new culture. In some cases, successful adaptation may consist in parents learning new ways of living and changing some of their previous attitudes and values by being receptive to the lessons their children have to offer.

Immigrant socialization also provides a useful metaphor for understanding parental adaptation to ongoing historical change during the parents' lifetime. Ongoing changes in society challenge adults to adapt as new situations arise and old definitions and strategies no longer apply. To some extent, parents will always find themselves in the role of intergenerational immigrants steeped in the values, customs, technology, music of their own generation but backward in the cultural practices and values of their children's generation. Not all parents succeed in this periodic resocialization. Many take advantage of the age-stratified nature of society and by isolating themselves in "generational ghettos" avoid adapting to change.

Although adults have many means at their disposal to keep abreast of changes, parents can use their interactions with their children to top up their cultural socialization. Some evidence of such a process comes from a study by Peters (1985) who interviewed parents of undergraduates to determine specific areas where parents thought they had been influenced by their children. Among these parents, 81% reported some attitudinal changes, 60% reported change in participation levels, and 56% reported behavioral changes. Adolescents had considerable influence in such areas as sports, personal care, and leisure activities and somewhat less in areas such as religion and politics. Moreover, parents reported that they were influenced to change their views toward youth in such areas as sexuality, tolerance toward minorities, and the handicapped.

Managing the Context of Other Working Models

Earlier in this chapter, the ecological context of working models was considered as having an important influence on the working models constructed by parents and children. In this section, the reverse direction of influence will be considered. The arrows from parents and children to other working models suggest that exchanges with the surrounding culture are bidirectional and that, in essence, individual parents and children can effect changes in society (Valsiner, 1988). Here, the focus will remain on socialization and the ways by which parents and children modify each others' experience of the ecological context of other working models.

Parents' Management of Other Working Models

Although parents' management of other perspectives has always been an important part of their role, there is little research on this aspect of parenting. Holden (1985) provided a framework for guiding initial explorations of such interactions with the concept of pro-active parenting. Proaction is a category of anticipatory and future-oriented strategies whereby parents attempt to prevent undesirable events from occurring. Some of Holden's examples of proactive strategies for very young children included attempts to manage the influence of other working models. Warning the child in advance, monitoring the child in dangerous settings, providing opportunities for desirable peer interactions, selecting good schools, and living in a good neighborhood are all examples of proactive management of other sources of influence. Research has also documented that parents may actively manage their children's peer relationships during early childhood by facilitating contacts, providing supervision, and coaching their children during interaction (Bhavnagri & Parke, 1991; Ladd, Profilet, & Hart, 1992; Lollis, Ross, & Tate, 1992).

In addition to providing generic good environments that minimally do not undermine parental influences, some parents actively manage the external environment so that it re-inforces their ideas. For example, as children's television has become increasingly violent, some parents have chosen to censor certain television shows. Similarly, parents may teach their children not to speak with strangers or have chosen to shrink the physical boundaries within which their children can play. A comprehensive form of management of the ecological context of working models has been used by members of traditional cultures, nations, and immigrant groups concerned with maintaining the purity of their heritage. To accomplish this, attempts are made to isolate entire communities from competing perspectives. Peters (1990) notes that Greeks and Arabs in Canada are predominantly endogamous, and a son or daughter who marries a non-Greek or non-Arab is considered "lost." Old Order Mennonite families have maintained their distinctive lifestyle by isolating their children from outside influences. However, Louv (1990) suggests that when used to an extreme degree this type of parental strategy can sometimes " . . . drive family life deeper into itself, reduces public trust, replaces real community with walls and gates, and isolates children" (p. 36).

Additionally, parents sometimes behave as on-site managers of outside influences. An example of this is the viewing of television. Most children watch television with their parents (Van Evra, 1990), although coviewing decreases across adolescence (Sang, Schmitz, & Tasche, 1993). Parent-child coviewing and discussion of television content supplies children with background information; helps children distinguish categories of programs (documentaries from fantasy); helps them decipher the difference between television content and reality; and teaches them to evaluate media information as good or bad, right or wrong (Austin, Roberts, & Nass, 1990; Messaris, 1986).

For parents interested in fostering specific values managing external social influences is becoming increasingly important as a socialization process. By means of such strategies as preventing access to or interpreting incompatible perspectives or exposing children to compatible perspectives parents may prevent, for a time, subversion of their own influences on their children's working models.

Children's Management of Other Working Models

Considering children's agency in socialization provides a counterforce to overly opti-mistic portrayals of proactive parenting. Despite parents' best efforts at anticipating and managing outside influences, children and adolescents determine how much management they will accept from their parents. For example, research on televison viewing (Buckingham, 1994) suggests that children are not passive either with regard to the messages that television has to offer or with parental attempts to mediate its effects. Children's reports indicate that they actively use television to make sense of their social lives, and actively negotiate with and often resist the messages that television makes available to them. Moreover, young children are knowledgeable about parental theories concerning television's potential harmful effects and, nevertheless, portray themselves as successfully evading parental attempts at regulation.

As a second example, it is consistently reported in the empirical literature that parents who are adept at monitoring the whereabouts and friends of their adolescents, have adolescents who are less involved in a variety of high-risk behaviors such as smoking and drug use. Although such studies imply that monitoring is a strategy that parents "do" to children, parental monitoring often requires children's active cooperation. A recent qualitative study of high-risk youth (Schell, 1996) found that adolescents are particularly adept at "counteranticipating" their parents' monitoring strategies by using proactive strategies that, in essence, managed the external context that was accessible to parents. During interviews, high-risk youth indicated that they routinely thwarted their parents' attempts to monitor their whereabouts. As one youth said, "My mom always hunts me down at my friends' house . . . she just pops in on me and my friends when I don't expect it, so I've learned to lie about where I'm going and to jump from house to house . . . we're like the hunter and the hunted" (female, age 14). The proactive and management techniques of parents occur in tandem with proactive management techniques of their children.

Children also have complex reciprocal interactions with the context of other working models that shape the content of values and messages that are expressed there. An example concerns the process by which children shape the products, services, and values provided by consumer-driven industries. Children are a major consumer force in North America, which has led to an advertising and marketing industry that is very responsive to children's values and preferences (Marney, 1993). Market researchers (Graham & Hamdan, 1989) study the changing consumer habits of children and youth because of their impact on the clothing, food, and music industries. Because children's spending power comes from personal earnings and from allowances, their influence on the economy is, in part, managed by parental control over allowances. However, children have been found to influence their parents' buying practices. Thus, multiple reciprocal interactions between children, parents, and industry determine in an important way the content of the working models that form the cultural context of their socialization.

CONCLUSION: EXPANDING THE IDEA OF SOCIALIZATION

The chapter began with a depiction of a "unidirectional model of parenting" that emphasized assumptions of parental causality, parental agency and power, and static transmission of characteristics from parents to children. Although such a model has never existed in a formal sense, one or more of its assumptions are implicit in traditional conceptions of socialization. The unidirectional model unnecessarily constrained research to questions having to do with children's conformity to parent-determined goals and intergenerational transmission of similarity. A comprehensive bidirectional perspective was presented that encompassed assumptions of bidirectional causality, parents and children as agents, a relational perspective on power asymmetry and an emphasis on socialization as a process.

Bidirectionality provides an enlarged perspective on the parental role in socialization by placing the traditional emphasis of intergenerational transmission of similarity in a bidirectional context. The model suggests that parents fulfill their responsibility as socializing agents in a context where children act as agents and have considerable resources—themselves—to influence their parents. Moreover, parental influence occurs in a larger ecological and cultural system with alternative values that often compete with parental goals. Presumably, parents who are concerned about "transmitting" some degree of similarity in values could do so more successfully by taking into account, rather than ignoring, the bidirectional reality of socialization. Recent models of parental behavior (Grusec & Goodnow, 1994) including many of the perspectives represented in this book, are beginning to consider how parents navigate their roles in a context where bidirectional influence and the agency of the child are givens. There is much to the art of designing disciplinary interventions that dispose an agentic child to be receptive to parental messages. Besides such direct influence strategies, other parental actions such as managing the parent-child relationship or managing the context of other working models are also highlighted by a bidirectional approach to socialization.

A bidirectional perspective also provides a positive framework for studying intergenerational change and transformation of values. In the unidirectional perspective, intergenerational differences tended to be regarded as a kind of "failure" of socialization (Rowe, 1994). In a bidirectional perspective, however, differences between parents and children or between two siblings in the same family are regarded as normative, to be expected, outcomes. Opportunities for transformation and change in values occur at every level of the parent-child socialization system: the internal constructive processes of the parent, the internal constructive processes of the child, their social interactions with each other and the reciprocal influences between the parent-child dyad and the ecological context of other working models. Moreover, parents may often condone intergenerational change or actively foster differences between their own socialization attainments and those of their children (Goodnow, 1994).

Another expansion in the idea of socialization comes from looking at the "big picture" of socialization from a bidirectional perspective. Looking at the bidirectional model as a whole (Figure 2.2), it is apparent that internalization is a continuing lifespan process not a static end point of development. The activity of the parent and the child, developmental change, social change are just a few of the dynamic features of socialization context that were neglected in unidirectional models. Bidirectionality suggests that parents struggle with the products of their own internalization even as they attempt to foster their children's socialization. Both parents and their children must recurrently update their working models of internalization in the light of their transactions with each other and with the changing context.

By encouraging researchers to examine assumptions that have long been taken for granted, bidirectionality provides a sometimes unsettling perspective on socialization in the family. However, in the process, important and challenging questions emerge. What is a successful outcome in socialization if not transmission? How do parents help children transcend their own preparation for social life? How do parents accomplish their roles as socialization agents in a bidirectional context?

REFERENCES

Adams, G. R., & Jones, R. M. (1983). Female adolescents' identity development: Age comparisons and perceived child-rearing experience. *Developmental Psychology, 19,* 249–256.

Alwin, D. (1988). From obedience to autonomy: Changes in traits desired in children, 1924–1978. *Public Opinion Quarterly, 52,* 33–52.

Alwin, D. (1990). Historical changes in parental orientations to children. *Sociological Studies of Child Development, 3,* 65–86.

Ambert, A. M. (1992). *The effect of children on parents.* New York: Haworth Press.

Anthony, E. J. (1982). Afterward. In S. Cath, A. Gurwitt, & J. M. Ross (Eds.), *Father and child: Developmental and clinical perspectives* (pp. 569–585). Boston: Little, Brown.

Austin, E. W., Roberts, D. F., & Nass, C. I. (1990). Influences of family communication on children's television-children's interpretation processes. *Communication Research, 17,* 545–564.

Bandura, A. (1969). A social-learning theory of identificatory processes. In D. A. Goslin (Ed.), *Handbook of socialization theory and research* (pp. 213–262). Chicago: Rand McNally.

Bandura, A. (1977). *Social learning theory.* Englewood Cliffs, NJ: Prentice-Hall.

Baranowski, M. D. (1978). Adolescent's attempted influence on parental behaviors. *Adolescence, 13,* 585–604.

Baumeister, R. F. (1991). *Meanings of life.* New York: Guilford Press.

Baumrind, D. (1971). Current patterns of parental authority. *Developmental Psychology Monographs, 4*(1, Pt. 2).

Bell, R. Q. (1968). A reinterpretation of the direction of effects in studies of socialization. *Psychological Review, 75,* 81–95.

Bell, R. Q., & Harper, L. V. (1977). *Child effects on adults.* New York: Erlbaum.

Bernard, J. (1972). *The future of marriage.* New York: World.

Bhavnagri, N., & Parke, R. D. (1991). Parents as direct facilitators of children's peer relationships: Effects of age of child and sex of parent. *Journal of Abnormal Child Psychology, 8,* 423–440.

Blos, P. (1982, December 17). *Son and father.* Plenary lecture presented at the meeting of the American Psychoanalytic Association, New York.

Bowlby, J. (1980). *Attachment and loss: Vol. 3. Loss, sadness and depression.* New York: Basic Books.

Bretherton, I., Biringen, Z., & Ridgeway, D. (1991). The parental side of attachment. In K. Pillemer & K. McCartney (Eds.), *Parent-child relations throughout life* (pp. 1–24). Hillsdale, NJ: Erlbaum.

Bronfenbrenner, U. (1989). Ecological systems theory. In R. Vasta (Ed.), *Annals of child development* (Vol. 6, pp. 185–246). Greenwich, CT: JAI Press.

Bruch, H. (1978). *The golden cage: The enigma of anorexia nervosa.* Cambridge, MA: Harvard University Press.

Buckingham, D. (1994). Television and the definition of childhood. In B. Mayall (Ed.), *Children's childhoods: Observed and experienced* (pp. 79–96). Washington, DC: Falmer Press.

Bugental, D. B. (1992). Affective and cognitive processes within threat-oriented family systems. In I. E. Sigel, A. V. McGillicuddy-DeLisi, & J. J. Goodnow (Eds.), *Parental belief systems: The psychological consequences for children* (pp. 219–248). Hillsdale, NJ: Erlbaum.

Chornesky, A. (1991). Ghosts in the nursery revisited. Paternal images, reworking experiences and parental awareness among fathers of latency-age children. *Smith College Studies in Social Work, 61,* 275–292.

Cooper, C. (1994). Cultural perspectives on continuity and change in adolescents' relationships. In R. Montemayor, G. R. Adams, & T. P. Gullotta (Eds.), *Advances in adolescent development: Personal relationships during adolescence* (Vol. 6, pp. 78–100). Thousand Oaks, CA: Sage.

Corsaro, W., & Eder, D. (1990). Children's peer cultures. *Annual Review of Sociology, 16,* 197–220.

Crockenberg, S., & Litman, C. (1990). Autonomy as competence in 2-year-olds: Maternal correlates of child defiance, compliance, and self-assertion. *Developmental Psychology, 26,* 961–971.

Daly, K. (1992). Toward a formal theory of interactive resocialization: The case of adoptive parenthood. *Qualitative Sociology, 15*(4), 395–417.

Dawber, T., & Kuczynski, L. (1996, August 13). *The question of "ownness": Parent-child interactions in the context of relationships.* Paper presented at the 14th Biennial International Society for the Study of Behavioral Development Conference, Quebec, Canada.

Dunn, J. (1993). *Young children's close relationships: Beyond attachment.* London: Sage.

Dunn, J., & Plomin, R. (1990). *Separate lives: Why siblings are so different.* New York: Basic Books.

Eisenberg, A. R. (1992). Conflicts between mothers and their young children. *Merrill-Palmer Quarterly, 38,* 21–44.

Eisenberg, N., Miller, P., Shell, R., McNalley, S., & Shea, C. (1991). Prosocial development in adolescence: A longitudinal study. *Developmental Psychology, 27,* 849–857.

Epston, D., White, M., & Murray, K. (1992). A proposal for a re-authoring therapy: Rose's revisioning of her life and a commentary. In S. McNamee & K. J. Gergen (Eds.), *Therapy as social construction* (pp. 96–115). Newbury Park, CA: Sage.

Feiring, C., & Lewis, M. (1993). Do mothers know their teenagers' friends? Implications for individuation in early adolescence. *Journal of Youth and Adolescence, 22,* 337–354.

Ferree, M. M. (1990). Beyond separate spheres: Feminism and family research. *Journal of Marriage in the Family, 52,* 866–884.

Fraiberg, S., Adelson, E., & Shapiro, B. (1975). Ghosts in the nursery: A psychoanalytic approach to the problems of impaired mother-infant relationships. *Journal of the American Academy of Child Psychiatry, 14,* 387–421.

Frankel, J. (1991). On being reared by your children: State of art as reflected in the literature. *Free Inquiry in Creative Sociology, 19,* 193–200.

Gaskins, S., Miller, P. J., & Corsaro, W. A. (1992). Theoretical and methodological perspectives in the interpretive study of children. In W. A. Corsaro & P. J. Miller (Eds.), *Interpretive approaches to children's socialization* (pp. 5–23). San Francisco: Jossey-Bass.

Geasler, M. L., Dannison, L. L., & Edlund, C. J. (1995). Sexuality education of young children: Parental concerns. *Family Relations, 44,* 184–188.

Gergen, K. J. (1991). *The saturated self: Dilemmas of identity in contemporary life.* New York: Basic Books.

Glass, J., Bengston, V. L., & Dunham, C. C. (1986). Attitude similarity in three generational families: Socialization, status inheritance or reciprocal influence? *American Sociological Review, 51,* 685–698.

Goodnow, J. J. (1994). Acceptable disagreement across generations. *New Directions for Child Development, 66,* 51–63.

Goodnow, J. J., & Collins, W. A. (1990). *Development according to parents: The nature, sources, and consequences of parents' ideas.* Hillside, NJ: Erlbaum.

Graham, L., & Hamdan, L. (1989). *Youthtrends: Capturing the $200 billion youth market.* Toronto, Ontario: McClelland and Stewart.

Grotevant, H. D., & Cooper, C. H. (1985). Patterns of interaction in family relationships and the development of identity exploration in adolescents. *Child Development, 56,* 415–428.

Grusec, J. E., & Goodnow, J. J. (1994). Impact of parental discipline methods on the child's internalization of values: A reconceptualization of current points of view. *Developmental Psychology, 30,* 4–19.

Grusec, J. E., Rudy, D., & Martini, T. (this volume). Parenting cognitions and child outcomes: An overview and implications for children's internalization of values. In J. E. Grusec & L. Kuczynski (Eds.), *Parenting and children's internalization of values: A handbook of contemporary theory.* New York: Wiley.

Harris, J. R. (1995). Where is the child's environment? A group socialization theory of development. *Psychological Review, 102,* 458–489.

Hartup, W. L. (1996). The company they keep: Friendships and their development significance. *Child Development, 67,* 1–13.

Hildebrandt, N., & Kuczynski, L. (1996). *Children's views of their own influence in the parent-child and other adult-child relationships.* Unpublished manuscript, University of Guelph, Department of Psychology.

Hinde, R. A. (1979). *Towards understanding relationships.* New York: Academic Press.

Hoffman, L. W. (1988). Cross-cultural differences in child-rearing goals. In R. A. LeVine, P. M. Miller, & M. M. West (Eds.), *Parental behavior in diverse societies* (pp. 99–122). San Francisco: Jossey-Bass.

Hoffman, L. W. (1991). The influence of the family environment on personality: Accounting for sibling differences. *Psychological Bulletin, 110,* 187–203.

Hoffman, M. L. (1970). Moral development. In P. H. Mussen (Ed.), *Carmichael's manual of child psychology* (Vol. 2, pp. 261–360). New York: Wiley.

Hoffman, M. L. (1975). Moral internalization, parental power, and the nature of parent-child interaction. *Developmental Psychology, 11,* 228–239.

Holden, G. W. (1985). How parents create a social environment via proactive behavior. In T. Garling & J. Valsiner (Eds.), *Children within environments* (pp. 193–215). New York: Plenum Press.

Hunter, F. T. (1984). Socializing procedures in parent-child and friendship relations during adolescence. *Developmental Psychology, 20,* 1092–1099.

Inkeles, A. (1955). Social change and social character: The role of parental mediation. *Journal of Social Issues, 11,* 12–23.

Kochanska, G., & Kuczynski, L. (1991). Maternal autonomy granting: Predictors of normal and depressed mothers' compliance with the requests of 5-year-olds. *Child Development, 62,* 1449–1459.

Kohn, M. L. (1983). On the transmission of values in the family: A preliminary reformulation. *Research in Sociology of Education and Socialization, 4,* 1–12.

Kuczynski, L. (1997, April 4). *Power asymmetry revisited: Power in the context of relationships.* Paper presented at the biennial meeting of the Society for Research in Child Development, Washington, DC.

Kuczynski, L., & Kochanska, G. (1990). The development of children's noncompliance strategies from toddlerhood to age 5. *Developmental Psychology, 26,* 398–408.

Kuczynski, L., Kochanska, G., Radke-Yarrow, M., & Girnius-Brown, O. (1987). A developmental interpretation of young children's noncompliance. *Developmental Psychology, 23,* 799–806.

Kuczynski, L., & Lollis, S. (in press). *Parenting process.* New York: Guilford Press.

Kuczynski, L., Zahn-Waxler, C., & Radke-Yarrow, M. (1987). Development and content of imitation in the second and third year of life: A socialization perspective. *Developmental Psychology, 23,* 276–282.

Ladd, G. W., Profilet, S. M., & Hart, C. H. (1992). Parents' management of children's peer relations: Facilitating and supervising children's activities in the peer culture. In R. D. Parke & G. W. Ladd (Eds.), *Family-peer relationships, modes of linkage* (pp. 215–253). Hillsdale, NJ: Erlbaum.

Laursen, B. (1993). Conflict management among close friends. In B. Laursen (Ed.), *Close friendships in adolescence: New directions for child development* (pp. 39–54). San Francisco: Jossey-Bass.

Laursen, B., & Collins, W. A. (1994). Interpersonal conflict during adolescence. *Psychological Bulletin, 115,* 197–209.

Lawrence, J., & Valsiner, J. (1993). Conceptual roots of internalization: From transmission to transformation. *Human Development, 36,* 150–167.

Leonard, R. (1993). Mother-child disputes as arenas for fostering negotiation skills. *Early Development and Parenting, 2,* 157–167.

Lewis, M. (1990). Models of developmental psychology. In M. Lewis & S. Miller (Eds.), *Handbook of developmental psychopathology* (pp. 15–28). New York: Plenum Press.

Lewis, M., & Feinman, S. (Eds.). (1992). *Social influences and socialization in infancy.* New York: Plenum Press.

Lewis, M., & Painter, L. (1974). An interactional approach to the mother-infant dyad. In M. Lewis & L. A. Rosenblum (Eds.), *The effect of the infant on its caregiver.* New York: Wiley.

Lollis, S. P., Ross, H. S., & Tate, E. (1992). Parents' regulation of their children's peer interaction: Direct influences. In R. D. Parke & G. W. Ladd (Eds.), *Family-peer relationships: Modes of linkage.* Hillsdale, NJ: Erlbaum.

Lopata, H., & Thorne, B. (1978). On the term "sex roles." *Signs, 3,* 718–721.

Louv, R. (1990). *Childhood's future.* Boston: Houghton Mifflin.

Lytton, H. (1990). Child and parent effects in boys' conduct disorder: A reinterpretation. *Developmental Psychology, 26,* 683–697.

Maccoby, E. E. (1992). The role of parents in the socialization of children: An historical overview. *Developmental Psychology, 28,* 1006–1017.

Maccoby, E. E., & Martin, J. A. (1983). Socialization in the context of the family: Parent-child interaction. In E. M. Hetherington (Ed.), *Handbook of child psychology: Socialization, personality and social development* (Vol. 4, pp. 1–101). New York: Wiley.

Main, M., Kaplan, N., & Cassidy, J. (1985). Security in infancy, childhood and adulthood: A move to the level of representation. In I. Bretherton & E. Waters (Eds.), *Growing points in attachment* (Monographs of the Society for Research in Child Development, 50(1/2, Serial No. 209), 66–106). Chicago: University of Chicago Press.

Marcia, J. E. (1966). Development and validation of ego-identity status. *Journal of Personality and Social Psychology, 3,* 551–558.

Marcia, J. E. (1994). The empirical study of ego identity. In H. A. Bosma, T. L. G. Graafsma, H. D. Grotevant, & D. J. deLevita (Eds.), *Identity and development: An interdisciplinary approach* (pp. 67–80). Thousand Oaks, CA: Sage.

Marney, J. (1993). Youthful shoppers can be savvy and skeptical. *Marketing, 98,* 26.

Mayall, B. (1994). Children in action at home and school. In B. Mayall (Ed.), *Children's childhoods: Observed and experienced.* Washington, DC: Falmer Press.

McLaughlin, E., Karp, S., & Herzog, D. (1985). Sense of ineffectiveness in women with eating disorders: A clinical study of anorexia nervosa and bulimia. *International Journal of Eating Disorders, 4,* 511–523.

Messaris, P. (1986). Parents, children, and television. In G. Gumpert & R. Cathcart (Eds.), *Inter/media. Interpersonal communication in a media world* (3rd ed., pp. 519–536). New York: Oxford University Press.

Miller, G. R., & Steinberg, M. (1975). *Between people: A new analysis of interpersonal communication.* Chicago: Science Research Associates.

Newberger, C. M. (1980). The cognitive structure of parenthood: Designing a descriptive measure. *New Directions for Child Development, 7,* 45–67.

Parpal, M., & Maccoby, E. E. (1985). Maternal responsiveness and subsequent child compliance. *Child Development, 56,* 1326–1334.

Patterson, G. (1982). *Coercive family process.* Eugene, OR: Castalia Press.

Patterson, G. (this volume). Performance models for parenting: A social interactional perspective. In J. E. Grusec & L. Kuczynski (Eds.), *Parenting and children's internalization of values: A handbook of contemporary theory.* New York: Wiley.

Patterson, G., Reid, J., & Dishion, T. (1992). *Antisocial boys: Vol. 4. A social interactional approach.* Eugene: Oregon Social Learning Center.

Perry, D. G., & Bussey, K. (1979). The social learning theory of sex differences: Imitation is alive and well. *Journal of Personality and Social Psychology, 37,* 1699–1712.

Peters, J. (1985). Adolescents as socialization agents to parents. *Adolescence, 20,* 921–931.

Peters, J. (1990). Cultural variations: Past and present. In M. Baker (Ed.), *Families: Changing trends in Canada* (2nd ed., pp. 166–191). Toronto, Ontario: McGraw-Hill Ryerson.

Piaget, J. (1965). *The moral judgment of the child* (M. Gabain, Trans.). New York: Free Press. (Original work published 1932)

Plomin, R., & Daniels, D. (1987). Why are children in the same family so different from one another? *Behavioral and Brain Sciences, 10,* 1–22.

Rawlings, W. (1989). Rehearsing the margins of adulthood: The communicative management of adolescent friendship. In J. F. Neussbaum (Ed.), *Lifespan communication: Normative processes* (pp. 223–259). Hillsdale, NJ: Erlbaum.

Rheingold, H. L., Cook, K. V., & Kolowitz, V. (1987). Commands activate the behavior and pleasure of 2-year-old children. *Developmental Psychology, 23,* 146–151.

Rogoff, B. (1990). *Apprenticeship in thinking.* New York: Oxford University Press.

Rotenberg, K., & Mann, L. (1986). The development of the norm of the reciprocity of self-disclosure and its function in children's attraction to peers. *Child Development, 57,* 1349–1357.

Rowe, D. (1994). *The limits of family influence: Genes, experience, and behavior.* New York: Guilford Press.

Russell, A., & Russell, G. (1988). Mothers' & fathers' explanations of observed interactions with their children. *Journal of Developmental Psychology, 9,* 421–440.

Sameroff, A. (1975). Transactional models of early social relations. *Human Development, 18,* 65–79.

Sang, F., Schmitz, B., & Tasche, K. (1993). Developmental trends in television coviewing of parent-child dyads. *Journal of Youth and Adolescence, 22,* 531–542.

Scarr, S. (1993). Biological and cultural diversity: The legacy of Darwin for development. *Child Development, 64,* 1333–1353.

Schaffer, H. R. (1984). *The child's entry into a social world.* Orlando, FL: Academic Press.

Schell, K. (1996). *Family peer linkages: Adolescence and high risk behavior.* Unpublished doctoral dissertation, University of Guelph.

Seltzer, V. (1982). *Adolescence social development: Dynamic functional interaction.* Lexington, MA: Heath.

Shantz, C. (1987). Conflicts between children. *Child Development, 50,* 283–305.

Sigel, I. E., McGillicuddy-DeLisi, A. V., & Goodnow, J. J. (1992). *Parental belief systems: The psychological consequences for children.* Hillsdale, NJ: Erlbaum.

Siegel, M., & Barclay, M. S. (1985). Children's evaluation of fathers' socialization behavior. *Developmental Psychology, 21,* 1090–1096.

Siegel, M., & Cohen, J. (1984). Appraisals of intervention: The mother's versus the culprit's behavior as determinants of children's evaluation of discipline techniques. *Child Development, 55,* 1760–1766.

Skolnick, A. S. (1988). Socialization: Generational politics. In *The intimate environment: Exploring marriage and the family* (pp. 363–392). Boston: Little, Brown.

Smetana, J. G., & Asquith, P. (1994). Adolescents' and parents' conceptions of parental authority and personal autonomy. *Child Development, 65,* 1147–1162.

Stone, E. (1988). *Black sheep and kissing cousins. How our family stories shape us.* London: Penguin Books.

Strauss, C. (1992). Models and motives. In R. G. D'Andrade & C. Strauss (Eds.), *Human motives and cultural models* (pp. 1–20). New York: Cambridge University Press.

Tesson, G. (1987). Socialization and parenting. In K. L. Anderson (Ed.), *Family matters* (pp. 87–111). Agincourt, Ontario: Methuen.

Valsiner, J. (1988). Ontogeny of co-construction of culture within socially organized environmental settings. In J. Valsiner (Ed.), *Child development within culturally structured environments: Vol. 2. Social co-construction and environmental guidance in development* (pp. 283–297). Norwood, NJ: ABLEX.

Van Evra, J. (1990). *Television and child development.* Hillsdale, NJ: Erlbaum.

Vasta, R. (1982). Physical child abuse: A dual-component analysis. *Developmental Review, 2,* 125–149.

Wenar, C. (1982). On negativism. *Human Development, 25,* 1–23.

Wrong, D. H. (1961). The oversocialized conception of man in modern sociology. *American Sociological Review, 26,* 183–193.

Youniss, J. (1994). Rearing children for society. In J. G. Smetana (Ed.), *Beliefs about parenting: Origins and developmental implications* (pp. 37–50). San Francisco: Jossey-Bass.

Youniss, J., & Smollar, J. (1985). *Adolescent relations with mothers, fathers, and friends.* Chicago: University of Chicago Press.

PART II

Developmental Context of Parenting Strategies and Value Internalization

CHAPTER 3

The Emergence and Development of Conscience in Toddlerhood and Early Childhood

GRAZYNA KOCHANSKA and ROSS A. THOMPSON

To function successfully in society, children must be inducted into the social system of rules, values, norms, and standards of conduct. They must develop internal regulators of behavior—psychological mechanisms that can reliably guide their actions not only when they are supervised and externally controlled, but also when they are on their own, without surveillance and not immediately accountable to any authority. Because of its critical importance for the individual and for the society, the development of conscience has been long recognized as one of the main objectives of socialization. The development of conscience interests and challenges researchers because conscience is at the very nexus of multiple developing systems, such as affect, cognition, motivation, the emerging self, self-regulation, temperament, and the organization of conduct, with each contributing to its emergence.

In this chapter, the origins of conscience in the toddler and early childhood years will be considered. Reflecting renewed research interest in the sociomoral development of young children, we discuss the many catalysts to moral internalization of this period that guide how values are adopted by the young child. We also consider the factors that account for individual differences in conscience development, including temperamental individuality and features of the relationship shared by parent and child. We argue that any thorough consideration of moral internalization must begin with the toddler and early childhood period, and offer suggestions for new research directions in early sociomoral development.

We begin by defining conscience, and outline the multiple developmental systems involved in the emerging internalization of conduct rules by young children. We then discuss the core contributors to conscience development starting with basic developmental processes such as the growth of self-understanding; social referencing; emergent skills in cognition, memory, and representation; sensitivity to standards; and temperament. Next, we focus on the role of relational processes by considering the importance of a secure attachment, a mutually responsive parent-child orientation, the influence of parent-child discourse, and parental control and discipline practices. We then explore the developmental interactions between the qualities of the child and parental socialization. The chapter ends with suggestions for several directions for future research.

Grazyna Kochanska was supported by the grants from the National Science Foundation (DBS-9209559 and SBR-9510863), from the National Institute of Mental Health (KO2 MH01446-01), and the University of Iowa Faculty Scholar Award.

DEFINING CONSCIENCE

Conscience is a broad concept that refers to the development, maintenance, and application of generalizable, internal standards of conduct for one's behavior. Developmental scholars have long recognized the complexity and the multifaceted quality of this system of internal regulation of conduct. In our view, conscience organizes four components that are essential to moral self-regulation but also contribute to other behavioral processes: emotion (particularly the moral emotions associated with compliance and misbehavior), self-control capacities, motivational processes (that assist in the internalization of values), and cognitive facets of the awareness and understanding of behavioral standards. Each of these components not only highlights the early beginnings of conscience development, but also its links to other aspects of psychosocial growth.

The emotional processes most relevant to early conscience development include the emotions associated with the consequences of one's conduct, such as anxiety, guilt, remorse, and discomfort triggered by actual or contemplated wrongdoing, and pride from acting in accord with one's standards (Kochanska, DeVet, Goldman, Murray, & Putnam, 1994). Young children also show emotional responses to others' wrongdoing (and, more generally, to standard violations) that include upset, interest, and amusement (Dunn, 1988; Kagan, 1981; Lamb, 1993). Included within this domain of moral emotions are also young children's affective responses to others' misfortune that may have empathic as well as egoistic bases (Eisenberg, 1992; Radke-Yarrow, Zahn-Waxler, & Chapman, 1983; Zahn-Waxler, Radke-Yarrow, Wagner, & Chapman, 1992). Each of these emotional underpinnings of conscience begins to emerge during the second year.

The behavioral self-control processes—the emerging capacity to suppress prohibited acts and sustain socially desirable acts without surveillance or immediate external control—constitute the "executive" component of conscience that encompasses emerging self-regulation and the capacity to carry out a caregiver's early "dos" and "don'ts." As Kopp (1982, 1987; Kopp & Wyer, 1994) has pointed out, the growth of behavioral self-control and self-regulation is itself a painstaking developmental process in the early years, entailing the development of self-awareness as an autonomous, agentic individual, a capacity for self-initiated modifications of behavior resulting from remembered parental guidelines, and the ability continuously to monitor one's behavior according to these guidelines in diverse circumstances. Not surprisingly, the capacity for competent self-control is, according to Kopp, an achievement of the third year of life, with self-regulatory capacities emerging somewhat later.

The motivational component of conscience refers to young children's relatively enduring stance toward the caregiver's values and standards, or their receptiveness to socialization (Maccoby, 1984). Some children are generally oriented positively and eagerly toward their caregivers' socialization agenda: they wish to accept, embrace, and endorse caregivers' values. Other children, however, early tend to reject or are reluctant to accept those values. This difference in a core component of conscience may be associated with the security of the attachment relationship formed between parent and child in infancy, as well as continuing influences of parenting practices as children mature; it may also involve differences in children's temperamental profiles.

Finally, cognitive processes encompass young children's awareness, understanding, and sensitivity to standards. Developmental researchers are realizing that this is far more than the internalization of parental values as it has been traditionally conceived, and requires consideration of how young children progressively assimilate and construct moral values in relation to their understanding of self, others, and of causality, as well as their capacities to remember and represent behavioral standards in the context of other life experiences. The manner in which children acquire and adopt standards of conduct also extends far beyond the discipline encounter, and it reflects the various ways that parents use to help offspring to reconstruct, remember, and interpret the daily experiences that contribute to event representation, prototypical knowledge (including knowledge of behavioral norms), and autobiographical memory of personally meaningful experiences of misbehavior as well as of compliance. Taken together, the cognitive constituents of conscience are part of a much broader process of appropriating understanding through observation, conversation, and diverse other kinds of shared experiences with family members (cf. Rogoff, 1990), rather than merely internalizing values as they are learned from discipline encounters with parents. There is evidence that this process is also inaugurated in the second and third years of life.

Not only do all these processes begin to emerge in the first three years of life, but they also predict different developmental trajectories in conscience development and its later outcomes. Thus, early childhood is a critical developmental context for future moral development.

THE IMPORTANCE OF TODDLERHOOD AND EARLY CHILDHOOD

The past 10 to 15 years have been an exciting time in the history of research on conscience. Several noteworthy shifts in conceptual and empirical approaches to early morality have influenced contemporary views of conscience development.

First, after many years in which moral development research focused largely on the judgment and reasoning processes of older children, researchers now share the view that conscience emerges surprisingly early—in fact, toddlerhood and early childhood are now seen as the critical context for moral development. In many respects, renewed attention to the growth of conscience in early childhood revisits the concerns of many developmentalists in the post-World War II era when, inspired by psychoanalytic theory, researchers explored the child-rearing influences on young children's guilt, self-control, identification, and morality (e.g., Radke-Yarrow, Campbell, & Burton, 1968; Sears, Maccoby, & Levin, 1957; Sears, Rau, & Alpert, 1965). Other researchers of that era, applying instead learning principles, explored conscience as the outgrowth of anxiety-based conditioning processes (e.g., Aronfreed, 1968; Parke, 1974). In each case, the influence of parent-child interaction on conscience development in the preschool years was the focus. With the discovery of Piaget's theory in subsequent years and its applications to moral judgment by Kohlberg (1969) and others (see also Piaget, 1932), however, attention shifted to cognitive aspects of morality in older children because of the presumed egocentrism of preschoolers and the conclusion that they were essentially amoral, complying to avoid punishment and obtain rewards rather than because of genuinely moral or humanistic considerations.

The contemporary return of scholarly interest to early conscience revisits earlier theoretical concerns about the influence of parent-child relationships on early morality, therefore, but within a broader and more complex conceptual landscape. For example, attachment theory now provides potentially valuable insights into the motivational bases of early moral compliance, and advances in temperamental theory highlight the importance of a young child's behavioral individuality for the internalization of values. Recent research on early parent-child interaction reveals the multifaceted ways that children acquire knowledge of morality and emotion both within and outside the discipline encounter. Additional contemporary insights derive from allied research fields, such as new perspectives on the growth of young children's psychological understanding of others (known currently as "theory of mind") and their representations of self and others, which show that preschoolers are decidedly nonegocentric in many features of social cognition that inform early conscience. Altogether, it now appears that many emergent capabilities of the second and third years of life—including an early appreciation of standards, a rapidly developing network of self-conscious emotions, the growth of self-understanding, and emerging restraint and self-control—fuel early moral development.

Second, accompanying a return of scholarly interest to early childhood is renewed attention to the affective, motivational, and self-regulatory facets of conscience development. By contrast with the predominant emphasis on cognitive features of moral judgment in research with older children, students of early childhood have revealed how closely conscience development is tied to affective processes in self (e.g., salient experiences of pride, shame, and guilt) or another (signaling approval or disapproval of the child's actions or intentions). Moreover, as young children strive to manage their self-care, emotion regulation, and peer sociability, self-regulation of compliance, like rules of conduct, is also a salient concern. Consequently, the toddler and preschool years are an important arena for studying conscience development because it highlights central components of moral growth prior to the emergence of sophisticated moral cognition. Furthermore, a contemporary focus on the affective and motivational features of conscience has also drawn attention to individual differences in these characteristics, particularly with regard to temperamental individuality and its potentially important role in the development of internalized regulators of conduct.

Finally, renewed attention to early childhood has also caused researchers to revisit questions about the importance of close relationships to conscience development. Although most contemporary researchers do not draw explicitly on psychoanalytic formulations, the relational processes they examine—a secure attachment, a mutually responsive parent-child relationship, the quality of parent-child discourse, as well as adult actions in the discipline encounter—are each consistent with the analytic legacy and, more importantly, point to the diverse relational experiences that contribute to conscience development. For many reasons, therefore, the toddler and early preschool years constitute a critically important period for the foundation of conscience and morality.

BASIC PROCESSES IN EARLY CONSCIENCE DEVELOPMENT

The emergence of conscience is based on multiple developing systems. Several early developmental processes associated with self-understanding, social referencing, memory, and the awareness of behavioral standards constitute the necessary antecedents of conscience, and temperamentally based individual differences contribute to variation in early internalization.

The Growth of Self-Understanding

The growth of self-awareness and self-understanding during the second year is necessary for conscience because it permits children to view the self as an object of evaluation and as a causal agent in activity that is appraised as right or wrong. Even infants experience themselves as causal agents, especially in the context of social and nonsocial contingency. It is not until the end of the second year, however, that young children acquire a sense of themselves as autonomous agents in a temporal context (Thompson, in press-a). When this occurs, they begin to associate past experiences with present circumstances and future outcomes and can, with guidance, evaluate past actions in the present moment (Nelson, 1993). As self-understanding continues to mature during the preschool years, young children begin to connect personal experiences to broader representations of their abilities, characteristics, and past experiences in constructing a sense of personal history, or autobiographical memory (Welch-Ross, 1995). Consequently, their sense of self becomes more deeply associated with the behaviors that evoke others' approval or disapproval (Stipek, Recchia, & McClintic, 1992). Thus in many respects, the growth of self-understanding and of conscience are mutually influential in early childhood as emerging new forms of self-awareness permit more competent self-regulation, and as experiences of moral socialization (and of compliance and disobedience) become integrated with the child's self-concept and autobiographical memory.

The growth of self-understanding has other significant implications for conscience development. An empathic capacity flourishes during the second year as young children begin to differentiate and associate external events, emotional expressions, and subjective experiences of emotion in themselves and others (Thompson, in press-b; Zahn-Waxler & Radke-Yarrow, 1990). Empathy provides a catalyst for conscience that is, in many ways, independent of compliance-based moral socialization (Hoffman, 1983). Moreover, some scholars (Lewis, Sullivan, Stanger, & Weiss, 1989) argue that self-awareness is also a necessary precondition for the growth of self-referent or "moral emotions" such as guilt, shame, and pride (although other emotion theorists do not hold this view, arguing instead that parental socialization of pride, guilt, and other self-referent emotions fosters the young child's self-awareness; see Barrett, 1995). Regardless, the second year also witnesses growing indications that young children experience guilt, shame, pride, embarrassment, and related self-referent emotions in appropriate circumstances, which may be associated with their greater capacities to appraise the self's actions in a more sophisticated fashion. As these self-referent emotions become enlisted into recurrent experiences of moral socialization by parents and other authorities, the child's motivation to comply becomes associated with the desire to regard the self with an affectively positive valence, which is one of the crucial components of moral internalization.

Social Referencing

Late in the first year of life, infants acquire a capacity for social referencing: They respond to novel or uncertain situations based on the emotional expressions they detect in others. Although there is currently controversy over whether social referencing at this age reflects genuine information seeking or is a by-product of affective sharing, comfort seeking, or other facets of secure-base behavior (see Baldwin & Moses, 1996), the social referencing literature indicates that late in the first year, infants are fairly good consumers of emotional information from others and can use it in their own action tendencies (Thompson, in press-a). More generally, social referencing indicates how early young children can acquire understanding from the distal emotional communications of others. As this capacity becomes progressively accompanied by the child's growing language capabilities, it can provide an important foundation for moral socialization in the early years of life. Because of the salience of the emotional signals of others, in other words, referencing provides an important avenue by which these emotional cues become moral incentives.

One way that social referencing contributes to conscience development is through the multimodal cues by which parents signal disapproval in circumstances in which young children may be unaware or uncertain of prohibited acts. As social referencing theory predicts, infants and young children are most likely to look to caregivers for cues when they are uncertain of how to respond (see Feinman, Roberts, Hsieh, Sawyer, & Swanson, 1992), but the caregiver's cues may also have a significant impact even when children are not particularly seeking them (especially when both salient facial and vocal cues are used). Thus social referencing helps to endow acts with affective valence for the child, and this becomes even more influential when the parents' emotional cues are accompanied by language. Moreover, there is evidence that social referencing becomes enlisted by parents for purposes of behavioral control shortly after infants have become mobile during the first year (Zumbahlen & Crawley, 1996).

Another way that social referencing is influential, at somewhat older ages, is to provide for nonverbal negotiation between parent and child over permitted and prohibited actions through the exchange of looks, expressions, and gestures (e.g., the toddler progressively approaches the VCR while glancing toward his or her parents; Emde & Buchsbaum, 1990). This kind of checking and rechecking the parent's emotional message may be an important avenue toward the growth of genuine self-control as the process of comparing contemplated behavior with a behavioral standard becomes internalized. The internalization of the parent's approving or disapproving expressions when young children are considering action in the parent's absence may link social referencing to the progressive emergence of conscience. In "referencing the absent parent," young children spontaneously evoke the caregiver's expected reaction to behavior that they know is permitted or prohibited (Emde, Biringen, Clyman, & Oppenheim, 1991; Emde & Buchsbaum, 1990).

Early Cognition, Memory, and Representation

As Kopp (1982, 1987; Kopp & Wyer, 1994) has noted, a young child's compliance is contingent on the intellectual capacities required for attending and responding to an adult's prohibitions, understanding and recalling standards of conduct, and applying these standards to one's behavior in diverse situations. As these constituents of self-regulation slowly develop, behavioral compliance can occur for very different reasons at different ages. A 12-month-old may avoid prohibited acts (such as touching forbidden objects) because of simple associative learning or a conditioned response to past disapproval, and a toddler may resist acting in a prohibited manner because of imitative learning. In neither instance, however, does compliance derive from an internalized behavioral standard that is generalizable, and thus it is unclear whether these actions may be truly regarded as "moral."

The beginnings of an understanding of behavioral standards may emerge late in the second year and in the third year, however, with the growth of prototypical knowledge structures by which young children strive to represent and understand common, recurrent experiences, as well as to predict their outcomes. Such prototypical structures—commonly called "scripts"—form a bedrock for event representation by enabling young children inclusively to represent familiar experiences and to integrate them with other knowledge systems (see Hudson, 1993; Nelson, 1978; Nelson & Gruendel, 1981). Because many behavioral standards (both moral and conventional) are based on routine events and are repeatedly conveyed in these circumstances—whether they entail prohibitions from touching dangerous objects at home, self-control with respect to waiting, sharing, and eating, participation in family routines, or the use of simple manners (see Gralinski & Kopp, 1993)—it would be surprising if simple rules did not become incorporated into young children's early scripted knowledge systems. Moreover, to the extent that children use such scripts for their representations of novel events also (e.g., using a familiar bedtime script to describe the specific events of the previous night), knowledge of the behavioral standards embedded within such scripts is likely to become well integrated into children's memory and representation of many of their personal experiences. The incorporation of behavioral standards into prototypical knowledge structures is especially important because of young children's use of these scripts to predict their outcomes: It is important to know, for example, what happens when you fail to cooperate with rules about playing with forbidden objects as well as what happens when you comply.

There has been little research into the development of prototypical knowledge structures pertinent to standards of conduct, although research by Smetana (Chapter 7; 1989) indicates that, in their interactions, both parents and children make distinctions among behavioral standards, rules, and values in different domains (e.g., pertaining to social relationships, conventions, or safety). There are interesting suggestions in this literature, moreover, that parents assume a significant role in establishing the content, as well as the organization and structure, of such scripts by how they prompt the child's memory retrieval. In the context of shared discourse that begins as soon as children can participate meaningfully in simple conversation, parents help to review, reconstruct, and consolidate young children's memory of generalized routines as well as of their specific experiences (Fivush, 1994; Fivush & Hamond, 1990; Hudson, 1990). In this way, the child's understanding of recurrent (as well as novel) events is defined and organized. Moreover, parents differ in their styles for doing so, with some parents (labeled "elaborative") providing considerable embellishment on their children's efforts at recall and representation during shared conversations, while others (labeled "pragmatic" or "repetitive") act in a more directive, focused manner (Fivush, 1991; Hudson, 1990; Reese & Fivush, 1993).

Although these variations in parents' styles of guiding emergent representation have been related to children's memory for the past, how they might affect the developing conscience is poorly understood. Perhaps each fosters its development in different ways. The pragmatic, directive style may communicate basic behavioral standards clearly and somewhat forcefully, whereas the elaborative style may instill a broader moral orientation toward others, reminiscent perhaps of Hoffman's (1970a) "humanistic orientation." No research, however, has directly addressed this topic.

Similarly, researchers have not yet explored other dimensions of variability that may affect the valence of children's recall of personal experiences. It seems likely that parents who help reconstruct their children's memory for past events of disobedience using heightened emotion and emphasizing negative outcomes would differentially affect children's representations of such experiences compared with parents who help children recall these events using a more benign affective tone. These individual differences would likely have an important effect on conscience development. For example, parents who help young children reconstruct past experiences of misbehavior while emphasizing the guilt inherent in misconduct are likely to heighten young children's compliance compared with parents whose event reconstructions emphasize the benign intent of children's misbehavior. Such an hypothesis remains, however, for future exploration.

With further growth in representation, the young child's grasp of behavioral standards becomes more multifaceted. Rules that had earlier been tied to specific situations may now be generalized to similar circumstances in other settings (e.g., keeping hands off delicate or dangerous objects in settings outside the home). A growing awareness and anticipation of causal relations enables young children better to grasp the significance of many behavioral expectations and also permits their application elsewhere (e.g., avoiding strangers or resisting scaling high or precarious places). Later, with the growth of a more sophisticated understanding of others' thoughts, feelings, emotions, and desires, children begin to understand the humanistic rationale for behavioral standards that entail respect for another's well-being. Finally, as young children begin constructing a valenced sense of self in the fourth year that entails personal evaluations of one's actions, compliance with behavioral standards becomes one of the avenues for others' approval or disapproval and, as a consequence, of positive or negative self-image.

Sensitivity to Standards and Their Violations

Kagan (1981) and Lamb (1993) have described another important maturational phenomenon that emerges in the second half of the second year. At that time, children begin to notice instances when standards (of wholeness, intactness, etc.) have been violated, such as when they see missing buttons, torn pages, trash on the floor, or misplaced objects. They pay attention to these violations of the norm, and they show both negative and positive emotional responses to them. Even though those events share no common perceptual qualities, young children's behavior strongly indicates that a flaw is a salient and affectively laden occurrence. Kagan and Lamb interpreted this phenomenon as a marker of the emerging sensitivity to and appreciation of standards, but their evidence was anecdotal or based on very few cases.

In a study of a large group of 2- and 3-year-old toddlers, one of us (G.K.) examined that conclusion empirically (Kochanska, Casey, & Fukumoto, 1995b). First, we explored in a systematic fashion children's responses to flawed objects. During a home visit, each child was presented with four pairs of play objects (toy bears, beds, blankets, and Sesame Street cups). In each pair, one object was whole and one was visibly flawed (i.e., broken or stained). The children's responses were videotaped and coded, including their answers to the examiner's standard questions, physical acts on the objects, and the manner of play with all eight objects. The findings indicated that young toddlers clearly responded to the flawed/whole quality. They showed significantly more interest in and concern about the flawed objects, although they declared strong preference for the whole ones. They were clearly aware of the violations of standards that the flawed objects embodied, and they repudiated the flaws; at the same time, however, they were fascinated with them. Dunn (1988) described similar, affectively complex reactions of young children to norm violations, such as their responses to the transgressions of siblings.

In the same study, we also examined Kagan's proposal that sensitivity to flaws is a marker of a more general system of internal standards. During a laboratory visit several weeks later, the same children were led to believe, on two occasions, that they had committed an act of wrongdoing that resulted in serious damage to an object that was valued by the examiner (i.e., broke a large doll, stained a new T-shirt). The situations were contrived so that the damage occurred while the child was handling the object. The children exhibited multiple verbal, affective, and behavioral signs of distress following the mishaps, including attempts at reparation. Moreover, those reactions were correlated significantly with the child's sensitivity to flawed objects assessed previously. Children who appeared more sensitive to the flawed/whole quality of those objects were also more distressed and concerned following the mishaps, supporting Kagan's proposal that both sets of responses reflect an early sense of right and wrong and an emerging system of internal standards.

Temperamental Underpinnings

Temperament has received very little attention in research on conscience and internalization. This gap is quite surprising, in view of the fact that biological contributions to internalization have been long acknowledged. For example, the fundamental role of emotions of fear or anxiety in the development of conscience has been implicated in the classic psychoanalytic model, as well as in the early learning approaches to internalization and in research on psychopathy (Fowles, 1993, 1994; Lykken, 1957; Quay, 1993). Until recently, however, there has been no systematic research addressing the implications of individual differences in fearfulness and other temperamental qualities for the early development of internalization. We have begun to examine the temperamental foundations that make internalization possible, as well as qualities of temperament that account for individual differences in early conscience.

Successful internalization often requires restraint—the suppression or inhibition of desired but prohibited acts, and the production or sustinance of socially desirable acts. Therefore, two temperamental inhibitory systems appear particularly relevant to emerging internalized regulators of conduct: a passive inhibition system (anxiety, fearfulness) and an active inhibition system (inhibitory or effortful control).

The first system (passive inhibition, or fearfulness) has been long believed to be an important mediator of internalization and conscience. The classic learning models had proposed that when children are punished for transgressions, they experience anxiety and other aversive states, and they come to associate anxiety with actual or potential deviation (Mowrer, 1960). Fear or anxiety contributes to internalization, in this view, because it underpins children's apprehension, anxiety, or discomfort associated with an actual or even contemplated transgression (Parke, 1974). Similar views have been long endorsed by researchers studying psychopathy. Since the classic work by Lykken (1957), substantial experimental evidence in research on psychopathy has documented that antisocial individuals with grossly impaired conscience differ significantly from those without such impairments in the weaker regulatory role of fear and anxiety or, more generally, a weaker Behavioral Inhibition System (Fowles, 1988, 1993). Therefore, whereas most people refrain from destructive or antisocial acts due to apprehension, anticipatory anxiety, and other negative emotions associated with the potential consequences of wrongdoing, in many psychopaths this process is undermined by their physiologically based hyporesponsiveness to signals of punishment—the deficit of fear.

To the extent that temperamental fearfulness is involved in emerging internalization, variations in fearfulness should be associated with the differential outcomes in early conscience. Fearful children may feel salient remorse and upset after wrongdoing, may be quite concerned about its potential negative consequences, and may experience discomfort even while considering future wrongdoing. They may, therefore, become well internalized. In contrast, relatively fearless children are likely to be less concerned about rule violations and less prone to transgression-related discomfort, and consequently, become less well internalized.

Data from several laboratories support this model. Rothbart, Ahadi, and Hershey (1994) reported that 6- to 7-year-old children who were described by their parents as high on moral traits, such as empathy and guilt, had been highly fearful when they had been observed in standardized assessments in the laboratory as infants. Kochanska (1995) found that fearful toddlers, who responded with distress and withdrawal in laboratory situations that presented them with novel and mildly "risky" events and stimuli, were also more internalized on several independent observational measures that involved the inhibition of prohibited behavior and execution of behavior consistent with parental values, compared with fearless toddlers who readily approached novel and risky stimuli. In another study (Kochanska, DeVet, Goldman, Murray, & Putnam, 1994), using maternal reports to assess children's temperament and conscience, fearfulness was associated with girls' tendency to experience guilt and other negative affects after transgressions. Asendorpf and Nunner-Winkler (1992) reported that fearful, shy, and inhibited children cheated less while playing a game without surveillance.

The second system (inhibitory or effortful control) is also associated with a temperamental quality that has only recently become the subject of systematic research (Derryberry & Reed, 1994; Rothbart, 1989; Rothbart & Ahadi, 1994). In contrast to fearfulness—which represents the reactive aspect of temperament—inhibitory control represents its self-regulatory aspect. Rothbart (1989) considers this capacity to be fundamental to the emerging ability voluntarily to suppress or initiate responses. In earlier research (e.g., Block & Block, 1980), similar qualities were considered part of ego-control, an important individual difference variable, but only recently has effortful/inhibitory control been explicitly defined in the context of a more general model of temperament that includes its developmental course and its psychophysiological and neuroanatomical underpinnings (Rothbart, Derryberry, & Posner, 1994).

Although we are only beginning systematically to examine inhibitory or effortful control, new data already strongly support its fundamental role in the development of internalization. Using newly developed behavioral batteries, Kochanska and her colleagues recently assessed inhibitory control in a large group of toddlers and preschool children. The tasks involved several (highly coherent) functions that are theoretically the components of inhibitory or effortful control, such as delaying, slowing down motor activity, suppressing/initiating activity to alternating signals, lowering voice, and reflective information processing. The same children were also observed in multiple paradigms assessing internalization of rules of conduct, and were rated by their mothers on several dimensions of early conscience. The findings indicated that, both contemporaneously and longitudinally, children who had high scores on the inhibitory control dimension of temperament were also highly internalized on observational and mother-reported measures, whereas those who performed poorly on the temperament battery were less internalized (Kochanska, Murray, Jacques, Koenig, & Vandegeest, 1996). In another study, Rothbart, Ahadi, et al. (1994) found that an early antecedent of inhibitory control, latency to grasp in infancy, predicted moral traits in middle childhood. In yet another study (Kochanska et al., 1994), inhibitory control assessed by mothers' reports was strongly linked to children's internalization.

RELATIONAL INFLUENCES ON EARLY CONSCIENCE DEVELOPMENT

As researchers have increasingly come to appreciate the importance of early childhood in the emergence of conscience, they have also begun to reevaluate the critical role of early parent-child relationships. Most developmentalists now agree that the first values and standards are conveyed and enforced in the context of the child's early relationships in the family.

Hoffman's work (1963, 1970a, 1970b, 1983) is best known for his emphasis on the importance of the parent-child relationship in moral internalization, focusing not only on their interaction in the discipline encounter but also the warmth and reciprocity characterizing their relationship, and the extent to which offspring identified with parents and their values. But Hoffman's research focused mostly (although not exclusively) on parent-child relations in the late school-age years and adolescence, when many of the foundations of conscience have already become established. By contrast, contemporary researchers approach the study of conscience with a renewed appreciation of the importance of very early parent-offspring relations and the orientation they instill in young children to cooperate and comply, or to resist and reject, parental values. In this respect, contemporary researchers build on much earlier studies concerned with the impact of parental warmth on young children's conscience (e.g., Sears et al., 1957; Sears et al., 1965).

However, relational influences on moral internalization begin, but do not end, with parent-child interaction. As Piaget (1932) himself noted, and as subsequent researchers have confirmed, peer relationships and interactions with other authorities (such as preschool teachers, the parents of peers, etc.) provide important catalysts for moral development.

Security of Attachment

Contemporary interest in early parent-child relationships has been enlivened by attachment theory, which emphasizes the growth of the child's security and trust in the parent during the first year of life as an important cornerstone for sociopersonality development (see Ainsworth, Blehar, Waters, & Wall, 1978; Bowlby, 1969/1982; Bretherton, 1985; Lamb, Thompson, Gardner, & Charnov, 1985). Consistent with theoretical predictions, attachment research has shown that the sensitivity and warmth of maternal care during the first year contribute to the development of secure attachment, which is also affected by the extent of stress and social support within the broader family environment (Thompson, in press-a).

A secure attachment at 12 months is thus an important indicator of harmony in the parent-infant relationship, with the infant capable of relying on the parent for support when it is needed, based on a history of reasonably sensitive care. By contrast, infants who are insecurely attached at this age respond to the parent more angrily or avoidantly, partly owing to a history of less consistent sensitivity by the caregiver. It is not surprising, therefore, that secure attachment in infancy leads to more harmonious parent-child interaction in subsequent years. Children who as infants were securely attached respond more cooperatively and compliantly, and with greater enthusiasm and positive emotion, during encounters with their mothers in short-term follow-up assessments. Their mothers, in turn, were also more supportive, sensitive, and helpful in later observations than were the mothers of insecurely attached infants (see Thompson, in press-a, for a comprehensive review). Because a secure attachment in infancy paves the way for a more harmonious parent-child relationship in early childhood, researchers have begun to explore Bowlby's (1973) provocative view that, over an extended period, these relationships contribute to the development of internal representations (or working models) of self and relationships that have broader consequences for sociopersonality development.

The security of attachment thus has several important implications for conscience development. First, to the extent that securely attached infants and young children participate in more harmonious encounters with parents, the opportunities for observational learning, reinforcement of behavioral standards, and the broader transmission of norms and expectations within a positive relational context are expanded. In other words, not only are there greater opportunities for the transmission of values, but the child's receptiveness to these values may be enhanced by a secure attachment and the sensitive, responsive care associated with it (a view anticipated by Stayton, Hogan, & Ainsworth, 1971).

Second, to the extent that a secure attachment in infancy paves the way for subsequent relational influences that contribute to the child's development of self-representations of worth, approval, and competence—and to representations of the attachment figure as reliable, loving, and supportive—it provides another foundation for young children's receptivity to parental values and the arousal of uncomfortable affect when violating those standards (each of which is a crucial contributor to moral internalization). Finally, to the extent that a secure attachment appears also to enable young children to enter more successfully into other close relationships, such as with peers, in the preschool years (see Thompson, in press-a), it provides additional positive relational contexts for the growth of conscience in interpersonal interaction.

Taken together, these considerations suggest that a secure attachment provides a foundation for more positive, harmonious relationships in early childhood and the incentives they provide for the development of conscience. These outcomes are contingent on the maintenance of harmonious parent-offspring relations from infancy to early childhood when the growth of self-understanding, sensitivity to standards, and representational capacities provide additional catalysts to moral internalization. Studies have shown that when parent-child relationships change over this period, a secure attachment does not provide later benefits (see Egeland, Kalkoske, Gottesman, & Erickson, 1990; Erickson, Sroufe, & Egeland, 1985). But the view that attachment security is significant to early conscience development because it provides a foundation for a mutually positive parent-child orientation is consistent with other views of moral internalization to be reviewed in this chapter.

The Mutual Interpersonal Orientation between Parent and Child

Maccoby (1983, 1984) has proposed that, within each individual parent-child dyad, a mutual interpersonal orientation of distinct valence emerges as a result of their repeated transactions during the early years of life. She conceptualized parent-child socialization as the process of inducting the child into a system of reciprocity—the formation of a mutually binding, reciprocal, and mutually responsive relationship. Such relationships are often described as "communal" in social psychology (Clark, 1984). Briefly, two partners in a communal or mutually reciprocal relationship feel invested in and responsible for each other's welfare; one feels concern for and acts responsively to the other's needs, and at the same time, one comes to expect the other to be responsive to one's needs and to be concerned about one's welfare. Not all parent-child relationships develop, however, along the trajectory of increasing communality or mutual responsiveness, as is well known from common knowledge and clinical literature. Sometimes, they progress along an adversarial developmental path (Maccoby, 1984; Patterson, DeBaryshe, & Ramsey, 1989).

As suggested by the attachment literature, the degree of mutual reciprocity, cooperation, or responsiveness appears to be an important quality of the parent-child relationship that differentiates individual dyads, and it serves as a foundation for a host of outcomes central in successful socialization. At this point, it is not yet clear how such orientation emerges. Two influences appear central, both also consistent with attachment theory. One factor is the parent's responsiveness to the child's signals of distress, bids for attention, influence attempts, or need for assistance. The other factor is the history of their mutually enjoyable interactions, infused with shared positive affect. Other qualities of parent-child relationship also may prove important in the consolidation of a mutually cooperative dyadic set. According to Maccoby, the history of such experiences contributes to the child's commitment to the relationship with the parent, and an internally felt obligation to reciprocate the parent's cooperative behavior.

The first study to test Maccoby's formulations was by Parpal and Maccoby (1985). In that study, 3- to 4-year-old children's cooperation with their mothers in three groups was compared. In each group, the mothers had played with their children in somewhat different ways prior to the assessment of the child's cooperation. In one group, mothers had been trained to be responsive to their children's bids (and had practiced doing so at home during the week preceding this assessment), and consequently they engaged in responsive play in which they followed the child's suggestions and expressed enjoyment. The other conditions involved free play that had not been preceded by any training to heighten maternal responsiveness. After the brief play session, mothers requested that the children clean up the toys using standard commands. As expected, even after that brief experience of mutual reciprocity, children in the responsive play group were significantly more willing to cooperate with their mothers in the cleanup task than the children in the free-play condition (see also Lay, Waters, & Park, 1989).

A mutually responsive orientation between parent and child, with its shared commitment to each other, constitutes a critical context for early moral socialization. Because in mutually responsive, cooperative dyads the child acquires a receptive, eager, or enthusiastic stance toward the parent, he or she is much more likely to embrace the parent's values and standards, and to accept them as his or her own. Children's compliance in such mutually cooperative dyads is more likely to have a self-regulated, internalized quality—"committed compliance"—that may be contrasted with "situational compliance" that entails cooperation without any feeling of internal obligation by the child. In the recent work of one of us (G.K.), we examined young children's committed compliance more closely. We found that, indeed, it was significantly related to the shared positive affect in the mother-child dyads (Kochanska & Aksan, 1995). This finding parallels Lytton's (1977) report that higher frequency of mother-child play (presumably mutually enjoyable) was associated with toddlers' higher "rudimentary conscience," or spontaneous self-correction or reversal of a misbehavior.

Encouraged by those findings, one of us (G.K.) examined a more general prediction that a mutually responsive, positive parent-child orientation also promotes the child's broad internalization of parental values. This prediction was tested in a longitudinal study on conscience development, in which data were collected from a large group of mothers and their young children in toddlerhood and again at preschool age (Kochanska, 1997b). Based on multiple observations of mother-child interaction in routines, chores, discipline, and play contexts at each age, we created a composite measure of mutually responsive orientation that encompassed various assessments (both molecular and global) of the mother's and the child's mutual responsiveness to each other and of their history of shared positive affect. We also collected multiple observational and mother-reported measures of the child's internalization of the mother's rules and values. The findings strongly supported Maccoby's views on the influence of a mutually responsive parent-child orientation on the child's internalization of the parent's norms and values. Children from the dyads characterized by such an orientation showed significantly higher internalization scores, both on the contemporaneous and longitudinal measures. Thus, they seemed to have developed strong feelings of internal obligation regarding maternal goals, values, and standards for conduct. This obligation derived, it seems, from the genuinely harmonious and responsive relationship between mother and child, established early in their interactions.

Those results, although preliminary, encourage further exploration of the parent-child relationship as an ongoing context for the successful development of conscience. In particular, the roles of secure attachment, parental warmth (MacDonald, 1992), shared positive affect or "positive distal interaction" (Kochanska & Aksan, 1995; Maccoby & Jacklin, 1983), and maternal compliance to child (Parpal & Maccoby, 1985) deserve attention as possible contributors to the kind of relational harmony that fosters moral internalization.

Parent-Child Discourse

Relationships provide a context for many kinds of shared activity, and with the growth of language the parent-child relationship also becomes an arena for shared conversations about the child's experiences. Developmental researchers have devoted considerable attention to early parent-child discourse and its influence on event representation, scripted knowledge structures, and autobiographical memory, as well as its role in the socialization of self-understanding and the child's knowledge of emotion and morality (e.g., Hudson, 1990; Miller, 1994; Miller, Potts, Fung, Hoogstra, & Mintz, 1990; Nelson, 1993). They have discovered, in short, that many lessons are included in how parents help children to review, reconstruct, and interpret their everyday experiences.

To illustrate, consider a brief conversation between a 21-month-old and his mother about an event that occurred earlier in the day (Dunn & Brown, 1991, p. 97):

CHILD: Eat my Weetabix. Eat my Weetabix. Crying.

MOTHER: Crying, weren't you? We had quite a battle. "One more mouthful, Michael." And what did you do? You spat it out!

CHILD: (pretends to cry).

Like many simple conversations shared by young children and their parents, this one includes many things: In response to the child's prompt, the mother provides an explicit, verbal representation of the shared experience that includes the causal sequence of events leading to the child's emotional reaction and lessons about the self in the context of a moral evaluation. Such shared recounting not only contributes to the content and structure of the child's event representation, but also embeds lessons about the self in the context of information about relationships, emotion, and morality—and thus, according to some researchers, shapes early autobiographical memory. It is likely that recurrent experiences of shared conversations like these about the child's everyday experiences are central to the development of representations (or "working models") of self, relationships, and other people, as well as the child's understanding of others' thoughts, feelings, beliefs, and motives—as they are construed and interpreted by parents in shared dialogue with the child (Thompson, in press-a).

It is also likely that shared discourse provides valuable lessons about morality, since the content of many early conversations centers on a child's (or a sibling's) compliance or misbehavior, and its consequences. Thus how a parent interprets and construes the events of the child's life provides opportunities for transmitting implicit values concerning acceptable and unacceptable behavior. There are important cultural differences, for example, in how parents structure conversational exchanges with young children in relation to the values of the culture. Miller and her colleagues (Miller, Fung, & Mintz, 1996; Miller et al., 1990) have noted that Chinese and Chinese American mothers stress moralistic themes when they discuss with 2-year-olds the experiences of the day, and also emphasize the shame inherent in misbehavior. By contrast, American mothers tended to deemphasize the child's misbehavior, or attribute it to the child's spunk or mischievousness. It is likely that these differences in discourse patterns are associated with differences in young children's compliance with parental prohibitions and, in particular, with the arousal of certain emotions (e.g., shame) associated with misbehavior. There are also differences in how parents help to recount and interpret the experiences of their young sons and daughters, with a greater emphasis on emotion and its relational contexts with daughters (Fivush, 1993, 1994). Thus lessons about morality are embedded not only directly in the discipline encounter, but also indirectly in the shared recounting of everyday experiences in early parent-child conversation.

In this light, it is not surprising to find that during the second and third years of life, young children who converse more frequently with their mothers about feelings and their causes are more competent on later measures of emotional understanding (Brown & Dunn, 1996; Dunn, Brown, & Beardsall, 1991; Dunn, Brown, Slomkowski, Tesla, & Youngblade, 1991). Similarly, 2- to 3-year-old children whose mothers use reasoning and humanistic concerns in resolving conflict with them are more advanced in measures of moral understanding in assessments in kindergarten and first grade (Dunn, Brown, & Maguire, 1995). In each case, shared discourse—often centered on experiences that are personally meaningful to the child—provides important lessons that shape the growth of conscience. Much more research is needed, however, to elucidate how parent-child discourse has this influence, and the individual differences in parental conversational styles that may have important implications for variations in early conscience development.

Control and Discipline

The actual process of conveying and enforcing standards in the family has been long viewed as the critical context in which children's internalization develops (Hoffman, 1970b, 1983). In general, parental use of power-assertive or forceful techniques to effect children's compliance has been considered detrimental to the development of internalization (Kochanska, Padavich, & Koenig, 1996). Discipline based on psychological methods and deemphasizing power, such as reasoning-based induction, has been found most effective in promoting internalization, although complexities involved in those bodies of research findings have also been pointed out (Grusec & Goodnow, 1994; Perry & Perry, 1983).

Hoffman's (1983) model of early discipline and internalization is particularly important to understanding early conscience development. The model proposes that anxiety or discomfort is essential in determining the effectiveness of parental discipline for the internalization of values. When children misbehave, parents intervene using a variety of techniques that vary in their forcefulness or reliance on the parent's power over the child. The degree of forcefulness results in varying degrees of discomort, anxiety, or arousal in the child. To be effective, the child's arousal must be optimal. Discipline practices that are completely devoid of force are ineffective because they elicit insufficient anxiety to signal the importance of the parental intervention, to orient the child to the message, and to provide the motivation to change.

Too much force, however, can also be detrimental to moral internalization. Power-oriented, forceful discipline elicits very high anxiety or arousal in the child and it interferes with the effective processing of the parental message about behavioral standards, and thus undermines internalization. According to Hoffman, under conditions of high arousal, the child is likely to store the encounter in episodic memory (along with salient situational features, extraneous to the actual socialization message) rather than in semantic memory where it can provide a lasting behavioral guide. Furthermore, even if the child complies, he or she likely attributes compliance to the external cause (the parent's exertion of power), rather than to internal factors, such as rules and values. Finally, the child often experiences resentment and anger toward the parent when forced to comply, and thus might tend to reject any parental message or value.

Hoffman concludes that discipline that uses only the minimal amount of power and employs rational induction and nonassertive methods of influence elicits a more optimal arousal level in the child. Under these conditions, the child attends to the parental intervention and is likely to store the socialization message in semantic memory "stripped" of extraneous situational details; thus the message becomes part of an internalized system of rules, later experienced as one's own. Attributions for compliance are likely to be internal, and thus the discipline encounter is more likely to promote future rule-compatible behavior without surveillance.

This formulation, where parental power assertion is linked to the storage of the socialization message in episodic or semantic memory system, is consistent with the research on early memory and internalization reviewed earlier. Additionally (from a depth-of-processing perspective), parental use of power may interfere with internalization also because it may be associated with the child's more shallow processing of the message. A child's retention of the content of the parent's prohibition may be impaired when power assertion is employed because the heightened affect generated by the parent's power-oriented discipline limits the child's capacity, at that moment, to reflect on the moral rule as the event is retained in memory. More broadly, it is possible to generalize Hoffman's formulations beyond the discipline encounter itself to other situations when parents and offspring converse about earlier instances of disobedience or misbehavior (such as the Weetabix encounter previously described). Insofar as forceful discipline inhibits a deeper processing of the parent's moral message at the moment that misbehavior occurs, so also the parent's reliance on denigrating, threatening, or demeaning interpretations of that event during subsequent conversations may have the same effect, as we suggested earlier while considering parent-child discourse. Conversely, a parent who uses rational explanations when discussing the child's earlier misbehavior may better facilitate the depth of processing required for effective storage and retrieval of the adult's moral message in appropriate circumstances.

THE INTERACTION OF CHILD TEMPERAMENT AND PARENTAL SOCIALIZATION

Earlier, we described the direct associations between child temperament and the developing conscience. We have also described several processes of early socialization that capitalize on different motivational incentives in the child to promote moral internalization. One process, associated with the mutually cooperative, responsive parent-child orientation, capitalizes on the positive feelings between parent and child. The other process, associated with rationally oriented discipline and the arousal it creates (as described in Hoffman's model), capitalizes on negative motivation, fear, or anxiety.

One of the most interesting questions in recent research on early internalization concerns the relative effectiveness of these two socialization processes in the development of conscience in children with different individualities. One of us (G.K.) has recently proposed that considering children's temperament as a factor that moderates the impact of parental socialization may contribute to an effective integration of these two socialization processes that promote early conscience (Kochanska, 1993, 1995, 1997a). In particular, individual differences in children's temperamental fearfulness appear critical for understanding how different mechanisms of moral socialization may promote conscience in children with varying temperaments.

A closer analysis of Hoffman's model, which portrays the pathway to internalization as capitalizing on the child's anxiety, suggests that it may be particularly well suited for children who are temperamentally relatively fearful and anxiety prone. Such children are likely to respond with optimal, moderate arousal even to subtle parenting techniques. They may, in fact, experience anxiety associated with wrongdoing even before parents intervene. Their parents, if they resort to non-power-oriented, rationally oriented discipline techniques, often capitalize on that discomfort, using gentle strategies of influence that, in turn, foster internal attributions and a deeper processing of the socialization message.

In contrast, children who are relatively fearless and are not anxiety prone may not experience such spontaneous discomfort and may not react with sufficient arousal to parents' rational interventions. Thus, for them, gentle discipline may not be equally effective in fostering internalization. Simply increasing parental power—which parents of fearless children may be often tempted to do, as pointed out first by Bell (1968)—may not be effective either. Highly power-assertive discipline is uniformly detrimental to internalization due to the child's resentment toward parents, external attributions, and the shallow processing of parental message (Hoffman, 1983; Maccoby, 1983). We are thus faced with a provocative question: How then, do fearless children become morally internalized?

We propose that for temperamentally fearless children, the alternative pathway to internalization capitalizes on the positive motivation that derives from a mutually responsive, cooperative parent-child orientation, rather than from discomfort or anxiety (Maccoby, 1983). For example, for those children, secure attachment may be particularly important in fostering internalization because it inaugurates such a harmonious mutual orientation.

The first empirical study that suggested—but did not test—this possibility was the previously described study by Parpal and Maccoby (1985) on situationally induced maternal responsiveness and its consequences for the child's cooperation. Whereas the findings, in general, supported the importance of the mutually responsive mother-child orientation for children's cooperation, there was also a hint in the results that such an orientation was most beneficial for children who were rated by mothers and teachers as difficult. In our terms, these children were most likely relatively fearless in their temperamental profile.

Consequently, one of us (G.K.) pursued that possibility at a greater depth in further research. In a preliminary study, 58 children and their mothers were studied first at toddler age (Kochanska, 1991). Children's fearfulness was observed during their encounter with an unfamiliar adult in an unfamiliar laboratory setting, and their responses were coded using categories typically indicative of fear or anxiety proneness, such as proximity to mother, reluctance to explore, and distress and withdrawal from the stranger. Children were then divided into relatively fearful and relatively fearless groups using a median split procedure. Mothers' discipline style was assessed also, using self-reports and observations of interactions with their toddler children during lengthy videotaped sessions. Finally, children's conscience was assessed at the age of 8 to 10 by eliciting their narrative endings to several semiprojective stories that depicted moral transgressions. These responses were subsequently scored for the general affective/moral orientation (yielding an overall internalization score), and themes of reparation and distress tied to wrongdoing.

As expected, children's temperamental fearfulness moderated the influence of maternal socialization style. For the relatively fearful children, toddler-age maternal discipline that deemphasized power (from both observational and self-report measures) significantly predicted more internalized conscience in middle childhood, consistent with Hoffman's model. For the relatively fearless children, however, there were no such relations.

In a subsequent study, an ongoing longitudinal project on conscience development, we pursued those issues much more extensively with a large group of children and mothers studied at toddler, preschool, and kindergarten age. Children's fearfulness was asssessed in an observational battery that included several standardized encounters with unfamiliar and mildly scary objects and events (e.g., getting into an unusual-looking car, putting the hand inside a big black box, interacting with a clown), as well as using mothers' reports. Again, children were classified into relatively fearless and fearful. Mothers' discipline style was assessed using a number of self-reports and was observed in lengthy home and laboratory contexts focused on control issues, such as toy cleanups and not touching attractive objects near the child. In addition, the study included assessment of socialization processes expected to promote conscience in the relatively fearless children, including the security of attachment (using the Attachment Q-Set; Waters, 1987) and maternal responsiveness, both of which reflect a mutually cooperative parent-child relationship. Multiple maternal reports and observational measures were used to assess children's conscience, as described before: rule-abiding conduct while alone with prohibited toys, committed compliance, maternal descriptions of the child's internalization of rules in their daily lives.

The same children were seen again when they were approximately 4 years old. At that time, measures of conscience included game playing without surveillance where winning was impossible without cheating, in which their rule-abiding or rule-violating behaviors were coded, and children's narratives produced to hypothetical moral story stems, in which morally-relevant themes were coded. They also returned to the lab one more time at age 5 to 5½ years, and were observed again while playing a game that occasioned cheating, as well as while responding to hypothetical moral dilemmas that yielded cognitive measures of morality, mostly involving choices of actions—prosocial and moral versus antisocial and selfish (Eisenberg-Berg, 1979; Nunner-Winkler & Sodian, 1988).

The findings provided powerful support, in both contemporaneous and longitudinal relations and across multiple conscience measures, for our model of the complex interplay of child temperament and parental socialization in the emergence of internalization. For the children who had been relatively fearful as toddlers, mothers' gentle discipline deemphasizing power was associated with strong conscience, both at toddler age and at preschool age (Kochanska, 1995, 1997a). We speculate that for fearful children, low-key maternal interventions are sufficient to elicit the optimal level of discomfort and arousal, promoting deeper semantic processing and encoding, as described by Hoffman. Because those interventions are subtle, children are likely to form internal attributions for that discomfort, which is another factor promoting internalization. As expected, for the children who were relatively fearless, such low-key maternal discipline was less effective in promoting conscience, presumably because the level of discomfort it elicited fell short of optimal. For such children, different influences that capitalized on positive motivation rather than on anxiety, fostered internalization. In particular, a mother-child mutually cooperative, positive, responsive orientation was associated with strong conscience development at toddler and preschool age.

An interesting question posed by those findings concerns the relatively lower effectiveness (in terms of fostering conscience) of the mother-child mutually responsive orientation in fearful children. Although this question deserves more attention, at least two interpretations are possible. First, perhaps the mechanism based on internal discomfort and anxiety indeed is the primary one involved in internalizing prohibitions, as implied in the psychopathy literature. Only when it fails, due to the child's constitutionally low anxiety, alternative mechanisms may come into play. Second, perhaps secure attachment (which we view as one form of the mutually responsive orientation) serves two developmental functions for the child: providing "felt security" (Sroufe & Waters, 1977) and creating a "preparedness for socialization" (Kochanska, 1995). The relative importance of these functions may depend on the child's temperament: perhaps for fearful children, particularly concerned with issues of security, the first function dominates over the second one, whereas for fearless children the reverse is true—the second function dominates over the first. Future research will help clarify such possibility.

CONCLUSION

This is an exciting time in the study of early conscience. There is converging evidence that the early years may hold the key to our understanding of the foundations of morality and its future developmental trajectories. Moreover, contemporary research on conscience begins to cross traditional domains of inquiry, as multiple windows appear to provide insights into its early development—the study of early temperament, moral emotion, cognition, emerging self, and early parent-child relationships.

Several future directions of research appear particularly promising. First, new research points to compelling interfaces between biologically founded temperamental individuality and the qualities of socialization. Mapping the complex interactions between the child's temperament and his or her experiences in relationship with parents may enable researchers to make considerable progress in understanding the traditional nature-nurture question as it pertains to moral development. They may become better able to understand both moral emotions (e.g., guilt or shame) and behavioral control processes (e.g., restraint) involved in internalization. They will also gain new insights in the early combinations of both sets of influences that may create potentially adaptive pathways to conscience or, in contrast, contribute to early vulnerability in moral development.

Second, several strands of research point to the rich complexities involved in the early parent-child relationship that await integration. Attachment scholars' compelling notion of internal working models of self and relationships may be reconsidered in the context of multiple processes embedded within that relationship, such as parent-child discourse, parental discipline and control, and the emergence of the mutually responsive and cooperative—or adversarial—parent-child orientation. Taken together with the work on temperamental influences, one implication of this chapter is that temperament may affect not only the behavioral styles to which parents must respond in their discipline practices, but also the cognitive styles by which children construct working models from relational experience. Such a view may elucidate how the earliest understandings of self and morality are co-constructed by the child and the parent, and what multiple pathways this process may follow (Thompson, in press-a).

Third, a related direction is exploring the early development of the child's internal representation of moral values. An intriguing task will be to elucidate how early memory and information processing are influenced by diverse features of the child's experiences during which the values are conveyed (discipline encounters, parent-child discourse) and later remembered and applied. It is likely that the context of both the actual discipline encounters and of the later shared reviews of those encounters by the parent-child dyad affect how the information about moral values and rules is processed and stored.

Progress in many areas of developmental psychology has invigorated research on early conscience. The time is thus particularly conducive for future integrative investigations that will highlight the origins of internalized regulators of conduct.

REFERENCES

Ainsworth, M. D. S., Blehar, M. C., Waters, E., & Wall, S. (1978). *Patterns of attachment.* Hillsdale, NJ: Erlbaum.

Aronfreed, J. (1968). *Conduct and conscience.* New York: Academic Press.

Asendorpf, J. B., & Nunner-Winkler, G. (1992). Children's moral motive strength and temperamental inhibition reduce their egoistic behavior in real moral conflicts. *Child Development, 63,* 1223–1235.

Baldwin, D. A., & Moses, L. J. (1996). The ontogeny of social information-processing. *Child Development, 67,* 1915–1939.

Barrett, K. C. (1995). A functionalist approach to shame and guilt. In J. P. Tangney & K. W. Fischer (Eds.), *Self-conscious emotions* (pp. 25–63). New York: Guilford Press.

Bell, R. Q. (1968). A reinterpretation of the direction of effects in studies of socialization. *Psychological Review, 75,* 81–95.

Block, J. H., & Block, J. (1980). The role of ego-control and ego-resiliency in the organization of behavior. In W. A. Collins (Ed.), *Development of cognition, affect, and social relations. Minnesota Symposia on Child Psychology* (Vol. 13, pp. 39–101). Hillsdale, NJ: Erlbaum.

Bowlby, J. (1973). *Attachment and loss: Vol. 2. Separation: Anxiety and anger.* New York: Basic Books.

Bowlby, J. (1982). *Attachment and loss: Vol. 1. Attachment* (2nd ed.). New York: Basic Books.

Bretherton, I. (1985). Attachment theory: Retrospect and prospect. In I. Bretherton & E. Waters (Eds.), Growing points of attachment theory and research. *Monographs of the Society for Research in Child Development, 50*(Serial No. 209), 3–35.

Brown, J. R., & Dunn, J. (1996). Continuities in emotional understanding from 3 to 6 years. *Child Development, 67*, 789–802.

Clark, M. S. (1984). Record keeping in two types of relationships. *Journal of Personality and Social Psychology, 47*, 549–557.

Derryberry, D., & Reed, M. A. (1994). Temperament and the self-organization of personality. *Development and Psychopathology, 6*, 653–676.

Dunn, J. (1988). *The beginnings of social understanding.* Oxford, England: Blackwell.

Dunn, J., & Brown, J. (1991). Relationships, talk about feelings, and the development of affect regulation in early childhood. In J. Garber & K. A. Dodge (Eds.), *The development of emotion regulation and dysregulation* (pp. 89–108). Cambridge, England: Cambridge University Press.

Dunn, J., Brown, J., & Beardsall, L. (1991). Family talk about feeling states and children's later understanding of others' emotions. *Developmental Psychology, 27*, 448–455.

Dunn, J., Brown, J. R., & Maguire, M. (1995). The development of children's moral sensibility: Individual differences and emotion understanding. *Developmental Psychology, 31*, 649–659.

Dunn, J., Brown, J., Slomkowski, C., Tesla, C., & Youngblade, L. (1991). Young children's understanding of other people's feelings and beliefs: Individual differences and their antecedents. *Child Development, 62*, 1352–1366.

Egeland, B., Kalkoske, M., Gottesman, N., & Erickson, M. F. (1990). Preschool behavior problems: Stability and factors accounting for change. *Journal of Child Psychology and Psychiatry, 31*, 891–909.

Eisenberg, N. (1992). *The caring child.* Cambridge, MA: Harvard University Press.

Eisenberg-Berg, N. (1979). Development of children's prosocial moral judgment. *Developmental Psychology, 15*, 128–137.

Emde, R. N., Biringen, Z., Clyman, R. B., & Oppenheim, D. (1991). The moral self of infancy: Affective core and procedural knowledge. *Developmental Review, 11*, 251–270.

Emde, R. N., & Buchsbaum, H. K. (1990). "Didn't you hear my Mommy?" Autonomy with connectedness in moral self emergence. In D. Cicchetti & M. Beeghly (Eds.), *The self in transition: Infancy to childhood* (pp. 35–60). Chicago: University of Chicago Press.

Erickson, M. F., Sroufe, L. A., & Egeland, B. (1985). The relationship between quality of attachment and behavior problems in preschool in a high-risk sample. In I. Bretherton & E. Waters (Eds.), Growing points of attachment theory and research. *Monographs of the Society for Research in Child Development, 50*(Serial No. 209), 147–166.

Feinman, S., Roberts, D., Hsieh, K.-F., Sawyer, D., & Swanson, D. (1992). A critical review of social referencing in infancy. In S. Feinman (Ed.), *Social referencing and the social construction of reality in infancy* (pp. 15–54). New York: Plenum Press.

Fivush, R. (1991). The social construction of personal narratives. *Merrill-Palmer Quarterly, 37*, 59–81.

Fivush, R. (1993). Emotional content of parent-child conversations about the past. In C. A. Nelson (Ed.), *Memory and affect in development. Minnesota Symposia on Child Psychology* (Vol. 26, pp. 39–77). Hillsdale, NJ: Erlbaum.

Fivush, R. (1994). Constructing narrative, emotion, and self in parent-child conversations about the past. In U. Neisser & R. Fivush (Eds.), *The remembering self: Construction and accuracy in the self-narrative* (pp. 136–157). Cambridge, England: Cambridge University Press.

Fivush, R., & Hamond, N. R. (1990). Autobiographical memory across the preschool years: Toward reconceptualizing childhood amnesia. In R. Fivush & J. A. Hudson (Eds.), *Knowing and remembering in young children* (pp. 223–248). Cambridge, England: Cambridge University Press.

Fowles, D. C. (1988). Psychophysiology and psychopathology: A motivational approach. *Psychophysiology, 25*, 373–391.

Fowles, D. C. (1993). Electrodermal activity and antisocial behavior: Empirical findings and theoretical issues. In J. C. Roy, W. Boucsein, D. Fowles, & J. Gruzelier (Eds.), *Progress in electrodermal research* (pp. 223–237). New York: Plenum Press.

Fowles, D. C. (1994). A motivational theory of psychopathology. In W. Spaulding (Ed.), *Nebraska Symposium on Motivation: Integrated views of motivation and emotion* (Vol. 41, pp. 181–228). Lincoln: University of Nebraska Press.

Gralinski, J. H., & Kopp, C. B. (1993). Everyday rules for behavior: Mothers' requests to young children. *Developmental Psychology, 29*, 573–584.

Grusec, J. E., & Goodnow, J. J. (1994). The impact of parental discipline methods on the child's internalization of values: A reconceptualization of current points of view. *Developmental Psychology, 30*, 4–19.

Hoffman, M. L. (1963). Childrearing practices and moral development: Generalizations from empirical research. *Child Development, 34*, 295–318.

Hoffman, M. L. (1970a). Conscience, personality, and socialization techniques. *Human Development, 13*, 90–126.

Hoffman, M. L. (1970b). Moral development. In P. H. Mussen (Ed.), *Carmichael's handbook of child psychology* (3rd ed.) (Vol. 2, pp. 261–359). New York: Wiley.

Hoffman, M. L. (1983). Affective and cognitive processes in moral internalization. In E. T. Higgins, D. Ruble, & W. Hartup (Eds.), *Social cognition and social development: A sociocultural perspective* (pp. 236–274). New York: Cambridge University Press.

Hudson, J. A. (1990). The emergence of autobiographical memory in mother-child conversation. In R. Fivush & J. A. Hudson (Eds.), *Knowing and remembering in young children* (pp. 166–196). Cambridge, England: Cambridge University Press.

Hudson, J. A. (1993). Understanding events: The development of script knowledge. In M. Bennett (Ed.), *The child as psychologist: An introduction to the development of social cognition* (pp. 142–167). New York: Harvester Wheatsheaf.

Kagan, J. (1981). *The second year: The emergence of self-awareness.* Cambridge, MA: Harvard University Press.

Kochanska, G. (1991). Socialization and temperament in the development of guilt and conscience. *Child Development, 62*, 1379–1392.

Kochanska, G. (1993). Toward a synthesis of parental socialization and child temperament in early development of conscience. *Child Development, 64*, 325–347.

Kochanska, G. (1995). Children's temperament, mothers' discipline, and security of attachment: Multiple pathways to emerging internalization. *Child Development, 66*, 597–615.

Kochanska, G. (1997a). Multiple pathways to conscience for children with different temperaments: From toddlerhood to age five. *Developmental Psychology, 33*, 228–240.

Kochanska, G. (1997b). Mutually responsive orientation between mothers and their young children: Implications for early socialization. *Child Development, 68*, 94–112.

Kochanska, G., & Aksan, N. (1995). Mother-child mutually positive affect, the quality of child compliance to requests and prohibitions, and maternal control as correlates of early internalization. *Child Development, 66*, 236–254.

Kochanska, G., Aksan, N., & Koenig, A. L. (1995a). A longitudinal study of the roots of preschoolers' conscience: Committed compliance and emerging internalization. *Child Development, 66*, 852–868.

Kochanska, G., Casey, R. J., & Fukumoto, A. (1995b). Toddlers' sensitivity to standard violations. *Child Development, 66*, 643–656.

Kochanska, G., DeVet, K., Goldman, M., Murray, K., & Putnam, S. P. (1994). Maternal reports of conscience development and temperament in young children. *Child Development, 65,* 852–868.

Kochanska, G., Murray, K., Jacques, T. Y., Koenig, A. L., & Vandegeest, K. (1996). Inhibitory control in young children and its role in emerging internalization. *Child Development, 67,* 490–507.

Kochanska, G., Padavich, D. L., & Koenig, A. L. (1996). Children's narratives about hypothetical moral dilemmas and objective measures of their conscience: Mutual relations and socialization antecedents. *Child Development, 67,* 1420–1436.

Kohlberg, L. (1969). Stage and sequence: The cognitive-developmental approach to socialization. In D. A. Goslin (Ed.), *Handbook of socialization theory and research* (pp. 347–480). Chicago: Rand McNally.

Kopp, C. B. (1982). Antecedents of self-regulation: A developmental view. *Developmental Psychology, 18,* 199–214.

Kopp, C. B. (1987). The growth of self-regulation: Caregivers and children. In N. Eisenberg (Ed.), *Contemporary topics in developmental psychology* (pp. 34–55). New York: Wiley.

Kopp, C. B., & Wyer, N. (1994). Self-regulation in normal and atypical development. In D. Cicchetti & S. L. Toth (Eds.), Disorders and dysfunctions of the self. *Rochester Symposium on Developmental Psychopathology* (Vol. 5, pp. 31–56). Rochester, NY: University of Rochester Press.

Lamb, M. E., Thompson, R. A., Gardner, W., & Charnov, E. L. (1985). *Infant-mother attachment: The origins and developmental significance of individual differences in Strange Situation behavior.* Hillsdale, NJ: Erlbaum.

Lamb, S. (1993). First moral sense: An examination of the appearance of morally related behaviours in the second year of life. *Journal of Moral Education, 22,* 97–109.

Lay, K.-L., Waters, E., & Park, K. A. (1989). Maternal responsiveness and child compliance: The role of mood as a mediator. *Child Development, 60,* 1405–1411.

Lewis, M., Sullivan, M. W., Stanger, C., & Weiss, M. (1989). Self-development and self-conscious emotions. *Child Development, 60,* 146–156.

Lykken, D. T. (1957). A study of anxiety in the sociopathic personality. *Journal of Abnormal and Social Psychology, 55,* 6–10.

Lytton, H. (1977). Correlates of compliance and the rudiments of conscience in two-year-old boys. *Canadian Journal of Behavioral Science, 9,* 242–251.

Maccoby, E. E. (1983). Let's not over-attribute to the attribution process: Comments on social cognition and behavior. In E. T. Higgins, D. Ruble, & W. Hartup (Eds.), *Social cognition and social development: A sociocultural perspective* (pp. 356–370). New York: Cambridge University Press.

Maccoby, E. E. (1984). Socialization and developmental change. *Child Development, 55,* 317–328.

Maccoby, E. E., & Jacklin, C. N. (1983). The "person" characteristics of children and the family as environment. In D. Magnusson & V. L. Allen (Eds.), *Human development: An interactional perspective* (pp. 75–91). New York: Academic Press.

MacDonald, K. (1992). Warmth as a developmental construct: An evolutionary analysis. *Child Development, 63,* 753–773.

Miller, P. J. (1994). Narrative practices: Their role in socialization and self-construction. In U. Neisser & R. Fivush (Eds.), *The remembering self: Construction and accuracy in the self-narrative* (pp. 158–179). Cambridge, England: Cambridge University Press.

Miller, P. J., Fung, H., & Mintz, J. (1996). Self-construction through narrative practices: A Chinese and American comparison of early socialization. *Ethos, 24,* 237–280.

Miller, P. J., Potts, R., Fung, H., Hoogstra, L., & Mintz, J. (1990). Narrative practices and the social construction of self in childhood. *American Ethnologist, 17,* 292–311.

Mowrer, O. H. (1960). *Learning and behavior.* New York: Wiley.

Nelson, K. (Ed.). (1978). *Event knowledge: Structure and function in development.* Hillsdale, NJ: Erlbaum.

Nelson, K. (1993). The psychological and social origins of autobiographical memory. *Psychological Science, 4,* 7–14.

Nelson, K., & Gruendel, J. (1981). Generalized event representations: Basic building blocks of cognitive development. In M. Lamb & A. Brown (Eds.), *Advances in developmental psychology* (pp. 131–158). Hillsdale, NJ: Erlbaum.

Nunner-Winkler, G., & Sodian, B. (1988). Children's understanding of moral emotions. *Child Development, 59,* 1323–1338.

Parke, R. D. (1974). Rules, roles, and resistance to deviation: Recent advances in punishment, discipline, and self-control. In A. D. Pick (Ed.), *Minnesota Symposia on Child Psychology* (Vol. 8, pp. 111–143). Minneapolis: University of Minnesota Press.

Parpal, M., & Maccoby, E. E. (1985). Maternal responsiveness and subsequent child compliance. *Child Development, 56,* 1326–1334.

Patterson, G. R., DeBaryshe, B. D., & Ramsey, E. (1989). A developmental perspective on antisocial behavior. *American Psychologist, 44,* 329–335.

Perry, D. G., & Perry, L. C. (1983). Social learning, causal attribution, and moral internalization. In J. Bisanz, G. L. Bisanz, & R. Kail (Eds.), *Learning in children: Progress in cognitive development research* (pp. 105–136). New York: Springer-Verlag.

Piaget, J. (1932). *The moral judgment of the child.* New York: Harcourt, Brace.

Quay, H. C. (1993). The psychobiology of undersocialized Aggressive Conduct Disorder: A theoretical perspective. *Development and Psychopathology, 5,* 165–180.

Radke-Yarrow, M., Campbell, J. D., & Burton, R. V. (1968). *Child rearing: An inquiry into research and methods.* San Francisco, CA: Jossey-Bass.

Radke-Yarrow, M., Zahn-Waxler, C., & Chapman, M. (1983). Children's prosocial dispositions and behavior. In P. H. Mussen (Series Ed.) & E. M. Hetherington (Vol. Ed.), *Handbook of child psychology: Vol. 4. Socialization, personality, and social development* (pp. 469–545). New York: Wiley.

Reese, E., & Fivush, R. (1993). Parental styles of talking about the past. *Developmental Psychology, 29,* 596–606.

Rogoff, B. (1990). *Apprenticeship in thinking.* New York: Oxford University Press.

Rothbart, M. K. (1989). Temperament and development. In G. A. Kohnstamm, J. E. Bates, & M. K. Rohtbart (Eds.), *Temperament in childhood* (pp. 187–247). New York: Wiley.

Rothbart, M. K., & Ahadi, S. A. (1994). Temperament and the development of personality. *Journal of Abnormal Psychology, 103,* 55–66.

Rothbart, M. K., Ahadi, S. A., & Hershey, K. L. (1994). Temperament and social behavior in childhood. *Merrill-Palmer Quarterly, 40,* 21–39.

Rothbart, M. K., Derryberry, D., & Posner, M. I. (1994). A psychobiological approach to the development of temperament. In J. E. Bates & T. D. Wachs (Eds.), *Temperament: Individual differences at the interface of biology and behavior* (pp. 83–116). Washington, DC: American Psychological Association.

Sears, R. R., Maccoby, E. E., & Levin, H. (1957). *Patterns of child rearing.* Evanston, IL: Row-Peterson.

Sears, R. R., Rau, L., & Alpert, R. (1965). *Identification and child rearing.* Stanford, CA: Stanford University Press.

Smetana, J. G. (1989). Toddlers' social interactions in the context of moral and conventional transgressions in the home. *Developmental Psychology, 25,* 499–508.

Sroufe, L. A., & Waters, E. (1977). Attachment as an organizational construct. *Child Development, 48,* 1184–1199.

Stayton, D. J., Hogan, R., & Ainsworth, M. D. S. (1971). Infant obedience and maternal behavior: The origins of socialization reconsidered. *Child Development, 42,* 1057–1069.

Stipek, D., Recchia, S., & McClintic, S. (1992). Self-evaluation in young children. *Monographs of the Society for Research in Child Development, 57* (1, Serial No. 226).

Thompson, R. A. (in press-a). Early sociopersonality development. In W. Damon (Ed.) & N. Eisenberg (Vol. Ed.), *Handbook of child psychology: Vol. 3. Social, emotional, and personality development* (5th ed.). New York: Wiley.

Thompson, R. A. (in press-b). Reflections on early empathy. In S. Braten (Ed.), *Intersubjective communication and emotion in ontogeny: A sourcebook.* Cambridge, England: Cambridge University Press.

Waters, E. (1987). *Attachment Behavior Q-Set* (Revision 3.0). Unpublished instrument, State University of New York, Department of Psychology.

Welch-Ross, M. K. (1995). An integrative model of the development of autobiographical memory. *Developmental Review, 15,* 338–365.

Zahn-Waxler, C., & Radke-Yarrow, M. (1990). The origins of empathic concern. *Motivation and Emotion, 14,* 107–130.

Zahn-Waxler, C., Radke-Yarrow, M., Wagner, E., & Chapman, M. (1992). Development of concern for others. *Developmental Psychology, 28,* 126–136.

Zumbahlen, M., & Crawley, A. (1996, April). Infants' early referential behavior in prohibition contexts: The emergence of social referencing? In R. A. Thompson (Chair), *Taking perspective on social referencing: New viewpoints.* Symposium conducted at the meeting of the International Conference on Infant Studies, Providence, RI.

CHAPTER 4

Internalization, Autonomy, and Relationships: Development during Adolescence

W. ANDREW COLLINS, TRACY GLEASON, and ARTURO SESMA, JR.

Adolescence has long been viewed as a period of tension between two developmental tasks: increasing conformity to societal expectations, while attaining autonomy from the influences of others. Psychological theories about these dual tasks often have emphasized the competencies and motives of individuals (Cooper, 1994) and, thus, have paralleled classical views of internalization (Grusec, this volume). In these conceptions, the function of internalization is to permit self-regulated action in accord with the expectations of others. In theories of adolescence, this emphasis has been dealt with in terms of three constructs: autonomy, identity, and morality.

An intraindividual bias is apparent in the traditional view of all three. *Autonomy* has been regarded as a process of striving to gain freedom from parents and other influences (for a review, see Hill & Holmbeck, 1986). *Identity* has been viewed as a sense of coherence in impressions of the self across time and in current beliefs and commitments (Erikson, 1968; Marcia, 1980). *Morality* has been regarded as mastery of intrapsychic impulses toward self-gratification and arousal of empathy toward others, acquisition of appropriate contingencies for and models of appropriate behavior, or achievement of a universal sense of justice or concern for reciprocity (Bandura, 1969; Hoffman, 1980; Kohlberg, 1969).

This emphasis on individual processes now is being expanded because of increasing evidence that competencies associated with autonomy, identity, and morality are embedded in extensive social interdependencies. The shift underscores the centrality of interpersonal relationships to individual functioning. Hill and Holmbeck (1986) proposed that autonomy refers not to freedom *from* others (e.g., parents), but freedom *to* carry out actions on one's own behalf while maintaining appropriate connections to significant others. Autonomous functioning requires skills for interacting effectively with others. A recent definition holds that autonomy comprises "capacities for taking responsibility for one's own behavior, making decisions regarding one's own life, and maintaining supportive relationships" (Crittenden, 1990, p. 162). Similarly, identity increasingly is viewed in terms of the interpersonal experiences that encourage and support individuation vis-à-vis others (e.g., Adams, Gullotta, & Montemayor, 1992; Grotevant & Cooper, in press); and morality more often is regarded as a socially and culturally influenced process (Miller & Bersoff, 1992; Shweder, 1982; Snarey, 1985; Thoma & Ladewig,

Preparation of the manuscript was supported in part by the Center for Research on Interpersonal Relationships, University of Minnesota, and by the Graduate School of the University of Minnesota.

1993). Autonomy and internalization thus have come to be viewed less as independence, in the sense of distancing and separation from others, and more as the result of behavioral regulation arising in interdependent patterns of interaction with other persons.

The focus of this chapter is the linkages between internalization and changes in adolescents and in their significant social relationships. The chapter is divided into three major sections. In the first section, we briefly describe research findings on internalization during adolescence, with a focus on the constructs of autonomy, identity, and morality and social responsibility and the normative changes that occur in these from childhood to adolescence. The second section is a discussion of normative changes in interpersonal relationships that may be important to the development of behavioral regulation. These include both transformation in existing relationships (e.g., with parents) and expansion of the network of relationships in which adolescents participate. The third section outlines empirical evidence linking relationships with parents and peers during adolescence to individual markers of autonomy, identity, and morality and social responsibility. In addition, the section includes a discussion of two general trends in ideas about the impact of others on internalization during adolescence: shifts from views that emphasize independence to views that emphasize interdependency; and shifts from unilateral to bilateral models that incorporate interactions with others. In the final section, we address several implications of developmental changes and the role of relationships for further understanding of internalization during adolescence. One implication is the need for an expanded view of the competencies required for internalization. A second implication is the need for models that incorporate changing capacities of adolescents. A third implication encompasses other significant relationships besides those with parents as contexts for internalization.

INTERNALIZATION AND DEVELOPMENT
DURING ADOLESCENCE

Theories of adolescent development have given little explicit attention to internalization in the sense of self-regulation, emphasizing instead the degree to which individuals manifest conformity to the behaviors and attitudes endorsed by adults. The central concern in this formulation is the degree of similarity between parents and children, and the primary metaphor is the unidirectional, unilateral transmission of values from the older to the younger generation. Internalization, in the sense of self-directed competence, has been a relatively minor theme in this literature (Hill & Holmbeck, 1986). Exceptions are the emphasis on *achieved* identities, compared with foreclosure on beliefs and commitments advocated by parents (Erikson, 1968; Marcia, 1991), and on individually reasoned judgments posited in the literature on moral development (e.g., Kohlberg, 1969; Rest, 1983).

This general emphasis on conformity is evident in speculations about the implications of the transition from childhood to adolescence. Hormonal and physiological changes of puberty are viewed as sources of disruption in individual emotional equilibrium and also in the interpersonal power balance between parents and children (e.g., Blos, 1979; A. Freud, 1969; S. Freud, 1923/1949). Both changes have traditionally been viewed as threatening adherence to adult values. Cognitive and social changes have been construed as both advantageous and disadvantageous to increasing conformity. Development of more abstract, complex concepts of relationships and more elaborated reasoning processes is credited both with increasing tendencies to discount the superior wisdom of parents and one's obligations to them (e.g., Blos, 1967, 1979; Keating, 1990; Selman, 1980) and with fostering socially responsible behavior through increased interpersonal understanding, more mature concepts of rights and responsibilities, and enhanced capacities for negotiating interpersonal difficulties (see Laursen & Collins, 1988, for a critical review of these formulations). Similarly, the rapid expansion of social networks experienced by most adolescents provides opportunities to engage in self-direction, although the wider variety of tasks and settings also may make it more difficult to maintain self-regulation (e.g., Simmons & Blyth, 1987), especially when pressures toward conformity are strong (e.g., Berndt, 1979).

Research findings imply that adolescence generally is a period of increasing self-regulation of behavior (for reviews, see Hill, 1987; Steinberg, 1990). In this section, the focal question is, what are the normative patterns associated with self-regulation of behavior during adolescence? This evidence will be reviewed for the three core constructs identified in the first section of the chapter: autonomy, identity, and morality.

Autonomy

Autonomy includes both intrapsychic and interpersonal dimensions (Hill & Holmbeck, 1986) and implies independence and greater self-determination in three domains: behavior, emotion, and cognition. These domains have been defined and studied separately.

Behavioral autonomy refers to "active, overt manifestations of independent functioning, including the regulation of one's own behavior and decision-making" (Sessa & Steinberg, 1991, p. 42). Behavioral autonomy frequently has been operationalized as independence of thought and self-governance of action in relationships with parents (e.g., choosing how to spend money, which clothes to buy, and which friends to go out with; Amato, 1987; Dornbusch, Ritter, Mont-Reynaud, & Chen, 1990; Feldman & Quatman, 1988; Feldman & Rosenthal, 1991; Poole & Gelder, 1984) and peers (Steinberg & Silverberg, 1986). Age-related increases have been documented in both seeking and receiving greater independence from parental control (e.g., Collins & Luebker, 1994). Skills involved in behavioral autonomy, such as awareness of risk and long-term consequences and choices of reliable consultants for problem-solving (e.g., Lewis, 1981; Young & Ferguson, 1979) and feelings of self-reliance (e.g., Greenberger, 1982; Steinberg & Silverberg, 1986), also increase during adolescence. These changes mark not only the transition from childhood to adolescence, but also further development from early to later adolescence.

Emotional autonomy refers to a sense of individuation from parents and relinquishing dependence on them (Blos, 1967; Steinberg & Silverberg, 1986). With increasing age, adolescents have been found more likely to feel individuated, less likely to idealize their parents, and less likely to express childish dependency on them (Steinberg & Silverberg, 1986).

Cognitive autonomy refers to a "sense of self-reliance, a belief that one has control over his or her own life, and subjective feelings of being able to make decisions without excessive social validation" (Sessa & Steinberg, 1991, p. 42). A key criterion is that judgments and choices are derived from one's own individually held principles, rather than from the expectations of others (Douvan & Adelson, 1966). Subjective sense of autonomy has been found to increase from preadolescence to adolescence (Greenberger, 1982, 1984; Greenberger & Sorenson, 1974).

Identity

Identity refers to "one's sense of coherence of personality and continuity over time" (Grotevant & Cooper, in press). Although identity development is a lifelong process, adolescence traditionally has been regarded as crucial because of the convergence of physical, cognitive, and social changes. In adolescence, identity encompasses not only one's ideas about and feelings about the self, but also the prospect for convergence between these ideas and feelings and one's potential adult roles (e.g., occupational options, relationships, beliefs, and values). Identity is important as a construct of behavioral regulation because of repeated findings that identity difficulties are associated with diverse problems, such as higher levels of conformity to counternormative behavior by peers (e.g., Toder & Marcia, 1973; Waterman, 1992), difficulties in intimate relationships (Fitch & Adams, 1983; Tesch & Whitbourne, 1982), substance use (e.g., Jones & Hartmann, 1988; Jones, Hartmann, Grochowski, & Glider, 1989), and sexual intercourse without protection against the possibility of HIV infection (Hernandez & Diclemente, 1992).

Identity issues appear to be most salient in the late teenage years and early 20s (Waterman, 1985). Early adolescents reveal little engagement in active exploration of identity issues (Archer & Waterman, 1983). In late adolescence, however, gradually increasing proportions of individuals express concerns about integrating self-perceptions of physical changes, sexual feelings, evaluations of competencies, and current or anticipated roles with the sense of self that persists from earlier developmental periods (Grotevant, 1992; Marcia, 1991; Waterman, 1985). As with autonomy transitions, these normative patterns reflect increasing reliance on the self, rather than on compliance and conformity to others. Sizable individual differences occur, however, in the timing and trajectory of identity development (Archer & Waterman, 1983; Grotevant, 1992).

Morality and Responsibility

Morality and social responsibility refer, behaviorally, to "both 'doing good' and 'not doing bad' (as well as ameliorating the negative consequences of one's misbehavior)" (Hartup & Van Lieshout, 1995, p. 675). Both imply autonomous action carried out in the service of internally held principles.

Prosocial behaviors such as helping, sharing, donating, and comforting generally increase during middle childhood and adolescence (Eisenberg, Miller, Shell, McNalley, & Shea, 1991; Underwood & Moore, 1982). Parallel to these behavioral patterns is a stronger emphasis on abstract values and moral principles (e.g., Rest, Davison, & Robbins, 1978), and greater concern for others and adherence to values in reasoning about moral dilemmas (Eisenberg et al., 1991). Similarly, correlations between maturity of reasoning and prosocial behavior and empathy toward others increase during late childhood and adolescence (Eisenberg et al., 1991; Ford, Wentzel, Wood, Stevens, & Siesfeld, 1989; Underwood & Moore, 1982). Feelings of responsibility for the welfare of others become more normative as well (Peterson, 1983). Thus, adolescents increasingly engage in behavior and endorse views and report feelings that are consistent with internalized social values.

Taken together, these findings indicate a developmental pattern that is contrary to popular stereotypes of degeneracy among the young. Normatively, adolescence appears to be a period of strengthening orientation to and mastery of self-directed, competent action, apart from the regulation of others.

CHANGING RELATIONSHIPS AS A CONTEXT
FOR INTERNALIZATION

Although normative psychological and social changes of adolescence often are viewed as direct functions of pubertal maturation, current evidence is consistent with indirect links between the two: Biological maturation appears to elicit different expectations by others and by adolescents themselves; and these expectations, rather than hormonal surges or reproductive physiology, mediate psychological and interpersonal changes (Brooks-Gunn & Reiter, 1990; Buchanan, Eccles, & Becker, 1992; Hill, 1988; Paikoff & Brooks-Gunn, 1991). For example, when a child becomes a teenager or shows signs of the adolescent growth spurt, others often change their expectations about and reactions to the adolescent's behavior; and these altered expectations and reactions, rather than physiological changes per se, contribute to behavioral and emotional changes in early adolescence. Of special significance for internalization are adults' intensifying concerns about the degree to which adolescents have adopted conventional social values and moral standards in preparation for assuming adult roles and responsibilities. These expectations for altered behavior often generate both personal stress and interpersonal difficulties (e.g., Collins, 1990, 1995; Petersen & Hamburg, 1986; Simmons & Blyth, 1987; Smetana, 1995). Thus, understanding internalization during adolescence requires attention to interpersonal relationships, as well as to developmental changes.

Changes in Relationships

Relationships are defined as more or less enduring ties or connections between two individuals, comprising frequent, highly interdependent action sequences across diverse settings and tasks (Kelley et al., 1983). These interdependencies are natural products of the shared histories and complementary roles that emerge over time in both familial or close extrafamilial relationships (e.g., friendships; Collins & Repinski, 1994).

Relationships during childhood and adolescence are marked by both continuity and change (for reviews, see Collins & Russell, 1991; Parker & Gottman, 1989). In most parent-adolescent relationships, emotional bonds and patterns of mutual influence are maintained during this transition, but signs of greater individuation appear as well. Feelings of positive regard increase between childhood and adolescence, especially toward mothers; perceptions of reciprocity with and acceptance by parents become more frequent (Youniss & Smollar, 1985); and adolescents' perceptions of self and others increasingly converge with those of parents (Alessandri & Wozniak, 1987) and friends (Furman & Bierman, 1984). At the same time, feelings of acceptance and satisfaction with family life and decision making generally are lower in middle adolescence than in childhood or young adulthood; and both parents and adolescents report more expressions of negative emotion, more instances of disagreement, and lower expressions of positive emotions and feelings of closeness in early and middle adolescence (for reviews, see Collins & Russell, 1991; Steinberg, 1990).

In adolescents' friendships, intimacy, defined as reciprocal feelings of self-disclosure and engagement in activities, becomes more frequent across the years from middle childhood to middle adolescence (Berndt, 1982; Bigelow & LaGaipa, 1975; Buhrmester, 1990; Furman & Bierman, 1984; Furman & Buhrmester, 1992; Sharabany, Gershoni, & Hofmann, 1981). Intimacy is closely related to satisfaction with friendships during early and middle adolescence (for reviews, see Hartup, 1993, 1996). Paradoxically, conflicts also are more likely between friends than between acquaintances in both childhood and adolescence. During adolescence, conflicts between friends increasingly are likely to be resolved effectively, and conflicts between friends are less likely to disrupt friendships (for reviews, see Hartup, 1993; Savin-Williams & Berndt, 1990).

The coexistence of continuity and discontinuity in relationships often has been viewed as fostering the development of appropriate levels of individuation and autonomy as adolescents mature (Collins, 1990, 1995; Collins & Luebker, 1994; Grotevant & Cooper, 1986; Laursen, 1995; Wynne, 1984). Continuities in emotional bonds make it possible for parents to continue to influence adolescents despite less time together, adolescents' greater autonomy in some activities and responsibilities, and frequent violations and realignments of interpersonal expectancies during periods of rapid individual change (Collins & Luebker, 1994). A key issue in studying internalization during adolescence is identifying the mechanisms through which significant relationships contribute to the development and maintenance of appropriate self-regulated behavior.

Expansion of Relationship Networks

Changes in the nature and course of relationships are accompanied by increasing differentiation among adolescents' close relationships. Relationships in adolescence are more extensive and diverse than those of childhood (Blyth, 1982; Csikszentmihalyi & Larson, 1984). Although family relationships remain salient during adolescence, an increasing proportion of time is devoted to interactions with nonfamily members (Csikszentmihalyi & Larson, 1984). Adolescents establish a wider range of casual friendships than children do, perhaps because of the more numerous possibilities available in school and at work. Romantic relationships also become common.

These diverse relationships serve both complementary and overlapping functions in the development of behavioral regulation (see reviews by Collins & Russell, 1991; Hartup, 1996). Relationships with family members may be described as *closed-field,* in that they are partly defined and constrained by kinship or legal definitions and associated norms and environmental pressures (Berscheid, 1985). Closed-field relationships entail long interaction histories and extensively routinized interactional scripts that militate against autonomy and in favor of internalization of parental expectations and values. Outside the family, adolescents participate in *open-field* interactions and can form and dissolve relationships without the biological or legal constraints that apply to family members. In these less restrictive circumstances, autonomy is more probable, but so is the pressure to conform to conventions of the reference group (Collins, Laursen, Mortensen, Luebker, & Ferreira, 1997; Laursen & Collins, 1994).

The dyadic variability of pressures toward autonomy and internalization thus reflects both social and psychosocial processes. Attention to these processes, as well as to the multiple persons with whom adolescents may form relationships, is important to understanding the potential significance of relationships to internalization during adolescence.

RELATIONSHIP PROCESSES IN INTERNALIZATION

Three broad themes regarding the role of relationships in the development of behavioral regulation have emerged from the research findings reviewed in earlier sections. The first theme is that what have been regarded heretofore as individual traits are inherent in regulatory processes that occur within significant relationships; thus, behavioral regulation is *relational,* rather than intraindividual. The second theme is that the processes of interest are *bilateral* in nature, in contrast to the unilateral mechanism of transmission from one person to another implied by earlier views of internalization. The third theme is that multiple relationships are involved in self-regulatory processes during adolescence. For each of these trends, we summarize evidence on the significance of familial and extrafamilial relationships in the development of autonomy, identity, and morality and social responsibility.

From Individualistic to Relational Views of Outcomes

Although internalization is commonly associated with individual traits, a long tradition of research on correlates of internalization has implicated parent-child relationships, particularly their affective quality. In classic psychoanalytic perspectives, parental warmth and degree of control were seen as conducive to optimal impulse control and formation of object relations (e.g., Blos, 1979; A. Freud, 1969; S. Freud, 1923/1949). Behaviorist viewpoints emphasized the greater effectiveness of socializing agents who had established nurturant relationships with children (e.g., Bandura, 1969; Hartup, 1958). In a different tradition, Vygotsky (1978) and more recent writers (e.g., Rogoff, 1990) have emphasized interpersonal collaboration with agemates, as well as with responsive adults, in acquiring individual competencies. During the past decade, increasing attention has been given to the distinctive qualities of internalization that occur in relationships with parents and with peers.

Familial Relationships

Current models (e.g., Grotevant & Cooper, 1986; Hauser, Powers, & Noam, 1991) posit that the quality of parent-child exchanges and shared decision making, over and above the specific content of parental teaching, contribute to the development of competencies that are more or less compatible with autonomous, responsible behavior. Among these competencies are role-taking skills and advanced ego development and identity exploration. More mature levels of these individual competencies are associated with parent-adolescent relationships marked by behaviors that encourage both individuation (holding and expressing autonomous views, being one's "own person") and connectedness (feeling a bond with other family members).

This correlational pattern is evident in findings about autonomy (for reviews, see Hill & Holmbeck, 1986; Steinberg, 1990). The most extensive evidence comes from research on Baumrind's (1991) conceptualization of parental patterns of control (e.g., Dornbusch, Ritter, Leiderman, Roberts, & Fraleigh, 1987; Lamborn, Mounts, Steinberg, & Dornbusch, 1991; Steinberg, Elmen, & Mounts, 1989). In these studies, primary attention is given to *authoritative* parent-child relationships, marked by parents' expectations of mature behavior in combination with interpersonal warmth, accepting attitudes, bidirectional communication, and an emphasis on training social responsibility and concern for the impact of one's action on others. These characteristics of parent-child relationships are correlated during childhood and adolescence with higher levels of age-appropriate personal maturity and with socially desirable and responsible behavior (Baumrind, 1991; Lamborn et al., 1991). By contrast, patterns characterized as *neglectful,* consisting of relatively few expectations, low involvement with the child, and a rejecting, unresponsive, parent-centered attitude, are associated with relatively higher levels of antisocial delinquency and drug use and with lower levels of personal maturity and achievement (e.g., Lamborn et al., 1991; Steinberg et al., 1989). The association between parent-adolescent relationships and adolescent competence becomes more pronounced over time, as shown in a one-year longitudinal study following students from age 16 to age 17 (Steinberg, Lamborn, Mounts, Darling, & Dornbusch, 1994).

Similar relational correlates are found in research on morality and identity. In studies of moral development and social responsibility, prosocial behavior is correlated with clearly communicated parental expectations for appropriate behavior, combined with warmth and moderate power and presented with reasoning and explanation (for reviews, see Eisenberg, 1990; Hartup & Van Lieshout, 1995). These same characteristics are associated with the higher levels of self-confidence and autonomously chosen values that characterize mature identity. For example, Enright and colleagues (Enright, Lapsley, Drivas, & Fehr, 1980) reported that 7th-grade and 11th-grade adolescents from democratic families were more likely to show a mature identity than were adolescents from autocratic families. Among late adolescents, research findings (Bosma & Gerrits, 1985; Quintana & Lapsley, 1987) have shown that identity achievement was lowest when parents were perceived to attempt to control adolescents' behavior to a great degree.

Longitudinal studies have shown that high levels of bidirectional communication and acceptance in parent-child relationships during childhood and early adolescence are correlated positively with psychosocial maturity in later adolescence. Allen, Hauser, Bell, and O'Connor (1994) followed adolescents in two-parent families who had been observed at age 14 in a revealed differences laboratory interaction task. The task required participants to reconcile their different preferences for a hypothetical family activity. Measures of ego development and self-esteem were taken both at age 14 and at age 16, at the time of Allen's follow-up. The key variable for this analysis was qualities of parent-adolescent relationships that encouraged autonomy, or individuation, *and* relatedness. Examples include encouraging the expression of disagreement, explanations for one's position, confidence in one's position, validation and agreement with another's position, and attending to another's statements. A low score reflects frequent behaviors that make it more difficult for family members to discuss their own reasons for preferring one option over others. Parents' (especially fathers') behaviors of this type were highly correlated with decreases in adolescents' ego development and self-esteem between the ages of 14 and 16. In a similar study, Walker and Taylor (1991) observed parent-adolescent discussions about both hypothetical and real-life moral dilemmas. Parents varied in the degree to which they accommodated to the current moral-reasoning level of their offspring during the discussions. When children's moral-reasoning levels were assessed two years later, movement to a higher level was best predicted by earlier parent-child interactions characterized by supportive, but cognitively challenging, discussions of moral issues (Walker & Taylor, 1991).

These correlational findings leave open the question of how associations between variations in family relationships and manifestations of internalization come about. Several possibilities have been proposed. One is that parents' child-rearing behaviors provide models of different patterns of social responsibility and concern for others. Authoritative parents exemplify socially responsible, caring behavior, whereas neglectful parents model self-absorption and low responsibility for the welfare of others

(Baumrind, 1991). Older siblings may represent another source of modeling and reinforcement of values endorsed by parents (Amato, 1989).

A second possibility is that different parenting styles engender differentially effective skills for autonomous, responsible behavior. Grotevant and Cooper (1986) and Hauser et al. (1991) propose that parents who encourage both individuation and connectedness foster the development of capabilities for more socially responsible, competent behavior. In this respect, parent-child relationships may provide continuities between childhood learning and the new demands of adolescence and adulthood that facilitate the integration of past and future roles.

Third, sensitive, responsive parental treatment of children and adolescents may engender positive emotional bonds that make the values and behaviors of parents more salient and attractive to adolescents. Research findings indicate that adolescents' perceptions of warmth and security in relationships with parents are correlated positively with self-confidence, exploration of issues related to identity, and comfort in interactions with others (Jackson, Dunham, & Kidwell, 1990; Kamptner, 1988). In Grotevant and Cooper's (1985) observational studies of parent-adolescent interaction, adolescents from families marked by high encouragement for expressing and developing one's own point of view disproportionately showed higher levels of identity exploration. These findings imply that the characteristically warm, accepting relationships in authoritative families may increase the likelihood of positive parental influences on adolescents (Barnes & Olson, 1985; Darling & Steinberg, 1993). This principle may apply to sibling relationships as well. Adolescents regard their siblings as relatively important sources of companionship, intimacy, and affect (Buhrmester, 1990). These feelings may provide inducements for coordinating goals and sharing. Turn-taking with siblings may foster both prosocial behavior patterns and self-control (Amato, 1989).

The three possibilities outlined here are not mutually exclusive. The existence of multiple mechanisms implies a more complex causal process than the simple transmission of parents' values. Internalization is facilitated by certain parental behaviors, but the operative processes almost certainly include dynamic properties of relationships between parent and child that foster the adolescents' desire or willingness to be influenced (Darling & Steinberg, 1993).

Extrafamilial Relationships

Peer contributions to behavioral regulation likewise are affected by relationship qualities. Piaget (1932/1977) proposed that the horizontal power structures of peer relationships make them especially important contexts for the development of moral decision making. Research findings confirm that social participation is both the source of most moral issues for adolescents and the context for decisions about such issues (e.g., Haan, 1978, 1985). Recent findings from a sample of high-school students showed that the majority, when asked to cite a dilemma they personally had faced, described moral conflicts in the context of relationships, usually involving friends (Johnston, Brown, & Christopherson, 1990). Peers also contribute to key aspects of identity formation. In Erikson's (1968) view, identity achievement includes both bringing oneself into accord with the social group and becoming comfortable with some differences between oneself and one's peers. Individuals facing identity difficulties may use the social group to define themselves because they lack internally held standards or an adequate sense of self (Grotevant, 1992; Waterman, 1992).

The impact of peers varies, however, as a function of relationship qualities. Just as parent-child relationships marked by emotional warmth and reciprocity are especially efficacious contexts for internalization, peer relationships marked by greater closeness, frequency of interaction, and positive emotional expression are more influential in the development of internalized values and behaviors than less close relationships (Haan, 1985; Nelson & Aboud, 1985). In adolescence, increasing capacities for intimacy and negotiation may enhance the potential impact of close relationships on the development of moral reasoning.

Links between peer relations and internalization follow a complex trajectory. Whereas autonomy in parent-adolescent relationships is characterized by a gradual linear increase in distance and independence, autonomy in peer contexts follows a curvilinear pattern. Autonomy from peers is relatively high in middle childhood, such that parental influences predominate for most children (Hartup, 1983). In early adolescence, by contrast, autonomy from parents increases and peer influence becomes more prevalent. Brown and colleagues (Brown, 1989, 1990; Brown, Eicher, & Petrie, 1986; Brown, Mory, & Kinney, 1994) posit that peer groups furnish stable and intimate relationships that partly replace the psychological dependence on parents. As autonomy from peers reaches its nadir, early adolescent peer groups foster conformity by providing alternative norms and expectations that adolescents can adopt temporarily before achieving a mature, autonomous identity.

Autonomy from peers is higher during late adolescence than during early adolescence (Brown et al., 1986; Clasen & Brown, 1985). The reasons for this relative increase, however, almost certainly are different than the reasons for the relative difference between middle-childhood and early-adolescent autonomy from peers. One reason may be the end of secondary schooling, which is the context for much peer-group activity. Another possible reason is that older adolescents increasingly view peer group pressures as threatening their greater individuality and autonomy.

From Unilateral to Bilateral Processes

In early research on adolescence, as in the study of other developmental periods, relationships were viewed primarily as sources of directly transmitted behavior patterns and values. These *social-mold theories* (Hartup, 1983) attributed variations in adolescent behavior to variations in parental behavior. In classic psychoanalytic perspectives, parental warmth and degree of control were seen as conducive to optimal impulse control and formation of object relations (e.g., Blos, 1979; A. Freud, 1969; S. Freud, 1923/1949). Behaviorist viewpoints emphasized the need for appropriate contingencies and effective models of self-control (e.g., Bandura, 1969). Current models of behavioral regulation imply bilateral influences, although adolescents are not depicted as having an impact equal to that of parents. Baumrind's (e.g., 1991) typological model emphasizes parental actions, but also acknowledges the importance of responsiveness to the child as a basis for continuing influence. Bilateral individual functioning may become increasingly significant during adolescence, when the child's greater competence potentially permits more extensive contributions to decision making and behavioral regulation.

Familial Relationships

These relational conceptions of individual competence carry two important implications. One is that effective socialization is likely to entail a gradual, rather than abrupt, process of developmental change. Maccoby (1984) has argued that the development of autonomy moves from parent regulation in early life, to increasingly shared decision making between parent and child in childhood and adolescence, to self-regulation in adulthood. In this view, coregulation provides essential training for effective interdependence, rather than independence. In her words, parenting that is attentive to training for autonomy ". . . inducts the child into a system of reciprocity" (Maccoby, 1992, p. 1013).

A second implication is that parent-child influence may occur on multiple levels. Research findings now indicate that the outcomes for adolescents are most positive when parents practice child-centered patterns of discipline, accompanied by clearly communicated demands, parental monitoring, and an atmosphere of acceptance toward the child (authoritative parenting; Baumrind, 1991; Darling & Steinberg, 1993; Maccoby, 1984; Maccoby & Martin, 1983). Darling and Steinberg (1993) distinguish between parental *styles,* which are global attitudes and emotional stances that influence the quality of relationships with children, and parental *practices,* which are specific strategies for gaining children's compliance, maintaining control, and enforcing expectations. *Style* is regarded as having motivational effects on the child's receptiveness to specific practices.

Extrafamilial Relationships

Peer influences also reflect these bidirectional and multidirectional processes. Friendships are, by definition, bilateral relationships between individuals. Friends typically are concordant in both demographic and individual attributes (Hartup, 1996). Consequently, interactions between friends are likely to strengthen existing patterns of behavior and values in both members of the dyad. One reason for this is that similarity to friends enhances one's sense of well-being; another is that interpersonal discrepancies challenge and threaten the bases for continuing the relationship and may interfere with shared goals between the two friends (Hartup, 1992). Longitudinal findings (e.g., Dishion, Duncan, Eddy, Fagot, & Feltrow, 1994; Kandel, 1978) indicate that friends become more similar to one another over time. This tendency toward greater similarity is stronger in pairs who are later found to have maintained their friendship than in pairs whose friendship will be terminated in the near future. Increases in similarity also are greater for friendships with many positive features (Berndt & Keefe, 1995). Perhaps, as the network of extrafamilial relationships expands, peer affiliations can be more sharply differentiated on the basis of relationship qualities.

From Relationships to Relations among Relationships

Current views of the development of behavioral regulation incorporate the bidirectional processes between friends and those between parents and children, as well as the interrelations between the two (e.g., Patterson, DeBaryshe, & Ramsey, 1989). Although traditional conceptualizations have placed peer influences in opposition to parental values, recent findings have shown that extrafamilial relationships work in conjunction with parent-adolescent relationships in predicting behavior.

Two lines of research illustrate how interrelated parent and peer processes support the regulation of behavior. In both cases, the internalized patterns of interest are deviant behaviors. One line of work comes from Dishion's confluence model (Dishion, Patterson, & Griesler, 1994) of how friendships between deviant peers serve to maintain or increase deviant behaviors in adolescence, over and above the effects associated with parental influences (Dishion, Patterson, Stoolmiller, & Skinner, 1991). According to this model, peer rejection limits the pool of available peers from which an adolescent can select friends. Because of attraction among similar others (Kandel,

1978), children and adolescents with antisocial traits tend to befriend others with antisocial traits (Dishion, Andrews, & Crosby, 1995); and these friendship dyads display higher rates of conversation about antisocial behavior and substance abuse in an effort to elicit positive reinforcement and more firmly establish common ground between the interactants. Thus, interactions in dyads formed on the basis of similarity in antisocial traits constitute "deviancy training."

The second line of research arises from a similar model, although the focus is peer-group norms and pressures, rather than friendship processes. Brown and colleagues (Brown, Mounts, Lamborn, & Steinberg, 1993; Durbin, Darling, Steinberg, & Brown, 1993) posit that particular parenting practices (e.g., emphasis on academic achievement, parental monitoring, and facilitation of joint parent-child decision making) and parenting styles (e.g., variations along dimensions of demandingness and responsiveness) are associated with certain adolescent behaviors and predispositions. These behaviors then guide adolescents into particular peer groups, such as "brains," "jocks," or "druggies." Like Dishion, Brown assumes that like-minded peers gravitate toward one another. Once adolescents affiliate with a peer group, peer norms reinforce the behavioral styles that were the impetus for the affiliation. Thus, parents indirectly affect their children's peer group association through their influence on certain personality traits and behaviors in their child.

The interplay between familial and extrafamilial influences thus is moderated partly by qualities of parent-child relationships that are undergoing change during adolescence. Fuligni and Eccles (1993) have demonstrated links between the degree and direction of change in parent-child relationships during early adolescence and the likelihood of orientation to peers as sources of information and influence. Following a sample of 1,771 children from sixth to seventh grade, they found that an increasing degree of extreme orientation to peers over time is a positive function of perceptions of parental strictness and a negative function of opportunities for decision making affecting the self.

Summary

Although familial influences, especially from parents, have been dominant in much of the research on autonomy, identity, and morality, the research reviewed here documents that parent-child relationships implicate extrafamilial influences as well. This may become more apparent from developmental studies. With the expansion of social networks during adolescence, the interrelated influences of family and peers are likely to be especially significant in behavioral regulation. To date, this possibility has been addressed primarily in studies of antisocial behavior, and research is needed to examine interrelated influences in other aspects of internalization.

TOWARD RELATIONAL PERSPECTIVES ON INTERNALIZATION

Findings on self-direction and self-regulation in adolescence imply a broader framework for future research on internalization. At a minimum, this framework should provide an expanded view of the competencies under the rubric of *internalization*. In addition, the framework should take account of developmental changes in these competencies during and following the transition from childhood to adolescence. Finally, the framework should recognize the contributions of adolescents' experiences in multiple relationships to internalization.

Expanding the Construct of Internalization

Theorists and researchers long have recognized that internalization incorporates multiple aspects of human functioning. The constructs discussed in this chapter—autonomy, identity, and morality—themselves represent facets of internalization during adolescence, and each has been construed in terms of multiple components (i.e., behavior, cognition, and affect). Research findings on adolescents, moreover, show that these components are manifested more diversely than has traditionally been recognized.

The broader range of relevant behaviors comes in part from the relational nature of internalization. In contrast to traditional views of internalization as independence from others, research on adolescents depicts self-regulatory functioning as embedded in the interdependencies between self and others. Consequently, internalization research must include not only competencies for individual action, but also skills for participating in the varied relationships that contribute to behavioral regulation.

These skills go beyond the acquisition of socially approved behavior patterns to capabilities for mature judgments and for interpersonal coordination and collaboration (e.g., role-taking, empathy, negotiation). Grusec and Goodnow have proposed a useful model of socialization conditions that foster these core competencies. As a primary condition they posit characteristics of relationships that encourage attentiveness to the other and enhance clarity of exchanges (e.g., Goodnow, 1994; Grusec & Goodnow, 1994).

The greater salience of this richer set of competencies during adolescence comes about for several reasons. One reason is that multiple skills may become more obvious because of the opportunity and necessity to adapt to a wider range of settings (cf. Higgins & Parsons, 1983). A second reason is that skills themselves may more closely approximate adult competence and, thus, may become relatively more important for forming adults' expectations and their appraisal of the degree to which internalization has been accomplished. An example of the latter is negotiation, which is more common during adolescence and for which competence is significantly greater in adolescence than in childhood (for a review, see Laursen & Collins, 1994).

The salience of multiple competencies also may reflect different issues associated with self-regulation during adolescence. Compared with younger children, adolescents view many issues as matters of personal choice, rather than as matters of either morality or conventionality. In their view, many autonomy transitions, therefore, are not subject to the authority of parents or society (Smetana, 1995). At the same time, many activities that are typically initiated during adolescence (e.g., sexual activity, use of alcohol and drugs, driving a car) may involve more serious long-term consequences (Ford, 1991; Ford et al., 1989). As a result, parents may be less willing to recognize them as solely personal matters. Consequently, conflicts over autonomy transitions may result from issues of competence to undertake more complex judgments, as well as from noncompliance (Smetana, 1989, 1995).

The proposal for a broader conceptualization of internalization readily accommodates cultural diversity regarding internalization. Growing evidence documents cultural variations in expectations for behavioral regulation during adolescence (for reviews, see Cooper, 1994; Grotevant & Cooper, in press; Snarey, 1985). For example, Cooper (1994) has argued that autonomy from family members is not a salient developmental expectation in non-European cultural groups (see also Feldman & Quatman, 1988; Feldman & Rosenthal, 1991). Moreover, expectations regarding the conduct of familial relationships constrain adolescents' attitudes toward parents and siblings. Consequently, variations in parent-child relationships that are associated with distinctive patterns of behavior in adolescents of European descent may not manifest similar links in non-European groups (e.g., Rohner & Pettengill, 1985). The emotional and behavioral implications of these differences for internalization need further study.

Recognizing Developmental Changes in Capacities for Self-Regulation

Examining a wider range of competencies is complicated by developmental changes in skills for behavioral regulation. Cognitive competencies provide an example. Internalization requires grasping the implications of thoughts and actions conveyed by other persons. Several aspects of developmental changes during adolescence potentially affect this aspect of internalization. Increasing capabilities for abstract thinking and logical reasoning are manifested in social relations (e.g., Keating, 1990; Selman & Shultz, 1989; Smetana, 1989). Mature moral judgments require integration of several different pieces of information. Moral development is partly a growing ability to generalize from one moral situation to the next and to apply established principles to unfamiliar events (Smetana, 1995). Moreover, with development, moral issues center less on the welfare of others and more on a balance between the rights of multiple individuals (Eisenberg et al., 1991; Smetana, 1995).

Growth in moral judgment parallels the development of competencies for coordinated action and for beneficent acts toward others. Improved perspective-taking skills, problem-solving, and increased empathy are associated with increased prosocial behavior during middle childhood and adolescence (Eisenberg, 1990; Eisenberg et al., 1991; Underwood & Moore, 1982). Conceptual advances regarding relationships with parents and friends also enhance competencies for internalization (e.g., Selman, 1980; Selman & Schultz, 1989).

The developmental trajectories of component skills for internalization in earlier periods of life have been studied little more than change during adolescence (for an exception, see Kuczynski, Zahn-Waxler, & Radke-Yarrow, 1987). A developmental perspective on a greater range of competencies thus may encourage researchers to examine the roots of these competencies in earlier periods of life and their implications for behavioral regulation beyond adolescence.

Recognizing Multiple Relational Contexts

The evidence of interrelations among significant relationships necessitates a broader interpersonal context for internalization. Studies largely have addressed varying levels of parent-adolescent-peer relationships (e.g., the interrelation of parent-adolescent relationships with an adolescent's closest associates vs. general peer group involvement). These studies have undermined some traditional views of the social influences impinging on adolescents. For example, examining links between parent and peer contributions to antisocial behavior (e.g., DeBaryshe, Patterson, & Capaldi, 1993; Dishion, 1990; Dishion et al., 1991; Patterson, Reid, & Dishion, 1992; Vuchinich, Bank, & Patterson, 1992) has challenged the simplistic but widely held view that adolescents turn away from parents toward peers. More consistent with the evidence is a formulation in which both are elements of an expanding network of relationships and in which their influences are interrelated and complementary.

Research findings also indicate that socially appropriate behavior patterns often attributed to individual dispositions actually vary across individuals and contexts. For example, prosocial behavior may differ in the context of the peer group and in the company of adults (Eisenberg, 1990): Prosocial behavior among peers may include coalition formation or intimacy, as well as instrumental helping and support; whereas prosocial behavior with adults more appropriately includes instrumental assistance, but not intimacy. The conditions under which influences from parents and peers contradict each other and the circumstances in which parent and peer influences contribute to the same developmental outcomes are central questions for future internalization research.

CONCLUSION

Research with adolescents challenges traditional theoretical and methodological approaches to internalization. Conceptually, findings imply that internalization, like many other putatively individual changes, can be understood more fully in the context of relationships with significant others (Collins et al., 1997). Methodologically, the findings imply the need for broadening the construct of internalization to incorporate interpersonal competencies and developmental changes in them. The key task is to understand not only the developing individual, but the interplay between individual growth and change and the nature and developmental significance of relationships with others. This broader perspective thus may allow for a more comprehensive understanding of internalization and its developmental course.

REFERENCES

Adams, G. R., Gullotta, T. P., & Montemayor, R. (1992). *Adolescent identity formation.* Newbury Park, CA: Sage.

Alessandri, S. M., & Wozniak, R. H. (1987). The child's awareness of parental beliefs concerning the child: A developmental study. *Child Development, 58,* 316–323.

Allen, J. P., Hauser, S. T., Bell, K. L., & O'Connor, T. G. (1994). Longitudinal assessment of autonomy and relatedness in adolescent-family interactions as predictors of adolescent ego development and self-esteem. *Child Development, 65,* 179–194.

Amato, P. (1987). Family processes in one-parent, stepparent, and intact families: The child's point of view. *Journal of Marriage and the Family, 49,* 327–337.

Amato, P. (1989). Family processes and the competence of adolescents and primary school children. *Journal of Youth and Adolescence, 18,* 39–53.

Archer, S. L., & Waterman, A. (1983). Identity in early adolescence: A developmental perspective. *Journal of Early Adolescence, 3,* 203–214.

Bandura, A. (1969). *Principles of behavior modification.* New York: Holt, Rinehart and Winston.

Barnes, H., & Olson, D. (1985). Parent-adolescent communication and the circumplex model. *Child Development, 56,* 438–447.

Baumrind, D. (1991). Effective parenting during the early adolescent transition. In P. A. Cowan & M. Hetherington (Eds.), *Family transitions* (pp. 111–163). Hillsdale, NJ: Erlbaum.

Berndt, T. J. (1979). Developmental changes in conformity to peers and parents. *Developmental Psychology, 15,* 608–616.

Berndt, T. J. (1982). The features and effects of friendship in early adolescence. *Child Development, 53,* 1447–1460.

Berndt, T. J., & Keefe, K. (1995). Friends' influence on adolescents' adjustment to school. *Child Development, 66*(5), 1312–1329.

Berscheid, E. (1985). Interpersonal attraction. In G. Lindzey & E. Aronson (Eds.), *Handbook of social psychology* (3rd ed., pp. 413–484). New York: Random House.

Bigelow, B. J., & LaGaipa, J. J. (1975). Children's written descriptions of friendship: A multidimensional analysis. *Developmental Psychology, 11,* 857–858.

Blos, P. (1967). The second individuation process of adolescence. *The Psychoanalytic Study of the Child, 22,* 162–168.

Blos, P. (1979). *The adolescent passage.* New York: International Universities Press.

Blyth, D. A. (1982). Mapping the social world of adolescents: Issues, techniques, and problems. In F. Serafica (Ed.), *Social cognitive development in context* (pp. 240–252). New York: Guilford Press.

Bosma, H. A., & Gerrits, R. S. (1985). Family functioning and identity status in adolescence. *Journal of Early Adolescence, 5,* 69–80.

Brooks-Gunn, J., & Reiter, E. O. (1990). The role of pubertal processes. In S. S. Feldman & G. R. Elliott (Eds.), *At the threshold: The developing adolescent* (pp. 16–53). Cambridge, MA: Harvard University Press.

Brown, B. B. (1989). The role of peer groups in adolescents' adjustment to secondary school. In T. J. Berndt & G. W. Ladd (Eds.), *Peer relationships in child development* (pp. 188–215). New York: Wiley.

Brown, B. B. (1990). Peer groups and peer cultures. In S. S. Feldman & G. R. Elliott (Eds.), *At the threshold: The developing adolescent* (pp. 171–196). Cambridge, MA: Harvard University Press.

Brown, B. B., Eicher, S. A., & Petrie, S. (1986). The importance of peer group affiliation in adolescence. *Journal of Adolescence, 9,* 73–96.

Brown, B. B., Mory, M. S., & Kinney, D. (1994). Casting adolescent crowds in a relational perspective: Caricature, channel, and context. In R. Montemayor, G. R. Adams, & T. P. Gullotta (Eds.), *Personal relationships during adolescence* (pp. 123–167). Newbury Park, CA: Sage.

Brown, B. B., Mounts, N., Lamborn, S. D., & Steinberg, L. (1993). Parenting practices and peer group affiliation in adolescence. *Child Development, 64,* 467–482.

Buchanan, C. M., Eccles, J. S., & Becker, J. B. (1992). Are adolescents the victims of raging hormones: Evidence for activational effects of hormones on moods and behavior at adolescence. *Psychological Bulletin, 111,* 62–107.

Buhrmester, D. (1990). Intimacy of friendship, interpersonal competence, and adjustment during preadolescence and adolescence. *Child Development, 61,* 1101–1111.

Clasen, D. R., & Brown, B. B. (1985). The multidimensionality of peer pressure in adolescence. *Journal of Youth and Adolescence, 14*(6), 451–568.

Collins, W. A. (1990). Parent-child relationships in the transition to adolescence: Continuity and change in interaction, affect, and cognition. In R. Montemayor, G. Adams, & T. Gullotta (Eds.), *From childhood to adolescence: A transitional period?* (pp. 85–106). Beverly Hills, CA: Sage.

Collins, W. A. (1995). Relationships and development: Family adaptation to individual change. In S. Shulman (Ed.), *Close relationships and socioemotional development* (pp. 129–155). New York: ABLEX.

Collins, W. A., Laursen, B., Mortensen, N., Luebker, C., & Ferreira, M. (1997). Conflict processes and transitions in parent and peer relationships: Implications for autonomy and regulation. *Journal of Adolescent Research, 12,* 178–198.

Collins, W. A., & Luebker, C. (1994). Parent and adolescent expectancies: Individual and relational significance. In J. G. Smetana (Ed.), *New directions for child development* (Vol. 66, pp. 65–80). San Francisco: Jossey-Bass.

Collins, W. A., & Repinski, D. J. (1994). Relationships during adolescence: Continuity and change in interpersonal perspective. In R. Montemayor, G. Adams, & T. Gullotta (Eds.), *Advances in adolescent development: Vol. 5. Personal relationships during adolescence* (pp. 7–36). Beverly Hills, CA: Sage.

Collins, W. A., & Russell, G. (1991). Mother-child and father-child relationships in middle childhood and adolescence: A developmental analysis. *Developmental Review, 11,* 99–136.

Cooper, C. R. (1994). Cultural perspectives on continuity and change in adolescents' relationships. In R. Montemayor, G. R. Adams, & T. P. Gullotta (Eds.), *Personal relationships during adolescence* (pp. 78–100). Thousand Oaks, CA: Sage.

Crittenden, P. M. (1990). Toward a concept of autonomy in adolescents with a disability. *Children's Health Care, 19,* 162–168.

Csikszentmihalyi, M., & Larson, R. (1984). *Being adolescent.* New York: Basic Books.

Darling, N., & Steinberg, L. (1993). Parenting style as context: An integrative model. *Psychological Bulletin, 113*(3), 487–496.

DeBaryshe, B. D., Patterson, G. R., & Capaldi, D. M. (1993). A performance model for academic achievement in early adolescent boys. *Developmental Psychology, 29,* 795–804.

Dishion, T. J. (1990). The family ecology of boys' peer relations in middle childhood. *Child Development, 61,* 874–892.

Dishion, T. J., Andrews, D. W., & Crosby, L. (1995). Antisocial boys and their friends in early adolescence: Relationship characteristics, quality, and interactional process. *Child Development, 66,* 139–151.

Dishion, T. J., Duncan, T. E., Eddy, J. M., Fagot, B. I., & Feltrow, R. (1994). The world of parents and peers: Coercive exchanges and children's social adaptation. *Social Development, 3*(3), 255–268.

Dishion, T. J., Patterson, G. R., & Griesler, P. C. (1994). Peer adaptations in the development of antisocial behavior: A confluence model. In L. R. Huesmann (Ed.), *Aggressive behavior: Current perspectives* (pp. 61–95). New York: Plenum Press.

Dishion, T. J., Patterson, G. R., Stoolmiller, M., & Skinner, M. L. (1991). Family, school, and behavioral antecedents to early adolescent involvement with antisocial peers. *Developmental Psychology, 27*(1), 172–180.

Dornbusch, S. M., Ritter, P. L., Leiderman, P. H., Roberts, D. F., & Fraleigh, M. J. (1987). The relation of parenting style to adolescent school performance. *Child Development, 58,* 1244–1257.

Dornbusch, S. M., Ritter, P. L., Mont-Reynaud, R., & Chen, Z. (1990). Family decision making and academic performance in a diverse high school population. *Journal of Adolescent Research, 5,* 143–160.

Douvan, E., & Adelson, J. (1966). *The adolescent experience.* New York: Wiley.

Dunn, J., & Munn, P. (1986). Siblings and prosocial development. *International Journal of Behavioral Development, 9,* 265–284.

Durbin, D. L., Darling, N., Steinberg, L., & Brown, B. B. (1993). Parenting style and peer group membership among European-American adolescents. *Journal of Research on Adolescence, 3*(1), 87–100.

Eisenberg, N. (1990). Prosocial development in early and midadolescence. In R. Montemayor, G. Adams, & T. Gullotta (Eds.), *From childhood to adolescence: A transitional period?* (pp. 240–268). Newbury Park, CA: Sage.

Eisenberg, N., Miller, P. A., Shell, R., McNalley, S., & Shea, C. (1991). Prosocial development in adolescence: A longitudinal study. *Psychological Bulletin, 27*(5), 849–857.

Enright, R., Lapsley, D., Drivas, A., & Fehr, L. (1980). Parental influences on the development of adolescent autonomy and identity. *Journal of Youth and Adolescence, 9,* 529–545.

Erikson, E. H. (1968). *Identity: Youth and crisis.* New York: Norton.

Feldman, S. S., & Quatman, T. (1988). Factors influencing age expectations for adolescent autonomy: A study of early adolescents and parents. *Journal of Early Adolescence, 8,* 325–343.

Feldman, S. S., & Rosenthal, D. A. (1991). Age expectations of behavioral autonomy in Hong Kong, Australian and American youth: The influence of family variables and adolescents' values. *International Journal of Psychology, 26,* 1–23.

Fitch, S., & Adams, G. R. (1983). Ego identity and intimacy status: Replication and extension. *Developmental Psychology, 19,* 839–845.

Ford, M. (1991). Social intelligence in adolescence. In R. M. Lerner, A. C. Petersen, & J. Brooks-Gunn (Eds.), *Encyclopedia of adolescence* (Vol. 2, pp. 1066–1071). New York: Garland.

Ford, M., Wentzel, K., Wood, D., Stevens, E., & Siesfeld, G. (1989). Processes associated with integrative social competence: Emotional and contextual influences on adolescent social responsibility. *Journal of Adolescent Research, 4,* 405–425.

Freud, A. (1969). Adolescence as a developmental disturbance. In G. Caplan & S. Lebovici (Eds.), *Adolescence: Psychological perspectives* (pp. 5–10). New York: Basic Books.

Freud, S. (1949). *Collected papers: Vol. 2. The infantile genital organization of the libido.* London: Hogarth Press. (Original work published 1923)

Fuligni, A. J., & Eccles, J. S. (1993). Perceived parent-child relationships and early adolescents' orientation toward peers. *Developmental Psychology, 29,* 622–632.

Furman, W., & Bierman, K. (1984). Children's conceptions of friendship: A multimethod study of developmental changes. *Developmental Psychology, 20,* 925–931.

Furman, W., & Buhrmester, D. (1992). Age and sex differences in perceptions of networks of personal relationships. *Child Development, 63,* 103–115.

Goodnow, J. J. (1994). Acceptable disagreement across generations. In J. G. Smetana (Ed.), *New directions for child development: Vol. 66. Social cognitive models of parenting* (pp. 51–64). San Francisco: Jossey-Bass.

Greenberger, E. (1982). Education and the acquisition of psychosocial maturity. In D. C. McClelland (Ed.), *The development of social maturity* (pp. 155–189). New York: Irvington.

Greenberger, E. (1984). Defining psychosocial maturity in adolescence. In P. Karoly & J. Steffen (Eds.), *Adolescent behavior disorders: Foundations and contemporary concerns* (pp. 54–81). Lexington, MA: Heath.

Greenberger, E., & Sorenson, A. (1974). Toward a concept of psychosocial maturity. *Journal of Youth and Adolescence, 3,* 329–358.

Grotevant, H. (1992). Assigned and chosen identity components: A process perspective on their integration. In G. R. Adams, T. P. Gullotta, & R. Montemayor (Eds.), *Adolescent identity formation* (pp. 73–90). Newbury Park, CA: Sage.

Grotevant, H., & Cooper, C. (1985). Patterns of interaction in family relationships and the development of identity exploration in adolescence. *Child Development, 56,* 415–428.

Grotevant, H., & Cooper, C. (1986). Individuation in family relationships. *Human Development, 29,* 82–100.

Grotevant, H. D., & Cooper, C. R. (in press). Individuality and connectedness in adolescent development: Review and prospects for research on identity, relationships, and context. In E. Skoe & A. von der Lippe (Eds.), *Personality development in adolescence: A cross national and life span perspective.* London: Routledge & Kegan Paul.

Grusec, J. E., & Goodnow, J. J. (1994). Impact of parental discipline methods on child's internalization of values: A reconceptualization of current points of view. *Developmental Psychology, 30,* 4–19.

Haan, N. (1978). Two moralities in action contexts: Relationships to thought, ego regulation, and development. *Journal of Personality and Social Psychology, 36*(3), 286–305.

Haan, N. (1985). Processes of moral development: Cognitive or social disequilibrium? *Developmental Psychology, 21*(6), 996–1006.

Hartup, W. W. (1958). Nurturance and nurturance-withdrawal in relation to the dependency behavior of young children. *Child Development, 29,* 191–201.

Hartup, W. W. (1983). Peer relations. In P. H. Mussen (Series Ed.) & E. M. Hetherington (Vol. Ed.), *Handbook of child psychology: Vol. 4. Socialization, personality and social development* (4th ed., pp. 103–196). New York: Wiley.

Hartup, W. W. (1992). Friendships and their developmental significance. In H. McGurk (Ed.), *Contemporary issues in childhood social development* (pp. 175–205). London: Routledge & Kegan Paul.

Hartup, W. W. (1993). Adolescents and their friends. In B. Laursen (Ed.), *New directions for child development: Vol. 60. Close friendships in adolescence* (pp. 3–22). San Francisco: Jossey-Bass.

Hartup, W. W. (1996). The company they keep: Friendships and their developmental significance. *Child Development, 67,* 1–13.

Hartup, W. W., & Van Lieshout, C. F. M. (1995). Personality development in social context. *Annual Review of Psychology, 46,* 655–687.

Hauser, S. T., Powers, S., & Noam, G. (1991). *Adolescents and their families: Paths of ego development.* New York: Free Press.

Hernandez, J. T., & Diclemente, R. J. (1992). Self control and ego identity development as predictors of unprotected sex in late adolescent males. *Journal of Adolescence, 15,* 437–447.

Higgins, E. T., & Parsons, J. E. (1983). Social cognition and the social life of the child: Stages as subcultures. In E. T. Higgins, D. N. Ruble, & W. W. Hartup (Eds.), *Social cognition and social development: A sociocultural perspective* (pp. 15–62). New York: Cambridge University Press.

Hill, J. P. (1987). Research on adolescents and their families: Past and prospect. In C. E. Irwin, Jr. (Ed.), *New directions for child development: Vol. 37. Adolescent social behavior and health* (pp. 13–32). San Francisco: Jossey-Bass.

Hill, J. P. (1988). Adapting to menarche: Familial control and conflict. In M. R. Gunnar & W. A. Collins (Eds.), *Minnesota symposia on child psychology: Vol. 21. Development during the transition to adolescence* (pp. 43–77). Hillsdale, NJ: Erlbaum.

Hill, J. P., & Holmbeck, G. N. (1986). Attachment and autonomy during adolescence. *Annals of Child Development, 3,* 145–189.

Hoffman, M. L. (1980). Moral development in adolescence. In J. Adelson (Eds.), *Handbook of adolescent psychology* (pp. 295–343). New York: Wiley.

Jackson, E., Dunham, R., & Kidwell, J. (1990). The effects of gender and of family cohesion and adaptability on identity status. *Journal of Adolescent Research, 5,* 161–174.

Johnston, D., Brown, L., & Christopherson, S. (1990). Adolescents' moral dilemmas: The context. *Journal of Youth and Adolescence, 19,* 615–622.

Jones, R. M., & Hartmann, B. R. (1988). Ego identity: Developmental differences and experimental substance abuse among adolescents. *Journal of Adolescence, 11,* 347–360.

Jones, R. M., Hartmann, B. R., Grochowski, C. O., & Glider, P. (1989). Ego identity and substance abuse: A comparison of adolescents in residential treatment with adolescents in school. *Personality and Individual Differences, 10,* 625–631.

Kamptner, N. (1988). Identity development in late adolescence: Causal modeling of social and familial influences. *Journal of Youth and Adolescence, 17,* 493–514.

Kandel, D. B. (1978). Similarity in real-life adolescent friendship pairs. *Journal of Personality and Social Psychology, 36,* 302–312.

Keating, D. P. (1990). Adolescent thinking. In S. S. Feldman & G. R. Elliott (Eds.), *At the threshold: The developing adolescent* (pp. 54–89). Cambridge, MA: Harvard University Press.

Kelley, H. H., Berscheid, E., Christensen, A., Harvey, J. H., Huston, T. L., Levinger, G., McClintock, E., Peplau, L. A., & Peterson, D. R. (1983). *Close relationships.* New York: Freeman.

Kohlberg, L. (1969). State and sequence: The cognitive-developmental approach to socialization. In D. Goslin (Eds.), *Handbook of socialization theory and research.* Chicago: Rand McNally.

Kuczynski, L., Zahn-Waxler, C., & Radke-Yarrow, M. (1987). Development and content of imitation in the second and third years of life: A socialization perspective. *Developmental Psychology, 23*(2), 276–282.

Lamborn, S. D., Mounts, N. S., Steinberg, L., & Dornbusch, S. M. (1991). Patterns of competence and adjustment among adolescents from authoritative, authoritarian, indulgent, and neglectful families. *Child Development, 62,* 1049–1065.

Laursen, B. (1995). Conflict and social interaction in adolescent relationships. *Journal of Research on Adolescence, 5,* 55–70.

Laursen, B., & Collins, W. A. (1988). Conceptual changes during adolescence and effects upon parent-child relationships. *Journal of Adolescent Research, 3*(2), 119–140.

Laursen, B., & Collins, W. A. (1994). Interpersonal conflict during adolescence. *Psychological Bulletin, 115*(2), 197–209.

Lewis, C. (1981). How adolescents approach decisions: Changes over grades seven to twelve and policy implications. *Child Development, 52,* 538–544.

Maccoby, E. E. (1984). Middle childhood in the context of the family. In W. A. Collins (Ed.), *Development during middle childhood: The years from six to twelve* (pp. 184–239). Washington, DC: National Academy Press.

Maccoby, E. E. (1992). The role of parents in the socialization of children: An historical overview. *Developmental Psychology, 28,* 1006–1017.

Maccoby, E. E., & Martin, J. A. (1983). Socialization in the context of the family: Parent-child interaction. In P. H. Mussen (Ed.), *Handbook of child psychology* (Vol. 4, pp. 1–101). New York: Wiley.

Marcia, J. E. (1980). Identity in adolescence. In J. Adelson (Ed.), *Handbook of adolescent psychology* (pp. 159–187). New York: Wiley.

Marcia, J. E. (1991). Identity and self-development. In R. M. Lerner, A. C. Petersen, & J. Brooks-Gunn (Eds.), *Encyclopedia of adolescence* (Vol. 1, pp. 529–533). New York: Garland.

Miller, J. G., & Bersoff, D. M. (1992). Cultural and moral judgment: How are conflicts between justice and interpersonal responsibilities resolved? *Journal of Personality and Social Psychology, 62*(4), 541–554.

Nelson, J., & Aboud, F. E. (1985). The resolution of social conflict between friends. *Child Development, 56,* 1009–1017.

Paikoff, R. L., & Brooks-Gunn, J. (1991). Do parent-child relationships change during puberty? *Psychological Bulletin, 110,* 47–66.

Parker, J. G., & Gottman, J. M. (1989). Social and emotional development in a relational context: Friendship interaction from early childhood to adolescence. In T. J. Berndt & G. W. Ladd (Eds.), *Peer relationships in child development* (pp. 95–131). New York: Wiley.

Patterson, G. R., DeBaryshe, B. D., & Ramsey, E. (1989). A developmental perspective on antisocial behavior. *American Psychologist, 44,* 329–335.

Patterson, G. R., Reid, J. B., & Dishion, T. J. (1992). *Antisocial boys.* Eugene, OR: Castalia Press.

Petersen, A. C., & Hamburg, B. (1986). Adolescence: A developmental approach to problems and psychopathology. *Behavior Therapy, 17,* 480–499.

Peterson, L. (1983). Influence of age, task competence, and responsibility focus on children's altruism. *Developmental Psychology, 19,* 141–148.

Piaget, J. (1977). *The moral judgment of the child.* New York: Free Press. (Original work published 1932)

Poole, M. E., & Gelder, A. J. (1984). Family cohesiveness and adolescent autonomy in decision making. *Australian Journal of Sex, Marriage and the Family, 5,* 65–75.

Quintana, S. M., & Lapsley, D. K. (1987). Adolescent attachment and ego identity: A structural equations approach to the continuity of adaptation. *Journal of Adolescent Research, 2,* 393–409.

Rest, J. (1983). Morality. In P. Mussen (Ed.), *Handbook of child psychology* (4th ed.) (Vol. 3, pp. 556–629). New York: Wiley.

Rest, J., Davison, M., & Robbins, S. (1978). Age trends in judging moral issues: A review of cross-sectional, longitudinal, and sequential studies of the Defining Issues Test. *Child Development, 49,* 263–279.

Rogoff, B. (1990). *Apprenticeship in thinking: Cognitive development in social context.* New York: Oxford University Press.

Rohner, R. P., & Pettengill, S. M. (1985). Perceived parental acceptance-rejection and parental control among Korean adolescents. *Child Development, 56,* 524–528.

Ryan, R. M., & Lynch, J. H. (1989). Emotional autonomy versus detachment: Revisiting the vicissitudes of adolescence and young adulthood. *Child Development, 60,* 340–356.

Savin-Williams, R. C., & Berndt, T. J. (1990). Friendship and peer relations. In S. S. Feldman & G. R. Elliott (Eds.), *At the threshold: The developing adolescent* (pp. 277–307). Cambridge, MA: Harvard University Press.

Selman, R. L. (1980). *The growth of interpersonal understanding.* New York: Academic Press.

Selman, R. L., & Schultz, L. H. (1989). Children's strategies for interpersonal negotiation with peers: An interpretive/empirical approach to the study of social development. In T. J. Berndt & G. W. Ladd (Eds.), *Peer relationships in child development* (pp. 371–406). New York: Wiley.

Sessa, F. M., & Steinberg, L. (1991). Family structure and the development of autonomy during adolescence. *Journal of Early Adolescence, 11,* 38–55.

Sharabany, R., Gershoni, R., & Hofman, J. (1981). Girlfriend, boyfriend: Age and sex differences in intimate friendship. *Developmental Psychology, 27,* 800–808.

Shweder, R. A. (1982). Beyond self-constructed knowledge: The study of culture and morality. *Merrill-Palmer Quarterly, 28,* 41–69.

Simmons, R. G., & Blyth, D. A. (1987). *Moving into adolescence: The impact of pubertal change and school context.* New York: Aldine de Gruyter.

Smetana, J. G. (1989). Adolescents' and parents' reasoning about actual family conflict. *Child Development, 60,* 1052–1067.

Smetana, J. G. (1995). Conflict and coordination in parent-adolescent relationships. In S. Shulman (Ed.), *Close relationships and socioemotional development* (pp. 155–184). Norwood, NJ: ABLEX.

Smetana, J. (1995). Morality in context: Abstractions, applications, and ambiguities. In R. Vasta (Ed.), *Annals of child development* (Vol. 10, pp. 83–130). London: Jessica Kingsley.

Snarey, J. R. (1985). Cross-cultural universality of social-moral development: A critical review of Kohlbergian research. *Psychological Bulletin, 97,* 202–232.

Steinberg, L. (1990). Interdependency in the family: Autonomy, conflict, and harmony in the parent-adolescent relationship. In S. Feldman & G. Elliot (Eds.), *At the threshold: The developing adolescent* (pp. 255–276). Cambridge, MA: Harvard University Press.

Steinberg, L., Elmen, J. D., & Mounts, N. S. (1989). Authoritative parenting, psychosocial maturity, and academic success among adolescents. *Child Development, 60,* 1424–1436.

Steinberg, L., & Lamborn, S. D. (1992, March). Autonomy redux: Adolescent adjustment as a joint function of emotional autonomy and relationship security. In S. J. Frank (Chair), *Adolescent autonomy: Is it all it's cracked up to be?* Symposium conducted at the biennial meeting of the Society for Research on Adolescence, Washington, DC.

Steinberg, L., Lamborn, S. D., Mounts, N. S., Darling, N., & Dornbusch, S. M. (1994). Over-time changes in adjustment and competence among adolescents from authoritative, authoritarian, indulgent, and neglectful families. *Child Development, 65,* 754–770.

Steinberg, L., & Silverberg, S. B. (1986). The vicissitudes of autonomy in early adolescence. *Child Development, 57,* 841–851.

Tesch, S., & Whitbourne, S. (1982). Intimacy and identity status in young adults. *Journal of Personality and Social Psychology, 43,* 1041–1051.

Thoma, S. J., & Ladewig, B. H. (1993, March). *Close friendships, friendship networks, and moral judgment development during the college years.* Poster presented at the meeting of the Society for Research in Child Development, New Orleans, LA.

Toder, N. L., & Marcia, J. E. (1973). Ego identity status and response to conformity pressure in college women. *Journal of Personality and Social Psychology, 2,* 287–294.

Underwood, B., & Moore, B. (1982). Perspective taking and altruism. *Psychological Bulletin, 91,* 143–173.

Vuchinich, S., Bank, L., & Patterson, G. R. (1992). Parenting, peers, and the stability of antisocial behavior in preadolescent boys. *Developmental Psychology, 28,* 247–257.

Vygotsky, L. S. (1978). *Mind in society.* Cambridge, MA: Harvard University Press.

Walker, L., & Taylor, J. (1991). Family interactions and the development of moral reasoning. *Child Development, 62,* 264–283.

Waterman, A. (Ed.). (1985). *New directions for child development: Identity in adolescence: Processes and contents* (Vol. 30). San Francisco: Jossey-Bass.

Waterman, A. (1992). Identity as an aspect of optimal psychological functioning. In G. R. Adams, T. P. Gullotta, & R. Montemayor (Eds.), *Adolescent identity formation* (pp. 50–72). Newbury Park, CA: Sage.

Wynne, L. (1984). The epigenesis of relational systems: A model for understanding family development. *Family Process, 23,* 297–318.

Young, H., & Ferguson, L. (1979). Developmental changes through adolescence in the spontaneous nomination of reference groups as a function of decision context. *Journal of Youth and Adolescence, 8,* 239–252.

Youniss, J., & Smollar, J. (1985). *Adolescent relations with mothers, fathers, and friends.* Chicago: University of Chicago Press.

PART III

Parenting Strategies and Child Outcomes

CHAPTER 5

Attachment and the Transmission of Values

INGE BRETHERTON, BARBARA GOLBY, and EUNYOUNG CHO

Despite deep roots in psychoanalytic theory, attachment theory as formulated by John Bowlby does not include an explicit and systematic treatment of parents' role in moral development. In his attachment trilogy, Bowlby (1969, 1973, 1980) reworked the classic psychoanalytic themes of mother-child relatedness, separation anxiety, mourning, defense, trauma, and sensitive periods during early development in light of then emerging insights from ethology, cybernetics, and research on emotion and cognition. But although he was able to shed new light on the intergenerational transmission of child-parent attachment patterns, his theorizing touched only briefly on the intergenerational transmission of familial, community, and societal values, a topic that played a central role in Freud's conception of the superego.

Yet Bowlby's early work contains a number of interesting statements that link the parent-child relationship to moral development. In his article "Forty-four Affectionless Thieves, Their Characters and Home Life," Bowlby (1944) noted that children who have experienced maternal separation and deprivation frequently develop an affectionless personality and engage in delinquent behavior. He went on to conclude, "The failure of super-ego development in these cases" follows "a failure in the development for the capacity for object-love (p. 55)." Elaborating on the same theme from a positive perspective in his 1951 report to the World Health Organization about the mental health of institutionalized children, Bowlby drew attention to parents' role in fostering a child's capacity for self-regulation and openness to socialization. Still employing the psychoanalytic terminology he later abandoned, Bowlby first discussed the emergence and role of the superego:

> Because one of our foremost long-term needs is to remain on friendly terms with others, we must keep their requirements firmly in the front of our minds; and so important is this for us that we differentiate within our ego machinery especially designed for the purpose—our conscience or super-ego. (Bowlby, 1951, p. 52)

He then reflected on the maternal role in socialization:

> It is evident that both ego and super-ego are absolutely dependent for their functioning on our ability to maintain an abstract attitude and it is not surprising that during infancy

---

The study by Golby (1995), from which extensive findings are presented in this chapter, was supported by grant R01 HD267766 from the National Institutes of Health (NIH) awarded to the first author. We would like to thank the mothers who shared their experiences with us.

and early childhood these functions are either not operating at all or are doing so most imperfectly. During this phase of life, the child is therefore dependent on his mother performing them for him. She orients him in space and time, provides his environment, permits the satisfaction of some impulses, restricts others. She is his ego and his super-ego. Gradually he learns these arts himself, and, as he does so the skilled parent transfers these roles to him. This is a slow, subtle and continuous process, beginning when he first learns to walk and feed himself and not ending completely until maturity is reached. Ego and super-ego development are thus inextricably bound up with the child's primary human relationships; only when these are continuous and satisfactory can his ego and super-ego develop. (Bowlby, 1951, pp. 52–53)

Bowlby's is a very different normative conception of self-regulation and socialization than the oedipal story proposed by Freud (e.g., 1940). According to Bowlby, the child cooperates with parental demands because the parent is valued, not because the parent is feared. Furthermore, the capacity for internalized morality develops gradually and continuously as the parent supports the growing child's ability to cope with conflicting impulses. Making parental values one's own, according to this perspective, is not the result of identification derived from fear of punishment, but is based on an increasing capacity for self-regulation achieved through the supportive quality of parent-child interactions.

In this chapter, we will present an attachment perspective on internalization, discussing how the quality of parent-child communication becomes reflected in a child's internal working models (representations) of secure and insecure attachment relations. Parental and parenting values underlying the concept of secure (optimal) attachment will also be considered. A review of empirical studies follows, demonstrating that secure attachment patterns are associated with more cooperative, prosocial child behavior both in the context of the parent-child relationship and with others. We interpret this cooperative capacity as a reflection of internalized relationship values acquired in a secure attachment. We then discuss the compatibility of specific parenting styles from the socialization literature with secure attachment relations and consider how the roles of attachment and authority figure can be optimally integrated. This section includes data from a qualitative study.

AN ATTACHMENT PERSPECTIVE ON INTERNALIZATION

Socialization theorists (e.g., Grusec & Goodnow, 1994; Hoffman, 1970, 1983, 1994) interested in children's acquisition of familial and societal values have placed great emphasis on the concept of internalization, defined as children's adherence to parental commands without surveillance. Although the term internalization seems to have crept into socialization theory through the psychoanalytic construct of the superego (that is, an internalized authority relationship), the current meaning of internalization applies more narrowly to a child's ability to resist temptation and to engage in unselfish or other societally approved behaviors even in the absence of the parent or other socializing agent. Under attachment theory, by contrast, the term internalization denotes an internalized relationship regardless of its optimal or nonoptimal quality.

To talk about the internalization of relationships, Bowlby (1969) borrowed the term "internal working model" from Craik (1943), through the writings of the eminent neurobiologist J. Z. Young (1964). Craik had proposed that internal working models of the environment provide an organism with greater behavioral flexibility, because alternative behavioral strategies can be tried out mentally without exposure to physical danger. Bowlby liked the term working models because it connoted dynamic "working" mental structures on which an individual could operate to "model" alternative courses of action. However, to make the concept fit the requirements of attachment theory, Bowlby had to adapt and substantially extend Craik's ideas in several ways.

Craik's writings had focused on internal working models of the physical world, whereas Bowlby (1973) was interested in the internalization of interaction patterns that develop in the early mother-child relationship. Because the affective-cognitive schema systems that constitute internal working models emerge in the context of interpersonal interaction patterns, Bowlby saw working models of self and attachment figure as complementary, so that—taken together—they represent both sides of the relationship (see also Sroufe and Fleeson, 1986). Hence infants cared for by an emotionally available, sensitive and responsive figure, are likely to develop a positive internal working model of the parent and a reciprocal internal working model of self as valued and self-reliant.

For internal working models constructed in the context of rejecting relationships, however, Bowlby envisioned a somewhat different process. Infants whose parents fairly consistently rebuff bids for comfort or interfere with efforts at mastery and exploration are likely to form *two competing* and *contradictory* working models of the same relationship (Bowlby, 1973). One of these models—accessible to awareness and eventually to verbal discussion—represents the parent as good and the parent's rejecting behavior as a justifiable response to the "badness" of the child. The other model—defensively excluded from awareness—represents the rejecting or disappointing side of the parent. But although these defensive processes protect the individual (in this case, the child) from experiencing the unbearable mental pain, confusion, or conflict associated with feeling devalued by an attachment figure, they offer only limited protection. In the long run, they are likely to impede the adequate development of internal working models.

Bowlby also differed from Craik in the functions he ascribed to internal working models. In addition to enabling mental trial and error, Bowlby envisaged internal working models as guides for the interpretation of ongoing experience and interaction with attachment figure(s). Hence internal working models are seen as governing a child's interpersonal attributions or meaning-making in ongoing interactions with parents and later with others.

Third, unlike Craik, Bowlby had to account for developmental changes in internal working models that first emerge in the parent-child relationship as affective-cognitive schemas of interaction. For this, he borrowed Piaget's notion of sensorimotor development (1951) according to which past schemas guide future behavior, but are then accommodated, integrated, and ultimately internalized. Two factors, according to Bowlby, enhance the relative stability of internal working models: (a) Familiar, oft-repeated interaction patterns tend to become less accessible to awareness as they become habitual and automatic, and (b) dyadic patterns of relating tend to be more resistant to change than individual patterns because reciprocal expectancies govern each partner's interpretation of the other's behavior (Bowlby, 1973). Thus, infants are not likely to instantly accommodate their internal working models of the relationship to abrupt changes in a parent's sensitivity or rejecting behavior (see Sroufe, 1988). Assimilation of the present to schemas of past interactive experience means that a certain degree of distortion in processing new relationship information is expectable.

Nevertheless, in the long run, internal working models must be accommodated to developmental and environmental changes if they are to adequately fulfill their function (Bowlby, 1980). The interference of defensive processes in this updating process is likely to have detrimental consequences for mental health. Contradictory conscious and unconscious working models of the same relationship hamper the appropriate affective and cognitive processing of interpersonal information, resulting in working models that remain ill adapted to reality (Bretherton, 1990), or as Crittenden (1990) has so aptly put it, working models that are not working well, and are hence not readily adaptable to relationship changes and to new relationships.

The organization and flexibility of infants' emerging working models stem—at least in part—from working models of self and attachment figures that the parents developed in their own families of origin. Responsive parents who are supportive when called on, but also permit and encourage autonomy tend themselves to have experienced supportive parenting in childhood. According to Bowlby (1973, p. 323), such parents not only respond sensitively to their children's bids for reassurance and comfort, but engage in fairly frank communication of their own working models of self, of their child and of others. In addition, they tend to *"indicate to the child that these working models are open to questioning and revision."* The intergenerational transmission of secure attachment patterns is dependent on parents' ability to engage in emotionally open, sensitive but honest communication. Under this view, the parental role of secure base includes a representational function, not just the provision of physical safety. By providing a child with a framework for interpreting the meaning of experience and relationships, a parent serves as representational secure base (for further discussion, see Bretherton, 1993, 1995; see also Thompson, in press).

An important factor in serving as representational secure base, according to Bowlby, is the appropriate acknowledgment of infants' and children's emotions, in particular their negative emotions:

> Nothing helps a child more, I believe, than being able to express hostile and jealous feelings candidly, directly, and spontaneously, and there is no parental task more valuable, I believe, than being able to accept with equanimity such expressions of filial piety as "I hate you, mummy" or "Daddy, you're a beast." By putting up with these outbursts we show our children that we are not afraid of hatred and that we are confident it can be controlled; moreover, we provide for the child the tolerant atmosphere in which self-control can grow. . . . As in politics, so with children. In the long run tolerance of opposition pays handsome dividends. (1979, p. 12)

In the context of this tolerant parental attitude, Bowlby (1951) claims, the emotions of anxiety and guilt will develop in a moderate and organized way. By contrast, when parental feelings toward a child are distorted by unconscious conflicts stemming from family of origin experiences, a parent is unlikely to be able to acknowledge and help modulate the child's negative emotions. A parent who has not experienced empathic parenting him- or herself, is less likely to feel and express empathy in response to his or her own child's negative emotions and to discuss distress situations supportively and openly with the child. This may lead the child to experience incomprehensible feelings of anxiety, guilt, and hostility and ultimately to engage in oppositional behavior or to exhibit withdrawn behavior (Bowlby, 1973; see also Fraiberg, Adelson & Shapiro, 1975).

From an attachment perspective, then, a child who habitually engages in forbidden behavior in the absence of the parent, has internalized a nonresponsive, rejecting, and coercive relationship in which cooperation is not willingly given. From the perspective of socialization theorists like Grusec and Goodnow (1994) and Hoffman (1970, 1994), however, this child has not internalized anything because the term internalization refers only to societally valued behaviors such as altruism and resistance to temptation.

The values considered important in attachment theory are those underpinning a secure attachment, rather than societal values in general. Whereas even severely maltreated children become attached to parents (Cicchetti & Rizley, 1980) and internalize this attachment relationship, the optimal pattern of attachment is associated with parental commitment, empathy, cooperation, perspective-taking, open communication, and respect for the uniqueness of the child, because not every child is likely to require the same type of responsiveness. In a secure relationship, a child is exposed to and embedded in these qualities, which are valued because within a relationship exemplifying them the child is believed to attain a sense of self-worth and the capacity to develop close, cooperative, and empathic relations with others.

ATTACHMENT QUALITY AND CHILD COOPERATION/COMPLIANCE: EMPIRICAL EVIDENCE

Seminal Studies

In her pioneering study of 26 infants and their families in Baltimore, Ainsworth and her colleagues (Ainsworth, Blehar, Waters, & Wall, 1978) observed wide variations in the quality of mother-infant interaction and communication patterns that corroborated many of Bowlby's ideas. When mothers responded sensitively to their infants' signals during feeding (Ainsworth & Bell, 1969), face-to-face play (Blehar, Lieberman, & Ainsworth, 1977), physical contact (Ainsworth, Bell, Blehar, & Main, 1971), and distress episodes (Bell & Ainsworth, 1972) in the first three months of life, their infants later cried less but had a larger communicative repertoire (Ainsworth, Bell, & Stayton, 1974; Bell & Ainsworth, 1972), demanded close bodily contact less often but enjoyed it more (Ainsworth, Bell, Blehar, & Main, 1971), and—most importantly in the context of this chapter—also cooperated more readily with their mothers' verbal requests and commands (Stayton, Hogan, & Ainsworth, 1973).

In line with the ethological-evolutionary principles on which Bowlby (1969) drew during the formulation of attachment theory, Stayton et al. hypothesized that human infants may be biologically predisposed to cooperate with an attachment figure's safety-related commands because such obedience is survival-enhancing.

To assess infant compliance, the authors used narrative records of naturalistic home observations during the last quarter of the first year. They tallied the frequency of mothers' verbal commands, the percentage of commands with which the infant actually complied, either immediately or after a slight delay, and the number of mothers' physical interventions. They also recorded infant behaviors indicative of nascent internalization in the socialization sense (i.e., self-inhibition in the face of temptation).

In addition, the authors made global ratings of the mothers' sensitivity, acceptance, and cooperation as opposed to insensitivity, rejection, and interference. Sensitivity, in this context, was defined as prompt and appropriate responding to infant signals (see Ainsworth, Bell, & Stayton, 1974). Acceptance referred to a mother's ability to assume the responsibility of caring for her infant without feeling overwhelmed by the restrictions this imposed on her own activities, while rejection, denoted angry and resentful feelings toward the infant, whether voiced openly and displayed in behavior.

Cooperation was defined as a mother's ability to align her own activities and schedules with the needs of her infant, whereas interference referred to a mother's assumption that she could or should arbitrarily impose her will without regard for the infant's mood or current activities.

When mothers had high scores on sensitivity, acceptance, and cooperation, their infants were significantly more likely to comply with verbal commands (e.g., "No! No!," "Don't touch," "Give it to me," "Come"). Perhaps as a consequence of their infants' high rate of compliance, these mothers tended to make fewer physical interventions (such as dragging their infants away from a forbidden area, slapping them in response to touching a forbidden object, or forcing them into a particular posture). Cooperative, acceptant, and sensitive mothers had more cooperative infants, and in turn, infants who cooperated more readily with their mothers' verbal commands were also more likely to self-inhibit acts that had been forbidden in the past. For example, they might shake the head "no" when standing in front of a prohibited object.

Although Stayton et al. (1973) conclude that attachment fosters willingness to comply, strictly speaking their actual findings were both more general and more limited than they claim. More general, because the infants' disposition to comply was not limited to danger situations, and more limited because infants complied most readily with mothers whose behaviors toward their infants were more sensitive, acceptant, and cooperative. Their findings undermine the notions of psychoanalysts such as Hartman, Kris, and Loewenstein (1946) and Spitz (1957) who also associated moral development with the mother-infant bond, but believed that compliance is mediated by fear of loss of love. Stayton et al.'s findings suggest that sensitive and cooperative mothering induces greater willingness to cooperate with maternal requests.

ATTACHMENT QUALITY AND CHILDREN'S COOPERATIVE DISPOSITION

When subsequent researchers became interested in examining the impact of parental responsiveness to infants on child cooperativeness during the preschool years, they did not undertake frequent and lengthy home observations across the infant's first year of life as Ainsworth and her colleagues had done. Instead, they relied on more standardized and somewhat less time-consuming, validated procedures that can serve as indices of responsive parenting and secure attachment.

Procedures for Assessing Attachment Quality

The first and most widely used assessment is the Ainsworth Strange Situation, which became the benchmark for all that followed (Ainsworth, Bell, & Stayton, 1971). Infants' behavior in this situation was strongly correlated with mother-infant interaction patterns at home (Ainsworth et al., 1978). As a result, this 20-minute laboratory procedure has become the technique *par excellence* for assessing individual differences in the quality of infant-parent attachment and, by inference, the cooperative and harmonious nature of the relationship (see also Ainsworth et al., 1974).

The Ainsworth Strange Situation is a miniature drama comprising a standard sequence of seven 3-minute episodes, videotaped in a laboratory playroom. Of special importance are three distinct patterns of infant reunion behavior that were observed after the mother had twice left the room briefly and then returned. These patterns could be predicted from maternal behavior to infants during the first 3 months of life and the harmony of the relationship during fourth quarter of the first year of life.

When mothers had responded more sensitively during feeding, crying, holding, and face-to-face play episodes at home during the first 3 months, their 1-year-olds approached them readily on reunion in the Strange Situation, sought interaction or close bodily contact, responded relatively quickly to soothing and then returned to exploration. These infants were labeled secure (group B). When mothers had been rated insensitive and rejecting of close bodily contact at home, infants snubbed them, looked, turned, or walked away, or rebuffed interaction bids during Strange Situation reunions (insecure-avoidant or group A). When mothers had inconsistently responded to their infants' signals at home, but did not reject close bodily contact, infants exhibited conflicted behavior (group C) during reunions in the Strange Situation, simultaneously wanting to be held and displaying angry distress that was not easily calmed (see Ainsworth et al., 1978). More recently, Main and Solomon (1990) identified a fourth Strange Situation reunion pattern, labeled insecure-disorganized (group D). Infants assigned to this group combine avoidance and resistance and/or show a variety of puzzling behaviors that indicate fleeting fear of the parent.

Two additional ABCD classification systems for assessing attachment quality in children older than 24 months have been created and validated against infancy Strange Situations, one for 6-year-olds (Main & Cassidy, 1988) and the other for 3- to 5-year-olds (Cassidy, Marvin, & the MacArthur Working Group on Attachment, 1989). Classification criteria were adjusted to take account of preschoolers' increased ability to communicate verbally, but bear a family resemblance to infant Strange Situation criteria. An exception were children classified as insecure-disorganized in infancy. As preschoolers, these children took a controlling role-reversing stance, acting as either as disciplinarians or caregivers of their parents upon reunion.

To facilitate and standardize home observations, Waters and Deane (1985; Waters, 1987) devised a Q-sort for examining 1- to 3-year-olds' use of the parent as secure base to explore (see also Waters, Vaughn, Posada, & Kondo-Ikemura, 1995). The Q-sort is preferably performed by trained observers after spending several hours in the family's home, but can be performed by mothers. The 90 Q-items consist of short descriptions of secure base behaviors that are sorted into nine categories, ranging from "definitely applies" to "does not at all apply." Placement of the card in a category determines its score, and a child's scores for the whole Q-sort are then correlated with expert-sorted scores for " the ideal secure child." The resulting correlation coefficient is a reflection of how strongly a particular child resembles the secure prototype and predicts secure reunion behavior in the Strange Situation.

In addition to these observational procedures, attachment researchers have developed a number of representational assessments to reflect an individual's working model of self and other in attachment relationships. In a groundbreaking study, Main, Kaplan, and Cassidy (1985) discovered that parents' responses to an interview that explored their own childhood attachments were systematically related to their infants' Strange Situation classifications.

During the Adult Attachment Interview or AAI (George, Kaplan, & Main, 1985), mothers of secure infants were at ease in talking about the influence of attachment-related experiences on their own development. Importantly, this held whether or not they recalled a secure childhood. These parents, labeled *autonomous-secure* or *free to evaluate* gave coherent, consistent, and emotionally open accounts of their childhood attachments. In contrast, parents with avoidant infants claimed that early attachment experiences had had little or no effect on their own development. These parents, labeled *dismissing,* frequently gave idealized global descriptions of their own parents in childhood but then said that they could not recall specific episodes. Attachment memories that emerged later in their interview, however, often portrayed their own parents as rejecting. Moreover, dismissing parents seemed unaware of these contradictions. Parents with insecure-ambivalent infants, on the other hand, gave the impression of being *preoccupied* with or *entangled* in family of origin attachments. These parents recalled many, often extremely detailed, conflict-ridden incidents about childhood attachments, but could not stand back and integrate them into a consistent overall picture of the relationship. Both the dismissing and preoccupied/entangled parents found it difficult to portray their childhood attachments coherently. Finally, parents with insecure-disorganized infants showed various confusions of speech and thought when discussing unresolved childhood bereavements (Ainsworth & Eichberg, 1991; Main & Hesse, 1990) or other traumas such as physical or sexual abuse (Lyons-Ruth & Block, 1996).

Inspired by the AAI, several investigators created similar interviews in which parents were asked to describe the attachment-relationship with their child (Aber, Slade, Berger, Bresgi, & Kaplan, 1985; Benoit, Zeahnah & Barton, 1989; Bretherton, Biringen, Ridgeway, Maslin, & Sherman, 1989; George & Solomon, 1989, 1996). Ratings and classifications modeled on the AAI predicted other attachment measures, including child assessments of attachment representations.

Representational attachment measures for young children rely on pictures of separation situations or on attachment story completions enacted with small family figures. Kaplan (1984) adapted Klagsbrun and Bowlby's (1976) picture-based Separation Anxiety Test for 6-year-olds. Children classified as secure with mother in infancy gave coherent, elaborated, and open responses to drawings of mild and stressful parent-child separation scenes, whereas those earlier judged insecure-avoidant described the pictured children as sad, but were at a loss when asked what the children could have done in the situation. Children classified as disorganized/disoriented in infancy tended to be completely silent or to give irrational or bizarre responses involving catastrophes and disasters (Main et al., 1985; see also Slough & Greenberg, 1990, who developed a further adaptation of the SAT).

Building on findings with the SAT, Bretherton, Ridgeway, and Cassidy (1990) developed an Attachment Story Completion Task for even younger children. Three-year-olds whose story-completions addressed attachment story-issues openly, and supplied benign resolutions were also assessed as more secure in a separation-reunion situation evaluated with the Cassidy et al. (1989) system for 3- to 5-year-olds. Children with irrelevant or bizarre story resolutions or who avoided the story issue, tended to be classified as insecure in the separation-reunion observation.

These observational and representational assessments of attachment quality have become important and effective shortcuts for the assessment of attachment quality. Beyond their methodological significance as indices of responsive and cooperative parent-child relationships, they also reveal that the emotionally open, mutual responsive communication pattern characteristic of secure dyad relationships in Ainsworth's Baltimore study (Ainsworth et al., 1978) is reflected in adults' and children's ability to present attachment issues openly and coherently when talking to others (see Bretherton, 1990). Emotionally open communication, in turn, is likely to be an important factor in facilitating continued cooperative relations with the attachment figure, and in engaging with others.

Attachment Quality and Child Cooperation with Parents, Peers, and Teachers

Mother-Child Cooperation

Londerville and Main (1981) examined toddlers' compliance with maternal requests during play in the laboratory at 21 months in relation to infant attachment patterns in the Strange Situation at 12 months. Consistent with Stayton et al. (1973), they found that secure toddlers complied with maternal requests more often and actively disobeyed their mothers less often than insecure toddlers. In addition, secure children showed greater evidence of internalized controls (visibly self-inhibiting a behavior that the mother had prohibited earlier in the session). Mothers of secure toddlers were less likely to use force and more likely to use a warmer tone of voice during their interventions, whereas mothers of insecure toddlers tended to describe their toddlers' personality as more troublesome.

Finally, insecure toddlers cooperated less readily with the requests of two unfamiliar testers, even though these women interacted with them warmly and sensitively. Londerville and Main cite this finding as evidence that children's ability to cooperate with others is, at least during a first encounter, primarily governed by their relationship history with their mothers.

Insecure children are not invariably noncompliant. Indeed, Crittenden and DiLalla (1988) report that maltreated children are sometimes extremely compliant, but their hypervigilant and fearful compliance differs greatly from the willing compliance with maternal requests observed in the attachment studies previously reviewed.

Cooperation with Peers and Teachers Related to Infancy Attachment Classifications

This section provides a new perspective on studies reporting links between attachment quality and children's prosocial behavior, cooperation, and self-regulation in extrafamilial contexts. These were based on the assumption that secure attachment fosters the self-confidence, trust, and social skills required for entering into friendly relationships with others (peers and teachers). By contrast, insecure children, feeling less highly valued by attachment figures, would tend to expect and elicit more negative responses from companions. These studies support our claim that secure attachment fosters openness to socialization outside the family context.

In the first such study, Waters, Wippman, & Sroufe (1979) reported that 15-month-olds judged secure in an adaptation of the Strange Situation, were more likely as preschoolers to be self-directed, act as peer leaders and behave empathically to peers. Similar findings were obtained in an exhaustive longitudinal study of disadvantaged children in Minnesota whose attachment to mother had been classified in infancy. As preschoolers, these children were observed in two experimental preschool classrooms staffed with highly trained teachers not privy to the children's infancy attachment classifications. Secure children were better liked by peers and were less likely to be perceived as having behavior problems by their teachers (Erickson, Sroufe, & Egeland, 1985). When observed in pairs, secure children did not victimize the pairmate nor were they themselves victimized. Avoidantly attached children, however, were likely to be victimizers, whereas ambivalently attached children tended to be victimized by avoidantly attached children.

Not all children in the Minnesota study conformed to this picture. To shed light on exceptions to the rule, Erickson et al. (1985) performed a more fine-grained analysis in which they discovered that the small number of children with secure infant attachments, but preschool behavior problems, had mothers with depressive symptoms who had become less supportive than predicted when observed with their children at 24 and 42 months. These findings suggest that changes in the quality of maternal care and attachment came to be reflected in these preschoolers' behavior with peers and teachers. Following the Minnesota children into elementary school, Egeland, Pianta, and O'Brien (1993) were able to predict their internalizing and externalizing behavior problems in first grade from infancy attachment quality. In addition, maternal hostility assessed when children were 3 years of age also foreshadowed behavior problems and teacher-rated aggression in the first three grades.

In a later study, also with disadvantaged families, Lyons-Ruth, Alpern, and Repacholi (1993) found that insecure disorganized attachment in combination with maternal psychosocial problems such as depression, strongly predicted hostile-aggressive behavior problems in kindergarten. In a second study, Lyons-Ruth, Easterbrooks, & Cibelli (in press) noted deviant levels of internalizing behavior in children with disorganized infant attachments if they concurrently had a low IQ score. Furthermore, children with avoidant and disorganized infancy classifications were rated as more internalizing and externalizing at age 7.

Suess, Grossmann, & Sroufe (1992) found associations of mother- and father-infant attachment classifications with later preschool behavior in middle-class German children, though mother attachment was a better predictor. Secure children managed to resolve more peer conflicts in the preschool on their own, whereas insecure children had numerous behavior problems. In addition, secure children tended to give realistic and well-meaning interpretations to cartoons depicting peer conflict whereas avoidant children's interpretations tended to be negative or unrealistic. Finally, Lewis, Feiring, McGuffog, & Jaskir (1984) using a modified Strange Situation also reported links between insecure attachment and later behavior problems rated by mothers, but Bates, Maslin, & Frankel (1985) found no such relationships with mother- and teacher-rated behavior problems when children were 3 years of age. There is, then, considerable though not entirely consistent evidence that infant attachment classifications are a significant predictor of a child's cooperative behavior in the preschool.

Greenberg and Speltz (1988) explained the continuity between earlier Strange Situation classifications and later cooperativeness with their mothers, peers, and teachers in transactional terms—as deriving from continuity in parents' and the children's internal working models of secure relatedness. Discontinuity (i.e., favorable preschool outcomes despite early insecurity, or unfavorable outcomes despite early security) are attributed to positive or negative changes in the quality of caregiving and the reflection of these changes in children's internal working models. For example, a mother's supportive new partner may engender positive change, whereas a family member's physical or mental illness or dire economic circumstances may lead to negative change (Sroufe, 1983). Secure infant attachment does not inoculate individuals or relationships against adverse change, but rather acts as a buffering factor.

Cooperation with Peers and Teachers Related to Concurrent Attachment Classifications

In line with Greenberg and Speltz's transactional model (1988), several researchers have examined preschoolers' prosocial and aggressive behaviors in relation to concurrent attachment quality. In the first such study, Lieberman (1977) found that securely attached 3-year-olds engaged in more sharing, less physical aggression and fewer verbal threats than children classified as insecure with mother on the basis of home observations. More recently, Cohn (1990) reported that preschoolers judged secure in the Main and Cassidy (1988) procedure, were less aggressive and better liked by peers, though the findings were stronger for boys than girls. Similarly, Greenberg, Speltz, DeKlyen, and Endriga (1993) found that 3- to 5-year-old clinic-referred boys diagnosed with significant disruptive behavior problems were far more likely to be judged insecure when assessed with the Cassidy et al. (1989) or Main and Cassidy systems (1988) than a matched group of nonclinic boys. Moreover, mothers' Adult Attachment Interview classifications were impressively concordant with their children's secure and insecure reunion classifications (DeKlyen, 1991). Also relevant in this context are Lieberman and Pawl's (1990) observations with clinically referred insecure, severely rejected toddlers who repeatedly engaged in reckless and accident-prone behavior such as leaving the house alone, wandering off, or repeatedly getting hurt. Lieberman and Pawl viewed this seemingly disobedient behavior as a counterphobic defense against anxiety as toddlers managed "their uncertainty over the mother's availability as a protector by taking off on their own and courting danger, rather than seeking protection from a source they perceive as unreliable (p. 333)." Alternatively, these children may be attempting to mobilize parents' protective behavior.

Studies using representational measures of attachment quality for children (the Slough & Greenberg version of the Separation Anxiety Test [SAT], 1990) reported similar findings. The semiprojective SAT, based on children's responses to pictures of mild and severe separations from parents, yields scores for attachment, self-reliance, and avoidance. Kim (1992) reported that 5-year-olds with high scores on the attachment and self-reliance scales of the SAT were rated low on the hostility/aggression, anxiety, and hyperactivity/distractibility scales of the Behar Preschool Behavior Checklist (1977) by their teachers, whereas the converse was true of children with high avoidant SAT scores. In the second study, Cho (1994; personal communication, 1995) found similar correlations between the Slough and Greenberg (1990) version of the SAT and teacher ratings based on the Kohn Social Competence Scale (1988). Furthermore, although both Kim and Cho reported child gender differences with respect to the SAT, their findings remained significant when child gender was controlled.

Maternal responsiveness as a predictor of children's cooperativeness has also attracted the attention of socialization researchers, though their arguments tend to be based on studies of mother-child interaction and child compliance, rather children's behavior with peers and teachers (for a detailed review, see Maccoby & Martin, 1983). Maccoby and Martin distinguished a child's receptive or willing compliance with parental requests from situational compliance, which is parentally coerced, based on fear, and does not predict parent-child cooperation in the long run. They contended that children comply with parents when parents comply with children and hence questioned the necessity of the attachment contruct in explaining child cooperativeness.

Drawing on Maccoby and Martin's ideas, Kochanska (1995) found that toddlers showed more "committed" compliance with maternal requests during a toy cleanup task when the affective tone of mother-toddler interaction was positive. The same toddlers were also better able to resist the temptation to touch and play with attractive forbidden toys when left alone in the playroom (internalization in the socialization sense). When observed again as preschoolers, the children's earlier and later committed compliance and internalization were correlated. However, girls engaged in higher levels of these behaviors than boys.

Based on these findings, Kochanska (1995) concluded that committed compliance is more adequately explained in terms of the history of the parent-child relationship than in terms of parental power, because maternal responsiveness facilitates a mutually cooperative mode of interaction in which the child is more likely to accede to maternal requests. Richters and Waters (1992) voiced similar ideas from an attachment perspective, noting that in a secure attachment relationship the child learns to engage in "prosocial commerce." However, in their discussions of children's cooperative and prosocial behavior neither Maccoby and Martin, nor Kochanska or Richters and Waters include any overt discussion of parental authority, though they allude to it implicitly by using the word "committed" as in committed compliance.

AN ATTACHMENT PERSPECTIVE ON AUTHORITY

The Attachment Figure as "Stronger and Wiser"

Parental authority, though not an explicit part of attachment theory, is implied in Bowlby's (1979, p. 292) definition of attachment as an affectional bond to a discriminated protective figure who is "usually considered stronger and/or wiser." As long as the protective function of attachment is observed in situations that may frighten an infant or young child but are not considered dangerous by the parent (such as the Strange Situation), the authority aspect of attachment is less visible. It takes center stage, however, when a parent interprets a situation as threatening and when protection of the infant requires not only comforting, but warnings, commands, physical retrieval, and/or leaving the scene with the child.

Likewise, "stronger and wiser" parental authority is manifest in situations that call for parental reassurances or explanations to help a child make sense of and cope with feelings of sadness, distress, anxiety, and fear (Bretherton, 1993, 1995). Although Bowlby only briefly touches on parents as a psychological or representational secure base, he extensively warns of the damaging consequences likely to ensue when parents deliberately misinterpret or distort a child's perceptions. This can occur, for example, when a parent is ashamed about his or her own neglecting, rejecting, or abusive behavior or prefers the child not to know about a traumatic situation that the child has actually witnessed or heard about. Citing work by Cain and Fast (1972), Bowlby (1980) maintained that mismatches between a child's own memory of a traumatic experience and a parent's subsequent innocuous reinterpretation or denial of that experience can cause damaging intrapsychic conflict and confusion. Ultimately, such conflict becomes reflected in disorganized internal working models of the relationship, especially when parents place a taboo on further discussion of the event.

Finally, Bowlby (1973) alluded to the role of authority in attachment indirectly, by warning of situations when parents "invert the relationship" and rely on the child as attachment figure. He notes that, in many cases, school phobia—often regarded as a disciplinary issue—is due to an anxious parent's desire to retain the child at home as companion and/or the child's fear that, unless he or she remains at home to prevent it, some dreadful event may befall the parent. Implicitly, Bowlby is thereby suggesting that, in optimal attachment relationships, the child should see the parent as in charge of providing protection rather than the reverse. In support of Bowlby, Lieberman, and Pawl (1990) reported that when a clinically depressed parent is emotionally unavailable but not hostile, even toddlers may become overresponsible, precociously taking charge of the relationship. Similarly, as already noted, Main et al. (1985) found that children, assessed as insecure-disoriented/disorganized in the Strange Situation in infancy, treat their parents in a separation-reunion procedure at age 6 as if the parents were in need of care or control. In these cases, the children's controlling behavior is interpreted as a coverup for anxiety.

Integrating the Roles of Attachment and Authority Figure

Although attachment theory speaks to parental authority in situations that require protection, reassurance, and comforting of the child and despite studies showing that secure attachment predicts less aggressive, more prosocial behavior in young children, attachment theorists have tended to neglect the parents' role as authority figures or socialization agents who have the task of facilitating the child's acquisition of family, community, and societal rules.

One reason socialization has not been greatly emphasized by students of attachment may be that so much of the early home observational research centered on infants. It is in the second year that toddlers more fully assert their will (Emde & Buchsbaum, 1990; Erikson, 1950; Spitz, 1957) while also becoming more aware of behavioral standards (Kagan, 1981; Kochanska, Casey, & Fukumoto, 1995). During this period, parents make stronger demands on children for prosocial behavior, and compliance with family rules (do's) and self-regulation (don'ts). When we interviewed parents of preschoolers between 2.5 and 6 years of age about attachment-related topics, all dwelt at length on issues related to cooperation, limit-setting, and power struggles (Bretherton et al., 1989; Golby, 1995) though families differed in how these issues were resolved.

Although research efforts on childrearing/socialization and on attachment have proceeded on somewhat separate paths (Richters & Waters, 1992), there are substantial conceptual overlaps between the two literatures. Bowlby (1973) himself noted that aspects of the parenting style described as *authoritative* in the socialization literature (e.g., Baumrind, 1967, 1971) are compatible with the sensitive, accepting, and cooperative parenting behaviors held up as optimal by attachment theory and research. Authoritative parents resembled responsive attachment figures in paying attention to their children's needs and point of view, and tended to use persuasion, negotiation, and reasoning to engage their children's cooperation. In addition, authoritative parents were firm, self-confident, and did not allow themselves to be coerced by their children. They acted as leaders, but not dictators. Baumrind did not report how well these children cooperated with their authoritative parents, but in preschool observations they behaved very much like the securely attached preschoolers observed in Minnesota and elsewhere.

In contrast, the coercive style Baumrind defined as *authoritarian* seems incompatible with secure attachment. The authoritarian parents Baumrind studied tried to shape their children according to an absolute set of standards, valued obedience for its own sake, restricted the child's autonomy, discouraged verbal give-and-take, and did not allow children to express their needs or negative feelings. In addition, authoritarian parents discouraged what they regarded as infantile behavior (perhaps attachment behavior?), but without encouraging their children's independence. Baumrind (1967, 1971) does not report whether and to what extent the authoritarian style led to child compliance at home. In the preschool, however, children of authoritarian parents cooperated less and were more aggressive, behaving somewhat like the insecure preschoolers described earlier. Moreover, irrespective of the undesirable preschool behavior associated with this style, it is difficult to see how a parent who consistently used coercion to control the child through fear, could simultaneously provide a sense of emotional security.

Despite obvious conceptual overlaps between the literatures on child rearing or disciplinary styles and attachment, only a very small number of researchers have so far examined them empirically. Focusing on correlations among attachment security (assessed with the Waters Q-sort), maternal discipline and child temperament, Kochanska (1995) failed to find the expected straightforward associations. Only temperamentally fearless children with higher attachment security scores displayed more committed compliance with maternal requests and higher levels of internalization in the mother's absence. By contrast, temperamentally fearful-inhibited children, were more resistant to temptation when their mothers used gentle discipline (reasoning, polite requests, positive incentives, distractions), but their attachment security scores were unrelated to moral internalization. These findings are puzzling from an attachment perspective, and thus need replication. (But see van IJzendoorn's, in press, explanation)

In a related study, Cho (1994) relied on the Block Child Rearing Practices Report or CRPR (1965) to evaluate mothers' child-rearing behaviors and used the Slough and Greenberg (1990) version of the Separation Anxiety Test to assess attachment quality in 4- to 5-year-olds at the representational level. Block (1965) and Kochanska, Kuczynski, & Radke-Yarrow (1989) had validated the CRPR against observed parenting practices, and the SAT had been validated against infant Strange Situations or childhood separation-reunion procedures (Main et al., 1985; Shouldice & Stevenson-Hinde, 1992; Slough & Greenberg, 1990).

Following Kochanska et al. (1989), Cho grouped items from the 21 CRPR subscales into an *authoritative* and *authoritarian* domain. The authoritative domain included the subscales for open expression of affect, rational guidance, and encouragement of independence, but Cho added the scale for encouraging openness of expression because it fit Baumrind's descriptions of the authoritative style. The *authoritarian* CRPR subscales included strict control, supervision of the child, and control through anxiety induction. For reasons of conceptual fit, Cho also included the scales for emphasis on early training and overprotectiveness.

Cho found that two of the authoritative CRPR scales (encouraging openness of expression and open expression of affect) and three of the authoritarian CRPR scales (authoritarian control, overprotectiveness of the child, and early training) correlated significantly with the children's SAT responses, even after controlling for maternal education, psychological wellbeing, marital satisfaction, and child gender. Mothers who saw themselves as encouraging openness of expression, including expression of affect, had children with higher attachment and self-reliance scores on the SAT. By contrast, mothers with higher authoritarian scores had children who scored lower on the attachment and self-reliant scales and higher on the avoidance scale of the SAT.

In addition, children's SAT attachment and self-reliance scores were positively related to maternal ratings of the child's compliance/obedience and negatively related to maternal ratings of child detachment/distancing (based on the Mother's Report of Child Relationship and Personality; Schaefer, Sayers, Clair, & Burnett, 1987). Mothers' authoritarian CRPR scores also predicted teacher-rated preschool problem behavior, specifically anger/defiance and apathetic/withdrawn behavior.

Finally, George and Solomon (1989), used their "Experiences of Mothering Interview" to study the caregiving behavior of 32 middle-class mothers whose children who were about to enter school. The interview explored mothers' thoughts and feelings about situations that might pose real and/or psychological threats to the child, including kindergarten entry, separations, maternal psychological unavailability, and disciplinary confrontations. The authors devised a *secure base* scale to evaluate the degree to which mothers mentioned strategies that showed sensitivity to the child's needs while respecting the mothers' own needs. The authors also created a competence scale to rate the mother's descriptions of her child as capable, industrious, and striving for autonomy, and of herself as taking a prominent teaching role by making demands for mature behavior, using authoritative discipline, encouraging the child to think about transgressions, and supporting autonomy through self-regulation. Maternal scores for the secure base and competence scales were highly correlated, and high scores on both predicted ratings of the child's security in the separation-reunion procedure devised by Main and Cassidy (1988); whereas low scores predicted ratings of the child's avoidant and controlling behavior during reunion. Surprisingly, correlations between the secure-base and competence ratings from the interview and a specially developed Q-sort based on home observations of mothers and children were few and moderate. In this study, George and Solomon subsume discipline and teaching associated with parental authority under the protective role, and hence do not explicitly distinguish between parents as attachment figures and socialization agents.

Mothers' Self-Descriptions of Limit-Setting and Control in Relation to the Values Underlying Secure Attachment

Taking a somewhat different approach to this topic, we used a qualitative study based on interviews with 71 divorced mothers of 4.5-year-old children (Golby, 1995) to explore what types of parental control or guidance may be compatible with secure attachment. The Parent Attachment Interview (Bretherton et al., 1989) is based on a series of open-ended questions designed to elicit a parent's thoughts and feeling about the parent-child attachment relationship. In responding to the questions, parents are encouraged to describe memories of actual situations. Like the Adult Attachment Interview (George et al., 1985), the PAI is transcribed verbatim.

Despite the PAI's focus on attachment issues, mothers spontaneously offered so much material related to cooperation, guidance, negotiation, control, and other discipline issues, that a decision was made to examine this aspect of the interview separately. During this analysis, it became evident that potentially conflicting attachment and discipline issues often arise in the same situation (such as comforting and insistence on adherence to rules).

The analysis proceeded in two steps. The first step was to extract all sections from the transcripts in which mothers talked about cooperation, conflict, negotiation, compromise, and discipline. This included both concrete descriptions of actual situations or events (i.e., how mothers engaged their children's cooperation or handled their demands and noncompliance) as well as descriptions of mothers' thoughts and feelings when their children were either cooperative and "listened," or were uncooperative, manipulative, or defiant. The second step was to read through the extracted transcripts, identify individual vignettes or ideas, assign each an initial descriptive code, and print them out on separate pieces of paper. Using a modified grounded theory method to identify underlying themes (Glaser & Strauss, 1967; Strauss, 1987), the vignettes were then repeatedly sorted without regard to the particular transcript from which they came.

The following general themes emerged from this iterative sorting process: (a) firmness-demandingness versus laxness-nondemandingness; (b) flexibility versus inflexibility; (c) sensitivity in communication about feelings versus insensitivity; and (d) sense of effectiveness versus ineffectiveness. Although the grounded theory method does not require conventional reliability checks, a second reader checked the categorizations made by the first and discussed disagreements.

Examining the vignettes from an attachment perspective, it becomes quite evident that flexibility, sensitivity in communication about feelings, and sense of effectiveness are compatible with the parental values underlying secure attachment (that is, parental empathy, role-taking, sensitivity to signals, and being in charge), whereas inflexibility, insensitivity in communication about feelings, and a sense of ineffectiveness are not compatible. We are not arguing that mothers can be categorized as inflexible, not in charge, or insensitive on the basis of a single vignette. No mother is invariably effective or ineffective, sensitive or insensitive, just as no child is invariably cooperative and willingly compliant. Thus, when reading the following vignettes, it should be firmly borne in mind that we are using the vignettes as illustrations. The claims made for particular vignettes apply only to parenting in which such behaviors or attitudes are pervasive.

Flexibility

Flexibility was exemplified by the following vignette in which a mother described her decision-making strategy about whether or not to give in to her child's demand to be carried (which could also be seen as attachment behavior):

> If we're coming back from a playground and she's tired and she could probably make it but we'll both be miserable by the time we get home, I just pick her up. It's no big deal. I guess I measure it. If she's being a wimp and she can make it and I can talk to her about it, I'll try to get her to do it. But if I just think it's going to be a war of wills, I tend to just do it.

In another vignette classified as flexible, a mother discussed how she compromised in a situation that could easily have turned into an escalating power struggle. This mother successfully integrated her role as protector with promoting her child's autonomy:

> . . . using a knife at the table . . . he insists on doing it himself. I say, "No, knives are very sharp." We compromise and I say, "We'll get you a special knife for little boys at the table." So then the next day, we will go out and buy a special one. We normally talk back and forth of what would work the best.

A third vignette in the flexible category describes a mother's approach to obtaining cooperation by not pushing too hard:

> He can tie his shoes and sometimes he won't do it. Or if I get in the pool and I want him to swim, he won't do it. He just will not, refuses to do it. . . . But then a little while later he'll do it if I don't push the issue and drop it. . . . I usually try not to push the issue. I don't want to get into it like that.

Sense of Effectiveness

There were many vignettes in which mothers spontaneously evaluated their own effectiveness. For most mothers, perceptions of effectiveness were based on whether or not they experienced themselves as successful in achieving their socialization goals. Some mothers explained that their children "listened" to maternal requests and responded to maternal demands. Others talked about how pleased they were that their children went to bed at night with relatively little resistance. Yet others commented that their children followed rules such as picking up toys after play or that they complied with safety-related rules about not running in the street highlighting the role of rules in protecting the child:

> He knows that there are rules. He knows he doesn't go run in the street. He respects them. He knows . . . when you flag up the word "rule," he's good with that. He is very good. I'm proud of him for that.

Mothers who saw themselves as effective generally conveyed a sense of command over the difficult situations they described, emphasizing positive changes such as seeing their children's stubborn and demanding behavior improve. They also spoke insightfully of how changes in their own behavior helped to bring about positive interactions, thus evaluating both themselves and their children:

> Sometimes it's kind of hard when we disagree about something. Usually it's a real tug-of-war about who is going to win because he is very stubborn and so am I . . . But we both learn from being stubborn, too; somebody's got to give in, and he's learning that too. He's getting better at giving it, and I am too.

> If I'm sitting on the couch and somebody is standing by the sink, he will come to me and say, "Will you get me a drink of water?" Of course, now we have gotten to the point where he does it himself. But, um, he would go through a point where he was real, "Mommy, you do this for me. Mommy, you do 'everything' for me," and with time, of course, he's out-grown that . . .

Others conveyed their satisfaction with their children or with the relationship in general, by giving an overall assessment of their children's behavior or of their interactions:

> . . . we have a good relationship. It's getting better and better and better.

> . . . she listens pretty well . . . she is usually a pretty cooperative kid . . .

These mothers did not idealize the relationship; rather, their narratives had an open quality as they talked about problems and frustrations. But the overriding sentiment was one of confidence.

Sensitivity in Communication about Feelings

Vignettes were categorized as sensitive when mothers showed an awareness, acceptance, or understanding of their children's feelings, especially their negative feelings. Many mothers discussed children's anger in the context of misbehavior. How the mothers handled their children's anger largely depended on what they believed the source of the anger to be. For example, anger expressed in response to requests to perform an undesirable task was often not accommodated. If, however, the mother believed there was a deeper reason why her child might be acting out, many mothers showed more acceptance:

> I've very rarely, maybe once a month, had to send him to his room, you know, on my own: "Alright, that's it. Mom's had enough, away you go." But a lot of times if he's that out of it, part of it's your fault. He hasn't gotten a nap, you're off your schedule a little bit,

maybe dinner's late, he's starving to death, you know? . . . So I kind of excuse that a little bit for that.

The more I've been a parent, the more I've learned that her actions all depend on how her day goes. Like if she hasn't had her nap, if she's hungry. Then they get tired, they get ornery. It's like, you know, you just gotta realize they're acting this way because, you know, there's a reason behind it.

One mother had successfully adopted techniques suggested by her therapist:

This therapist that I've gone to, he gave me some really good skills about talking to the kids . . . they can't articulate [what's wrong], so what I can do is label things. I'll have no idea what's wrong, and I'll start naming the teacher, kids at school, the babysitter, missing the TV show, "oh no, oh no." But when you hit on it, you know, like dinner wasn't very good, "Yes, I'm still hungry." . . . So that's been really helpful because I'd get real frustrated. I'd go, "You don't need to cry, there's nothing wrong," that's how I used to be. "Why are you so upset?" But now it's like, if they're crying, even if it's nothing that I think is reasonable, [I know] there's something wrong.

Another mother was very creative in her efforts to help her child work through difficulties in communicating:

What I have started to do with her, I was in Arizona and got these little trouble dolls. . . . I bought each of the kids one, I thought that would give her something to talk to maybe. So I told her, "At bedtime you tell them your troubles, and you know, you have to try to help yourself but they will try to help you too." She will whisper into them. Actually that was part of the start because she would ask them to help her sleep in her own bed, and stuff like that . . .

One of the mothers explained how she dealt with the child's disappointment about the long hours she had to work:

He disagrees with my having to work long hours. He doesn't like that at all. So we really talk about these things. He very much holds his own in the conversation. He still doesn't like it, and I tell him that I really understand that and that he's entitled to that, but I still have to do it.

Another mother described how she helped her child cope when the child did not understand why her younger sibling had been disciplined.

There are times where I discipline [sibling] and she will be very upset about it, so I'll sit down and talk to her about it, explain to her why I did that, and if those kinds of situations were to happen with her, that we might have to take, you know, disciplinary actions like that, and this is why. It's sort of amazing in that way because she can sort of see both sides of the story if you tell her both. If you just leave it and say, "I just did it because I'm the mom and that's what I do," then she would say, "Well, that's not fair." She really has the capability of understanding both.

Whereas maternal flexibility, a sense of effectiveness and sensitive communication about emotion accord well with the values associated with secure attachment, inflexibility, extreme laxness, a sense of ineffectiveness, and insensitivity in communicating about emotion do not.

Inflexibility

In vignettes categorized as inflexible, mothers often explained that they "won't tolerate" misbehavior, and talked about giving ultimatums instead of choices:

> He is a lousy eater . . . he likes the junk food . . . I took 13 months of saying, "You're not getting anything else, kitchen is closed, and this is still sitting on the table and you're going to eat it," and he will.

> . . . sometimes like zipping up her coat and I know she can do it because she has done it before and all of a sudden she says, "I can't do it, I can't do it." I just tell her, "Well, it's like this: You're doing it or you can just suffer," you know [laugh]? She will start whining and stuff and if we're not in a hurry she will go to her room, otherwise I let her go out the door without it zipped and if you freeze it's your problem . . .

Many, although not all, mothers who portrayed themselves as inflexible had a tendency to talk repeatedly about escalating power struggles that ensued when neither the mother nor the child would give in. Some of these mothers said they had to use physical force to prevail:

> It was bedtime and she didn't want to go to bed and she just . . . I mean it was to the point where I had to wrap my arms and legs around her and say, "It is bedtime and we are staying in this bed." I mean it was like physical, hold her down. She was just determined, "No, I am not going to do it and you're not going to make me."

> If he finishes drinking his Kool-Aid and he sets it on the table, I says, "Now go put that in the kitchen." "No, you do it, Mom. I don't want to do it. I'm too tired." He'll say, "I'm too tired." He'll justify that way. [I: What do you do?] I don't do it. I just keep on him and tell him to go do it. . . . It's almost like I have a power struggle with him. . . . That little turd, he can go put it in the sink himself [laugh]. *He's supposed to be my slave* [laugh]. You know what I mean? It's almost comical sometimes the way he, you know, is like, "No Mom, you do it, I'm too tired." Like I'm not tired. He just played all day, that's his job, you know?

> Yesterday he wanted to watch a movie and I told him, "No," because he wasn't behaving very well. He started putting the movie into the VCR: "I want to watch this movie!" I said, "No, you can't." "But I want to watch it, Mom!" It kept going back and forth: "I want to watch it!" "No you can't!" you know. I said, "If you say it one more time, you're going to your room." I didn't even get that whole sentence out and he was saying it again. I tried to send him to his room and he wouldn't go so I had to drag him to his room, and when he got in there he screamed and kicked his feet, "But I want to see the movie!"

> If I'm mad at him and him and I are butting heads about something, I get just as much resistance from him as I give him. So that's kind of like a stalemate. Of course, since I'm mom and I'm bigger and I'm older, I can last a lot longer than he can, so usually I'll still win, but we'll butt heads and he'll, he'll be just as mad at me.

Laxness under Pressure

Lax maternal responding, if pervasive, also seems inconsistent with provision of a secure base. Vignettes were categorized as lax when mothers expressed feelings of irritation, frustration, and helplessness about their inability at eliciting cooperation. They talked about giving in because it was easy or because they could not tolerate their children's behavior, and then described feeling weak or "like a pushover":

Sometimes you just give in so they don't have that temper tantrum . . . it's like, well I guess I'll feed her and keep her shut up.

A lot of times I'm tired 'cause I've got a house and my other daughter and it's just like, fine, it's just easier just to give in.

I don't do anything about it . . . It's like I just let them out [of time-out] so they'll shut up . . . Now he's teaching his little brother to be the same way, "Just keep on her, she'll give in."

Some mothers who talked quite openly about their tendency to give in too much felt unable to change, mostly because of being fatigued or overwhelmed. As one mother stated, "The more I give in, the more he knows he can play the game with me." Another mother tried unsuccessfully to get her child to sleep in her own room by buying her a brand-new bedroom set, including her own VCR. Several mothers planned to become more consistent and firm after an upcoming event ("when school starts," "when we move into the new apartment"), but when faced with time constraints, fatigue, and high levels of frustration, giving in was the easiest way to get things done. As one mother confessed:

They usually pretty much get what they want, unfortunately. I gotta try to get them used to, you know, not always getting their way and to be happy with when I say, "No." But it doesn't always work that way. When I'm tired at night, "Okay, you can have it. Get whatever you want. Let's just go home and get ready for bed."

Ineffectiveness and Lack of Confidence

Many mothers expressed feelings of frustration and dissatisfaction with their everyday interactions. These mothers said they had no control over their children, that their children showed complete disregard for their authority by ignoring them, mimicking them, and even belittling them with derogatory remarks. As one mother explained, "She just acts like I'm not even there, and that really ticks me off." Although they were exhausted and angry, these mothers did not know what to do to improve their situation, for no matter what they tried, they could not gain their children's cooperation. In several vignettes categorized as portraying ineffectiveness, mothers implied that the problem was not just with the target child, but with several or all of the children, a fact that seemed to exacerbate the situation:

A lot of times I'm annoyed when they [child and sibling] gang up on me . . . it's hard to get at both of them. I'm there by myself. I'm like chasing the other one, the other one's running and . . . [laugh] It happens almost every night.

[Mother describes child as "mouthy"] . . . if I try to discipline him sometime and he doesn't, like . . . he'll come back with a snide comment, all the time. I think he gets it from his brother, too . . . sometimes I catch him swearing. . . . There was one time (his dad used to threaten me all the time), one time I told [child] that he needed to do something, he called me a bitch . . . so.

In some vignettes, mothers explained that the reason for their ineffectiveness was their children's lack of motivation to behave in a desirable fashion. Neither the mothers' praise for good behavior, nor their anger over poor behavior seemed to move the children to change their ways:

He's harder to motivate to do what you want him to do . . . it's real hard to get him to want to keep his room clean. He just doesn't care, he just doesn't care . . . he doesn't seem to need pleasing a lot, you know, he does things because he wants to do them because it makes him feel good, rather than, I'm going to clean my room and please Mom. That's not what motivates him, and that frustrates me. I don't quite know how to get him to do certain things like that.

Some mothers spoke of their children's manipulative and controlling behavior. Although they recognized the problem, and sometimes even contemplated possible solutions, they did not mention any improvements in the relationship:

I think I'm falling right into what he wants me to do, you know, giving him all this attention because when he does it I yell at him and it goes on all day long, and no matter what I do it doesn't seem to stop the behavior.

They will pretty much ignore me. I mean, I have not found a way to get mad yet, whether it's quietly or loudly or whatever that makes either one of them respond. They just do what they are going to do, and they don't care if I'm mad or not, or they don't seem to.

In other vignettes that focused on ineffectiveness, mothers described themselves as not sure about their judgments or decisions, suggesting that their lack of self-confidence was hindering their ability to parent with authority. Whereas some mothers felt they gave in too easily, were inconsistent, and let their children walk all over them, others felt guilty, were afraid they were not good mothers, and feared their behavior was negatively affecting their children's emotional development. Many struggled with finding a balance between letting their children express their feelings and setting limits on negative behavior. For some, their uncertainty was reflected in the vacillating manner in which they spoke:

. . . his stubbornness frustrates me sometimes. I can't always get a handle on it. I'm not sure how to . . . what exactly to do sometimes in discipline, as far as how much I should let him get away with. Sometimes I'm real lax and other times, "No, you will not do this," you know, it's, where do you draw the line? You know, what's right and what's wrong and, I don't know that there is a right or a wrong, and every situation is different. That's somewhat frustrating. I wish that there's a book that could tell you all the answers to everything.

Like getting dressed in the morning . . . not quite half the time probably, usually I'll say, "Now look, you know you're a good boy. Get dressed or you can't watch your show," . . . acting too much like I'm manipulating him too much by doing that. But, yeah, he expects me to do a lot of things. Sometimes I give in and sometimes I just say, "No, Look here," and sometimes I worry about that because there isn't enough consistency, you know? Sometimes I don't feel like I have a whole lot of consistency, that I'm not a very consistent person, and I worry about what that's doing to them.

I have mixed feelings as to how I should discipline him when he is naughty, you know, when he's out of my control. I mean, I don't want him to be my robot, but I just want him to be good, you know, "Don't be so rotten."

A few mothers expressed fear in anticipation of not being able to control their children (especially sons) as they grew older and bigger and stronger:

It's kind of scary to think if he's like what he is now, I'm going to have a handful because sometimes, not that a parent should control a child . . . but sometimes I feel like he's going to try to run me over, you know? Like, there's many times when he won't even listen to me now. What's going to happen ten years down the road when he's developed all these other tools of manipulation [laugh] and, you know, be really rotten?

Some mothers talked about ineffectiveness when asked to compare themselves with their own parents. These mothers remembered being more fearful and more respectful of their parents than they felt their own children were of them. Still, they seemed puzzled as to why they could not elicit the same response from their children that their own parents had been able to generate from them:

She [the mother's own mother] had this look, I mean, that can wilt a linebacker . . . Oh, if I could generate one tenth of that look to keep my children in control, I would [laugh].

You just did whatever my dad said. It was like, how did that ever come about? You just did. I can't explain why. You just did. Sometimes it was out of respect, sometimes it was just because my dad said it, you just did it. I'd like her to do that once in a while [laugh]. But that just wouldn't be her [laugh . . . I try to do that [and] it just doesn't work [laugh].

Another factor that may have contributed to these mothers' sense of ineffectiveness was their feeling that their ex-spouses were undermining the legitimacy of their authority by telling the children that they did not need to listen to what their mother said.

Insensitivity in Communicating about Emotions

Also incompatible with providing an effective secure base is insensitivity in communicating about emotions, especially disavowing or brushing aside the child's negative emotions. The following quotes show how discipline situations and attachment situations are often intertwined:

What I usually do is if she's crying, you know, I'll, you know, either go up and poke at her or tickle her, or just say something . . . try to get her mind off it.

I also try to ask him, "Why?" and try to figure out why he is mad, and he will tell me, he'll explain. If I don't think it's a good enough reason to my own judgment, "You shouldn't have to be mad. It's just the way it is." Or I try to get him to think about something else.

If she wants to do something and I tell her, "No," she will pout. I'm not real big on spanking . . . I'll send her to her room or say, "Stop crying or you'll . . . " and I always want to say, "Or I'll give you something to cry about," because that's what I heard every day when I was growing up from my father . . . I'll say, "Go to your room and cry," or, "I don't want to hear it," you know. "I don't like to hear little girls crying. There's no reason for you to be crying. Why are you crying?" She gets stubborn and frustrated at that point and she will go in her room and lay down once in a while, she'll go and she'll find a corner and she'll like kind of hide . . .

We call him our little crybaby sometimes. "I'm not a crybaby." It's, "Go to your room. Here's a tissue. When you come back, I hope that you're feeling better."

In some vignettes categorized as insensitive, mothers explained that they did try to talk to their children about their anger or undesirable behavior. But for these mothers, talking was described more as lecturing their children on the reasons why they should not misbehave. Some mothers would ask their children to explain their behavior in such a way as to put them on the defensive:

> Sometimes he'll try and argue back with me. . . . Other times he won't do anything. If I'm mad at him about something and, you know, ask him, "Why did you do this? How come this happened?" or whatever, he'll be like, "Well, Mom, because," and he'll come up with some lame, off-the-wall excuse, and it's like . . . "Just because, because I wanted to. Because I felt like it." . . . Sometimes it's hard. Like yesterday, when I like cut him off from TV, he didn't want to talk, would not talk to me. It's like, "Why did you do this at school?" Wouldn't say a word. Just would not talk.

A number of vignettes categorized as insensitive centered on children's sadness or hurt feelings. The mothers seemed unable to get past the behavior, and thus appeared not to think about the source of the children's actions. In trying to change or set up rules, they often ignored their children's feelings. One mother described a time when she dealt with her child's undesirable behavior by trying to make him understand another perspective. But she seemed to be unaware of the child's own experience of the situation for which he was being reprimanded:

> I just told him, "That's 'cause you're mean. Nobody wants to play with someone who slaps and pokes fun and hits people and stuff. Nobody wants to play with anybody like that." I said, "How would you like it if I was slapping you and poking at you all the time?" . . . I said, "You have to treat people the way you would like them to treat you." "I will, Mom." I just talk, I guess I just talk to him, try to make him understand . . .

Nondemandingness by Choice

In these vignettes, mothers showed less interest in standards than firm/demanding or even lax mothers, though it would be a mistake to say that nondemanding mothers had no standards at all. Most embraced low demands as part of their child-rearing philosophy and felt confident in their decisions. In several vignettes, mothers said they enjoyed doing things for their children, even things they knew their children could do themselves:

> People tell me that I lolly-cog him or that I'm too easy on him and that he is a mama's boy and it's probably true, but that's my relationship with him. He's my baby. He's the last baby I'm going to have and he's still little, so if he wants to be little for a little while longer I'm going to let him. So I do let him suck his fingers and play with my hair if he wants to, and I do little things for him that people think I shouldn't because he's almost 5. But I think he really appreciates that I do those things for him. . . . Our relationship is a lot like that, though. I spoil him, I think that's it. I don't like to see him unhappy.

Although nondemanding (permissive by choice) parenting is not consistent with descriptions of the authoritative style, whether or not it is consistent with secure attachment depends on the underlying parental motivation (wanting the child to be or remain a baby versus greater leniency or flexibility). For example, the following two examples of leniency, categorized as nondemanding, do not seem inconsistent with providing a secure attachment:

> It happens a lot in the morning, she will want me to dress her, and simply because it saves time, you know, I do. Some mornings I think, you really shouldn't be doing this, but, you

know, I don't think it's hindering her from dressing herself, it just makes life easier. So in that case I just go ahead with it.

I think that I tend to run things in a more kind of, I hate to say loving, but it's just, it's a softer relationship I guess [compared with the child's father]. Their dad has more expectations of, sort of, you know, the "grow up," you know. Always put on your own clothes because you can do it, you know, you can do that so you do it type of thing. Move on in life. Whereas, it's like this morning he wanted me to dress him. That's fine, you know. Or we play a game at bedtime where he wants me to say, "OHHH!" when I take his socks off like everything smells, and it's a fun game. I know he can take all his clothes off, but I don't always have him do it, you know.

Firmness and Demandingness

Firmness and demandingness define an authoritative style, and—like nondemanding parental behaviors—present a quandary concerning their compatibility with secure attachment. In Golby's study, only vignettes in which mothers portrayed themselves as following through on their demands in a relatively nonpunitive manner were categorized as firm and demanding (otherwise they were categorized as inflexible). A wide range of firmness is compatible with the values underlying attachment theory, but only inasmuch as firmness is tempered by flexibility, sensitivity, and a sense of effectiveness or being in charge.

In some of the vignettes categorized as firm, mothers explained that they did not give in to their children's demands even when the children were said to have violent temper tantrums or used more subtle forms of manipulation. In the following example, a mother talked about what she did when her child would not put on her shoes:

I know she knows how to put her shoes on and sometimes when we are in a hurry, and I'll say, "Will you help Mommy put your shoes on?" she will say, "No." I will say, "Okay, I'm going to go and get my coat, and when I come back I want to see those shoes on your feet." Most of the times she will do it, but if she is really stubborn about it, you know, if I want her to do something that she doesn't want to do, if she is having a real, you know, crying fit, I usually just leave the room, and she seems to calm down, and then she will do it . . . but I find it better if I just leave her alone . . .

Some mothers said they felt that it was important their children have the security of knowing that they, the parent, were in charge:

I'm able to be, whether I am on the inside or not, put across the appearance of, this is the decision, I made it, this is what we're going for. I'm confident in my decision. So that she can see a strong parental unit that way. "Oh, Mom made this decision, this is what we're doing, cool, let's go for it."

In vignettes categorized as firm, mothers did not describe themselves as intimidated by their children or afraid to make demands. One way in which they exercised their authority was by establishing generational boundaries. Unlike mothers who were not firm, these mothers did not feel subject to the same rules and restrictions they placed on their children:

Usually I'll say, "Two minutes bedtime," or I'll say, "Two minutes to get your pajamas on," and then he will slowly and surely get his pajamas on and I help him put on his pajama top and then he is usually pretty good. He'll say, "Well after I get my pajamas on can I play or watch TV for a few more minutes?" I'll say either yes or no. If I say no, I get some resistance. Then it's like, "Well, why is it bedtime, you always get to stay up later than me," and I'll just explain, "Well, I'm an adult and you're not." He's actually pretty good.

When talking about firmness, mothers felt themselves to be in control even when things did not work out the way they planned, and they were open in their evaluations of themselves and their children:

> I just get real upset with him and I say, "You realize that you know how to clean up, and I'm not expecting you to clean up more than what you made, I'm not expecting you to clean up my mess . . . but I want the toys picked up now" . . . if he still refuses . . . I say, "Alright, I'm very disappointed and I want you to go to bed right now." . . . I've been trying to reevaluate that situation to see how I can approach that in a better way because I don't think what I'm doing is working.

Safety Issues

Lastly, and consistent with attachment theory, one issue about which most mothers tended to agree more closely was to act swiftly and decisively when their children were in danger. Many mothers, even some who described themselves as lax or nondemanding under other circumstances, said they would not hesitate to enforce rules if they felt their children's safety was compromised.

Summary

Vignettes compatible with secure attachment describe flexible, sensitive, and firm or demanding maternal behavior attuned to the child's developmental level, and effective in gaining children's cooperation. Vignettes not compatible with secure attachment portray lax or inflexible behavior not attuned to children's feelings and ineffective in gaining the child's compliance or having to coerce it. Relationship quality, however, may be more important in these families than specific parental techniques. Attempts to use authoritative persuasion, reasoning, and negotiation may not be effective when the child is basically unwilling to regard parental authority as reasonable, legitimate, or fair.

CONCLUSION

Although attachment research has not systematically explored the role of parents as authority figures or socialization agents, closer examination of the attachment literature leads to the following proposals:

- A secure attachment relationship is associated with a child's disposition toward willing or "committed compliance." This makes disciplinary encounters in secure attachment relationships less necessary. In such relationships, the teaching or scaffolding component of authority may be more striking than the control component.
- Children who derive a sense of security from the relationship with their parents may also be more likely to regard parental control as legitimate even when they test it.

- Children who are securely attached to parents also appear to be more cooperative and less aggressive with their preschool peers, carrying the cooperative attitude over into extrafamilial contexts, and thus lessening the amount of control their teachers need to exercise.

- A flexible and sensitive style of parental guidance, accompanied by a sense of effectiveness (Golby, 1995), is highly compatible with secure attachment. Cho's (1994) finding that only the expressive components of the *authoritative* parenting domain were related to a representational measure of attachment quality, suggest that a wide range of parental firmness is compatible with secure attachment, provided the underlying parental motive is child-oriented (Dix, 1992) and attuned to the child's developmental level.

- Parental behavior defined as *authoritarian* by socialization theorists would, in many instances, be identified as rejection under attachment theory. Cho's (1994) finding that maternal beliefs in authoritarian control are negatively related to children's representation of secure attachment supports the notion that arbitrary authoritarian control in conjunction with emotional coldness, perhaps even hostility, is likely to undermine security by arousing fear of the parent.

- Parental rejection is also likely to induce covert or overt resentment and hostility toward the parent. This resentment may manifest itself in deliberate misbehavior against the parent, peers, and others outside the family. Hence, parental attempts to control a child in an arbitrary and nonempathic way may foster the very behavior the parent is trying to prevent. Children of maltreating parents may compulsively comply with them, checking vigilantly for signs of parental loss of control (Crittenden & DiLalla, 1988), but they may then engage in antisocial behavior against vulnerable others, such as peers. As Richters and Waters (1992) have speculated, frequent threats and acts of love withdrawal as well as arbitrary control undermine the relationship. They may also lead the child to deliberately defy and circumvent parental authority, or to comply only if monitored.

- The use of parental techniques regarded as optimal by socialization theorists (e.g., Hoffman, 1970), such as explanation, induction, and other forms of authoritative guidance, may become ineffective in the context of highly insecure and mutually unrewarding relationships. The success of these techniques requires mutual trust and caring.

- Pervasive parental laxness (as defined by Golby, 1995), may also elicit a child's provocative and manipulative behavior in an attempt to elicit parental protective responses (Greenberg & Speltz, 1988). Thus an attachment-theory guided approach to socialization is quite different from the "taming" approach implicit in a number of socialization theories in which a parent's disciplinary task is to subdue and regulate children's selfish impulses (see Richters & Waters, 1992). Attachment theorists propose that some antisocial behaviors originate from disappointments within the relationship.

The moderate size of the correlations between parent-child or peer cooperation and early or concurrent attachment measures suggests that factors other than attachment quality and the associated parental responsivity also foster or impede children's willingness to cooperate with family and societal rules (see Thompson, in press, for further discussion on this point). Much remains to be learned about these other factors, be they individual, familial, extrafamilial, or societal.

Nevertheless, secure attachment relationships emerge time and again as central in the development of children's cooperative, empathic behavior and "committed compliance" with parents who, as attachment figures, offer emotional support and protection and, as authority figures, provide flexible, understanding guidance, and exercise firmness that does not overtax the child's developmental capabilities. According to attachment theory, internal working models of self and parent that children form in such relationships are also the vehicles whereby conventional, moral, and ethical rules are initially transmitted. Various stresses and strains on parents, children, and the family can impede and undermine this process. Parents' ability to provide their children with sensitive support and responsive discipline is best fostered when extended families, neighborhoods, communities, and societal institutions acknowledge and respect the values underlying secure attachment relations.

REFERENCES

Aber, J. L., Slade, A., Berger, B., Bresgi, I., & Kaplan, M. (1985). *The parent development interview.* Unpublished manuscript, Columbia University, Barnard College, New York.

Ainsworth, M. D. S., & Bell, S. M. (1969). Some contemporary patterns in the feeding situation. In A. Ambrose (Ed.), *Stimulation in early infancy* (pp. 133–170). London: Academic Press.

Ainsworth, M. D. S., Bell, S. M., Blehar, M. C., & Main, M. (1971, April). *Physical contact: A study of infant responsiveness and its relation to maternal handling.* Paper presented at the biennial meeting of the Society for Research in Child Development, Minneapolis, MN.

Ainsworth, M. D. S., Bell, S. M., & Stayton, D. J. (1971). Individual differences in Strange Situation behaviour of one-year-olds. In H. R. Schaffer (Ed.), *The origins of human social relations* (pp. 17–57). London: Academic Press.

Ainsworth, M. D. S., Bell, S. M., & Stayton, D. (1974). Infant-mother attachment and social development. In M. P. Richards (Ed.), *The introduction of the child into a social world* (pp. 99–135). London: Cambridge University Press.

Ainsworth, M. D. S., Blehar, M. C., Waters, E., & Wall, S. (1978). *Patterns of attachment: A psychological study of the strange situation.* Hillsdale, NJ: Erlbaum.

Ainsworth, M. D. S., & Eichberg, D. (1991). Effect on infant-mother attachment of mother's unresolved loss of an attachment figure or other traumatic experience. In C. M. Parkes, J. Stevenson-Hinde, & P. Marris (Eds.), London: Routledge & Kegan Paul.

Bates, J., Maslin, C., & Frankel, K. A. (1985). Attachment security, mother-child interaction, and temperament as predictors of behavior-problem ratings at age three years. In I. Bretherton & E. Waters (Eds.), Growing points of attachment theory and research. *Monographs of the Society for Research in Child Development, 50*(1/2, Serial No. 209).

Baumrind, D. (1967). Child care practices anteceding three patterns of preschool behavior. *Genetic Psychology Monographs, 75,* 43–88.

Baumrind, D. (1971). Current patterns of parental authority. *Developmental Psychology Monographs, 4,* 1–103.

Baumrind, D. (1994). The social context of maltreatment. *Family Relations, 43,* 360–368.

Behar, L. B. (1977). The Preschool Behavior Questionnaire. *Journal of Abnormal Child Psychology, 5,* 265–275.

Bell, S. M., & Ainsworth, M. D. S. (1972). Infant crying and maternal responsiveness. *Child Development, 43,* 1171–1190.

Benoit, D., Zeahnah, C., & Barton, M. L. (1989). Maternal attachment disturbances in failure to thrive. *Infant Mental Health Journal, 10,* 185–202.

Blehar, M. C., Lieberman, A. F., & Ainsworth, M. D. S. (1977). Early face-to-face interaction and its relation to later infant-mother attachment. *Child Development, 48,* 182–194.

Block, J. (1965). *The Child Rearing Practices Report (CRPR): A set of Q items for the description of parental socialization attitudes and values.* Berkeley: University of California, Institute for Human Development.

Bowlby, J. (1944). Forty-four juvenile thieves: Their characters and home life. *International Journal of Psycho-Analysis, 25,* 19–52.

Bowlby, J. (1951). *Maternal health and mental health.* Geneva: World Health Organization Monograph Series, No. 2.

Bowlby, J. (1969). *Attachment and loss: Vol. l. Attachment.* New York: Basic Books.

Bowlby, J. (1973). *Attachment and loss: Vol. 2. Separation.* New York: Basic Books.

Bowlby, J. (1979). *The making and breaking of affectional bonds.* London: Tavistock.

Bowlby, J. (1980). *Attachment and loss: Vol. 3. Loss, sadness and depression.* New York: Basic Books.

Bowlby, J. (1988). *A secure base.* New York: Basic Books.

Bretherton, I. (1990). Open communication and internal working models: Their role in the development of attachment relationships. In R. A. Thompson (Ed.), *Nebraska Symposium on Motivation: Socioemotional development* (pp. 59–113). Lincoln: University of Nebraska Press.

Bretherton, I. (1993). From dialogue to representation: The intergenerational construction of self in relationships. In C. A. Nelson (Ed.), *Minnesota Symposia for Child Development: Memory and affect in development* (Vol. 26, pp. 237–263). Hillsdale, NJ: Erlbaum.

Bretherton, I. (1995). Attachment and developmental psychopathology. In C. Cicchetti & S. Toth (Eds.), *Emotion and representation in developmental psychopathology.* Rochester, NY: Rochester University Press.

Bretherton, I., Biringen, Z., Ridgeway, D., Maslin, C., & Sherman, M. (1989). Attachment: The parental perspective. *Infant Mental Health Journal, 10,* 203–221.

Bretherton, I., Ridgeway, D., & Cassidy, J. (1990). Assessing internal working models of the attachment relationship: An attachment story completion task for 3-year-olds. In D. Cicchetti, M. Greenberg, & E. M. Cummings (Eds.), *Attachment during the preschool years* (pp. 272–308). Chicago: University of Chicago Press.

Cain, A. C., & Fast, I. (1972). Children's disturbed reactions to parent suicide. In A. C. Cain (Ed.), *Survivors of suicide* (pp. 93–111). Springfield, IL: Thomas.

Cassidy, J. (1988). The self as related to child-mother attachment at six. *Child Development, 59,* 121–134.

Cassidy, J., Marvin, R., & the MacArthur Working Group on Attachment. (1989). *Attachment organization in three and four year olds: Coding manual.* Unpublished scoring manual.

Cho, E. (1994). *Mothers' authoritative and authoritarian parenting: Attitudes related to preschoolers' attachment representations and teacher-rated social competence.* Unpublished doctoral dissertation, University of Wisconsin-Madison.

Cicchetti, D., & Rizley, R. (1980). Developmental perspectives on the etiology, intergenerational transmission, and sequelae of child maltreatment. *New Directions for Child Development, 11,* 31–35.

Cohn, D. A. (1990). Child-mother attachment of six-year-olds and social competence at school. *Child Development, 61,* 152–162.

Cohn, D. A. (1991). The family and children's peer relations. *Journal of Social and Personal Relationships, 8,* 315–346.

Craik, K. (1943). *The nature of explanation.* Cambridge, England: Cambridge University Press.

Crittenden, P. (1990). Internal representational models of attachment relationships. *Infant Mental Health Journal, 11,* 259–277.

Crittenden, P., & DiLalla, D. L. (1988). Compulsive compliance: The development of an inhibitory coping strategy in infancy. *Journal of Abnormal Child Psychology, 16,* 585–599.

DeKlyen, M. (1991). *Disruptive behavior disorder and the internal representation of attachment of preschool boys and their mothers.* Paper presented at the biennial meeting of the Society for Research in Child Development, Seattle, WA.

Dix, T. (1992). Parenting on behalf of the child: Empathic goals in the regulation of responsive parenting. In I. E. Sigel, A. V. McGillicuddy-Delisi, & J. Goodnow (Eds.), *Parental systems* (pp. 319–346). Hillsdale, NJ: Erlbaum.

Egeland, B., Pianta, R., & O'Brien, M. A. (1993). Maternal intrusiveness in infancy and child maladaptation in early school years. *Development and Psychopathology, 5,* 359–370.

Emde, R. N., Biringen, Z., Clyman, R. C., & Oppenheim, D. (1991). The moral self of infancy: Affective core and procedural knowledge. *Developmental Review, 11,* 251–270.

Emde, R. N., & Buchsbaum, H. K. (1990). "Didn't you hear my Mommy?" Autonomy with connectedness in moral self emergence. In D. Cicchetti & M. Beeghly (Eds.), *The self in transition: Infancy to early childhood* (pp. 35–60). Chicago: University of Chicago Press.

Erikson, E. H. (1950). *Childhood and society.* New York: Norton.

Erickson, M., Sroufe, L. A, & Egeland, B. (1985). The relationship between quality of attachment and behavior problems in preschool in a high risk sample. In I. Bretherton & E. Waters (Eds.), Growing points of attachment theory and research. *Monographs of the Society for Research in Child Development, 50* (1/2, Serial No. 209), 147–166.

Fonagy, P., Steele, H., & Steele, M. (1991). Maternal representations of attachment during pregnancy predict the organization of infant-mother attachment at one year of age. *Child Development, 62,* 891–905.

Fraiberg, S., Adelson, E., & Shapiro, V. (1975). Ghosts in the nursery: A psychoanalytic approach to the problems of impaired infant-mother relationships. *Journal of the American Academy of Child Psychiatry, 14,* 387–421.

Freud, S. (1940). An outline of psycho-analysis (J. Strachey, Trans.). *International Journal of Psychoanalysis, 21,* 27–82.

George, C., Kaplan, N., & Main, M. (1985). *The Berkeley Adult Attachment Interview.* Unpublished manuscript, University of California-Berkeley, Department of Psychology.

George. C., & Solomon, J. (1989). Internal working models of caregiving and security of attachment at age six. *Infant Mental Health Journal, 10,* 222–237.

George, C., & Solomon, J. (1996). Representational models of relationships: Links between caregiving and attachment. *Infant Mental Health Journal, 17,* 198–216.

Glaser, B., & Strauss, A. (1967). *The discovery of grounded theory.* New York: Aldine.

Golby, B. (1995). *Divorced mothers' narratives on childrearing: A qualitative analysis.* Unpublished master's thesis, University of Wisconsin-Madison.

Gordon, T. (1975). *Parent effectiveness training.* New York: New American Library.

Greenberg, M., & Speltz, M. (1988). Attachment and the ontogeny of conduct problems. In J. Belsky & T. Nezworski (Eds.), *Clinical implications of attachment* (pp. 177–218). Hillsdale, NJ: Erlbaum.

Greenberg, M., Speltz, M., DeKlyen, M., & Endriga, M. C. (1993). Attachment security in preschoolers with externalizing behavior problems: A replication. *Development & Psychopathology, 3,* 413–430.

Grossmann, K., Fremmer-Bombik, E., Rudolph, J., & Grossmann, K. (1988). Maternal attachment representations as related to patterns of infant-mother attachment and maternal care during the first years. In R. Hinde & J. Stevenson-Hind (Eds.), *Relationships within families: Maternal influences* (pp. 241–260). Oxford, England: Oxford University Press.

Grusec, J., & Goodnow, J. J. (1994). Impact of parental discipline methods on the child's internalization of values: A reconceptualization of current points of view. *Developmental Psychology, 30,* 4–19.

Hartman, H., Kris, E., & Loewenstein, R. (1946). Comments on the formation of psychic structure. *Psychoanalytic Study of the Child,* 10–36.

Hoffman, M. L. (1970). Moral development. In P. H. Mussen (Ed.), *Carmichael's handbook of child psychology* (3rd ed.) (Vol. 2, pp. 261–359). New York: Wiley.

Hoffman, M. L. (1983). Affective and cognitive processes in moral internalization. In E. T. Higgins, D. Ruble, & W. Hartup (Eds.), *Social cognition and social development* (pp. 236–274). New York: Cambridge University Press.

Hoffman, M. L. (1994). Discipline and internalization. *Developmental Psychology, 30,* 26–28.

Kagan, J. (1981). *The second year: The emergence of self-awareness.* Cambridge, MA: Harvard University Press.

Kaplan, N. (1984). *Individual differences in six-year-olds' thoughts about separation: Predicted from attachment to mother at age one.* Unpublished doctoral dissertation, University of California-Berkeley.

Kim, S. (1992). *Early daycare and the family as predictors of children's socio-emotional development.* Unpublished doctoral dissertation, University of Wisconsin-Madison.

Klagsbrun, M., & Bowlby, J. (1976). Responses to separation from parents: A clinical test for young children. *British Journal of Professional Psychology, 21,* 7–21.

Kobak, R., & Holland, C. (1994). Attachment and meta-monitoring: Implications for adolescent autonomy and psychopathology. In D. Cicchetti & S. L. Toth (Eds.), *Rochester Symposium on Developmental Psychopathology: Disorders and dysfunctions of the self* (Vol. 5). Rochester, NY: University of Rochester Press.

Kochanska, G. (1995). Children's temperament, mother's discipline, and security of attachment: Multiple pathways to emerging internalization. *Child Development, 66,* 597–615.

Kochanska, G., Casey, R., & Fukumoto, A. (1995). Toddlers' sensitivity to standard violations. *Child Development, 66,* 643–656.

Kochanska, G., Kuczynski, L., & Radke-Yarrow, M. (1989). Correspondence between mothers' self-reported and observed child-rearing practices. *Child Development, 60,* 56–63.

Kohn, M. (1988). *Kohn Problem Checklist/Kohn Social Competence Scale.* New York: Harcourt Brace Jovanovich.

Kuczynski, L., & Kochanska, G. (1995). Developmental function and content of maternal demands: Early demands for competent action. *Child Development, 66,* 616–628.

LaFreniere, P., & Sroufe, L. A. (1985). Profiles of peer competence in the preschool: Interrelations between measures, influence of social ecology, and relation to attachment history. *Developmental Psychology, 21,* 56–69.

Lewis, M., Feiring, C., McGuffog, C., & Jaskir, J. (1984). Predicting psychopathology in six-year-olds from early social relations. *Child Development, 60,* 146–156.

Lieberman, A. F. (1977). Children's competence with a peer: Relations with attachment and peer experience. *Child Development, 48,* 1277–1287.

Lieberman, A. F., & Pawl, J. H. (1990). Disorders of attachment and secure base behavior in the second year of life: Conceptual issues and clinical intervention. In M. T. Greenberg, D. Cicchetti, & E. M. Cummings (Eds.), *Attachment in the preschool years* (pp. 375–397). Chicago: University of Chicago Press.

Londerville, S., & Main, M. (1981). Security of attachment, compliance, and maternal training methods in the second year. *Developmental Psychology, 17,* 289–299.

Lyons-Ruth, K. (1992). Maternal depressive symptoms, disorganized infant-mother attachment relationship and hostile-aggressive behavior in the preschool classroom: A prospective longitudinal view from infancy to age five. In D. Cicchetti & S. Toth (Eds.), *Developmental perspectives on depression* (pp. 131–169). Rochester, NY: University of Rochester Press.

Lyons-Ruth, K., Alpern, L., & Repacholi, B. (1993). Disorganized infant attachment representation and maternal psychosocial problems as predictors of hostile-aggressive behavior in the preschool classroom. *Child Development, 64,* 572–585.

Lyons-Ruth, K., & Block, D. (1996). The disturbed caregiving system: Relations among childhood trauma, maternal caregiving and infant affect and attachment. *Infant Mental Health Journal, 17,* 257–275.

Lyons-Ruth, K., Easterbrooks, M. A., & Cibelli, C. D. (1997). Infant attachment strategies, infant mental lag, and material depressive symptoms: Predictors of internalizing and externalizing symptoms at age 7. *Developmental Psychology, 33*(4).

Maccoby, E. E., & Martin, J. A. (1983). Socialization in the context of the family: Parent-child interaction. In E. M. Hetherington (Ed.), *Handbook of child psychology: Vol. 4. Socialization, personality, and social development* (pp. 1–101). New York: Wiley.

Main, M., & Cassidy, J. (1988). Categories of response to reunion with the parent at age six: Predicted from infant attachment classifications and stable over a one-month period. *Developmental Psychology, 24,* 415–426.

Main, M., & Hesse, E. (1990). The insecure disorganized/disoriented attachment pattern in infancy: Precursors and sequelae. In M. Greenberg, D. Cicchetti, & E. M. Cummings (Eds.), *Attachment during the preschool years: Theory, research, and intervention* (pp. 161–182). Chicago: University of Chicago Press.

Main, M., Kaplan, K., & Cassidy, J. (1985). Security in infancy, childhood and adulthood: A move to the level of representation. In I. Bretherton & E. Waters (Eds.), Growing points of attachment theory and research. *Monographs of the Society for Research in Child Development, 50*(1/2, Serial No. 209), 66–104.

Main, M., & Solomon, J. (1990). Procedures for identifying as disorganized/disoriented during the Ainsworth Strange Situation. In M. T. Greenberg, D. Cicchetti, & E. M. Cummings (Eds.), *Attachment in the preschool years* (pp. 121–161). Chicago: University of Chicago Press.

Matas, L., Arend, R. A., & Sroufe, L. A. (1978). Continuity and adaptation in the second year: The relationship between quality of attachment and later competence. *Child Development, 49,* 547–556.

Piaget, J. (1951). *The origins of intelligence in children.* New York: Norton.

Radke-Yarrow, M., Cummings, E. M., Kuczynski, L., & Chapman, M. (1985). Patterns of attachment in two- and three-year-olds in normal families and families with parental depression. *Child Development, 56,* 884–893.

Reid, M., Landesman-Ramey, S., & Burchinal, M. (1990). Dialogues with children about their families. In I. Bretherton & M. Watson (Eds.), *New directions in child development: Vol. 48. Children's perspectives on the family* (pp. 5–28). San Francisco: Jossey-Bass.

Richters, J. E., & Waters, E. (1992). Attachment and socialization: The positive side of social influence. In M. Lewis & S. Feinman (Eds.), *Social influences and behavior* (pp. 185–214). New York: Plenum Press.

Schaefer, E. S., Sayers, S. L., Clair, K. L., & Burnett, C. K. (1987, August). *Mothers' reports of child relationship with mother and of child personality.* Paper presented at the annual meeting of the American Psychological Association, New York.

Shouldice, A., & Stevenson-Hinde, J. (1992). Coping with security distress: The separation anxiety test and attachment classification at 4.5 years. *Journal of Child Psychology and Psychiatry, 33,* 331–348.

Slough, N., & Greenberg, M. (1990). 5-year-olds representations of separation from parents: Responses for self and a hypothetical child. In W. Damon (Series Ed.) & I. Bretherton & M. Watson (Vol. Eds.), *New directions for child development: Vol. 48. Children's perspectives on the family* (pp. 67–84). San Francisco: Jossey-Bass.

Spitz, R. A. (1957). *No and yes: On the genesis of human communication.* Madison, CT: International Universities Press.

Sroufe, L. A. (1983). Infant-caregiver attachment and patterns of adaptation in the preschool: The roots of competence and maladaptation. In M. Perlmutter (Ed.), *Minnesota Symposia in Child Development, Vol. 16* (pp. 41–83). Hillsdale, NJ: Erlbaum.

Sroufe, L. A. (1988). The role of infant-caregiver attachment in adult development. In J. Belsky & T. Nezworski (Eds.), *Clinical implications of attachment* (pp. 18–38). Hillsdale, NJ: Erlbaum.

Sroufe, L. A., & Fleeson, J. (1986). Attachment and the construction of relationships. In W. Hartup & Z. Rubin (Eds.), *Relationship and development* (pp. 51–71). Hillsdale, NJ: Erlbaum.

Stayton, D., Hogan, R., & Ainsworth, M. D. S. (1973). Infant obedience and maternal behavior: The origins of socialization reconsidered. *Child Development, 42,* 1057–1070.

Strauss, A. (1987). *Qualitative analysis.* New York: Cambridge University Press.

Suess, G. J., Grossmann, K. E., & Sroufe, L. A. (1992). Effects of infant attachment to mother and father on quality of adaptation in preschool: From dyadic to individual organization of self. *International Journal of Behavioral Development, 15,* 43–65.

Thompson, R. (in press). *Early sociopersonality development. Handbook of child psychology.* New York: Wiley.

Troy, M., & Sroufe, L. A. (1987). Victimization among preschoolers: The role of attachment relationship history. *Journal of the American Academy of Child Psychiatry, 26,* 166–172.

Van IJzendoorn, M. (in press). Attachment, morality and criminality. *International Journal of Development.*

Waddington, C. H. (1960). *The ethical animal.* Chicago: University of Chicago Press.

Waters, E. (1987). *Attachment Behavior Q-set (Revision 3.0).* Unpublished instrument, State University of New York at Stony Brook, Department of Psychology.

Waters, E., & Deane, K. E. (1985). Defining and assessing individual differences in attachment relationships: Q-methodology and the organization of behavior in infancy and early childhood. In I. Bretherton & E. Waters (Eds.), Growing points of attachment theory and research. *Monographs of the Society for Research in Child Development, 50*(1/2, Serial No. 209), 41–65.

Waters, E., Kondo-Ikemura, K., Posada, G., & Richters, J. (1990). Learning to love: Mechanisms and milestones. In M. Gunner & L. A. Sroufe (Eds.), *Minnesota Symposia on Child Psychology* (Vol. 23, pp. 217–255). Hillsdale, NJ: Erlbaum.

Waters, E., Vaughn, B. E., Posada, G., & Kondo-Ikemura, K. (1995). Caregiving, cultural and cognitive perspectives on secure-base behavior and working models: New growing points of attachment theory and research. *Monographs of the Society for Research in Child Development, 60*(2/3, Serial No. 244).

Waters, E., Wippman, J., & Sroufe, L. A. (1979). Child-rearing and children's prosocial initiations towards victims of distress. *Child Development, 50,* 319–330.

Young, J. Z. (1964). *A model for the brain.* London: Oxford University Press.

Zahn-Waxler, C., & Radke-Yarrow, M. (1990). The origin of empathic concern. *Motivation and Emotion, 14,* 107–120.

CHAPTER 6

Internalization within the Family: The Self-Determination Theory Perspective

WENDY S. GROLNICK, EDWARD L. DECI, and RICHARD M. RYAN

The study of familial socialization is concerned with how children acquire the motives, values, and behavior patterns that allow them to function within the larger society (Maccoby, 1984; Zigler & Child, 1973). Although the term *socialization* may conjure up a picture of powerful parents forcing standards and behaviors onto passive or resistant children, effective socialization requires something more than behavior in accord with parental demands. It involves an inner adaptation to social requirements so that children not only comply with these requirements but also accept and endorse the advocated values and behaviors, experiencing them as their own. Thus, although socializing agents can force children to carry out behaviors, the real goal is for children to carry them out volitionally. Whereas socializing agents can "teach" their children the values and attitudes they hold dear, the important thing is having the children "own" those values and attitudes.

The development of volition (as opposed to mere compliance) with regard to socialized behaviors thus requires a transformation of internal structures by which the child fully assimilates the values underlying the behaviors. In a sense, this points to a potential contradiction between the forces of socialization that attempt to promote compliance with culturally transmitted behaviors and attitudes, and the children's need to actively assimilate new values and behaviors if they are to accept them as their own. Insofar as socializers force behaviors onto children they may, unwittingly, stifle the very assimilatory tendencies required for successful socialization. Indeed, within self-determination theory (Deci & Ryan, 1985; Ryan, Deci, & Grolnick, 1995), we assume that children have a natural motivational propensity to take in extant social values and behaviors and to make them their own, but socializers often forestall this occurrence. From our viewpoint, therefore, socializing agents such as parents and teachers face the important challenge of how to mobilize, facilitate, and support a child's natural tendency to internalize cultural values, attitudes, and behaviors. It is the challenge of how to promote socially sanctioned behaving without killing the spirit of the child, without diminishing the child's natural curiosity, vitality, and excitement.

Preparation of this chapter was facilitated by a Faculty Scholars Award from the William T. Grant Foundation to the first author and by a research grant from the National Institute of Child Health and Human Development (HD-19914) to the Human Motivation Program, Department of Psychology, University of Rochester.

According to the self-determination perspective, another challenge has been highlighted by recent theory-guided research. New research has indicated that the internalization of some socially promulgated values and goals is associated with well-being, whereas the internalization of others is associated with ill-being. Thus the content being internalized also seems to affect whether the socialization represents healthy adaptation.

One of the remarkable findings from numerous investigations of internalization is that children appear more likely both to fully internalize societal values and behaviors (i.e., make them their own) and also to focus on the values and behaviors that are congruent with their intrinsic nature when less, rather than more, pressure is applied from without. An understanding of these phenomena, and thus of effective socialization, requires a consideration of the motivational processes involved in the child's tendency to internalize aspects of the social world.

INTERNALIZATION AS A DEVELOPMENTAL PROCESS

Self-determination theory employs an *organismic* perspective, beginning with the assumption that humans are active agents who engage their surroundings in an attempt not only to master and assimilate aspects of the social and inanimate environments but also to accommodate to interesting and important aspects of those environments (Blasi, 1976; Ryan, 1993). Development is understood as moving in the directions of increased complexity, differentiation, and refinement, and at the same time, of increased coordination, cohesion, and unity (Piaget, 1971; Werner, 1948). Psychological development thus entails individuals' working to elaborate or expand themselves while striving to maintain or enhance integration and harmony among all aspects of themselves (Ryan, 1991). We refer to this general developmental process as *organismic integration*, suggesting that it is an innate process which operates at all phases of development. In this sense, self-determination theory is a developmental theory even though it pays relatively little attention to age-related changes in socialization contents and practices.

One corollary of the assumption that individuals are naturally inclined to elaborate themselves over the life span is that they have a readiness to absorb and accept socially transmitted values and practices as they develop a more complex and unified self (Deci & Ryan, 1991; Ryan, 1995). This process of accepting values and behaviors by actively transforming them is typically referred to as *internalization* (Kelman, 1961; Meissner, 1981; Schafer, 1968). For us, then, internalization is theorized to be a natural developmental process in which children (as well as adolescents and adults) progressively integrate societal values and proscriptions into a coherent sense of self.

Internalization does not always function optimally, however. To the extent that the natural process of internalizing and integrating societal behaviors or values is impeded rather than supported, a partial or less effective form of internalization will occur, resulting in less adaptive regulatory processes. Furthermore, if the cultural values being internalized are overly discordant with the individual's intrinsic nature, less adaptive outcomes are also to be expected. Accordingly, our view of optimal internalization as a natural, active process of integrating aspects of the social world with one's intrinsic self—a process that can either be facilitated or forestalled—provides a basis for explaining why different types and contents of socialization represent differentially healthy psychological development.

SELF-DETERMINATION THEORY AND DEVELOPMENT

Although the organismic perspective maintains that development occurs naturally through the dual processes of differentiating psychological structures and processes and then integrating those elements into coherent organizational units and networks (Piaget, 1971; Werner, 1948), this organismic integration does not happen automatically. Indeed, it requires sustained, motivated activity. Both the behaviors that provide inputs to development and the psychological processes through which that development occurs must be energized and directed—they must be *motivated*. A full understanding of development therefore requires consideration of the motivational processes that underlie it and the social conditions that encourage rather than hinder those motivational processes. Self-determination theory addresses these very issues (Ryan, Deci, & Grolnick, 1995).

The theory employs the distinction between two broad types of motivation: *intrinsic* and *extrinsic*. Intrinsic motivation comprises both behavioral and psychological activities that do not require external prompts or reinforcement contingencies. These are activities that people do freely and for which the only "rewards" are the inherent satisfactions that accompany them. Intrinsically motivated actions are spontaneous and thus do not require internalization. Such activities are an expression of individuals' natural propensity to engage their environment, performing interesting tasks and undertaking optimal challenges. Intrinsic motivation encompasses curiosity and exploration, and it often energizes persistent task engagement. It thus represents an organismic tendency that plays an important role in development by energizing the activity necessary to elaborate one's capacities (Deci, 1975; Elkind, 1971; Ryan, 1991).

Extrinsic motivation, in contrast, refers to engagement in an activity that is instrumental to some separable consequence. When extrinsically motivated, people behave in order to attain some outcome different from the mere enjoyment of the activity itself. In terms of socialization, extrinsic motivation pertains to "acquired" motivations—to values or regulations that are initially advocated by an external source and thus must be internalized to become an enduring motivational propensity. Intrinsic and extrinsic motivation will be considered in turn.

Intrinsically Motivated Development

Intrinsic motivation encompasses the energization of both behavior and psychological processes. When applied to behavior, intrinsically motivated activity is often described as "autotelic" (Csikszentmihalyi, 1975), meaning that it is done "for its own sake" or, more accurately, for the satisfaction inherent in the activity itself (Deci, 1975). Intrinsic motivation thus refers to actions that are done out of *interest*. As adults, the tasks we do because they interest us are often quite circumscribed, but children find many activities interesting and they do them quite willingly, with no prods from socializing agents. They invent games, they manipulate objects, they mimic adults, and they do things that lead to responses from others. Such activities are integral to development for they represent inputs to the natural integrative tendency through which psychological processes and structures are elaborated and refined. Thus, many behaviors that provide inputs for development, as well as the natural developmental process through which these nutriments become part of the self, are intrinsically motivated. Like all natural processes, however, intrinsically motivated development can be either facilitated or hindered by the social context (Deci & Ryan, 1985, 1991). Stated differently, intrinsic motivational tendencies requires nutriments from the environment for their expression to be manifest. Specifically, the maintenance of intrinsic motivation, and the vitality and effectiveness of the activity it spawns, is dependent on the satisfaction of three primary *psychological needs*—competence, autonomy, and relatedness (Ryan, 1995; Ryan, Deci, & Grolnick, 1995).

Psychological Needs

White (1959) first discussed the desire to feel effectance or *competence* in dealing with the environment. This psychological need underlies a variety of selective, directed, and prolonged behaviors that result in mastery. The experience of competence can therefore be viewed as one type of intrinsic satisfaction that people freely pursue and that promotes learning and development.

A second psychological need that subserves intrinsic motivation is the need for *autonomy*. DeCharms (1968), using Heider's (1958) construct of *perceived locus of causality* argued that a basic human propensity is to be an "origin" or agent with respect to action: People fundamentally desire to experience an internal locus of initiation and regulation for their behavior. According to deCharms, people must experience a sense of choice to maintain high intrinsic motivation. Similarly, Deci and Ryan (1985) have argued that factors that enhance one's experience of autonomy facilitate intrinsic motivation, whereas those that promote a sense of being controlled (i.e., of an external perceived locus of causality) diminish it.

The third fundamental psychological need is for *relatedness*. As Harlow (1958) argued, individuals need to experience love and interpersonal contact to develop optimally—they need to experience warmth and affection. Similarly, Bowlby (1969) has emphasized the importance of children's feeling a sense of security with respect to parents. Although MacDonald (1992) has noted differences between security and affection, the concept of a need for relatedness encompasses both. Considerable research on attachment (Ainsworth, Blehar, Waters, & Wall, 1978) has demonstrated that if infants and young children do not experience security in their primary relationships, exploratory activity is diminished and various adjustment problems are likely to follow. In this sense, intrinsic motivation flourishes only when there is a backdrop of relatedness to others. This is not just true in infancy, however; the exploratory spirit in all humans is most robust when persons are operating from a "secure base" (Bowlby, 1979) or sense of relatedness (Ryan, Deci, & Grolnick, 1995).

The active tendency inherent in intrinsic motivation—to do, to assimilate, to seek and master challenges—is theorized to occur primarily under conditions that allow satisfaction of the intrinsic needs to feel competent, autonomous, and related. By contrast, conditions that diminish these crucial experiences interfere with intrinsically motivated processes, thereby undermining the natural developmental tendencies. As such, the specification of innate psychological needs provides a basis for making predictions about what social-contextual conditions will facilitate versus undermine healthy psychological development.

Beyond Intrinsic Motivation: Internalization

Whereas intrinsically motivated behaviors are undertaken for the spontaneous satisfaction that accompanies them, extrinsically motivated behaviors are instrumental to some separable, rewarding condition. When a boy hangs up his coat to get his mother's approval, he is extrinsically motivated, as is a girl when she plays the piano to get a surprise from her grandfather.

Many behaviors that socializing adults would like children to do are not intrinsically interesting and thus not likely to occur spontaneously (e.g., memorizing number facts or cleaning up after an art project). Indeed, children may not be intrinsically interested in many of the activities adults consider "good for them." Even prosocial behaviors such as sharing may not be intrinsically motivated in spite of the fact that children have the innate propensity to feel related to others. All these behaviors, as well as the values and attitudes consistent with them, thus fall within the domain of extrinsic motivation, for they must, at least initially, be externally prompted. These are the behaviors, attitudes, and values for which internalization is necessary if children are to fully accept them.

As mentioned, the term *extrinsic motivation* refers to any behavior in which the "reward" or desired consequence is separable from the activity, whether administered interpersonally or intrapsychically. Extrinsic motivation subsumes instances in which children behave as a direct function of rules, demands, threats, or proffered rewards, as well as instances in which children behave to maintain a fragile sense of self-esteem, or simply because they think it is important for their health or well-being. Thus, not all extrinsic motives involve external control; the source for some is inside the person.

A critical dimension on which extrinsic motives vary is the extent to which they are self-determined versus regulated by externally imposed constraints, rewards, or punishments (Ryan, Connell, & Deci, 1985). According to self-determination theory, individuals become increasingly autonomous or self-determined for extrinsic activities as the process of internalization functions more fully and effectively to bring the initially external regulations into coherence with one's self.

Internalization Defined

Internalization, as we view it, concerns the processes by which individuals acquire beliefs, attitudes, or behavioral regulations from external sources and progressively transform those external regulations into personal attributes, values, or regulatory styles (Ryan, Connell, & Grolnick, 1992). Three aspects of this definition merit discussion because they diverge from various other viewpoints.

First, while internalization is often discussed only in terms of moral or prosocial values, the concept applies to any values, attitudes, and behavioral regulations that were originally external and have been "taken in" by the person. Our work has focused on internalization of regulations for a variety of behaviors such as doing schoolwork (Ryan & Connell, 1989), performing chores around the house (Grolnick & Ryan, 1989), attending religious functions (Ryan, Rigby, & King, 1993), and maintaining weight loss (Williams, Grow, Freedman, Ryan, & Deci, 1996). Further, we have explored the internalization of various cultural values, ranging from materialism to health, and the conditions associated with their adoption (e.g., Kasser, Ryan, Zax, & Sameroff, 1995; Williams & Deci, 1996).

Second, this definition highlights that full or optimal internalization involves not only taking in a value or regulation but also integrating it with one's sense of self—that is, making it one's own—so the resulting behavior will be fully chosen or *self*-regulated.

When values have personal meaning and behaviors are willingly emitted, they are not only internally initiated but they are experienced as autonomous.

This definition of internalization thus differs from various others that refer only to whether the attitude, value, or behavior is regulated internally or externally. That use of the internal/external spatial metaphor as a simple dichotomy between whether a behavior is initiated by the person, or alternatively by external prompts, contingencies, or demands, fails to differentiate between different *degrees* or *types* of internalization. It fails to consider whether a value or regulation that has been taken in by the person has been fully integrated and thus has what we, like deCharms (1968), refer to as an internal (rather than an external) perceived locus of causality. If a behavior is experienced as fully chosen and autonomously undertaken, it would have an internal perceived locus of causality, whereas if it is experienced as pressured or coerced by an internal force, it would have an external perceived locus of causality. In the latter case, the regulatory process would be within the person but would not have been fully integrated.

Think about a boy who feels an intense pressure and a sense of having to do well on an exam to prove his self-worth and gain some imagined approval from a generalized other. The cause of the boy's trying to do well is inside him, but according to our theory it is not internal to his sense of self. It is as if he were being forced to behave by a contingency that has been imposed on him, even though the contingency is now within him. He has partially internalized a regulation, has taken it in without accepting it as his own. As such, he would lack a sense of willingness and choice and instead would feel pressure, anxiety, and a sense of "should." This form of regulation differs greatly from that of a child who tries hard because the achievement is what he wants for himself, because it is central to his future goals and personal values. According to our definition, internalization is thus not an all-or-none phenomenon. Rather, it concerns the degree to which an activity initially regulated by external sources is perceived as one's own and is experienced as self-determined. Internalized regulations can thus vary in their levels of autonomy and integration.

Third, our definition, which views internalization as a developmental process, implies that internalization is an expression of the organismic integration tendency and is energized by the intrinsic needs for competence, autonomy, and relatedness. Through internalization, a child is able to cope more effectively with environmental demands. At the same time, the child will feel more autonomous as he or she moves from the conflicts of external control toward a more flexible, volitional self-regulation. The experience will then be one of activity and willingness rather than passivity and control (Meissner, 1981). Finally, as a child internalizes culturally sanctioned regulations, he or she will experience a greater sense of shared values, and of belonging (Goodenow, 1992) and closeness with the socializing agent or group.

The assumption, then, is that the *process* of internalization of behavioral regulations and values is intrinsically motivated by the three basic psychological needs, even though the behaviors themselves are extrinsically motivated. The importance of this assumption is that it provides a means for predicting what factors in the interpersonal context will enhance versus diminish internalization. Those that allow satisfaction of the basic needs will facilitate internalization, whereas those that thwart satisfaction will forestall it. These phenomena, of internalization being motivated by the three psychological needs and thus being facilitated or forestalled by conditions in the social context, are understood to operate across the life span. Although the competencies one is acquiring and the content being internalized may vary systematically with age, the fundamental processes and needs are theorized to be operative at all ages (Ryan, Deci, & Grolnick, 1995).

A Continuum of Internalization

One of the features of our theory of internalization is its postulate of a continuum describing how fully a value or behavior has been internalized. Initially, what motivates behaviors in the extrinsic domain are *external* contingencies such as requests, rewards, and demands administered by caretakers. This type of regulation requires only that the person anticipate these contingencies and regulate accordingly. A somewhat greater degree of internalization is seen in *introjected* regulation, where externally imposed regulations have been "taken in" by the person but are maintained in essentially their original form. The resulting source of regulation is within the person, but it has not been integrated with the self and is thus a source of tension and inner conflict. Regulation is not perceived as one's own, but instead as controlling and coercive. The boy who pressures himself to do well on a test provides an example of introjected regulation.

A third form of extrinsic regulation, which lies further along the internalization continuum, is regulation through *identification*. Here, the person identifies with the value of the behavior and sees it as important for his or her own goals. With identified regulation, the person experiences a greater degree of choice and personal valuing. An example of identified regulation might be a man who exercises regularly because it is important to him to be cardiovascularly healthy.

Finally, a still more mature form of regulation resulting from an even fuller internalization happens when the identification has been *integrated* or reciprocally assimilated with other aspects of one's self; that is, with one's unified and coherent system of values, goals, and motives (Deci & Ryan, 1991; Ryan, Connell, & Deci, 1985). For example, if the man's identification with exercise were integrated, he would also refrain from smoking and eating excessively fatty foods—both behaviors being directly related to cardiovascular functioning. But if he does smoke regularly, that would be evidence that the identification of exercising is not integrated.

Accompanying the structural changes represented by movement along the internalization continuum is a corresponding change in experience. As organismic integration functions more fully, individuals experience greater degrees of volition and choice—they perceive the locus of causality to become more internal. The internalization continuum thus distinguishes experientially as well as structurally among these forms of regulation that differ in terms of autonomy, integration, and self-determination. The control-to-autonomy continuum, with each of the forms of internalized regulation is displayed schematically in Figure 6.1.

Substantial research has explored the antecedents and consequences of different degrees of internalization. The research is typically done within domains (Ryan, 1995), suggesting that individuals can be relatively autonomous in one domain (e.g., schoolwork) while being relatively controlled in another (e.g., chores around the house), although it is possible to explore integration in personality as a more generalized individual difference, which theoretically is as if one aggregated across domains (Koestner, Bernieri, & Zuckerman, 1992).

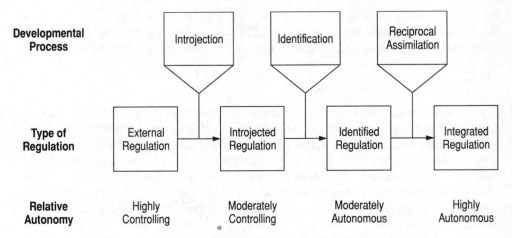

Figure 6.1   Styles and Descriptors of Regulation Resulting from
Different Degrees of Organismic Integration

Research on the Internalization Continuum

In a preliminary investigation of the self-regulation continuum, Chandler and Connell (1987) interviewed children between the ages of 5 and 13 about doing "chores," such as picking up their rooms, going to bed on time, and doing homework. The researchers reported that external reasons (contingencies in the environment) decreased with age while transitional reasons (general rules and maxims, which we here call "introjects") and internalized reasons (achievement of a self-determined goal, which we here call "identifications") increased with age, thus suggesting a general movement along the internalization continuum as children grow older.

Ryan and Connell (1989) developed a self-report measure of regulatory styles based on the internalization continuum, which assesses three of the four forms of internalized regulation: external, introjected, and identified. The questionnaire assesses reasons why individuals do particular classes of behaviors, such as schoolwork. *External* reasons include behaving because of constraints, rewards, or punishments externally imposed by a teacher or parent. A sample item would be, "I do my homework because I'll get in trouble if I don't." *Introjected* reasons include behaving because the child would feel unworthy if he or she did not. A sample item would be, "I try to do well in school because I would feel bad about myself if I don't." *Identified* reasons include valuing learning and education, and a sample item would be, "I do my classwork because I want to understand the subject."

This academic self-regulation scale does not include the integrated style for two reasons. First, the scale was designed for middle childhood and the integrated style is a more developmentally advanced form of self-regulation than would be expected for these children. Second, an identified reason is not appreciably different from an integrated reason. What differentiates these two forms of regulation is not why one is doing them, but rather whether the identified reason is integrated with other values and behaviors. The academic self-regulation questionnaire does, however, assess intrinsic motivation because children do vary in the extent to which they are intrinsically motivated to engage in school activities. An example of an *intrinsic* reason would be, "I do my homework because it is interesting and fun."

Data confirmed that the four subscales of the measure formed a simplex-like pattern (higher correlations between scales that theoretically are more closely related), indicating that these regulatory styles can be ordered along an underlying dimension of autonomy. Although intrinsic motivation is innate and thus does not result from internalization, it correlates more strongly with identified regulation than with introjected regulation suggesting that the more fully assimilated a regulation becomes, the more closely its qualities approximate intrinsic motivation, which is characterized by felt autonomy.

Ryan and Connell (1989) found that, in the academic domain during middle childhood, more autonomous styles (identified and intrinsic) were correlated with positive affect and proactive coping, whereas less autonomous styles (external and introjected) were correlated with negative affect and maladaptive coping. Introjection, in particular, was highly correlated with anxiety and with anxiety amplification following failure.

Ryan and Connell (1989) also found that 10- to 12-year-old children reporting more autonomous regulation in the prosocial domain displayed greater empathy, more mature moral reasoning, and more positive relatedness to others. Support for the existence of an internalization continuum, with more positive outcomes being associated with more self-determined forms of regulation, has been further provided by research using the self-regulation model with widely varying age groups in several domains, including religion (Ryan et al., 1993), sport (Pelletier et al., 1995), aging (Vallerand, O'Connor, & Hamel, 1995), relationships (Blais, Sabourin, Boucher, & Vallerand, 1990), and health care (Ryan, Plant, & O'Malley, 1995; Williams et al., 1996).

Internalization of Values: Content Matters

The work on internalization thus far discussed concerns the regulation of particular behaviors within specifiable domains such as school, work, and sport. Another line of research has focused on internalization of cultural values or aspirations. In particular, this work has considered seven different life aspirations: wealth (i.e., financial success), image (i.e., physical attractiveness), fame (i.e., social recognition), self-acceptance (i.e., personal growth), affiliation (i.e., meaningful relationships), community contribution (i.e., social responsibility), and health (i.e., physical fitness).

Factor analytic studies have indicated that the first three of these values load together, forming an *extrinsic* aspirations factor, so labeled because all three are considered instrumental (Kasser & Ryan, 1996). Wealth, image, and fame do not constitute basic psychological satisfactions in their own right but instead are means for obtaining some other tangible or psychological outcome. The other four life values (self-acceptance, affiliation, community, and health) load on a second factor, which Kasser and Ryan labeled *intrinsic* aspirations, for they are typically rewarding in their own right and are closely related to the three fundamental psychological needs (i.e., competence, autonomy, and relatedness). Simply stated, they are congruent with one's intrinsic nature.

Of course, individuals can engage in behaviors that promote health, affiliation, and community for instrumental, even controlled, reasons. However, the two groups of values seem to have a very different character and research indicates that they have quite different correlates.

Several studies have indicated that adolescents and young adults who place particularly strong emphasis on the extrinsic aspirations for wealth, fame, and image were more likely to experience various forms of ill-being, including depression, anxiety, narcissism, negative affect, and physical symptoms (Kasser & Ryan, 1993, 1996). Similarly, Kasser and Ryan found that placing particularly strong emphasis on these same extrinsic aspirations was negatively associated with the well-being indicators of vitality, positive affect, and self-actualization.

In contrast, the research by Kasser and Ryan (1993, 1996) indicated that placing strong emphasis on the intrinsic aspirations was positively associated with the well-being indicators and negatively associated with the ill-being indicators. It seems that when people are more focused on intrinsic than on extrinsic aspirations, they will experience more positive and less negative affect, more vitality and less depression, and a greater sense of self-actualization.

Because financial success, fame, and physical attractiveness are culturally advocated values (at least within the ubiquitous media), the socialization of children within our culture could easily result in their strongly holding these aspirations. However, the data indicate quite clearly that when these values are particularly strong within one's overall value configuration, individuals are likely to have poorer psychological adjustment. It is, however, important to note that the negative correlates of extrinsic aspirations appear primarily when the strength of those aspirations is unusually high—that is, when the extrinsic aspirations are out of balance with the intrinsic aspirations. When they are more moderate in strength, it is quite possible that they are more integrated and thus would not be associated with ill-being.

Ryan, Sheldon, Kasser, and Deci (1996) have suggested that people are more likely to strongly adopt these extrinsic values if they have an underlying insecurity, a fragile sense of self that must be continually bolstered by outward indicators of worth. Because our culture seems to value wealth and image, the developing individual who lacks the solid foundation of a well-integrated self will be vulnerable to internalizing these values strongly and relying heavily on them as a way to get affirmation and maintain self-worth. The problem, however, is that this self-worth is contingent and requires one to continually prove one's self, to continually accumulate or accomplish (Deci & Ryan, 1995). Thus, as the data now show, achieving self-worth in this contingent way appears not to be an effective strategy for attaining psychological well-being (Greenier, Kernis, & Waschull, 1995).

This negative relation between strong extrinsic aspirations and well-being is undoubtedly bidirectional. In other words, people will be more likely to strongly adopt extrinsic values when they have deficits in the development of self. In turn, having strong extrinsic aspirations will likely interfere with individuals' satisfying their inherent psychological needs for competence, autonomy, and relatedness, resulting in still greater ill-being.

This work has thus confirmed that the content of internalization does indeed make a difference in terms of its psychological consequences. Internalizing all of society's values does not represent healthy development; suggesting that a differentiated view of socialization is necessary.

EFFECTS OF THE SOCIAL CONTEXT

Maintenance and enhancement of intrinsically motivated behaviors and psychological processes are theorized to require satisfaction of the innate needs for competence, autonomy, and relatedness (Ryan, 1995). Thus, our research on the social-contextual conditions that maintain intrinsic motivation, facilitate the integrated internalization of behavioral regulations, and promote acceptance of the intrinsic values associated with well-being has focused on environmental dimensions that are expected to allow (vs. thwart) satisfaction of the basic needs (Deci & Ryan, 1985, 1991). This section begins with a review of context effects on intrinsic motivation.

Socialization and Intrinsic Motivation

Although intrinsic motivation does not have to be internalized, its expression is strongly affected by social contextual forces. Considerable research has indicated that performing an inherently interesting activity in the presence of events or interpersonal contexts that are controlling results in reduced intrinsic motivation (Amabile, DeJong, & Lepper, 1976; Deci, 1971; Ryan, Mims, & Koestner, 1983), whereas the same activity performed in the presence of events or interpersonal contexts that support autonomy results in enhanced intrinsic motivation (Zuckerman, Porac, Lathin, Smith, & Deci, 1978). Deci and Ryan (1985) suggested that events such as rewards (Deci, 1971; Lepper, Greene, & Nisbett, 1973), deadlines (Amabile et al., 1976), threats (Deci & Cascio, 1972), surveillance (Lepper & Greene, 1975; Pittman, Davey, Alafat, Wetherill, & Kramer, 1980), and evaluations (Smith, 1974), as well as pressuring language and a demanding interpersonal style (Ryan, 1982) tend to be experienced as controlling and thus to undermine intrinsic motivation as the perceived locus of causality for the behavior shifts from internal to external (deCharms, 1968). Opportunities for autonomy or choice, on the other hand, have been found to enhance intrinsic motivation while promoting a shift toward a more internal perceived locus of causality (Zuckerman et al., 1978).

These findings from laboratory experiments with children, adolescents, and college students have clear applicability to parent-child interactions, as additional research has shown. For example, Grolnick, Frodi, and Bridges (1984), in a study of infant mastery motivation, found that infants whose mothers were more autonomy supportive evidenced more exploration and persistence in a play task than infants whose mothers were more controlling. Similarly, Deci, Driver, Hotchkiss, Robbins, and Wilson (1993) videotaped 5- and 6-year-old children doing construction tasks (Legos® and Lincoln Logs®) with their mothers in a free-play situation. Maternal vocalizations were coded as autonomy supportive or controlling, and a summary score was calculated for each mother. Children's intrinsic motivation for the target activity was assessed with the free-choice behavioral measure and with the children's reports of interest/enjoyment. Results revealed that the level of maternal autonomy support was positively correlated with the children's intrinsic motivation.

Several studies within school contexts have also explored the effects of autonomy-supportive interpersonal styles on children's intrinsic motivation. Deci, Nezlek, and Sheinman (1981), for example, found that teachers' orientations toward supporting autonomy (vs. controlling behavior) were positively related to late-elementary students' intrinsic motivation, perceived competence, and self-esteem. Autonomy-supportive teachers, who encourage children to take initiative and try to solve their own problems, tended to enhance the children's intrinsic motivation, whereas controlling teachers, who pressure children to behave by using sanctions and comparisons with other children, tended to undermine children's intrinsic motivation (Deci, Schwartz, Sheinman, & Ryan, 1981).

Ryan and Grolnick (1986) similarly found that children's perceptions of their class-rooms as affording opportunities to be autonomous were predictive of their intrinsic motivation, perceived competence and perceived control. In particular, the more autonomy supportive the children perceived their classroom to be, as assessed by both self-report and projective measures, the more they believed that they could control successes and failures in school and the less they reported that the sources of control were unknown or in the hands of powerful others (e.g., the teacher). This study, although not examining internalization, suggests that autonomy support facilitates children's seeing themselves as being more in control of outcomes, a factor that is associated with greater responsibility for behavior.

A second relevant aspect of contexts, in addition to autonomy support versus control, is the extent to which they promote and signify competence versus incompetence. Of particular importance for motivation is the concept of *optimal challenge* (Deci, 1975). When tasks are just slightly beyond a child's capabilities, the tasks are likely to be preferred and to motivate the child to master the task (Harter, 1974). Further, several studies have indicated that positive competence feedback, when presented in the context of experienced self-determination, enhances intrinsic motivation (e.g., Fisher, 1978). Yet, when adults use rewards or external controls to promote behavior, children shy away from optimal challenges and prefer easier tasks, a finding supported by both experiments (Danner & Lonky, 1981) and field studies (Deci, Schwartz, et al., 1981).

Finally, the third relevant aspect, although it has been less thoroughly investigated, is the extent to which there is a backdrop of relational support. This finding, as noted earlier, derives from Bowlby's (1969) theory of attachment and suggests that when parents provide positive involvement and responsiveness—the interpersonal elements necessary for a secure attachment—infants will be more exploratory and mastery oriented. In fact, Frodi, Bridges, and Grolnick (1985) found that secure attachments, in addition to mothers' being autonomy supportive, did relate to infants' mastery motivation. The issue of relatedness and intrinsic motivation is interesting in that intrinsically motivated activity may well be solitary, so it does not necessarily require proximal support for relatedness the way it requires relatively proximal support for autonomy and competence. Nevertheless, there is indication that intrinsic motivation is more likely to flourish if individuals have the security of distal relational support.

To summarize, contexts that enhance intrinsically motivated activity are those that afford autonomy and promote competence. When these affordances occur in conjunction with relational support, even if only distally present in the form of supportive "object representations" (Ryan, Stiller, & Lynch, 1994), the conditions will be optimal for promoting intrinsic motivation.

Social Context and Internalization

According to self-determination theory, internalization is a developmental process that leads toward greater integration and felt autonomy. When functioning effectively, people take in aspects of their interpersonal world and work to bring them into a harmonious or integrated relation with other aspects of the self. The issue of promoting internalization, while similar in many respects to that of promoting intrinsically motivated behavior is also somewhat different. Intrinsically motivated behavior is spontaneous and flourishes under autonomy-supportive conditions, but regulations that are to be internalized must typically be introduced to the child by a socializing agent who has some relationship with

that child. Thus, although autonomy support is extremely important for integrated internalization, socializing agents must also provide the structures that are to be internalized,
and they must have the type of positive relatedness or involvement that leaves a child willing to engage these structures. For internalization, therefore, relational support from parents must be more proximal and the structures provided must be more extensive than is
the case for intrinsic motivation. Thus, in research on internalization, we have focused on
three social-contextual dimensions: interpersonal involvement, structure, and autonomy
support. These dimensions are elaborated in Figure 6.2.

Involvement refers to the parental dedication of resources to the child. Involved parents put more effort into child-rearing, spend more time with their child, and know more
about their child's daily life. *Structure* refers to the provision of guidelines and constraints on behavior. It involves communicating social expectations, explaining why they
are important, delineating the consequences of meeting or not meeting these expectations, and consistently following through. This could, for example, involve providing a rationale for a request, such as explaining how a playmate might feel if the child grabbed
a toy away. It also involves ensuring that the requested action is appropriate for the child's

Autonomy Support	Providing choice that is developmentally appropriate
	Encouraging self-initiation
	Minimizing use of controls
	Acknowledging the other's perspective and feelings
Structure	Communicating expectations that are optimally challenging
	Providing a rationale
	Explaining and consistently administering consequences
	Providing informational feedback
Interpersonal Involvement	Devoting time and resources to the child with respect to the target agendas
	Taking interest in the child's activities
	Providing warmth and caring

Figure 6.2   The Central Dimensions of a Facilitating Parental Context

capacities. A request to engage in a behavior will not be optimally challenging if there is not a match between the regulatory demand and the child's capacity to understand and carry out the action (Ryan et al., 1992). Efforts to socialize a child too early, for example, generate excessive conflict and anxiety.

It is very important to distinguish between structure and control, however. Structure refers to information about the relation between behaviors and outcomes. Conveying information about socially sanctioned behaviors and naturally occurring consequences to various behaviors are examples of providing structure. But such structure can be provided in either an autonomy supportive or a controlling manner. Language that pressures children and close surveillance to ensure compliance make the structure controlling, but simply conveying information in a reasoned and empathic way allows the structure to provide guidance while at the same time supporting autonomy.

In the first study examining this model, Grolnick and Ryan (1989) conducted individual interviews with 114 mothers and fathers of third- through sixth-grade children about how they motivate their children to engage in school- and home-related activities such as doing homework, going to bed on time, and doing chores. The hour-long interviews were scored by independent raters, and summary scores were generated for parental autonomy support, involvement, and structure.

Autonomy support was operationally defined as the degree to which parents value and use techniques that encourage choice, self-initiation, and participation in making decisions; whereas its opposite, control, was viewed as motivating the child by using controlling techniques and emphasizing obedience and compliance. Involvement was operationally defined as the extent to which the parent is interested in, knowledgeable about, and actively participates in the child's life concerning the target activities. Finally, structure was operationally defined as the clarity and consistency of rules, expectations, and limits.

Data from the parent interviews were then related to children's data collected in their classrooms. Results showed that parental autonomy support was positively related to children's reports of autonomous self-regulation (i.e., greater internalization), teacher ratings of the children's competence and adjustment, and the children's grades and achievement scores. Parental provision of structure was positively related to the children's reporting greater understanding of how to control their successes and failures in school and in general. Finally, maternal involvement was positively related to teacher-rated competence and adjustment, and to school grades and achievement.

Grolnick, Ryan, and Deci (1991) used children's self-reports of their parents' autonomy support and involvement to test whether children's self-related perceptions and motivations mediate between the parenting environment and school outcomes. Findings indicated that children who perceived their mothers and fathers as more involved and as providing greater autonomy support exhibited more autonomous regulation in school, higher perceived competence, and a greater understanding of the sources of control of school outcomes. These self-relevant motives and perceptions, in turn, predicted school achievement.

Finally, Avery and Ryan (1988) related late-elementary children's reports of parental involvement and autonomy support to their projectively measured "object representations" of their parents. They found that both dimensions were significantly related to more nurturant object representations, which in turn were associated with better classroom adjustment among a group of largely urban, minority, children.

In other research, Grolnick and Slowiaczek (1994) found that both mother and father involvement predicted their children's internalization. Further, Ryan et al. (1994)

found that the quality of relatedness of junior high and high school students to their parents and teachers was associated with greater internalization with respect to school-related activities, and with their sense of well-being. These findings are congruent with the results of attachment research showing that when parents are warm and contingent in their responding to infants, the children are likely to respond more positively to parent requests in subsequent years (Sroufe & Fleeson, 1986), and to be less aggressive (Cohn, 1990) and less oppositional (Greenberg, Kusche, & Speltz, 1991), thus suggesting greater internalization.

Deci, Eghrari, Patrick, and Leone (1994) took a different approach to exploring the effects of autonomy support and structure on internalization. They performed a laboratory experiment to investigate how three specific behaviors that represent autonomy support and structure would affect internalization of the regulation for a nonintrinsically interesting activity. Participants were asked to engage in a highly boring task in one of eight conditions, formed by the factorial crossing of the presence versus absence of three facilitating behaviors: providing a meaningful rationale for doing the task; providing an acknowledgment of the participants' feelings of finding the task boring; and emphasizing choice. The dependent variables were the amount of time participants voluntarily spent with the task in a later session when they were alone and had not been asked to do it, and participants' reports of feeling free, enjoying the task, and finding it important. Results indicated that participants in conditions with more of the facilitating conditions spent more subsequent free time with the task and reported more positive feelings than those in conditions with fewer facilitating factors. It therefore appears that supporting individuals' self-determination by explaining the reasons for a requested behavior, validating their feelings about it, and minimizing controls increases the likelihood that a regulation will be internalized.

There was an even more interesting finding in this study. Participants in the supportive conditions showed a strong positive correlation between the amount of free time they spent on the task and their self-reports of freedom, enjoyment, and importance, thus suggesting integration of the regulation, whereas subjects in the nonsupportive conditions showed a *negative* correlation between their free-time behavior and the same self-reports, thus suggesting a lack of integration. It appears, then, that if people do internalize behavior regulations in circumstances that are controlling, the internalization that occurs will take the form of introjection rather than identification or integration. They will perform the behavior because they think they should, despite not liking it and not feeling free. This stands in sharp contrast to the individuals who internalized the regulation under autonomy-supportive conditions and came to enjoy the task and felt free in performing it.

In general, then, the results of these studies on internalization of regulations are consistent and complementary with the results of studies on promoting intrinsic motivation in children. They suggest that parents who provide an environment characterized by autonomy support, structure, and involvement facilitate children's internalizing regulations and displaying both greater competence and healthier adaptation. Variables related to these parenting dimensions have been found to predict child outcomes as widely varied as moral reasoning, behavioral adjustment, and self-regulation in school.

Parenting and the Content of Internalization

Having considered the effects of socializing contexts on the degree to which norms and regulations are internalized we turn to a consideration of the effects of socializing contexts on the profile of values that children internalize. A study by Kasser et al. (1995)

explored the parental antecedents of developing strong extrinsic aspirations, relative to intrinsic aspirations. This seems particularly important in light of the new findings that holding strong extrinsic aspirations is negatively associated with well-being, whereas holding strong intrinsic aspirations is positively associated with well-being (Kasser & Ryan, 1996).

In the Kasser et al. (1995) study, 140 eighteen-year-olds from mixed SES backgrounds completed various questionnaires (including the life aspirations questionnaire) and were interviewed by a clinician. In addition, the mothers of these teenagers provided interview and questionnaire data, and a composite variable of maternal nurturance was created, consisting of items indicating high autonomy support, involvement, and warmth. Results revealed that when mothers were more nurturant, the children tended to value the intrinsic aspirations of personal growth, meaningful relationships, and community contributions more than the extrinsic aspiration of financial success. By contrast, children who were reared by more controlling, cold, or uninvolved mothers were relatively more focused on material acquisition than on prosocial or growth-related values. That profile of value content, as has been presented earlier, tends to be associated with unhealthy adaptation. We suggest that parenting which is unresponsive to basic psychological needs of the child creates an insecurity that promotes this inner emphasis on exterior signs of worth such as wealth or appearance.

To summarize our diverse research on the socializing context, findings have consistently indicated that when social and familial contexts are more autonomy supportive, provide optimal structure, and have warm, involved socializing agents, they promote healthy adaptation as indexed by more intrinsic motivation, greater internalization and integration of behavioral regulations, and the adoption of intrinsic life values.

OTHER WORK ON PARENTING

This section provides a discussion of other research on internalization within the family, beginning with research relevant to the concept of control.

Within the parenting literature, many theories include a variable related to control. For example, Becker (1964) spoke of restrictive parenting, Schaefer (1959) described controlling parenting, and Baldwin (1955) discussed an autocratic style of parenting. These terms apply to parents who place paramount value on compliance. Children of parents high on these attributes have been found to be obedient (Baldwin, 1955) as well as dysphoric and disaffiliated (Baumrind, 1967), while also being less likely to turn to their parents for support (Solky, 1995) and being low in social interaction and dominated by peers (Baldwin, 1955).

In research on socialization, among the most studied techniques associated with the construct of control is power assertion (Hoffman, 1960). Power-assertive techniques such as direct commands, threats, deprivations, and physical force put direct coercive pressure on the child to immediately change his or her ongoing pattern of behavior. Hoffman demonstrated that the more mothers used unqualified power assertion in dealing with their children, the more the children were hostile and power assertive toward other children, and the more they were resistant to influence attempts by teachers and other children. Thus, power assertion, when it is extreme, can have the effect of producing resistance (rather than obedience), resulting in the forestalling of internalization and a rejection of socialization attempts.

Lytton (1980) demonstrated a negative effect of control with young children. In his work, the focus was on child outcomes of internalization and compliance, which were based on parents' ratings of whether they had to remind the child to obey and whether the child exhibited self-restraint. Using observations of mother-child interactions, it was shown that mothers who were more controlling and scolding had children with poorer internalization scores than children of mothers who were less scolding and helped the children do things independently.

Research based on attribution theory has also found evidence that superfluous controls hinder internalization. Theorists such as Lepper (1983) and Grusec (1981) argue that internalization requires an internal, as opposed to an external, attributional justification for a behavior that is externally prompted. For example, Lepper (1983) reviewed studies showing that when pressure is just sufficient to obtain compliance, children will attribute their compliance to internal factors such as liking the activity (rather than external demands such as being told to do it), and they will therefore be more likely to continue the behavior in the absence of external surveillance. As such, the prescription from attribution theory is to minimize the use of superfluous controls to maximize internalization.

Interestingly, parents seem to intuitively understand that controlling approaches are less likely to facilitate long-term compliance. Kuczynski (1984) demonstrated that parents tended to choose less controlling discipline methods such as reasoning more often when they were told their child would have to demonstrate compliance at a later time than if they were not given such information.

Although we agree that minimizing the use of external control facilitates internalization, the attribution theory of internalization does not distinguish between introjected versus integrated types of internalization. As such, an attribution to guilt avoidance (an internal factor) could facilitate internalization, but from our perspective it would result in a regulatory style that is internally controlling rather than autonomous.

It is also worth noting that although several theorists have anchored one end of a continuum with being controlling (or an equivalent concept), the other end of the continuum is often not well specified. Thus, for example, attribution theory addresses the need to minimize superfluous controls, but it does not encompass a theoretical explication of what parents would do instead of controlling. In our theory, the answer is support autonomy, which is akin to what Baldwin (1955) labeled democratic parenting.

Several studies have found comparable results regarding the effects of parental control on children's moral development. Dunton (1988) showed that parental restrictiveness was negatively related to moral development. Powers (1982; Powers, Hauser, Schwartz, Noam, & Jacobson, 1983) examined parents' behavior during family discussions of moral dilemmas. Her findings showed, in contrast to what might be intuitively predicted, that it was not how cognitively stimulating the parents' discussions were that predicted high levels of moral development in the children, but rather how supportive versus interfering the parents were in these discussions. Parents who were more supportive and less likely to interfere in their children's communications had children who were more advanced in their moral reasoning. Walker and Taylor (1991), building on this work, found that the discussion style resulting in the greatest increases in moral reasoning over a 2-year time span was one in which the parents elicited the child's opinion, asked clarifying questions, and checked the child's understanding. Such a style is consistent with an autonomy-supportive stance in which the parent attempts to take the child's perspective and support his or her initiations. In contrast, a style that directly challenged and criticized the child and one in which the parent simply provided his or her opinions (which was described as resembling "lecturing") were associated with lesser increases in moral reasoning over the 2-year span. These styles would be conceptualized as controlling.

Patterns of Parenting

Within the parenting literature, there have been several attempts to describe the effects on children of parents' overall approach to interacting with and motivating their children. Baumrind (1967) was among the first to define and empirically examine approaches to parenting and their impact on the developing child. In this section, we briefly discuss her work, pointing out that general patterns of parenting can be understood in terms of the three parenting dimensions we have outlined.

Baumrind (1971), in her complex study of parenting approaches, made the important distinction between the authoritative and authoritarian patterns of parenting. The *authoritative* style involves parents' encouraging their children's independence and individuality while at the same time expecting mature behavior, firmly enforcing rules and standards, communicating openly, and respecting both parents' and children's rights. In our conceptualization, this parenting approach would be described as a combination of high autonomy support and high structure. The *authoritarian* pattern, in contrast, involves parents' valuing obedience and compliance, attempting to shape and control the child in accordance with an absolute set of standards, and discouraging verbal give-and-take. Using our conceptual model, the authoritarian style involves high levels of both control and structure.

Findings of the Baumrind (1967, 1971) research indicated that children from authoritative homes tended to be the most self-reliant and independent. In contrast, girls with parents characterized as authoritarian tended to be dependent, whereas boys with such parents tended to be aggressive. These two contrasting styles can be conceptualized as opposite reactions to controls. In one case (passive, compliant), the child relies excessively on controls from others, and in the other case (aggressive, reactive) the child actively rebels against controls. In both cases, however, the child exhibits a lack of integrated internalization, so regulation remains tied to the external world.

Discipline Techniques: Inconsistent Findings

Substantial research on parenting has focused on the effects of particular discipline techniques such as reasoning and withdrawal of love. However, a review of this literature by Grusec and Goodnow (1994) indicates that research relating discipline techniques to internalization outcomes has yielded inconsistent and noncompelling evidence. These authors have suggested various factors, such as the nature of the misdeed, that should be taken into account in evaluating the effectiveness of various techniques.

From the self-determination perspective, two important considerations can help disentangle the complex findings concerning the relations between discipline techniques and internalization. First, using the differentiated conception of internalization, based on the internalization continuum, would provide a basis for considering whether a particular technique has led a value or behavior to be only introjected or, alternatively, to be more fully integrated. This in turn would allow for prediction of the accompanying qualities and affects. Second, we suggest that an understanding of the effects of various discipline techniques requires a consideration of the interpersonal context and relationship within which they are administered. We consider each point in turn.

Discipline and Types of Internalization

Many approaches to discipline have advocated strict socialization practices such as making clear demands and using consistently administered reinforcements or punishments. From our theoretical perspective, these techniques tend to be controlling, and yet there is evidence that some internalization does occur under such conditions. For example, Lamborn, Mounts, Steinberg, and Dornbusch (1991) found that children reared in authoritarian families did well on measures of obedience and conformity suggesting that they had internalized parental demands.

The problem in interpreting these results and reconciling them with the results of other studies which show that less controlling methods promote more internalization concerns the outcome measures one uses to assess internalization. Typically, the outcome is whether the child engages in (or refrains from performing) some particular behavior. However, as delineated earlier, an individual can behave (or refrain from behaving) in either an easy, flexible way, with little or no internal conflict, or alternatively in a pressured way with considerable internal conflict. Even though the outward behaviors might look the same, the consequences of the different underlying regulatory processes for adjustment and self-esteem are quite different. The case of the child's being flexible and unconflicted suggests that the regulation is identified, whereas the case of pressure and conflict suggests that it has been only introjected.

Because we hypothesize that internalization resulting from relatively controlling techniques and authoritarian approaches will be only introjected, we suggest that it is important to use outcome measures that are more complex than just behavior. This could be done, for example, by having children complete the self-regulation questionnaire (Ryan & Connell, 1989) indicating why they engage in the target behaviors. Alternatively, a method such as that used by Deci et al. (1994) might be used. In that study, the introjection that occurred in the nonsupportive conditions and the greater integration that occurred in the autonomy-supportive conditions were distinguished by examining the correlations between the subsequent behavior and the feelings accompanying it. In fact, in the Lamborn et al. (1991) study, although authoritarian parenting led to behavioral obedience, it was also associated with low perceived ability and low social competence, suggesting that indeed the internalization which had occurred was poorly integrated.

An interesting case in point concerns the effectiveness of love withdrawal as a disciplinary technique, a technique that we would consider quite controlling. Research has shown that this technique leads to high compliance (Zahn-Waxler, Radke-Yarrow, & King, 1979) but also to unsophisticated moral reasoning (e.g., Hoffman, 1970). Using our theorizing, these findings indicate that the use of love withdrawal tends to promote introjected rather than identified or integrated forms of internalizations. Thus, a child from a home in which parents rely on this technique may act in parent-valued ways, but the behavior is likely to have negative affective consequences such as low self-esteem (Coopersmith, 1967).

Techniques and Parenting Contexts

The second important consideration in interpreting the research relating discipline techniques to internalization is that a particular technique may be administered within different relational contexts. For example, the technique of other-oriented induction (Hoffman, 1970) involves explaining to the child the effects that his or her behavior would have on another (e.g., the other might be hurt or angry). This technique may be used in relatively autonomy-supportive ways, which would involve minimizing pressure, listening to the child's perspective, and accepting the child's feelings, or the technique may be used in relatively controlling ways, which would involve emphasizing that the child should not do the behaviors that would hurt or anger the other. Our theory suggests that the effects of this technique used in the different ways would be quite different.

Considerable research has shown that the same technique can be experienced as autonomy supportive or alternatively as controlling, depending on the way it is introduced, expressed, or administered (e.g., Ryan, 1982; Ryan et al., 1983). For example, the language used in setting a limit or the tone of voice in reasoning with a child may determine how the child experiences that particular technique, and thus its effects. Studies that focus on a particular technique without attending to issues such as the parents' locution and whether the child's feelings are acknowledged may yield conflicting results.

This point is illustrated in a study by Koestner, Ryan, Bernieri, and Holt (1984), which examined the effects on first- and second-grade children of setting limits in a controlling or a noncontrolling manner. The limits were the same, but the style was different. The researchers reasoned that, to relieve the possible controlling pressure created by the existence of limits, it is important to avoid using controlling language and to acknowledge that the children might not want to conform to the limits. Results indicated that the children's intrinsic motivation and creativity were undermined by the controlling limits but not by the autonomy-supportive limits. This study therefore illustrates that the same techniques or structures can either facilitate or impede internalization depending on whether they are conveyed in an autonomy-supportive or controlling manner. In a discussion of the relation between parenting functions and children's motivation, Pomerantz and Ruble (in press) suggested that not only disciplining, but also other parenting functions such as praising, helping, and making decisions can have differential effects depending on whether they are used in ways that promote autonomy or control. Research by the authors indicated that mothers' being more controlling, rather than autonomy granting, was associated with children (particularly girls) making more maladaptive attributions.

The distinction between parenting techniques and the manner in which they are administered is important in considering suggestions by Maccoby (1984) and others that the effectiveness of certain parenting techniques change with children's age. We concur that as children develop greater cognitive capacities they will, for example, be more able to respond to techniques involving perspective taking that require more advanced cognitive abilities. However, whatever the technique, and whatever the child's age, the use of the technique in an autonomy-supportive (rather than controlling) way would be adaptive.

Darling and Steinberg (1993) made a similar distinction when they emphasized the difference between parenting techniques or practices, which refer to relatively specific parenting behaviors, and what they call parenting style, which includes attitudes toward the child and the emotional climate in which the parent's behavior is expressed. Parent style, as the term is used by Darling and Steinberg, can be understood as referring to the ongoing relationship that is evident across a wide range of situations. Thus, they suggested that parenting techniques and practices are used within a general parent-child relationship that may involve respect for the child or lack of respect, connectedness with the child or disengagement from parenting, and support for the child's autonomy or control of the child's behavior. Accordingly, this suggests that the effect on internalization of a particular technique will depend both on the manner in which it is used and on the more generalized quality of the ongoing relationship that the parent has created with the child.

Darling and Steinberg suggested that parenting style affects internalization in two ways. First, a positive context may render the child more open to communications from the parent, and second, such a context may make the techniques themselves more effective. Within self-determination theory, a positive parenting style would have autonomy support as a central feature.

Promoting Autonomy Not Independence

The concept of supporting autonomy means encouraging children to be self-initiating and volitional in their actions. It means providing the supports necessary for children to feel ownership of their actions, to feel as if their actions were emanating from themselves. It does not, however, mean making children wholly self-reliant, independent, or detached.

Although the concepts of *autonomy* and *independence* are frequently fused or confused (e.g., Kashima et al., 1995; Steinberg & Silverberg, 1986), important conceptual distinctions can be drawn between the two terms. Independence means not relying on others; it means behaving on one's own and not depending on others for help. Autonomy does not, however, convey this sense of detachment or nonreliance. One can be volitional or autonomous while still depending or relying on others for support. To be related to others means that one will be emotionally reliant on them, and that reliance can serve to support one's sense of autonomy. Whereas independence or detachment may result from parents being cold, distant, or unreliable, autonomy results from support rather than nonsupport. Research by Ryan and Lynch (1989) indicates that adolescents who rely on their parents for emotional support display more positive mental health indicators than those who are nonreliant and detached. It seems clear from the network of findings that children who are both autonomous and related to (or reliant on) their parents are likely to display healthier psychological development (Ryan & Solky, 1996).

CREATING THE SOCIAL CONTEXT: A TRANSACTIONAL PROCESS

In previous sections, we have provided evidence that characteristics of the social context—autonomy support, structure, and involvement—promote internalization and integration. Although these findings are well supported, it is important to recognize the transactional nature of the relation between parenting contexts and internalization. Children are active participants in determining their social context (Bell, 1968; Grolnick & Ryan, 1989; Ryan & Grolnick, 1986). Thus, parenting can be seen as a dynamic process in which the parents' behavior and style are affected by their children's behavior and by other contextual factors operating on them (e.g., Bronfenbrenner, 1986; Grolnick, Benjet, Olson, & Apostoleris, in press).

More specifically, children help create their own parenting context because parents use their children's behavior as a regulator of their own action (Maccoby, Snow, & Jacklin, 1984). When children are more difficult or resistant, for example, parents tend to find the interactions less satisfying and more aversive, and research has shown that they may respond either by being more controlling (Grolnick, Weiss, McKenzie, & Wrightman, 1996) or by withdrawing from contact (Grolnick et al., 1996).

Children's level of internalization with respect to a particular domain will undoubtedly affect parents' strategies within that domain. Children who rely on external controls to regulate their actions will elicit more control from adults, whereas those who identify with values or regulations originally imposed by socializers will tend to receive more support and less control. In fact, a study by Pelletier and Vallerand (in press) showed that when teachers were told that some children were intrinsically motivated and others were extrinsically motivated, even though there were no actual differences in the children's motivation, the teachers were more controlling with the children who had been labeled as extrinsic than with those who had been labeled intrinsic. The challenge for caretakers is, therefore, to break these ongoing cycles of control by providing structure in an autonomy-supportive manner, even when the children's behavior seems to "pull" for control.

Much socialization occurs under adverse circumstances, whether it be family adversities or large classes, creating stress for parents and teachers and leading them to use controls to change behavior in the moment rather than focusing on long-term socialization. Research has confirmed that parents or teachers who have experienced high levels of recent stresses tend to provide less structure (Grolnick et al., 1996) and lower levels of involvement with their children (Grolnick et al., in press), and to be more controlling (Deci, Spiegel, Ryan, Koestner, & Kauffman, 1982). To be sure, parents and teachers need support, both tangible and emotional, in providing an involved, autonomy-supportive socializing context that will be conducive to children's healthy psychological development—to children's maintaining intrinsic motivation, internalizing and integrating behavioral regulations, and acquiring the values or aspirations associated with well-being.

To conclude, the self-determination approach to parenting and socialization emphasizes that individuals are active organisms who need to feel competent, autonomous, and related to develop in the direction of greater integrity and psychological coherence. Nutriments provided by parents in the form of autonomy support, structure, and involvement are the means through which their children's needs can be satisfied, and yet the provision of these nutriments is itself a dynamic, interactive process. Sadly, when children's behavior makes it harder for the parents to be supportive or when the parents are experiencing other stressors, the children are less likely to experience the need satisfaction that is crucial for their continued healthy development.

REFERENCES

Ainsworth, M. D. S., Blehar, M. C., Waters, E., & Wall, S. (1978). *Patterns of attachment.* Hillsdale, NJ: Erlbaum.

Amabile, T. M., DeJong, W., & Lepper, M. R. (1976). Effects of externally imposed deadlines on subsequent intrinsic motivation. *Journal of Personality and Social Psychology, 34,* 92–98.

Avery, R. R., & Ryan, R. M. (1988). Object relations and ego development: Comparison and correlates in middle childhood. *Journal of Personality, 56,* 547–569.

Baldwin, A. L. (1955). *Behavior and development in childhood.* New York: Dreyden Press.

Baumrind, D. (1967). Child care practices anteceding three patterns of preschool behavior. *Genetic Psychology Monographs, 75,* 43–88.

Baumrind, D. (1971). Current patterns of parental authority. *Developmental Psychology Monographs, 4,* 1–102.

Becker, W. C. (1964). Consequences of different kinds of parental discipline. In M. L. Hoffman & L. W. Hoffman (Eds.), *Review of child development research* (Vol. 1, pp. 169–208). New York: Russell-Sage Foundation.

Bell, R. Q. (1968). A reinterpretation of the direction of effects in studies of socialization. *Psychological Review, 75,* 81–95.

Blais, M. R., Sabourin, S., Boucher, C., & Vallerand, R. J. (1990). Toward a motivational model of couple happiness. *Journal of Personality and Social Psychology, 59,* 1021–1031.

Blasi, A. (1976). Concept of development in personality theory. In J. Loevinger (Ed.), *Ego development* (pp. 29–53). San Francisco: Jossey-Bass.

Bowlby, J. (1969). *Attachment.* New York: Basic Books.

Bowlby, J. (1979). *The making and breaking of affectional bonds.* London: Tavistock.

Bronfenbrenner, U. (1986). Ecology of the family as a context for human development: Research perspectives. *Developmental Psychology, 22,* 723–742.

Chandler, C. L., & Connell, J. P. (1987). Children's intrinsic, extrinsic and internalized motivation: A developmental study of children's reasons for liked and disliked behaviours. *British Journal of Developmental Psychology, 5,* 357–365.

Cohn, D. A. (1990). Child-mother attachment of six-year-olds and social competence at school. *Child Development, 61,* 152–162.

Coopersmith, S. (1967). *The antecedents of self-esteem.* San Francisco: Freeman.

Csikszentmihalyi, M. (1975). *Beyond boredom and anxiety.* San Francisco: Jossey-Bass.

Danner, F. W., & Lonky, E. (1981). A cognitive-developmental approach to the effects of rewards on intrinsic motivation. *Child Development, 52,* 1043–1052.

Darling, N., & Steinberg, L. (1993). Parenting style as context: An integrative model. *Psychological Bulletin, 113,* 487–496.

deCharms, R. (1968). *Personal causation: The internal affective determinants of behavior.* New York: Academic Press.

Deci, E. L. (1971). Effects of externally mediated rewards on intrinsic motivation. *Journal of Personality and Social Psychology, 18,* 105–115.

Deci, E. L. (1975). *Intrinsic motivation.* New York: Plenum Press.

Deci, E. L., & Cascio, W. F. (1972, April). *Changes in intrinsic motivation as a function of negative feedback and threats.* Paper presented at the meeting of the Eastern Psychological Association, Boston.

Deci, E. L., Driver, R. E., Hotchkiss, L., Robbins, R. J., & Wilson, I. M. (1993). The relation of mothers' controlling vocalizations to children's intrinsic motivation. *Journal of Experimental Child Psychology, 55,* 151–162.

Deci, E. L., Eghrari, H., Patrick, B. C., & Leone, D. R. (1994). Facilitating internalization: The self-determination theory perspective. *Journal of Personality, 62,* 119–142.

Deci, E. L., Nezlek, J., & Sheinman, L. (1981). Characteristics of the rewarder and intrinsic motivation of the rewardee. *Journal of Personality and Social Psychology, 40,* 1–10.

Deci, E. L., & Ryan, R. M. (1985). *Intrinsic motivation and self-determination in human behavior.* New York: Plenum Press.

Deci, E. L., & Ryan, R. M. (1991). A motivational approach to self: Integration in personality. In R. Dienstbier (Ed.), *Nebraska Symposium on Motivation: Vol. 38. Perspectives on motivation* (pp. 237–288). Lincoln: University of Nebraska Press.

Deci, E. L., & Ryan, R. M. (1995). Human autonomy: The basis for true self-esteem. In M. Kernis (Ed.), *Efficacy, agency, and self-esteem* (pp. 31–49). New York: Plenum Press.

Deci, E. L., Schwartz, A. J., Sheinman, L., & Ryan, R. M. (1981). An instrument to assess adults' orientations toward control versus autonomy with children: Reflections on intrinsic motivation and perceived competence. *Journal of Educational Psychology, 73,* 642–650.

Deci, E. L., Spiegel, N. H., Ryan, R. M., Koestner, R., & Kauffman, M. (1982). The effects of performance standards on teaching styles: The behavior of controlling teachers. *Journal of Educational Psychology, 74,* 852–859.

Dunton, K. J. (1988). Parental practices associated with their children's moral reasoning development (Doctoral dissertation, Stanford University, 1988). *Dissertation Abstracts International, 49,* 3306A. (University Microfilms No. 8826133)

Elkind, D. (1971). Cognitive growth cycles in mental development. In J. K. Cole (Ed.), *Nebraska Symposium on Motivation* (Vol. 19, pp. 1–31). Lincoln: University of Nebraska Press.

Fisher, C. D. (1978). The effects of personal control, competence, and extrinsic reward systems on intrinsic motivation. *Organizational Behavior and Human Performance, 21,* 273–288.

Frodi, A., Bridges, L., & Grolnick, W. S. (1985). Correlates of mastery-related behavior: A short-term longitudinal study of infants in their second year. *Child Development, 56,* 1291–1298.

Goodenow, C. (1992). Strengthening the links between educational psychology and the study of social contexts. *Educational Psychologist, 27,* 177–196.

Greenberg, M. T., Kusche, C. A., & Speltz, M. (1991). Emotional regulation, self-control, and psychopathology: The role of relationships in early childhood. In D. Cicchetti & S. L. Toth (Eds.), *Internalizing and externalizing expressions of dysfunction* (pp. 21–56). Hillsdale, NJ: Erlbaum.

Greenier, K. D., Kernis, M. H., & Waschull, S. B. (1995). Not all high (or low) self-esteem people are the same: Theory and research on stability of self-esteem. In M. Kernis (Ed.), *Efficacy, agency, and self-esteem* (pp. 51–71). New York: Plenum Press.

Grolnick, W. S., Benjet, C., Olson, C., & Apostoleris, N. A. (in press). *Predictors of parents' involvement in children's schooling. Journal of Educational Psychology.*

Grolnick, W. S., Frodi, A., & Bridges, L. (1984). Maternal control styles and the mastery motivation of one-year-olds. *Infant Mental Health Journal, 5,* 72–82.

Grolnick, W. S., & Ryan, R. M. (1989). Parent styles associated with children's self-regulation and competence in school. *Journal of Educational Psychology, 81,* 143–154.

Grolnick, W. S., Ryan, R. M., & Deci, E. L. (1991). The inner resources for school achievement: Motivational mediators of children's perceptions of their parents. *Journal of Educational Psychology, 83,* 508–517.

Grolnick, W. S., & Slowiaczek, M. L. (1994). Parents' involvement in children's schooling: A multidimensional conceptualization and motivational model. *Child Development, 65,* 237–252.

Grolnick, W. S., Weiss, L., McKenzie, L., & Wrightman, J. (1996). Contextual, cognitive, and adolescent factors associated with parenting in adolescence. *Journal of Youth and Adolescence, 25,* 33–54.

Grusec, J. E. (1981). Socialization processes in the development of altruism. In J. P. Rushton & R. M. Sorrentino (Eds.), *Altruism and helping behavior* (pp. 65–90). Hillsdale, NJ: Erlbaum.

Grusec, J. E., & Goodnow, J. J. (1994). Impact of parental discipline methods on the child's internalization of values: A reconceptualization of current points of view. *Developmental Psychology, 30,* 4–19.

Harlow, H. F. (1958). The nature of love. *American Psychologist, 13,* 673–685.

Harter, S. (1974). Pleasure derived by children from cognitive challenge and mastery. *Child Development, 45,* 661–669.

Heider, F. (1958). *The psychology of interpersonal relations.* New York: Wiley.

Hoffman, M. L. (1960). Power assertion by the parent and its impact on the child. *Child Development, 31,* 129–143.

Hoffman, M. L. (1970). Moral development. In P. H. Mussen (Ed.), *Carmichael's manual of child psychology* (Vol. 2, pp. 261–359). New York: Wiley.

Kashima, Y., Yamaguchi, S., Kim, U., Choi, S.-C., Gelfand, M. J., & Yuki, M. (1995). Culture, gender, and self: A perspective from individualism-collectivism research. *Journal of Personality and Social Psychology, 69,* 925–937.

Kasser, T., & Ryan, R. M. (1993). A dark side of the American dream: Correlates of financial success as a central life aspiration. *Journal of Personality and Social Psychology, 65,* 410–422.

Kasser, T., & Ryan, R. M. (1996). Further examining the American dream: Differential correlates of intrinsic and extrinsic goals. *Personality and Social Psychology Bulletin, 22,* 281–288.

Kasser, T., Ryan, R. M., Zax, M., & Sameroff, A. J. (1995). The relations of maternal and social environments to late adolescents' materialistic and prosocial values. *Developmental Psychology, 31,* 907–914.

Kelman, H. C. (1961). Processes of attitude change. *Public Opinion Quarterly, 25,* 57–78.

Koestner, R., Bernieri, F., & Zuckerman, M. (1992). Self-determination and consistency between attitudes, traits, and behaviors. *Personality and Social Psychology Bulletin, 18,* 52–59.

Koestner, R., Ryan, R. M., Bernieri, F., & Holt, K. (1984). Setting limits on children's behavior: The differential effects of controlling versus informational styles on intrinsic motivation and creativity. *Journal of Personality, 52,* 233–248.

Kuczynski, L. (1984). Socialization goals and mother-child interaction: Strategies for long-term and short-term compliance. *Developmental Psychology, 20,* 1061–1073.

Lamborn, S. D., Mounts, N. S., Steinberg, L., & Dornbusch, S. M. (1991). Patterns of competence and adjustment among adolescents from authoritative, authoritarian, indulgent, and neglectful families. *Child Development, 62,* 1049–1065.

Lepper, M. R. (1983). Social-control processes and the internalization of social values: An attributional perspective. In E. T. Higgins, D. N. Ruble, & W. W. Hartup (Eds.), *Social cognition and social development* (pp. 294–330). New York: Cambridge University Press.

Lepper, M. R., & Greene, D. (1975). Turning play into work: Effects of adult surveillance and extrinsic rewards on children's intrinsic motivation. *Journal of Personality and Social Psychology, 31,* 479–486.

Lepper, M. R., Greene, D., & Nisbett, R. E. (1973). Undermining children's intrinsic interest with extrinsic rewards: A test of the "overjustification" hypothesis. *Journal of Personality and Social Psychology, 28,* 129–137.

Lytton, H. (1980). *Parent-child interaction: The socialization process observed in twin and singleton families.* New York: Plenum Press.

Maccoby, E. E. (1984). Socialization and developmental change. *Child Development, 55,* 317–328.

Maccoby, E. E., Snow, M. E., & Jacklin, C. N. (1984). Children's dispositions and mother-child interaction at 12 and 18 months: A short-term longitudinal study. *Developmental Psychology, 28,* 459–472.

MacDonald, K. (1992). Warmth as a developmental construct: An evolutionary analysis. *Child Development, 63,* 753–773.

Meissner, W. W. (1981). *Internalization in psychoanalysis.* New York: International Universities Press.

Pelletier, L. G., Fortier, M. S., Vallerand, R. J., Tuson, K. M., Brier, N. M., & Blais, M. R. (1995). Toward a new measure of intrinsic motivation, extrinsic motivation, and amotivation in sports: The Sport Motivation Scale (SMS). *Journal of Sport & Exercise Psychology, 17,* 35–53.

Pelletier, L. G., & Vallerand, R. J. (in press). Supervisors' beliefs and subordinates' intrinsic motivation. *Journal of Personality and Social Psychology.*

Piaget, J. (1971). *Biology and knowledge.* Chicago: University of Chicago Press.

Pittman, T. S., Davey, M. E., Alafat, K. A., Wetherill, K. V., & Kramer, N. A. (1980). Informational versus controlling verbal rewards. *Personality and Social Psychology Bulletin, 6,* 228–233.

Pomerantz, E. M., & Ruble, D. N. (in press). The multidimensional nature of control: Implications for the development of sex differences in self-evaluation. In J. Heckhausen & C. S. Dweck (Eds.), *Motivation and self-regulation across the life span.* New York: Cambridge University Press.

Powers, S. I. (1982). *Family environments and adolescent moral development: A study of psychiatrically hospitalized and non-patient adolescents.* Unpublished doctoral dissertation, Harvard University.

Powers, S. I., Hauser, S. T., Schwartz, J., Noam, G. G., & Jacobson, A. M. (1983). Adolescent ego development and family interaction: A structural-developmental perspective. *New Directions for Child Development, 22,* 5–25.

Ryan, R. M. (1982). Control and information in the intrapersonal sphere: An extension of cognitive evaluation theory. *Journal of Personality and Social Psychology, 43,* 450–461.

Ryan, R. M. (1991). The nature of the self in autonomy and relatedness. In J. Strauss & G. R. Goethals (Eds.), *The self: Interdisciplinary approaches* (pp. 208–238). New York: Springer-Verlag.

Ryan, R. M. (1993). Agency and organization: Intrinsic motivation, autonomy and the self in psychological development. In J. Jacobs (Ed.), *Nebraska Symposium on Motivation: Developmental perspectives on motivation* (Vol. 40, pp. 1–56). Lincoln: University of Nebraska Press.

Ryan, R. M. (1995). Psychological needs and the facilitation of integrative processes. *Journal of Personality, 63,* 397–428.

Ryan, R. M., & Connell, J. P. (1989). Perceived locus of causality and internalization: Examining reasons for acting in two domains. *Journal of Personality and Social Psychology, 57,* 749–761.

Ryan, R. M., Connell, J. P., & Deci, E. L. (1985). A motivational analysis of self-determination and self-regulation in education. In C. Ames & R. E. Ames (Eds.), *Research on motivation in education: The classroom milieu* (pp. 13–51). New York: Academic Press.

Ryan, R. M., Connell, J. P., & Grolnick, W. S. (1992). When achievement is *not* intrinsically motivated: A theory of self-regulation in school. In A. K. Boggiano & T. S. Pittman (Eds.), *Achievement and motivation: A social-developmental perspective* (pp. 167–188). New York: Cambridge University Press.

Ryan, R. M., Deci, E. L., & Grolnick, W. S. (1995). Autonomy, relatedness, and the self: Their relation to development and psychopathology. In D. Cicchetti & D. J. Cohen (Eds.), *Developmental psychopathology: Vol. 1. Theory and methods* (pp. 618–655). New York: Wiley.

Ryan, R. M., & Grolnick, W. S. (1986). Origins and pawns in the classroom: Self-report and projective assessments of individual differences in children's perceptions. *Journal of Personality and Social Psychology, 50,* 550–558.

Ryan, R. M., & Lynch, J. (1989). Emotional autonomy versus detachment: Revisiting the vicissitudes of adolescence and young adulthood. *Child Development, 60,* 340–356.

Ryan, R. M., Mims, V., & Koestner, R. (1983). Relation of reward contingency and interpersonal context to intrinsic motivation: A review and test using cognitive evaluation theory. *Journal of Personality and Social Psychology, 45,* 736–750.

Ryan, R. M., Plant, R. W., & O'Malley, S. (1995). Initial motivations for alcohol treatment: Relations with patient characteristics, treatment involvement and dropout. *Addictive Behaviors, 20,* 279–297.

Ryan, R. M., Rigby, S., & King, K. (1993). Two types of religious internalization and their relations to religious orientations and mental health. *Journal of Personality and Social Psychology, 65,* 586–596.

Ryan, R. M., Sheldon, K. M., Kasser, T., & Deci, E. L. (1996). All goals were not created equal: An organismic perspective on the nature of goals and their regulation. In P. M. Gollwitzer & J. A. Bargh (Eds.), *The psychology of action: Linking motivation and cognition to behavior* (pp. 7–26). New York: Guilford Press.

Ryan, R. M., & Solky, J. A. (1996). What is supportive about social support? On the psychological needs for autonomy and relatedness. In G. R. Pierce, B. R. Sarason, & I. G. Sarason (Eds.), *Handbook of social support and the family* (pp. 249–267). New York: Plenum Press.

Ryan, R. M., Stiller, J., & Lynch, J. H. (1994). Representations of relationships to teachers, parents, and friends as predictors of academic motivation and self-esteem. *Journal of Early Adolescence, 14,* 226–249.

Schaefer, E. S. (1959). A circumplex model for maternal behavior. *Journal of Abnormal and Social Psychology, 59,* 226–235.

Schafer, R. (1968). *Aspects of internalization.* New York: International Universities Press.

Smith, W. E. (1974). *The effects of social and monetary rewards on intrinsic motivation.* Unpublished doctoral dissertation, Cornell University.

Solky, J. (1995). *Emotional reliance: The development of a new measure.* Unpublished manuscript, University of Rochester.

Sroufe, L. A., & Fleeson, J. (1986). Attachment and the construction of relationships. In W. Hartup & Z. Rubin (Eds.), *Relationships and development* (pp. 51–76). Hillsdale, NJ: Erlbaum.

Steinberg, L., & Silverberg, S. (1986). The vicissitudes of autonomy in adolescence. *Child Development, 57,* 841–851.

Vallerand, R. J., O'Connor, B. P., & Hamel, M. (1995). Motivation in later life: Theory and assessment. *International Journal of Aging and Human Development, 41,* 221–238.

Walker, L. J., & Taylor, J. H. (1991). Family interactions and the development of moral reasoning. *Child Development, 62,* 264–283.

Werner, H. (1948). *Comparative psychology of mental development.* New York: International Universities Press.

White, R. W. (1959). Motivation reconsidered: The concept of competence. *Psychological Review, 66,* 297–333.

Williams, G. C., & Deci, E. L. (1996). Internalization of biopsychosocial values by medical students: A test of self-determination theory. *Journal of Personality and Social Psychology, 70,* 767–779.

Williams, G. C., Grow, V. M., Freedman, Z., Ryan, R. M., & Deci, E. L. (1996). Motivational predictors of weight loss and weight-loss maintenance. *Journal of Personality and Social Psychology, 70,* 115–126.

Zahn-Waxler, C., Radke-Yarrow, M., & King, R. A. (1979). Childrearing and children's prosocial initiations toward victims of distress. *Child Development, 50,* 319–330.

Zigler, E. F., & Child, I. L. (1973). *Socialization and personality development.* Reading, MA: Addison-Wesley.

Zuckerman, M., Porac, J., Lathin, D., Smith, R., & Deci, E. L. (1978). On the importance of self-determination for intrinsically motivated behavior. *Personality and Social Psychology Bulletin, 4,* 443–446.

CHAPTER 7

Parenting and the Development of Social Knowledge Reconceptualized: A Social Domain Analysis

JUDITH G. SMETANA

Although they differ on many issues, socialization theories and structural-developmental theories of moral and social development have converged on one important observation: The power relationships between parents and children are unequal. However, these theories differ radically on the implications of this observation for development. Socialization theorists have proposed that moral internalization stems primarily from parents' influence on children and thus have focused on the parenting practices, styles, and disciplinary strategies that lead to the internalization of values. Structural-developmental theorists (Damon, 1977; Piaget, 1932/1965; Youniss, 1980), in contrast, have proposed that the hierarchical nature of parent-child relationships constrains children's moral development and therefore have focused on the formative role of peers in moral reasoning development. In this chapter, parenting is reconceptualized from the social domain perspective (Nucci, 1996; Smetana, 1983, 1995b; Tisak, 1995; Turiel, 1983, in press; Turiel, Killen, & Helwig, 1987). This approach is structural-developmental in origin but departs in significant ways from previous theorizing. The proposition made here is that the internalization of values needs to be considered in the context of children's varied social experiences with both parents and peers and through processes of active construction rather than direct assimilation of adult values. Furthermore, inequalities in power relationships between parents and children (or other relationships, such as between men and women) are aspects of children's social world that children observe, interpret, and use in the construction of social knowledge. The chapter begins with a brief overview of different ways that parents' contributions to development have been viewed.

Socialization theories have proposed that differences in the strength of moral internalization stem from individual differences in parenting styles or disciplinary strategies (Brody & Shaffer, 1982; Grusec & Goodnow, 1994). The prevailing assumption is that parents consistently use the same parenting practices when intervening in their children's misdeeds. Hoffman (1970; Hoffman & Saltzstein, 1967) has asserted that greater parental reasoning, sometimes combined with power assertion, is associated with more internalized moral values. Similarly, Baumrind (1978, 1989, 1991) has proposed that authoritative parenting, which entails setting clear standards while being responsive to

I am grateful to Charles Helwig, Barbara Ilardi, Melanie Killen, Larry Nucci, and Elliot Turiel for their comments on earlier versions of this chapter.

the child's needs, is associated with greater child competence, including more mature moral values (Baumrind, 1978, 1989; Steinberg, Mounts, Lamborn, & Dornbusch, 1991). Two assumptions are central to these views: that the direction of influence in moral socialization is from parent to child and that socialization is due to functionally stable individual differences in parenting. Indeed, Hoffman (1975) has asserted that parents must influence children, as there is insufficient evidence that aspects of the child's behavior (or development) influence parents.

In contrast, most structural-developmental theories (Colby & Kohlberg, 1987; Damon, 1977; Kohlberg, 1969, 1976; Piaget, 1932/1965; Youniss, 1980) have viewed moral internalization as occurring through interaction with peers. Piaget (1932/1965) proposed that young children are heteronomous and view rules as sacred and unchangeable. With age and social experiences with peers, children develop an autonomous orientation to morality, where rules are viewed as changeable by general agreement or social consensus. As stated by Piaget (1932/1965): "Adult authority, although it constitutes a necessary moment in the moral evolution of the child, is not sufficient to create a sense of justice. This can develop only through the progress made by cooperation and mutual respect . . . between children" (pp. 319–320). Therefore, Piaget viewed parental authority and demands for compliance as inhibiting (rather than facilitating) moral development, particularly among young children. Although Kohlberg (1969, 1976) modified Piaget's stance and viewed parents as contributing positively to development, their contributions were not seen as unique. Like peers, parents were seen to provide the child with the role-taking opportunities that are necessary, in Kohlberg's model, for moral development to occur.

The evidence reviewed here suggests that both traditional socialization theories and structural-developmental theories provide incomplete accounts of values internalization. Although a great deal of research has examined the socialization theory claim that parents have a unidirectional influence on children, the evidence is largely correlational and replete with conflicting findings (Grusec & Goodnow, 1994; Maccoby & Martin, 1983). Alternatively, others have proposed that characteristics of the child such as temperament or habits may influence parental practices and that the influence is bidirectional (Bell, 1968). However, this view also does not fully account for the research evidence. Although structural-developmentalists' focus on peers as the context for moral development may be an undervalued and important corrective to socialization theories, which have overemphasized the role of parental power, these theories give parents' contributions to children's social development short shrift.

Social domain theory provides a third alternative. The proposition made here is that situations or types of act (rather than parental styles or child temperament) generate different parental responses. Parents have a large repertoire of disciplinary strategies. In some situations, they may appeal to rules and issue sanctions, whereas in other situations, they may reason and provide explanations (Grusec & Goodnow, 1994). Parents' choice of disciplinary strategy depends on the situation or transgression and the child's developmental level. The social domain analysis described in this chapter provides a conceptual framework for understanding differences in parents' goals, behaviors, and strategies and correspondingly, children's moral and social development. The analysis presented here is informed by the structural-developmental assumption that the process of moral development entails the construction (rather than the reproduction) of social knowledge from children's social interactions. This proposition differs from socialization theories, which have proposed that internalization entails the transmission of values, which are incorporated as given. As Kohlberg

(1969) has documented extensively, however, parents' and children's values typically do not match in ways that socialization theories would predict.

The current analysis also departs from previous structural-developmental theories on several points. First, research from the distinct domain perspective indicates that young children's moral concepts are not heteronomous (Piaget, 1932/1965) or "pre-moral" (Kohlberg, 1969, 1976). The results of many studies indicate that even very young children do not view moral rules as sacred, unchangeable, and contingent on the demands of adult authority. Second, Piaget and Kohlberg have focused primarily on middle childhood and early adolescence, when the child's social world begins to broaden beyond the confines of the family. This differs from social learning theory's and psychoanalytic theory's focus on the formative role of early social experiences in the family. In the view presented here, parents play an important role in the child's development throughout childhood and adolescence. Finally, interactions with parents are seen as facilitating children's moral and social development, although not in the ways described by either social learning or psychoanalytic theories. In prohibiting actions, giving instructions, and responding to transgressions, parents are an important (and because of their emotional bonds to their children, valued) source of children's social experiences that may lead to the formation of social concepts throughout childhood and adolescence.

Models of internalization have varied in their focus on emotional, behavioral, or cognitive processes. Recent emotionally based nonrational approaches to moral development have focused on the regulatory aspects of guilt and conscience (Emde, Johnson, & Easterbrooks, 1987; Kochanska, 1993), whereas social learning theories traditionally have stressed the behavioral components of moral internalization, as indexed by resistance to temptation or reparation after transgression. Structural-developmental theories, in contrast, have examined individuals' moral reasoning and decision making; these typically have been described in terms of global developmental stages that vary qualitatively with age and social experience (Colby & Kohlberg, 1987; Kohlberg, 1969, 1976; Piaget, 1932/1965). Differences in attitudes and decisions thus are viewed in the context of developmental differences in moral reasoning.

In keeping with the moves away from global conceptions of stages to more domain-specific views of development (Carey, 1991; Damon, 1977; Keil, 1986), the position presented in this chapter is that parents' (and children's) thinking about the social world is characterized by heterogeneity and coexistence of different social orientations, motivations, and goals (rather than global reasoning stages) and that analyses of parents' actions need to consider these different orientations, which are described here in terms of domains of social knowledge. Furthermore, it is assumed that analyses of parenting need to be informed by theories of child development and the types of social knowledge that children develop. As with these earlier approaches, however, a major assumption of the present analysis is that there still are compelling reasons for focusing on moral and social understanding rather than emotional regulation or moral behavior (see Smetana, 1995b; Turiel, 1983, in press, for elaborations of this argument). According to the social domain view, behavioral situations can be understood only in terms of the interrelations of domains of social judgments and cultural content in those situations (Turiel & Smetana, 1984). Therefore, an understanding of decisions and actions in social situations must be informed by analyses of social judgments (Turiel & Smetana, 1984), which are the central focus of this chapter.

The points of departure from socialization and structural-developmental theories and the major assumptions to be elaborated in this chapter are the following:

- Traditional theories of socialization have paid insufficient attention to the content of the values to be internalized. Social domain theory assumes that the social world is not unitary and that children (and parents) make distinctions among different types of social rules, knowledge, and actions. Therefore, parents' goals and children's responsiveness differ vis-à-vis these different domains of knowledge and action.

- Traditional theories of socialization focus on parents as the primary socializing agents. Although the role of others, such as teachers, other adults, the media, and culture, are sometimes acknowledged, the role of children's interactions with peers typically is ignored. The domain approach focuses on the child's active construction of knowledge from varied social experiences and different interaction partners, including peers as well as adults.

- Socialization theories assume a unidirectional process from adult (typically the parent) to child. The social domain approach focuses attention on reciprocal relations between parents and children and on how children interpret, negotiate, and sometimes challenge the rules, norms, and standards that are part of their social experiences. (Because the term *socialization* is identified with perspectives that view development as proceeding unilaterally from adult to child, this term is not employed here; *development* or *acquisition* is used instead.)

- Traditional theories of internalization have paid insufficient attention to the child's developmental status. The domain approach asserts that the child's developmental status must be considered. In turn, this suggests that developmentalists need to focus on children's differential experiences across a broad age range, not just early childhood, as has been the focus of traditional theories of internalization, or middle childhood and early adolescence, as has been the focus of other structural-developmental theories (Colby & Kohlberg, 1987; Kohlberg, 1969; Piaget, 1932/1965).

- Traditional theories of internalization have varied in their focus on affect, cognition, and behavior. Although social domain theory focuses on social-cognitive development, affect is viewed here as an inseparable aspect of children's social experience that leads to the construction of social knowledge. Furthermore, behavior is seen as related to social cognition, although in complex ways.

Each of these points will be elaborated in this chapter. It is proposed here that an understanding of parenting must be informed by a theory of child development and the types of social knowledge that children develop. Therefore, the next two sections describe theory and research from the social domain perspective on the forms that development takes and the nature of children's social experiences. Parents' contributions to children's moral and social development are considered in more detail in the second half of this chapter, after general theoretical issues have been discussed.

THE STRUCTURE OF SOCIAL KNOWLEDGE AND THE NATURE OF SOCIAL EXPERIENCE

Although traditional (e.g., psychoanalytic and social learning) theories have provided detailed accounts of the processes that lead to moral internalization, these approaches have left the content of the values to be internalized largely unspecified. This is because socialization is seen as pertaining to the acquisition of society's rules and standards, however those may be defined by the particular society or social system under consideration. Therefore, few distinctions are made in the types of rules, norms, and standards that children acquire.

In contrast, within social domain theory, the social world is not unitary and children have qualitatively different social interactions with different classes of rules, events, or actions. These differentiated social interactions lead to the construction of different types of social knowledge systems, or domains of social knowledge (Turiel, 1979, 1983, in press; Turiel & Davidson, 1986). They also inform parents' actions, goals regarding their children's behavior, social rules, and responses to transgressions, as described in the following section.

Domains of Social Knowledge

A major concern of parents is with ensuring their child's welfare, protecting their rights, and helping the child learn how to relate to others. According to social domain theory, these concerns all are aspects of the moral domain. Morality pertains to the system of rules that regulates the social interactions and social relationships of individuals within societies. Morality is based on concepts of welfare (harm), trust, justice (comparative treatment and distribution), and rights and is defined as individuals' prescriptive understanding of how individuals ought to behave toward each other. Moral judgments are proposed to be obligatory, universalizable, unalterable, impersonal, and determined by criteria other than agreement, consensus, or institutional convention (see Smetana, 1983, 1995b; Turiel, 1983, in press; Turiel & Davidson, 1986; Turiel et al., 1987 for an elaboration).

Although morality is socially constructed, not all social concepts are moral. In addition to concerns with children's welfare and rights, parents also are concerned with maintaining appropriate social behavior and facilitating social interactions so that they function smoothly and efficiently. According to social domain theory, these concerns, which pertain to individuals' understanding of social systems, social organizations, and social conventions, are conceptually and developmentally distinct from an understanding of morality (Davidson, Turiel, & Black, 1983; Nucci, 1981; Smetana, 1983, 1995b; Turiel, 1979, 1983, in press; Turiel & Davidson, 1986; Turiel et al., 1987). Conventions have been defined as the arbitrary, consensually determined rules, uniformities, and behaviors that coordinate the interactions of individuals within social systems. They represent shared knowledge among members of society or a social unit and provide individuals with a set of expectations regarding appropriate behavior. Conventions are hypothesized to be alterable, contextually relative, and contingent on the rules and dictates of authority (see Helwig, Tisak, & Turiel, 1990; Smetana, 1995b; Turiel et al., 1987, for review).

Parents' concerns with harm are not restricted to children's social interactions and social relationships. Similar concerns also arise in nonsocial contexts. According to social domain theory, prudential issues include nonsocial harm to the self, safety, comfort, and health (Shweder, Turiel, & Much, 1981; Smetana & Asquith, 1994; Tisak, 1993; Tisak & Turiel, 1984) and are also of great concern to parents. Like moral rules, prudential rules regulate acts with physical consequences to persons. Whereas morality pertains to interactions among people, however, prudence pertains to acts with immediate negative consequences to the self that are directly perceptible to the actor (e.g., harm occurring through carelessness; Shweder et al., 1981).

Finally, there are other issues that fall beyond the realm of conventional regulation and moral concern but are relevant to family life. Personal issues have been defined as pertaining only to the actor and entailing preference and choice about such issues as friends or activities, the state of one's body, and privacy (Nucci, 1981, 1996; Nucci & Lee, 1993; Nucci & Weber, 1995; Smetana, 1983; Tisak, 1993; Turiel, 1983). Personal issues form boundaries between the self and the social world (Nucci, 1996; Nucci & Lee, 1993), and these boundaries may be actively negotiated within families. Maintaining an arena of personal discretion is seen as representing an important aspect of the individual's autonomy or distinctiveness from others (Nucci, 1981).

Experiential Origins of Children's Social Knowledge

According to social domain theory (and consistent with other structural-developmental theories), these different forms of social knowledge are constructed from children's interactions with the environment (Turiel, 1983, in press). Other structural-developmental theories (Colby & Kohlberg, 1987; Kohlberg, 1969, 1976; Piaget, 1932/1965) have described moral development as a process of increasing differentiation; with age and social experience, children are hypothesized to distinguish concepts of justice from nonmoral concepts, such as convention, prudence, and pragmatics. In contrast, in the social domain view, social knowledge domains are seen as separate, self-regulating developmental systems that are not developmentally ordered. Rather, they are hypothesized to coexist from early childhood on. However, concepts in each domain are seen to change qualitatively with age.

The proposition is that an important aspect of how children develop prescriptive moral judgments is from their experiences as victims and observers of transgressions (Smetana, 1983, 1995b; Turiel, 1979, 1983). Consider the following examples:

Tammy and Nina are washing the table where brownies were mixed. Agnes comes to help. Tammy [says] "I'm sorry, but you can't help." Alice comes over from her painting and intervenes. Alice [says] "She can help. You don't have to be rude." Tammy begins to cry. Teacher (approaching) [says] "What's the matter?" Tammy [says] "She pinched me." Teacher (to Alice), "Why?" Alice: "She wouldn't let Agnes help." Teacher: "That's not your business. I told Tammy to clean the table. I'm very angry that you hurt Tammy." Alice cries. The teacher kneels down and comforts her until she stops. (Much & Shweder, 1978, p. 28)

A group of children are playing on the floor with toy cars. David, who has been coloring nearby, approaches and sees Michael's bright red car. When Michael looks away, David grabs it. Michael begins to cry and screams, "Mine! Mine!" (Smetana, 1983, p. 134)

A salient aspect of both of these examples is the pain or perceived injustice experienced by the victims of the moral transgressions. Such experiences are central to the development of moral concepts. Young children have ample social experiences with physical and psychological harm, fair distribution, and the violation of rights through their experiences of rule violations, misdeeds, and conflicts. Numerous studies have documented that young children's peer conflicts pertain to aggression (hitting and hurting), possession of objects (taking a toy or not sharing), teasing, and name calling (Ross & Conant, 1992), all moral interactions as defined by social domain theory. Young children may respond to these events by fussing, protesting, crying, whining, grabbing, claiming objects as their own ("Mine!"), and denying the request (all common among toddlers and preschoolers), as well as leaving the interaction, challenging assertions, disagreeing, postponing, contradicting, threatening, proposing means to repair the breach, and reasoning (more common among older children; Ross & Conant, 1992).

These attempts to understand such social experiences lead children to construct abstract notions of fair and unfair, right and wrong. Children generate an understanding of the wrongness of moral conflicts and rule violations from their experiences of the intrinsic features of acts, such as the harm or unfairness the acts caused. These experiences may be highly affectively charged, and negative emotional reactions from parents, siblings, and peers may contribute to the construction of moral knowledge. Children's experiences can include observations or direct experiences (e.g., as victims or participants) with harm or the perceived violations of rights, as in Tammy's and Michael's reactions in the preceding examples. In addition, comments or reactions from others, such as the teacher's attempt to focus Alice on the harm done to Tammy, or from parents can help focus children on the consequences of the acts for others.

As children develop, the social experiences that facilitate children's understanding of morality may change. Concepts of morality first may be applied to concrete and immediate personal experiences, such as the young child's direct experiences of harm and unfairness with siblings or other family members. With age and increasing development, children may apply moral criteria to a broader range of social events, including those that are unfamiliar, more abstract (such as issues of rights), more symbolically mediated (such as issues of psychological harm as a consequence of others' actions), or that pertain to unfamiliar individuals or groups or cultures who are more removed historically or culturally (e.g., victims of the Holocaust, the plight of the Bosnians).

In contrast to moral judgments, which arise from the consequences of actions, the basis for understanding social conventions is in the social system. Conventional violations are not intrinsically wrong. The acts are arbitrary in that alternate actions could serve the same functions:

> Children are greeting a teacher who has just come into the nursery school. A number of children go up to her and say "Good morning, Mrs. Jones." One of the children says "Good morning, Mary." (Turiel, 1983, p. 41)

> It is snack time, and the teachers instruct everyone to sit in their seats. Cindy is kneeling in her chair. The teacher tells her, "Cindy, bottoms have to be on the chair before children can have their snack." Cindy sits down; the other children pay no attention. (Smetana, 1983, p. 135)

There is no intrinsic basis for knowing that it is wrong for children to address their teachers by their first name or that children must be seated before a snack is served. Rather, this knowledge is based on an understanding of social conventions (in the former case) and school regulations (in the latter case). Although these examples were drawn from preschools, similar examples of conventional breaches abound in family life. Conventional knowledge is generated from an understanding of the prohibitions regarding acts rather than from the acts themselves. Social-conventional knowledge is empirical, descriptive knowledge based on a recognition of the uniformities in the social environment, differences in expectations across settings, and the social context surrounding acts (Smetana, 1995b; Turiel, 1979, 1983).

Understanding within the personal domain is also empirical, descriptive knowledge. Unlike social interactions regarding moral and conventional events, however, which are hypothesized to entail explicit social messages demanding or expecting behavioral change, social interactions with parents and other adults regarding personal issues focus on the needs and choices of the child (Nucci & Weber, 1995). These may include specific claims to the child's freedom of choice and resistance to the demands of authority. Although culture and context have been hypothesized to determine the scope and content of the personal domain, an arena of personal choice is viewed as expressing a fundamental human need to differentiate self from others (Nucci, 1996; Nucci & Weber, 1995).

As the foregoing discussion suggests, the development of social knowledge depends less on who the social interactions are with than on the social interactions. Social knowledge is acquired from interactions with qualitatively different social events, actions, and experiences. Nevertheless, some types of social interactions or responses to events may be more likely with different interaction partners. Parents and other adults may be more invested than children in enforcing social conventions, maintaining social institutions, and keeping social order. Therefore, interactions regarding conventional regularities may be more likely with (but are not restricted to) adults, especially when the regularities pertain to adult conventions. As children grow older, however, they, too, might be expected to notice, comment on, enforce, and respond to events and misdeeds in the conventional domain. On the other hand, because morality pertains to social relationships, some kinds of moral interactions may more likely be initiated with (but are not exclusive to) peers, although both adults and children may observe and respond to those events. In the following section, research that bears on these claims for the experiential origins of moral and conventional knowledge is considered.

RESEARCH ON THE EXPERIENTIAL ORIGINS OF SOCIAL KNOWLEDGE

Before considering parents' role in the development of social knowledge, three types of evidence in support of the claim that children construct social knowledge from their social experiences are discussed in this section. First, observational research on children's social interactions is presented. Then, research on children's affective reaction to transgressions is discussed. Finally, studies addressing the issue of active construction are considered.

Observational Studies of Children's Social Interactions

The proposition that social interactions form the experiential basis for the development of social knowledge has been tested by examining children's naturally occurring social interactions. Researchers have looked for systematic patterns of social interactions that parallel hypothesized distinctions in social concepts. Correspondences between social interactions and social judgments are seen as demonstrating that social interactions provide the experiential basis for the construction of social knowledge (Smetana, 1995b; Turiel, Smetana, & Killen, 1991).

The results of observational studies are consistent with Piaget (1932/1965) in demonstrating that conflicts over possessions, rights, taking turns, hurting, aggression, psychological harm, and unkindness (all moral issues) occur primarily in interactions with peers (Smetana, 1989b) and siblings (Dunn, Brown, & Maguire, 1995; Dunn & Munn, 1985, 1987; Dunn & Slomkowski, 1992) in free-play settings (Nucci & Nucci, 1982a; Nucci & Weber, 1995; Smetana, 1989b). Research suggests that peer conflicts pertain primarily to the possession and sharing of objects (see Ross & Conant, 1992, for a review), whereas these types of conflict are relatively infrequent between parents and children (Smetana, 1989b). Studies also indicate that children actively negotiate issues of fairness and rights and that even young children are able to respond positively to other children's justice claims (Killen, 1995; Killen & Nucci, 1995). Furthermore, research demonstrates that when children use reasoning and justify their initial position in a dispute, their partners are less likely to pursue the dispute (Ross & Conant, 1992), perhaps because they are able to make their perspective on the dispute clear. This is consistent with the finding that children are more likely to endorse working conflicts out on their own without adult intervention as the preferred means of resolving moral conflicts (Killen & Turiel, 1991). Such experiences are likely to provide an important context for children's moral development. As others have speculated (Damon, 1977; Piaget, 1932/1965; Youniss, 1980), children appear to acquire notions of reciprocity through their interactions with peers. In addition, research indicates that children who resolve conflicts using negotiation and compromise rather than more aggressive strategies are liked by their peers and that rejected children are lacking in just these skills (see Killen, 1995; Ross & Conant, 1992, for a review).

In contrast, conflicts over physical harm and aggression are relatively rare among peers (Ross & Conant, 1992; Shantz, 1987) but occur somewhat more frequently with mothers, although the rates are still low (Shantz, 1987; Smetana, 1989b). Gralinski and Kopp (1993) found that among mothers of toddlers, prohibitions regarding interpersonal issues (including both the expression of prosocial behaviors, such as sharing and being nice, and the inhibition of aggressive behaviors directed toward parents and others) accounted for only a small proportion of the total prohibitions mothers reported.

Once initiated, both adults and children respond to moral disputes and conflicts. Research on naturally occurring social interactions among toddlers (Dunn & Munn, 1985, 1987; Dunn & Slomkowski, 1992; Smetana, 1984, 1989b), preschoolers (Killen & Smetana, 1996; Much & Shweder, 1978; Nucci & Turiel, 1978; Nucci, Turiel, & Gawrych, 1983; Nucci & Weber, 1995; Ross, 1996; Ross, Tesla, Kenyon, & Lollis, 1990; Tisak, Nucci, & Jankowski, 1996) and school-age children (Blumenfeld, Pintrich, & Hamilton, 1987; Nucci & Nucci, 1982a, 1982b) are consistent with the claim that adults' and children's (primarily the victims') responses to moral transgressions provide feedback about the effects of acts for others' rights or welfare. Adult responses to moral disputes (such as hitting, pushing, and not sharing objects) typically focus on evaluations of rights and on requests to take the victim's perspective. Children also initiate responses to moral transgressions with statements of injury or loss, emotional reactions, and evaluations of rights, as well as with physical retaliation and commands to cease the offending behavior (Dunn & Munn, 1987; Much & Shweder, 1978; Nucci & Turiel, 1978; Nucci & Nucci, 1982a, 1982b; Ross, 1996; Ross et al., 1990; Smetana, 1984, 1989b). Children too may respond with statements that focus on others' rights and welfare; in one study, such other-oriented responses emerged between 33 and 47 months of age and were more frequent during arguments with peers than with mothers or siblings (Dunn, Slomkowski, Donelan, & Herrera, 1995). Although parental requests and prohibitions regarding moral issues appear to increase between the second and third year of life (Gralinski & Kopp, 1993), adult interventions appear to decrease from the preschool years to middle childhood and differ markedly according to setting.

Two aspects of these findings should be noted. First, moral transgressions frequently occur and are resolved in the absence of parents or other adults. Although this observation provides little evidence for the relative efficacy of parental versus peer responses in facilitating moral development or in inhibiting moral misdeeds, it indicates that both parents and peers are part of children's social experience of moral transgressions. Second, even when parents are present, studies indicate that children are active participants in negotiating and resolving moral disputes. Such evidence challenges the view of young children as passive recipients of adult values.

Sequential analyses of responses to moral transgressions help illuminate how both adult and peer responses may contribute to children's understanding of morality. In one such analysis of responses to toddlers' naturally occurring interactions in preschool classrooms (Smetana, 1984), two patterns of responses were observed. One was that adults interceded to control the transgressor's behavior with power assertion, such as commands and physical restraint. Such responses have been found in other research to be effective in terminating unwanted behavior, but they do not lead to moral internalization (Kuczynski, 1984). The other pattern was that child victims responded to the transgression with emotional reactions or statements of injury or loss, followed in turn by adult responses that focused the transgressor on the harm or injury caused (e.g., through statements of rights or requests to take the victim's perspective). These adult responses appeared to amplify and elaborate on the messages children received from the victims.

Research also demonstrates that until middle childhood, adults primarily respond to children's violations of school rules and familial conventions (Nucci & Turiel, 1978; Smetana, 1984, 1989b). Their responses generally focus on commands to cease the behavior, and less frequently, focus on aspects of social organization, such as statements about rules, sanctions, and the disorder the act creates (Blumenfeld et al., 1987; Much & Shweder, 1978; Nucci & Nucci, 1982a, 1982b; Nucci & Turiel, 1978; Smetana, 1984, 1989b).

Although preschool children do not appear to respond to more contextualized rules and regulations, they have been found to respond when the conventions are generated by the children themselves (Killen, 1989) or when they pertain to breaches of cultural conventions (Much & Shweder, 1978; Nucci et al., 1983). Whereas young children do not initiate responses to all conventional events, research indicates that they understand such events and that their responses differ from their responses to moral events. With age, children respond more to school conventions, with the greatest increase in response occurring between the second and fifth grades (Nucci et al., 1983). Children respond to other children's conventional transgressions with sanctions and statements of ridicule (Nucci & Nucci, 1982a, 1982b). Responses to conventional transgressions focus on the expected regularities in the social system, including information about what is acceptable in different contexts and what is not.

Observational studies also indicate that social interactions in the context of moral and prudential events differ, both in the home (Gralinski & Kopp, 1993; Smetana, 1990) and the preschool (Tisak et al., 1996). Adult responses to prudential rule violations typically focus on statements about the risks of the child's actions, rationales pertaining to safety or prudence, and less frequently, commands to cease the behavior and statements of rules (Gralinski & Kopp, 1993; Nucci & Weber, 1995; Smetana, 1990; Tisak et al., 1996). Therefore, adults respond in ways that focus the child on the consequences of their actions for their health or safety.

Finally, two studies (Killen & Smetana, 1996; Nucci & Weber, 1995) demonstrate that during the preschool years, interactions about personal issues differ from interactions about moral, conventional, or prudential events. Mothers negotiated more over personal issues than other events, and both mothers and preschool teachers were more likely to give children indirect or tacit social messages about personal issues in the form of offering choices (Killen & Smetana, 1996; Nucci & Weber, 1995). These findings suggest that adults respond differentially to events in the personal domain and recognize the need to grant the child an arena of personal discretion. However, children did not merely assimilate adults' tacit social messages about what is personal; they actively negotiated and challenged their mothers to gain more control and assert their perspectives on these issues. In contrast, they rarely challenged mothers over moral or prudential issues (Nucci & Weber, 1995).

The Role of Affect

As proposed earlier, affect is a highly salient aspect of children's social experiences in the family that contributes to the early development of moral concepts. A series of intriguing studies by Arsenio and his colleagues (Arsenio, 1988; Arsenio, Berlin, & O'Desky, 1992; Arsenio & Ford, 1985; Arsenio & Kramer, 1992) indicate that affective information may be used to understand, differentiate, and remember moral and other types of social events. Arsenio and Ford (1985) found that young children judge moral events as affectively negative, whereas they judge conventional transgressions as affectively neutral; affect ratings were found to be highly correlated with judgments of the obligatoriness and alterability of moral events. Furthermore, in a 3-week posttest, these investigators found that children more easily remembered negative moral events than conventional events. Arsenio and Ford speculate that differences in the tendency of moral and conventional events to elicit emotional arousal may lead to differential encoding of these events. Highly arousing moral events may be considered "immoral" in part because they are more affectively salient than less arousing events. In an extension of this study, Arsenio (1988) found that elementary school-age children employed information about situational affective consequences (e.g., whether actors or victims were happy, sad, angry, fearful, or neutral) to correctly infer whether initiating events were moral, conventional, or personal. These expectancies regarding the likely emotional consequences of different moral and conventional events were found to be highly differentiated and to increase in complexity with age (Arsenio et al., 1992).

These studies indicate that affective reactions are not only a salient, but an inseparable feature of children's experiences of transgressions employed in the construction of abstract judgments of right and wrong. This assertion is consistent with Hoffman's (1984, 1991) proposal that empathy typically is aroused in witnessing another individual in distress. In Hoffman's theory (1984, 1991), however, empathy is transformed developmentally with age. In the social domain view, emotions, including empathy, are grist for the social-cognitive mill. Children's affective experiences are part of and influence children's understanding and encoding of moral transgressions, but conceptual knowledge, not emotional responses, is transformed with age.

The assertion here is *not* that domain distinctions are based solely on the degree of affective reactions or arousal to events. Distinctions between morality and social convention are based on qualitative differences in the acts, of which affect is one dimension. One study provides convincing evidence in support of this proposition. Tisak and Turiel (1988) compared children's judgments of a major conventional event (wearing pajamas to school) with judgments about moral transgressions having major consequences (hitting someone) and minor consequences (stealing an eraser). A pilot study indicated that the conventional transgression was highly affectively charged for children (e.g., resulted in a great deal of ridicule). Although the majority of children stated that individuals would be more likely to commit a minor moral transgression than a major conventional misdeed, they evaluated the major conventional transgression as less wrong than the moral transgressions on the grounds that the moral transgressions would result in negative consequences for others. Furthermore, when asked what would be the right thing to do, children chose the major conventional transgression over either the major or minor moral transgression. The results of this study therefore support the assertion that affective reactions are an aspect of children's social experiences that helps to differentiate (but does not define distinctions in) the domains.

The research reviewed earlier indicated that moral conflicts and transgressions are a common feature of young children's social interactions. If children consistently judge moral transgressions as prescriptively wrong and attribute negative emotions (sad, angry, or scared) to the victims of those transgressions (Arsenio & Kramer, 1992), why are moral conflicts so frequent among young children? Several studies on attributions regarding affective reactions to transgressions (Arsenio & Kramer, 1992; Nunner-Winkler & Sodian, 1988) provide some clues. These studies indicate that children attribute positive emotions (e.g., happiness) to transgressors, a finding that has been called the "happy victimizer" effect (Arsenio & Lover, 1995). Indeed, Arsenio and Kramer (1992) found that nearly all young children (e.g., 4- and 6-year-olds) and a majority of 8-year-olds attributed happiness to victimizers. By 6 years of age, children also attributed conflicting emotions (happiness as well as negative emotions) to victimizers. In other words, children judged that children would feel happy after transgressing due to their gains as a result of their behavior, while they would also feel negative emotions due to their recognition of their victim's plight. Children did not attribute conflicting emotions to victims of moral transgressions, however; regardless of age, their attributions regarding victims were consistently negative.

How, then, do children come to view victimization as negative? In an interesting analysis based on Piaget's account (1954/1981) of affectivity and intelligence, Arsenio and Lover (1995) argue that it is due to affective decentration. Children shift from viewing victimizers as feeling strictly happy to focusing on the negative consequences for the victim. Like Piaget (1954/1981), Arsenio and Lover (1995) ground their account in the pattern of children's social relationships. Children whose social relationships are characterized by positive feelings and reciprocal goodwill are more likely to transform their initial views of victimization and shift from viewing transgressors as happy to focusing on concern for the victim, whereas children whose peer relationships are weak or dysfunctional may lack the emotional connections to make this shift. Thus, stable individual differences in children's peer relationships combine with developmental changes to affect children's moral understanding.

The research on happy victimizers thus far has focused on children's attributions regarding hypothetical victimizers' emotions. Recent research (Smetana, Toth, Cicchetti, Bruce, Kane, & Daddis, 1997) also indicates that young children (ages 3–6) also are "happy victimizers" in real-life situations. Research on happy victimizers provides one explanation for discrepancies between moral judgments and actions. It suggests that until children view victimizers as experiencing negative rather than positive emotions, there may be discrepancies between their prescriptive judgments of the wrongness of moral transgressions (and the negative emotions ascribed to victims) and children's own behavior as transgressors. Children may judge moral transgressions as wrong, but this may not be sufficient to inhibit immoral behavior because such behavior is seen as leading to positive gains and emotional consequences. With age and positive social experiences with peers, children would be expected to coordinate their moral concepts with their behavior and to inhibit moral misdeeds (Turiel & Smetana, 1984).

Children's Inferences from Their Social Interactions

The studies discussed in the previous sections indicate that naturally occurring responses to transgressions differ and that affect is an important aspect of these experiences. Studies also indicate that children make moral judgments based on their inferences from their social experiences. In one study (Smetana, 1985), the content of familiar transgressions was separated from associated features hypothesized to distinguish moral and conventional actions. Preschool children evaluated stories that manipulated different features of moral and conventional interactions but in which the events themselves were unspecified (through the use of nonsense words). Thus, the features of interactions that generate differentiated judgments were examined independent of children's knowledge of the content of specific events. In particular, the stories varied the consistency of the prohibitions regarding the events and the types of responses to the actions, both attributes associated with the moral and conventional domains. As expected, preschool children differentiated between familiar moral and conventional transgressions in their reasoning and judgments. Preschool children focused on the nature of the acts when reasoning and making judgments about events that were depicted as affecting others ("moral" acts), whereas they focused on the presence of rules when the events did not describe apparent harm or violations of rights ("conventional" acts).

A more recent study (Zelazo, Helwig, & Lau, 1996) elaborates on these findings. Preschool children's judgments were assessed in different conditions in which actors' intentions, as well as the relation between acts and their associated outcomes, were varied. For example, children were asked to consider conditions under which hitting causes harm (a normal or canonical causal relation) or hitting causes pleasure (an unusual or noncanonical causal relation) and where the actors either intended or did not intend to cause harm. Although young children had more difficulty with noncanonical than canonical causal relations, most children's judgments of act acceptability were based on the outcomes (whether or not someone got hurt), rather than on the canonical acceptability of the acts or the actor's intentions. Thus, children's judgments were not found to be based on associations between specific acts (such as hitting) and factors external to the acts, such as punishment or adult sanctions. Children's judgments of the acts were based on their outcomes. The results of these two studies are consistent with the findings from Arsenio (1988) that children use the sociomoral consequences of acts in making judgments and support the contention that children construct generalizable moral judgments from specific features of moral actions, such as whether they cause harm. Therefore, these studies support the proposition that children actively interpret their social experiences and construct social knowledge.

The theory and research presented in this section indicate that both adults and children respond differentially to misdeeds in various domains and that emotional responses are aspects of children's experiences that help children differentiate, interpret, and remember such acts. It was hypothesized (and the results of two experimental studies provided evidence) that these responses to transgressions lead to the construction of moral and social knowledge; children appear to make inferences from their social experiences in theoretically predictable ways. In the following sections, the implications of these findings for parents' contributions to moral and social development are considered in more detail.

EFFECTIVE PARENTING FROM THE SOCIAL DOMAIN PERSPECTIVE

In this section, the implications of the social domain view for parents' role in development are elaborated. First, the types of message parents use are considered. Research on induction (reasoning) and power assertion are reinterpreted from the social domain perspective. Then, the importance of the domain and developmental appropriateness of messages are discussed. In a subsequent section, factors that may affect children's acceptance or rejection of the message are examined.

The Role of Reasoning and Explanations

The theory and research presented thus far have several implications for understanding parents' contributions to moral and social development. First, the domain analyses of children's social knowledge suggest that parents' understanding of social rules and children's behaviors and misdeeds likewise is differentiated. The proposition that children distinguish among different kinds of events, rules, and transgressions also pertains to parents; parents would be expected to distinguish moral, social-conventional, prudential, and personal rules, events, and transgressions in their reasoning and judgments. Strong evidence for this assertion has been obtained in a number of studies (Nucci & Smetana, 1996; Nucci & Weber, 1995; Smetana, 1988a, 1995c; Smetana & Asquith, 1994).

Second, the evidence suggests that parents may be differentially concerned about and involved in events in different domains and that their involvement and concern may shift as a function of their child's age. Studies of mothers with young toddlers indicate that mothers are primarily concerned with safety (prudence) as their children become increasingly mobile and that they are somewhat less concerned about interpersonal issues (morality); they make relatively few social-conventional demands of these children (Gralinski & Kopp, 1993). Furthermore, Gralinski and Kopp (1993) report that mothers of toddlers are more proactive in preventing nonsocial (e.g., prudential) harm than in preventing harm toward others; the majority of mothers' reported prohibitions and requests to their young children appeared to focus on safety and self-care. However, as children grow older, concerns with prudence may decline somewhat (at least until adolescence, when problem behaviors increase), whereas concerns with conventional and moral behavior increase (Gralinski & Kopp, 1993; Smetana, 1989b). The research on peer conflict also suggests that many moral interactions occur outside adults' purview and may be resolved by children without adult intervention (Killen & Nucci, 1995; Killen & Turiel, 1991; Ross & Conant, 1992).

Third, parents' contributions to development may differ by conceptual domain. The evidence reviewed previously indicates that children may obtain information about the wrongness of transgressions from varied sources, including observations and direct experiences. Children may construct moral notions of right and wrong from their experiences as victims and observers to moral transgressions. Likewise, children can construct an understanding of conventions from their observations of regularities in the environment and differences in regularities across contexts (e.g., boys wear blue and girls wear pink; teachers typically are not addressed by their first name). Children also can acquire prudential understanding through direct experiences, such as touching hot stoves, wearing summer clothes in winter, and falling off high places.

Such direct experiences are not the only sources of development, and they may not always be the most desirable or effective source. The value or efficacy of direct experience may vary by conceptual domain. Adults may wish to protect children from some types of experiences, or may view it as their duty or obligation to do so. Most parents see themselves as having a duty or obligation to protect their children from prudential harm (Gralinski & Kopp, 1993; Nucci & Smetana, 1996; Smetana & Asquith, 1994). Furthermore, although children can construct an understanding of conventions from their observations of regularities in their social environments and differences in expectations across varying contexts, this may not always be the most efficient way of acquiring this knowledge. For example, it may be less trying on parents' patience to inform children about expectations regarding appropriate table manners than to wait for them to construct this knowledge through their observations of regularities in behavior or differences in expectations across contexts. Children also may lack the information or social-cognitive abilities to make certain associations. Many prudential issues related to health and safety may require knowledge or understanding that is beyond the child's capability or understanding. Ample research has demonstrated that young children's conceptions of illness, birth, sexuality, and death differ qualitatively from adults' understanding (see Bibace & Walsh, 1981, for examples). Therefore, it may be necessary (or certainly more effective) to tell children to use tissues to wipe their noses to prevent spreading colds than to rely on the development of their understanding of germs!

Parents can facilitate children's understanding and development in each of these domains. Although this may sound contradictory to a structural-developmental position, it is not. At issue is how such parental messages and responses are seen as affecting children's development. In the social domain view, parents' communications are one source of knowledge about different classes of events or transgressions. Through reciprocal social interactions with their children, parents can facilitate children's social judgments by providing information or knowledge about the domain of the action or event in question and by stimulating children to think reflectively about their actions. As discussed in greater detail in subsequent sections, however, this does not mean that children will internalize the message as given; how children assimilate parents' messages is affected by many factors, including children's developmental level, their domain appropriateness, and children's goals for the situation. As should be evident, this view differs from internalization theories, which have argued that children directly internalize parents' rules and standards. In the domain view, parents' communications are aspects of children's social experiences that are used in the construction of social knowledge; these constructions are not direct copies of parents' messages, rules, standards, and values, but are new constructions.

The assertion that parents facilitate development by providing domain-relevant information (e.g., Nucci, 1984) implies, in turn, that how explicit parental messages are on this dimension (as well as their developmental appropriateness) may affect their effectiveness. The more explicit parents are about the nature of the event and why a behavior is expected or a misdeed is wrong, the more effective such messages might be, particularly for young children (but see Goodnow, 1988, or Grusec & Goodnow, 1994, for some exceptions). This suggests that reasoning, explanations, and rationales will be more effective than other types of disciplinary strategies in facilitating children's development in different domains. This assertion is consistent with the findings on authoritative parenting (Baumrind, 1978, 1989, 1991), as authoritative parents appear to rely on reasoning and explanations more than do other parents.

Although a great deal of developmental research has advocated the use of reasoning as a disciplinary strategy, critics (Grusec & Goodnow, 1994; Maccoby & Martin, 1983) have noted that reasoning is a broad and poorly defined "amorphous category" (Maccoby & Martin, 1983, p. 51). The social domain view adds specificity to our understanding of reasoning as an effective parenting practice. It suggests that reasoning would be expected to be effective only if it is coordinated with the domain of the act under consideration (more will be said about this later), because only such explanations would provide the child with information about that domain.

More specifically, explanations and responses to moral violations would need to highlight the consequences of the acts for others' rights and welfare. The research reviewed previously indicates that parental responses to moral transgressions typically focus on evaluations of rights, requests to take the victim's perspective, and statements about the harm or unfairness caused by the acts. This is consistent with other studies, which have indicated that parental reasoning, and in particular, other-oriented reasoning (Hoffman, 1970), is associated with greater moral internalization and the development of concern for others (Hoffman & Saltzstein, 1967; Zahn-Waxler & Chapman, 1982; Zahn-Waxler, Radke-Yarrow, & King, 1979). Kuczynski (1982) has found that statements focusing on actions' consequences for others are more effective in promoting resistance to temptation than are appeals regarding the consequences of antisocial behavior for the self. Other research (Grusec & Kuczynski, 1980; Trickett & Kuczynski, 1986; Zahn-Waxler & Chapman, 1982) also has indicated that mothers reason more in response to misdeeds pertaining to fairness, psychological harm, aggression, lapses in consideration to others, and violations of others' rights (all moral issues) than other issues. Research from the social domain perspective has not directly examined the effectiveness of different types of parental responses on the development of moral concepts or behavior. However, unpublished analyses from a study of mothers and toddlers (Smetana, 1989b) indicate that mothers who reason more about the intrinsic consequences of acts had children who committed fewer moral transgressions.

Distinctions also need to be made between reasoning and negotiation. Others have observed that although reasoning may facilitate development, it does not lead to immediate child compliance (Chapman & Zahn-Waxler, 1982; Ross & Conant, 1992). Ross and Conant (1992) speculate that parental reasoning may make the parents' perspective clearer to the child but also may encourage negotiation and counterproposals rather than compliance. The notion that parental explanations make parents' perspectives clearer is consistent with the position taken here about the importance of providing explanations. Other research, however, indicates that parents (Nucci & Weber, 1995) and preschool teachers (Killen & Smetana, 1996) typically employ direct statements and do not negotiate moral and conventional issues, whereas they use more indirect statements and negotiate more with children regarding personal issues. These latter modes of communication (e.g., "Could you help me clean up?") have been associated with greater child resistance and child negotiation (Grusec, 1995; Kuczynski, 1984). Therefore, whether parental communications are direct or indirect needs to be distinguished conceptually and empirically from reasoning or explanations. Likewise, Walker and Taylor (1991) found that statements asking for clarifications or critiquing the other's point of view (operational statements in their scheme) did not facilitate children's moral development. Although they interpreted these results as indicating that such statements may have been perceived by children as hostile or critical, it is also possible that asking children to clarify their position implies that the position is negotiable and that the moral expectation therefore is not obligatory or prescriptive.

Parent-child relations also may influence children's social understanding in more subtle ways. As others have noted (Okin, 1989; Turiel, in press), families comprise complex social arrangements that entail hierarchical social roles and power relationships. In most families, there are gender (as well as parent-child) inequalities in the distribution of power, the way resources are allocated, and the way opportunities (e.g., for work or recreation) are encouraged or discouraged (Okin, 1989; Turiel, in press). These social experiences may inform children's conventional notions of the forms that social authority may take in different cultural contexts. This does not mean, however, that children (and adults) necessarily accept these structural arrangements as given. An emerging body of cross-cultural research (see Turiel, in press, for a review) suggests that children and adults also construct notions of the fairness of different social arrangements and that these evaluations depend on where in the social hierarchy one stands. Those in more subordinate roles (e.g., females), who may experience greater restrictions in their choices and freedoms as a function of their social position, tend to evaluate social practices as more unfair than do those in more dominant positions, who may be accorded greater entitlements and choices (Wainryb & Turiel, 1994). Thus, children receive many tacit social messages that they may use in constructing moral and social knowledge. The results provide further evidence for the proposition that individuals do not unquestioningly accept the social messages they receive.

The Role of Parental Warmth and Affect

Does the nature of the adult-child relationship matter? Other structural-developmental theorists such as Kohlberg (1969, 1976) have viewed parents as contributing positively but not uniquely to development. Kohlberg (1976, p. 399) stated, "Family participation is not unique or critically necessary for moral development." However, a great deal of research suggests that the quality of the parent-child bond and the degree of warmth in the relationship (Bretherton & Waters, 1985) affect children's development in many domains. Although research from the social domain perspective has not examined the role of children's attachment to parents in the development of social knowledge, it is likely that a warm, supportive bond between parents and children would enhance the likelihood that children are motivated to listen and respond to parents. This is consistent with Piaget's (1981) view of affect as providing the motivation (or "energetics") of action. One of the most consistent (and least anticipated) findings from research on family interactions that facilitate Kohlbergian moral reasoning stages is that parental warmth, involvement, and support are related to moral reasoning development (Hart, 1988; Powers, 1988; Walker & Taylor, 1991). Therefore, the quality of the parent-child relationship may affect children's motivation to listen to parental messages and, consequently, their social development. Children may be more likely to construct domain-differentiated understandings within the context of more positive parent-child relationships.

In addition, studies reviewed in a previous section indicate that affective reactions are an inseparable aspect of children's experiences of transgressions and that situations differ in their propensity to elicit emotional arousal. Parental affective reactions in particular situations, in conjunction with reasoning, may facilitate children's understanding and encoding of moral and social rules. The results of previous research indicate that maternal responses to moral transgressions accompanied by intense feelings lead to greater reparation among children than when cognitive messages are not so embellished (Grusec, Dix, & Mills, 1982; Zahn-Waxler et al., 1979). The evidence reviewed previously also suggests that parents are more likely to employ negative affect, including dramatizations of distress (Zahn-Waxler & Chapman, 1982) and greater anger (Grusec et al., 1982) in response to moral than other transgressions. Such affective responses, used in conjunction with explanations that focus on others' welfare and rights, may increase the effectiveness of reasoning because it helps focus the child on the harm or injustice their actions caused. However, too much anger may be too negatively arousing and therefore have the opposite effect; it may inhibit the child's focus on others' feelings. This speculation is consistent with a great deal of recent work on vicarious emotional arousal, which has distinguished between other-oriented emotional reactions (sympathy) and self-oriented, aversive emotional reactions (Eisenberg et al., 1988). This research indicates that too much emotional arousal leads to self- rather than other-oriented reactions.

The Effects of Power Assertion

Conversely, previous studies (Grusec, 1995; Hoffman & Saltzstein, 1967; Zahn-Waxler et al., 1979) have indicated that power assertion is associated with poorer moral internalization. However, power assertion, like reasoning, is an overly broad and poorly defined category. Power-assertive responses have included parental sanctions ranging from physical punishment to deprivation of privileges, coercive statements, harshness and criticism, expressions of anger, commands, and statements indicating general disapproval of the child's behavior. The relative effectiveness (or ineffectiveness) of power assertion may depend on the form of the power-assertive response, as well as the domain to which it is applied.

Some forms of power-assertive responses, such as commands to do or cease to do an act, with no explanations as to why the act is expected or wrong, may be ineffective in inhibiting antisocial behavior or facilitating the development of social understanding simply because they are indirect or lack informational value. This might be particularly problematic for conventional requests or misdeeds, where there is no other basis for determining the actions' wrongness. The results of several observational studies indicate that the majority of adult responses to preschool children's conventional transgressions are undifferentiated commands (Nucci & Turiel, 1978; Smetana, 1984, 1989b). The prevalent use of such responses to conventional events may explain the consistent finding that young children's understanding of social conventions lags behind their understanding of morality (Nucci & Turiel, 1978; Smetana, 1981, 1985; Smetana & Braeges, 1990; see Smetana, 1995b, for a review).

Other forms of power assertion, such as statements of rules, references to parental authority, and some types of sanctions, may not facilitate children's moral development for the same reason: They fail to communicate the reasons for the rule or prohibition and do not focus the child on the effects of the actions for others' welfare or rights. This speculation is consistent with the assertion that power assertion may successfully terminate unwanted behavior and induce short-term compliance but does not facilitate moral development (Kuczynski, 1984).

However, the effectiveness of rule statements, references to parental authority, and sanctions may vary by conceptual domain and children's developmental status. These same responses may inform children's understanding of social conventions to the extent that they provide information about expected regularities in the environment, including the presence of rules and the expectations of authority. Statements such as, "There's a rule that we line up in school" informs the child that there is a school rule governing the act and also implies that lining up is mandatory in school but may not be required elsewhere.

Finally, more extreme forms of power assertion would be expected to hinder children's development, moral or otherwise. For instance, responses that are extremely negative, angry, or coercive may scare the child and threaten the child's sense of security (Grusec & Goodnow, 1994). Such responses are also likely to promote aversive emotional reactions, such as anxiety or discomfort, which do not promote moral development (Eisenberg et al., 1988). Little research has examined parents' views of power assertion in different conceptual domains. The results of a study on middle-class mothers' judgments of corporal punishment (Catron & Masters, 1993), however, suggest that mothers endorse domain-differentiated harshness in response to transgressions, most likely because their child-rearing goals differ by conceptual domain. Mothers of young children (4- and 5-year-olds) endorsed more (and relatively harsh) spanking for serious prudential than moral and conventional transgressions; the latter were not seen as deserving of corporal punishment at all. These analyses suggests that power assertion may be too global a category. Future research needs to distinguish different types of power assertion (e.g., Grusec, 1995), and their effects on social development in different domains for children at different ages need to be examined.

Parents' Informational Assumptions

Parental reasoning facilitates children's moral development by encouraging reflection on their actions. But parents' explanations also may influence moral development by providing children with information, in the form of beliefs or theories about the social world, that are relevant to making moral judgments (Wainryb & Turiel, 1993). Research has demonstrated that apparent differences in moral evaluations are due to differences in relevant informational assumptions, or descriptive concepts about the nature of reality (Wainryb, 1991).

Wainryb (1991) compared adolescents' and young adults' judgments about prototypical moral violations (e.g., a father spanking his son who has done nothing wrong) with judgments about similar acts, which were described as performed in the context of potentially legitimate goals (e.g., a father who spanks his son for repeatedly misbehaving). Descriptions of these latter events also included information about how children learn and the efficiency of spanking as a teaching method. As expected, all subjects evaluated the prototypical moral acts as wrong. However, manipulating subjects' informational assumptions (by presenting subjects with information counter to the position they held) changed their evaluations of the goal-directed events by changing the meaning of the acts. Subjects judged that they would evaluate these events differently if they were convinced that the facts were different from what they actually believed. Therefore, Wainryb's research suggests that much of what is considered to be moral variation is due to differences in informational assumptions.

There has been little research on the origins of different informational assumptions, but they are most likely culturally variable (Wainryb & Turiel, 1993). Others have asserted that beliefs about children and child rearing are culturally determined and differ by historical periods, social class, and cultural settings (Goodnow, 1988; Wertsch & Youniss, 1987; Youniss, 1994). Goodnow (1985) has suggested that individuals acquire beliefs about what goals should be valued, what children are like at different ages, and what parenting strategies work from their culture. Likewise, Wainryb and Turiel (1993) have proposed that in many cultures, scientific "facts" and theories, as well as religion, are important sources of individuals' informational assumptions. Therefore, moral evaluations stem from children's social experiences and are constructed from social interactions, whereas the theories, beliefs, and assumptions that inform moral evaluations may be acquired from parents, teachers, and other cultural informants, including scientific or religious teachings.

It is possible that what may sometimes be seen as failures in internalization are due to different cultural or subcultural variations in factual beliefs or assumptions about the natural and social world. A case in point is ethnic and social class differences in the use of power assertion, severe discipline, and corporal punishment (Hoffman & Saltzstein, 1967; Kelley, Power, & Wimbush, 1992). Differences in practices may stem from cultural differences in beliefs about the efficacy of such methods, rather than from differences in moral evaluations about whether harming the child is morally justified.

The Domain-Appropriateness of Messages

The observational studies of responses to transgressions indicated that adults naturally coordinate their explanations with the nature of the misdeed (or provide undifferentiated commands). Adults rarely focus on the intrinsic consequences of acts for others in response to conventional events, nor do they reason about social order in response to moral transgressions. But these findings alone do not indicate that children necessarily perceive responses as more appropriate when they are coordinated with the domain of the transgression.

The results of three studies suggest that children actively evaluate social messages in terms of their domain appropriateness. In one study, 8- to 14-year-olds rated teacher responses to moral and conventional transgressions that were concordant, discordant, or undifferentiated with respect to the domain of the transgression (Nucci, 1984). Children evaluated statements focusing on the intrinsic features of acts (e.g., the harm or injury they caused) in response to moral or conventional transgressions (considered a domain-appropriate or domain-inappropriate response, respectively). Conversely, they evaluated statements indicating that the act was creating disorder in response to moral transgressions (domain-inappropriate) or conventional transgressions (domain-appropriate). Children aged 10 years and older rated domain-appropriate teacher responses (and the teachers themselves) more favorably than domain-inappropriate or domain-undifferentiated teacher responses (and teachers). Similar findings were obtained in a more recent study of preschool children's evaluations of teacher responses to peer conflicts (Killen, Breton, Ferguson, & Handler, 1994) and replicated in a study of Japanese preschoolers in Tokyo (Killen & Sueyoshi, 1995). Therefore, these studies indicate that from across ages, children make prescriptive judgments about adults as social agents and evaluate adult messages in terms of their domain appropriateness.

These findings and the research reviewed previously on reasoning provide an additional explanation for the consistent associations found between authoritative parenting and moral internalization (Baumrind, 1978, 1989, 1991; Steinberg et al., 1991). Recent research indicates that authoritative, authoritarian, and permissive parents differ in the domain appropriateness of their social judgments (Smetana, 1995c). In contrast to other parents, authoritarian parents of adolescents were found to moralize social-conventional acts in their judgments and justifications and to treat personal, friendship, and prudential issues as conventional and legitimately subject to their authority. These findings are consistent with Baumrind's description of authoritarian parents as moralizing, overintrusive, and valuing obedience as a virtue (Baumrind, 1989). Permissive parents, in contrast, were more likely than other parents to treat personal, prudential, and friendship issues as personal for the child.

Only authoritative parents drew clear boundaries between moral, conventional, and personal issues in ways that were consistent with domain-theoretical expectations. These parents distinguished moral and conventional regulations, but they also were responsive to the child's need for an arena of personal control and choice. This is consistent with Baumrind's (1989, 1991) assertion that authoritative parents negotiate more with their children, but it also suggests that negotiation occurs primarily in the personal domain. Interestingly, authoritative parents were found to be relatively restrictive in their definition of what is personal for the child.

This study did not examine parents' actual communications with their children. Children may be more receptive to authoritative parents because their demands and expectations are more consistent with children's own understanding and construction of events, as well as because they provide more explicit messages about the domains in question than do other parents. Authoritative parents appear to set clear standards about moral and conventional issues but are more willing to negotiate other issues. In addition, these parents appear to use explanations and reasoning more than do other parents. Of course, children may respond more positively to authoritative parents because they differ on other dimensions such as warmth, coerciveness, firm control, and communicativeness (Darling & Steinberg, 1993; Maccoby & Martin, 1983). Although these issues deserve greater investigation, the findings suggest that the effectiveness of parents' messages also should be examined in terms of the different domains in which parents exert authority and grant autonomy (Smetana, 1995c), as well as their propensity to provide explicit messages in different domains.

The Developmental Appropriateness of Messages

Social domain theory also suggests that effective parental reasoning needs to consider the child's developmental status. At the most basic level for parental reasoning to be effective, young children must develop the verbal capacities to comprehend such messages. Studies suggest that during the second year of life, parents shift from employing physical strategies for intervening in children's transgressions to employing verbal strategies (Dunn & Munn, 1987; Kuczynski, Kochanska, Radke-Yarrow, & Girnius-Brown, 1987). These findings suggest that parents naturally respond to developmental changes in children's comprehension; they also may reflect parents' increasing expectations for morally and conventionally appropriate behavior (Kuczynski, 1984; Smetana, 1989b).

According to social domain theory, reasoning or level of conceptual understanding within each domain changes qualitatively with age (see Smetana, 1995b; Turiel, 1983; Turiel & Davidson, 1986, for an analysis of how this view differs from other structural-developmental theories of moral development). Although few studies from the social domain perspective have focused specifically on age-related changes in moral reasoning, the results of several studies suggest that moral reasoning develops from a focus primarily on others' welfare to reasoning that includes a notion of reciprocity between individuals' rights (Davidson et al., 1983; Tisak & Turiel, 1988) and that children's thinking about distributive justice becomes increasingly informed by an understanding of benevolence, equality, and reciprocity (Damon, 1977). In contrast, social-conventional knowledge develops through a sequence of seven levels of increasingly sophisticated concepts of social convention (Turiel, 1979, 1983). Development in the conventional domain progresses toward an understanding of social systems as hierarchically organized and a view of social systems as functioning to coordinate social interactions.

Structural-developmentalists have provided evidence that reasoning slightly above the child's own level stimulates development, although research has varied as to the optimal degree of discrepancy. Although the traditional view is that one stage above the child's level (+1 reasoning) represents the optimal mismatch (e.g., Blatt & Kohlberg, 1975; Turiel, 1966), others (Berkowitz, Gibbs, & Broughton, 1980) found that +⅓ stage was most effective, whereas Walker (1982) found that +2 reasoning was equally effective. Regardless of the optimal discrepancy, the findings suggest that parents' messages need to be somewhat more sophisticated than children's level of understanding, but not so much above that children will assimilate parental messages to their own level. Research also indicates that parents typically do accommodate their level of reasoning to their child's level when reasoning about actual moral dilemmas in their children's lives (Walker & Taylor, 1991).

CHILDREN'S EVALUATIONS OF EVENTS AND PARENTAL MESSAGES

Although parents' explanations and responses to misdeeds may facilitate children's moral and social development, children also evaluate the messages they receive. This section considers aspects of children's judgments and evaluations that may affect their acceptance or rejection of parental messages.

A great deal of the research on socialization has focused on young children's compliance with parental demands and expectations (e.g., Kochanska & Aksan, 1995; Kuczynski, 1984; Kuczynski et al., 1987; Minton, Kagan, & Levine, 1971). This research assumes, either explicitly or implicitly, that submissiveness to parental rules and requests indicates successful socialization (although distinctions are made as to whether acquiescence is externally coerced or freely chosen). Whereas conformity to parental rules may be desirable in many circumstances, there may be instances when adults' demands are unjust or cause cruelty, when the adult does not have the authority to issue the command, or when the child's goals or developmental needs differ from parents' demands. Therefore, greater compliance may not always indicate greater moral maturity or child competence (indeed, such instances may indicate the opposite).

Others have recognized more recently that compliance may be only one of many goals parents have for their children (Grusec & Goodnow, 1994). Parents may wish their child to develop autonomy rather than conformity or to express autonomy in acceptable ways (Kuczynski et al., 1987). This issue has been raised in a slightly different way by Goodnow (1994), who has questioned whether agreement between parents and children is the only good developmental outcome and has analyzed the conditions under which parents might tolerate disagreements from their children. Parents may rely on certain strategies to avoid confrontations and maintain their relationship (Goodnow, 1994; Grusec & Goodnow, 1994), or parents may wish their children to develop different strengths and skills than the ones they possess. The complexity of compliance as a construct also has been recognized in behavioral attempts to distinguish among young children's defiance, compliance, and self-assertion (Crockenberg & Litman, 1990) and between committed compliance and external compliance (Kochanska & Aksan, 1995; Kochanska, Aksan, & Koenig, 1995). Although such behavioral distinctions are useful, they do not explicitly assess either parents' or children's evaluation of situations in which compliance is requested.

Research from the social domain perspective indicates that children's view of parental authority differs according to social knowledge domain and as a function of the particular acts prescribed. Numerous studies indicate that from early childhood to late adolescence, nearly all children judge both moral and conventional issues as legitimately regulated by adults, except under specified circumstances (see Smetana, 1995a, for a review). For example, research demonstrates that children judge that adult authority does not legitimately extend to causing harm, prescribing immoral acts, or being unjust or unfair (Damon, 1977; Laupa & Turiel, 1986, 1993; Weston & Turiel, 1980). Under these conditions, children might be expected to reject adult demands for compliance.

Children's judgments of the legitimacy of adult authority also depend on the domain of the act. Children and adolescents are more equivocal about adults' authority to regulate prudential and personal issues. Parents view the regulation of prudential issues ranging from whether children dress warmly (Nucci & Smetana, 1996; Nucci & Weber, 1995) to drug and alcohol use and cigarette smoking (Smetana, 1995c; Smetana & Asquith, 1994) as not only within the realm of their legitimate authority, but as obligatory, based on concerns with the child's comfort, safety, and health. Children, however, are more likely to view these issues as personal and within the individual's discretion (Smetana & Asquith, 1994). Studies also indicate that American children and adolescents consistently view personal issues as beyond the bounds of legitimate parental authority (Nucci, 1981; Nucci & Weber, 1995; Smetana, 1988a; Smetana & Asquith, 1994), nor do they see themselves as obligated to comply with attempts to regulate the personal domain once those rules have been established (Smetana & Asquith, 1994). Thus, children and adolescents view any type of parental intervention in the personal domain as inappropriate.

Many parents also endorse the view that children and adolescents should have personal jurisdiction over some issues, such as choice of food, clothes, friendships, and activities (Nucci & Smetana, 1996; Nucci & Weber, 1995; Smetana, 1988a, 1995c; Smetana & Asquith, 1994), although across studies, a sizable minority of parents viewed themselves as retaining control over these areas. Parents consistently viewed themselves as having more authority to control personal issues than their children were willing to grant them (Smetana, 1988a; Smetana & Asquith, 1994). Indeed, research indicates that the same issues that parents profess to be under their child's personal discretion are the ones that cause conflict in their relationships, not only among parents and their adolescents (Smetana, 1989a), but among mothers and young children as well (Nucci & Smetana, 1996). This suggests that disagreement and rejection of parents' regulation of personal issues are characteristic of children's social relations with parents throughout childhood and adolescence. Children and adolescents actively claim events as personal, resisting regulation and challenging adult authority. Traditional socialization theories may view such behavior as blatantly noncompliant and as indicating failures in internalization. In contrast, in the social domain view, interactions in the personal domain are seen as leading to the development of autonomy. Children's active assertions of personal choice serve to increase personal agency and enlarge the sphere of personal action (Nucci, 1996; Smetana, 1995a). Thus, conflict over what is personal allows children to renegotiate the boundaries between the self and the social world.

CONCLUSION

In this chapter, it was proposed that children's reciprocal interactions with parents as well as agemates lead to the construction of moral and social knowledge. Although parents are not exclusive influences on children's development, they are centrally important by virtue of their concern with their child's development and welfare, their affective relationship and extensive interaction history with their child, and their ability to provide the types of interaction that may facilitate development. Parents facilitate children's moral and social understanding by providing domain-appropriate and developmentally sensitive reasoning and explanations, often affectively charged, about different aspects of the child's social world. In turn, children act on the information they receive, assimilating, evaluating, negotiating, and challenging it. Such interactions stimulate moral and social development.

A great deal of research from a variety of perspectives was brought to bear on these propositions. However, research from the social domain perspective needs to test many of these propositions directly. For example, structures of thinking were hypothesized to interact with features of the environment, such as parental responses, to produce differentiated moral and social concepts. Observational studies of social interactions in the context of transgressions and conflicts in different domains provide some support for these hypotheses, but the proposition that these social interactions lead to the construction of moral and social concepts in ontogenesis needs to be tested directly, preferably through longitudinal research. Such research also needs to further examine the effects of domain- and developmentally appropriate parental reasoning on children's moral and social understanding and behavior.

In addition, it would be fruitful to examine how individual differences in the quality of children's relationships with parents and peers affect children's moral development and behavior. Arsenio and Lover (1995) raise interesting questions about how differences in children's social relationships interact with the construction of social knowledge to affect children's development. Greater elaboration and more research from the social domain perspective is needed on how cultural beliefs and values influence parenting and in particular, on how differences in informational assumptions about parenting and child rearing influence parents' moral and social judgments and children's development in different domains. This chapter focused primarily on children's commission of negative acts, or on what Tisak (1995) has referred to as inhibitory morality. Further discussion of parenting from the social domain perspective needs to consider children's judgments for positive or prosocial acts. Finally, the analysis presented here suggests that research on parenting needs to move beyond assessments of the consistencies between parental and child values to pay greater attention to the discrepancies, contradictions, and mismatches between parents and children and their positive role in children's development.

REFERENCES

Arsenio, W. F. (1988). Children's conceptions of the situational affective consequences of sociomoral events. *Child Development, 58,* 1611–1622.

Arsenio, W. F., Berlin, N., & O'Desky, I. (1992). *Children's and adults' expectancies regarding the emotional consequences of sociomoral events.* Unpublished manuscript, Yeshiva University.

Arsenio, W. F., & Ford, M. E. (1985). The role of affective information in social cognitive development: Children's differentiation of moral and conventional events. *Merrill-Palmer Quarterly, 31,* 1–17.

Arsenio, W. F., & Kramer, R. (1992). Victimizers and their victims: Children's conceptions of the mixed emotional consequences of victimization. *Child Development, 63,* 915–927.

Arsenio, W. F., & Lover, A. (1995). Children's conceptions of sociomoral affect: Happy victimizers, mixed emotions, and other expectancies. In M. Killen & D. Hart (Eds.), *Morality in everyday life* (pp. 87–128). Cambridge, England: Cambridge University Press.

Baumrind, D. (1978). Parental disciplinary patterns and social competence in children. *Youth and Society, 9,* 239–276.

Baumrind, D. (1989). Rearing competent children. In W. Damon (Ed.), *Child development today and tomorrow* (pp. 349–378). San Francisco: Jossey-Bass.

Baumrind, D. (1991). Effective parenting during the early adolescent transition. In P. A. Cowan & E. M. Hetherington (Eds.), *Advances in family research* (Vol. 2, pp. 111–163). Hillsdale, NJ: Erlbaum.

Bell, R. Q. (1968). A reinterpretation of the direction of effects in studies of socialization. *Psychological Review, 75,* 81–95.

Berkowitz, M. W., Gibbs, J. C., & Broughton, J. M. (1980). The relation of moral judgment stage disparity to developmental effects of peer dialogues. *Merrill-Palmer Quarterly, 26,* 341–357.

Bibace, R., & Walsh, M. E. (Eds.). (1981). *New directions for child development: Children's conceptions of health, illness, and bodily functions* (Vol. 14). San Francisco: Jossey-Bass.

Blatt, M., & Kohlberg, L. (1975). The effects of classroom moral discussion upon children's level of moral judgment. *Journal of Moral Education, 4,* 129–163.

Blumenfeld, P. C., Pintrich, P. R., & Hamilton, V. L. (1987). Teacher talk and students' reasoning about morals, conventions, and achievement. *Child Development, 58,* 1389–1401.

Bretherton, I., & Waters, A. (Eds.). (1985). Growing points of attachment theory and research. *Monographs of the Society for Research in Child Development, 50,* (Serial No. 29). Chicago: University of Chicago Press.

Brody, G. H., & Shaffer, D. R. (1982). Contributions of parents and peers to children's moral socialization. *Developmental Review, 2,* 31–75.

Carey, S. (1991). Knowledge acquisition: Enrichment or conceptual change? In S. Carey & R. Gelman (Eds.), *The epigenesis of mind* (pp. 257–291). Hillsdale, NJ: Erlbaum.

Catron, T. F., & Masters, J. C. (1993). Mothers' and children's conceptualizations of corporal punishment. *Child Development, 64,* 1815–1828.

Chapman, M., & Zahn-Waxler, C. (1982). Young children's compliance and noncompliance to parental discipline in a natural setting. *International Journal of Behavioral Development, 5,* 81–94.

Colby, A., & Kohlberg, K. (Eds.). (1987). *The measurement of moral judgment* (Vols. 1–2). New York: Cambridge University Press.

Crockenberg, S., & Litman, C. (1990). Autonomy as competence in 2-year-olds: Maternal correlates of child defiance, compliance, and self-assertion. *Developmental Psychology, 26,* 961–971.

Damon, W. (1977). *The social world of the child.* San Francisco: Jossey-Bass.

Darling, N., & Steinberg, L. (1993). Parenting style as context: An integrative model. *Psychological Bulletin, 113,* 487–496.

Davidson, P., Turiel, E., & Black, A. (1983). The effect of stimulus familiarity on the use of criteria and justifications in children's social reasoning. *British Journal of Developmental Psychology, 1,* 49–65.

Dunn, J., Brown, J. R., & Maguire, M. (1995). The development of children's moral sensibility: Individual differences and emotion understanding. *Developmental Psychology, 31,* 649–659.

Dunn, J., & Munn, P. (1985). Becoming a family member: Family conflict and the development of social understanding in the second year. *Child Development, 56,*764–774.

Dunn, J., & Munn, P. (1987). The development of justifications in disputes. *Developmental Psychology, 23,* 781–798.

Dunn, J., & Slomkowski, C. (1992). Conflict and the development of social understanding. In C. U. Shantz & W. Hartup (Eds.), *Conflict in child and adolescent development* (pp. 70–92). Cambridge, England: Cambridge University Press.

Dunn, J., Slomkowski, C., Donelan, N., & Herrera, C. (1995). Conflict, understanding and relationships: Developments and differences in the preschool years. *Early Education and Development, 6,* 303–316.

Eisenberg, N., Fabes, R. A., Bustamante, D., Mathy, R. M., Miller, P. A., & Lindholm, E. (1988). Differentiation of vicariously induced emotional reactions in children. *Developmental Psychology, 24,* 237–246.

Emde, R. N., Johnson, W. F., & Easterbrooks, M. A. (1987). The do's and don'ts of early moral development: Psychoanalytic tradition and current research. In J. Kagan & S. Lamb (Eds.), *The emergence of morality in young children* (pp. 245–276). Chicago: University of Chicago Press.

Goodnow, J. J. (1985). Change and variation in ideas about childhood and parenting. In I. E. Sigel (Ed.), *Parent belief systems: The psychological consequences for children* (pp. 235–270). Hillsdale, NJ: Erlbaum.

Goodnow, J. J. (1988). Parents' ideas, actions, and feelings: Models and methods from developmental and social psychology. *Child Development, 59,* 286–320.

Goodnow, J. J. (1994). Acceptable disagreement across generations. In J. Smetana (Ed.), *New directions for child development: Vol. 66. Beliefs about parenting: Origins and developmental implications* (pp. 51–64). San Francisco: Jossey-Bass.

Gralinski, H. H., & Kopp, C. B. (1993). Everyday rules for behavior: Mothers' requests to young children. *Developmental Psychology, 29,* 573–584.

Grusec, J. E. (1995, April). *The impact of negotiation, reasoning, and power assertion on children's feelings of empowerment.* Paper presented at the biennial meeting of the Society for Research in Child Development, Indianapolis, IN.

Grusec, J. E., Dix, T., & Mills, R. (1982). The effects of type, severity, and victim of children's transgressions on maternal discipline. *Canadian Journal of Behavioural Science, 14,* 276–289.

Grusec, J. E., & Goodnow, J. J. (1994). Impact of parental discipline methods on the child's internalization of values: A reconceptualization of current points of view. *Developmental Psychology, 30,* 4–19.

Grusec, J. E., & Kuczynski, L. (1980). Direction of effect in socialization: A comparison of parent vs. the child's behavior as determinants of disciplinary techniques. *Developmental Psychology, 16,* 1–9.

Hart, D. (1988). A longitudinal study of adolescents' socialization and identification as predictors of adult moral judgment development. *Merrill-Palmer Quarterly, 34,* 245–260.

Helwig, C. C., Tisak, M. S., & Turiel, E. (1990). Children's social reasoning in context. *Child Development, 61,* 2060–2078.

Hoffman, M. L. (1970). Moral development. In P. H. Mussen (Ed.), *Carmichael's manual of child psychology* (Vol. 2, pp. 261–300). New York: Wiley.

Hoffman, M. L. (1975). Moral internalization, parental power, and the nature of parent-child interaction. *Developmental Psychology, 11,* 228–239.

Hoffman, M. L. (1984). Empathy, its limitations, and its role in a comprehensive moral theory. In W. M. Kurtines & J. L. Gewirtz (Eds.), *Morality, moral behavior and moral development* (pp. 283–302). Hillsdale, NJ: Erlbaum.

Hoffman, M. L. (1991). Empathy, social cognition, and moral action. In J. L. Gewirtz & W. M. Kurtines (Eds.), *Handbook of moral behavior and development: Vol. 1. Theory* (pp. 275–301). Hillsdale, NJ: Erlbaum.

Hoffman, M. L., & Saltzstein, H. D. (1967). Parent discipline and the child's moral development. *Journal of Personality and Social Psychology, 5,* 45–57.

Keil, F. (1986). On the structure dependent nature of stages of cognitive development. In I. Levin (Ed.), *Stage and structure: Reopening the debate* (pp. 144–163). Norwood, NJ: ABLEX.

Kelley, M. L., Power, T. G., & Wimbush, D. D. (1992). Determinants of disciplinary practices in low-income Black mothers. *Child Development, 63,* 573–582.

Killen, M. (1989). Context, conflict, and coordination in early social development. In L. T. Winegar (Ed.), *Social interaction and the development of children's understanding* (pp. 114–136). Norwood, NJ: ABLEX.

Killen, M. (1995). Conflict resolution in early social development. *Early Education & Development, 6,* 297–302.

Killen, M., Breton, S., Ferguson, H., & Handler, K. (1994). Preschoolers' evaluations of teacher methods of intervention in social transgressions. *Merrill-Palmer Quarterly, 40,* 399–415.

Killen, M., & Nucci, L. (1995). Morality, autonomy, and social conflict. In M. Killen & D. Hart (Eds.), *Morality in everyday life* (pp. 52–86). Cambridge, England: Cambridge University Press.

Killen, M., & Smetana, J. G. (1996). *Social interactions in preschool classrooms and the development of young children's conceptions of autonomy.* Unpublished manuscript, University of Maryland, College Park.

Killen, M., & Sueyoshi, L. (1995). Conflict resolution in Japanese social interactions. *Early Education and Development, 6,* 317–334.

Killen, M., & Turiel, E. (1991). Conflict resolution in preschool social interactions. *Early Education and Development, 2,* 240–255.

Kochanska, G. (1993). Toward a synthesis of parental socialization and child temperament in early development of conscience. *Child Development, 64,* 325–347.

Kochanska, G., & Aksan, N. (1995). Mother-child mutually positive affect, the quality of child compliance to requests and prohibitions, and maternal control as correlates of early internalization. *Child Development, 66,* 236–254.

Kochanska, G., Aksan, N., & Koenig, A. L. (1995). A longitudinal study of the roots of preschoolers' conscience: Committed compliance and emerging internalization. *Child Development, 66,* 1752–1769.

Kohlberg, L. (1969). Stage and sequence: The cognitive-developmental approach to socialization. In D. Goslin (Ed.), *Handbook of socialization theory and research* (pp. 347–480). Skokie, IL: Rand McNally.

Kohlberg, L. (1976). Moral stages and moralization: The cognitive-developmental approach. In T. Lickona (Ed.), *Moral development and behavior: Theory, research, and social issues* (pp. 31–53). New York: Holt, Rinehart and Winston.

Kuczynski, L. (1982). Intensity and orientation of reasoning: Motivational determinants of children's compliance to verbal rationales. *Journal of Experimental Child Psychology, 34,* 357–370.

Kuczynski, L. (1984). Socialization goals and mother-child interaction: Strategies for long-term and short-term compliance. *Developmental Psychology, 20,* 1061–1073.

Kuczynski, L, Kochanska, G., Radke-Yarrow, M., & Girnius-Brown, O. (1987). A developmental interpretation of young children's noncompliance. *Developmental Psychology, 23,* 799–806.

Laupa M., & Turiel, E. (1986). Children's conceptions of adult and peer authority. *Child Development, 57,* 405–412.

Laupa M., & Turiel, E. (1993). Children's concepts of authority and social contexts. *Journal of Educational Psychology, 85,* 191–197.

Maccoby, E. E., & Martin, J. A. (1983). Socialization in the context of the family: Parent-child interaction. In E. M. Hetherington (Ed.), *Handbook of child psychology: Vol. 4. Socialization, personality, and social development* (pp. 1–102). New York: Wiley.

Minton, C., Kagan, J., & Levine, J. A. (1971). Maternal control and obedience in the two-year-old. *Child Development, 42,* 1873–1894.

Much, N., & Shweder, R. A. (1978). Speaking of rules: The analysis of culture in breach. In W. Damon (Ed.), *New directions for child development: Vol. 1. Moral development* (pp. 19–40). San Francisco: Jossey-Bass.

Nucci, L. P. (1981). The development of personal concepts: A domain distinct from moral or societal concepts. *Child Development, 52,* 114–121.

Nucci, L. P. (1984). Evaluating teachers as social agents: Students' ratings of domain appropriate and domain-inappropriate teacher responses to transgressions. *American Educational Research Journal, 21,* 367–378.

Nucci, L. P. (1996). Morality and personal freedom. In E. Reed, E. Turiel, & T. Brown (Eds.), *Knowledge and values* (pp. 41–60). Hillsdale, NJ: Erlbaum.

Nucci, L. P., & Lee, J. (1993). Morality and personal autonomy. In G. G. Noam & T. Wren (Eds.), *The moral self: Building a better paradigm* (pp. 123–148). Cambridge, MA: MIT Press.

Nucci, L. P., & Nucci, M. S. (1982a). Children's responses to moral and social-conventional transgressions in free-play settings. *Child Development, 53,* 1337–1342.

Nucci, L. P., & Nucci, M. S. (1982b). Children's social interactions in the context of moral and conventional transgressions. *Child Development, 53,* 403–412.

Nucci, L. P., & Smetana, J. G. (1996). Mothers' conceptions of personal issues. *Child Development, 67,* 1870–1886.

Nucci, L. P., & Turiel, E. (1978). Social interactions and the development of social concepts in preschool children. *Child Development, 49,* 400–407.

Nucci, L. P., Turiel, E., & Gawrych, G. (1983). Children's social interactions and social concepts: Analyses of morality and convention in the Virgin Islands. *Journal of Cross-Cultural Psychology, 14,* 468–487.

Nucci, L. P., & Weber, E. K. (1995). Social interactions in the home and the development of young children's conceptions of the personal. *Child Development, 66,* 1438–1452.

Nunner-Winkler, G., & Sodian, B. (1988). Children's understanding of moral emotions. *Child Development, 59,* 1323–1338.

Okin, S. M. (1989). *Justice, gender, and the family.* New York: Basic Books.

Piaget, J. (1965). *The moral judgment of the child.* New York: Free Press. (Original work published 1932)

Piaget, J. (1981). *Intelligence and affectivity: Their relationship during child development.* Palo Alto, CA: Annual Reviews Monograph. (Original work published 1954)

Powers, S. I. (1988). Moral judgment development within the family. *Journal of Moral Education, 17,* 209–219.

Ross, H. (1996). Negotiating principles of entitlement in sibling property disputes. *Developmental Psychology, 32,* 90–101.

Ross, H., & Conant, C. (1992). The structure of early conflict: Interaction, relationships, and alliances. In C. U. Shantz & W. Hartup (Eds.), *Conflict in child and adolescent development* (pp. 153–185). Cambridge, England: Cambridge University Press.

Ross, H., Tesla, C., Kenyon, B., & Lollis, S. (1990). Maternal intervention in toddler peer conflict: The socialization of principles of justice. *Developmental Psychology, 26,* 994–1003.

Shantz, C. (1987). Conflicts between children. *Child Development, 58,* 283–305.

Shweder, R. A., Turiel, E., & Much, N. (1981). The moral intuitions of the child. In J. H. Flavell & L. Ross (Eds.), *Social-cognitive development: Frontiers and possible futures* (pp. 288–305). Cambridge, England: Cambridge University Press.

Smetana, J. G. (1981). Preschool children's conceptions of moral and social rules. *Child Development, 52,* 1333–1336.

Smetana, J. G. (1983). Social-cognitive development: Domain distinctions and coordinations. *Developmental Review, 3,* 131–147.

Smetana, J. G. (1984). Toddlers' social interactions regarding moral and conventional transgressions. *Child Development, 55,* 1767–1776.

Smetana, J. G. (1985). Preschool children's conceptions of transgressions: The effects of varying moral and conventional domain-related attributes. *Developmental Psychology, 21,* 18–29.

Smetana, J. G. (1988a). Adolescents' and parents' conceptions of parental authority. *Child Development, 59,* 321–335.

Smetana, J. G. (1988b). Concepts of self and social convention: Adolescents' and parents' reasoning about hypothetical and actual family conflicts. In M. R. Gunnar & W. A. Collins (Eds.), *Minnesota Symposium on Child Psychology: Development during the transition to adolescence* (Vol. 21, pp. 79–122). Hillsdale, NJ: Erlbaum.

Smetana, J. G. (1989a). Adolescents' and parents' reasoning about actual family conflicts. *Child Development, 60,* 1052–1067.

Smetana, J. G. (1989b). Toddlers' social interactions in the context of moral and conventional transgressions in the home. *Developmental Psychology, 25,* 499–508.

Smetana, J. G. (1990). *Toddlers' social interactions in the context of harm.* Unpublished manuscript, University of Rochester.

Smetana, J. G. (1995a). Context, conflict, and constraint in adolescent-parent authority relationships. In M. Killen & D. Hart (Eds.), *Morality in everyday life* (pp. 225–255). Cambridge, England: Cambridge University Press.

Smetana, J. G. (1995b). Morality in context: Abstractions, ambiguities, and applications. In R. Vasta (Ed.), *Annals of child development* (Vol. 10, pp. 83–130). London: Jessica Kinglsey.

Smetana, J. G. (1995c). Parenting styles and conceptions of parental authority during adolescence. *Child Development, 66,* 299–316.

Smetana, J. G., & Asquith, P. (1994). Adolescents' and parents' conceptions of parental authority and adolescent autonomy. *Child Development, 65,* 1147–1162.

Smetana, J. G., & Braeges, J. L. (1990). The development of toddlers' moral and conventional judgments. *Merrill-Palmer Quarterly, 36,* 329–346.

Smetana, J. G., Toth, S. L., Cicchetti, D., Bruce, J., Kane, P., & Daddis, C. (1997). *Maltreated and nonmaltreated preschoolers' conceptions of hypothetical and actual transgressions.* Unpublished manuscript, University of Rochester.

Steinberg, L., Mounts, N. S., Lamborn, S. D., & Dornbusch, S. M. (1991). Authoritative parenting and adolescent adjustment across varied ecological niches. *Journal of Research on Adolescence, 1,* 19–36.

Tisak, M. S. (1993). Preschool children's judgments of moral and personal events involving physical harm and property damage. *Merrill-Palmer Quarterly, 39,* 375–390.

Tisak, M. S. (1995). Domains of social reasoning and beyond. In R. Vasta (Ed.), *Annals of child development* (Vol. 11, pp. 95–130). London: Jessica Kingsley.

Tisak, M. S., Nucci, L. P., & Jankowski, A. M. (1996). Preschool children's social interactions involving moral and prudential transgressions: An observational study. *Journal of Early Education and Development, 17,* 137–148.

Tisak, M. S., & Turiel, E. (1984). Children's conceptions of moral and prudential rules. *Child Development, 55,* 1030–1039.

Tisak, M. S., & Turiel, E. (1988). Variation in seriousness of transgressions and children's moral and conventional concepts. *Developmental Psychology, 24,* 352–357.

Trickett, P., & Kuczynski, L. (1986). Children's misbehaviors and parental discipline strategies in abusive and nonabusive families. *Developmental Psychology, 22,* 115–123.

Turiel, E. (1966). An experimental test of the sequentiality of developmental stages in the child's moral judgment. *Journal of Personality and Social Psychology, 3,* 611–618.

Turiel, E. (1979). Distinct conceptual and developmental domains: Social convention and morality. In H. E. Howe & C. B. Keasey (Eds.), *Nebraska Symposium on Motivation, 1977: Social cognitive development* (Vol. 25, pp. 77–116). Lincoln: University of Nebraska Press.

Turiel, E. (1983). *The development of social knowledge: Morality and convention.* Cambridge, England: Cambridge University Press.

Turiel, E. (in press). Moral development. In W. Damon (Series Ed.) & N. Eisenberg (Vol. Ed.), *Handbook of child psychology: Vol. 3. Social, emotional, and personality development* (5th ed.). New York: Wiley.

Turiel, E., & Davidson, P. (1986). Heterogeneity, inconsistency, and asynchrony in the development of cognitive structures. In I. Levin (Ed.), *Stage and structure: Reopening the debate* (pp. 106–143). Norwood, NJ: ABLEX.

Turiel, E., Killen, M., & Helwig, C. (1987). Morality: Its structure, functions, and vagaries. In J. Kagan & S. Lamb (Eds.), *The emergence of morality in young children* (pp. 155–243). Chicago: University of Chicago Press.

Turiel, E., & Smetana, J. G. (1984). Social knowledge and social action: The coordination of domains. In J. L. Gewirtz & W. M. Kurtines (Eds.), *Morality, moral development, and moral behavior* (pp. 261–282). Hillsdale, NJ: Erlbaum.

Turiel, E., Smetana, J. G., & Killen, M. (1991). Social contexts in social-cognitive development. In J. L. Gewirtz & W. M. Kurtines (Eds.), *Handbook of moral behavior and development: Vol. 2. Research* (pp. 307–332). Hillsdale, NJ: Erlbaum.

Wainryb, C. (1991). Understanding differences in moral judgments: The role of informational assumptions. *Child Development, 62,* 840–851.

Wainryb, C., & Turiel, E. (1993). Conceptual and informational features in moral decision making. *Educational Psychologist, 28,* 205–218.

Wainryb, C., & Turiel, E. (1994). Dominance, subordination, and concepts of personal entitlements in cultural contexts. *Child Development, 66,* 390–401.

Walker, L. (1982). The sequentiality of Kohlberg's stages of moral development. *Child Development, 53,* 1330–1336.

Walker, L., & Taylor, J. H. (1991). Family interactions and the development of moral reasoning. *Child Development, 62,* 264–283.

Wertsch, J. V., & Youniss, J. (1987). Contextualizing the investigator: The case of developmental psychology. *Human Development, 30,* 18–31.

Weston, D., & Turiel, E. (1980). Act-rule relations: Children's concepts of social rules. *Developmental Psychology, 16,* 417–424.

Youniss, J. (1980). *Parents and peers in social development: A Sullivan-Piaget perspective.* Chicago: University of Chicago Press.

Youniss, J. (1994). Rearing children for society. In J. Smetana (Ed.), *New directions for child development: Vol. 66. Beliefs about parenting: Origins and developmental implications* (pp. 37–50). San Francisco: Jossey-Bass.

Zahn-Waxler, C., & Chapman, M. (1982). Immediate antecedents of caretakers' methods of discipline. *Child Psychiatry and Human Development, 12,* 179–192.

Zahn-Waxler, C., Radke-Yarrow, M., & King, R. A. (1979). Child rearing and children's prosocial initiations towards victims of distress. *Child Development, 50,* 319–330.

Zelazo, P. D., Helwig, C. C., & Lau, A. (1996). Intention, act, and outcome in behavioral prediction and moral judgment. *Child Development, 67,* 2478–2492.

CHAPTER 8

Performance Models for Parenting: A Social Interactional Perspective

GERALD R. PATTERSON

Three decades ago, Frank (1965) could assert that there was no solid evidence for a link between family variables and child pathological outcomes. The title for this volume suggests that researchers now believe that an empirical linkage exists between what parents do and child adjustment as an outcome. This chapter examines this linkage between parent and child behaviors from a social interactional perspective; the stated goal is to construct a theory that accounts for most of the variance in measures of both parents' and child's performance. This chapter might best be viewed as a snapshot of an in-progress strategy for building a developmental model for children's antisocial behavior.

In the first part of the chapter, I briefly examine the questions addressed by a social interactional perspective. The theory operates at two very different but interrelated levels. The first level consists of a multimethod- and multiagent-defined macromodel that describes in very general terms how parenting behaviors correlate with negative child outcomes. The second level is based on observations of parent-child interactions and used to explain in detail how parents and children change each other's behavior over time. The general strategy is a dynamic one in that new variables can be added if a means of measurement is available and their place in the model can be specified. As part of the bootstrapping strategy, the discussions will include brief overviews of current efforts to embed emotional and social-cognitive variables in a social interactional perspective. Finally, the implications of this social interactional perspective will be considered for the question of what the child internalizes during this process.

Building a performance theory requires researchers to provide models that account for a major portion of the variance in child adjustment (or parenting behavior; Patterson, Reid, & Dishion, 1992). The social interaction perspective, however, also requires specifying the contributions of contextual variables such as divorce, depression, or poverty on family process. The theory becomes a developmental one to the extent that the models can account for both stability across time and settings as well as changes in the form of child behaviors over time. The utility of the models in addressing these issues will be briefly examined.

I gratefully acknowledge the accumulative contributions emerging from a series of discussions with Ken Dodge, Jim Snyder, and Tom Dishion. I also acknowledge the support provided by Grants R37 MH 37940 from the Center for Studies of Violent Behavior and Traumatic Stress at the National Institute of Mental Health (NIMH), U.S. Public Health Service (PHS); P50 MH 46690 from the Prevention Research Branch, NIMH, U.S. PHS; and R01 MH 38318 from the Prevention Research Branch, Division of Epidemiology and Services Research, NIMH, U.S. PHS.

The traditional explanation by developmentalists and social scientists, in general, involves cognitive mechanisms. Antisocial behavior can be understood and changed only by exploring what goes on in the presumably rational minds of parents and children. Ideas about internalized mechanisms and rational choice form the capstones of our legal and educational agencies as well as the cornerstone for modern theories about economics. Nevertheless, some of our confidence in this perspective may be misplaced. Studies to be reviewed here show that measures of childhood emotions and social cognitions simply do not connect that strongly to measures of social behavior. Even when they do correlate, the amount of variance accounted for is limited; and the evidence for causal status of these cognitions remains to be established (Patterson, 1986). Alternatively, I hypothesized that the reinforcing contingencies embedded in social interaction are actually the direct determinants for children's aggression. Presumably emotion and social-cognitive variables play key roles, not as direct causes, but rather as indirect contributors.

In this chapter, the beginning assumption is that the bulk of the determinants for aggression are not to be found "in" the mind of the child but rather in the reactions provided by the social environment. To some extent, the social environment is selected by the child; furthermore, the child shapes those environments that are selected (i.e., the child is an active agent). This perspective places a heavy emphasis on what can be observed and counted. Each model is evaluated in terms of the amount of variance accounted for in measures of childhood antisocial behavior. The long-term goal is to build replicated models that account for at least half the variance in the outcome measures. Models that describe the trajectory for the development of antisocial behavior are expected to inform society about how and when to intervene in order to successfully deflect emerging trajectories to an antisocial lifestyle.

A PERFORMANCE MODEL OF PARENTING

Performance theory evolved as a flexible and pragmatic approach to building a theory of parenting (Patterson et al., 1992). Essentially, each stage in the developmental model requires that measures be tailored to fit the key parenting and child adjustment concepts. Success in building the models is evaluated by the simple expedient of calculating the variance accounted for in multimethod and -agent indicators that define various aspects of child adjustment.

Three general requirements must be met when adopting this strategy. First, the estimates of variance accounted for should be contaminated as little as possible with shared method variance. This is the "glop problem" discussed in detail in Bank, Dishion, Skinner, and Patterson (1990). Dornbusch, Ritter, Leiderman, Roberts, and Fraleigh (1987) showed that adolescent ratings of authoritarian parenting styles the boys had experienced were correlated −.18 (males) and −.23 (females) with the adolescents' ratings of their academic standing. However, how does one interpret the 5.3% of the variance accounted for in this model? Does it reflect only shared method variance, or does the correlation also reflect a real relationship between parenting and adolescent achievement? Given an abiding concern with method bias, the strategy adopted assesses all major concepts with indicators that sample across methods and agents. My colleagues and I at the Oregon Social Learning Center (OSLC) assumed that in combining information across indicators, we would be more likely to get better leverage on estimating "true scores" (Bank et al., 1990).

Second, a great deal of variance may be accounted for by stuffing an endless supply of independent measures into the equation (i.e., the well-known "shrinkage" problem). For this reason, when building a performance theory, replication becomes a key issue. In studies reviewed later, the evaluation will rest in part on how well the results stand up in across-sample and across-site replications.

Evaluating the causal status of key variables is a third characteristic of performance models. This is, perhaps, both the most important and yet the most difficult to carry out. For example, only experimental manipulations can give credence to statements about the causal status of parenting variables. Forgatch (1991) proposed that the experiments be tailored to answer specific questions about the causal status of parenting practices to child outcomes. This requires (a) a random assignment design, where some families in a prevention trial receive extended training and supervision in their parenting practices and others receive a set of placebo procedures; and (b) follow-up data demonstrating that children in the experimental group reduced their antisocial behavior, whereas those in the comparison group did not. Studies now available that test this hypothesis will be reviewed in a later section.

A SOCIAL INTERACTIONAL PERSPECTIVE

Theory building is analogous to Meehl's (1954) bootstrapping process. Where to start depends entirely on which of the relevant variables can be measured. As the process proceeds, other variables are added as they become available. During the 1960s, observers in the homes of clinical families could see that children's aggressive behavior often seemed quite functional (e.g., it often deflected an ongoing attack by another family member). In these studies, researchers at OSLC were also very much aware of the ubiquitous presence of negative emotions, such as anger, fear, and contempt (Patterson & Brodsky, 1966). However, we had no way of adequately assessing these variables. We could sense that negative attributions and other social cognitions played important roles in the process, but without a means of measurement, it was not possible to determine what the function of negative emotions and social cognitions might be. Because appropriate measures are now available for both emotion and social cognitions, research can begin a new stage in the bootstrapping operation.

Gradually, we came to the view that we must build two parallel theories, one about the contingencies that control prosocial and deviant behaviors and the other about the parenting practices that controlled the contingencies. The social interactional perspective in building the parallel theories emerged from two very different scientific traditions in psychology. Roger Barker's (1963) injunction to observe child behavior in natural context powerfully influenced my thinking about how and where to begin. In fact their techniques for collecting such data served as the starting point for the development of our own observation procedures (Patterson & Brodsky, 1966; Reid, 1978, 1982).

The idea of functional analyses was the basis for outlining what to look for in the sequential observation data. As Skinner (1969) pointed out, all social behavior has a function. One prime function of social behavior is to produce predictable reinforcing reactions and to avoid aversive outcomes from the social environment. Our interest in studying functions led us directly to observations in the home and the school settings.

As the work proceeded, it soon became evident that to fit the phenomena, we had to expand our ideas about both context and contingencies. In the initial studies, the term "context" simply described the behavior of the other person (Patterson & Cobb, 1971). However, the measures of context gradually expanded to include measures of daily levels of stress and depression experienced by the mother (Patterson, 1983). Eventually, context was expanded to include stressors such as divorce and poverty (Forgatch, Patterson, & Ray, 1996; Larzelere & Patterson, 1990). In a similar vein, earlier views about reinforcement were expanded to include the broader perspective taken in the modern work on learning theory that views reinforcement effects from the intraindividual perspective. In the matching law (McDowell, 1988; Snyder & Patterson, 1995), payoffs for deviant behaviors are examined in the context of payoffs for all other behaviors that occur in that situation. From the intraindividual perspective of equilibrium theory, selectively reinforcing a response must be understood in the context of the individuals existing repertoire (Timberlake, 1995).

Within a few years, it was also becoming apparent that the exchanges between parents and children were bidirectional in their effects (Patterson, 1976). Dyads who engaged in repeated interactions could become increasingly deviant over time; this effect was found for many different dyads other than just parent and child (e.g., husband and wife, child and peer or sibling (Barkley, 1981; Bugental, Blue, & Lewis, 1990; Dishion, Patterson, & Griesler, 1994; Vuchinich, Bank, & Patterson, 1992). What this means is that family processes can change very quickly. Its presence also makes experimental tests for causal status imperative.

The main characteristics of a social interactional perspective on the socialization process are: (a) longitudinal observations collected in natural settings; (b) functional analyses of the key concepts; (c) analyses of the contribution of context to parental and child behaviors; (d) bidirectional perspective; (e) across-site replication of models; and (f) experimental manipulations to demonstrate causal status.

MACROTHEORY ABOUT PARENTING

The details of the macrotheory of parenting are summarized in the book *Antisocial Boys* (Patterson et al., 1992); recent applications of the models to longitudinal data sets are detailed in Forgatch et al. (1996) and Patterson, Yoerger, and Stoolmiller (in press). The concepts found in the parenting models emerged from several decades of efforts to clinically intervene with families of antisocial boys. The observations in the homes of families referred for treatment of antisocial children showed that the parents were relatively noncontingent in their use of support for prosocial child behaviors (Patterson, 1982). When problem behaviors occurred, parents were most likely to respond with scolding and threats. But these threats were seldom backed up by effective punishment. A long series of laboratory studies reviewed by Wells (1995) demonstrated that such noncontingent reactions were associated with high rates of oppositional behavior. Even in normal families, the failure to back up reasoning with punishment is associated with antisocial behavior (Larzelere, Schneider, Larson, & Pike, 1996).

Thus, although most studies find strong positive correlations between harsh punishment (scolding, threatening, and occasional hitting) and oppositional behavior, the direction of causality is complex. In clinical samples, the oppositional child plays a major role in shaping the parent to scold, threaten, command, and coerce at high rates. If scolding and threats (harsh discipline) caused the oppositional behavior, all we would have to do is teach the parent to stop scolding and the child would improve.

In these early treatment studies, we trained parents to be more contingent in their use of support for prosocial behavior and effective punishment for deviant behaviors (Patterson, McNeal, Hawkins, & Phelps, 1967). We also learned that each family has its own set of implicit rules about what is valued and what should be punished, but families differed a great deal in the clarity with which the rules were spelled out. Effective discipline requires that the existing rules be spelled out and consistently applied, not only to the target child but to the siblings as well (Patterson, 1982). As the child develops, the new rules must also be negotiated in some fashion. Training in family problem-solving skills was designed to facilitate these negotiations (Forgatch, 1989). It was also apparent that unsupervised time with deviant peers was a key component in training for deviancy. Many of the parents in our clinical samples had only the most rudimentary information about the whereabouts of their children, what they were doing, or who they were with. Thus, we developed techniques to train parents to monitor and track their child's behavior. Over time, Parent Training Therapy included not only contingency skills but monitoring and family problem-solving skills as well.

A study of normal families supported by the National Institute of Mental Health (NIMH) generated a battery of indicators for each of the key concepts in the parenting models (Patterson, 1982). The psychometric analyses were replicated and extended in the at-risk Oregon Youth Study (OYS; Capaldi & Patterson, 1989). To be included in a definition, each indicator had to demonstrate a factor loading of .30 or greater. For example, the indicators for the monitoring construct included data from a child interview (six items), plus the mean of six telephone interviews with parents, and a general observer rating from the interview with parents. The information described how well the parents keep track of the child's activities (where the child is, with whom, and doing what) outside the home (evenings, weekends, and when parent is working). All the indicators for the discipline construct are based on observation data, usually sessions collected in the home. Our repeated efforts to use child or parent interview reports of discipline practices produced only equivocal results. Our recent studies no longer include such indicators. The observation data generate three different indicators. Nattering consists of the likelihood the parent reacts in a negative manner during interaction with the child. The abusive parenting indicator consists of the likelihood of a parental threat to hit or actual hitting when the parent is interacting with the target child. The observers' global ratings of discipline practices (six items) describes consistency and follow-through during discipline confrontations. The family problem-solving construct was based on videotapes of the parents and child attempting to resolve a series of family problems listed as hot issues in a prior interview. Coders rated the solutions to each of the three problems on six different scales (e.g., quality of proposed solutions, extent of resolution, and likelihood of implementation; Forgatch, DeGarmo, & Knutson, 1997).

The measurement of parental discipline, family problem solving, and monitoring skills defined what we meant by macrolevel parenting models. The reinforcement construct is defined by sequential analyses of interactions such as those carried out in the matching law studies (Snyder & Patterson, 1995).

Macromodels of Parenting

We believed that faulty measurement had been the chief impediment to the development of an empirically based theory of socialization. As noted earlier, efforts to construct theories based on maternal reports could not be replicated (Schuck, 1974). Contemporary emphasis on structural equation modeling (SEM) made a strong case for multimethod and -agent measurement of the key concepts (Hoyle, 1995). We agreed with this point of view and argued that multimethod and -agent definitions would increase our ability to replicate structural models of parenting across samples and sites (Patterson & Bank, 1987). We received 2 years of NIMH support to develop the first set of multiagent and -method indicators for each of the parenting, child adjustment, and contextual concepts in the model. We estimated that it would take up to 20 hours of assessment to fulfill these requirements. The data from a normal sample of adolescents and their families showed significant correlations between police arrest data and parental monitoring (.55) as well as parental discipline (.30; Patterson & Stouthamer-Loeber, 1984).

This was a promising beginning, but some of the constructs seemed to have borderline psychometric qualities. A revised assessment battery was then used in a longitudinal study of 206 at-risk families in the OYS. The boys were in the fourth grade during the first wave of data collection and have been assessed biannually through high school and young adult years. Details of recruitment for the OYS procedures and demographics are presented in Capaldi and Patterson (1987). Psychometric studies of the indicators for each parenting construct used in the OYS are detailed in Capaldi and Patterson (1989) and Patterson et al. (1992). It was assumed that the care given to the measurement of parental and child behaviors would be repaid in two different ways: (a) The resulting models would be more generalizable (i.e., replicate across samples and sites); and (b) the resulting performance models would account for much more of the variance in the criterion measures.

The data in Figure 8.1 illustrate the procedure for defining two key parenting skills, Monitoring and Discipline (Patterson & Bank, 1987). It can be seen that the latent construct for Discipline loads very differently on each of the four indicators that define it. For example, the construct loaded −.94 on the Nattering indicator (mother aversive given she was interacting with child), whereas the loading for mother interview was a borderline −.35. Examining the corresponding factor loadings for the Monitoring construct yielded only one strong indicator, one borderline, and two marginal. The findings suggest that further work is needed on the Monitoring construct.

With the constructs as they stand, several interesting questions can be addressed. For example, parents who tended to be less skilled in monitoring were also less skilled in their discipline practices. As a general case, a matrix of constructs for different types of parenting skills will tend to be intercorrelated. For the OYS, the median correlation among parenting practices was .25 (Patterson et al., 1992). The bivariate correlation between the Discipline and Monitoring composites in Figure 8.1 was .57 ($p < .01$).

A confirmatory factor analysis compared a one-factor (Good-Bad parenting) solution with a two-factor (Monitoring and Discipline) solution. The chi-square value of 28.25 ($p < .001$) showed that the two-factor solution provided the better fit. Parental discipline could be significantly differentiated from parental monitoring. A confirmatory factor analysis demonstrated that constructs for Family Problem-Solving, Positive Reinforcement, and Parent Involvement represent three different parenting skills rather just Good versus Bad parenting (Patterson et al., 1992, p. 87).

As noted earlier, the primary function of both micro- and macrotheories is to account for variance in criterion measures of childhood social behaviors. To test the status of the parenting model as a performance theory, a structural equation model (SEM) was used to demonstrate that Discipline and Monitoring contributed significantly to a

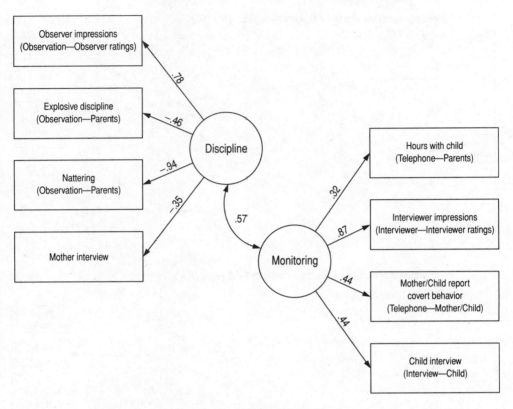

Figure 8.1 One Factor or Two?

From "When Is a Nomological Network a Construct?" by G. R. Patterson and L. Bank, 1987. In D. R. Peterson and D. B. Fishman (Eds.), *Assessment for Decision* (pp. 249–279). New Brunswick, NJ: Rutgers University Press. Copyright © 1987 Rutgers University Press. Reprinted with permission.

latent construct for childhood antisocial behavior. The model was examined separately for three different at-risk samples. Figure 8.2a summarizes the findings from the OYS. The theoretical model states that the two parenting skills should account for a significant portion of the variance in the measure of antisocial behavior. The first point of interest concerns the fit of the data to the a priori model. This value is expressed as a chi-square of 37.83. If there was a lack of fit between theory and data, the chi-square would be significant. Therefore, the nonsignificant $p < .22$ defines an acceptable fit. The second matter of interest concerns the magnitude of the path coefficients between parenting behavior and child outcomes. The path coefficient for Monitoring was .32 ($p < .01$). It specifies that even after the contribution of discipline was partialed out, parental monitoring made a significant and unique contribution. The data indicate that disruptions in either parenting skill place the child at significant risk for deviant behavior. The zeta value immediately below the Antisocial construct was .70. One minus this value provides an estimate of the joint contribution of the two parenting practices. For the OYS, the parenting model accounted for 30% of the variance in antisocial behavior and in so doing meets our requirements for a performance theory.

Model A. Parenting model for at-risk boys aged 9–10 years (*N* = 201)

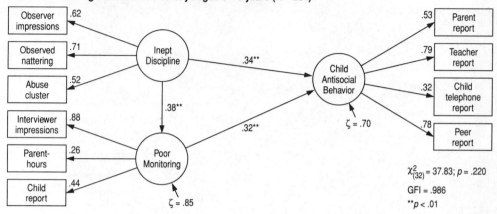

Model B. Parenting model for boys of divorced parents 9–12 years (*N* = 96)

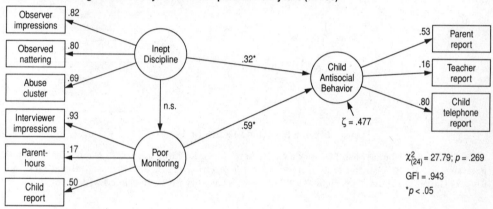

Model C. Parenting for clinical sample of boys and girls aged 5–12 (*N* = 71)

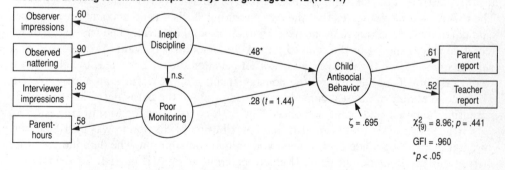

Figure 8.2   Replicated Model for Parental Discipline and Parental Monitoring Practices

From "The Clinical Science Vortex: A Developing Theory of Antisocial Behavior," by M. S. Forgatch, 1991. In D. J. Pepler and K. H. Rubin (Eds.). *The Development and Treatment of Childhood Aggression* (pp. 291–315). Hillsdale, NJ: Erlbaum. Copyright © 1991 Lawrence Erlbaum Associates. Reprinted with permission.

Replication and Causal Status

Our approach requires that key models be replicated across equivalent samples and sites. Forgatch (1991) addressed this task with data from three different at-risk samples that employed similar measuring procedures. In Figure 8.2b she used her own data from a longitudinal study of separated and divorced families. Again a nonsignificant chi-square value shows that the parenting model provided a good fit to this data set, and this was interpreted to mean that the model was robust. Again, the path coefficients from both parenting skills to the latent construct for antisocial behavior were significant. One minus the zeta value of .48 showed that the parenting model accounted for 52% of the variance in the criterion construct.

Figure 8.2c contains data from a clinical sample referred for treatment. What was interesting was that the sample included both boys and girls and included a much wider age range. The nonsignificant chi-square indicates an acceptable fit of the data to the a priori model. The parenting model accounted for about 30% of the variance. The fact that the general findings held even though the measures used in the different samples varied somewhat also speaks to the robustness of the general parenting model. More recently, the model has been shown to provide acceptable fits to data from normal samples of both adolescents (Metzler & Dishion, 1992) and preschool boys and girls (Eddy & Fagot, 1991).

The most conservative test for the generalizability assumption involved an across-site replication of a complex parenting model designed to account for child adjustment (Conger, Patterson, & Gé, 1995). Of the 11 indicators used to define the model in Oregon and in Iowa, only one was exactly the same in the two studies. Nevertheless, the a priori model provided acceptable fits to both data sets. Structural invariance obtained for two of the three paths. The power of these findings rested on the fact that it was possible to use somewhat different indicators to define the same abstract latent construct at the two sites. Recent studies have been designed to test for the replicability of models based on parental skills manifest during family problem-solving with data from the Oregon and Iowa sites. Rueter and Conger (1995) provided a cross-site replication of Forgatch's (1989) earlier findings.

Passive longitudinal designs can provide descriptions of growth and covariates for growth that are very useful in building a theory of socialization. For example, Forgatch et al. (1997) showed worsening family problem-solving outcomes were associated with increases in childhood antisocial behavior. These findings generate some fascinating hypotheses but reveal very little about cause and effect. As a more direct test, Forgatch (1991) argued for random assignment field trials. Here, families assigned to the experimental group received specific training in parenting skills and comparison groups did not. Follow-up comparison of experimental and control groups determined whether or not the manipulation increased parenting skills, and these in turn were associated with reduced antisocial behavior. The first study of this type by Dishion, Patterson, and Kavanagh (1992) was based on a sample of preadolescents thought to be at risk of substance abuse. Follow-up showed significant improvements in parental discipline practices in the experimental as contrasted with the control group; and teacher ratings showed significant reductions in antisocial behavior for the former but not the latter. The SEM showed that the measures of discipline at termination correlated significantly with the changes in antisocial behavior. Three additional random assignment studies are currently underway at OSLC, all were designed to test the causal status of various components of correlational models about development.

The necessary descriptive studies examining the way in which parenting differences vary as a function of gender of child and parent and with age of child are just beginning. The Oregon parenting studies summarized thus far have primarily focused on the interval from 10 to 18 years of age as it occurs in at-risk families living in a medium-size metropolitan setting. For that limited window, the findings suggest that psychologists are well on the way to constructing a performance theory that not only accounts for a substantial portion of the variance in antisocial childhood behavior but, in addition, significantly predicts early onset and chronic offending (Patterson, Forgatch, Yoerger, & Stoolmiller, 1997).

Effects of Context on Parenting

One question to be answered by a theory of parenting concerns the impact of context (social disadvantage, divorce, parental stress, parental depression, and parental antisocial behavior) on child adjustment outcomes. Each of these variables might be assumed to contribute directly to increased risk for adjustment. From a social-interactional perspective, such variables produce negative outcomes for child adjustment only if they cause disruptions in the social interchanges between parent and child. In the first test of this hypothesis, Patterson (1983) showed daily variations in maternal stress covaried with observed daily variations in mother's irritable reactions to the child. The pilot study had failed to address the connection between increased maternal irritability and increases in negative child outcomes. However, a subsequent Snyder (1991) study showed that daily variations in levels of maternal stress covaried with disruptions in discipline practices and this in turn with increases in child problem behaviors.

Outside stressors can disrupt parenting, not only at the microsocial level (e.g., observed irritability), but even at the level of macromeasures of parenting. The disrupted interaction hypothesis has been tested at least a dozen times using macromodels on a range of contextual variables such as divorce, social disadvantage, parental depression, and antisocial behavior. In each case, we assumed that the impact of the contextual variable on child adjustment would be mediated by the impact on parenting practices. For example, models testing the effect of poverty on delinquency (Larzelere & Patterson, 1990; Laub & Sampson, 1988), the impact of school failure and rejection by peers on boys' depressed mood (Patterson & Stoolmiller, 1991), and the effect of divorce on antisocial behavior (Forgatch et al., 1996) demonstrated that the effects of negative context on child outcomes were mediated by parenting practices.

EXTENDING THE MACROMODEL OF PARENTING

A performance model can be a flexible affair that expands as the studies proceed. Studies demonstrate that parenting practices determine childhood antisocial behaviors. The next question might then be: What determines whether parents will employ effective or ineffective practices? The researcher is moving from a concern with immediate or proximal determinants to a deeper level of concern with what it is that controls the proximal determinants. This section provides a brief description of our efforts to move to this second level of concerns by examining variables measuring emotion and social cognitions.

The working hypothesis is that parenting practices and contingencies directly control both prosocial and deviant behaviors of the child; measures of emotion and social cognition in turn play a key role in determining parenting practices and contingencies. Emotion and social-cognitive variables are cast in the role of indirect contributors to deviant outcomes.

Emotions as Causes for Aggression

An extensive literature review by Dix (1991) suggested that families with problem children are characterized by high levels of conflict and negative emotions together with low levels of warmth and positive emotions. In his review, Feshbach (1979) also noted that aggressive children are often found to be angry and frustrated. The correlations presented in these reviews are in keeping with the hypothesis that frustration and anger are major causes for aggressive behavior. Alternatively, it may be that although these emotions are ubiquitous components of family interactions, they are products rather than direct causes for aggressive and delinquent behaviors.

Experience in treating families of aggressive children put us in close agreement with the findings from the Dix (1991) review. The *most* salient feature of clinical contacts with families of antisocial boys was the ubiquitous presence of negative emotions, such as irritability, anger, contempt, fear, and perhaps sadness. Of these, irritability seemed to occur most frequently. However, in the mid-1960s when these studies began, we had no means, other than self-report, of measuring emotion variables. In the past decade, two procedures for directly assessing emotion in family interaction have been developed. One approach is to require observers not only to give a sequential description of the content of social exchange but also to rate positive and negative changes from neutral emotion. In the home, such ratings were entered in real time into small computers held by the observers (Dishion, Gardner, Patterson, Reid, & Thibodeaux, 1983). More recently, the coding of facial affect from videotapes was brought into the Oregon Center by Marion Forgatch. Her studies were based on the Specific Affect Coding System (SPAFF) developed by Gottman, McCoy, Coan, and Collier (1996), who based their work on the earlier studies by Ekman and Freisen (1975).

In keeping with our clinical impressions, observer ratings of family interactions showed that negative emotion was a frequent event. Mothers in a clinical sample were coded as displaying negative affect in 31.1% of their interactions compared with 16.5% for mothers from the OYS at-risk sample (Patterson et al., 1992). The comparable figures on aversive behaviors for boys in the clinical and at-risk OYS samples were 16.3% and 10.4% respectively.

One of the best settings for the study of emotions was provided in videotapes of family problem-solving sessions. Capaldi, Forgatch, and Crosby (1994) studied OYS problem-solving sessions repeated from Grade 8 through Grade 10, coded according to the Gottman et al. (1996) SPAFF. The findings showed that about a third of parents' reactions and about half of the adolescents' reactions tended to be emotionally toned. With age, there was a significant increase in the growth of adolescent contempt and affection but a decrease in behavior rates for sadness and humor.

We hypothesized that the impact of emotion on child adjustment would be mediated by parenting practices. If this is true, then emotional variables will correlate with disrupted parenting. Observers' ratings of negative emotions made during family problem-solving were significantly correlated with disrupted family problem-solving outcomes

(Forgatch, 1989). The next study went on to demonstrate that the effect of adolescent negative emotion on delinquency was mediated through disrupted monitoring. It is simply more difficult to supervise an angry and contemptuous adolescent. Less monitoring means greater involvement with deviant peers and a corresponding increase in risk of delinquent behavior and substance use (Dishion, Duncan, Eddy, Fagot, & Fetrow, 1994). Forgatch also found that mothers' use of humor contributed to increased effectiveness in monitoring.

Typically, it is assumed that a lack of parental warmth causes deviant behavior in children (Dix, 1991). Alternatively, we assumed that deviant child behavior leads to a lack of warmth and to parental rejection (Patterson, 1986). A structural equation analysis by Patterson and Dishion (1988) supported the idea that the aversive quality of the child's behavior may diminish parental warmth. Most likely, the relation between child adjustment and parental warmth is bidirectional. An initial lack of maternal warmth may also be a cause for parental noncontingent reactions in the first place.

Figure 8.3 projects our future strategy for fitting emotion and social-cognition (and biology as well) variables into a larger model. As long as the data support the hypothesis, we will continue to think of the proximal causes in the macromodel as being parenting skills. Emotional (and social-cognitive and biological) variables may help to explain why some parents at some times become ineffective. For example, divorce produces child adjustment problems primarily in families where the parenting practices become disrupted (Forgatch et al., 1996). In a similar vein, the main effects of parent antisocial behavior, poverty, and social disadvantage on childhood antisocial outcomes are mediated through disrupted parenting practices (Bank, Forgatch, Patterson, & Fetrow, 1993; Conger, McCarty, Yang, Lahey, & Kropp, 1984; Laub & Sampson, 1988).

I hypothesized that emotion, social-cognitive, and biological variables may also play an important role by explaining the relationship between context and parenting practices. In Figure 8.3, there is a hypothesized indirect path from context variables to emotion and social cognitive variables and a direct path to disrupted parenting. The model implies that emotions, cognitions, and biological variables may be helpful in understanding more precisely when parent practices will break down and when they will not. For example, a failure to control negative emotion will be a significant predictor

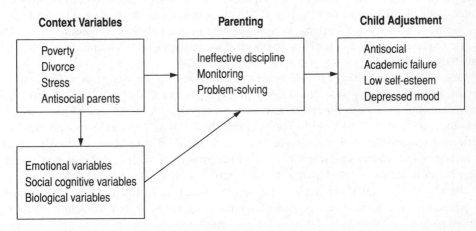

Figure 8.3　Emotion as Indirect Causal Agent in Parenting Model

of accompanying ineffective parenting practices. In turn, the risk for these emotional reactions is likely to be greater for antisocial, depressed, and socially disadvantaged parents. This more complex model has immediate implications for prevention trials. It suggests that teaching mothers more effective means for controlling negative emotions might enhance treatment outcomes based on training in parenting practices alone (Patterson, Dishion, & Chamberlain, 1993).

Parental Social-Cognition Variables as Causes

In the past decade, research has focused on social-cognitive variables that might explain why parents behave as they do (Darling & Steinberg, 1993). Our own clinical studies also suggested a correlation between faulty parental perceptions and poor child adjustment. Programmatic observational studies of abused children and their families showed that abusive parents were extremely biased in their perceptions of what constitutes deviant child behavior (Reid, Kavanagh, & Baldwin, 1987; Reid, Patterson, & Loeber, 1982). Abusive parents tended to rate their children as being significantly more deviant than did parents in other at-risk samples, even though abused children did not differ significantly from other at-risk children in their observed behavior. Parental negative attributions might be measured by the discrepancy between what observers code and what the mother perceives to be child deviant behaviors. Modeling this measure of negative attribution could show whether this contributes above and beyond what is measured as parenting skill to predict future antisocial outcomes.

Laboratory studies provided further confirmation for the importance of this variable. In these studies, parents of problem and nonproblem children were asked to classify ongoing responses from videotapes of children as to deviant or nondeviant status. Parents of problem children tended to be overly inclusive in that they classified as deviant what observers and other parents would classify as neutral or prosocial (Holleran, Littman, Freund, & Schmaling, 1982; Lorber, 1981; Schmaling & Patterson, 1984). Moreover, the cognitive variable "overly inclusive" correlated significantly with the mothers' observed rates of aversive behavior in the home.

Maternal perceptions about themselves might also contribute to parenting practices but not directly to child adjustment. Greenwald (1989) used the OYS data to demonstrate that maternal reports of their own irritability correlated with maternal reports of stress. However, the contribution to child outcomes was entirely mediated through the discipline construct (observations of what parents do).

These correlations do not establish what is cause and what is effect. We hypothesized that parental distortion in the perception of deviancy was one determinant for disrupted parenting practices. As parents and as investigators, we assumed that our beliefs, values, and reports about what we do *must* have some impact on child adjustment. There is an emerging consensus, however, that the impact of these cognitions on child adjustment is mediated through parenting practices. Consistent with the social interactional point of view, Darling and Steinberg's (1993) proposed that the effect of parental beliefs and values on child adjustment is mediated by what parents actually do. This means that given a path coefficient of say .3 between beliefs and parenting practices and a second path coefficient of .3 between parenting and child adjustment, then the correlation of beliefs with adjustment would be only about .09. Sigel and his colleagues at Educational Testing Service carried out programmatic studies on this problem. These studies on parental cognitions have found the relation between child outcomes and parental beliefs, values, and cognitions to be negligible (Hess & McDevitt, 1986; Sigel, 1985, 1986). The mediation model proposed in this chapter and by Darling and Steinberg (1993) is also consistent with findings from studies by Kochanska, Kuczynski, and Radke-Yarrow (1988) and Luster, Rhoades, and Haas (1989).

Measures of parental emotion and cognitions make important contributions to our understanding of antisocial behavior in children. However, the findings are consistent with the hypothesis that the contribution of these variables to child adjustment is indirect rather than direct.

Child Cognitions as Causes

Studies of the impact of children's cognitions on child adjustment have introduced procedures that differ from those used in studies of parental cognitions. For this reason, the two sets of findings are reviewed in different sections. Most of the studies of child cognitions are focused on measures of internalized mechanisms (attitudes, delay of gratification, executive impairment) that have something to do with either self-control or negative attributions.

Two issues focus the discussion. One has to do with the inadequacy of measures of child internal processes and the other with their status as direct causes for antisocial behavior. This brief review will examine studies that employ measures of self-esteem, antisocial attitudes, verbal IQ as a measure of impaired executive functioning and social-information processing.

Studies have repeatedly shown that child self-esteem correlates with police arrests, achievement, and deviant peer involvement. There is a strong presumption that increasing self-esteem will cause an increase in achievement (Gardner, 1992). We hypothesize that self-esteem is a correlate but not a cause. Bank, Burraston, and Patterson (1996) used a longitudinal design to test this hypothesis and showed that although self-esteem correlated with achievement, it did not account for changes in achievement. The findings replicate earlier findings from longitudinal studies of self-esteem by Bachman and O'Malley (1977). The findings are also consistent with those from a cross-sectional design by Ryan, Corville-Smith, and Adams (1995).

We hypothesized that although measures of child cognition might correlate with adjustment outcomes, their contribution will become nonsignificant when compared in multivariate designs with the contribution of parenting practices. In our first study of this type, adolescent reports of attitudes about school, authority, and antisocial behavior were used to predict school dropout for the OYS longitudinal study (Patterson & Yoerger, 1995). The measure of internalized attitudes was based on the Elliott, Huizinga, and Ageton (1985) effort to test Gottfredson and Hirschi's (1990) social-control theory. In that theory, a failure to internalize parental and societal values, beliefs, and attitudes supportive of academic achievement would predict future school dropout. Alternatively, the Oregon parenting model hypothesizes that ineffective parenting and antisocial childhood behavior are the primary predictors for school dropout. Antisocial behavior with its core of noncompliance directly causes academic slowdown as shown in studies by Cobb and Hops (1973); DeBaryshe, Patterson, and Capaldi (1993); and Shinn, Ramsey, Walker, Stieber, and O'Neill (1987). In the Oregon model, antischool attitudes are seen as a byproduct of the same process that produced the antisocial behavior.

As a test of this model, grade-school measures of antisocial attitudes, context, parenting practices, and child adjustment were used to predict school dropout by 18 years of age. The data from the boys in the OYS longitudinal data set for at-risk families showed that 51% of the sample had dropped out of school by 18 years of age. A univariate logistic regression analysis showed that each of the attitude measures and all the contextual, parenting, and child adjustment variables assessed at Grade 4 significantly predicted later school dropout. These findings are in accord with predictions from both the social control and the parenting theory. The composite measure of antisocial attitudes continued to make a significant prediction even after the contribution of social disadvantage (education + occupation) and parental IQ had been partialed out. However, its contribution had been reduced from .93 to .79. In keeping with our prediction, the contribution of the attitude measure became nonsignificant when the parenting measures were introduced; this means that ineffective parenting makes a contribution that includes the information contained in the measure of child internalized attitudes. As expected, when the composite score for antisocial behavior was introduced, the contribution of all the prior variables became nonsignificant.

The findings suggest that the impact of internalized attitudes on child adjustment is entirely mediated by parenting practices. We can only guess at what the function of antisocial attitudes might be. For example, it may constitute a prerequisite for entrance into a deviant peer group but is not a direct cause of school dropout. The findings do not support assumptions made by Gottfredson and Hirschi's social control theory.

Moffitt and Silva (1988) hypothesized that impaired executive capacity is an important causal variable for delinquent acts. They, along with Quay (1987), and Wilson and Herrnstein (1985) hypothesized that measures of child verbal IQ could serve as a marker variable for an impaired executive function. These theorists noted that there are literally hundreds of studies showing antisocial boys score about a standard deviation lower than the general population on measures of verbal IQ (Quay, 1987). Studies show that delinquents score significantly higher on performance than on verbal measures of IQ.

From a social interactional perspective, it is assumed that antisocial childhood behaviors lead to lower achievement, and reduce verbal IQ scores, but leave performance measures relatively unaffected. Patterson and Yoerger (1995) used data from the OYS to test this assumption. They showed, as expected, that all childhood measures—context, verbal IQ, parenting, antisocial child, and deviant peers—correlated significantly with early arrest. However, in the multivariate analysis when measures of parenting and child antisocial behavior were entered, the contribution of child verbal IQ became nonsignificant. The findings are consistent with the hypothesis that reduced verbal IQ scores are a product of the process rather than a cause.

Several decades of findings attest to the significant relation between antisocial behavior and the inability to delay gratification (Kochanska, 1991, 1995; Krueger, Caspi, Moffitt, White, & Stouthamer-Loeber, 1996; Mischel, 1976; Scaramella, 1994). I propose that observations of toddler noncompliance and coerciveness will predict measures of delay of gratification. In fact, this effect has been shown in studies by Funder, Block, and Block (1983) and Bem and Funder (1978). Kochanska and Aksan (1995) found a correlation of .45 between the child's observed compliance and the laboratory task measure of resistance to temptation. Lytton and Zwirner (1975) also found a correlation of .44 between observers' ratings of compliance and their ratings of internalization of standards suggesting that one variable is simply a surrogate of the other.

A test of this hypothesis requires a longitudinal study that begins at the toddler stage with provision for observations of parenting, compliance-coercion, and delay of gratification at 24, 48, and 72 months. At Grade 3, ratings by teachers and parents together with peer nomination data on antisocial behavior would serve as the criterion variables. Do the measures of delay of gratification account for unique variance in predicting later antisocial behavior? The cognitive position implies that measures of the process by which rules are internalized should account for more variance than simple measures of compliance-coercion. Although most developmental theorists agree on the importance of the outcome for compliance training during the toddler stage, they would tend to see it as a necessary but not sufficient condition for effective socialization. The social interactional perspective would take the position that noncompliance plus coercion sets the stage for a developmental progression that is devastating for the child. From this point of view, noncompliance plus coercion constitute necessary and sufficient conditions for entrance to a progression to increasing deviance. The stages in the progression include rejection by peers, parents, and teachers; and school failure, depressed moods, and eventual risk for early entrance into the juvenile justice system (Patterson et al., 1992). Some modern studies, such as Kochanska's longitudinal studies, have high-quality data that could be used to test the proposed model; yet to my knowledge, no multivariate studies have been undertaken to do that.

As detailed in Patterson (1996), attachment theory would be another likely candidate for inclusion in a performance model although it does not correlate consistently with measures of child adjustment. Fagot and Kavanagh (1990, 1993) catalog their own failure and that of others to predict child adjustment from measures of attachment based on the Strange Situation test. According to their review, significant findings obtain only for boys, not for girls, and only for at-risk families, not for normal families. Finally, the amount of variance accounted for tends to be less than 10%. This is hardly a robust set of findings for developmental psychology's premier effort to construct a parenting model based on internalized mechanisms. From a social interactional point of view, it would be important to compare the contribution of parenting skills and attachment scores in predicting future adjustment. Does the attachment measure contribute beyond what is obtained from measures of parenting skill? We do not know.

In a more positive vein, however, Paley, Conger, and Harold (in press) used data from the Iowa Youth Study to demonstrate that adolescents' negative perceptions of fathers contributed unique variance in predicting adolescent adjustment behavior 2 years later. Adolescents' perceptions of negative aspects of fathers contributed above and beyond observed fathers' negative behaviors.

Dodge, Pettit, Bates, and Valente (1995) test direct and indirect effects of social-information-processing variables in predicting future aggressive behavior for children. In this study, mothers of 584 families were interviewed when the children were in kindergarten to estimate the likelihood of child abuse. In a direct effect model, the path coefficient from this surrogate measure of parenting to teacher ratings of externalizing at Grades 3 and 4 was .24. Early abuse was also significantly correlated with social-information-processing variables assessed consecutively over the 4-year period. Two of these cognitive variables were significantly related to child abuse and ratings of externalizing behavior. In the mediational model, the path from parenting to externalizing was reduced by 33% but remained significant. Clearly, this is a mediational effect and a case for the unique contribution of cognitive variables.

However, there are concerns about this model related to measurement issues. The mediational model accounts for only 5% of the variance in measures of antisocial behavior suggesting that measures of both parenting and social-information-processing variables are very weak. For example, the parenting variable correlates only .15 with the initial teacher ratings of externalizing. The parenting practices variable is assessed by interviews, something that does not work well in our studies, further buttressing this concern. We are currently planning to replicate the design and to correct some of these flaws.

It seems that some measures of child internalized processes, such as antisocial attitude or verbal IQ, do not make direct outcomes to school dropout or to delinquency. However, several findings suggest that childhood negative attributions about family members and peers may make both direct and indirect contributions to negative outcomes.

MICROTHEORY ABOUT PARENTING: WHY DOES THE CHILD CHANGE?

Macrotheories of parenting fail to illuminate three different processes that are central to socialization. First, knowing that ineffective parental discipline, monitoring, and family problem-solving are related to negative child adjustment outcomes does not explain how these practices bring about changes in the child. Darling and Steinberg (1993) pointed out that the study of processes associated with parenting has been a major omission; none of the parenting theories clearly define testable mechanisms that could explain change in the child. Second, these macromodels cannot satisfactorily explain why the child maintains these behaviors across time and across settings. Third, and most important, macromodels cannot address the key developmental question: How does child behavior change its form? Questions such as these require a microlevel analysis of parent-child interactions.

The microsocial theory attempts to explain the dynamics of how dyads change each other over time. Most of our studies were comparisons of observed interactions for problem and nonproblem samples. The studies tended to be narrowly focused on the development of coercive behaviors in marital partners (Hops, Sherman, & Biglan, 1990) and children's interactions with family members (Snyder & Patterson, 1995) and peers (Dishion, Duncan, et al., 1994). The mechanism most frequently studied has been applications of escape conditioning (negative reinforcement) arrangements to ongoing, observed social-interaction sequences. Other studies of special environments, such as permissive nursery schools, correctional institutions, and laboratory studies of social exchanges among deviant peers had a focus on positive payoffs (Dishion, French, & Patterson, 1995; Patterson, Littman, & Bricker, 1967) for antisocial behavior.

The child is viewed as an active seeker and selector rather than a passive recipient of contingencies provided by others. The child contributes by selecting family members with whom to interact and actively seeks, selects, and shapes the behavior of persons in the immediate surround (Patterson, 1976). The selections are based on what the environment provides. After several hundred trials, the child's behaviors and others' reactions become overlearned patterns that require little or no active cognitive processing for employment.

The principal mechanism for teaching the child to use coercive behaviors is based on payoffs provided by parents and siblings during conflict episodes. Problem families are highly selective in what they pay off for during conflict episodes; they tend not to pay off for prosocial behaviors but provide higher payoffs than do normal families for coercive behaviors (Snyder & Patterson, 1995). In a sense, problem families function as simple short-term maximizing systems that inadvertently contribute to their own long-term misery.

Brief History

In order to build a performance theory, one must have a theory. However, each major theory of child aggression (frustration, modeling, social-cognitive, and reinforcement) was obviously fatally flawed (Patterson, 1996) when set to the task of explaining child aggression as it occurred in natural settings. The problem with reinforcement theory was that laboratory studies consistently failed to show a linear relation between reinforcement density and response strength (Herrnstein, 1974). This meant that a reinforcement theory could not account for observed individual differences in performance of aggression. Even so, it seemed to OSLC researchers that information about contingencies was essential in analyzing the function of child aggression.

In the mid-1960s, OSLC began building a microsocial-based performance model for children's aggressive behavior, studying its function as aggression occurred in nursery schools (Patterson, Littman, & Bricker, 1967). These very first field studies showed that the kind of functions served by child aggression varied depending on setting (home or school) and the person (parent, sibling, or peer) interacting with the child. The reinforcement in families was analogous to escape conditioning, where the child tended to select the behaviors that most effectively terminated a conflict episode with other family members. In other settings such as a permissive nursery school, however, the payoffs for overt aggression might include the victim giving up a disputed toy (Patterson, Littman, & Bricker, 1967). If the victim protested or counterattacked and the initiator escalated his or her attack thus winning the toy, then the payoff was more analogous to the escape conditioning found in homes. In this setting, both positive reinforcement and escape conditioning provided rich schedules of support for aggressive behavior. Observing interactions in institutional settings provides many examples like this, where the tough adolescent gets what he or she wants. Even more interesting, both the staff and the adolescent peer group in that setting are more likely to pay off for deviant behavior than for prosocial behavior (Buehler, Patterson, & Furniss, 1966; Sanson-Fisher, Seymour, Montgomery, & Stokes, 1978).

Age, Agents, Settings, and Contingencies

As already noted, much of the training in the family setting for children's coercive behaviors, such as noncompliance, yelling, whining, teasing, temper tantrums, and hitting, took place in conflict situations (Patterson, 1982). During conflict episodes, the child might try a number of things before selecting one that "worked" (i.e., it was followed by termination of the conflict). Unpublished data from the study by Snyder and Patterson (1995) showed that the utility for child coercive behaviors was on the average .35 in normal families compared with .59 for problem boys from distressed families. Coercive child behavior was significantly ($p < .01$) more likely to be followed by termination of conflict in problem than in nonproblem families. This three-step dance (conflict, coercive reaction, termination of conflict) defines what is meant by escape conditioning or negative reinforcement in the operant literature.

Several small-scale experiments demonstrated that even a few trials with this kind of reinforcement produced dramatic changes in both prosocial and deviant behaviors (Patterson, 1982). Observations of preschool mother-child dyads showed that distressed families had nearly twice as many conflicts as did nondistressed families (Snyder & Patterson, 1995). In distressed families, such conflicts took up about 4% of the dyads' interactions. Many of the events that started conflicts in families were readily identified as "aversive" (e.g., a sibling teases or hits or a mother scolds; Patterson & Cobb, 1971, 1973).

To some extent, what is aversive may vary from one individual to another and at the extremes may become an idiosyncratic affair. For example, Carr's 1988 programmatic studies showed that some reacted to a request to do homework or chores as if the request were aversive (i.e., it would precipitate a conflict). Handicapped children learned several techniques for escaping from such aversive conditions; these included temper tantrums, physical attacks on staff, and self-injurious behavior. If one reaction didn't alter the behavior of the staff person, the child would often escalate to higher amplitude behaviors. Carr and Horner and Day's (1991) systematic observations and experiments constitute some of the most convincing existing evidence for the contribution of the escape conditioning arrangement to the development of both coercive and prosocial behavior.

During a series of conflicts, a child is likely to use a whole range of behaviors (Snyder & Patterson, 1995). To understand the impact of reinforcement on a child behavior such as "whining," researchers must begin by calculating the relative payoffs for all of the other behaviors that the child tried during conflict. In one column, the frequencies of everything the child did during conflict are listed; the adjoining column lists the frequency each response was followed by the termination of the conflict. The analysis begins at this molecular intraindividual level. The question is straightforward. During a conflict episode, which is more successful in terminating the conflict, negotiating, using humor, temper tantrum, and so on? Listing the relative frequencies for what the child does during conflict (the repertoire) should be a reliable reflector of social environmental payoffs. Assuming that the individual is selectively shopping (from settings, persons, and activities) to maximize the payoffs, then his or her relative rates of behaviors are expected to match the relative rates of payoffs provided in this family. Behaviors with the highest frequency of payoffs should occur most frequently, and those with the lowest relative rate of payoff should occur infrequently. The match can be expressed as a correlation coefficient. For example, in highly controlled laboratory settings, a correlation of .9 to 1.0 is expected. In the Snyder and Patterson (1995) study, the average match for the boys was .59. The mother's behavior reflected a similar correlation between the relative rates for her behaviors to payoffs provided by the child. The formulation is based in part on the contributions of Herrnstein's (1961) matching law to modern reinforcement theory (e.g., Davison & McCarthy, 1988).

The data from the Snyder and Patterson (1995) study of preschool sons and their mothers showed that in distressed families, only coercive child behaviors were related to effective conflict resolution; whereas in nondistressed families, boys' prosocial and coercive behaviors were significantly related to termination of conflict. This is a critical finding, because it may explain why antisocial boys tend to also be socially unskilled.

As noted earlier, because reinforcement schedules are not linearly related to response strength, a reinforcement theory cannot account for individual differences in children's aggression. By itself, the analysis of intraindividual relative rates of payoffs and relative rates of behavior does not solve that problem. Consider a family with only four conflict episodes that were successfully terminated by the child. A temper tantrum led to successful termination for one of these; so the relative payoff was 25%. Compare this with a child from a distressed family where 100 conflicts were successfully terminated by the child, and 25% of these payoffs followed the child's temper tantrum. To predict individual differences, information is needed both about the relative payoffs and the number of training trials. Frequency of conflict defines what is meant by training trials. We assumed that in a multiple regression analysis, information for the relative payoffs for coercive behaviors and frequency of family conflict would both make significant and unique contributions in accounting for variance in measures of antisocial outcomes. The two variables were used to predict observed child deviancy rates a week later (Snyder & Patterson, 1995). The multiple correlation showed that the reinforcement and frequency of conflict variables accounted for 65% of the variance in the criterion measure. Differences in reinforcement history accounted for individual differences in child coerciveness.

Snyder, Schrepferman, and St. Peter (1997) have replicated the findings using a larger sample of 5- to 15-year-old boys and girls referred for treatment because of antisocial behavior problems. The baseline observation data were collected in the home prior to treatment. The criterion consisted of a composite measure of police arrest and out-of-home placement that occurred during a 2-year follow-up. The two reinforcement variables accounted for 38% of the variance in predicting the data from community records. We concluded that a microsocial-based performance theory may function as successfully as does the macroparenting model in predicting negative child outcomes. Assuming that these criterion variables have reliabilities in the .6 to .8 range suggests that for both the macro- and the microtheories, we may be accounting for the majority of the available variance.

The driving assumption behind the microsocial theory has been that during conflict episodes both parents and siblings provide payoffs that shape a wide range of prosocial and coercive behaviors. We are now in a position to begin the study of positive payoffs for prosocial behaviors during nonconflict exchanges. The framework is also being expanded to study the simultaneous contributions of parents, siblings, and deviant peers (Bank, Patterson, Burraston, & Shortt, 1995; Dishion, Andrews, & Crosby, 1995).

Why Are Traits Stable across Settings and Time?

Numerous studies have established that given adequate measures, childhood aggressive behaviors are surprisingly stable across time (Olweus, 1979) and settings (Wright, 1983). For example, Ramsey, Patterson, and Walker (1990) used data from multiple agents assessed in the home at Grade 4 to define an antisocial construct. At Grade 5, data from teachers, peers, and observers in classroom and playground defined the antisocial construct for the school setting. The across-time and -setting path coefficient was .72. Furthermore, growth in antisocial behavior is suspected to be more the exception than the rule. For example, the data suggest a great deal of growth in antisocial behavior during the preschool years (Patterson, 1992) with new cases added during elementary school. The new addition seems to come primarily from families in transition.

The question for the developmental theorist is, how are these stabilities to be explained? We believe that these stabilities can only be explained at the microsocial level. The child is essentially constructing a system that is stable across settings and across time. The coercive style and limited set of social survival skills produce predictable reactions from the social environment. What the child is doing and reactions to these behaviors are highly stable over time. For example, longitudinal data shows that the stabilities for child adjustment and for parenting are both high and parallel in magnitude (Patterson & Bank, 1989). Within a social interactional framework, we hypothesized that the relative rates of reinforcement for prosocial and for deviant behaviors provide the mechanism that determines these stabilities.

Reinforcement theory makes it clear that behavior under the control of reinforcing contingencies will return to baseline level in short order if the contingencies are withdrawn. As pointed out by Maccoby (1992), given the presumed differences in reinforcement from one setting to another, how then does one explain stability? The answer lies in reconsidering the role of the child as an active agent in both selecting and shaping the social environment. A common failing of the early developmental models of parenting (Darling & Steinberg, 1993) was that they didn't take into account the child's active contribution to the process. In any given setting, the child actively selects the behaviors that work best in maximizing immediate payoffs. He or she selects among settings and among activities and individuals within settings. For example, even casual observations suggest that antisocial boys tend to avoid playground activities that are adult supervised and organized. Alternatively, children select corners of the playground that are not readily under adult surveillance (D. Pepler, personal communication, October 4, 1995).

The selectivity hypothesis involves three separate hypotheses:

1. Children tend to select children who are most like them. Thus, antisocial boys are significantly more likely to select antisocial boys to hang out with as demonstrated in longitudinal studies, such as Dishion, Andrews, and Crosby (1995) and Cairns and Cairns (1991).

2. Boys who are similar mutually reinforce one another at higher levels than dissimilar boys. Thus, antisocial boys should tend to reinforce each other but be less likely to reinforce normal boys; conversely, normal boys should be more reinforcing to normal boys and less reinforcing to antisocial boys. Studies of preschool (Snyder, West, Stockemer, Gibbons, & Almquist-Parks, 1996) and adolescent peers (Dishion, Andrews, & Crosby, 1995) showed that this was indeed true. For example, Dishion's coding of videotapes showed that deviant dyads were more likely to reinforce each other contingent on "rule-breaking talk." Structurally, one boy's rule-breaking talk was reciprocated by the second boy.

3. Children select as friends those who maximize payoffs. Snyder et al. (1996) tested this hypothesis by using observation data collected in a nursery school setting for a high-risk sample. He showed that children selected as friends also tended to be those children who maximized the target child's relative payoffs. The average correlation between expressed preference and payoff ratios (positive/negative) ranged from .69 to .83.

Finally, one further aspect of stability should be introduced. Studies by Timberlake (1995) and the earlier work by Premack (1965) emphasize that the structure of child behaviors, as reflected in ranking by relative rates, also defines the child's point of equilibrium. Components of structure can be used to either inhibit or facilitate change; but change at any point means shifting the entire structure. Future studies of stability should be framed in part by these considerations from equilibrium theory. These studies will be based on longitudinal data sets that include microsocial variables; such data do not now exist.

What Determines Changes in the Form of Antisocial Behavior?

Children who remain in the coercion process show marked changes in the form of aversive behaviors as a function of age (Patterson, 1995; Patterson et al., 1992). The amplitude or severity of the coercive antisocial behaviors increases with age. Childish forms of hitting become fighting, and stealing from mother's purse is transformed to shoplifting. We assumed that in some families escalation would be more likely to pay off in that it would increase the likelihood the other person would terminate the conflict. We found that the problem child and the mother were most likely to escalate during conflict (Patterson, 1980). The data also showed that problem families were much more likely to escalate in the amplitude of their coercive behaviors during conflict exchanges than were members of nonproblem families (Snyder, Edwards, McGraw, Kilgore, & Holton, 1994). Moreover, when a member of problem families escalated coercive behaviors, the other family members were more likely to back off. Escalation works. Reid, Patterson, and Lorber (1981) showed that escalation to hitting was more likely to occur during longer conflict bouts, with the risk increasing markedly at about 18 s duration in at-risk families. The mean duration of conflicts was about 65 s for at-risk families in the OYS and 74 s for a sample of families of aggressive children referred for treatment. The findings suggest rich reinforcement opportunities for the progression from noncompliance to temper tantrums and hitting in young toddlers (Patterson, 1992).

As the child moves into the elementary grades, he or she usually has selected or formed a deviant peer group. The powerful microsocial processes within these groups are thought to be the mechanism that determines the metamorphosis from childish antisocial acts to juvenile offenses. The direct cause for early involvement with deviant peers lies in the lack of supervision provided by parents (e.g., the child is allowed on the streets at a very early age without adult supervision) as shown in the studies by Stoolmiller (1994). Patterson (1993) demonstrated that those boys who were the first to experiment with new forms of antisocial behavior had also been among the first to be heavily involved with deviant peers. Growth in new forms of antisocial behavior (e.g., substance use, truancy) were directly related to increased growth for involvement with deviant peers and in unsupervised time spent out of the home. As noted earlier, Dishion's work showed that the positive reinforcement for deviancy provided by deviant peers is a key mechanism driving new forms of antisocial behavior.

If the behavior is changing in form, how do researchers know that it is still the same thing? Patterson (1993) showed that over time each new form of problem behavior loaded on the same general deviancy factor. In a sense, stability and orderly change are part of the same process.

WHAT IS INTERNALIZED?

Summaries of Experiential History

In the earlier discussion of macro- and micromodels, measurement issues entirely guided the selection of cognitive variables and broader considerations about what a child might internalize. In this speculative context, historic and reconstructed historic accounts are examined as potential candidates for inclusion within a performance model. Finally, the most promising of the internalized variables will be considered: delay of gratification or resistance to temptation. These laboratory-based procedures are placed within the framework of mediated performance models.

History and Reconstructions of History

Most theories about economics, crime, child behavior, and education are based on some variation of rational choice theory. Human behavior is assumed to be governed by a series of decisions and choices. This process is occasionally overwhelmed by emotional forces. However, investigators of rational behavior (Dawes, 1988; Piliavin, Hardyck, & Vadum, 1968; Slovic, Fischoff, & Lichtenstein, 1977) caution us that the empirical base for our societal faith in this model is far from solid. Dawes pointed out in his brilliant summary of a decade of work in the cognitive science that, even under the best of conditions, the individual is capable of only very limited types of rational thought. He suggested the phrase "shallow psychology" as an appropriate label for a rational-choice-based theory of human behavior. If human behavior is not governed by rational thought and occasionally by emotional upwellings, then what does govern behavior? We maintain our hold on the idea of "rational humans" because, even if it doesn't work very well as a theory, it is all we have.

An alternative perspective on human behavior and cognitions begins with Herbert Simon's (1982) work on bounded rationality. He points out that each individual is equipped with a biological computer that is inherently limited in the number of channels available at any given time for processing information. This limitation means that the complexity of moment-by-moment social experience is simply more than can be handled by active processing mechanisms. In our early observation codes for a dyad, four events were coded every 6 s. In an extremely simple dyadic exchange, that would provide 2,400 pieces of information per hour. In a normal but slightly more complex setting such as a car trip, the individual would have to process a multitude of additional new stimuli on a second-by-second basis. According to Tversky and Kahneman (1974), the flood of incoming information forces each individual to develop shortcuts in storing and representing experience. These considerations set limits or constraints on the processing of information from ongoing social behaviors. Within these constraints, some limited subset of all the person's social behaviors may be directly processed, whereas some other significant subsets are stored under various heuristics. Still other sets are not processed either directly or indirectly.

The reinforcing contingencies that control coercive behaviors are embedded in social exchanges. When the contingency occurs, there is good reason to believe that the event is not actively processed. This would be particularly true during conflict where much of this conflict behavior is overlearned and behaviors are shaped without the individual being aware of the process, as demonstrated in studies by Gewirtz and Boyd (1977) and Rosenfeld and Baer (1969). This position runs counter to the position taken by some cognitive theorists that all reinforcing events are cognitively processed such that if the expectancies do not occur, then the behavior will not be affected by contingencies (Bandura, 1981).

A future theory of social interaction will require a focus on the entire tripartite mix of overlearned social behaviors, cognitions, and emotions. Existing theories about any one of the three are too simplistic to be of much use in constructing a performance theory of ongoing interaction. We need a generation of young investigators who can move beyond an either-or position to address the far more complex question of how these three things work together in ongoing social interactions. In this context, Newtson (1990, 1993) offers some brilliant speculations about how a waveform theory could integrate all three pieces of information in describing ongoing dyadic interactions.

From this perspective, one would not expect the individual to be able to reconstruct an accurate accounting of his or her own history. Although present, the child failed to actively process most of it. Nevertheless, it is reasonable to examine the question: How much variance can we account for by studying individual reconstructions of past history?

Self-History and Rule-Governed Behavior

Child self-reports—whether of disciplinary confrontations, internal process, or personality traits—have been the cornerstone used to build socialization theories. However, when we attempted to use them as indicators for constructs in a performance theory, these measures became problematic.

A brief review of these contributions by OSLC's investigators revealed that prior to adolescence, children's self-reports about parenting or child adjustment variables simply do not converge very well with other measures of the same variable. The correlation of child report with teacher, parent, and observer data is usually in the range of .2 or less (Patterson & Capaldi, 1990; Patterson et al., 1992) and is further detailed in the psychometric studies by Capaldi and Patterson (1989). Parent reports about child-rearing history, discipline practices, and marital satisfaction seem to be of equally limited value (Patterson et al., 1992).

It could be said that measures of beliefs, values, and attitudes represent a reconstruction or higher order of organization for experiential history. Bella (1995a, 1995b) hypothesized that each individual builds a series of stories to explain self-identity and self-behavior. Some part of these stories and the specific values and beliefs reflected in them are probably modeled and explicitly taught by parents. It would be surprising then to find that self-reports of attitudes and beliefs accurately summarize experiential history or serve as valid predictors of future behavior (e.g., our own failed effort to use adolescent attitudes to predict school dropout). The lack of correspondence between attitude and performance has plagued social psychology for decades; but it may be that the strategy used to test the idea was too simplistic. Our own strategy would be to add a construct that measures whether or not the parent actually taught the skills necessary to comply with the beliefs and attitudes. For example, most parents of antisocial boys want their child to go to college; however, they neglect to teach him how to study and to do homework (DeBaryshe et al., 1993; Forgatch & Ramsey, 1994). Parents of antisocial boys believe it is good for children to do chores, but they fail to teach their child how to do them. In a similar manner, parents may believe that children should keep their word but fail to support them for "doing" what they "said" they would do. Risley and Twardosz (1976) demonstrated that a person learns to keep his or her word by being directly reinforced for doing what was committed to. I assumed that parent's beliefs and values correlate only moderately with the parent's disposition to actually teach the child the skills necessary to fulfill the requirements of the parent's values. Skills training would in turn correlate significantly with child outcome variables. Here, again, the cognitive variables make an important indirect but not a direct contribution to child outcome.

An examination of rules and rule-governed behavior might give studies a much more specific focus. Parents could be observed actually labeling ongoing experiences as exemplars of rules. Alternatively, researchers could ask what the child thinks the rules are. For example, antisocial children can verbalize the rule that aggression works (Perry, Perry, & Rasmussen, 1986). The child also believes that aggression is acceptable and legitimate and that it leads to increased status (Slaby & Guerra, 1988). All these variables have been shown to correlate significantly with children's antisocial behavior. If used in mediational models that included effective measures of parenting or reinforcement variables, would these effects be mediated by the child's self-reported "rule" variables? I don't think so, but researchers should find out.

The possibility should also be examined that, under some conditions, rule-governed behavior may impede behavior change. Skinner (1969) and Hayes (1988) showed that for those who possess language, rule-governed behavior may be both an asset and a potential liability. Having an accurate rule for what the payoffs are then makes it possible to shift behaviors very rapidly to maximize payoffs. But there is an extremely interesting flip side to rule-governed behavior (Hayes). If the contingencies supplied by the social environment change, then earlier rules are no longer functional. In this situation, the individual who is rule governed is less sensitive to changes in the social environment. This phenomenon is often apparent during treatment; it applies both to the child and the parent. The effect is to produce dramatic increases in resistance to change (Patterson & Chamberlain, 1994). We hypothesized that one important function served by historic accounts was to provide a significant basis for resisting behavior change. The individual's "story" may function like a cocoon protecting the person from the necessity for change. For example, Bella (1995a, 1995b) details the process by which tobacco corporate executives and slave owners selectively organized information to support their positions. This strategy effectively neutralizes counterinformation and, in so doing, effectively resists the necessity for change. In like fashion, family members' reconstructions of history may also retard change and maintain the continuity of pathology in a family.

Negative Attributions

A salient candidate for an effective internalized mechanism would be the variable, "negative attribution," as assessed in the social-information-processing model (Dodge et al., 1995). To assess this variable, the child responds to a set of vignettes about what a child would do who finds him- or herself in a series of ambiguous situations. A key finding is that in an ambiguous situation, aggressive children report that there is a high likelihood of being attacked by peers. Dodge et al. interpreted this report as a measure of bias or negative attribution. They also demonstrated that it correlates with measures of antisocial behavior.

OSLC's observation data showed that the aggressive child at home is four to five times more likely (than normal children) to be blindsided (e.g., attacked without provocation; Patterson, 1982). The child has a similar experience in the school yard (Shinn et al., 1987). This means that in the Dodge studies, child reports of a high likelihood of attack by peers is a measure of current history rather than attributional bias. In another study where peers reacted to Dodge-type vignettes, they agreed that in an ambiguous situation, a teacher or peer is most likely to go after the aggressive child (i.e., he or she gets blindsided; Trachtenberg & Viken, 1994). These findings also support the history rather than the bias hypothesis. To earn status as "bias," it would seem necessary to first partial out observation data that describe the likelihood of the child being blindsided at home or on the playground.

Intrinsic Reinforcers

As development unfolds, it becomes increasingly apparent that there are massive individual differences in what it is that each individual finds to be reinforcing. This is also one of the least understood aspects of internalized processes. There are individual differences in responsiveness even to primary reinforcers, such as food, sex, and so forth. But, what determines responsiveness to art, music, or work itself? One can see the fine hand of biology in this enterprise, but surely experience also contributes to these activities that seem to function as intrinsic reinforcers for some individuals but not for most people. For example, my good friend Irene is a musician who plays Celtic music hour after hour on her fiddle. How she finds this reinforcing is a deep mystery to me. One could say her public appearances and audience reactions are reinforcers, but that ignores the likelihood Irene would continue even if external reinforcers became few and far between.

The decade of work on intrinsic reinforcement might have addressed these issues; but, this work has been almost totally focused on a flawed effort to demonstrate that extrinsic reinforcement destroys intrinsic motivation (Lepper & Dafoe, 1979). Reviews of this prodigious effort showed that external reinforcement had little to do with changes in intrinsic motivation (Cameron & Pierce, 1994). Sadder still, these studies failed to identify what the antecedents for intrinsic motivation might be. Although there are enormous individual differences in what individuals find to be reinforcing, current research does little to explain how this comes about.

CONCLUSION

Psychologists need to construct empirically based models that contain the best measures of contingencies, emotions, and social cognitions that the social sciences have to offer. Due perhaps to limitations in training or vision, most researchers have been content to work at constructing simple theories that focus only on one set of variables. It is inconceivable to have a theory of socialization that doesn't include, at some point, an analysis of what children actually do in the real world. A theory about coercive behavior that leaves out direct measures of negative emotion or negative attributions is by definition terribly incomplete. Leaving emotion and thinking out of the account is to ignore much of what psychologists mean by "human" behavior. Alternatively, how could psychologists have a theory that contains only cognitive variables when the bulk of children's coercive reactions are overlearned and, therefore, not under immediate cognitive control?

It is not logic that stands in the way of building an integrated model of parenting. The villain is inertia and the stress induced when a student (of any age) must learn new ideas and master a new literature. Most of us read the same restricted set of journals each year and feel that we can barely keep up with even these. But even the developmental theory about contingencies and overlearned behaviors described here required the parallel development of both macro- and microtheories. The macrotheory helps in understanding the interaction between contextual variables and family process such as what the contribution of deviant peers might be to transforming childhood antisocial behaviors into juvenile offenses. With only a microsocial perspective, we will miss the contributions of forces outside the family. However, a singular focus on macrovariables will prevent our understanding the mechanisms that directly change child behaviors. If we do not understand these mechanisms, we will not understand the determinants for stability and change.

The advent of a performance model that uses multivariate analyses and multimethod and -agent indicators to define concepts about contingencies, emotions, and social cognitions provides a framework for expanding theoretical perspectives about socialization. No one of us can become experts simultaneously in both micro- and macrotheory and methodology for all three of these substantive areas. The implication is that it will require a consortium of investigators, each with a rather different set of skills. However this is to be done, it is time to begin longitudinal studies that will compare the function of the contingencies, emotions, and social cognitions as they account for variance in measures of child outcome.

In a very real sense, this chapter is not so much about a theory of parenting as it is a presentation of a strategy for building one. It is more of a continuous bootstrapping operation focused on tailoring measures to fit concepts than it is deductive. I suppose what is missing is mystery. The approach has all the elegance of an assembly line for putting together a Ford automobile. However, the performance theory has three things that recommend it as a strategy for the study of children's antisocial behavior. First, it has generated both a microtheory and a macrotheory; each of them accounts for 30% to 50% of the variance in criterion measures of childhood antisocial behavior. To our knowledge, no competing developmental theories are this successful in accounting for performance in natural settings. Second, the parallel micro- and macromodels have provided an empirical base that addresses questions about both stability and change. Third, the same variables that explain children's performance of aggressive acts also define the main components for intervention and prevention trials that effectively reduce antisocial behavior. To our knowledge, parenting-based therapies for antisocial children are the only ones that have consistently been shown to be effective.

REFERENCES

Bachman, J. G., & O'Malley, P. M. (1977). Self-esteem in young men: A longitudinal analysis of the impact of educational and occupational attainment. *Journal of Personality and Social Psychology, 35,* 365–380.

Bandura, A. (1981). In search of pure unidirectional determinants. *Behavior Therapy, 12,* 30–40.

Bank, L., Burraston, B., & Patterson, G. R. (1996, March). *Adjustment outcomes as a function of self-esteem and antisocial behavior in adolescent boys.* Poster displayed at the Society for Research in Adolescence, Boston, MA.

Bank, L., Dishion, T. J., Skinner, M. L., & Patterson, G. R. (1990). Method variance in structural equation modeling: Living with "glop." In G. R. Patterson (Ed.), *Depression and aggression in family interaction* (pp. 247–279). Hillsdale, NJ: Erlbaum.

Bank, L., Forgatch, M. S., Patterson, G. R., & Fetrow, R. A. (1993). Parenting practices of single mothers: Mediators of negative contextual factors. *Journal of Marriage and the Family, 55,* 371–384.

Bank, L., Patterson, G. R., Burraston, B., & Shortt, J. W. (1995, December). *Contributions of negative sibling interactions in the prediction of poor adjustment outcomes.* Paper presented at the conference on "Revising the Model," Oregon Social Learning Center, Eugene, OR.

Barker, R. G. (1963). The stream of behavior as an empirical problem. In R. G. Barker (Ed.), *The stream of behavior: Explorations of its structure and content* (pp. 1–22). New York: Appleton-Century-Crofts.

Barkley, R. A. (1981). The use of psychopharmacology to study reciprocal influences in parent-child interaction. *Journal of Abnormal Child Psychology, 9,* 303–310.

Bella, D. A. (1995a). *The systemic distortion of information.* Unpublished manuscript, Oregon State University, Corvallis, OR.

Bella, D. A. (1995b). *In the system, but not of it: Spirit lessons from American slavery.* Corvallis, OR: Desperate Scholar's Press.

Bem, D. J., & Funder, D. C. (1978). Predicting more of the people more of the time: Assessing the personality of situations. *Psychological Review, 85,* 485–501.

Buehler, R. E., Patterson, G. R., & Furniss, J. M. (1966). The reinforcement of behavior in institutional settings. *Behaviour Research and Therapy, 4,* 157–167.

Bugental, D. B., Blue, J., & Lewis, J. (1990). Caregiver beliefs and dysphoric affect directed to difficult children. *Developmental Psychology, 26,* 631–638.

Cairns, R. B., & Cairns, B. D. (1991). Social cognition and social networks: A developmental perspective. In D. J. Pepler & K. H. Rubin (Eds.), *The development and treatment of childhood aggression* (pp. 249–278). Hillsdale, NJ: Erlbaum.

Cameron, J., & Pierce, W. D. (1994). Reinforcement, reward, and intrinsic motivation: A meta-analysis. *Review of Educational Research, 64,* 363–423.

Capaldi, D. M., Forgatch, M. S., & Crosby, L. (1994). Affective expression in family problem-solving discussions with adolescent boys: The association with family structure and function. *Journal of Adolescent Research, 9,* 28–49.

Capaldi, D. M., & Patterson, G. R. (1987). An approach to the problem of recruitment and retention rates for longitudinal research. *Behavioral Assessment, 9,* 169–177.

Capaldi, D. M., & Patterson, G. R. (1989). *Psychometric properties of fourteen latent constructs from the Oregon Youth Study.* New York: Springer-Verlag.

Carr, E. G. (1988). Functional equivalence as a mechanism of response generalization. In R. H. Horner, G. Dunlap, & R. L. Koegel (Eds.), *Generalization and maintenance: Life-style changes in applied settings* (pp. 194–219). Baltimore: Brookes.

Cobb, J. A., & Hops, H. (1973). Effects of academic survival skill training on low achieving first graders. *Journal of Educational Research, 67,* 108–113.

Conger, R. D., McCarty, J. A., Yang, R. K., Lahey, B. B., & Kropp, J. P. (1984). Perception of child, childrearing values, and emotional distress as mediating links between environmental stressors and observed maternal behavior. *Child Development, 55,* 2234–2247.

Conger, R. D., Patterson, G. R., & Gé, X. (1995). It takes two to replicate: A mediational model for the impact of parents' stress on adolescent adjustment. *Child Development, 66,* 80–97.

Darling, N., & Steinberg, L. (1993). Parenting styles as context: An integrative model. *Psychological Bulletin, 113,* 487–496.

Davison, M., & McCarthy, D. (1988). *The matching law: A research review.* Hillsdale, NJ: Erlbaum.

Dawes, R. N. (1988). *Rational choice in an uncertain world.* San Diego, CA: Harcourt Brace Jovanovich.

DeBaryshe, B. D., Patterson, G. R., & Capaldi, D. M. (1993). A performance model for academic achievement in early adolescent boys. *Developmental Psychology, 29,* 795–804.

Dishion, T. J., Andrews, D. W., & Crosby, L. (1995). Antisocial boys and their friends in adolescence: Relationship characteristics, quality, and interactional processes. *Child Development, 66,* 139–151.

Dishion, T. J., Duncan, T. E., Eddy, J. M., Fagot, B. I., & Fetrow, R. (1994). The world of parents and peers: Coercive exchanges and children's social adaptation. *Social Development, 3,* 255–268.

Dishion, T. J., French, D. C., & Patterson, G. R. (1995). The development and ecology of antisocial behavior. In D. Cicchetti & D. Cohen (Eds.), *Developmental psychopathology: Vol. 2. Risk, disorder, and adaptation* (pp. 421–471). New York: Wiley.

Dishion, T. J., Gardner, K., Patterson, G. R., Reid, J. B., & Thibodeaux, S. (1983). *The family process code: A multidimensional system for observing family interactions.* Unpublished technical manual, Oregon Social Learning Center, Eugene.

Dishion, T. J., Patterson, G. R., & Griesler, P. C. (1994). Peer adaptation in the development of antisocial behavior: A confluence model. In L. R. Huesmann (Ed.), *Current perspectives on aggressive behavior* (pp. 61–95). New York: Plenum Press.

Dishion, T. J., Patterson, G. R., & Kavanagh, K. A. (1992). An experimental test of the coercion model: Linking theory, measurement, and intervention. In J. McCord & R. Tremblay (Eds.),

The interaction of theory and practice: Experimental studies of intervention (pp. 253–282). New York: Guilford Press.

Dix, T. (1991). The affective organization of parenting: Adaptive and maladaptive processes. *Psychological Bulletin, 110,* 3–25.

Dodge, K., Pettit, G. S., Bates, J. E., & Valente, E. (1995). Social-information-processing patterns partially mediate the effect of early physical abuse on later conduct problems. *Journal of Abnormal Psychology, 104,* 632–643.

Dornbusch, S. M., Ritter, P. O., Leiderman, P. H., Roberts, D. F., & Fraleigh, M. J. (1987). The relation of parenting style to adolescent school performance. *Child Development, 58,* 1244–1257.

Eddy, M., & Fagot, B. I. (1991, April). *The coercion model of antisocial behavior: Generalization to 5-year-old children and their parents.* Paper presented at the Society for Research in Child Development, Seattle, WA.

Ekman, P., & Freisen, W. V. (1975). *Unmasking the human face.* Englewood Cliffs, NJ: Prentice-Hall.

Elliott, D. S., Huizinga, D., & Ageton, S. S. (1985). *Explaining delinquency and drug use.* Beverly Hills, CA: Sage.

Fagot, B. I., & Kavanagh, K. (1990). The prediction of antisocial behavior from avoidant attachment classifications. *Child Development, 61,* 864–873.

Fagot, B. I., & Kavanagh, K. (1993). Parenting during the second year: Effects of children's age, sex, and attachment classification. *Child Development, 64,* 258–271.

Feshbach, S. (1979). The regulation and modification of aggression: Commonalities and issues. In S. Feshbach & A. Fraczek (Eds.), *Aggression and behavior change: Biological and social processes* (pp. 171–286). New York: Praeger.

Forgatch, M. S. (1989). Patterns and outcome in family problem solving: The disrupting effect of negative emotion. *Journal of Marriage and the Family, 5,* 115–124.

Forgatch, M. S. (1991). The clinical science vortex: A developing theory of antisocial behavior. In D. J. Pepler & K. H. Rubin (Eds.), *The development and treatment of childhood aggression* (pp. 291–315). Hillsdale, NJ: Erlbaum.

Forgatch, M. S., DeGarmo, D. S., & Knutson, N. M. (1997). *Influences of change during the transition into adolescence.* Manuscript in preparation.

Forgatch, M. S., Patterson, G. R., & Ray, J. A. (1996). Divorce and boys' adjustment problems: Two paths with a single model. In E. M. Hetherington (Ed.), *Stress, coping, and resiliency in children and families* (pp. 67–105). Mahwah, NJ: Erlbaum.

Forgatch, M. S., & Ramsey, E. (1994). Boosting homework: A videotape link between families and schools. *School Psychology Review, 23,* 472–484.

Forgatch, M. S., & Stoolmiller, M. (1994). Emotions as contexts for adolescent delinquency. *Journal of Research on Adolescence, 4,* 601–614.

Frank, G. H. (1965). The role of family in the development of psychopathology. *Psychological Bulletin, 64,* 191–205.

Funder, D. C., Block, J. H., & Block, J. (1983). Delay of gratification: Some longitudinal personality correlates. *Journal of Personality and Social Psychology, 44,* 1198–1213.

Gardner, R. A. (1992). *Self-esteem problems in children.* Palo Alto, CA: Consulting Psychologists Press.

Gewirtz, J. L., & Boyd, E. F. (1977). Experiments on mother-infant interaction underlying mutual attachment acquisition: The infant conditions the mother. In T. Alloway, P. Pliner, & L. Krames (Eds.), *Attachment behavior* (pp. 109–143). New York: Plenum Press.

Gottfredson, M. R., & Hirschi, T. (1990). *A general theory of crime.* Stanford, CA: Stanford University Press.

Gottman, J. M., McCoy, K., Coan, J., & Collier, H. (1996). *The Specific Affect Coding System (SPAFF).* In J. M. Gottman (Ed.), *What predicts divorce? The measures.* Mahwah, NJ: Erlbaum.

Greenwald, R. (1989). *Abusive parenting: A mediated model.* Unpublished doctoral dissertation, University of Oregon, Eugene.

Hayes, S. C. (1988). *Rule-governed behavior: Cognition, contingencies, and instructional control.* New York: Plenum Press.

Herrnstein, R. J. (1961). Relative and absolute strength of response as a function of frequency or reinforcement. *Journal of Experimental Analysis of Behavior, 4,* 267–272.

Herrnstein, R. J. (1974). Formal properties of the matching law. *Journal of the Experimental Analysis of Behavior, 21,* 486–495.

Hess, R. D., & McDevitt, T. M. (1986). Some antecedents of maternal attributions about children's performance in mathematics. In R. D. Ashmore & D. M. Brodzinsky (Eds.), *Thinking about the family: Views of parents and children* (pp. 95–118). Hillsdale, NJ: Erlbaum.

Holleran, P. A., Littman, D. C., Freund, R., & Schmaling, K. B. (1982). A signal detection approach to social perception: Identification of negative and positive behaviors by parents of normal and problem children. *Journal of Abnormal Child Psychology, 10,* 547–557.

Hops, H., Sherman, L., & Biglan, A. (1990). Maternal depression, marital discord and children's behavior: A developmental perspective. In G. R. Patterson (Ed.), *Depression and aggression in family interactions* (pp. 185–208). New York: Erlbaum.

Horner, R. H., & Day, H. M. (1991). The effects of response efficiency on functionally equivalent competing behaviors. *Journal of Applied Behavior Analysis, 24,* 719–732.

Hoyle, R. H. (1995). *Structural equation modeling: Concepts, issues, and applications.* Thousand Oaks, CA: Sage.

Kochanska, G. (1991, April). *Child compliance and noncompliance in the origins of conscience.* Paper presented at the Society for Research in Child Development, Seattle, WA.

Kochanska, G. (1995). Children's temperament, mothers' discipline, and security of attachment: Multiple pathways to emerging internalization. *Child Development, 66,* 597–615.

Kochanska, G., & Aksan, N. (1995). Mother-child mutually positive affect, the quality of child compliance to requests and prohibitions, and maternal control as correlates of early internalization. *Child Development, 66,* 236–254.

Kochanska, G., Kuczynski, L., & Radke-Yarrow, M. (1988, April). *Correspondence between childrearing attitudes and actual discipline practices in mothers of young children.* Paper presented at the 6th Biennial International Conference on Infant Studies, Washington, DC.

Krueger, R. F., Caspi, A., Moffitt, T. E., White, J., & Stouthamer-Loeber, M. (1996). Delay of gratification, psychopathology, and personality: Is low self-control specific to externalizing problems. *Journal of Personality, 64,* 107–129.

Larzelere, R. E., & Patterson, G. R. (1990). Parental management: Mediator of the effect of socioeconomic status on early delinquency. *Criminology, 28,* 301–324.

Larzelere, R. E., Schneider, W. N., Larson, D. B., & Pike, P. L. (1996). The effects of discipline responses in delaying toddler misbehavior recurrences. *Child and Family Behavior Therapy, 18,* 35–57.

Laub, J. H., & Sampson, R. J. (1988). Unraveling families and delinquency: A reanalysis of the Gluecks' data. *Criminology, 26,* 355–380.

Lepper, M. R., & Dafoe, J. L. (1979). Incentives, constraints, and motivation in the classroom. In I. H. Frieze, D. Bar-Tal, & J. S. Carroll (Eds.), *New approaches to social problems* (pp. 309–336). San Francisco: Jossey-Bass.

Lorber, R. (1981). *Parental tracking of childhood behavior as a function of family stress.* Unpublished doctoral dissertation, University of Oregon, Eugene.

Luster, T., Rhoades, K., & Haas, B. (1989). The relation between parental values and parental behavior: A test of the Kohn Hypothesis. *Journal of Marriage and the Family, 51,* 139–147.

Lytton, H., & Zwirner, W. (1975). Compliance and its controlling stimuli observed in a natural setting. *Developmental Psychology, 11,* 769–779.

Maccoby, E. E. (1992). The role of parents in the socialization of children: An historical overview. *Developmental Psychology, 28,* 1006–1017.

McDowell, J. J. (1988). Matching theory in natural human environments. *The Behavior Analyst, 11,* 95–109.

Meehl, P. (1954). *Clinical versus statistical prediction: A theoretical analysis and a review of the evidence.* Minneapolis: University of Minnesota Press.

Metzler, C. E., & Dishion, T. J. (1992, November). *A model of the development of youthful problem behaviors.* Paper presented at the 18th Annual Convention for Association for Behavior Analysis, Boston, MA.

Mischel, W. (1976). *Introduction to personality* (2nd ed.). New York: Holt, Rinehart and Winston.

Moffitt, T. E., & Silva, P. A. (1988). Self-reported delinquency, neuropsychological deficit, and history of Attention Deficit Disorder. *Journal of Abnormal Child Psychology, 16,* 553–569.

Newtson, D. (1990). Alternatives to representation or alternative representations: Comments on the ecological approach. *Contemporary Social Psychology, 14,* 163–174.

Newtson, D. (1993). The dynamics of action and interaction. In L. B. Smith & E. Thelen (Eds.), *A dynamic systems approach to development: Applications.* Cambridge, MA: MIT Press.

Olweus, D. (1979). Stability of aggressive reaction patterns in males: A review. *Psychological Bulletin, 86,* 852–875.

Paley, B., Conger, R. D., & Harold, G. T. (in press). The role of parental affect and adolescent cognitive representations of parent/child relations in the development of adolescent social functioning. *Child Development.*

Patterson, G. R. (1976). The aggressive child: Victim and architect of a coercive system. In E. J. Mash, L. A. Hamerlynck, & L. C. Handy (Eds.), *Behavior modification and families: 1. Theory and research: 2. Applications and developments* (pp. 267–316). New York: Brunner/Mazel.

Patterson, G. R. (1980). Mothers: The unacknowledged victims. *Monographs of the Society for Research in Child Development, 45*(5, Serial No. 186).

Patterson, G. R. (1982). *A social learning approach: Vol. 3. Coercive family process.* Eugene, OR: Castalia Press.

Patterson, G. R. (1983). Stress: A change agent for family process. In N. Garmezy & M. Rutter (Eds.), *Stress, coping, and development in children* (pp. 235–264). New York: McGraw-Hill.

Patterson, G. R. (1986). Performance models for antisocial boys. *American Psychologist, 41,* 432–444.

Patterson, G. R. (1992). Developmental changes in antisocial behavior. In R. D. Peters, R. J. McMahon, & V. L. Quinsey (Eds.), *Aggression and violence throughout the life span* (pp. 52–82). Newbury Park, CA: Sage.

Patterson, G. R. (1993). Orderly change in a stable world: The antisocial trait as a chimera. *Journal of Consulting and Clinical Psychology, 61,* 911–919.

Patterson, G. R. (1995). Coercion as a basis for early age of onset for arrest. In J. McCord (Ed.), *Coercion and punishment in long-term perspective* (pp. 81–105). New York: Cambridge University Press.

Patterson, G. R. (1996). Some characteristics of a developmental theory for early onset delinquency. In M. F. Lenzenweger & J. J. Haugaard (Eds.), *Frontiers of developmental psychopathology* (pp. 81–124). New York: Oxford University Press.

Patterson, G. R., & Bank, L. (1987). When is a nomological network a construct? In D. R. Peterson & D. B. Fishman (Eds.), *Assessment for decision* (pp. 249–279). New Brunswick, NJ: Rutgers University Press.

Patterson, G. R., & Bank, L. (1989). Some amplifying mechanisms for pathologic processes in families. In M. R. Gunnar & E. Thelen (Eds.), *The Minnesota Symposia on Child Psychology: Systems and development* (pp. 167–209). Hillsdale, NJ: Erlbaum.

Patterson, G. R., & Brodsky, G. (1966). A behaviour modification programme for a child with multiple problem behaviours. *Journal of Child Psychology and Psychiatry, 7,* 277–295.

Patterson, G. R., & Capaldi, D. (1990). A mediational model for boys' depressed mood. In J. E. Rolf, A. Masten, D. Cicchetti, K. Nuechterlein, & S. Weintraub (Eds.), *Risk and protective factors in the development of psychopathology* (pp. 141–163). New York: Cambridge University Press.

Patterson, G. R., & Chamberlain, P. (1994). A functional analysis of resistance during parent training therapy. *Clinical Psychology: Science and Practice, 1,* 53–70.

Patterson, G. R., & Cobb, J. A. (1971). A dyadic analysis of "aggressive" behaviors. In J. P. Hill (Ed.), *Minnesota Symposia on Child Psychology* (Vol. 5, pp. 72–129). Minneapolis: University of Minnesota.

Patterson, G. R., & Cobb, J. A. (1973). Stimulus control for classes of noxious behaviors. In J. F. Knutson (Ed.), *The control of aggression: Implications from basic research* (pp. 144–199). Chicago: Aldine.

Patterson, G. R., & Dishion, T. J. (1988). Multilevel family process models: Traits, interactions, and relationships. In R. A. Hinde & J. Stevenson-Hinde (Eds.), *Relationships within families: Mutual influences* (pp. 283–310). Oxford, England: Clarendon.

Patterson, G. R., Dishion, T. J., & Chamberlain, P. (1993). Outcomes and methodological issues relating to treatment of antisocial children. In T. R. Giles (Ed.), *Handbook of effective psychotherapy* (pp. 43–88). New York: Plenum Press.

Patterson, G. R., Forgatch, M. S., Yoerger, K., & Stoolmiller, M. (1997). *Variables that initiate and maintain an early-onset trajectory for juvenile offending.* Manuscript in preparation.

Patterson, G. R., Littman, R. A., & Bricker, W. (1967). Assertive behavior in children: A step towards a theory of aggression. *Monographs of the Society for Research in Child Development, 32*(5), 1–43.

Patterson, G. R., McNeal, S., Hawkins, N., & Phelps, R. (1967). Reprogramming the social environment. *Child Psychology and Psychiatry, 8,* 181–195.

Patterson, G. R., Reid, J. B., & Dishion, T. J. (1992). *A social interactional approach: Vol. 4. Antisocial boys.* Eugene, OR: Castalia Press.

Patterson, G. R., & Stoolmiller, M. (1991). Replications of a dual failure model for boys' depressed mood. *Journal of Consulting and Clinical Psychology, 59,* 491–498.

Patterson, G. R., & Stouthamer-Loeber, M. (1984). The correlation of family management practices and delinquency. *Child Development, 55,* 1299–1307.

Patterson, G. R., & Yoerger, K. (1995). Two different models for adolescent physical trauma and for early arrest. *Criminal Behaviour and Mental Health, 5,* 411–423.

Patterson, G. R., Yoerger, K., & Stoolmiller, M. (in press). A developmental model for late-onset delinquency. In D. W. Osgood (Ed.), *Motivation and delinquency.* Lincoln: University of Nebraska Press.

Perry, D. G., Perry, L. C., & Rasmussen, P. (1986). Cognitive social learning mediators of aggression. *Child Development, 57,* 700–711.

Piliavin, I. M., Hardyck, J. A., & Vadum, A. C. (1968). Constraining effects of personal costs on the transgressions of juveniles. *Journal of Personality and Social Psychology, 10,* 227–231.

Premack, D. (1965). Reinforcement theory. In D. Seime (Ed.), *Nebraska Symposium on Motivation* (Vol. 13, pp. 123–180). Lincoln: University of Nebraska Press.

Quay, H. (1987). Intelligence. In H. C. Quay (Ed.), *Handbook of juvenile delinquency* (pp. 106–117). New York: Wiley.

Ramsey, E., Patterson, G. R., & Walker, H. M. (1990). Generalization of the antisocial trait from home to school settings. *Journal of Applied Developmental Psychology, 11,* 209–223.

Reid, J. B. (Ed.). (1978). *A social learning approach to family intervention: 2. Observation in home settings.* Eugene, OR: Castalia Press.

Reid, J. B. (1982). Observer training in naturalistic research. In D. P. Hartmann (Ed.), *New directions for methodology of social and behavioral science: No. 14. Using observers to study behavior* (pp. 37–50). San Francisco: Jossey-Bass.

Reid, J. B., Kavanagh, K. A., & Baldwin, D. V. (1987). Abusive parents' perceptions of child problem behaviors: An example of parental bias. *Journal of Abnormal Child Psychology, 15,* 457–466.

Reid, J. B., Patterson, G. R., & Loeber, R. (1982). The abused child: Victim, instigator, or innocent bystander? In D. Bernstein (Ed.), *Response structure and organization* (pp. 47–68). Lincoln: University of Nebraska Press.

Reid, J. B., Patterson, G. R., & Lorber, R. (1981). The treatment of multiple-offending young adolescents using family treatment based on social learning principles. In N. Berlin (Ed.), *Children and our future.* Albuquerque: University of New Mexico Press.

Risley, T. R., & Twardosz, S. (1976). The preschool as a setting for behavioral intervention. In H. Leitenberg (Ed.), *Handbook of behavior modification and behavior therapy* (pp. 453–474). Englewood Cliffs, NJ: Prentice-Hall.

Rosenfeld, H. M., & Baer, D. M. (1969). Unnoticed verbal conditioning of an aware experimenter by a more aware subject: The double agent effect. *Psychological Review, 76,* 425–432.

Rueter, M. A., & Conger, R. D. (1995). Interaction style, problem-solving behavior, and family problem-solving effectiveness. *Child Development, 66,* 98–115.

Ryan, B. A., Corville-Smith, J., & Adams, G. R. (1995, April). *The effect of family process variables on the relationship between self-esteem and achievement.* Poster presented at the annual meeting of the American Educational Research Association, San Francisco.

Sanson-Fisher, R. W., Seymour, F. W., Montgomery, W., & Stokes, T. F. (1978). Modifying delinquent's conversations using reinforcement of self-recorded behavior. *Journal of Behavior Therapy and Experimental Psychiatry, 9,* 163–168.

Scaramella, L. V. (1994). *An examination of the development of delinquency in middle childhood.* Unpublished doctoral dissertation, University of Arizona, Tempe.

Schmaling, K. B., & Patterson, G. R. (1984, November). *Maternal classification of deviant and prosocial child behavior and reactions to the child in the home.* Paper presented at the annual meeting of the Association for the Advancement of Behavior Therapy, Philadelphia, PA.

Schuck, J. R. (1974). The use of causal nonexperimental models in aggression research. In J. DeWit & W. W. Hartup (Eds.), *Determinants and origins of aggressive behavior* (pp. 381–389). The Hague: Mouton.

Shinn, M. R., Ramsey, E., Walker, H. M., Stieber, S., & O'Neill, R. E. (1987). Antisocial behavior in school settings: Initial differences in an at risk and normal population. *Journal of Special Education, 21,* 69–84.

Sigel, I. E. (1985). A conceptual analysis of beliefs. In I. E. Sigel (Ed.), *Parental belief systems: The psychological consequences for children* (pp. 345–371). Hillsdale, NJ: Erlbaum.

Sigel, I. E. (1986). Reflections on the belief-behavior connection: Lessons learned from a research program on parent belief systems and teaching strategies. In R. D. Ashmore &

D. M. Brodzinski (Eds.), *Thinking about the family: Views of parents and children* (pp. 35–65). Hillsdale, NJ: Erlbaum.

Simon, H. A. (1982). *Models of bounded rationality.* Cambridge, MA: MIT Press.

Skinner, B. F. (1969). *Contingencies of reinforcement: A theoretical analysis.* New York: Appleton-Century-Crofts.

Slaby, R. G., & Guerra, N. G. (1988). Cognitive mediators of aggression in adolescent offenders: 1. Assessment. *Developmental Psychology, 24,* 580–588.

Slovic, P., Fischoff, B., & Lichtenstein, S. (1977). Behavioral decision theory. *Annual Review of Psychology, 28,* 40.

Snyder, J. (1991). Discipline as a mediator of the impact of maternal stress and mood on child conduct problems. *Development and Psychopathology, 3,* 263–276.

Snyder, J., Edwards, P., McGraw, K., Kilgore, K., & Holton, A. (1994). Escalation and reinforcement in mother-child conflict: Social processes associated with the development of physical aggression. *Development and Psychopathology, 6,* 305–321.

Snyder, J., & Patterson, G. R. (1995). Individual differences in social aggression: A test of a reinforcement model of socialization in the natural environment. *Behavior Therapy, 26,* 371–391.

Snyder, J., Schrepferman, L., & St. Peter, C. (1997). Origins of antisocial behavior: Negative reinforcement and affect dysregulation of behavior as socialization mechanisms in family interaction. *Behavior Modification, 21,* 187–215.

Snyder, J., West, L., Stockemer, V., Gibbons, S., & Almquist-Parks, L. (1996). A social learning model of peer choice in the natural environment. *Journal of Applied Developmental Psychology, 17,* 215–237.

Stoolmiller, M. (1994). Antisocial behavior, delinquent peer association, and unsupervised wandering for boys: Growth and change from childhood to early adolescence. *Multivariate Behavioral Research, 29,* 263–288.

Timberlake, W. (1995). Reconceptualizing reinforcement: A causal-system approach to reinforcement and behavior change. In W. O'Donohue & L. Krasner (Eds.), *Theories of behavior therapy: Exploring behavior change* (pp. 59–96). Washington, DC: American Psychological Association.

Trachtenberg, S., & Viken, R. J. (1994). Aggressive boys in classroom: Biased attributions or shared perceptions? *Child Development, 65,* 829–835.

Tversky, A., & Kahneman, D. (1974). Judgment under uncertainty: Heuristics and biases. *Science, 185,* 1124–1131.

Vaughn, M. (1989). Rule-governed behavior in behavior analysis: A theoretical and experimental history. In S. C. Hayes (Ed.), *Rule-governed behavior: Cognition, contingencies and instructional control* (pp. 97–118). New York: Plenum Press.

Vuchinich, S., Bank, L., & Patterson, G. R. (1992). Parenting, peers, and the stability of antisocial behavior in preadolescent boys. *Developmental Psychology, 28,* 510–521.

Wells, K. D. (1995, August). *Discussion of "time out for timeout? Its place in today's behavior therapy."* Paper presented at the annual meeting of the American Psychological Association, New York.

Wilson, J. Q., & Herrnstein, R. J. (1985). *Crime and human nature.* New York: Simon & Schuster.

Wright, J. C. (1983). *The structure and perception of behavioral consistency.* Unpublished doctoral dissertation, Stanford University, Stanford, CA.

CHAPTER 9

Models of Conformity and Resistance in Socialization Theory

LEON KUCZYNSKI and NEIL HILDEBRANDT

The study of socialization and internalization in the context of the family entails assumptions about conformity, resistance, and authority in parent-child social interactions. Although it is generally accepted that children develop capacities for self-regulation (Kochanska, 1991; Kopp, 1982), basic orientations toward authority (Dubin & Dubin, 1963), and an initial store of values during interactions with parents, assumptions about the core processes that underlie socialization vary considerably across theories. Early theories of moral development (Kohlberg, 1969) and socialization (Aronfreed, 1969; Gewirtz, 1969) shared a conception of conformity as the child's immediate compliance to unilateral parental authority. Baumrind's (1971) model of authoritative parenting legitimized a degree of assertion in children's responses to parents who were firm but willing to engage in give-and-take with their children. In Vygotskian frameworks on the development of cognitive competence (Rogoff, 1990), implicit assumptions can be found about a "benign and relatively neutral" family context where parents are "willing teachers" and children are "eager learners" and where the motives of power and resistance play no role (Goodnow, 1990). Such explicit and implicit assumptions about the nature of children's conformity form the core ideas of major theoretical perspectives on socialization. They encapsulate each theory's model of children's competence and also its model of the kind of parenting required for the optimal socialization of children.

The purpose of this chapter is to outline major perspectives on children's conformity that guide contemporary research on socialization and internalization. Four theoretical perspectives on children's conformity and resistance to parental influence will be presented. These are external control theories, internal control theories, relational theories, and contextual theories of socialization (Figure 9.1). The first two perspectives represent well-established models of children's conformity that originated in early theories of socialization and internalization developed prior to the 1970s. However, since that time there have been major developments in theory and research on socialization. Bidirectional models of causality in the family have mostly replaced unidirectional assumptions and a large body of research now exists on parent-child relationships and parent-child interactions. Although these developments have been reflected in contemporary versions of external control and internal control perspectives, they have also led to two additional perspectives on socialization. Thus the relational perspective and the contextual perspective will be presented as formulations of two new models of children's conformity that have emerged.

External Control Theories

Compliance/Noncompliance*

*within 15 seconds of parental command

Internal Control Theories

"mere compliance"
Internal Control*

*in parents' absence

Relational Theories

Accommodation/Negotiation*

*in close relationships

Contextual Theories

Compliance*
Internal Control†
Accommodation‡

*institutional, hierarchical, coercive contexts
†moral and high value contexts
‡close relationship contexts

Figure 9.1   Models of Conformity in Socialization Theory

Each perspective will be discussed in terms of (a) its general assumptions about socialization, (b) its model of children's conformity and resistance to parental demands, and (c) its models of parental competence and the parent-child relationship context. It will be argued that the external control, the internal control and the relational perspectives make distinctive assumptions about the nature of child and parental competence. The contextual perspective, however, offers a framework for considering the different models of conformity as complementary perspectives. In the final section of the chapter, the cultural and historical context of current models of conformity will be considered. We suggest that the emphasis on children's autonomy and the relationship context of socialization that can be found in current theories reflects social changes in child-rearing values and parents' relationships with children.

EXTERNAL CONTROL PERSPECTIVES

The external control perspective on socialization is represented by two different conceptual frameworks: behavior theory and traditional authoritarianism. Although the two perspectives have different origins, they have similar orientations toward children's conformity and parental competence. Behavior theory and traditional authoritarianism are applied perspectives whose models of parenting and child behavior can be found in parent-education and parent-training manuals. Both emphasize immediate compliance as a focus of parental socialization efforts and both emphasize external contingencies such as reward and punishment as techniques for managing children's behavior.

Behavior Theory

The behavioral perspective on conformity (Forehand & MacMahon, 1981; Patterson, 1982) has conceptual roots in operant theory and functional analysis, which emphasize observable parent and child behaviors and immediate antecedants and consequences as causes of behavior. A trademark of the behavioral perspective is that it avoids the inference of internal mental constructs such as "internalization," "internal motivation," "autonomy," "will," and "relationship." There are various reasons for this stance to theory and research. A legacy of operant theory is that inferences of internal processes are assumed to distract researchers from powerful external contingencies that parents and children provide each other in their immediate environments (Gewirtz, 1969). It has also been argued (Aronfreed, 1969) that social behavior is overdetermined by external supports and sanctions and, therefore, it is misleading to emphasize internal motives as explanations: "Many forms of conduct may have their value continually reinstated by external social reinforcements which are not easily observable. A person's behavior may be externally controlled not only by explicit reward and punishment, but also by various subtle indicators of social approval or disapproval which are conveyed in the behavior of others" (p. 266). Moreover, research on coercive family processes (Patterson, this volume; Patterson, Reid, & Dishion, 1992) also suggests a stronger causal role for external behavioral contingencies than for internal cognitions. Patterson suggests that most social interactions occur at an automatic level and that it is impossible for parents and children to be aware of, or consciously process, the multitude of contingencies that occur during their moment-to-moment interchanges.

The behavioral perspective on children's conformity is also shaped by a clinical focus on conduct-disordered children whose presenting problems include severe noncompliance and defiance. Patterson (1982; Patterson, DeBarsyshe, & Ramsey, 1989) suggests that noncompliance is a foundation for the development of aggression and delinquency. Antisocial behavior is assumed to originate in parental mishandling of ordinary acts of noncompliance during early childhood. If noncompliant behavior is not checked, it may become part of a causally interconnected chain of events that escalates the child's involvement in antisocial behavior throughout development. This is because noncompliance contributes to the bidirectional dynamics of coercive family interactions and to impairments in parents' ability to manage their children's behavior (Patterson, 1982). Thus, the noncompliant child may learn to use coercion as an influence strategy with parents during early childhood. Coercion then sets the stage for academic failure, parental rejection and poor peer relationships in middle childhood, depression and involvement in deviant peer groups in adolescence, and maladaptive outcomes in adulthood.

Model of Children's Conformity

Children's conformity in the behavioral perspective is conceived as immediate compliance or noncompliance following a parental request or command (Figure 9.1). Current operational definitions of the compliance construct emphasize the timing of the child's response but do not consider the form or function of the behavior. Compliance or noncompliance with a parental request is scored within a specified time criterion such as 5 seconds for 3- to 8-year-old children (Forehand & MacMahon, 1981) or 15 seconds for adolescents (Patterson, 1982; Patterson & Forgatch, 1987). This focus on simple operational criteria and absence of concern for motivation or context means that the measurement of compliance is not as much a problem for the behavioral perspective as it is for the other perspectives in this chapter (Chamberlain & Patterson, 1995). Nevertheless, there is room for additional refinement in the measurement of compliance for the operational definition to coincide more adequately with existing theoretical statements about the construct. For example, in coercive process theory, noncompliance is conceived as one of a larger class of coercion, a category that includes such aversive behaviors as negative commands, crying, and hitting. However, behavioral definitions of noncompliance do not distinguish between forms of noncompliance that are perceived as aversive by the parent and forms of resistance that are perceived as appropriately assertive or positive in tone (e.g., Crockenberg & Litman, 1990; Kuczynski & Kochanska, 1990). Moreover, in Forehand and MacMahon's (1981) behavior management model, parents are taught to label a broad range of behaviors as noncompliance—not only failure to carry out an instruction immediately for the first time, but also transgressions against long-standing rules from the past. Thus, their definition does not strictly adhere to the operational criteria of immediate compliance and conceptually muddies the distinction between immediate compliance and the domain of long-term conformity considered by the internal control perspective (Kuczynski, 1984).

Model of Parental Competence

Behavioral interventions in families of noncompliant children are designed to train parents to manage children's behavior by the effective but noncoercive application of external contingencies. This seemingly paradoxical goal requires parents to firmly enforce compliance to their demands without engaging in ineffectual aversive behaviors such as yelling or "nattering" (Patterson, 1982) and without using physical punishment. In general, parent training programs (e.g., Forehand & MacMahon, 1981; Patterson & Forgatch, 1987) have a number of child management strategies in common. Parents are taught to track noncompliance in their interactions with children and to monitor their children's behavior outside the home. They are taught to deliver clear, direct, forceful commands as antecedants for compliance. They are taught to administer contingent positive consequences such as attention, praise, or material rewards for compliance and contingent but noncoercive punishment such as time-out or work chores for noncompliance. Of these, the techniques for confronting noncompliance are the most central. According to Patterson (1982), "If I were allowed to select only one concept to use in training parents of antisocial children, I would teach them how to punish more effectively" (p. 111).

Despite discouraging the use of physical punishment, the behavioral model of parental skill almost exclusively relies on the use of external controls for managing children's behavior. Indeed, admonishments can be found that discourage parents from using low power strategies such as reasoning and explanation (Forehand & MacMahon 1981; Patterson, 1982; Reid, 1982). The assumption is that explanations are, at best, ineffectual in terms of eliciting immediate compliance and, therefore, have little place in parental repertoires of child-rearing skills.

Until recently, behavioral models of parenting have not included an independent conceptualization of the parent-child relationship. In general, behavioral models do not distinguish between the immediate behaviors and strategies exchanged by parents and children during social interaction and the long-term affective and cognitive context of the parent-child relationship. Some aspects of Patterson's (1982) coercive process theory appear to be compatible with the notion that parents and children form relationship expectancies about each other's behavior based on past experiences of interaction. However, explanations in coercive process theory generally emphasize immediate contingencies of social interaction and eschew the construct of relationship. Thus, quality of relationship is often equated with the frequency of positive and negative behaviors exchanged between parents and children. Moreover, behavioral clinical interventions generally give priority to behavior management over relationship enhancement on the assumption that good relationships follow children's compliance rather than set the stage for compliance. However, there are signs that training in relationship enhancement and communication skills are beginning to be included as components in recent parent-training programs (Eyberg & Boggs, 1989; Forehand & Long, 1996).

Traditional Authoritarianism

In the recent developmental literature, the concept of authoritarianism has become associated with incompetent or coercive forms of parenting (Maccoby & Martin, 1983). This relatively recent use of the term has obscured that authoritarianism also has another meaning that represents a culturally normative parenting ideology with an explicit theory of socialization and of children's competence. The ideological basis of authoritarianism was apparent in Baumrind's (1971, 1991) definition of the Authoritarian parent type:

> Authoritarian parents attempt to shape, control, and evaluate the behavior and attitudes of their children in accordance with a set standard of conduct, usually an absolute standard, theologically motivated or formulated by a higher secular authority. They attempt to inculcate such conventional values as respect for authority, work, and preservation of order and traditional structure. They do not encourage give-and-take, believing that children should accept their parents' word for what is right. (p. 127)

Empirical literature has focused on cross-cultural manifestations of authoritarian parenting practices (Grusec, Rudy, & Martini, this volume) and on the influence of religious beliefs on authoritarian child-rearing values and parenting strategies (Ellison & Sherkat, 1993; Grasmick, Bursik, & Kimpel, 1991; Greven, 1990; Wiehe, 1990). The authoritarian perspective is considered here because it represents an influential external control perspective on children's conformity with considerable social and theoretical impact.

Because authoritarianism may take various cultural forms, the present discussion will be restricted to "traditional authoritarianism" (Osborne, 1995), an indigenous cultural parenting style in North America. The roots of traditional authoritarianism lies in Puritan Christianity of the 17th century (Greven, 1990; Osborne, 1995). It was the dominant philosophy of parenting in America prior to the 20th century (Alwin, 1988), and it persists in explicit form in current North American fundamentalist Christian religions. Thus, traditional authoritarianism is disseminated formally as a contemporary parent education perspective (Osborne, 1995), and it is frequently represented in social policy forums on such topics as firm discipline in home and school, parental authority and rights, and corporal punishment (Dobson, 1978; Gordon, 1990; Wald, Owen, & Hill, 1989).

The traditional authoritarian perspective on socialization is characterized by demands for rigid obedience and respect for authority, particularly, that of the father.

Parental correction for misbehavior emphasizes the inculcation of submission and respect for parental authority by the administration of corporal punishment and contingent parental affection and love. The theoretical underpinnings of this perspective on compliance rest on the theological construct of "willful disobedience" which was assumed to be a consequence of an innately evil human nature. A goal of parental socialization was to overcome defiance and ultimately gain submissiveness to parental authority and, eventually, God's authority through parental adoption of techniques that "break the child's will."

A statement of this perspective can be found in a sermon by John Wesley (1783/1973), the founder of Methodism:

> A wise parent . . . should begin to break their will, the first moment it appears. In the whole art of Christian education there is nothing more important than this. The will of a parent is to a little child in the place of the will of God. Therefore, studiously teach them to submit to this while they are children, that they may be ready to submit to his will when they are men. (pp. 59–60)

Model of Children's Conformity

The traditional authoritarian perspective on socialization has been formalized within a model of parent education by James Dobson in such books as *Dare to Discipline* (1970), *The Strong-Willed Child* (1978), and *Parenting Isn't for Cowards* (1987). The authoritarian conception of children's conformity and of parental skill as presented by Dobson is consistent with a unidimensional category of immediate compliance/noncompliance. Compliance is conceived as immediate, unquestioning obedience to parental instructions, whereas noncompliance is conceived as any failure to comply. The principal focus of parenting is on suppressing noncompliance as a manifestation of will. The various manifestations of will resemble such psychological constructs as "assertiveness," "expressing autonomy," and "negotiation."

Model of Parental Competence

The authoritarian conception of parental skill is captured by Dobson's idea of the parent as a "loving authority." This concept emphasizes the hierarchical status of the parent-child relationship, discipline of the child by means of external punishment, and contingent parental affection. Dobson advocates that parents maintain their authority and not surrender or bargain away their control to the child as a route to "shaping" the child's will.

Physical punishment, especially for young children, is one of the strategies for this shaping. However, corporal punishment should be reserved only for willful disobedience and should be administered only after the child has been provided sufficient explanations about the nature of the transgression. "In my opinion, spankings should be reserved for the moment a child (age 10 or less) expresses a defiant 'I will not' or 'You shut up!' When a youngster tries this kind of stiff-necked rebellion, you had better take it out of him, and pain is a marvelous purifier" (Dobson, 1970, p. 27).

The traditional authoritarian perspective on the role of the parent-child relationship context in socialization is also noteworthy for its psychological assumptions. First, Dobson proposes a developmental sequence where the creation of an authority relationship precedes the creation of a loving relationship. He suggests that much like the fearful image of God in the Old Testament precedes the loving image of God in the New Testament so too must children learn submission to parental authority before they can experience parental love. Second, parental love and affection are viewed as contingent rewards bestowed on the child by the parent for appropriate signs of submission after discipline. Thus, in the authoritarian perspective, child conformity is conceptualized as immediate and unquestioning compliance and noncompliance is considered to be an undesirable manifestation of will. The authoritarian model of parental skill consists of the ability to exert contingent external control in the context of a contingently affectionate relationship.

The behavioral and authoritarian perspectives differ considerably in their theories of socialization, their views about the origins of noncompliance, and about the place of physical punishment in parental repertoires of skills. However, both are influential proponents of an external control perspective on socialization and child conformity. Competent conformity is conceptualized as immediate compliance with the parents' agenda and parental competence consists in the use of external controls to suppress noncompliance. The parent-child relationship context has been a subsidiary concern in external control theories, regarded as a control strategy or a consequence of compliance rather than as a source of children's cooperation or a goal in itself.

INTERNALIZATION PERSPECTIVE ON SOCIALIZATION

The internalization perspective on child conformity encompasses many different frameworks, including cognitive developmental theories on moral development (Kohlberg, 1969; Piaget, 1932/1965) and motivational theories of internalization (Grolnick, Deci, & Ryan, this volume; Hoffman, 1970; Lepper, 1983). Despite their diversity, internalization theories share assumptions concerning the nature of conformity. One assumption is that different categories of conformity need to be distinguished on the basis of children's motivation for complying with parental directives, the most important distinction being between external control and internal control. The second assumption is that internal control is superior to external control or "mere compliance." In internalization theory, compliance is considered to be no more than an early precursor or necessary step on the way to internal control.

Motivational theories of internalization propose that there is a sequence in children's motivational development. Initially, children's compliance is maintained by external sources of control. At this stage, children would not comply unless compelled to do so by parental rewards or punishment and their compliance would cease in the absence of external surveillance. Gradually, with appropriate experiences, children develop internal motives for compliance and take over the task of regulating their own behavior. With the development of internalization, external inducements are no longer necessary to maintain conformity with parental demands, a development that makes the child's compliance more stable and durable over time.

Various motivational systems have been proposed as sources of children's internal control. Hoffman (1970) postulated that motivational resources such as guilt or empathic distress may be attached to children's acts of conformity with parental wishes. According to attribution theory, internal control may be motivated by a desire to behave consistently with self-attributed values and personality characteristics (Lepper, 1973, 1983). In self-determination theory (Deci & Ryan, 1987; Grolnick et al., this volume), it is assumed that internal motives themselves have intrapsychic counterparts to internal and external motivation. Several qualities of internal motives are distinguished on the basis of the quality of internal constraint versus autonomy underlying a person's conforming behavior.

A similar sequence was proposed in cognitive developmental theories of moral development (Kohlberg, 1969; Piaget, 1932/1965), where the idea can be found that compliance to external pressures is a less advanced level of self-regulation than internal control. In Piaget's theory, development proceeded from a morality of constraint where children feel an obligation to comply to rules because they are sacred and unalterable. It is only later that children proceed to a stage of moral cooperation where rules are maintained though reciprocal social agreements and are subject to negotiation. Experiential factors, in addition to cognitive development, were responsible for this shift. Piaget proposed that the shift coincided with a change in children's social experiences from interactions with parents, which he assumed to be hierarchical and power assertive, to interactions with peers where a relationship of equal power prevailed.

Kohlberg's (1969) theory also assumed that the earliest and most primitive stages of moral development are based on compliance to external parental socialization pressures. Thus, at Stage 1 children comply to avoid punishment and at Stage 2, children comply to obtain rewards. Relationship motives are considered at Stage 3, where children's compliance is assumed to be maintained by the parent's affection and social approval. It is only after leaving an environment dominated by the parent's power to reward and punish that children develop more mature stages of moral regulation such as regulation by social norms and, eventually, by autonomous principled reasoning.

Model of Children's Conformity

The internal control model of conformity is more differentiated than the behavioral model of compliance. Minimally, there are two categories of compliance to consider: external control and internal control (Figure 9.1). However, unlike external control theories, there is little independent conceptualization of "noncompliance," perhaps because parents' ability to secure compliance has been overestimated in internalization theory.

The distinction between internal and external control poses serious problems for measurement in internalization research because evidence is required to support the inference of the source of motivation for the child's behavior. The definition of immediate compliance as "compliance within 15 seconds" is ambiguous from a motivational standpoint. Although immediate compliance coincides with the idea of external control as "compliance in the parent's presence," children also may have internal motives for complying immediately with a parent's requests. Thus, many studies (Lytton, 1980; Stayton, Hogan, & Ainsworth, 1971) do find linkages between children's compliance rates and parental practices or other variables that suggest an internal or relational origin for the behavior.

One approach to assessing the child's motivation for control involves the use of indirect measures. Examples include projective measures of guilt, confession, or concern for others; moral judgments (Hoffman & Saltzstein, 1967; Kochanska, Padavich, & Koenig, 1996; Kohlberg, 1969); and behaviorally assessed signs of anxiety (Stayton et al., 1971) or positive affect (Kochanska & Aksan, 1995; Kuczynski, 1984; Rheingold, Cook, & Kolowitz, 1987) accompanying the child's conforming behavior.

Experimentally controlled contextual criteria have also been used to assess the internal versus external orientation of children's conformity behavior. For example, the resistance to deviation paradigm was used in laboratory settings to obtain data on the quality of children's compliance. In such studies, children's compliance with a prohibition was measured in the experimenter's absence under conditions where, from children's point of view, there was little risk of detection if they deviated.

The working assumption is that the amount of external control exerted by the socializing agent should decrease over time in the absence of surveillance and, therefore, the relative stability of compliance should indicate the extent to which the behavior is under internal versus external control. Several variations of this procedure have been used. One approach (Cheyne & Walters, 1969; Parke, 1969) was to assess children's compliance at three successive points in time during a 15-minute resistance to deviation test. A replicated finding is that children who received an unexplained prohibition tend to show decreases in compliance over time in the experimenter's absence, whereas children who receive an explanation for a prohibition tend to comply at a high and stable rate over time. Other approaches to measuring internally controlled compliance included testing children's long-term compliance after a 2-week delay (Leizer & Rogers, 1974) and measuring compliance in the experimenter's absence as the child's fear of detection was decreased by experimental manipulation (Kuczynski, 1983). Such studies illustrate that judgments regarding the effectiveness of a control strategy depend on how compliance is defined. Strategies such as power assertion and reasoning may be equally effective in the socializing agent's presence, under conditions of high external control. However, differences favoring inductive strategies emerge in the parent's absence when the external supports for children's compliance are removed.

Model of Parental Competence

Conceiving children's social competence as internal control has implications for a corresponding model of parental skill. Internalization theory emphasizes parenting behaviors and strategies that are opposite to those promoted by external control theories, a fact that has been the focus of a long-standing debate between the two perspectives (Gordon, 1990; Hoffman, 1970; Peterson, 1974). According to internal control theories, the child management strategies advocated by the traditional authoritarian and behavioral perspectives provide the ingredients for externally motivated compliance. Internalization theories, therefore, emphasize strategies such as minimal use of power (Lepper, 1973, 1983), character attributions (Grusec & Redler, 1980), choice and autonomy-enhancing strategies (Grolnick et al., this volume), and providing explanations (Hoffman, 1970; Kuczynski, 1982, 1983) as a way of promoting internal control of conformity.

Most early theories of internalization acknowledged the social relationship context of socialization although relationship was considered in diverse ways across theoretical accounts. In Piaget's theory, a relationship context where conflicts are resolved by negotiation rather than by exercise of superior power was considered to be beneficial for moral development. However, such give-and-take interactions were assumed to be more a characteristic of peer relationships than of parent-child relationships. Maintaining good interpersonal relationships was most explicitly considered as a motive for social regulation in Kohlberg's theory. However, as noted by Gilligan (1982), relationship was positioned as a relatively immature stage of moral development in Kohlberg's ranking of motives for conformity. In Hoffman's (1970) theory, relationship was represented by the variable of parental warmth, which was proposed to mediate the effects of other parenting strategies. Moreover, some of the strategies described by Hoffman such as other-oriented inductions and love withdrawal draw on motivational resources that have to do with relationships. However, Hoffman (1983) tended to emphasize the repercussions of such techniques for children's information processing of parental messages. Finally, various studies from the attribution theory perspective considered that social consequences such as praise and verbal rebuke were not as detrimental to the formation of intrinsic attributions as material consequences (Smith, Gelfand, Hartmann, & Partlow, 1979).

In summary, children's competent conformity in the internal control perspective is conceptualized as the superiority of internal control over immediate compliance. The models of parental competence that emerge from this view on conformity emphasize the subtle use of parental power and cognitive strategies such as reasoning and explanation. As with external control theories, the relationship context was a background consideration in early internal control theories; emphasis was placed on understanding the influence of discipline techniques. Conceptions of the relationship context did not venture much beyond the idea that the parent-child relationship was primarily an authority relationship. The relative emphasis on discipline techniques versus relationship is reversed in the next perspective to be considered.

RELATIONAL PERSPECTIVE ON SOCIALIZATION

The relational perspective emphasizes the long-term relationship context of parent-child interaction and of socialization. As was discussed earlier, the idea that socialization and social interactions occur in the context of relationships has always been in the background of research on socialization. In the relational perspective, however, the implications of the relationship context is a starting point for conceptualizations of socialization in the context of the family.

The perspective can be understood if it is considered that interactions between persons who have a close personal relationship follow different principles than interactions between unfamiliar individuals (e.g., Hinde, 1979; Laursen & Collins, 1994; Miller & Steinberg, 1975). The long-term relationship context gives a time dimension to parent-child interactions (Hinde, 1979; Lollis & Kuczynski, in press). Parents and children do not react only to the stimulus qualities of each others' immediate behaviors during interaction. They also react to mutual expectations formed during a previous history of interaction and to anticipations that their relationship will continue into the future. The parent-child relationship also involves a close interdependence of needs and goals (Kelly et al., 1983). Parents depend on their children to meet strong needs including needs for companionship and affection (L. W. Hoffman, 1988) just as children depend on their parents to meet their needs. The intimate knowledge that the relationship affords means that parents come to know their offspring as individual personalities rather than as generic children and children come to know their parents as individual personalities rather than as generic adults (Hildebrandt, 1996). Such relationship knowledge may contribute to parental attribution of agency, intentionality, and rights to their children (Hallden, 1991; Mayall, 1994). Thus, the relationship context is one in which parents and children are both powerful and vulnerable with regard to each other despite apparent differences in legitimate authority, individual capacities, and material resources. From a relational perspective, the traditional depiction of the parent-child relationship exclusively as a vertical power arrangement is a problematical one. Instead, many normative parent-child relationships, particularly in contemporary Western culture, resemble what Laursen and Collins (1994) have called a "mixed relationship" having some of the qualities of an authority relationship and some of the qualities of a friendship. This relationship context may promote an enhanced bidirectionality of influence that has been noted in the extraordinary degree of mutual cooperation (Fogel, 1993; Schaffer, 1984, 1991) and mutual resistance (Eisenberg, 1992; Patterson, 1982) that may occur in parent-child relationships.

Maccoby and Martin's (1983) review of research on parent-child interaction presaged many elements of a relational perspective on socialization. In contrast to earlier perspectives that emphasized parental discipline and authority, they traced the origins of socialization to the beginnings of relationship formation during the first year of life. Moreover, special emphasis was placed on social processes involving bidirectionality, mutual expectations, shared goals, and coregulation of behavior. Maccoby and Martin proposed that what is usually conceptualized as a shift of regulatory functions from the parent as an individual to the child as an individual can more accurately be described in terms of changes in coregulation. The concept of coregulation suggests that individuals are seldom truly "self"-regulating. Rather, individuals are always embedded in social systems in which they are influenced by others while simultaneously exercising influence on those others.

Research on maternal commands and children's compliance during the first years of life illustrates that it is possible to consider concepts such as compliance, self-regulation, and internal control as social and dyadic achievements rather than individual achievements. Kopp (1982) has described how young children's ability to independently carry out simple acts of self-regulation such as following a parent's request requires the development of underlying motor, attentional, and language capacities. Nevertheless, according to Schaffer (1984, 1991) 5-month-old infants manage to comply with maternal instructions at rates approaching 50% although their capacity for self-regulation is not fully developed. An examination of the context of mother-infant interaction reveals that the infant's compliance is not an individual behavior so much as a closely coordinated, mutually accomplished action (Fogel, 1993). Mothers sensitively time and adapt their verbal and physical behavior to the child's behavior so as to stimulate, fill in, and support the child's attempts at cooperation.

Evidence of similar social scaffolding of compliance also can be found during toddlerhood. For example, giving toddlers a command to pick up their toys often entails that the parent assist the child in carrying out the directive. Similarly, Kuczynski, Kochanska, Radke-Yarrow, and Girnius-Brown (1987) found that mothers' verbal commands to toddlers were frequently accompanied by touches and gestures and that mothers decreased these physical supports for their verbalizations as children developed. The phenomenon of early child compliance highlights the social and coregulated nature of children's performance. The parent and child accomplish together what they could not accomplish as individuals.

Maccoby and Martin (1983) suggest that although coregulation in the parent-child dyad occurs even in infancy, the degree to which the child is capable of participating in a coregulation system increases with age. The child's increasing capacity to function outside the parent-child dyad is only partly due to increases in self-regulation. Maccoby (1984) elaborated that between 6 and 12 years of age there is a gradual transfer in responsibility between the parent and the child from a coregulated system in which the parent assumes relatively immediate control over an aspect of children's lives to a coregulated system where parents adopt a more general supervisory role as children begin to exercise moment-to-moment self-regulation:

> The process of co-regulation if it is to be successful must be a cooperative one, with clarity of communication between the parent and the child of paramount importance. . . . Children must be willing to inform parents of their whereabouts, activities and problems so that parents can mediate and guide them when necessary; parents must keep informed about events occurring outside their presence and must coordinate agendas that link the daily activities of the parent and child. (pp. 191–192)

Empirical research is needed to explore the concept of coregulation. It is evident, however, that coregulation offers an alternative to conceptions of internalization as the movement from external control by others to autonomous or internal control. Past the childhood period, it may also be fruitful to consider that socialization may involve a shift from coregulation within relationships inside the family to coregulation within relationships with friends, spouses, and other persons outside the family of origin. Markus and Nurius (1984) suggest that mutual and reciprocal regulation may be a goal of socialization. As children "mature and are socialized, children's own needs, desires, goals, knowledge, skills, and expectations overlap or become the same as those of society, and co-regulation occurs" (p. 150). The embeddedness of social conformity and regulation within social relationships suggests that adaptive forms of social conformity may entail developing a stake in relationships rather than conformity to authority or to self-accepted autonomous motives .

The relational perspective also differs from the external and internal control perspectives in its views about the motivational foundations of socialization. In the control perspectives, the focus was on parents' management of power struggles so as to effectively force or persuade children to comply with parental commands (Hoffman, 1975; Schaffer, 1991). In the relational perspective, the primary focus is on the formation and management of the long-term relationship, a function that places constraints on the parent's use of coercive power.

Far from starting off as antisocial beings who must be coerced into sociability, children share a common heritage with their caretakers that impels them from infancy to adopt similar social goals (Schaffer, 1991). Mutual adaptation rather than conflict is the most frequent theme of parent-child interaction and constitutes the key context of the child's socialization. Consistent with this idea, Maccoby and Martin (1983) used the term "receptive" compliance to describe an early motive for compliance that stems from reciprocal expectations for cooperation that develop during the interaction history of the parent-child relationship. Other researchers have also noted the voluntary, affectively positive, sometimes enthusiastic, form that children's early compliance may take (Kochanska & Aksan, 1995; Rheingold, Cook, & Kolowitz, 1987).

Empirical support for the relational origins of receptive compliance comes from several sources. Compliance is related to maternal sensitivity, or compliance, to children's cues (e.g., Lytton, 1980; Stayton et al., 1971). Rocissano, Slade, and Lynch (1987) found that mothers who were skilled in following their toddler's leads in play fostered more synchronous exchanges with their children, who, in turn, were more compliant with maternal directives. Laboratory studies (Lay, Waters, & Park, 1989; Parpal & Maccoby, 1985) indicate that relatively short interventions designed to train mothers to follow their children's cues responsively during play sessions can enhance children's compliance. Research linking secure attachment to children's early compliance (Londerville & Main, 1981; Matas, Arend, & Sroufe, 1978) is also consistent with the construct of receptive compliance when it is considered that secure attachment may have origins in responsive interactions with parents.

These findings are challenging for older control perspectives on internalization. First, they suggest that some portion of children's cooperation is attributable not to specific parental control techniques but to the quality of parent-child interaction outside episodes of control. Second, they suggest that the long-accepted developmental sequence of external control followed by internal control may need to be reconsidered. The sequence emerging in the relationship literature is that initial dispositions toward cooperation are based on the early relationship developed between parent and child. External control and internal control may be later developments superimposed on, and, perhaps, undermining earlier relational motives for cooperation.

Besides highlighting the relevance of cooperative interactions for socialization, the relational perspective also provides a positive framework for understanding children's resistance and conflict. Close relationships within the family are a context for considerable conflict. The presence of noncompliant and assertive behavior in otherwise nondeviant parent-child dyads has attracted the attention of researchers for many years. Landauer, Carlsmith, and Lepper (1970) found that children were more obedient to an unfamiliar mother than their own mother, a finding they attributed to the children's ability to predict their mothers' lenient responses based on a prior history of interaction. Dumas and LaFreniere (1993) also found children to be more positive and cooperative with their own mothers than with unrelated mothers. Other researchers noted that children's responses to maternal control, while generally cooperative, are often accompanied by acts of noncompliance, assertion, whining, and argumentativeness (Kuczynski, 1984; Kuczynski & Kochanska, 1990; Vaughan, Kopp, & Krakow, 1984). Moreover, studies of nonclinic populations report that children disobey between 20% and 40% of the commands of their parents (Forehand, 1977) and noncompliance rates as high as 50% have been described as falling within reasonable bounds for 10- to 11-year-old boys (Patterson & Forgatch, 1987).

Matas et al. (1978) found positive associations between security of attachment assessed during infancy and children's competence in problem-solving at age 2 years. However, they also noted the nonexact nature of these children's cooperation with parents. "The competent 2-year-old as seen in this study is not the child who automatically complies with whatever the mother tells him/her. Rather, it is the child who shows a certain amount of noncompliance when requested to stop playing and clean up the toys, but who gradually cooperates with the mother" (p. 554). In contrast, Crittenden and DiLalla (1988) reported a compulsive and rigid form of compliance among infants of abusive parents.

Examining conflict from a relational perspective also raises many questions about traditional assumptions concerning parental authority. Eisenberg (1992) found that discipline and noncompliance represent only a subset of conflicts that occur regularly between mothers and their 4-year-old children. An emphasis on episodes of noncompliance underestimates the amount of conflict and the frequency of children's "wins" in normal relationships. Other interactions that precipitate conflicts include episodes where parents fail to comply with their children's requests, disagreements over statements of intent, and disagreements after factual and attitudinal assertions. Although behavioral compliance is not possible in such contexts, acquiescence and disagreeement in the context of verbal conflict is certainly relevant to the internalization of values.

When conflict is viewed in this larger perspective, resolutions do not reflect the picture of relatively high rates of child compliance (70%–80%) to parental demands that have been found for behavioral requests alone (Chamberlain & Patterson, 1995). Eisenberg (1992) found that although children complied twice as often as mothers, the proportions of compliance were 22% for children and 11% for mothers. Compromises were also rare (3%). Instead, the most frequent resolution of conflict was a standoff (64%) where the conflict is dropped in mutual opposition rather than in clear-cut conformity of one person to another. Very similar findings were also found for parent-child conflicts in late adolescence (Vuchinich, 1987, 1990). Vuchinich noted the puzzle that such findings pose for traditional ideas about power relations in the family:

> But what is surprising is that parents did not choose to—or were not able to—use their power to win most conflicts with their children. Parent-child conflicts ended in a stand-off three times more often (62 cases) than they ended in submission (21 cases). Parents did not usually "put their children in their place" in conflict closings. (p. 136)

Thus, research suggests that conflict is a frequent, sustained, and mutually tolerated feature of social interactions within parent-child relationships. Moreover, although mothers may have more power than their children, they do not exercise it by suppressing conflict or by demanding their children's submission as much as control perspectives on socialization might lead one to expect (Hoffman, 1975).

Model of Children's Conformity

A conception of conformity that fits the emerging relationship perspective is accommodation/negotiation (Figure 9.1). Unlike the idea of exact conformity implied by "compliance" and "internal control," the constructs of accommodation and negotiation suggest that a nonexact, mutually coregulated form of cooperation passes for compliance within relationships. Miller and Steinberg (1975) provided a useful distinction between two types of conformity, *compliance* and *conflict resolution* that has been influential in adult communication research. They suggest that in interactions between unfamiliar persons the goal is to obtain compliance, an exact match between the outcome and the desires of the communicator. In interactions within relationships where the participants know each other well, the goal is to obtain conflict resolution, some compromise of the original desires of the participants. In their view, successful outcomes are those that at least partially correspond with the communicators' original desires. Moreover, successful compromises may be accompanied by collateral physical, economic, or relational positive consequences.

It is likely that within close relationships even direct commands come to be understood as inviting accommodation rather than compliance. During a history of interaction, parents and children evolve shared understandings of what will pass for compliance in different situations. It is only on rare occasions that the shared understanding approximates the complete, immediate submission that is implied by "compliance within 15 seconds." More often, what parents accept as compliance, and what children understand to be compliance, is closer to the idea of "accommodation." Accommodation conveys both an expectation of a cooperative response, and also that the form of the cooperative response will be chosen by the recipient rather than by the sender of a request. Thus, an accommodating response by children may acknowledge that the parent has been heard, that children will attempt to coordinate the parent's wishes with their own plans or that children are willing to negotiate an alternative course of action.

Negotiation as a parenting practice was identified in Baumrind's (1971, 1991) identification of the authoritative parenting style, which was found to be associated with higher levels of social competence in both girls and boys than the authoritarian and permissive parenting styles. Authoritative parents were characterized as exercising firm control at points of parent-child divergence and holding high expectations for children's performance but willing to engage in responsive, give-and-take interactions with their children. The importance of negotiation and the creation of more symmetrical power relations between parents and children is especially emphasized in Baumrind's (1991) depiction of competent family transitions during adolescence: "Following puberty, a renegotiation of entitlements and obligations, and of roles and responsibilities among family members often will enable adolescents to accept reasonable parental control without sacrificing self-esteem and social assertiveness within the peer group" (p. 117).

The conceptualization of negotiation as a child practice has its recent origins in attempts to understand children's noncompliant behavior in normative families. A guiding assumption is that a moderate level of noncompliant behavior is a healthy manifestation of children's developing autonomy and assertiveness (Crockenberg & Litman, 1990; Kuczynski et al., 1987; Leavitt, 1991). Because children express their autonomy within the constraints of an interdependent relationship, it is possible to consider children's communication of resistance within a relational perspective. Thus, children's negotiations may be a counterpart to the concept of coregulation discussed earlier. Just as children must regulate their cooperative behaviors in a social context, they must also regulate their autonomous behaviors within a context that contains other individuals, including parents, whose choices clash with their own.

Autonomy development is a complex phenomenon that involves several interconnected systems. During the second and third years of life, children develop the capacity for self-regulation (Kopp, 1982) including the ability to follow verbal commands. Parents respond to such developments by increasing their socialization pressures toward their children (Dubin & Dubin, 1963; Gralinski & Kopp, 1993; Kuczynski & Kochanska, 1995). Moreover, during this time, children develop a sense of independent self and a motive to resist threats to their autonomy. This motivational change is manifested by a period of "negativism" or increased overt and active resistance to parental control (Wenar, 1982). Thus, at a time that children are more and more *able* to comply, they become less and less *willing* to comply. An early conception of the "terrible twos" or "negativism" was that it declined by the time the child entered school. However, similar forms of resistance have been studied as "reactance" (Brehm, 1981) and "counter-control" (Mahoney, 1974) during adulthood suggesting that the motive to defend one's autonomy from external control remains a theme throughout the life span (Kuczynski & Kochanska, 1990). Yet another developmental system concerns the expression of autonomy. Children gradually develop interpersonal negotiation strategies that enable them to defend their self interests in a way that takes into account the interests of other persons during conflict (Yeates & Selman, 1989).

Several studies explored the assertion dimension of children's resistance. Crockenberg and Litman (1990) distinguished between assertion as an appropriate manifestation of autonomy and noncompliance in the traditional sense of deviant or oppositional behavior. Their findings suggested that simple refusals are more competent and more autonomous forms of resistance than defiance because they have self-assertion rather than opposition as their primary goal.

Another approach has been to distinguish between assertive and unassertive forms of opposition (Kuczynski & Kochanska, 1990; Kuczynski et al., 1987). Active forms of noncompliance, which are accompanied by verbal and nonverbal indications of deliberate resistance, can be considered as more assertive than passive noncompliance that is not accompanied by signs of intent. Consistent with the autonomy development hypothesis, several studies have found that passive noncompliance becomes replaced by more active forms of resistance during the second and third years of life (Kuczynski et al., 1987; Vaughan, Kopp, & Krakow, 1984) and from the toddler period to age 5 (Kuczynski & Kochanska, 1990). Another focus of research has been on children's development of social skills for influencing parents during conflicts. This includes both compliance-gaining strategies, which are children's social strategies for persuading parents to comply with their requests (Becker, 1990; Delia, Kline, & Burleson, 1979; Garvey, 1975), and their strategies for avoiding compliance with parental requests (Dunn & Munn, 1987; Leonard, 1993; McQuillen, 1986). The latter have also been studied under the framework of "compliance-resisting strategies," which have been defined as verbal attempts to gain the agent's acceptance of the target's unwillingness to comply (McLaughlin, Cody, & Robey, 1980).

A substantial body of research indicates that children become more skillful in the use of compliance-resistance and negotiation strategies with development. In one approach, resistant behaviors were coded on the basis of the directness and aversiveness of the strategy for the parent (Kuczynski & Kochanska, 1990; Kuczynski et al., 1987). Using these criteria, strategies such as *passive noncompliance* (ignoring the parent), and *direct defiance* (temper tantrums, destructiveness, whining) were considered to be relatively unskillful as strategies, whereas *simple refusals* and *negotiation* (asking the parent to justify their request, providing an explanation, proposing compromises) were considered to be relatively more skillful. A cross-sectional study of children between the ages of 15 months and 51 months (Kuczynski et al., 1987) and a longitudinal study of the same children when they were followed up at age 5 years (Kuczynski & Kochanska, 1990) found that unskillful forms of noncompliance decreased in frequency with age, whereas socially skillful forms of resistance increased with age of child.

Other research (McQuillen, 1986; McQuillen, Higginbotham, & Cummings, 1984) indicates that the strategic quality of children's noncompliance continues to develop into adolescence. The use of four categories of compliance-resisting strategies was investigated in children attending Grade 1, Grade 4, and Grade 10. The strategies included *nonnegotiation:* inflexible, unapologetic refusal to assent to a request; *identity management:* indirect manipulation of the image of the agent or target or both; *justifying:* offering explanations for one's unwillingness to comply; and *negotiation:* proposal to engage in mutual talks that will result in maximized goals for both parties. Nonnegotiation, considered to be the riskiest strategy was found to decrease with age, whereas identity management and justifications increased with age. In a further study, McQuillen (1986) found that children became increasingly adaptive in their use of strategies with age, and chose different strategies depending on the target. Thus, 10th graders used more sophisticated strategies with their mothers than they did with their younger sibling or best friend. This finding indicates that skill involves more than just type of strategy it also involves how, when, and with whom the strategy is used.

Model of Parental Competence

The relational perspective on parental skill shifts the focus from the use of specific techniques for managing children's behavior to parental management of the parent-child relationship. Moreover, the perspective highlights a different set of issues in the etiology of children's behavior problems. Problems in socialization that may have more to do with relationship management rather than fostering control include the following:

1. Elevated levels of resistance may be a consequence of a poor relationship history. Although there is very little research on parental management of their relationships with children, several different aspects of the relationship may be implicated. These include insecurity in the attachment relationship (Bretherton, Golby, & Cho, this volume); deficiency in parental nurturance and warmth (MacDonald, this volume) and insufficient experience in reciprocal cooperation (Parpal & Maccoby, 1985).

2. Elevated resistance may also signal problems with children's autonomy development in the parent-child relationship (Rothbaum & Weisz, 1989). Adolescents may employ immature conflict negotiation strategies such as nonnegotiation (White, Pearson, & Flint, 1989) and attacking or withdrawing from conflict (Rubenstein & Feldman, 1993) in reaction to severe power imbalances with their parents. In this case, skillful parenting consists in promoting the child's sense of control within the parent-child relationship. Kuczynski and Kochanska (1990) suggest that skillful parents may deliberately permit their child to win conflicts and express dissent in appropriate situations as a way of promoting their children's sense of efficacy and power. Autonomy-enhancing strategies are also discussed by Grolnick et al. (this volume).

3. Children's failures in compliance may reflect problems of coregulation for acts of control that are developmentally challenging. Parental skill, in this case, may entail providing support or scaffolding for the mutual coregulation of complex actions (Schaffer, 1991).

4. Conduct problems may also reflect deficits in social skills for expressing resistance and negotiation. Children may be labeled noncompliant when the real problem is that they are expressing noncompliance at the skill level of a much younger child. A similar idea is reflected in Patterson's (1982) suggestion that the noncompliant child may show "arrested socialization." According to Patterson, ineffectual parental reactions such as coercion or withdrawal instead of firm enforcement may be responsible for training children to use such unskillful tactics. However, a consideration of what parenting practices may train positive social strategies suggests a paradoxical piece of parenting advice. A competent parent may wish to increase the skill level of their children's resistance. Both parental modeling of negotiation strategies (Kuczynski et al., 1987) and direct feedback and instruction (Leonard, 1993) might foster children's development of skillful negotiation strategies.

CONTEXTUAL PERSPECTIVES

Although the external control, internal control, and the relational perspectives developed as competing conceptualizations of the socialization process, it is possible to consider them as complementary processes in self-regulation. In this fourth perspective, socialization experiences and self-regulation are considered to occur within specific contexts that have different requirements. Standards of conformity that may be appropriate in one context may not be appropriate in others. In this perspective, the essence of social competence is the ability to adapt one's mode of functioning to meet the requirements of different situations.

Aronfreed (1969) was early to point out the situation-specific nature of the motivations underlying social behavior:

> External cues continue to determine internalized conduct not only through their control over the individual's selection of appropriate behavior, but also through their specification of whether a particular form of behavior will maintain its intrinsic value. Such discriminations are, of course, a pervasive feature of socialization. They serve to facilitate the accuracy with which the child's acquisition of internalized controls reflects social reality, since there are very few acts to which socializing agents will always respond in the same way regardless of the situational context in which they occur. (p. 267)

Therefore, Aronfreed suggests that motivation for individual acts of conformity should be considered as varying on a continuum of internal versus external orientation.

Model of Children's Conformity

A contextual perspective on social conformity would consider that external control, internal control, or relationship motives may each be called into play in different contexts (Figure 9.1). In some contexts, goals and strategies on the part of the parent and competent action on the part of the child may correspond to standards of conformity conceptualized as external control. For example, the behavioral standard of compliance/noncompliance may be appropriate and adaptive in nonintimate relationships and interactions in hierarchical institutional contexts (school, church, courts of law, police). Compliance may also be the most adaptive standard of conformity in the presence of coercive threats by an angry parent or a parent determined to enforce compliance.

In other situations, parent and child actions may correspond to the idea of self-regulation as internal control. Rigid forms of internal control involving severe guilt and remorse may be fostered by parents and may be adaptive for the child in specific settings that involve socially valued behavior, moral behavior, safety, and cultural and religious values. In such situations, parents and society may be invested in teaching children to cooperate with minimal surveillance and for internal motives. Similarly, it is likely that parents promote a looser standard of conformity, such as reciprocal accommodation and negotiation, for close interpersonal interactions. Rigid obedience or internal control is often neither appropriate nor adaptive in interpersonal interactions among intimates.

One source of support for this tripartite contextual classification of conformity behaviors comes from research on adult persuasion and compliance-gaining. Wheeless, Barraclough, and Stewart (1983) found that three broad classes of compliance-gaining strategies similar to the ones proposed here recur in adult communication research. These include strategies that make salient the *external consequences* associated with behavior (e.g., rewards and punishments), strategies that summon the target's *values and obligations* (e.g., inherent moral nature of the behavior and strategies that invoke the communicator's *relationship* with the target (e.g., empathy, liking, esteem, negotiation).

Similarly, Kelman (1961, 1974) described three classes of conformity behaviors: compliance, identification, and internalization. Each category was defined in a context-specific manner with distinct antecedents and processes that govern the performance of the behavior. Thus, *compliance* occurs when an individual accepts influence from another to gain reward, or avoid a punishment. Compliance is performed under conditions of surveillance by the influencing agent. *Internalization* occurs when an individual accepts influence to maintain congruence of actions and beliefs with an internal value system. Internalization is performed under conditions where an individual's values are relevant to a current issue. *Identification* occurs when an individual accepts influence to establish or maintain a desired relationship with another individual.

Although, the psychology of behaving in context is far from understood, the available research suggests that how adults approach a persuasive interaction depends on the situation. Communication strategies vary depending on such factors as the relationship of the participants, the goals and potential consequences of the persuasion situation, and other constraints operating in the situation (Cody et al., 1986; Dix, 1991; Grusec & Goodnow, 1994; Miller, Boster, Rolloff, & Siebold, 1977).

Research on parent-child interactions in natural contexts (Chapman & Zahn-Waxler, 1982; Lytton, 1980; Minton, Kagan, & LeVine, 1971; Trickett & Kuczynski, 1986) and research sampling parental responses across different categories of transgressions also indicates that parental reactions to children's transgressions are highly situation specific. Moreover, varying standards of conformity inherent in different situations appear to be one determinant of parental choice of strategy. Thus, Grusec and Kuczynski (1980) found that mothers of 4- and 8-year old children predominantly used power assertion for situations where immediate control seemed to be appropriate (arguing with peers, noisiness, playing ball in the living room, ignoring a call to dinner). Reasoning and explanation was a predominant strategy after transgressions that had long-term implications for the child and for which internal control seemed to be important (stealing from mother's purse, teasing an elderly man, running blindly into the street).

Kuczynski (1984) provided experimental evidence that parents use different influence strategies depending on the kinds of conformity required of children in particular situations. Mothers who were led to believe that children's immediate compliance in their presence was of interest, tended to use simple power-assertive strategies. However, mothers who believed that compliance that would persist in their absence was of interest, spontaneously used a pattern of strategies that included increased responsive play prior to the compliance task and a greater frequency of reasoning, positive character attributions, and conversation during the compliance task.

There is also evidence that a relational mode of conformity is more likely to occur in some situations than in others. Distinctions have been made between the coercive processes involved in disciplinary interactions versus the mutual regulation that occurs in play (Schaffer, 1984). Contexts of behavioral noncompliance have been distinguished from contexts of verbal conflict (Eisenberg, 1992). Other distinctions highlighting contexts for relational processes include interpersonal versus noninterpersonal communication (Miller & Sternberg, 1975); situational compliance versus receptive compliance (Maccoby & Martin, 1983); and interactions that follow requests for competent action versus interactions that follow prohibitions (Kuczynski & Kochanska, 1995).

Social domain theory (Smetana, this volume) also is consistent with the hypothesis that different forms of control are fostered in different contexts. Research in the domain perspective emphasizes that social knowledge develops around highly contextualized experiences. Children have been found to receive different kinds of environmental feedback for moral, prudential, conventional, and personal transgressions. Although parental control and child conformity are only a subset of the experiences that are considered by domain theory, these appear to overlap with contexts where the varying standards of compliance, internal control, and accommodation are appropriate. Thus, the moral and prudential domains, which involve long-term issues of conformity, correspond to the context of internal control, and as pointed out by Smetana, such contexts rarely involve negotiation. In contrast, transgressions in the personal domain tend to elicit interpersonal conflict and negotiation. Conventional transgressions are less clear from the perspective of parental socialization. It is possible that some parents may consider conventions as control issues requiring immediate compliance, and others may approach these as requiring the internalization of long-term values.

Model of Parental Competence

In a contextual perspective, children's social competence is judged by the situational appropriateness of children's standards of conformity. Similarly, the corresponding model of parental skill would consider situational appropriateness of parental control strategies (Hoffman, 1970; Trickett & Kuczynski, 1986).

Hoffman's (1970) early research on children's internalization identified two different patterns of internal control. One group, described as "conventional rigid," appeared to have an inflexible conscience and did not take extenuating circumstances into account in their moral reactions to transgressions. Another group, labeled "humanistic-flexible" had a more adaptive conscience and responded with internal controls but only in appropriate situations. An investigation of the disciplinary practices experienced by the two groups of children indicated that parents of humanistic-flexible children used various combinations of reasoning and power assertion in response to different transgressions, whereas parents of conventional-rigid children used reasoning in a less discriminating manner.

Similarly, Trickett, and Kuczynski (1986) compared the discipline strategies of child-abusing parents and a matched sample of non-child-abusing parents. In accord with previous findings, nonabusive parents tended to use power-assertive strategies for transgressions in which immediate compliance issues were salient (noisiness, noncompliance) but reserved reasoning strategies for transgressions where internal control was appropriate (e.g., moral transgressions and long-standing household rules). In contrast, child-abusing parents were less discriminating in their use of discipline strategies and used unexplained punishment regardless of the child's transgression. A contextual interpretation of these findings is that the failure of abusive parents to adapt their strategies to the requirements of different situations may be maladaptive because parents used short-term strategies for long-term purposes.

It is important to consider the relationship context in which these situationally discriminated experiences occur. Several findings mentioned earlier suggest that interactions occurring in different contexts may be bound by an encompassing relationship context. Correlations between parental play and child compliance (Lytton, 1980), responsive caretaking and child compliance, (Stayton et al., 1971) and parental nurturance and internalized conscience (Hoffman, 1970) suggest that there may be associations between interactions occurring in different child-rearing domains. Thus, parental handling of conformity issues in one context may well have implications for success of parental interventions in another. Moreover, parents appear to be aware of the cross-contextual implications of their behavior and incorporate these insights into their child-rearing strategies. In the study reported earlier (Kuczynski, 1984), mothers who had a goal of securing their children's long-term compliance spontaneously engaged in responsive play with their children before attempting to control their behavior. Thus they appeared to work on their relationship with their children as a resource for conformity in one context before attempting to foster control over their children's behavior in a different context.

THE SOCIAL AND HISTORICAL CONTEXT OF CURRENT MODELS OF COMPLIANCE

The preceding review indicated a change in the conceptualization of children's conformity. Early models of compliance and internal control were based on conceptions of the parent-child relationship as a hierarchical authority relationship. Furthermore, compliance to parental external control was assumed to be the foundation of outcomes such as successful socialization, internalization, and warmth in the parent-child relationship. In contrast, fear of punishment is rarely invoked as a motive in depictions of normative socialization in more recent research. Instead, concepts such as child assertion, parent-child conflict, negotiation, and mutuality document a shift toward egalitarian conceptions of the parent-child relationship. This shift may partially reflect a change in the knowledge base. There are now several decades of research on naturalistic parent-child interactions, especially during infancy and toddlerhood, that simply did not exist when the original, classic theories were proposed. Moreover, there has been a paradigmatic change from unidirectional to bidirectional conceptions of causality in socialization. Both of these shifts in the knowledge base facilitate more egalitarian and relational assumptions about socialization.

Changes in the cultural and historical context of the two phases of theorizing may also be responsible for the difference in emphasis of the newer models of child conformity. The conceptualizations of social scientists often reflect values prevalent in the surrounding culture (Kessen, 1979). Socialization theories proposed during the 1960s and 1970s were grounded in the socialization practices and personal experiences prevalent in Western culture during the first half of the 20th century, whereas more recent theories of socialized conformity are grounded in the socialization practices prevalent during the second half of the 20th century. Thus, the recent focus on relationship and on children's autonomy in theories of conformity may reflect social changes in child-rearing norms and values.

There is evidence that the attitudes of Western parents toward obedience as a child-rearing value have changed during the 20th century. Authors such as Miller (1983/1990) for the European context and Greven (1990) for the North American context documented the historical roots of authoritarian child-rearing beliefs and practices. They indicate that immediate, unquestioning compliance and coercive parental control persisted as child-rearing norms during the first part of the century. Alwin (1988, 1990) using data from the Middletown study documented a historical change in the value parents place on compliance and autonomy. Parents interviewed in 1924 noted that their values had shifted from the traditional authoritarian demand for strict obedience that characterized parenting during the Victorian era. However, child-rearing values continued to change during the period from 1924 to 1974. Respectful orientations toward authority such as strict obedience, loyalty toward church, patriotism, and good manners declined sharply, whereas values for independence, tolerance, and social-mindedness rose during the same period. Similar trends have been documented in other U.S. samples and in several European countries (Alwin, 1988, 1990). Consistent with these historical trends, only a minority of mothers have been found to report that they expect children to comply immediately with their requests (Newson & Newson, 1968; Sears, Maccoby, & Levin, 1957). Hallden (1991) found that mothers of 4-year-old children express contradictory attitudes toward obedience. They wish "to teach their children the difference between right and wrong" or "to learn to obey and to be considerate," but at the same time they wish "to promote the children's independence and self-reliance so that no one can walk all over them" (p. 342).

Western attitudes toward the value of children may also shape contemporary perspectives on child socialization and parent-child relations . In a cross-cultural study, L. W. Hoffman (1988) found that most Western parents value children because they satisfy needs for long-term relationship ties, affection, and companionship. Such relationship goals probably place constraints on parents' handling of disciplinary interactions. In an exploratory study, 40 mothers of children between the ages of 6 and 9 were asked open-ended questions concerning how they conceptualized their relationship with their children and what actions strengthened or hindered their relationships (Kuczynski, Blaine, & Dawber, 1995). The most frequent response, mentioned by 61% of mothers, characterized the meaning of the parent-child relationship in terms of friendship and intimacy. This category included ideas such as mutual respect, mutual understanding, mutual enjoyment, and shared activities in the parent-child relationship. Ideas concerning their roles as authorities and socialization agents featured in the responses of only 36% of mothers. Moreover, 56% thought that their use of power or authority might weaken the quality of their relationships with their children.

This line of research suggests that parents have a much more conflicted attitude toward children's compliance and their roles as socializing agents than was assumed by traditional conceptions of socialization. Contemporary parents may consider compliance and conformity to be a convenient characteristic to have in their children but may recognize that compliance represents only one of many socialization goals. Other issues that compete with compliance as a parental goal include fostering children's long-term acceptance of certain of their directives, supporting their children's developing autonomy, and promoting a positive and enduring relationship.

CONCLUSION

Research on socialization in the context of the family has been concerned with two broad issues. One has to do with the internalization of content—how children acquire parental values, beliefs, and attitudes. Elsewhere in this book (Kuczynski, Marshall, & Schell, Chapter 2), it has been argued that transformations in content due to rapid changes in society, negotiations during parent-child interaction, and processing at the level of the individual make it unrealistic to think of internalization as the current generation's conformity to the ideas and values of the previous generation. Socialization theory has also been concerned with the problem of fostering willingness to conform to certain expectations by others as a condition of communal living. To be adaptive, the degree of conformity, minimally, should serve to keep the individual within the bounds of what the family or society can tolerate. Although contemporary parents may not be invested in the exact transmission of their particular ideas, they continue to be invested in fostering positive orientations toward social conformity.

But how should social conformity be conceptualized? Four distinct models of conformity were described in this chapter. The external control perspective conceives conformity as exact compliance to external authority. The internal control perspective conceives conformity as deriving from an intrinsic, autonomous impulse. The relational perspective conceives conformity as a coregulated accommodation to other individuals in social relationships. The contextual perspective conceives conformity as a differentiated construct and considers that social competence may consist in individuals adapting their standards of conformity to the requirements of different situations.

As a future direction, we think that a contextual perspective, which considers the situational adaptiveness of behavior within the larger context of social relationships, affords the possibility of integrating earlier research in the separate perspectives. Accepting the assumption of situational specificity of socialized behavior will be a step toward understanding the child in context as well as the adaptive features of children's behavior across contexts. Moreover, a contextual perspective provides a route for understanding adaptive features of parental behavior. In a review of the literature on the measurement of parental attitudes, Holden and Edwards (1989) critiqued the static, traitlike models of parental behavior that persist in research. A similar critique could be made of research on socialization. Thus in external control theories, parental competence consists in using power assertion effectively; in internalization theories, parental competence consists in the predominant use of reasoning and rational persuasion; and in relational theories, a competent parent has an overriding concern about responsivity to children's needs. It is as if each theory considered the essence of competence to consist in the rigid use of a single solution for all situations that arise. Two decades of research on parental behavior in the natural environment suggest that competent parents are much more flexible and adapt their control strategies to the situation, their children's temperament, and stage of development. A lesson from research on parent-child interaction is that situational specificity and the discriminations made by parents and by children must become a part of future models of parent and child competence.

At the same time, it is important in this current stage of theory construction to consider both the parent's contextual choices and the child's contextual behavior as bounded by the context of their relationship. Sensitivity to the relationship context of socialization may make apparent linkages between parent and child behaviors across context and illuminate motivational dynamics of their interactions.

REFERENCES

Alwin, D. (1988). From obedience to autonomy: Changes in traits desired in children, 1924–1978. *Public Opinion Quarterly, 52,* 33–52.

Alwin, D. (1990). Historical changes in parental orientations to children. *Sociological Studies of Child Development, 3,* 65–86.

Aronfreed, J. (1969). The concept of internalization. In D. A. Goslin (Ed.), *Handbook of socialization theory and research* (pp. 263–324). Chicago: Rand McNally.

Baumrind, D. (1971). Current patterns of parental authority. *Developmental Psychology Monograph, 4*(1, Pt. 2).

Baumrind, D. (1991). Effective parenting during the early adolescent transition. In P. A. Cowan & M. Hetherington (Eds.), *Family transitions* (pp. 111–162). Hillsdale, NJ: Erlbaum.

Becker, J. A. (1990). Processes in the acquisition of pragmatic competence. In G. Conti-Ramsden & C. E. Snow (Eds.), *Children's language* (pp. 7–24). Hillsdale, NJ: Erlbaum.

Brehm, S. S. (1981). Oppositional behavior in children: A reactance theory approach. In S. S. Brehm, S. M. Kassin, & F. K. Gibbons (Eds.), *Developmental social psychology: Theory and research* (pp. 96–121). New York: Oxford University Press.

Bretherton, I., Golby, B., & Cho, E. (this volume). Attachment and the transmission of values. In J. E. Grusec & L. Kuczynski (Eds.), *Parenting and children's internalization of values: A handbook of contemporary theory.* New York: Wiley.

Chamberlain, P., & Patterson, G. R. (1995). Discipline and child compliance in parenting. In M. H. Bornstein (Ed.), *Handbook of parenting: Vol. 4. Applied and practical parenting* (pp. 205–226). Mahwah, NJ: Erlbaum.

Chapman, M., & Zahn-Waxler, C. (1982). Young children's compliance and noncompliance to parental discipline in a natural setting. *International Journal of Behavioural Development, 5,* 81–94.

Cheyne, J. A., & Walters, R. H. (1969). Intensity of punishment, timing of punishment, and cognitive structure as determinants of response inhibition. *Journal of Experimental Child Psychology, 7,* 231–244.

Cody, M. J., Greene, J. O., Marston, P. J., O'Hair, H. D., Baaske, K. T., & Schneider, M. J. (1986). Situation perception and message strategy selection. *Communication Yearbook, 9,* 390–420.

Crittenden, P. M., & DiLalla, D. L. (1988). Compulsive compliance: The development of an inhibitory coping strategy in infancy. *Journal of Abnormal Child Psychology, 16,* 585–599.

Crockenberg, S., & Litman, C. (1990). Autonomy as competence in 2-year-olds: Maternal correlates of child defiance, compliance, and self-assertion. *Developmental Psychology, 26,* 961–971.

Dawber, T., & Kuczynski, L. (1996, August 13). *The question of "ownness": Parent-child interactions in the context of relationships.* Paper presented at the 14th Biennial ISSBD Conference, Quebec City.

Deci, E. L., & Ryan, R. M. (1987). The support of autonomy and the control of behavior. *Journal of Personality and Social Psychology, 53,* 1024–1037.

Delia, J. G., Kline, S. L., & Burleson, B. R. (1979). The development of persuasive communication strategies in kindergartners through twelfth graders. *Communication Monographs, 46,* 241–246.

Dix, T. (1991). Parenting on behalf of the child: Empathic goals in the regulation of responsive parenting. In I. E. Sigel, A. V. McGuillicuddy-DeLisi, & J. J. Goodnow (Eds.), *Parental belief systems: The psychological consequences for children* (2nd ed., pp. 319–346). Hillsdale, NJ: Erlbaum.

Dobson, J. (1970). *Dare to discipline.* Wheaton, IL: Tyndale House.

Dobson, J. (1978). *The strong-willed child.* Wheaton, IL: Tyndale House.

Dobson, J. (1987). *Parenting isn't for cowards.* Waco, TX: Word.

Dubin, E., & Dubin, R. (1963). The authority inception period in socialization. *Child Development, 34,* 885–898.

Dumas, J. E., & LaFreniere, P. J. (1993). Mother-child relationships as sources of support or stress: A comparison of competent, average, aggressive, and anxious dyads. *Child Development, 64,* 1732–1754.

Dunn, J., & Munn, P. (1987). Development of justification in disputes with mothers and sibling. *Developmental Psychology, 23,* 791–798.

Eisenberg, A. R. (1992). Conflicts between mothers and their young children. *Merrill-Palmer Quarterly, 38,* 21–43.

Ellison, C. G., & Sherkat, D. E. (1993). Conservative Protestantism and support for corporal punishment. *American Sociological Review, 58,* 131–144.

Eyberg, S. M., & Boggs, S. R. (1989). Parent training for oppositional-defiant preschoolers. In C. E. Schaefer & J. M. Briesmeister (Eds.), *Handbook of parent training: Parents as cotherapists for children's behavior problems* (pp. 105–132). New York: Wiley.

Fogel, A. (1993). *Developing through relationships: Origins of communication, self, and culture.* Chicago: University of Chicago Press.

Forehand, R., & Long, N. (1996). *Parenting the strong-willed child: The clinically proven five-week program for parents of two-to-six-year-olds.* Chicago: Contemporary Books.

Forehand, R., & MacMahon, R. J. (1981). *Helping the noncompliant child: A clinician's guide to parenting.* New York: Guilford Press.

Garvey, C. (1975). Requests and responses in children's speech. *Journal of Child Language, 2,* 41–63.

Gewirtz, J. L. (1969). Mechanisms of social learning: Some roles of stimulation and behavior in early human development. In D. A. Goslin (Ed.), *Handbook of socialization theory and research* (pp. 57–212). Chicago: Rand McNally.

Gilligan, C. (1982). *In a different voice: Psychological theory and women's development.* Cambridge, MA: Harvard University Press.

Goodnow, J. J. (1990). The socialization of cognition: What's involved? In J. Stigler & R. Shweder (Eds.), *Cultural psychology* (pp. 259–286). Cambridge, England: Cambridge University Press.

Goodnow, J. J., & Collins, W. A. (1990). *Development according to parents: The nature, sources, and consequences of parents' ideas.* Hillside, NJ: Erlbaum.

Goodnow, J. J., & Warton, P. M. (1991). The social bases of social cognition: Interactions about work and their implications. *Merrill-Palmer Quarterly, 37,* 27–58.

Gordon, T. (1990). *Discipline that works: Promoting self-discipline in children.* New York: Plume, Penguin Books.

Gralinski, J. H., & Kopp, C. B. (1993). Everyday rules for behavior: Mothers' requests to young children. *Developmental Psychology, 29,* 573–584.

Grasmick, H. G., Bursik, R. J., & Kimpel, M. (1991). Protestant fundamentalism and attitudes toward corporal punishment of children. *Violence and Victims, 6,* 283–298.

Greven, P. (1990). *Spare the child: The religious roots of physical punishment and the psychological impact of physical abuse.* New York: Knopf.

Grolnick, W. S., Deci, E. L., & Ryan, R. M. (this volume). Internalization within the family: The self-determination theory perspective. In J. E. Grusec & L. Kuczynski (Eds.), *Parenting and children's internalization of values: A handbook of contemporary theory.* New York: Wiley.

Grusec, J. E., & Goodnow, J. J. (1994). Impact of parental discipline methods on the child's internalization of values: A reconceptualization of current points of view. *Developmental Psychology, 30,* 4–19.

Grusec, J. E., & Kuczynski, L. (1980). Direction of effect in socialization: A comparison of parent vs. child's behavior as determinants of disciplinary technique. *Developmental Psychology, 16,* 1–9.

Grusec, J. E., & Redler, E. (1980). Attribution, reinforcement, and altruism: A developmental analysis. *Developmental Psychology, 16,* 525–534.

Grusec, J. E., Rudy, D., & Martini, T. (this volume). Parenting cognitions and child outcomes: An overview and implications for children's internalization of values. In J. E. Grusec & L. Kuczynski (Eds.), *Parenting and children's internalization of values: A handbook of contemporary theory.* New York: Wiley.

Hallden, G. (1991). The child as project and the child as being: Parents' ideas as frames of reference. *Childhood and Society, 5,* 334–356.

Hildebrandt, N. (1996). *"Ownness" vs. "otherness": Children's sense of agency within parent-child and other adult-child relationships.* Unpublished masters thesis, University of Guelph, Department of Psychology.

Hinde, R. A. (1979). *Towards understanding relationships.* New York: Academic Press.

Hoffman, L. W. (1988). Cross-cultural differences in child rearing goals. In R. A. LeVine, P. M. Miller, & M. M. West (Eds.), *Parental behavior in diverse societies* (pp. 99–122). San Francisco: Jossey-Bass.

Hoffman, M. L. (1970). Moral development. In P. H. Mussen (Ed.), *Carmichael's manual of child psychology* (Vol. 2, pp. 261–360). New York: Wiley.

Hoffman, M. L. (1975). Moral internalization, parental power, and the nature of parent-child interaction. *Developmental Psychology, 11,* 228–239.

Hoffman, M. L. (1983). Affective and cognitive processes in moral internalization: An information processing approach. In E. T. Higgins, D. Ruble, & W. Hartup (Eds.), *Social cognition and social development: A sociological perspective* (pp. 236–274). Cambridge, England: Cambridge University Press.

Hoffman, M. L., & Saltzstein, H. C. (1967). Parent discipline and the child's moral development. *Journal of Personality and Social Psychology, 5,* 45–57.

Holden, G. W., & Edwards, L. A. (1989). Parental attitudes toward child rearing: Instruments, issues and implications. *Psychological Bulletin, 106,* 29–58.

Kelley, H. H., Berscheid, E., Christensen, A., Harvey, J. H., Huston, T. L., Levinger, G., McClintock, E., Peplau, L. A., & Peterson, D. R. (1983). Analysing close relationships. In H. H. Kelley, E. Berscheid, A. Christensen, J. H. Harvey, T. L. Huston, G. Levinger, E. McClintock, L. A. Peplau, & D. R. Peterson (Eds.), *Close relationships* (pp. 20–67). New York: Freeman.

Kelman, H. C. (1961). Processes of opinion change. *Public Opinion Quarterly, 25,* 57–78.

Kelman, H. C. (1974). Further thoughts on the processes of compliance, identification and internationalization. In J. T. Tedeschi (Ed.), *Perspectives on social power* (pp. 125–173). Chicago: Aldine.

Kessen, W. (1979). The American child and other cultural inventions. *American Psychologist, 34,* 815–820.

Kochanska, G. (1991). Socialization and temperament in the development of guilt and conscience. *Child Development, 62,* 1379–1392.

Kochanska, G., & Aksan, N. (1995). Mother-child mutually positive effect, the quality of child compliance to requests and prohibitions, and maternal control as correlates of early internalization. *Child Development, 66,* 236–254.

Kochanska, G., Devet, K., Goldman, M., Murray, K., & Putnam, S. P. (1994). Maternal reports of conscience development and temperament in young children. *Child Development, 65,* 852–868.

Kochanska, G., Padavich, D. L., & Koenig, A. L. (1996). Children's narratives about hypothetical moral dilemmas and objective measures of their conscience: Mutual relations and socialization antecedents. *Child Development, 67,* 1420–1436.

Kohlberg, L. (1969). Stage and sequence: The cognitive-developmental approach to socialization. In D. A. Goslin (Ed.), *Handbook of socialization theory and research* (pp. 347–480). Chicago: Rand McNally.

Kopp, C. B. (1982). Antecedents of self-regulation: A developmental perspective. *Developmental Psychology, 18,* 199–214.

Kuczynski, L. (1982). Intensity and orientation of reasoning: Motivational determinants of children's compliance to verbal rationales. *Journal of Experimental Child Psychology, 34,* 357–370.

Kuczynski, L. (1983). Reasoning prohibitions and motivations for compliance. *Developmental Psychology, 19,* 126–134.

Kuczynski, L. (1984). Socialization goals and mother-child interaction: Strategies for long-term and short-term compliance. *Developmental Psychology, 20,* 1061–1073.

Kuczynski, L. (1992). The concept of compliance in childrearing interactions. In J. Janssens & J. Gerris (Eds.), *Childrearing and the child's prosocial and moral development* (pp. 125–143). Lisse, The Netherlands: Swets & Zeitlinger.

Kuczynski, L., Blaine, J., & Dawber, T. (1995). *Mothers' conceptions of their relationships with their children*. Unpublished manuscript, University of Guelph, Department of Family Studies.

Kuczynski, L., & Kochanska, G. (1990). The development of children's noncompliance strategies from toddlerhood to age 5. *Developmental Psychology, 26,* 398–408.

Kuczynski, L., & Kochanska, G. (1995). Function and content of maternal demands: Developmental significance of early demands for competent action. *Child Development, 66,* 616–628.

Kuczynski, L., Kochanska, G., Radke-Yarrow, M., & Girnius-Brown, O. (1987). A developmental interpretation of young children's noncompliance. *Developmental Psychology, 23,* 799–806.

Kuczynski, L., Marshall, S., & Schell, K. (this volume). Value socialization in a bidirectional context. In J. E. Grusec & L. Kuczynski (Eds.), *Parenting and children's internalization of values: A handbook of contemporary theory.* New York: Wiley.

Landauer, T. K., Carlsmith, J. M., & Lepper, M. (1970). Experimental analysis of the factors determining obedience of four-year-old children to adult females. *Child Development, 41,* 601–613.

Laursen, B., & Collins, W. A. (1994). Interpersonal conflict during adolescence. *Psychological Bulletin, 115,* 197–209.

Lay, K. L., Waters, E., & Park, K. A. (1989). Maternal responsiveness and child compliance: The role of mood as a mediator. *Child Development, 60,* 1405–1411.

Leavitt, R. L. (1991). Power and resistance in infant-toddler day care centers. *Sociological Studies of Child Development, 4,* 91–112.

Leizer, J. I., & Rogers, R. W. (1974). Effects of method of discipline, timing of punishment, and timing of test on resistance to temptation. *Child Development, 45,* 790–793.

Leonard, R. (1993). Mother-child disputes as arenas for fostering negotiation skills. *Early Development and Parenting, 2,* 157–167.

Lepper, M. (1973). Dissonance, self-perception, and honesty in children. *Journal of Personality and Social Psychology, 25,* 65–74.

Lepper, M. (1983). Social control processes, attributions of motivation, and the internalization of social values. In E. T. Higgins, D. N. Ruble, & W. W. Hartup (Eds.), *Social cognition and social development: A sociological perspective* (pp. 294–330). Cambridge, England: Cambridge University Press.

Lollis, S., & Kuczynski, L. (in press). Beyond one hand clapping: Seeing bidirectionality in parent-child relations. *Journal of Social and Personal Relationships.*

Londerville, S., & Main, M. (1981). Security of attachment, compliance and maternal training methods in the second year of life. *Developmental Psychology, 17,* 289–299.

Lytton, H. (1980). *Parent-child interaction: The socialization process observed in twin and singleton families.* New York: Plenum Press.

Maccoby, E. E. (1984). Middle childhood in the context of the family. In W. Andrew Collins (Ed.), *Development during middle childhood, the years from six to twelve* (pp. 184–239). Washington, DC: National Academy Press.

Maccoby, E. E., & Martin, J. A. (1983). Socialization in the context of the family: Parent-child interaction. In P. H. Mussen (Series Ed.) & E. M. Hetherington (Vol. Ed.), *Handbook of child psychology: Vol. 4. Socialization, personality, and social development* (pp. 1–101). New York: Wiley.

MacDonald, K. (this volume). The coherence of individual development: An evolutionary perspective on children's internalization of parental values. In J. E. Grusec & L. Kuczynski (Eds.), *Parenting and children's internalization of values: A handbook of contemporary theory.* New York: Wiley.

Mahoney, M. J. (1974). *Cognition and behavior modification.* Cambridge, MA: Ballinger.

Markus, H. J., & Nurius, P. S. (1984). Self-understanding and self-regulation in middle childhood. In W. A. Collins (Ed.), *Development during middle childhood, the years from six to twelve* (pp. 147–183). Washington, DC: National Academy Press.

Matas, L., Arend, R., & Sroufe, L. (1978). Continuity of adaptation in the second year: The relationship between quality of attachment and later competence. *Child Development, 49,* 547–556.

Mayall, B. (1994). Children in action at home and school. In B. Mayall (Ed.), *Children's childhoods: Observed and experienced* (pp. 114–127). Washington, DC: Falmer Press.

McLaughlin, M. L., Cody, M. J., & Robey, C. S. (1980). Situation influences on the selection of strategies to resist compliance-gaining attempts. *Human Communication Research, 7,* 14–36.

McQuillen, J. S. (1986). The development of listener-adapted compliance-resisting strategies. *Human Communication Research, 12,* 359–375.

McQuillen, J. S., Higginbotham, D. C., & Cummings, M. C. (1984). Compliance-resisting behaviors: The effects of age, agent, and types of request. *Instructional Communication, 8,* 747–762.

Miller, A. (1990). *For your own good, hidden cruelty in child-rearing and the roots of violence.* New York: Noonday Press. (Original work published 1983)

Miller, G., Boster, F., Roloff, M., & Siebold, D. (1977). Compliance-gaining strategies: A typology and some findings concerning effects of situational differences. *Communication Monographs, 44,* 37–51.

Miller, G., & Steinberg, M. (1975). *Between people: A new analysis of interpersonal communication.* Chicago: Science Research Associates.

Minton, C., Kagan, J., & LeVine, J. A. (1971). Maternal control and obedience in the two-year-old. *Child Development, 42,* 1873–1894.

Newson, J., & Newson, R. (1968). *Four-year-old in an urban community.* Chicago: Aldine.

Osborne, P. (1995). The parenting experts. In R. D. Day, K. R. Gilbert, B. H. Settles, & W. R. Burr (Eds.), *Research and theory in family science* (pp. 320–333). Pacific Grove, CA: Brooks/Cole.

Parke, R. D. (1969). Effectiveness of punishment as an interaction of intensity, timing, agent nurturance and cognitive structuring. *Child Development, 40,* 213–236.

Parpal, M., & Maccoby, E. E. (1985). Maternal responsiveness and subsequent child compliance. *Child Development, 56,* 1326–1334.

Patterson, G. R. (1982). *Coercive family process.* Eugene, OR: Castalia Press.

Patterson, G. R. (this volume). Performance models for parenting: A social interactional perspective. In J. E. Grusec & L. Kuczynski (Eds.), Parenting and children's internalization of values: A handbook of contemporary theory. New York: Wiley.

Patterson, G. R., DeBarsyshe, B. D., & Ramsey, E. (1989). A developmental perspective on antisocial behavior. *American Psychologist, 44,* 329–335.

Patterson, G. R., & Forgatch, M. (1987). *Parents and adolescents: Living together.* Eugene, OR: Castalia Press.

Patterson, G. R., Reid, J., & Dishion, T. (1992). *Antisocial boys: Vol. 4. A social interactional approach.* Eugene: Oregon Social Learning Center.

Peterson, R. F. (1974). Power, programming, and punishment: Could we be overcontrolling our children? In E. J. Mash, L. A. Hamerlynck, & L. C. Handy (Eds.), *Behavior modification and families* (pp. 378–391). New York: Brunner/Mazel.

Piaget, J. (1965). *The moral judgement of the child* (Majorie Gabain, Trans.). New York: Free Press. (Original work published 1932)

Reid, J. (1982, April). *Social-interactional patterns in families of abused and nonabused children.* Paper presented at the Conference on Altruism and Aggression, Washington, DC.

Rheingold, H. L. (1982). Little children's participation in the work of adults: A nascent prosocial behavior. *Child Development, 53,* 114–125.

Rheingold, H. L., Cook, K. V., & Kolowitz, V. (1987). Commands activate the behavior and pleasure of 2-year-old children. *Developmental Psychology, 23,* 146–151.

Rocissano, L., Slade, A., & Lynch, V. (1987). Dyadic synchrony and toddler compliance. *Developmental Psychology, 23,* 698–704.

Rogoff, B. (1990). *Apprenticeship in thinking,* New York: Oxford University Press.

Rothbaum, F., & Weisz, J. R. (1989). *Child psychopathology and the quest for control.* Newbury Park, CA: Sage.

Rubenstein, J. L., & Feldman, S. S. (1993). Conflict-resolution behavior in adolescent boys: Antecedents and adaptional correlates. *Journal of Research on Adolescence, 3,* 41–66.

Schaffer, H. R. (1984). *The child's entry into a social world.* London: Academic Press.

Schaffer H. R. (1991). The mutuality of parental control in early childhood. In M. Lewis & S. Feinman (Eds.), *Social influences and socialization in infancy* (pp. 165–184). New York: Plenum Press.

Sears, R. R., Maccoby, E. E., & Levin, H. (1957). *Patterns of child rearing.* Evanston, IL: Row Peterson.

Smetana, J. (this volume). Parenting and the development of social knowledge reconceptualized: A social domain analysis. In J. E. Grusec & L. Kuczynski (Eds.). *Parenting and children's internalization of values: A handbook of contemporary theory.* New York: Wiley.

Smith, C. L., Gelfand, D. M., Hartmann, D. P., & Partlow, M. E. Y. (1979). Children's causal attributions regarding help giving. *Child Development, 50,* 203–210.

Stayton, D., Hogan, R., & Ainsworth, M. D. S. (1971). Infant obedience and material behavior: The origins of socialization reconsidered. *Child Development, 42,* 1057–1069.

Trickett, P. K., & Kuczynski, L. (1986). Children's misbehaviors and parental discipline strategies in abusive and non-abusive families. *Developmental Psychology, 22,* 115–123.

Vaughan, B. E., Kopp, C. B., & Krakow, J. B. (1984). The emergence and consolidation of self-control from 18–30 months of age: Normative trends and individual differences. *Child Development, 55,* 990–1004.

Vuchinich, S. (1987). Starting and stopping spontaneous family conflicts. *Journal of Marriage in the Family, 49,* 591–601.

Vuchinich, S. (1990). The sequential organization of closing in verbal family conflict. In A. Grimshaw (Ed.), *Conflict talk* (pp. 118–137). New York: Cambridge University Press.

Wald, K. D., Owen, D. E., & Hill, S. S. (1989). Habits of the mind? The problem of authority in the new Christian right. In T. G. Glen (Ed.), *Religion and political behavior in the United States* (pp. 93–108). New York: Praeger.

Wenar, C. (1982). On negativism. *Human Development, 25,* 1–23.

Wesley, J. (1973). Sermon on the education of children. In P. J. Greven (Ed.), *Child-rearing concepts, 1628–1861* (pp. 52–66). Itasca, IL: Peacock. (Original work published 1783)

Wheeless, L. R., Barraclough, R., & Stewart, R. (1983). Compliance-gaining and power in persuasion. *Communication Yearbook, 7,* 105–145.

White, K. D., Pearson, J. C., & Flint, L. (1989). Adolescents' compliance-resistance: Effects of parents' compliance strategy and gender. *Adolescence, 95,* 595–621.

Wiehe, V. R. (1990). Religious influence on parental attitudes toward the use of corporal punishment. *Journal of Family Violence, 5,* 173–185.

Yeates, K. O., & Selman, R. T. (1989). Social competence in the schools: Towards an integrative developmental model for intervention. *Developmental Review, 9,* 64–100.

PART IV

Parenting Cognitions: Implications for Parental Influence and Bidirectionality

CHAPTER 10

Parenting Cognitions and Child Outcomes: An Overview and Implications for Children's Internalization of Values

JOAN E. GRUSEC, DUANE RUDY, and TANYA MARTINI

Parents think as they socialize their children. They decide why their children are acting the way they are, they select goals they want to achieve, they reflect on the likelihood of achieving those goals. Positive or negative affect frequently accompanies this thinking. Both thoughts and affect are instrumental in determining socialization strategies and, hence, in determining the outcome of socialization. An understanding of parental cognitions is therefore an integral part of understanding the socialization of children and their internalization of values.

Parenting cognitions, which have been the object of empirical investigation for approximately the past 15 years, must be distinguished from broad-based parenting attitudes that have a comparatively long history of study in developmental psychology. Indeed, historically, the design of questionnaires to assess general parental attitudes, beliefs, and values has been a favored way of attempting to learn about the relation between parents' thoughts about child-rearing issues and child outcomes. By asking parents to respond to such questions as "Children should always treat adults with respect," "I enjoy being with my child," and "Sometimes I find being a parent an overwhelming and stressful experience," and relating their answers to measures of socialization outcome, researchers have attempted to gain insight into children's social development. For several reasons, the results of such studies have been far from promising. One reason is that many parenting cognitions are automatic rather than operative at a conscious, considered, or accessible level and so are not captured through the use of these traditional questionnaire and interview methods. Another is that the measures have been fraught with methodological problems, including questionable reliability and validity. Sigel (1992) has suggested that researchers may be looking at the wrong beliefs, selecting those with theoretical importance but with, in fact, less importance for parents. Finally, the general questions researchers have asked are abstract and require parents to extrapolate and draw summary conclusions from a wide range of disparate experiences. A detailed analysis of the measures and of their problems has been provided by Holden and Edwards (1989).

The study of parenting cognitions, however, attempts to overcome at least some of these problems. With the acknowledgment that in any parent-child interaction parents experience cognitions that are both automatic as well as considered has come a mapping of steps between child behaviors, particular parenting cognitions, associated affect, parenting behavior, and child outcomes. Much of the research has dealt with parenting cognitions in response to child misdeeds, and so has focused on the discipline process. For that reason, the following discussion will deal primarily with the socialization strategy of discipline. Wherever possible, however, the role played by cognitions in other reactive socialization strategies as well as in proactive strategies will be examined.

Parenting cognitions comprise ideas about many domains. Goodnow and Collins (1990) characterize them as having to do with directions and conditions of development. Directions of development include parents' goals for their children, their ideas about starting points for development, and beliefs about how it is that children develop. Under conditions of development, Goodnow and Collins list ideas about the relative contributions of internal as opposed to external events to development, the influence and responsibility of parents, and the methods parents can use to achieve various goals. This chapter will present an overview of research relevant to these cognitions.

The first part of the chapter is a summary of information about the impact of parenting cognitions on socialization strategies, particularly authoritarian and authoritative parenting styles, and child outcomes. Included are parents' attributions for children's behavior, their expectations about their own abilities to control child behavior, their schemas about attachment-related issues, the extent to which they both understand and share their children's point of view (that is, the extent to which cognitions are mutual), and the goals they have. All the research described has been done in an Anglo European or Western context. The remainder of the chapter addresses implications of the research on parenting cognitions for an understanding of parenting strategies and children's internalization of values. Thus the second part of the chapter moves to a consideration of relevant research from other cultures where the patterns of relations between parenting cognitions, parenting strategies, and child outcomes are quite different from those in Western contexts. This observation is used to argue that attention to a wider variety of parenting strategies than those most frequently considered by socialization researchers (authoritarian/punitive vs. authoritative/reasoning) is needed in our analyses of the socialization process. The cross-cultural research also raises the possibility that authoritarian and power-assertive parenting is not universally negative. In the third and final section of the chapter, the research on parenting cognitions is used to offer some hypotheses with respect to the controversy over whether values are transmitted or constructed.

PARENTING COGNITIONS, PARENTING BEHAVIORS, AND CHILD OUTCOMES

Attributions for Children's Behavior and Relationship Schemas

Attribution theory (e.g., Weiner, 1980; Jones & Davis, 1965) suggests that people look for reasons or explanations for their own behavior and that of others. Miller (1995) notes that parents should be especially likely to look for explanations for their children's behavior because the parent-child relationship involves several features that heighten such activity: expectation of continued interaction, desire for control, and the at least occasional occurrence of unexpected and possibly undesired outcomes. The reasons parents find (i.e., the attributions they make) have an impact on how they feel and what they do. People also have ideas about themselves and how they relate to others, including how they relate as parents to their children. These thoughts about relationships have an additional impact on how they feel and what they do when interacting with their children. In all these cases, ideas appear to be embedded in complex schemas that involve conscious and unconscious ideation, accompanied by strong affect. This affect occurs in response to cognitions as well as directs them by narrowing attentional processes, selectively guiding memory retrieval, and possibly interfering with reflective appraisal of and coping with the situation. This complex underpinning for behavior, as well as the possibility that at least some of these schemas have their origins in the parent's own childhood experiences, helps explain why parenting strategies may frequently be so difficult to change as well as why some parents cling so strongly to actions that they know are detrimental to the welfare of their children.

Attributions for Children's Behavior

The first parenting schema to be considered concerns the tendency of parents to search for the causes of their children's behavior. In this search, they may either hold their children accountable and attribute the behavior to their children's character (i.e., make a dispositional or internal attribution) or they may conclude that the children's actions were driven by circumstances (i.e., they make a situational, or external, attribution). These attributions have been related to parenting behavior and parenting affect. In the area of child maltreatment, it has been hypothesized that abuse arises from parental assumptions that noncompliance on the part of children is willful and therefore an indication of a "bad" disposition (Steele, 1970), although the empirical support for this contention is mixed (e.g., Bauer & Twentyman, 1985; Rosenberg & Reppucci, 1983). There has been considerable empirical research documenting the impact of parental attributions on parenting behavior and emotion in nonabusive families, mostly focused on the situation in which children are noncompliant or misbehaving.

Parents who attribute antisocial behavior to stable dispositional factors and who see it as intentional and under the child's control are likely to experience negative affect (Dix & Grusec, 1985; Dix, Ruble, Grusec, & Nixon, 1986). Moreover, they are also likely to be more punitive in their response, perhaps both because negative affect increases the probability of power-assertive responding and because our Western ethical system dictates that individuals who have behaved badly intentionally deserve more punishment than those whose bad behavior was unintentional (Dix, Ruble, & Zambarano, 1989). The implications for child outcomes are considerable. If behavior is in fact unintentional, resulting from lack of knowledge on the child's part, then punitive parental reactions without explanations will be ineffective in teaching the child more acceptable behavior. The finding that children who are highly aggressive (Dix & Lochman, 1990), socially withdrawn (Rubin & Mills, 1992), hyperactive (Sobol, Ashbourne, Earn, & Cunningham, 1989), or conduct-disordered (Baden & Howe, 1992) have mothers who make more negative attributions suggests that negative attributions may be contributing to maladaptive behavior because they lead to ineffective parenting practices. Thus parents who have distorted views of their child may contribute to their deviance. On the other hand, parental attributions may be a reflection of reality, a possibility that cannot be ruled out without longitudinal research.

Negative attributions can also affect children's behavior if these attributions are translated into verbal responses: the labeling that ensues may well promote continued undesirable responding on the child's part. Contrarily, dispositional attributions for good behavior would have positive outcomes, given that positive dispositional labeling of children (e.g., "You are a kind and helpful person") increases the probability of their acting in accord with that positive label (Grusec & Redler, 1980). Indeed, somewhat less is known about the attributions parents make for children's prosocial behavior. Both Gretarsson and Gelfand (1988) and Dix et al. (1986) report that mothers are more likely to see prosocial acts as intentional, dispositional, stable, and under the child's control than they are antisocial acts. A plausible explanation for this disparity is that different patterns of attributions for positive and negative child behaviors have a self-protective function, helping mothers to maintain self-esteem and feelings of self-efficacy. The impact of these attributions on parental affect and behavior, however, remains to be assessed.

Parents' attributions for children's misdeeds are, at least to some extent, the product of conscious, rational cognitive processes. Thus parents report that misbehaviors are more likely to be the result of dispositional factors when children are older and better able to control their behavior and understand its potential consequences (Dix et al., 1986; Dix et al., 1989; Fincham & Grych, 1991). Parents also appear to make use of well-established rules of inference, such as the discounting principle (Jones & Davis, 1965), being more likely to discount the child's disposition as the cause of the misdeed when alternative, situational forces over which the child has less control (e.g., the child was tired) appear to have been influencing their behavior (Dix & Lochman, 1990). Parents who endorse authoritarian ideologies are also more likely to make dispositional attributions for their children's misdeed (Dix et al., 1989).

Attributions for children's behavior appear also to be affected by factors that are less subject to conscious control and that guide the way parents process information about the child. Thus Dix, Reinhold, and Zambarano (1990) have demonstrated how the appraisals parents make are linked to the emotional state they are experiencing at the time. Mothers monitoring their mood at home were asked to watch videotapes of children responding to a parental request. Compared with mothers who were feeling affectively neutral, mothers who were experiencing a negative mood reported feeling more upset over noncompliance, were more inclined to blame their child, and indicated higher levels of disapproval. The chronic effects of affective disorders such as depression are also important determinants of parental appraisals. Depressed mothers, for example, are more likely to perceive their noncompliant children as being deviant (Sameroff, Seifer, & Elias, 1982).

Another cluster of variables that may operate outside awareness to influence parenting attributions is more stable over time. It includes strongly entrenched cognitions that are part of the parent's cultural surround, including beliefs about the inherent nature of children, differential valuation of character traits, and developmental timetables that indicate the age when specific characteristics are thought to emerge (Bornstein, 1989; Goodnow & Collins, 1990). These culturally determined cognitions may serve as a reference point for parental evaluation, having an impact on the likelihood that behavior will be seen as either dispositionally or situationally determined.

Relationship Schemas

Baldwin (1992) talks about relationship schemas as "cognitive maps" that "help individuals to navigate their social world" (p. 462). They involve expectations about interactions with others based on images of the self and of others. Two relationship schemas have been the focus of researchers interested in parenting. They are (a) ideas about the extent of the influence or power parents feel they have in dealing with their children, and (b) ideas about the extent to which parents believe others can be relied on to provide comfort and security.

The first relationship schema, ideas about power or ability to influence, appears in work on self-efficacy. Bandura (1977, 1986) proposes that domain-specific beliefs about abilities guide behavior by determining what people try to achieve and how much effort they put into their performance. When individuals have low self-efficacy, they become preoccupied with themselves as well as emotionally aroused, two conditions that distract from effective performance. In a test of this hypothesis in the child-rearing domain, Teti and Gelfand (1991) demonstrated that mothers who perceived themselves to be ineffective at parenting were less sensitive and warm, displayed flatness of affect, and were disengaged and angry during interactions with their infants. These mothers were also depressed, a manifestation of the negative affect accompanying feelings of inadequacy. The impact of mood on feelings of efficacy has also been addressed by Kochanska, Radke-Yarrow, Kuczynski, and Friedman (1987) who report that both unipolar and bipolar depressed mothers are more likely to attribute child outcomes to uncontrollable factors. They attribute this finding to the feelings of helplessness and cognitive distortions that are a crucial component of affective illness.

Some of the most comprehensive work on self-efficacy in the child-rearing domain has been done by Bugental and her associates. Building on a basis in attribution theory, Bugental (e.g., 1992; Bugental et al., 1993) noted that parents in a difficult child-rearing situation assign high or low levels of control to themselves and to their children. Bugental has been particularly concerned with parents who see themselves as having less control than their children in difficult child-rearing situations. In her analysis, these parents possess a relationship schema that is associated with harmful parenting behavior, negative affective reactions, and threat-focused and pessimistic conscious ideation. Bugental suggests that the experience of difficult child behavior activates a high threat schema that operates at an automatic, unaware level and puts these parents into a state of perceptual readiness to react to certain events in the environment. Stress produced by the child is filtered through preconscious cognitive schemas that influence both the affect experienced as well as more deliberate or aware ideation.

Behaviorally, low control/high threat mothers produce affectively confusing and inconsistent messages when dealing with their children. For example, they may deliver negative messages in a kidding, sarcastic, or condescending fashion, and neutral or positive messages with a voice quality that is inconsistent with the content (Bugental, Mantyla, & Lewis, 1989). Bugental suggests these messages reflect a "leakage" of the parents' feelings of low control and confuse the child because the verbal and affective content are discrepant. Low control mothers also are more likely to engage in abusive behavior (e.g., kicking, beating) and coercive discipline (Bugental, Blue, & Cruzcosa, 1989a). The confusing messages and power-assertive practices lead to slowing of responding, avoidance of the parent, and noncompliance with the parent's request on the part of the child. In this way, the parent's maladaptive thinking and inappropriate reactions are maintained. Affectively, low control mothers evidence sadness both facially and vocally. In addition, they report negative thoughts and show a physiological pattern of defensive arousal that is paired with difficulties in processing information and performing well on a cognitively demanding task (Bugental et al., 1993). The suggestion is that individuals with schemas of low relative control attend to their own heightened state of arousal when attempting to regulate the behavior of a difficult child and that this attention occurs at the expense of resources that could be used to meet the challenge of the difficult situation.

The second relationship schema emerges from work in attachment theory. According to attachment theory, children learn very early in development to expect either that their emotional needs will be dealt with in a satisfactory and comforting way or that such needs will be rejected or responded to only inconsistently (Ainsworth, Blehar, Waters, & Wall, 1978). These early childhood experiences, which exist outside conscious awareness (Bretherton, 1985), contribute to the development of a working model of relationships that guides behavior throughout the life course. The working models that manifest themselves in adulthood can be one of three types: secure, in which individuals expect that others will be reliable and capable of meeting their needs; dismissive, in which individuals expect rejection, victimization, and coercion; and preoccupied, in which individuals see themselves as unable to gain support from others who cannot give them what they want (Crittenden & Ainsworth, 1989; Main & Goldwyn, 1991).

The empirical evidence indicates that people with different working models do adopt different approaches to parenting. Dismissive parents, relative to secure ones, are less sensitive in interactions with their children, are cool and remote with a task-focused teaching style, use more commands, are less likely to accompany these commands with rationales, and are more likely to be physically abusive. Preoccupied parents provide inconsistent and confusing information when interacting with their children as well as being more likely to be neglecting. With respect to child outcomes, children of secure parents are affectionate, those of dismissive parents cool with subdued affect and responsivity to the needs of others, and those of preoccupied parents noncompliant, angry, and controlling (Crowell & Feldman, 1988, 1991; Grusec, Adam, Mammone, Walters, & Wilson-O'Halloran, 1996; Mammone, 1995).

Relation between Perceptions of Relative Control and Expectations of Responsivity from Others

Little attention has been paid to how different parenting cognitions are interrelated in the totality of parenting thought. Some preliminary work in the area of control and attachment schemas, however, indicates that parents who possess a relationship schema centered on beliefs that they are relatively powerless in difficult child-rearing situations and those who possess one centered on beliefs that they will be rejected and coerced both display authoritarian behavior in dealing with their children. This observation suggests at least an area of overlap. In fact, there is some evidence for a relation between these two schemas. Thus dismissive parents have the lowest scores for relative control over failure compared with secure and preoccupied parents, with the latter having the highest scores for relative control (Grusec, Adam, & Mammone, 1993). The implications of this relation between relative control and expectations of responsivity from others should begin to emerge as researchers learn more about ideation and affect surrounding attachment issues.

Mutual Cognitions

One of the most important determinants of successful interpersonal functioning is the ability of the individual to understand the other's point of view. The ability to understand events from the child's perspective is, therefore, an important feature of successful parenting. Presumably, such understanding makes it easier for a parent to persuade his or her child to behave in a way that is acceptable to the parent. As noted in the previous section, parents who correctly attribute misbehavior to a child's lack of knowledge will be able to provide that knowledge. The socialization literature suggests two possibilities, first, that agreement, or similar perceptions, on the part of parent and child is a significant feature of minimal disagreement and second, that parents who are knowledgeable about their children's thoughts and feelings are better able to achieve their child-rearing goals because they use their knowledge to promote them.

Agreement Is a Feature of Minimal Conflict

What is the function of similar perceptions in the reduction of conflict? Maccoby and Martin (1983) have argued that an important feature of harmonious parent-child inter-action is the extent to which parent and child share common goals. Goodnow and Collins (1990) speak, in more general terms, of "mutual cognitions" as essential for smooth in-teractions, which require parent and child to share a script. Smetana's (1988) analysis of parent-adolescent conflict provides an example of the importance of these mutual cogni-tions. She found conflict was most likely to occur in the case of "multifaceted" events that could be considered either as social conventions, subject to culturally dictated rules, or as personal issues falling only within the jurisdiction of the adolescent. (Keeping one's room clean is an example of such a multifaceted issue, because that room can be consid-ered either as part of the family house and subject to parental standards, or as personal territory subject only to the occupant's own standards.) Problems arose when parents saw the adolescent as violating a social convention while the adolescent saw the event in ques-tion as a personal issue. When both agreed in their assignment of the adolescent's behav-ior to a particular social domain, conflict was much less likely to occur. Interestingly, conflict was also reduced when the justifications adolescents presented for their behav-ior were sophisticated, presumably because parents recognized a similarity in the style of disagreement between themselves and their children even if the behavior itself was not per-ceived in the same fashion.

In a similar vein, Collins (1992; Collins & Luebker, 1994) locates conflict particu-larly at times and in situations where expectations for ideal adolescent behavior differ between adolescents and their parents. These differing expectations are especially likely to occur in early adolescence, when children may want to engage in activities such as use of tobacco or spirits or spend time with friends rather than family, and parents feel it is important that their children wait to engage in such activities. Thus Collins and Luebker (1994) suggest that conflict between generations is tied, not to the number of "older" be-haviors in which adolescents are engaging, but to disagreements about timing or appro-priateness of behavior. This is another example, then, of how dissimilar ways of viewing events augments conflict.

Knowledge Is Used to Increase Agreement

The second point is that parents who know how their children are thinking and feeling are more likely to be successful in minimizing conflict because they can use their knowl-edge to achieve a greater degree of mutuality in cognitions. Initial interest in parents' knowledge of the child came in the concern with "developmental timetables" and the idea that parents (and their children) will experience difficulty if parents' ideas of what to expect of a child are not attuned to the reality of the child. This concern appears in writings about child maltreatment where there is a proposal that physically abusive par-ents have unrealistically high expectations of their children that cannot be met. The child's failure to live up to expectations is attributed to intentionality and spitefulness, thereby leading to anger and strong physical intervention on the part of the parent (Twentyman, Rohrbeck, & Amish, 1984). However, although physically abusive mothers are likely to make malevolent attributions for their children's misdeeds, they do not appear to believe developmental milestones should be reached earlier than they are (Azar, Robinson, Hekimian, & Twentyman, 1984). Developmental researchers have been more successful in documenting beneficial effects of parents' accurate beliefs about their children's cognitive abilities. Several investigators (e.g., Hunt & Paraskevopoulous, 1980; Miller, 1988; Miller, Mondal, & Mee, 1991) have demonstrated that parents' accurate prediction of their children's cognitive performance is correlated with greater cognitive ability in their children, and one explanation for their findings is that parents who have accurate knowledge of their child's ability are better able to match teaching efforts to their child's developmental level.

In an extension of the work on children's cognitive functioning to the area of parent-child conflict, Hastings and Grusec (1997) addressed the extent to which parents were able to accurately identify the thoughts and feelings of their adolescents (as reported by the adolescents) in situations where the two were in disagreement about what was suitable behavior for the child. They found that accurate fathers had fewer conflicts with their children. Moreover, this relation existed independent of the type of discipline technique the father used. Hastings and Grusec suggest that fathers use the accurate information they have about their children's perceptions to avoid future conflicts, perhaps by anticipating problems or by knowing how to react to reduce the probability of interactions escalating into conflict. The results for mothers did not directly parallel those for fathers, although they still point to the importance of accurate knowledge in reducing conflict. For them, knowledge of their children's thoughts and feelings was linked to how satisfied they were with the outcome of the particular conflict under discussion. Knowledgeable mothers were less likely to be power assertive, and the suggestion is that accurate perception in this case served to achieve their goal of avoiding further escalation of the conflict in the specific situation (with reduced power assertion mediating the knowledge/outcome link).

These findings suggest, then, that knowing how a child is feeling and thinking plays a role in the socialization process. The question is what are the actions that follow from parental knowledge or lack of knowledge, and how do these actions lead to more or less successful parenting? At this point, we can only offer suggestions. But certainly parents who know their children do not understand that they have done something wrong can impart information. If they know their children believe they are being treated unfairly, they can attempt to change this perception, or they can change their own demands so they are perceived as fairer. Atkinson et al. (1995) have demonstrated that mothers who screen out information, or engage in avoidance behavior in stressful situations, are less sensitive and responsive to their infants. Lack of knowledge, then, may work at this basic level of impairing the quality of the attachment relationship between child and parent, thereby weakening attempts to internalize values.

Parenting Goals

The study of socialization has been primarily one of how children internalize societal values, or of how they develop a set of standards for behavior that is, in some sense, their own. Parents, however, have other goals in interactions with their children beyond the development of behavioral standards. Research on parenting cognitions reveals the nature of these additional goals.

By goals, researchers have meant the outcomes that parents wish to achieve as they interact with their children. Goals are different from values that parents try to instill in their children during the course of socialization, that is, those ideas that they value and that they wish their children to adopt. Values are enduring characteristics with a high degree of stability. Goals, on the other hand, pertain to what the parent hopes to accomplish in a particular child-rearing situation. Indeed, one of the goals a parent might have in a particular interaction would be to encourage a child to adopt a certain value, such as honesty or concern for others. But parents can have other goals as well and these may change across interactions or even within an ongoing interaction.

Parent-Centered versus Child-Centered Goals

Typically, researchers have differentiated parent- from child-centered goals. The assumption has been that child-centered goals, which underlie authoritative approaches to child rearing, are more likely to lead to the internalization of values than are parent-centered goals which underlie authoritarian approaches to child rearing (Maccoby & Martin, 1983). Parents who wish only to obtain compliance with their wishes will not achieve internalization because they do not employ the child-centered and egalitarian strategies appropriate for that latter goal. Another way of making the distinction is to suggest that authoritarian parents have short-term goals, whereas authoritative parents have long-term goals (Levine, 1974). Thus Kuczynski (1984) manipulated parenting goals by instructing mothers either to attempt to ensure that they would obtain immediate compliance from their children while they were with them, or to attempt to ensure continued compliance after they had left them. When they had been assigned a long-term goal, mothers were more nurturant with their children prior to setting the compliance task, used more varied explanations during the task, and praised and made more positive statements about the character of their children than did mothers who had been assigned a short-term goal. Moreover, children whose mothers had been provided with the long-term goal were more compliant in their mother's absence. Thus Kuczynski argued that mothers with different goals use different techniques to achieve those goals, and that these techniques are indeed generally effective in serving their aims. Holden (1983) has made a similar observation in studies of mothers who wanted to avoid conflict while shopping in the supermarket. Relative to mothers who did not have this goal, these mothers engaged in more proactive behaviors such as not setting out on shopping expeditions when their children were tired and distracting them through conversation or avoiding more tempting parts of the store. Their children, in turn, were better behaved during the shopping process than were children whose mothers did not have conflict avoidance as a goal.

An Expanded Set of Goals

Parents have even more goals, however, than obtaining short-term compliance, avoiding conflict, or promoting long-term internalization of societal values. The existence of these other goals means that all socialization interactions need to be considered not only in terms of the extent to which they successfully achieve internalization of values, but in terms of the extent to which other goals may be operative.

What are these other goals? Dix (1992) has provided some suggestions. He argues that child-centered goals are not unitary, and that they can be divided into two subsets: those designed to instill values, which he designates as socialization goals, and those designed to help the child reach outcomes that the child desires, which he designates as empathic goals. The latter require that parents understand the child's perspective as well as want to make the child happy. In all, then, he suggests the existence of three goals: parent-centeredness, child empathy, and child socialization. Grusec and Goodnow (1994) have argued that goals such as flexibility and initiative in the child's behavior rather than straightforward adoption of parental standards, or a concern with preventing damage to the child's self-esteem or the parent-child relationship, may be more important to parents under certain circumstances. For example, nonagreement with parents may be seen as a desirable outcome if it is accompanied by acceptable negotiation skills (Kuczynski & Kochanska, 1990), the use of sophisticated reasoning (Smetana, 1988), or the development of alternative value systems as long as there is similarity in some core values (Goodnow, 1992). The goal of maintaining family relationships has been identified as particularly important in other cultures (Conroy, Hess, Azuma, & Kashiwagi, 1980), although it is also among goals spontaneously identified as important by mothers (but not fathers) in our own culture (Hastings, 1995).

In an empirical expansion of these ideas, Hastings (1995) identified goals that are actually operative when parents are attempting to socialize their children, as well as established the links between these different goals and parenting socialization practices. Parents he interviewed about specific conflicts spontaneously generated four goals: parent-, child-, relationship-, and safety-centered. In addition, parents differentiated each of these goals in terms of whether they were long- or short-term (e.g., immediate suppression of behavior vs. assurance of future compliance, immediate happiness vs. teaching values, reaching a mutually satisfying outcome vs. building trust). What parenting behaviors were predicted by different parenting goals? As noted earlier, investigators have linked parent-centered goals to authoritarian behavior and child-centered goals to authoritative behavior. Hastings (1995) also found that parents who endorsed short- and long-term parent-centered goals were more power assertive with their children. In addition, he found that reasoning was linked by parents to long-term safety goals (a finding also reported by Gralinski & Kopp, 1993) and long-term relationship goals, while compromise, negotiation, and warmth were linked to short-term child-centered and short-term relationship-centered goals. Thus he found considerable support for the notion that goals and parenting behavior are related.

Hastings also addressed the question of what determines which goals are operative in a socialization situation. His parents reported that obtaining immediate compliance was the goal that predominated in a public setting, while long-term parent- and short- and long-term child-centered goals were more frequent when the conflict occurred in private. The preeminent demand of a public setting, presumably, is to demonstrate that one has control over one's child. As well, public settings are often arenas in which parents have other agendas to meet (e.g., getting their shopping done) and so they may have less time to entertain other, more cognitively demanding, goals. Parents also reported that relationship-centered short-term goals were more likely in the case of boys, a finding that accords with the observation that parents are more indulgent of the misbehavior of sons than of daughters (Zahn-Waxler, 1993).

Negotiation and Initiative-Taking as Goals

Hastings addressed the goals that parents report in situations where they are in conflict with their children and wish to change their behavior. Outside these situations of conflict, however, additional parenting goals have been identified. It is evident from a recent body of research that parents encourage autonomy, flexibility, and initiative in behavior (see, e.g., Kuczynski & Hildebrandt, this volume). The literature on parenting cognitions, however, directs attention to the specific conditions under which these goals are operative and those under which they are not.

According to Nucci and Smetana (1996) all mothers endorse the importance of a child's developing a sense of individuality, and they see themselves as having a role in the process of creating autonomy, competence, and uniqueness. They make it clear, however, that there are areas in which this sense of autonomy and uniqueness will be encouraged and others in which it will not. Nucci (1994), using a social domain approach to socialization (see Smetana, this volume), suggests that disagreement is tolerable in personal areas that pertain only to the child and hence are beyond the realm of regulation by others (e.g., form of fantasy play, friendship choice, choice of color in clothing). In the moral area (involving events that have to do with the welfare of others, trust, and equitable distribution of resources), the social conventional area (involving events that have consensually agreed-on behavior uniformities) and the prudential area (involving events that may be potentially or actually harmful to children) choice is less likely to be allowed (Nucci & Smetana, 1996; Smetana & Asquith, 1994).

Goodnow (1992, 1994, this volume), too, has addressed the issue of parental valuing of autonomy and negotiation, suggesting that there are levels of "acceptable disagreement," and asking when parents care about agreement between their values and those of their children, and when they accept or even value difference. She lists five conditions under which a difference between parent and child in the values they hold may be of concern to the parent. They are when the parent wishes for similarity or continuity in ideas, when the parent's position has little stretch (the only acceptable career is as a professional person), when a difference extends beyond the parent's bottom line, when a difference is not softened by acceptable forms of disagreement or when saving attributions cannot be made ("this is just a phase"), and when the difference is seen as an indication of a more general problem such as lack of success as a parent or an indication that the parent-child relationship is in difficulty.

Goodnow (e.g., 1994) speculates about the kinds of strategies that may be employed to indicate when difference is acceptable to the parent and when it is not. Drama or theater, for example, may be employed to signal that a particular message is something about which a parent really cares. In some cases, parents may not respond to noncompliance, an indication of a tolerance for disagreement. Empirical evidence comes from Nucci and Weber (1995) who note that mothers almost never negotiate with children in the realm of moral, conventional, or prudential forms of conduct, but they do in the realm of personal issues. Mothers also negotiate even more in areas of multifaceted events (those having both social conventional and personal features). When dealing with personal issues, mothers give few explicit messages (e.g., directly stating that what the child does is their choice), instead offering choices. Explicit messages, however, are characteristic of interactions in the moral, conventional, and prudential domains. This, then, is how mothers actually convey to their children a latitude of choice in their actions, as well as the criteria governing areas of behavior in which such choice is actually allowed.

Although all mothers endorse the importance of some degree of choice for their children, there are individual differences in the extent to which they allow it (Smetana, 1995). Smetana argues that differences in the willingness of parents to tolerate deviation depends on where they draw boundaries between moral, social conventional, prudential, and personal issues, and that the distinction between authoritarian, authoritative, and permissive parenting is, in fact, a distinction between these bound-aries. She reports that parents asked to make judgments about their right and their oblig-ation to make rules in the different domains differed as a function of their parenting style. Authoritarian and authoritative parents saw themselves as having a greater right to reg-ulate in all domains than did permissive parents, with authoritarian parents viewing rules about conventional and mixed or multifaceted domains as more obligatory than other par-ents. Moreover, authoritarian parents were the only ones not to differentiate among moral, social conventional, and mixed rules in terms of obligation: They "moralized nonmoral is-sues." For Smetana, then, the conditions under which disagreements make a difference have first of all to do with the nature of the domain under consideration, with the moral domain never being subject to negotiation. In other domains, however, disagreement be-comes acceptable to a degree that depends on characteristics of the parent. Some parents are better able to tolerate, or are more positively inclined toward, disagreement than oth-ers, and they can be identified using traditional divisions of parenting style.

Goals, Affect, and Other Parenting Cognitions

Some attention has been given to how goals, affect, and other cognitions interrelate. Dix (1992, 1993) speculates that the impact of goals is not directly on behavior but through causal attributions made for children's behavior. He suggests that parental at-tention is channeled by efforts to see whether a goal is being met. For empathic goals, attention would be on environmental events that would affect a child's happiness, and so attributions would tend to be external. For parent-centered goals, attention would be on conformity to parental wishes, thereby increasing the likelihood of internal or dis-positional attributions. Goals not successfully met produce negative emotion that in turn motivates a change of action or a change of goal. Empirical support for these specula-tions comes from Hastings' (1995) finding of a positive correlation between long-term parent-centered goals and internal attributions as well as a negative correlation between short-term safety-centered and short-term child-centered goals and internal attribu-tions, and from his observation that parents were more likely to change their goals when their original one had not been met.

Interrelationships Among Goals and Outcomes

The diverse goals that parents have during interactions with their children have legit-imacy in various contexts. The goals, nevertheless, may be served by actions that are different from those facilitating internalization. Compromise and negotiation, for ex-ample, may make children happier, although they obviously do not lead to the adop-tion of parental values. On the other hand, in some cases at least, certain goals may be important as "way stations" on the route to successful internalization. Values are more likely to be internalized, for example, if there is a positive relationship between parent and child, not only because the child may be more willing to comply with parental wishes but because the child may be more "present" both physically and psy-chologically to be exposed to those values. Parents who act to maintain harmony and a positive relationship may be creating conditions under which it is easier to demand compliance and internalization in areas where they are less willing to compromise. To ignore or yield at least partially to a child's inappropriate behavior, then, in the inter-est of not stressing the relationship, may make it easier to intervene in the case of other behaviors that are considered more important by the parent and to modify them to be more in accord with parental wishes.

PARENTING COGNITIONS IN CROSS-CULTURAL PERSPECTIVE

The research described to this point has all been conducted within an Anglo-European or Western cultural context. Moreover, the assumption has been that cognitions such as dispositional attributions, low estimations of self-efficacy, lack of sensitivity to the child's point of view, and parent-centered goals are detrimental to socialization because they promote authoritarian, power-assertive patterns of parent-child interaction that are ineffective in promoting the internalization of values. In this section, it is noted that authoritarian patterns of parenting are frequently accompanied in other cultures by more benign cognitions and that authoritative parenting is not always the most desirable strategy. These findings lead to the conclusion that assumptions about the universal negativity of authoritarian strategies and universal positivity of authoritative strategies are incorrect or, at least, that authoritarianism and authoritativeness are multifaceted constructs having both negative and positive features. The first part of the section focuses on authoritarianism and the second on authoritativeness.

Cross-Cultural Research and Implications for Understanding the Impact of Authoritarian Child-Rearing Strategies

The study of parents' attributional patterns and relationship schemas has assumed that dispositional attributions and low power and dismissive schemas are associated with power-assertive or authoritarian parenting practices, and that this is why these belief systems are detrimental for child outcomes. Thus anger, feelings of being threatened, low self-efficacy, and negative views of the child that are part of this set of cognitions are proposed to promote coercive and nonresponsive or authoritarian parenting behaviors. Authoritarian parents are seen, for example, as trying to establish their power over what they perceive to be willfully noncompliant children. Parents with more positive cognitive styles, on the other hand, exhibit more authoritative parenting, characterized by explanation, warmth, and responsivity. This more authoritative parenting is seen as desirable because it confirms the value of encouraging children's autonomy and responding to their emotional needs.

Consideration of practices and cognitions in non-Western cultures, however, casts a different light on this notion that authoritarian practices are always negative, particularly when these practices are not accompanied by the negative schemas that have been documented in Western cultures. It becomes apparent that authoritarian parenting need not always have detrimental outcomes for the child, particularly when the beliefs, thoughts, and emotions underlying authoritarian parenting are more positive than they characteristically are in Western culture. The conclusion is that the considerable emphasis on contrasting power-assertive/authoritarian and explanatory/authoritative approaches to parenting may have distracted us from looking at other behaviors associated with negative cognitions, and that it is important to consider these other behaviors along with the strategies to understand the full impact of parenting actions.

There are other reasons than the maintenance of parental power for the use of authoritarian practices. In collectivist Asian cultures, where interconnectedness of individuals and deference to authority are emphasized (Chao, 1994), it may be beneficial for children to learn to comply with a minimum of protest (a condition fostered by power assertiveness), thereby easing their integration into society later in life. Kelley, Power, and Wimbush (1992) have suggested that low-income African American mothers expect higher levels of obedience from their children because the consequences of disobedience in a low-income environment may be serious: Forceful methods are required to prevent involvement in activities harmful to the self and others. Consequently, while the parenting styles of Asian and low-income African American families have been described as strict and authoritarian, they may be conscious strategies, used to promote the interests of the child or of family harmony.

Authoritarian parenting practiced for the benefit of the child may differ in several important ways from authoritarian parenting practiced for the benefit of the parent (i.e., to maintain parental power). It may not be associated with a negative view of the child, the frequency of coercive parent-child exchanges thereby may be lower, parenting may be more conscious and considered in nature and less of an automatic reaction to the child, and parenting may be associated with higher levels of warmth. Each of these points is discussed in turn.

First, research suggests that authoritarian techniques in non-Western cultures tend not to be associated with a negative image of the child to the extent they are in Western cultures. Compared with American mothers, Japanese mothers expect obedience to parental wishes at an earlier age (Hess, Kashiwagi, Azuma, Price, & Dickson, 1980), and although they are more permissive and use more reasoning than American mothers, they are more likely to use physical punishment when the child directly confronts maternal authority (Power, Kobayashi-Winata, & Kelley, 1992). Relative to American mothers, Chinese mothers score high on measures of authoritarianism (Chao, 1994; Dornbusch, Ritter, Leiderman, Roberts, & Fraleigh, 1987), have been described as restrictive (Chiu, 1987; Kriger & Kroes, 1972), and are more likely to agree that when children continue to disobey, they deserve to be spanked (Chao, 1994). However, underlying these coercive features of Eastern parenting is a perception of the child as inherently good (Ho & Kang, 1984; Kojima, 1986). To the extent that children fulfill the expectations of their parents, it seems quite likely that the negative views accompanying authoritarianism in Anglo European cultures may be responsible for negative child outcomes, and that relatively positive expectations in Eastern cultures may facilitate positive outcomes. Thus children of authoritarian parents in collectivist societies may be less likely than those in individualistic societies to form a negative view of the self, and may act in ways that fulfill their parents' more positive expectations.

The second point follows from the first: Although non-Western collectivist and authoritarian parents may endorse coercive responses to child disobedience, they may be less likely to interpret ambiguous actions on the part of the child as willful disobedience because they do not have a generally negative view of the child. This is in contrast to Western authoritarian parents who interpret ambiguous information as deliberate and threatening (e.g., Dix et al., 1989), a way of thinking that leads to escalated interchanges and negative affect. Such escalation would be less likely to occur with parents who make more benign interpretations of their children's ambiguous actions. The positive environment engendered in this case is also likely to increase the willingness of the child to accept or internalize parental values.

The third point is that to the extent that authoritarian practices in the interests of the child are conscious strategies not derived from negative unconscious schemas, they should be more amenable to conscious reflection and less inflexible. Parents who employ authoritarian techniques in the child's interests may attend more effectively to various cues from the child, and the difficulties in information-processing associated with defensive arousal (Bugental, 1993) may not exist. They may be more accurate in their perceptions of the child being tired or bored, for example, and these perceptions may affect how the parents convey commands. They may also be more likely to make distinctions between the domains of parent-child disagreement and may be less likely automatically to interpret choices of the child in areas that the child considers under his or her own personal jurisdiction as a challenge to parental authority. And what of the evidence for these proposals? Two studies suggest that authoritarian strategies in non-Western cultures may be more purposeful, and less dependent on automatic, schema-based processing of information. First, whereas authoritarian parenting is associated with domination over children and a greater degree of hostility in Anglo-European cultures, Chao (1994) found that Asians equate such control with training their children, viewing their strictness as an "organizational type of control for the purpose or goal of keeping the family running more smoothly and fostering family harmony" (p. 1112). Second, Kelley et al. (1992) found that for lower-income African American mothers the use of power-assertive methods was not related to maternal attitudes toward child compliance. Mothers who endorsed authoritarian techniques were no more likely to value the child's obedience than were mothers who did not endorse these techniques, nor were they less likely to value the child's input or be responsive to it. It is possible that in these groups authoritarian mothers are not highly inflexible, and do not feel any more or less threatened or challenged by child noncompliance. Thus, they may be more rational and purposeful in dealing with noncompliance with maternal requests, and difficult interactions may be less likely to escalate as a result.

The last point is that parents engaging in authoritarian practices in collectivist cultures may not demonstrate the same affective characteristics as mothers in individualistic societies who are authoritarian: They may not necessarily be more detached (Baumrind, 1967) or angry with their children (Dix & Reinhold, 1991) than nonauthoritarian mothers. Bugental et al. (1989), as noted earlier, report that coercive and abusive mothers leak negative affect to difficult children, emitting hostile nonverbal cues that betray their attitude to the child. When this occurs, children perceive these cues and become more unresponsive, and coercive parent-child interactions escalate. If authoritarian parenting is engaged in for the benefit of the child, however, it is possible that children may detect more positive affective cues. Bartz and Levine (1978), for example, found that low SES African American parents preferred methods of child rearing that were more controlling than either European American or Hispanic parents, but also expressed greater agreement than the other two groups with parenting behaviors that were supportive of the child. Similarly, Rohner and Pettengill (1985) found a positive relationship between Korean children's ratings of their mothers and fathers on strict control and levels of warmth. (There was, however, also a relationship between strict parenting and ratings of maternal hostility.) In this case, the restrictive actions of their parents may be viewed by children more positively and, as a result, they may be more motivated to take on the values that the parents highlight as important as a result of this perceived warmth (Grusec & Goodnow, 1994).

The conclusion from these observations is that the study of parenting cognitions in other cultures suggests parents can behave in an authoritarian fashion and yet be quite successful in creating positive child-rearing conditions. If authoritarian parenting were pursued in Western culture in a similar manner then it ought to have less deleterious effects on child outcomes: The motives behind parental power assertion may substantially modify its effects. Thus the separation of parenting cognitions from parenting strategies becomes imperative. For a comprehensive understanding of socialization we need to look at other features of parenting behavior that may covary to some extent (particularly in Western culture) with authoritarianism but that may themselves be responsible for negative outcomes. It becomes necessary, then, to unravel the effects of power-assertive techniques from the effects of variables such as parental rejection, anger, low self-esteem, reactions to threat, and dislike of the child, features of parenting behavior that tend to be correlated with authoritarianism in our own culture but not necessarily in others. Indeed, they are not perfectly correlated in our culture or demonstrated relations between authoritarian/power-assertive parenting strategies and negative child outcomes would be strong and consistent, which they are not (see, e.g., Grusec & Goodnow, 1994).

Cross-Cultural Research and Implications for Understanding the Impact of Authoritative Child-Rearing Strategies

The argument for different parenting strategies serving different goals has also been made within the context of Western culture. It is now extended to a discussion of more general goals for socialization that are characteristic of different cultures. Here the suggestion is that authoritative parenting practices are the most effective way of socializing children when the ultimate goal of society is autonomy, but that this is not the case in other societies where the ultimate goal is interconnectedness. Authoritative practices are not necessarily inherently positive in their outcomes.

In Western, individualistic societies, the self is seen as relatively independent of its social context, and the individual as the basis of social action. Actions are believed to emanate from fairly stable dispositional sources: Westerners are therefore more comfortable characterizing themselves as having abstract attributes such as honesty that manifest themselves across different situations. In Western societies, then, autonomy is the valued end state of socialization (e.g., Osterweil & Nagano, 1991), a goal best achieved by the use of authoritative child-rearing strategies. Authoritative parenting, with its emphasis on encouraging independence and self-expression, encourages children to first be independent and assert themselves. The inculcation of prosocial values such as cooperation is secondary, and may have to be achieved by authoritative strategies such as reasoning or logical argument. Thus, because Western parents value autonomy, they may find it necessary to convince their children of the importance of prosocial values so their children will choose to adopt them. They may need to minimize the salience of external demands in order for good behavior to be attributed to an "inner self," so that children will continue to behave in accord with these standards when they exercise their autonomy.

Members of collectivist societies, in contrast to members of Western societies, are more likely to see themselves as being a part of a larger social group. They see their actions as determined by situational rather than dispositional factors (Cousins, 1989). In these cultures, individuals achieve their ends by aligning themselves with a larger social group, and trust that the group will work to meet their needs and desires (Markus & Kitayama, 1991). Self-restraint and self-effacement are valued, and self-interest is considered childish (Bond, Leung, & Wan, 1982; Hamaguchi, 1985): As a result, agents of socialization in collectivist cultures work to promote feelings of interdependence and cooperation in children in order to facilitate their effective integration into society. Authoritative parenting, with its emphasis on autonomy, is not the most effective way of reaching this goal. Rather, in one collectivist society at least (Japan), mothers maintain intensive physical contact with their children, as a means of promoting interdependence. Because of the child's sense of interdependence, discipline strategies that stress the continuity of familial relationships are particularly effective. Mothers will emphasize the consequences of children's misbehavior for the feelings of the mother and others, and will use threats to the continuity of familial relationships: Rather than being grounded, children may be threatened with being locked out of the house (Caudill & Weinstein, 1969; Conroy et al., 1980; Vogel & Vogel, 1961). This style of parenting ensures the acquisition of values such as cooperation and attending to the needs of others, because achieving these ends will serve to maintain a sense of self-worth and emotional security.

The collectivist approach to socialization may not require the use of authoritative discipline for several reasons. Because interdependence is a central aspect of a child's sense of self in collectivist cultures, there is less need to convince children, through logical arguments, of the importance of "taking in" prosocial values. Also, because counterarguments are not encouraged or expected, there is less need to use reasoning or logical argument. Finally, when interdependence is promoted and enduring dispositional factors are not emphasized, techniques that promote the conception of prosocial behavior as arising in response to the demands of the situation rather than in response to internalized norms may be less problematic.

These observations from a cross-cultural perspective serve to highlight again the important role that goals play in determining parenting behavior that is appropriate to what parents hope to achieve. They also bring home the point that, while autonomy appears as an ultimate goal in our own societal setting, it is not the ultimate goal in other settings. Thus, although authoritative and egalitarian practices may well be most appropriate for goals espoused in our own historical and cultural context, they do not represent what is inherently positive for human functioning.

PARENTING COGNITIONS AND THE
TRANSMISSION/CONSTRUCTION DEBATE

This final section also emerges from and enlarges on the argument that internalization of values is not the only goal that parents have when socializing their children. In so doing, it addresses a fundamental issue that has divided developmental researchers who have addressed the processes underlying the acquisition of values. The issue of how values are acquired, of whether they are transmitted from parent to child or whether they are constructed by the child, is addressed in several of the chapters in this volume. The discussion of negotiation and initiative-taking as goals in socialization provides the starting point for the present analysis. The argument is that values are sometimes transmitted and sometimes constructed; the question is under what conditions each of these outcomes occurs.

As noted earlier, parents are more likely to be flexible in their willingness to allow negotiation and compromise in specific areas. To use the language of social domain theory, moral, social conventional, and prudential issues are much less likely to be open to negotiation than are personal or multifaceted issues (Nucci & Weber, 1995). Goodnow (1994) adds to this list with the suggestion that negotiation and compromise may be more acceptable when the child employs mature lines of reasoning or when the parent interprets disagreement as manifestation of a relationship problem. In addition, there are individual differences in the extent to which parents are able to tolerate disagreement with their own point of view, possibly because they are inflexible in their own code of conduct or because they see disagreement as a threat to their own success as an authority figure (Smetana, 1995).

Goodnow (1994) suggests that notions about construction versus transmission may depend to a considerable extent on the content being considered. In some areas, values may be cared about more deeply and transmission therefore more important than in other areas where parents care less and where they are willing to allow the child to work out his or her own ideas. Goodnow notes that few parents " . . . are concerned about whether or not children acquire an understanding of conservation in the Piagetian sense. Most of the variance in children's understanding, then, can be attributed to factors within the child. For these topics, standard Piagetian theory works very well" (p. 53). Contrarily, she argues, when parents care about values such as honesty and fairness, it does not make sense to think of their children as constructing views of the world in relative isolation from the demands of that world.

Our general conclusion from this material, then, is that values are more likely to be transmitted—to be adopted with little if any change—when parents care about them, and that they are more likely to be constructed when parents care less about them. Authoritarian parents presumably tolerate less construction than authoritative or permissive parents. Overall, values involving personal and multifaceted issues may be more likely to be constructed than values involving moral, prudential, or social conventional issues. Thus child input may not be an inevitable feature of socialization, but one that is differentially encouraged by agents of socialization, with transmission typical when parents do not tolerate deviation from the standards they wish to impose and construction typical when parents are tolerant and even encouraging of change from their own position. It is important to note, however, that we have not speculated about the nature of the construction, that is, the processes underlying it. Bandura (1986), for example, notes that values may appear to have changed their form (i.e., to have been constructed), not because of a specific cognitive transformation undertaken by the child, but because children select from many sources in taking on a specific value. Selection is determined as well by such variables as differential expectations for reinforcement and feelings of self-efficacy in a particular domain. The argument here is meant only to suggest that under certain circumstances parents may be more willing to allow greater leeway in this selection than under others.

CONCLUSION

This chapter has presented the findings of a growing body of research suggesting that the thoughts parents have as they are interacting with their children have a substantial impact on their parenting strategies. Most frequently, the focus has been on the two parenting strategies of power assertion and reasoning. Negative attributions for children's behavior, feelings of ineffectiveness or inability to influence others, and parent-centered goals have been linked to the use of authoritarian parenting strategies and, therefore, ineffective internalization of values. Positive thoughts, on the other hand, have been linked to effective parenting interventions. In addition, research on mutual cognitions has been presented. Here identification of parenting strategies has been less precise. The suggestion is merely that parents who realize their children's ideas do not accord with their own can employ whatever strategies accomplish that outcome. Finally, the fact that internalization of values is not always the goal of parenting strategies has been documented, with the implication that strategies may be differentially appropriate in achieving these goals.

This overview of parenting cognitions widens, however, when one considers the limited, but nevertheless suggestive, cross-cultural research on parenting. In many cultural contexts, the link between negative cognitions and authoritarian behavior is less strong than in the Anglo-European context (where it is moderate at best). Moreover, authoritarian, power-assertive practices seem to be less detrimental to child development. The suggestion is that we need to look beyond the authoritarian/authoritative distinctions to other kinds of parenting characteristics that might be even more strongly linked to parenting cognitions. These include behavioral manifestations of like or dislike for the child, positive or negative expectations for future behavior, warmth or coldness and rejection, strength and success or failure of attempts to bring the child's understanding of the situation into line with that of the parent, behaviors resulting from the parents' own feelings of competence as a socializing agent, and features of parental information-processing and monitoring that are relevant to successful parenting strategies.

Consideration of cross-cultural research also widens thinking with respect to an assumed link in Western culture between internalization of values and parenting strategies that facilitate the development of autonomy and individuation. Here the conclusion is that autonomy and individuation are not universal expectations for child development, and that nonauthoritative strategies work better in more collectivist settings.

The final implication of the material on parenting cognitions for an understanding of parenting strategies and the internalization of values arises, not from a consideration of cross-cultural research, but from a consideration of parental willingness to negotiate and compromise at least in some areas in interactions with their children. The suggestion is that values are transmitted where parents do not tolerate compromise or construction, and that values are constructed when such construction is permitted or encouraged.

REFERENCES

Ainsworth, M. D. S., Blehar, M. C., Waters, E., & Wall, S. (1978). *Patterns of attachment: A psychological study of the Strange Situation.* Hillsdale, NJ: Erlbaum.

Atkinson, L., Chisholm, V., Dickens, S., Scott, B., Blackwell, J., Tam, F., & Goldberg, S. (1995). Cognitive coping, affective distress, and maternal sensitivity: Mothers of children with Down Syndrome. *Developmental Psychology, 31,* 668–676.

Azar, S. T., Robinson, D. R., Hekimian, E., & Twentyman, C. T. (1984). Unrealistic expectations and problem-solving ability in maltreating and comparison mothers. *Journal of Consulting and Clinical Psychology, 52,* 687–691.

Baden, A. D., & Howe, G. W. (1992). Mothers' attributions and expectancies regarding their conduct-disordered children. *Journal of Abnormal Child Psychology, 20,* 467–485.

Baldwin, M. J. (1992). Relational schemas and the processing of social information. *Psychological Review, 112,* 461–484.

Bandura, A. (1977). Self-efficacy: Toward a unifying theory of behavior change. *Psychological Review, 84,* 191–215.

Bandura, A. (1986). *Social foundations of thought and action: A social cognitive theory.* Englewood Cliffs, NJ: Prentice-Hall.

Bartz, K. W., & Levine, E. S. (1978). Child rearing by black parents: A description and comparison to Anglo and Chicano parents. *Journal of Marriage and the Family, 40,* 709–719.

Bauer, W. D., & Twentyman, C. T. (1985). Abusing, neglectful and comparison mothers' responses to child-related and non child-related stressors. *Journal of Consulting and Clinical Psychology, 53,* 335–343.

Baumrind, D. (1967). Child care practices anteceding three patterns of preschool behavior. *Genetic Psychology Monographs, 75,* 43–88.

Bond, M. H., Leung, K., & Wan, K. C. (1982). The social impact of self-effacing attributions: The Chinese case. *Journal of Social Psychology, 118,* 157–166.

Bornstein, M. H. (1989). Cross-cultural developmental psychology: The case of Japanese-American mother-infant comparisons: What do we know, what do we need to know, and why we need to know. *Developmental Review, 9,* 171–204.

Bretherton, I. (1985). Attachment theory: Retrospect and prospect. In I. Bretherton & E. Waters (Eds.), Growing points of attachment theory and research. *Monographs of the Society for Research in Child Development, 50*(1/2, Serial No. 209).

Bugental, D. B. (1992). Affective and cognitive processes within threat-oriented family systems. In I. E. Sigel, A. V. McGillicuddy-DeLisi, & J. J. Goodnow (Eds.), *Parental belief systems: Psychological consequences for children* (2nd ed., pp. 219–248). Hillsdale, NJ: Erlbaum.

Bugental, D. B. (1993). Communication in abusive relationships: Cognitive constructions of interpersonal power. *American Behavioral Scientist, 36,* 288–308.

Bugental, D. B., Blue, J., Cortez, V., Fleck, K., Kopeikin, H., Lewis, J., & Lyon, J. (1993). Social cognitions as organizers of autonomic and affective responses to social challenge. *Journal of Personality and Social Psychology, 64,* 94–103.

Bugental, D. B., Blue, J., & Cruzcosa, M. (1989). Perceived control over caregiving outcomes: Implications for child abuse. *Developmental Psychology, 25,* 532–539.

Bugental, D. B., Mantyla, S. M., & Lewis, J. (1989). Parental attributions as moderators of affective communication to children at risk for physical abuse. In D. Cicchetti & V. Carlson (Eds.), *Current research and theoretical advances in child maltreatment* (pp. 254–279). New York: Cambridge University Press.

Caudill, W., & Weinstein, H. (1969). Maternal care and infant behavior in Japan and America. *Psychiatry, 32,* 12–43.

Chao, R. K. (1994). Beyond parental control and authoritarian parenting style: Understanding Chinese parenting through the cultural notion of training. *Child Development, 65,* 1111–1119.

Chiu, L. H. (1987). Child-rearing attitudes of Chinese, Chinese-American, and Anglo-American mothers. *International Journal of Psychology, 22,* 409–419.

Collins, W. A. (1992). Parents' cognitions and changes in relationships during adolescence. In I. E. Sigel, A. V. McGillicuddy-DeLisi, & J. J. Goodnow (Eds.), *Parental belief systems: The psychological consequences for children* (2nd ed., pp. 175–197). Hillsdale, NJ: Erlbaum.

Collins, W. A., & Luebker, C. (1994). Parent and adolescent expectancies: Individual and relational significance. In J. Smetana (Ed.), *New directions for child development: Vol. 66. Beliefs about parenting: Origins and developmental implications* (pp. 65–80). San Francisco: Jossey-Bass.

Conroy, M., Hess, R. D., Azuma, H., & Kashiwagi, K. (1980). Maternal strategies for regulating children's behavior: Japanese and American families. *Journal of Cross-Cultural Psychology, 11,* 153–172.

Cousins, S. D. (1989). Culture and self-perception in Japan and the United States. *Journal of Personality and Social Psychology, 56,* 124–131.

Crittenden, P. M., & Ainsworth, M. D. S. (1989). Child maltreatment and attachment theory. In D. Cicchetti & V. Carlson (Eds.), *Child maltreatment: Theory and research on the causes and consequences of child abuse and neglect* (pp. 432–463). New York: Cambridge University Press.

Crowell, J. A., & Feldman, S. S. (1988). Mothers' internal models of relationships and children's behavioral and developmental status: A study of mother-child interaction. *Child Development, 59*, 1273–1285.

Crowell, J. A., & Feldman, S. S. (1991). Mothers' working models of attachment relationships and mother and child behavior during separation and reunion. *Developmental Psychology, 27*, 597–605.

Dix, T. (1992). Parenting on behalf of the child: Empathic goals in the regulation of responsive parenting. In I. E. Sigel, A. V. McGillicuddy-DeLisi, & J. J. Goodnow (Eds.), *Parental belief systems: The psychological consequences for children* (2nd ed., pp. 319–346). Hillsdale, NJ: Erlbaum.

Dix, T. (1993). Attributing dispositions to children: An interactional analysis of attribution in socialization. *Personality and Social Psychology Bulletin, 19*, 633–643.

Dix, T., & Grusec, J. E. (1985). Parent attribution processes in child socialization. In I. Sigel (Ed.), *Parent belief systems: Their psychological consequences for children* (pp. 201–233). Hillsdale, NJ: Erlbaum.

Dix, T., & Lochman, J. E. (1990). Social cognition and negative reactions to children: A comparison of mothers of aggressive and nonaggressive boys. *Journal of Social and Clinical Psychology, 9*, 418–438.

Dix, T., & Reinhold, D. P. (1991). Chronic and temporary influences on mothers' attributions for children's disobedience. *Merrill-Palmer Quarterly, 37*, 251–271.

Dix, T., Reinhold, D. A., & Zambarano, R. J. (1990). Mothers' judgments in moments of anger. *Merrill-Palmer Quarterly, 36*, 465–486.

Dix, T., Ruble, D. N., Grusec, J. E., & Nixon, S. (1986). Social cognition in parents: Inferential and affective reactions to children of three age levels. *Child Development, 57*, 879–894.

Dix, T., Ruble, D. N., & Zambarano, R. J. (1989). Mothers' implicit theories of discipline: Child effects, parent effects, and the attribution process. *Child Development, 60*, 1373–1391.

Dornbusch, S. M., Ritter, P. L., Leiderman, P. H., Roberts, D. F., & Fraleigh, M. J. (1987). The relation of parenting style to adolescent school performance. *Child Development, 58*, 1244–1257.

Fincham, F. D., & Grych, J. H. (1991). Explanations for family events in distressed and nondistressed couples: Is one type of explanation used consistently? *Journal of Family Psychology, 4*, 341–353.

Goodnow, J. J. (1992). Parents' ideas, children's ideas: The bases of congruence and divergence. In I. E. Sigel, A. V. McGillicuddy-DeLisi, & J. J. Goodnow (Eds.), *Parental belief systems: The psychological consequences for children* (2nd ed., pp. 293–318). Hillsdale, NJ: Erlbaum.

Goodnow, J. J. (1994). Acceptable disagreement across generations. In. J. Smetana (Ed.), *New directions for child development: Vol. 66. Beliefs about parenting: Origins and developmental implications* (pp. 51–64). San Francisco: Jossey-Bass.

Goodnow, J. J., & Collins, A. W. (1990). *Development according to parents: The nature, sources, and consequences of parents' ideas.* Hillsdale, NJ: Erlbaum.

Gralinski, H. H., & Kopp, C. B. (1993). Everyday rules for behavior: Mothers' requests to young children. *Developmental Psychology, 29*, 573–584.

Gretarsson, S. J., & Gelfand, D. M. (1988). Mothers' attributions regarding their children's social behavior and personality characteristics. *Developmental Psychology, 24*, 264–269.

Grusec, J. E., Adam, E., & Mammone, N. (1993, March). *Mental representations of relationships, parent belief systems, and parenting behavior.* Paper presented at the biennial meeting of the Society for Research in Child Development, New Orleans, LA.

Grusec, J. E., Adam, M., Mammone, N., Walters, G. C., & Wilson-O'Halloran, H. (1996). *The intergenerational transmission of control and protection strategies via mental representations of attachment relationships.* Unpublished manuscript, University of Toronto, Toronto, Canada.

Grusec, J. E., & Goodnow, J. J. (1994). Impact of parental discipline methods on the child's internalization of values: A reconceptualization of current points of view. *Developmental Psychology, 30,* 4–19.

Grusec, J. E., & Redler, E. (1980). Attribution, reinforcement, and altruism: A developmental analysis. *Developmental Psychology, 16,* 525–534.

Hamaguchi, E. (1985). A contextual model of the Japanese: Toward a methodological innovation in Japanese studies. *Journal of Japanese Studies, 11,* 289–321.

Hastings, P. (1995). *Parenting goals as organizing cognitions: The determinants and functions of parents' intentions.* Unpublished doctoral dissertation, University of Toronto, Toronto, Canada.

Hastings, P., & Grusec, J. E. (1997). Conflict outcome as a function of parental accuracy in perceiving child cognitions and affect. *Social Development, 6,* 76–90.

Hess, R. D., Kashiwagi, K., Azuma, H., Price, G. C., & Dickson, W. P. (1980). Maternal expectations for mastery of developmental tasks in Japan and the United States. *International Journal of Psychology, 15,* 259–271.

Ho, D. Y.F., & Kang, T. K. (1984). Intergenerational comparisons of child-rearing attitudes and practice in Hong Kong. *Developmental Psychology, 20,* 1004–1016.

Holden, G. (1983). Avoiding conflict: Mothers as tacticians in the supermarket. *Child Development, 54,* 233–240.

Holden, G., & Edwards, L. (1989). Parental attitudes toward child rearing: Instruments, issues, and implications. *Psychological Bulletin, 106,* 29–58.

Hunt, J. M., & Paraskevopoulos, J. (1980). Children's psychological development as a function of the inaccuracy of their mother's knowledge of their abilities. *Journal of Genetic Psychology, 136,* 285–298.

Jones, E. E., & Davis, K. E. (1965). From acts to dispositions: The attribution process in person perception. In L. Berkowitz (Ed.), *Advances in experimental social psychology* (Vol. 2, pp. 220–286). New York: Academic Press.

Kelley, M. L., Power, T. G., & Wimbush, D. D. (1992). Determinants of disciplinary practices in low-income black mothers. *Child Development, 63,* 573–582.

Kochanska, G., & Aksan, N. (1995). Mother-child mutually positive affect, the quality of child compliance to requests and prohibitions, and maternal control as correlates of early internalization. *Child Development, 66,* 236–254.

Kochanska, G., Radke-Yarrow, M., Kuczynski, L., & Friedman, S. L. (1987). Normal and affectively ill mothers' beliefs about their children. *American Journal of Orthopsychiatry, 57,* 345–350.

Kojima, H. (1986). Japanese concepts of child development from the mid-17th to mid-19th century. *International Journal of Behavioral Development, 9,* 315–329.

Kriger, S. F., & Kroes, W. H. (1972). Child-rearing attitudes of Chinese, Jewish, and Protestant mothers. *Journal of Social Psychology, 86,* 205–210.

Kuczynski, L. (1984). Socialization goals and mother-child interaction: Strategies for long-term and short-term compliance. *Developmental Psychology, 28,* 1061–1073.

Kuczynski, L., & Kochanska, G. (1990). Development of children's noncompliance from toddlerhood to age five. *Developmental Psychology, 26,* 398–408.

Levine, R. A. (1974). *Culture and personality: Contemporary readings.* Chicago: Aldine.

Maccoby, E. E., & Martin, J. A. (1983). Socialization in the context of the family: Parent-child interaction. In E. M.Hetherington (Ed.), *Handbook of child psychology* (4th ed.) (Vol. 4, pp. 1–102). New York: Wiley.

Main, M., & Goldwyn, R. (1991). *Adult attachment rating and classification systems.* Unpublished manuscript, University of California at Berkeley.

Mammone, N. (1995, April). *Mental representations of attachment relationships and parental control strategies and physical abuse.* Paper presented at the biennial meeting of the Society for Research in Child Development, Indianapolis, IN.

Markus, H. R., & Kitayama, S. (1991). Culture and the self: Implications for cognition, emotion, and motivation. *Psychological Review, 98,* 224–253.

Miller, S. A. (1988). Parents' beliefs about children's cognitive development. *Child Development, 59,* 259–295.

Miller, S. A. (1995). Parents' attributions for their children's behavior. *Child Development, 66,* 1557–1584.

Miller, S. A., Mondal, M., & Mee, L. L. (1991). Parental beliefs, parental accuracy, and children's cognitive performance: A search for causal relations. *Developmental Psychology, 27,* 267–276.

Nucci, L. (1994). Mother's beliefs regarding the personal domain of children. In J. G. Smetana (Ed.), *New directions for child development: Vol. 66. Beliefs about parenting: Origins and developmental implications* (pp. 81–90). San Francisco: Jossey-Bass.

Nucci, L. P., & Smetana, J. (1996). Mothers' conceptions of young children's areas of personal freedoms. *Child Development, 67,* 1870–1876.

Nucci, L. P., & Weber, E. K. (1995). Social interactions in the home and the development of young children's conceptions of the personal. *Child Development, 66,* 1438–1452.

Osterwiel, Z., & Nagano, K. N. (1991). Maternal views on autonomy: Japan and Israel. *Journal of Cross-Cultural Psychology, 22,* 362–375.

Power, T. G., Kobayashi-Winata, H., & Kelley, M. L. (1992). Child-rearing patterns in Japan and the United States: A cluster analytic study. *International Journal of Behavioral Development, 15,* 185–205.

Rohner, R. P., & Pettengill, S. M. (1985). Perceived parental acceptance-rejection and parental control among Korean adolescents. *Child Development, 56,* 524–528.

Rosenberg, M. S., & Reppucci, N. D. (1983). Abusive mothers: Perceptions of their own and their children's behavior. *Journal of Consulting and Clinical Psychology, 51,* 674–682.

Rubin, K., & Mills, R. S. L. (1992). Parents' thoughts about children's socially adaptive and maladaptive behaviors: Stability, change, and individual differences. In I. E. Sigel, A. V. McGillicuddy-DeLisi, & J. J. Goodnow (Eds.), *Parental belief systems: The psychological consequences for children* (2nd ed., pp. 41–69). Hillsdale, NJ: Erlbaum.

Sameroff, A. J., Seifer, R., & Elias, P. K. (1982). Sociocultural variability in infant temperament ratings. *Child Development, 53,* 164–173.

Sigel, I. E. (1992). The belief-behavior connection: A resolvable dilemma. In I. E. Sigel, A. V. McGillicuddy-DeLisi, & J. J. Goodnow (Eds.), *Parental belief systems: The psychological consequences for children* (2nd ed., pp. 433–456). Hillsdale, NJ: Erlbaum.

Smetana, J. (1988). Adolsecents' and parents' reasoning about actual family conflicts. *Child Development, 60,* 1052–1067.

Smetana, J. (1995). Parenting styles and conceptions of parental authority during adolescence. *Child Development, 66,* 299–316.

Smetana, J., & Asquith, P. (1994). Adolescents' and parents' conceptions of parental authority and adolescent autonomy. *Child Development, 65,* 1147–1162.

Sobol, M. P., Ashbourne, D. T., Earn, B. M., & Cunningham, C. E. (1989). Parents' attributions for achieving compliance from Attention-Deficit-Disordered children. *Journal of Abnormal Child Psychology, 17,* 359–369.

Steele, B. F. (1970). Parental abuse of infants and small children. In E. M. Anthony & T. Benedek (Eds.), *Parenthood, its psychology and psychopathology* (pp. 449–477). Boston: Little, Brown.

Teti, D. M., & Gelfand, D. M. (1991). Behavioral competence among mothers of infants in the first year: The mediational role of maternal self-efficacy. *Child Development, 62,* 918–929.

Twentyman, C. T., Rohrbeck, C. A., & Amish, P. L. (1984). A cognitive-behavioral model of child abuse. In S. Saunders (Ed.), *Violent individuals and families: A practitioner's handbook* (pp. 86–111). Springfield, IL: Thomas.

Vogel, E., & Vogel, S. H. (1961). Family security, personal immaturity, and emotional health in a Japanese sample. *Marriage and Family Living, 23,* 161–166.

Weiner, B. (1980). A cognitive (attribution)-emotion-action model of motivated behavior: An analysis of judgments of help-giving. *Journal of Personality and Social Psychology, 39,* 186–200.

Zahn-Waxler, C. (1993). Warriors and worriers: Gender and psychopathology. *Development and Psychopathology, 5,* 79–89.

CHAPTER 11

Co-Construction of Human Development: Heterogeneity within Parental Belief Orientations

JAAN VALSINER, ANGELA U. BRANCO, and CLAUDIA MELO DANTAS

In trying to make sense of human development, much of contemporary psychology is caught in the unproductive reliance on a dichotomy: Development is explained either by intrapersonal factors, or by the person's embeddedness in a social context. This dichotomy—even if phrased in cognitive and social terms—has the same underlying structure entailed by the traditions of the "nature-nurture" counterpositioning. Such dichotomies are intellectual impassés in psychology, and researchers try to find alternative general perspectives for conceptualization. Furthermore, a basic issue of construction of psychological novelty is in need of emphasis in psychology. In this chapter, we will look at issues of parental values and beliefs from a perspective that has become labeled by the unelegant term co-constructionism (Valsiner, 1994c). The term itself is merely a heuristic and metatheoretical device for establishing a focus on issues from a specifiable perspective. Its function is to maintain joint focus on the personal and social sides of human development.

WHAT IS A CO-CONSTRUCTIONIST PERSPECTIVE?

The co-constructionist perspective (Hermans & Kempen, 1993; Kurtines, Berman, Ittel, & Williamson, 1995; Valsiner, 1994a, 1994b, 1994c; Wozniak, 1986, 1993) is a growing effort to unite different classic ideas in developmental psychology into a framework of theories that emphasize personal construction within the field of social goal-directed conduct of other persons. It is a kind of sociogenetic personology (see also Eckensberger, 1995; Shweder, 1995), that preserves the uniqueness of individual persons as well as their interdependence within the culture. It has historical roots in the work of James Mark Baldwin, Jean Piaget, Lev Vygotsky, and William Stern (Valsiner, 1997).

This chapter was begun when the first author was a Visiting Professor at the Universidade de Brasilia in 1995 and was finished in 1996, thanks to the generous support from the Fulbright Foundation. Much of the work was accomplished in Berlin, thanks to the Alexander von Humboldt Stiftung, to whom the first author expresses his gratitude. The work in Brazil has been supported by grants from CNPq to Angela Branco and Claudia Melo Dantas, which are gratefully acknowledged. Teresa Mettel's productive suggestions at different phases of the development of the notion of belief orientation, and their extraction from narratives, played an important part in the present work. Editorial suggestions by Joan Grusec and Leon Kuczynski are acknowledged with gratitude.

The relatively cumbersome term co-construction is a semiotic mediating device that canalizes psychologists' thinking to simultaneously consider the personal construction of one's psychological development and its social guidance. The personal and the social in human psychological development are not mutually exclusive opposites, but complementary mechanisms that enable each other to proceed. Social guidance makes personal construction possible, and such construction modifies the social guidance of the others, and of oneself.

There exist different co-constructionist views on human development. In this chapter, the theoretical perspective of *bounded indeterminacy* will be explored (Valsiner, 1987, 1997). Development is bounded by temporary (context-based or intrapsychological) constraints that create the "bounded field" within which the actual course of development is not predictable. Furthermore, the boundaries of the field themselves are constantly renegotiated—the constraints once set are being continuously reset. Through the organization of constraints, the development is being directed, yet its actual course is not preset. Negotiation of constraints leads to the open-endedness of development, where novelty can emerge at any junction. Constraints create the basis for transcending them, and novel versions of developmental course emerge.

The co-constructionist perspective entails a focus on *bidirectional* and *reconstructive* transfer of cultural messages from adults' generations to those of following generations. Cultural messages are actively communicated (by parents) and equally actively reassembled by their recipient children, who are joint constructors of the new cultural knowledge through their constructive internalization/externalization process. Each new generation proceeds beyond the preceeding generation, as it transforms the cultural system. In their respective roles, both parents and children are active joint constructors of culture.

Unity in Diversity: Collective and Personal Cultures

Socialization in intergenerational culture transfer is a bidirectional process where both generations are active in the construction of their beliefs and values interdependently with others, yet in uniquely personal ways. The central aim of co-constructionist developmental psychology is to explain the processes involved in the construction of *personal culture* under the canalizing directions of the *collective culture* (Valsiner, 1989, pp. 47–48). The collective culture entails communally shared meanings, social norms, and everyday life practices. These meanings, norms, and practices are results of actions of particular persons, externalized into the collective domain, and maintained through social transaction and encoding in the human cultural environments. Symbolic architectural environments—temples, churches, cemeteries, opera houses—are all examples of personal externalizations of the meaning systems of the people involved in the initial design of these settings. The meaning system encoded into these architectural settings functions as a collective-cultural memory device, constraining the development of many next generations along the lines of some general values (e.g., historical identity—see the case of "the Castilian soul," in Del Río & Alvarez, 1995).

Individuals construct their idiosyncratic (personally meaningful) system of signs, practices, and personal objects, all of which constitute the personal culture. These cultures emerge from the collective culture; their function is to organize the intra- and interpersonal worlds of the person in ways that provide personal sense to the encounters with those worlds.

Semiogenetic Sufficiency

The emphasis on the semiotic construction of knowledge by the active person with the help of collective-cultural input gives dynamic form to the developmental process. On the one hand, the macrolevel ("collective culture") sets up myriad physical and semiotic forms—symbols, icons, and indices (to use C. S. Peirce's classification here)—thus including both verbal and figurative forms.

Because human beings construct (and reconstruct) signs, researchers can speak of the *semiogenetic* (sign-constructive) nature of human development. These signs are not set up in their final, fixed forms, but are characterized by some "semifinished"—therefore open to reconstruction—state of existence. Signs are open to modifications when a new context needs it; the meanings of signs are maintained in *complexes* rather than *concepts* (Vygotsky, 1935/1994). Semiotic mediation through complexes allows for flexible decontextualization and recontextualization of the mediating devices.

The Double Nature of Constructed Signs:
Half-Own, Half-Alien

The developing individual is constantly acting and constructing personal sense, utilizing the systems of signs available in the collective-cultural domain. He or she personally reconstructs, or adjusts, these signs in attempting to make sense of his or her new situation. Each moment in human life is necessarily new (even if it *resembles* a *similar* situation of the past), hence the need for constant reconstruction of the semiotic mediational devices.

Thus, collective-culturally maintained sign systems are necessarily open for new contextualizations giving them an important unfinished aspect—from the perspective of a person, a collective-cultural sign system has a double nature. The following statement by Mikhail Bakhtin is often used in sociocultural discourse:

> The word of language [*slovo iazyka*—in Russian]—is half alien [*chuzoye*—not belonging to me and unknown—in Russian] word. It becomes "one's own" when the speaker inhabits [*naselit,* in Russian] it with his intention, with his accent, masters [*ovladeet,* in Russian] the word, brings it to bear upon his meaningful and expressive strivings. Until that moment of appropriation [*prisvoenie* in Russian] the word is not existing in neutral and faceless language (as the speaker does not take the word from a dictionary!), but [it exists] on the lips of others, in alien contexts, in service of others' intentions: from here it has to be taken and made into one's own. (Bakhtin, 1934/1975, p. 106)

As the word is always "half-alien," it is simultaneously also constructed to be one's own, in the "other half." *Human development entails both,* and the perennial question is how the two sides reach a state of unity between persons who remain separate active agents. That they do not "fuse" into one superindividual being (a constructed psychological "Siamese twin," unified through language), remains an existential given. Furthermore, lack of such fusion makes development of novelty possible. For example, a parental social suggestion effort can include words whose meanings are unknown to the child. Likewise, human beings use words of open-ended generality (e.g., "beautiful," "good," "just," "bad," "wrong"). When words are used in a particular context by parents, the child co-constructs the other side of such open-ended or unknown meanings. Parents may have emphasized to their daughter the importance of "looking beautiful" ever since her childhood, yet are surprised when the girl, in adolescence, refuses to remove makeup that the parents think is awful—their daughter claims she looks beautiful exactly that way. Since "beautiful" is in principle an ill-defined term, its use has led to co-construction of a novel form of self-presentation that is far from "sharing" of values between parents and children.

Inconsistency of Social Worlds

The dynamic process of semiogenetic co-construction is necessary by the inevitable temporal heterogeneity of the developmental environments. Contrary to our usual tendency to describe environments in static terms that emphasize consistency, the reality (viewed from the point of view of the developing child) is very different. The world of a living human being is always uncertain and entails a semiotically overdetermined encoding of some aspects of the heterogeneous and constantly changing environment (Boesch, 1991; Obeyesekere, 1990). Using James Mark Baldwin's (1894) observation:

> The child begins to learn in addition the fact that persons are in a measure individual in their treatment of him, and hence that individuality has elements of uncertainty or *irregularity* about it. This growing sense is very clear to one who watches an infant in its second half-year. Sometimes the mother gives a biscuit, but sometimes she does not. Sometimes the father smiles and tosses the child; sometimes he does not. And the child looks for signs of these varying moods and methods of treatment. Its new pains of disappointment arise directly on the basis of that former sense of regular personal presence upon which its expectancy went forth. (p. 277)

The developing person moves around in a heterogeneous environment, being temporarily and conditionally open to its inputs. The result is relative functional autonomy of the person from the immediate social contexts. Although the person is always embedded in a context, yet the personal-cultural system allows for maintenance of a psychological distance from the given setting, while remaining a part of it. Psychological distancing is the main accomplishment of the reliance on semiotic mediation that has developed in the species of *Homo sapiens*. It is through the personal-cultural system that a person can maintain relative autonomy in heterogeneous social settings.

Linking Personal and Collective Cultures:
Internalization/ Externalization

Human development entails internalization and externalization of collective-cultural material within personal cultures (Lawrence & Valsiner, 1993). As a scientific term, the notion of internalization/externalization sets a focus on the boundary between a person and the social world. Internalization and externalization are mutually coordinated novelty-constructive processes. They involve a reciprocal cyclical process within which "personal sense" leads the construction of meanings, which are made available in the interpersonal domain.

Internalization is the process by which meanings that relate to phenomena and that are suggested for the individual by "social others"—who pursue their personal goals while assuming their social roles—are brought over into the individual's intrapsychological system. It is based on human (and other higher primates') openness to construction and use of signs (Tomasello, 1996; Toomela, 1996a, 1996b). Internalization/externalization processes use semiotic means that are personal ideational constructs, even when encoded in some material form.

Social roles of the other persons who surround the developing child guarantee heterogeneity of the social suggestions in the person's immediate surrounding. By "bringing over" into the intrapsychological field some of the suggestions, the person constructively modifies the brought-over material. The social suggestions are transformed into a personally meaningful form, which differs from the original suggestions. The reciprocal process of externalization connotes activities by which the once-social— but now-personal—set of meanings is constructively moved into novel contexts within one's self, as well as in the social environment. A co-constructionist view of socialization leads to a perspective on parenting that focuses on the active roles of *both* parents and children. This means that the role of children in parenting cannot be overlooked.

PARENTING: A THEME BETWEEN COMMON SENSE AND SCIENCE

When psychologists create their objects of investigation, they often borrow some aspects of their theoretical elaborations from ordinary language. Such borrowing may be related to the need to develop applied expertise in response to the social demands in a given culture at the given time. The construction of a scientific research object on the basis of society's culturally constructed focus of interest may run into conceptual problems since the common cultural knowledge is a historically particular phenomenon, whereas science is aimed at generality that transcends the particulars (Valsiner, 1985, 1994f). Many "hot topics" in child psychology pondered by researchers are cultural-historical inventions that represent the current narrative construction of a "problem" and may be only peripherally related to basic knowledge of human development.

PARENTING AS A CULTURAL INVENTION

Parenting is a word used often in English, yet it is even not translatable directly into other languages (e.g., Portuguese, Russian, German). Even in English it is a curious concept. A noun *(parent)* has been turned into a verb *(to parent* somebody = to act as a parent relative to somebody), from which the generic concept *parenting* is derived. That concept is supposed to reflect some process (ongoing activity) of an adult who acts in the role of a parent, relative to some child. Already in terms of semantics, it entails a unidirectional culture transmission perspective (see critique in Valsiner, 1989). As a scientific term, it retains that linguistically encoded unidirectionality. It would not fit with the co-constructionist assumptions outlined earlier, and therefore, it must be modified.

Psychology's Construction of Essential Concepts

It is characteristic of human ordinary language use to turn terms that are aimed at denoting processes into those that refer to entities supposedly present "in" the object in question. Thus, ordinary talk about parenting often turns into attributional assignment (e.g., "am I [is s/he] a good parent?" or "how can one be a good parent?"). In a similar vein, research on parenting in psychology often turns from the study of the issue as a process, to that of psychological features that are assumed to characterize a parent ("good," "bad," "at risk"). Hence, the potential uses of the English language invention of the word parenting—as reflective of process or activity—become unused, and translated back into the terminology of non-developmental psychology with its implicit ideologically value-ladden concerns about characteristics of different kinds of parents. Without denying the practical need for social practices, it remains important to emphasize that theoretical elaborations of psychology of parenting should be addressed in generic terms, distanced from practical applications.

Why Parenting? Selectivity of Focus

Parenting—in the sense of parental characteristics—has been approached from a number of angles by psychologists (Goodnow & Collins, 1990; Maccoby, 1992; McGillicudy-DeLisi, Siegel, & Johnson, 1982; Palacios, 1988, 1993). Behind studies of parenting is a certain ideology that there is something special and worthy of attention in the ways in which adults in their role of parents relate with children. This unique relationship is set up by culturally defined kinship relations, which include issues of "family," "marriage," "mothering," "fathering," "grandparenting," and other relational concepts. These terms reflect unidirectional power or responsibility assumptions: The "fathering" (or "mothering") adult is implied to have power and responsibility for the actions of the object of this described activity (i.e., the child), and not vice versa. This is further exemplified by the absence of action descriptions at the level of kinship relations where equal power relations are implicated (e.g., possible but unused, or awkward terms such as: "brothering," "sistering").

Different Versions of Role Relations

The asymmetry of power relations is part of such ideology. It is taken for granted that parents act in evaluative and directive ways (e.g., "disciplining" or "punishing") toward the children, and not vice versa. Likewise, parents are considered "responsible" for the actions of their children, but not the other way round. In reality, the child sometimes becomes responsible for the parent (see Vygotsky, 1935/1994, pp. 340–342 about the roles children of different ages could take relative to their alcoholic mother). Furthermore, mutual responsibility in parent-child relations may take different forms in different situations. Even if parents usually provide economic sources for children, this has not been always the case in history (e.g., children's work as provision of resources to family income, prior to legal prohibition of child labor). Nor is it the case in our "postmodern" world, where enterprising computer-fanatic adolescents may get high-paying jobs in former East European countries while their parents have lost their income-producing capacity, due to bankruptcy of their previous workplaces. The relative power role relations in such families become very different from the *assumed* norm of "parent as provider, child as provided for." It is not possible to take the latter assumed norm as the given, but rather as a special case of many possible parent-child role relations.

Parenting as a Derived Focus

The ideology of parenting is derived from the ways in which the parent-children role relations are differentiated out from the kinship network. This focus fits the Eurocentric middle-class worldview of the normative nature of nuclear and neolocal family life arrangements. The role of parents is notable where children live with their parents in living quarters separated by well-guarded locked doors, thick walls, and social rules against persons other than immediate family entering the "family territory" without explicit permission. Such a living arrangement, however, is a cultural-historical particular case and cannot be considered singularly normative. For example, in the context of the Indian joint family, the functional set of kinship relations that are important for organizing child-related activities can include other significant relations (e.g., "grandmother-child," "uncle-child," in parallel with the obvious relevance of mother-child and father-child relations).

Making Parenting into a "Task": Social Construction of Issues and Expert Roles

Widespread discourse about parenting has led psychologists to a selective focus on adults' different perspectives of children (e.g., "parenting" as a rational decision-making process, or as an affective process involving attachment), and on social institutionalization of an area of everyday expertise (part of informal knowledge) into formal expertise (e.g., representing parenting as involving selection of child-rearing "techniques" from a publicly known repertoire). Being a parent is no longer a personal, intuitive, and ordinary state of being, but rather a socially guided task that subordinates parents to the sets of social suggestions from authoritative institutional sources of expertise.

This institutionalizing focus carries traces of the cultural history of the researchers: Some domains of parent-child interaction have been emphasized that are usual topics in modern Western societies (e.g., eye contact, guidance of development, disciplinary tactics); whereas others (e.g., parents' teasing of children; Briggs, 1987, 1991; Loudon, 1970) have been overlooked by researchers' constructions of parenting. The whole range of possible psychological phenomena of parents that may accompany their movement into their roles is rarely given in all its complexity (Goodnow, 1988; Reichle & Montada, 1994). Instead, psychological literature on parenting is filled with discussions about typologies of parents (Smetana, 1994), and anthropological descriptions have linked parenting with cultural forms of organizing social lives (Harkness, 1990; Harkness & Super, 1992, 1994).

Psychological research is guided by the cultural-historical construction of its subject matter. Parenting is a good example here: As a species, *Homo sapiens* has emerged and developed in ways that require parents' care of the offspring over substantial periods of time, yet without any necessity to become involved in a *special activity* of "parenting." It may be that many grandmothers of our own—who may have brought up many more children in their lifetime than modern parents would ever expect to do—would question the necessity to talk about the issues of parenting (and even less to spend economic resources to study it!). For them, being a parent was a usual and expected part of human life, in all of its drama and pleasures. It is under the social-institutional takeover of control for aspects of ordinary life (e.g., childbearing, child rearing, expertise in knowledge; Del Río, 1996) that a semiotically directed focus on the "issue" appears in everyday talk. Parenting, dieting, money saving, brushing one's teeth, and so on, then become "problems" that require the assistance of special "experts," who are certified or at least accepted as such by social institutions. Such construction of problem areas leads to the mapping of scientific research efforts as social-institutional means of attention focusing on them. Not only must the problem area be treated by a specialist who is considered to be an expert, but the latter should rely on a corpus of knowledge that is labeled scientific, in the process of that treatment. In psychology, much of the empirically derived knowledge is actually a re-iterated version of knowledge that is already encoded in ordinary language. Hence the expertise of a grandmother need not differ from that of a child-rearing specialist. Psychology of parenting is merely one example of the social processes that reconstruct human everyday lives in modern (or postmodern) societies.

A CO-CONSTRUCTIONIST FOCUS: UNITY OF PARENTING AND FILIATING

The concept of *filiating* that will be introduced here reflects the complementarity in adult-child relations. Filiating refers to a process that complements parenting and is performed by the "parented" children. Any co-constructionist rendering of parenting must introduce such a term to counter the unidirectional implications of parenting.

Filiating entails a complex of phenomena that simultaneously reflect the constancy of the child's relationship with the parent, and the processes of active counterregulation of parenting efforts. From the basis of the guaranteed role of "the son or daughter of X," the child acts in goal-directed ways relative to parents' actions. The background frame of the particular relationship creates the field of possible actions toward parental efforts.

The basis for filiating cannot be reduced to "internal working models" of attachment perspectives. The latter are insufficiently differentiated as to the nature of the relationship (as those working models have become treated as properties of the child). Rather the filiating basis entails the child's basic feeling for how the relationship is organized. Surely that basis emerges in the ontogenetic history of the child-parent relations.

Organization of Filiating Bases: Conditional and Unconditional Love

An analysis of South Italian materials (Benigni & Valsiner, 1995) leads to an elaboration of the filiating basis. The child may self-construct a *feeling* that the consequence of his or her conduct will be either the parents' acceptance or rejection of him or her as their child. This condition can be described as the zone of conditional love (ZCL), and can be contrasted with its counterpart—the zone of unconditional love (ZUL). These feeling-zones are mutually related, much like the notion of "dependent independence" (Valsiner, 1984). Since any relation between persons is conditional to some mutual coordination, the ZCL includes ZUL, with the latter constituting a wider, or narrower area within the former. If ZUL is narrowed down, the child may constantly feel the ZCL conditions regulating the filiating process.

In this case, the child will constantly worry about whether his or her actions might lead to the parent's denouncing the child *in general*. Symbolic claims by parents that "you are no more my daughter [or son]" can be found in any society, and are often reflected in classical literature. Usually such claims are made in response to a child's major defiance—usually at adolescence—of basic social expectations of the parents. Typical scenarios include an adolescent's desire for marriage (or enactment via elopement) with an unsuitable or undesirable partner.

However, such generalizing threats from the parent can become related to *minor* everyday happenings in a child's life. A decision to create that linkage (or not insist on it) is the parent's; it belongs to his or her dominant role in the relationship with the child. A parent may use the threat of "withdrawal of love" in conjunction with a minor issue (e.g., "if you get less than the very best grade on your next exam at school, you are no longer my child"). Such "withdrawal of love" parenting tactic can become complemented by the child's acceptance of fear of such possible events, high (but fragmented) motivation to accomplish particular tasks (e.g., get the best grade on *this* test), and generalized intrapsychological mechanisms of guilt. Once the parenting/filiating system creates a ZCL/ZUL structure where the latter is minimized, and the former linked with a list of specific happenings in the child's life, the result may be a complicated and ambivalent relationship between the grown-up child and the (by then) elderly parent. It is probably no coincidence that the widespread use of "withdrawal of love" tactics (or narrowing of the ZUL inside ZCL, in present terminology) is reported mostly from the so-called "guilt cultures" (i.e., societies of European background which have successfully transferred capitalist economic thought to aspects of family relations), in contrast with so-called "shame cultures" (usually societies outside the Western cultural area). The distinction of "guilt" and "shame" cultures is more than questionable from any perspective of cultural psychology, yet the fact that children's guilt mechanisms are powerfully built up in many families in the world remains an important developmental phenomenon in need of further study.

Filiating as Buffering

Filiating makes it possible for the child to respond to the parenting efforts of the adult in ways that allow both maintenance of their relationship and relative distancing of the child's self from the particular actions of the parenting adult. Filiating—from the child's point of view—guarantees sufficient autonomy from goal-oriented parenting efforts, while retaining the particular child-parent basic relationship. Filiating grants the dialogicality of parent-child relations.

Dialogicality of interaction process leads to the construction of buffers against one (or the other) side's efforts. Psychological distancing within the frame of a maintained relationship becomes a means to constructively cope with challenging situations. Hence, filiating operates as an attenuator of the possibly excessive acts of parenting. For example, parents' efforts to control an adolescent's emerging heterosexual relations can be accepted by the youth ("Okay, if that's what they want, I comply, but in reality I do not care"); yet in his or her intrapsychological world, the adolescent can continue to build abstracted imaginary relations that remain hidden from the parents' control efforts. And when an adequate possibility emerges, the teenager may bring the imagined and desired relations to real life, and surprise the parents with actions that the latter thought had been eradicated from their child's psyche (e.g., the parents: "How awful [that the child acted in this way], we always strictly prohibited such behavior in our family").

In the process of parenting and filiating, both parents and their offspring build their culturally guided subjectivities—personal cultures—over the whole life span. These subjectivities entail beliefs and values that are used to regulate the actual process of human development. The unity of parenting and filiating processes in adult-child relations is a derivation from the general co-constructionist perspective on human development.

Processes of parenting and filiating are characterized by their future-oriented directionality, rather than by description of their ontological states. Human actions in any here-and-now situation are oriented both toward the present, and toward some future objective. When considering the activities of parents relative to their children and vice versa, this future orientation becomes relevant in the belief systems.

BELIEFS, VALUES, AND SEMIOTIC CONSTRUCTION OF PSYCHOLOGICAL FUNCTIONS

The future-oriented human development sets up the need to conceptualize personal-cultural mediating devices, such as beliefs and values, that are constructed by a person and that constrain development toward the future. Concepts such as beliefs and values are not easy to use in theoretical constructions in psychology. The complicated notion of belief is addressed by William James (1889):

> In the case of acquiescence or belief, the object is not only apprehended by the mind, *but is held to have reality.* Belief is thus the mental state or function of cognising reality. . . . (p. 321)
>
> . . . We shall presently see that we never disbelieve anything except for that the reason that we believe something else which contradicts the first thing. *Disbelief is thus an incidental complication to belief.* . . .
>
> The true *opposites of belief . . .* are *doubt and inquiry,* not disbelief. In both these states the content of our mind is in unrest, and the emotion engendered thereby, like the emotion of belief itself, perfectly distinct, but perfectly indescribable in words. (p. 322, emphases added)

Beliefs thus create relative mental stability for a person, by not letting the opposites—doubting and inquiring—take hold of conduct. If a person states "I believe that X is the case," a semiotic mediational device is created in the form of X. This belief constrains further mental actions, as the belief eliminates its opposites (doubt about X, and curiosity that would go beyond X). A statement about a belief which looks ontologically stable ("I believe X") actually occurs in some context of an ongoing process of "stream of future-oriented consciousness," and constitutes a semiotic vehicle for setting up a condition of virtual reality (an "as-if" state) of the desired future state. In this function, a belief is actually an orientation toward a future, desired state of affairs, rather than a description of actual reality.

For psychological conceptualization, the pair of concepts "belief" and "value" have posed major problems. A common solution has been to consider the latter as a generalized and staticized version of the former: Once constructed, beliefs may become values. A value is often defined as an "enduring belief that a specific mode of conduct or end state of existence is *personally or socially preferable to an opposite* or *converse mode* of conduct or end state of existence" (Rokeach, 1973, p. 5, emphasis added).

Again, a contrast with the opposite is evident. Rokeach's definition effort reflects the conceptual limitations of nondevelopmental psychology that has eliminated temporal organization of phenomena from its focus. The tentative talk about "mode of conduct" or "end state" reflects the necessity to consider value as time- and activities-bound. Nevertheless, the issue of time is not considered here in explicit terms (see the analysis of goal orientations later in this chapter).

Similarly, the distinction between belief and value is not clear. Rokeach unites "belief" and "value" (the latter being "enduring belief"—another allusion to temporal organization of conduct), and distinguishes between different values in terms of preferences (social, or personal). Thus, the world of human personalities may consist of unenduring "beliefs" and enduring "beliefs" (which are "values"), all available in their established forms (not constructed by the active believer or value-er), and selected on the basis of their oppositions with other beliefs and values.

Human Development as a Future-Oriented Process, and the Issue of Beliefs and Values

Rokeach's accepted view of beliefs and values is of little use in developmental psychology, and is particularly misfitting with the co-constructionist perspective. The joint construction of "relatively enduring" semiotic mediating devices that begin to regulate conduct is exactly what interests researchers about the latter perspective. Thus, the focus is on *construction*—as contrasted with *selection* (out of a ready-made set)—of beliefs or values in the process of social conduct, and in accordance with the constructors' (and co-constructors') goal orientations.

What is not considered by any nondevelopmental account of beliefs and values is the feed-forward nature of all developmental processes. Feed-forward regulation operates under the conditions of irreversible time, literally turning around the better-known feedback notion to face the future. A person at time X acts in way Z, and the result of that action provides some feed*back* to the person. This depiction fits the nondevelopmental perspectives on human action since the assumption of irreversibility of time is not relevant in their cases. Yet, when irreversibility of time is considered, then the feed*back* from the result of action Z necessarily reaches the person at time X + 1, thus constituting a feed-*forward* (relative to the time when Z was performed) signal, that organizes the person's next action (at time X + 1), which then provides further feed-forward signals (for time X + 2), and so on. Given the ongoing process of development, there is simply no possibility for any action to feed "back" to the previous state of the system, since the system is constantly moving forward to its next state. Hence the results of human action are always feed-forward regulators of either the immediate (next) future moment, or of some (indeterminate) moment in the future.

This future-orientedness of development sets up strict conditions for particular areas of investigation. First, the feed-forward nature of development leads to a focus on the processes by which *possibilities* of the indeterminate future are being facilitated in the present. The present state of affairs canalizes the possibilities for the making of the future. Any phenomenon of *anticipation* of something happening in the future reflects that orientation. Parents anticipate that if they act in way X, Y, or Z toward their child now, then the child might end up with one or another (desirable or undesirable) outcome later in life. Child-rearing experts tell stories about one or another outcome in the future if the parents act (or do not act) in a particular way now. The inevitable indeterminacy of the future creates a fertile basis for discursive construction of scenarios of anticipation.

Second, future-orientedness guarantees that human development is simultaneously continuous and discontinuous (or conservative and opportunistic), structured and open to novelties. Human life course allows for a range of possibilities, only one of which will become actualized by the given person. The move from multiplicity of future possibilities to the one that the person creates for him- or herself is the arena of co-construction, where constraints of various kinds are utilized. In this, the constraints are constructed *both* between persons (e.g., in parent-child interaction), and in the intrapsychological domains of each person. Constraining takes place in both action and feeling/thinking realms, with the result that the exact structure of constraints is constantly being renegotiated. Much of co-construction entails moving against existing constraints, removing them, constructing novelties, and setting up new constraints. Canalization through constraints allows for the emergence of both the constant and novel sides of development.

In the domain of parents' beliefs and values, it can be assumed that the beliefs are future-oriented local (i.e., personal-cultural) mediating devices. As such, they may constrain future actions, yet need not strictly determine them. From here follows that inconsistency between parents' beliefs and actions is the expected usual state of affairs. If there is consistency, it may be a situation-specific case where a particular event has led to the mobilization of the beliefs and actions into the same structure of unity of semiotic mediating devices and their direct control of action. This structure can dissipate once the event is over.

Alternatively, *generalized consistency* can exist within a parent's belief system. It may be labeled "value," but whether one or another label is attached to the phenomenon is less important than the focus on its generalized and semiotic consistency. Generalized assumptions about children (e.g., "little children are innocent" vs. "little children are devils and only strict education can change them into human beings") canalize parental understanding of children in one or another direction.

GOAL ORIENTATIONS AND BELIEF ORIENTATIONS

In this chapter, beliefs will be considered in terms of belief orientations. The notion of *orientation* maintains the canalizing function of beliefs in the reasoning of parents. The way psychology usually conceives a person's subjective representations does not take into account the dynamic character of developmental processes. The concepts presented here reflect the transformational quality at the core of developmental processes.

Goals and Goal Orientations

The existence of goals and their role in regulating individuals' actions has been proposed and discussed within a wide range of theoretical frameworks (Atkinson, 1982; Bandura, 1988; Eckensberger, 1994, 1995; Klein, Whitener, & Ilgen, 1991; Latham, 1991; Modell, 1990; Oppenheimer, 1987). Traditionally, goals tend to be conceptualized as an *end state that is to be achieved or accomplished* by the individual. A goal is a specific aim or defined direction that would guide the individual's conduct toward its accomplishment.

A goal-terminology can be useful in analyzing motivations as it describes the possible range of coordination of the person's conduct orientation within a certain context. Nonetheless, from a systemic approach, goals should not be considered a stable or definable state of expectations, but should suggest a flexible direction toward a desirable process or outcome. In the case of development, goals are necessarily ideal constructions the function of which is to lead the development of a person from a here-and-now situation toward some expected next state. As time-bound constructions, goals are constantly being reconstructed for the immediate future, following the fluidity of the individuals' interactions with his or her contexts, and therefore should be considered to exist *in a semideterminate state* at any specific time. The goals-system of a person at any time is not a strict set of mutually distinct goals, but a semistructured potpourri of goals with varying expected time spans (Kindermann & Valsiner, 1989). The system of goals is constantly being constructed and reconstructed as the person relates the here-and-now context with some imagined and desired future state. Terminology of goals may lead our thinking in the direction of certainty and finality in the description of the person's development.

The dynamic feature of human psychological functioning may be better described by the term *orientation*. In reference to goals, the notion of orientation frees our theoretical reasoning from having to assume the existence of future states, created by persons in the present. Such future states cannot be considered as existing in the present, and once they happen to come into existence in the next present (i.e., formerly future), they cannot be interpreted post factum as having been the goals the person actually had constructed in the past. In short—goals as such are not accessible.

The term *goal orientation* allows us to detect the direction of the persons' actions in the present, and interpret those as oriented toward one or another goal domain in the future. The goal orientations can be emerging, fluctuating, or changing; although their future-orientedness remains, their functions in the present are the actual participating events in the construction of the future. The emerging goal orientations are intertwined with the context of the ongoing actions and constitute the core for the organism's development leading to the use of present feedback for extrapolative actions for construction of the future. The term goal orientation, therefore, suggests such process quality of human psychological development, and can be tentatively defined as a kind of internal constraining system, semiotically mediated, that, by projecting into the future, constrains the individual's actions, feelings, and thoughts in the present time.

Goal Orientations and Belief Orientations

Goal orientations exist within a semiotic space, structured according to a systemic organization. That structure implies the existence of an interdependency and a hierarchical organization between the various goal orientations. The very nature of goal orientations—resulting from a continuous co-constructive process along the individual's interactions—entails a dynamic hierarchical configuration that will depend on the specific time and context within which the person is embedded. This structure is defined as a goal orientation system, an important component of the original, personal culture of each individual.

Theoretical considerations meant to counter the nondevelopmental features of traditional conceptualizations apply to psychological affect-ladden constructs such as beliefs and values. Their ever-changing nature, which emerges from co-constructive processes occurring in social interactions—must be well established. The notion of *belief orientations* (BO-s), and *belief orientation system (BOS)*, in analogical relation to the rationale presented to justify the term goal orientation, seems to be more appropriate to describe the flux of individuals' convictions and preferences.

Thoughts, ideas, and affective-cognitive elaborations over individuals' preferences and evaluations about life events are in fact actively co-constructed along the person's experiences. The belief orientation system is continuously being constructed and reconstructed. The person's goal orientations can be linked with belief orientations in a flexible way: Goal orientations may lead to reorganization of belief orientations, but some belief orientations may persevere at the face of changing goal orientations. This may explain the existence of a significant number of inconsistencies reflecting the emergence of novel patterns, the presence of an indeterminacy component typical of developmental processes (Ford & Lerner, 1992).

A belief orientation system (BOS) can include inherently contradictory BO-s, and some areas of content may be uncovered by specific belief orientations. Furthermore, different belief orientations may entail inherent relations with one another. The heterogeneity and frequently contradictory cultural suggestions represent a permanent source for change processes within belief orientation systems, but the affective dimension of psychological experience, on the other hand, exerts a kind of gravity influence on this ever-changing flow. The field of BOS (and values as a special case of belief orientations) entails internal temporary structure (e.g., Stern, 1917). This structure can be represented as BOS-field, within which different belief orientations are represented in their partially overlapping, oppositional, or mutually parallel forms of existence. Description of such a heterogeneous field is a formidable task for the methodology of parenting/filiating research.

Methodology of Investigation: Belief Orientations Constructed in Interviews

The co-constructionist perspective requires a new look at methodology in psychology (Branco & Valsiner, 1997; Valsiner, 1994e, 1995a). Methodology entails a systematic relationship between theories on the one hand, and data derivation processes, on the other. Theory determines the general direction in which data construction methods are being derived; the phenomenon under study adds specific constraints to the creation of methods.

Often the term "methodology" is habitually applied as a synonym for "methods," a language use that is unequivocally rejected in the context of the analysis in this chapter. Methodology entails the cyclical relationship between general worldviews, theories constructed on their basis, encounters with phenomena, construction of methods, and the context of research process as a whole. No methods—taken out of the context of the methodology cycle—can produce interpretable data (Branco & Valsiner, 1997).

In line with these expectations for methodology, an analysis of BOS in parental conduct entails a specific abstract (axiomatic) orientation, which the investigator coordinates with the phenomena. As emphasized earlier, a BOS entails belief orientations that at times contradict one another and that may be constructed in any here-and-now situation without obligatory determinative "effect" on conduct. Thus, interviewing of parents about their belief orientations in the content domain of parenting is itself a constructive process; these belief orientations may be constructed during the interview process, out of the parents' general experiences, which the interviewer influences in the direction of one or another generalization by the interviewee.

An Empirical Example: Constructing BO-Sentences in Interviews with Parents

The following examples come from a study of belief orientations in the reasoning of rural-background lower class mothers in one of the satellite cities of Brasilia (Melo Dantas, 1996). The study was based on a semistructured interview schedule, where different content domains of the experiences of parents (e.g., with child discipline, parents' social networks, reasoning about day-care centers and health facilities) were explored as the interviewer visited the interviewees in their home contexts. All interviews were tape-recorded and subsequently transcribed.

As is usual in semistructured interviews, the interviewees' speech can be rich in stylistic and content features, and does not constitute a simple answer to the questions. The question of extraction of relevant information from the text becomes crucial. It is exactly the process of interpretation of paragraph-length texts that led to the construction (by the investigators) of BO-sentences. The latter are sentence-length summaries of the major theme talked about by the interviewee. For example, from the following part of actual interview transcript:

> .eu fui criada muito mimada e eu me machuquei muito na vida por isso, que eu não tive preparo. Porque eu acho que você mimar uma criança ou bajular não vai adiantar de nada, vai chegar uma certa hora quando a criança estiver sozinha que não vai ter nem pai nem mãe para ajudar ele, ele vai ter que sozinho se defender.

> [. . . I was spoiled as a child and life has hurt me a lot on account of that, I wasn't prepared. Because I think that to spoil, to flatter a child won't help, there will be a time when the child is by himself he won't have dad or mom to help him, he will have to defend himself on his own.]

the following BO-sentence was generated:

> It is no good to spoil a child, to do everything he wants; a child needs to learn how to defend himself.

The construction of the BO-sentence here is the result of the investigator's synthesis of ideas—based on the interviewee's narrative—and need not represent the level of generalization that is available to the interviewee. Since the goal of research enterprise is abstracting knowledge from the richness of original context, such summarization is a necessary step. It entails a version of coding (that takes the form of a substantive sentence, rather than an abstract nominal code), where each encoded summary can be interpretable in its own terms. However, the adequacy of representation by BO-sentences of the complex phenomena (expressed in the transcript) is of central relevance.

A particular part of the transcript can give rise to more than one BO-sentence as in the following example:

> Com uma criança que era autista, né, mongol e quando ele estava meio agitado ele se isolava ele pegava uma pasta de soro, seringa, vidrinho e ficava lá brincando, sozinho. Eu aprendi com ele que quando ele estava nervoso ele se isolava, tentava se acalmar interiormente, eu acho que é por isso que eu me isolo quando eu estou nervosa. Foi nesse ponto que essa criança me ensinou.

> [With an autistic child, that is mongol (popular name for a child with Down's syndrome), when he was agitated he took a bag with serum, a syringe, and a little bottle and played with it. I learned with him that when he was nervous he isolated himself and tried to calm down internally, I think that's why I isolate myself when I am nervous. That's what this child taught me.]

The preceding passage leads to construction of two BO-sentences:

> When nervous or feeling stressed out, isolation and work help the person to feel relieved.
>
> The child teaches the adult a lot of things.

As can be seen, the BO-sentences constitute a summary—constructed by the investigator—of inductive translation of the explicated phenomena (i.e., parents' triggered thematic stories) into a set of common language sentences. The difference of this focus from the usual questionnaire-type methods is in the interpretive role of the investigator at each step of data construction. For example, the preceding statements could easily be constructed not from the interviews, but from the investigator's own imagination of what themes and meanings parents might utilize in their thinking. Such BO-sentences could then easily appear in a questionnaire to parents (e.g., asking them to endorse these items in "true" vs. "false" response format). However, getting parents to endorse some BO-sentence (as an item in a questionnaire) eliminates the possibility of coordinating the actual personal microgenetic generation context (i.e., the process of construction of the parent's utterance) with the extracted data. In the example given, the BO-sentences can be traced back to the mother's narration of a specific episode (of the child playing while agitated) that *she* inductively generalized as a learning event of her own. If the same mother had simply endorsed a "true" response to both of the BO-sentences embedded in a questionnaire, the generalization of similar kind would not have been hers to make, but socially suggested by the investigator. It is therefore not surprising that questionnaire-based research has to resort to the adoption of a unidirectional culture transmission model. In contrast, a co-constructionist perspective calls for methods that make it possible to examine the mother's active joint constructor role. The interview questions remain social suggestions by the investigator (similarly to questionnaire items), but instead of reducing the person's response options to forced choice between "true" and "false" (or to some enforced abstract numerical assignment as in a Likert scale), the interviewee is expected to generate an elaborate narrative of some kind in response to a question.

Certainly the extraction of BO-sentences is merely an inductive interpretive step in the process of data derivation. The value of such sentences for the researcher is not some abstract notion of the "data," but in the realm of how such derived data may allow us to characterize the whole mentality structure of the parent. It is at the next step beyond the BO-sentences that explicit theoretical assumptions about such mentality structure begin to figure prominently in the research process. The following are two such assumptions:

1. The parent's belief orientations are content-bound (can be characterized in relation to specific content domains).
2. Both within and between these content domains, belief orientations constitute a heterogeneous set, which includes contradictions.

On the basis of these assumptions, further data analyses would selectively look for heterogeneity in the BO-sentences. Given that direction, it is not surprising that this heterogeneity is found (as it was theoretically postulated to exist), yet what is *not* deductively predetermined is *where and in what concrete form* such heterogeneity might be found with particular parents.

Technically speaking, following the construction of BO-sentences, the individual parental profiles of BO-sentences of different content domains provide investigators with a description of the whole BOS. Each profile includes all the BO-sentences within the given content category.

Example 1

Content Domain: Discipline

BO-sentences:

It is necessary to beat the child when he disobeys you.

One should not beat a deficient child.

There is no point in punishing a rebellious child because he will repeat the bad behavior.

Each child should be disciplined in a different way.

A child should not be educated just by beating, that doesn't work.

As the child grows up, the way you discipline him has to change: to beat, to advise, to talk.

This individual profile of a mother's BO-sentences for the given category gives us a picture of belief orientations that is linked with the set of possible real-life disciplinary situation in a multitude of flexible ways. Each of the BO-sentences in this profile is reflecting *conditionality* of disciplinary techniques, starting from the conditions of when to punish (episodes of disobeying), but not beating a child who is deficient or punishing a rebellious child (i.e., it is assumed that the parent would decide in context whether the given child is "rebellious" or not). Differences between children, age-cohort specificities, and variation of educational techniques ("not . . . just by beating") are reflected in this profile.

We can now describe this inductively derived BOS by a generic narrative formula (which also indicates the "unfilled areas" of the field):

> Each child should be disciplined in a different way, and as the child grows, the disciplining must change. The distinction between deficient, rebellious, disobeying, x, y, z child, from which follows that a deficient child should not be beaten [but something else can be done], rebellious child need not be punished, but if a child is viewed as disobeying, he should be beaten, yet that is not the whole story as just beating doesn't work [what could work is not specified].

The given BOS "rules out" some actions under some conditions (leaving alternatives undifferentiated), and sets up a makeshift classification of children (or states of children). The BOS field is merely a dynamic anchor point for further specification of conditions, categorization of the state of affairs, and exclusions. It is very far from a full picture of a rational decision tree that would turn parenting into a task of calculated rationality (allowing for costs vs. benefits analysis).

The heterogeneity of the BOS leaves the options open to the filiating process. Thus, the actively filiating child can renegotiate the diagnosed characteristcs (e.g., "I am neither disobeying you or being rebellious, but X, Y, or Z"), or conditions ("I am rebellious but you know if you beat me I will do it again"). It is the BOS-texture that is constantly being renegotiated in the parenting/filiating process. This negotiation can differentiate further meaningful aspects of the BOS, and leave others without explicit formulation. The BOS is an immediate semiotic mediating device that is being co-constructed, rather than a set of "given" and "followed" rules for decontextual-ized parental actions.

Example 2

Content domain: Social Network

BO-sentences:

Other people's influence makes it difficult to educate a child: There are different modes of child education within a same community.

Neighbors disapprove/criticize, sometimes, the education you give to your child.

It is important to rely on your children's cooperation to take care of each other.

It is good to have the support from your neighbors to learn how to educate your children.

It is good to have someone to take care of the children (aunt, *mãe crecheira* [day-care provider, in a role uniting mother's and teacher's functions], an adolescent).

It is better to think about your children's problem by yourself: Don't look for external help.

Day care provides more freedom for the child to play.

A child raised by somebody else becomes difficult.

Here is a profile with inherent contradictions in the belief orientations set. The par-ticipation of "social others" in the parenting of a child is filled with uncertainties in this mother's BO-system. The neighbors and day-care providers are on the one hand a re-source of support, but on the other hand they intervene with the mother's own belief ori-entations about her own role. Day care provides the child with new opportunities, and with new influences. The picture of ambivalence that emerges in this mother's BO-system is not a particular case of that mother in a specific lower-class context of Brazil. It would repeat itself in many individual cases of parents in many social classes, since the issue of self-other differentiation in the role of parenting is inherently plurivalent. Thus, the same belief orientation system makes it possible to create a legitimate narra-tive account for a number of divergent parental action scenarios.

CONCLUSION

In this chapter, we outlined a co-constructionist perspective on parenting. That per-spective entails the view of two parallel processes—parenting and filiating—and of the study of semiotic mediational devices that regulate those processes, such as beliefs. Human beings are constantly creating new signs of greater or lesser permanence and fix-ity. The inevitable constraining of that process by irreversibility of time leads develop-ment to constantly work at the boundary between the present and the immediate future, and in person-environment relationships.

In the case of parenting and filiating, the constructed semiotic devices include a heterogeneous set of goal and belief orientations, that exist in the subjective worlds of adults in some incomplete form. This incompleteness is a vehicle of plasticity; a par-ticular belief orientation system (BOS) can be open to transformation when put into some unique activity context. In interaction with others, these belief orientations may obtain clearer forms, or dissipate. The subjective world of parents is not to be con-strued as a homogeneous or rational "calculation system" of how to act on the "tasks of parenting" to reach adequate solutions, but rather as a dynamically goals-oriented and -generating process. From that dynamic flow, a heterogeneous set of belief orientations emerges, and acquires relative autonomy. These belief orientations can be brought to regulate parental actions when necessary.

This dynamics of parental thinking and feeling set up demands for research methodology as the unfinished, open-systemic and semiautonomous nature of parental reasoning needs to be reflected in the data. In this chapter, we outlined a technique of constructing belief orientation sentences (BO-s) that would act as units of analysis in the profile of individuals' belief orientation systems (BOS). Our examples reveal the *locally constructed* structure of belief orientations: it cannot (and need not) be assumed that any specific BO-s in the empirical data remain constant in the personal-cultural world of the particular interviewed mothers. Instead, at every new instance, some version of such heterogeneous BOS becomes constructed de novo, either as a part of narrative about parental reflection (i.e., dissociated from action, as was the case with interview contexts), or guiding action in specific settings. Parental beliefs are not entities that remain existent when once constructed, but semiotic constructs that are constantly new, contradictory, and therefore powerful tools for regulating parents' reasoning and acting. Their study may benefit from descriptions of the fluidity of parental belief orientations over time, in dialogue with the parent. In such dialogue, the ways in which some belief orientations maintain relative stability (and others disappear, or are reconstructed) can be elaborated.

Can one look for immediate or long-term consequences of such dynamic belief orientation systems? From the perspective of bidirectional culture transmission models, any possible consequence of parental beliefs on child's immediate actions or development is mediated by the parenting/filiating system. All consequences are negotiated solutions, rather than unidirectional causal impacts. This leads to a necessary refocusing of specific research methods, in line with the consistency with the notion of methodology as a cycle (Branco & Valsiner, 1997). In general, it may be worth focusing investigations on *short-term* longitudinal investigation of parents and children moving through *a specifiable* life-course change together. The co-construction system can be visible for the investigator when challenged by real-life events, to which the investigator may be allowed to enter. The particular methods employed—whether these include questionnaires, interviews, or observations—need to bring out the heterogeneity of the phenomena in the data. Longitudinal contact with the parents and children should reveal both the fluidity and constancy in the belief-orientations system and its linkage with the processes of parent-child interaction.

It also follows from the co-constructionist perspective that there will always be some discrepancy between the domains of parental actions and their reflections on those actions. This discrepancy is usually viewed as invalidating either the evidence on parental reflection (if their actions are used as the "validation criterion") or on parental actions (if the "beliefs" are used as "validation criterion"). Such interpretation is unwarranted since *the semiotic process of human development necessarily produces some discrepancy between the levels of action and reflections.* The construction of externalized belief orientations (in social discourse) and immediate actions as parents (under demands of a particular context) are necessarily different kinds of phenomena, even if the same parent is involved in both situations.

These implications of the co-constructionist perspective throw new light on issues of parental beliefs and values. Parenting is thus a heterogeneous phenomenon of bidirectional cultural transformation, rather than unidirectional and unitary guidance of children toward adulthood. Research questions that may become productive include those of the dynamic nature of the construction of belief orientations, and the selective linking of those orientations with actual action. Both of these research directions would reveal the remarkable plasticity of the parenting and filiating system, which allows parents and children to develop sufficiently well under extremely varied (and varying) conditions. Human beings make themselves free to pursue their goals through semiotically organized flexibility.

REFERENCES

Atkinson, J. W. (1982). Old and new conceptions of how expected consequences influence actions. In N. T. Feather (Ed.), *Expectations and actions: Expectancy-value models in psychology.* Hillsdale, NJ: Erlbaum.

Bakhtin, M. M. (1975). Slovo v romane [Discourse in the novel]. In M. Bakhtin, *Voprosy literatury i estetiki* (pp. 73–232). Moscow: Khudozhestvennaya Literatura. (Original work published 1934)

Baldwin, J. M. (1894). Personality-suggestion. *Psychological Review, 1,* 274–279.

Bandura, A. (1988, August). *Self-regulation of motivation and action through goal systems.* Paper presented at the meeting of the 24th International Congress of Psychology, Sydney, Australia.

Bartkowski, J. P., & Ellison, C. G. (1995). Divergent models of childrearing in popular manuals: Conservative Protestants vs. the mainstream experts. *Sociology of Religion, 56*(1), 21–34.

Benigni, L., & Valsiner, J. (1995). "Amoral familism" and child development: Edward Banfield and the understanding of child socialization in Southern Italy. In J. Valsiner (Ed.), *Child development within culturally structured environments: Vol. 3. Comparative-cultural and constructivist perspectives* (pp. 83–104). Norwood, NJ: ABLEX.

Boesch, E. E. (1991). *Symbolic action theory and cultural psychology.* New York: Springer.

Branco, A. U., & Valsiner, J. (1992, July 20). *Development of convergence and divergence in joint actions of preschool children within structured social contexts.* Poster presented at the meeting of the 25th International Congress of Psychology, Brussels, Belgium.

Branco, A. U., & Valsiner, J. (1997). Changing methodologies: A constructivist study of goal-orientation in social interaction. *Psychology in developing societies, 9*(1), 35–64.

Briggs, J. L. (1987). In search of emotional meaning. *Ethos, 15*(1), 8–15.

Briggs, J. L. (1991). Expecting the unexpected: Canadian inuit training for an experimental lifestyle. *Ethos, 19*(3), 259–287.

Del Río, P. (1996). Building identities in a mass-communication world. *Culture & Psychology, 2*(2), 159–172.

Del Río, P., & Alvarez, A. (1995). Directivity: The cultural and educational construction of morality and agency. Some questions arising from the legacy of Vygotsky. *Anthropology & Education Quarterly, 26*(4), 384–409.

Eckensberger, L. H. (1994). Die Rolle von Analytizität und Empirie im Kontext einer entwicklungspsychologischen Kulturpsychologie. *Forum Kritische Psychologie, 34,* 23–35.

Eckensberger, L. H. (1995). Activity or action: Two different roads towards an integration of culture into psychology? *Culture & Psychology, 1*(1), 67–80.

Ford, D. H., & Lerner, R. M. (1992). *Developmental systems theory.* Thousand Oaks, CA: Sage.

Goodnow, J. J. (1988). Parents' ideas, actions, and feelings: Models and methods from developmental and social psychology. *Child Development, 59,* 286–320.

Goodnow, J. J., & Collins, W. A. (1990). *Development according to parents: The nature, sources, and consequences of parents' ideas.* Hillsdale, NJ: Erlbaum.

Harkness, S. (1990). A cultural model for the acquisition of language: Implications for the innateness debate. *Developmental Psychobiology, 23*(7), 727–740.

Harkness, S., & Super, C. M. (1992). Parental ethnotheories in action. In I. E. Siegel, A. McGillicudy-DeLisi, & J. J. Goodnow (Eds.), *Parental belief systems: The psychological consequences for children* (pp. 373–391). Hillsdale, NJ: Erlbaum.

Harkness, S., & Super, C. M. (1994). The developmental niche: A theoretical framework for analyzing the household production of health. *Social Science and Medicine, 38*(2), 217–226.

Hermans, H. J. M., & Kempen, H. J. G. (1993). *The dialogical self: Meaning as movement.* San Diego, CA: Academic Press.

James, W. (1889). The psychology of belief. *Mind, 55,* 321–352.

Kindermann, T., & Valsiner, J. (1989). Strategies for empirical research in context-inclusive developmental psychology. In J. Valsiner (Ed.), *Cultural context and child development* (pp. 13–50). Toronto-Göttingen-Bern: Hogrefe & Huber.

Klein, H. J., Whitener, E. M., & Ilgen, D. R. (1991). The role of goal specificity in the goal-setting process. *Motivation and Emotion, 14*(3), 179–193.

Kurtines, W. M., Berman, S. L., Ittel, A., & Williamson, S. (1995). Moral development: A co-constructivist perspective. In W. M. Kurtines & J. L. Gewirtz (Eds.), *Moral development: An introduction* (pp. 337–376). Boston: Allyn & Bacon.

Latham, G. P. (1991). Self-regulation through goal setting. *Organizational Behavior and Human Decision Processes, 50,* 212–247.

Lawrence, J. A., & Valsiner, J. (1993). Conceptual roots of internalization: From transmission to transformation. *Human Development, 36,* 150–167.

Loudon, J. B. (1970). Teasing and socialization on Tristan da Cunha. In P. Mayer (Ed.), *Socialization: The approach from social anthropology* (pp. 293–332). London: Tavistock.

Maccoby, E. E. (1992). The role of parents in the socialization of children: An historical overview. *Developmental Psychology, 28*(6), 1006–1017.

McGillicudy-DeLisi, A., Siegel, I., & Johnson, E. (1982). The family as a system of mutual influences: Parental beliefs, distancing behaviors, and children's representation. In M. Lewis & L. Rosenblum (Eds.), *The child and its family* (pp. 91–106). New York: Plenum Press.

Melo Dantas, C. (1996). *Crenças maternas sobre desenvolvimento e educação da criança en contexto de baixa renda.* Unpublished thesis, Universidade de Brasilia, Mestrado em Psicologia, Brasilia, D. F.

Modell, A. (1990). *Other times, other realities: Toward a theory of psychoanalytic treatment.* Cambridge, MA: Harvard University Press.

Obeyesekere, G. (1990). *The work of culture.* Chicago: University of Chicago Press.

Oppenheimer, L. (1987). Cognitive and social variables in the plan of action. In S. F. Friedman, E. K. Scholnick, & R. R. Cocking (Eds.), *Blueprints of thinking: The role of planning in cognitive development* (pp. 356–392). Cambridge, England: Cambridge University Press.

Palacios, J. (1988). *Las ideas de los padres sobre a educacion de suas hijos.* Seville: University of Seville, Instituto de Desarrolo Regional.

Palacios, J. (1993). *Parent's ideas about the development and education of their children: Answers to some questions.* Unpublished manuscript, University of Seville.

Reichle, B., & Montada, L. (1994). Problems with the transition to parenthood. In M. J. Lerner & G. Mikula (Eds.), *Entitlement and affectional bond: Justice in close relationships* (pp. 205–228). New York: Plenum Press.

Rokeach, M. (1973). *The nature of human values.* New York: Free Press.

Shweder, R. A. (1995). The confessions of a methodological individualist. *Culture & Psychology, 1*(1), 115–122.

Smetana, J. G. (Ed.). (1994). *New directions for child development: Vol. 66. Beliefs about parenting: Origins and developmental implications.* San Francisco: Jossey-Bass.

Stern, E. (1917). *Beiträge zur psychologie der wertung.* Strassburg: Schultz.

Tomasello, M. (1996). The child's contribution to culture: A commentary on Toomela. *Culture & Psychology, 2*(3), 307–318.

Toomela, A. (1996a). How culture transforms mind: A process of internalization. *Culture & Psychology, 2*(3), 285–306.

Toomela, A. (1996b). What characterizes language that can be internalized: A reply to Tomasello. *Culture & Psychology, 2*(3), 319–322.

Valsiner, J. (1984). *The childhood of the Soviet citizen: Socialization for loyalty.* Ottawa, Ontario, Canada: Carleton University Press.

Valsiner, J. (1985). Common sense and psychological theories: The historical nature of logical necessity. *Scandinavian Journal of Psychology, 26,* 97–109.

Valsiner, J. (1987). *Culture and the development of children's action.* Chichester, England: Wiley.

Valsiner, J. (1989). *Human development and culture.* Lexington, MA: Heath.

Valsiner, J. (1994a). James Mark Baldwin and his impact: Social development of cognitive functions. In A. Rosa & J. Valsiner (Eds.), *Explorations in sociocultural studies: Vol. 1. Historical and theoretical discourse* (pp. 187–204). Madrid: Fundación Infancia y Aprendizaje.

Valsiner, J. (1994b). Culture and human development: A co-constructionist perspective. In P. van Geert, L. P. Mos, & W. J. Baker (Eds.), *Annals of theoretical psychology* (Vol. 10, pp. 247–298). New York: Plenum Press.

Valsiner, J. (1994c). Co-constructionism: What is (and is not) in a name? In P. van Geert, L. P. Mos, & W. J. Baker (Eds.), *Annals of theoretical psychology* (Vol. 10, pp. 343–368). New York: Plenum Press.

Valsiner, J. (1994d). Irreversibility of time and the construction of historical developmental psychology. *Mind, Culture, and Activity, 1*(1/2), 25–42.

Valsiner, J. (1994e). Bidirectional cultural transmission and constructive sociogenesis. In W. de Graaf & R. Maier (Eds.), *Sociogenesis reexamined* (pp. 47–70). New York: Springer.

Valsiner, J. (1994f). Uses of common sense and ordinary language in psychology, and beyond: A co-constructionist perspective and its implications. In J. Siegfried (Ed.), *The status of common sense in psychology* (pp. 46–57). Norwood, NJ: ABLEX.

Valsiner, J. (1995a, September). *Meanings of "the data" in contemporary developmental psychology: Constructions and implications.* Invited lecture at 12. Tagung der Fachgruppe Entwicklungspsychologie der Deutschen Gesellschaft für Psychologie, Leipzig, Germany.

Valsiner, J. (1995b). Editorial: Discourse complexes and relations between social sciences and societies. *Culture & Psychology, 1*(4), 411–422.

Valsiner, J. (1997). *The guided mind: A sociogenetic approach to personality.* Cambridge, MA: Harvard University Press.

Vygotsky, L. (1994). The problem of the environment. In R. Van der Veer & J. Valsiner (Eds.), *The Vygotsky reader* (pp. 338–354). Oxford, England: Basil Blackwell. (Original work published 1935)

Wozniak, R. (1986). Notes toward a co-constructive theory of the emotion-cognition relationship. In D. J. Bearison & H. Zimiles (Eds.), *Thought and emotion: Developmental perspectives* (pp. 39–64). Hillsdale, NJ: Erlbaum.

Wozniak, R. (1993). Co-constructive metatheory for psychology. In R. Wozniak & K. Fischer (Eds.), *Development in context* (pp. 77–92). Hillsdale, NJ: Erlbaum.

PART V

Parental Influence in Social and Biological Context

CHAPTER 12

Value Transmission in an Ecological Context: The High-Risk Neighborhood

JAMES GARBARINO, KATHLEEN KOSTELNY, and FRANK BARRY

AN ECOLOGICAL PERSPECTIVE

Up to now, this book has viewed values transmission solely from a dyadic, or family perspective involving the child and the child's parent or other family members. In this chapter, we will explore the ecological dimension beyond the family, in particular, contexts where children are at risk for not acquiring prosocial values.

The importance of ecology on child outcomes was underscored by Lisbeth Schorr in her seminal book, *Within Our Reach* (1988). A 1993 study by Rosenbaum and colleagues powerfully demonstrated the effect of neighborhood on academic and vocational achievement by comparing children's accomplishments in two groups of families who left a violent inner city housing project for better living conditions. Some settled elsewhere in the same neighborhood while others moved to suburban locations. The children who grew up in the suburbs were roughly twice as likely to enter college and get jobs as those who moved elsewhere in the inner city. Since the choice of where to move was not made by the family but was dictated by the availability of housing through the Housing and Urban Development Section 8 program, both groups were considered similar, and the researchers attributed the differences to the community environment (Rosenbaum, Fishman, Brett, & Meaden, 1993).

While college entry and employment are not the same as a strong value system, they are in fact legitimate markers of one. Since values per se are extremely difficult to measure, it is perhaps more productive to identify and measure behaviors that positive values are presumed to produce. After all, if values are not reflected in behavior, do they really matter? We are interested in values primarily because they are presumed to affect behavior. It is hard to imagine inner-city children entering college and getting jobs without strong positive values.

The study of the ecological perspective in value transmission follows from two rather simple but fundamental assumptions:

1. Values are absorbed not only from family members, but also from sources outside the family, especially as the child grows old enough to spend more time out of the home. Some of these sources will be societal (television, movies, news reports, music) and some will be community based (school, friends, peers, neighbors, churches, and other community institutions).

2. The neighborhood environment can either help or hinder parents in the task of instilling positive values in their children. Residents of closely knit communities are likely to share strongly held values, which neighbors and relatives reinforce whenever a child flouts them. Neighborhoods with little communication between families cannot easily reinforce values taught by parents, and adults are less likely to intervene when a child behaves in an antisocial manner. (Maccoby, Johnson, & Church, 1958)

The neighborhood and societal environment in which children develop influences their value system both directly—by providing them with examples and information—and indirectly, by either reinforcing or subverting the efforts of parents to instill appropriate values. Where a strong positive community value system is lacking, the parental task is much harder, and the lack of support may undermine the parent's self-confidence in addition to providing conflicting information and role models. For parents, it is obviously much easier to instill positive values in a community where such values are expected than in a situation without support from neighbors or friends. It is simply easier to conform to expectations than to stand alone.

Values may be either positive or negative. We are naturally most interested in acquisition of positive values that promote hard work, responsibility for one's actions, responsible parenting, respect, compassion and caring for others, tolerance of differences, and responsibility to one's community and society. These are the values likely to produce behaviors that will sustain our civilization as opposed to undermining it. But children who grow up in negative family or community environments may develop negative values either because they are personally victimized, because they have no positive role models, because their parents demonstrate negative values, or because their associates outside the home demonstrate negative values. Such values may include responding to differences with force or violence, and devaluing the rights of others.

Ecological influences are critical in shaping children's value systems, and future research must reflect this if we are to develop a true and complete understanding of internalization. The first part of this chapter will explore the interaction between the developing child and its environment as seen through the lens of human ecology; the second part will examine the implications of this interaction for values internalization in high-risk neighborhoods. The final section will discuss ways to intervene to strengthen troubled community environments.

THE STUDY OF HUMAN ECOLOGY

An ecological perspective on any developmental issue directs attention simultaneously to two kinds of interaction. The first is the interaction of the child as a biological organism with the immediate social environment as a set of processes, events, and relationships. The second is the interplay of systems in the child's social environment. This dual mandate to look both outward to the forces that shape social contexts and inward to the day-to-day interaction of the child in the family is both the beauty and the challenge of human ecology. It demands much of investigators intellectually and ideologically, if it is to be more than an academic exercise. This first section will describe both the implications of this approach and the levels or "systems" within which these interactions occur.

Ecology is the study of relationships between organisms and environments. Ecologists explore and document how the individual and the habitat shape the development of each other. Like the biologist who learns about an animal by studying its habitat, sources of food, predators, and social practices, the student of human development must address how people live and grow in their social environment. And, while all students of animal ecology must accommodate to the purposeful actions of the organism, the human ecologist must go further and seek to incorporate the phenomenological complexity of the organism-environment interaction—the social and psychological maps that define human meaning.

Put this way, the habitat of the child includes family, friends, neighborhood, church, and school, as well as less immediate forces that constitute the social geography and climate (e.g., laws, institutions, and values), and the physical environment as well. Urie Bronfenbrenner's 1979 work *The Ecology of Human Development* provided a theoretical basis for understanding the effects of these factors, and his framework will be reviewed in some detail later. The interplay of these social forces and physical settings with the individual child defines the range of issues in the forefront of an ecological perspective. The most important characteristic of this ecological perspective is that it both reinforces investigators' inclination to look inside the individual and encourages them to look beyond the individual to the environment, for questions and explanations about individual behavior and development. It emphasizes development in context.

An ecological perspective is a constant reminder that child development results from the interplay of biology and society, from the characteristics children bring with them into the world and the way the world treats them, from nature and nurture. In this, it reflects what Pasamanick (1987) calls "social biology." In contrast to sociobiology which emphasizes a genetic origin for social behavior (Wilson, 1978), social biology concentrates on the social origins of biological phenomena (e.g., the impact of poverty on infant morbidity). Nevertheless, the two perspectives are not mutually exclusive. Indeed, sociobiologists see the historical (i.e., evolutionary) origins of biological phenomena (i.e., gene pool characteristics) in social phenomena (i.e., the differential life success of individuals) because of the social implications of their genetically based individual behavior (Wilson, 1978). They seek to explain how the social impact of biologically rooted traits affects the survival of organisms and thus the likelihood that those particular genetic patterns will be passed along to surviving offspring.

Children face different opportunities and risks for development because of their mental and physical makeup and because of the social environment they inhabit. Moreover, social environment affects the very physical makeup of the child. These effects may be negative (e.g., the impact of poverty on birth weight or the mutagenic influence of industrial carcinogens) or positive (e.g., intrauterine surgery or nutritional therapy for a fetus with a genetic disorder). When these social influences operate in psychological or sociological terms as opposed to physical terms, they are referred to as sociocultural opportunities and risks.

"Opportunities for development" refer to relationships in which children find material, emotional, and social encouragement compatible with their needs and capacities as they exist at a specific point in their developing lives. For each child, the best fit must be worked out through experience, within some very broad guidelines of basic human needs, and then renegotiated as development proceeds and situations change.

Risks to development can come both from direct threats and from the absence of normal, expectable opportunities. Besides such obvious biological risks as malnutrition or injury, there are sociocultural risks that impoverish the developing individual's world of essential experiences and relationships and thereby threaten development. For example, abandoned children may suffer from their lack of the family ties and diverse role models that enrich those who live in large close-knit families. Similarly, children who are born at the low point of an economic depression may receive fewer benefits from preventive services than those who are born during more economically auspicious times. Understanding the consequences of both sociocultural risks and opportunities, and the role of social support networks, is a central concern of human ecology.

Our goal here is to use a systems approach to clarify the complexity represented by the interplay of biological, psychological, social, and cultural forces in the transmission of values, particularly in a high-risk context.

An ecological systems approach helps investigators discover the connections among what might at first seem to be unrelated events and also helps them see that what often seems like an obvious solution may actually only make the problem worse. Forrester (1969) concludes that because systems are linked, and therefore influence each other ("feedback"), many of the most effective solutions to social problems are not readily apparent, and may even be "counterintuitive." According to Hardin (1966), the First Law of Ecology is, "You can never do just one thing." Intersystem feedback ensures that any single action will reverberate and produce unintended consequences.

As individuals develop, they play an ever more active role in an ever widening world. Newborns shape the feeding behavior of their mothers, but are confined largely to cribs or laps, and have limited means of communicating their needs and wants. Ten-year-olds, on the other hand, influence adults and other children in many different settings, and have many ways of communicating. The adolescent's world is still larger and more diverse, as is the ability to influence that world. Individuals and environments negotiate their relationships over time through a process of reciprocity. Neither is constant; each depends on the other. When asked, "Does X cause Y?" the answer is always, "It depends." We cannot reliably predict the future of one system without knowing something about the other systems with which it is linked. And even then it may be very difficult.

The individual's experiences can be seen as subsystems within systems within larger systems, "as a set of nested structures, each inside the next, like a set of Russian dolls" (Bronfenbrenner, 1979, p. 22). In asking and answering questions about development, investigators can and should always be ready to look at the next level of systems "beyond" and "within" to find the questions and the answers (Garbarino & Associates, 1992). If parents and visiting nurses are in conflict over the use of physical punishment in early childhood (the family system), it is necessary to look to the community that establishes laws and policies about child abuse as well as to the culture that defines physical force as an appropriate form of discipline in early childhood. But professionals must also look within the individual, as a psychological system that is affected by conscious and changing roles, unconscious needs, and motives, to know why and how each adjusts in ways that generate conflict. In addition, they must look "across" to see how the several systems involved (family, social services, social network, and economy) adjust to new conditions. Interaction among these social forces is the key to an ecological analysis of early developmental risk and development of values. They exist as linked social systems, implying that intervention can take place at each system level and that intervention at one level may well spill over to others.

This system approach examines the environment at four levels beyond the individual organism—from the "micro" to the "macro." These systems have been cataloged in detail elsewhere (Bronfenbrenner, 1979, 1986; Garbarino, Gaboury, Long, Grand-jean, & Asp, 1982). The goal here is to introduce them briefly to provide a context for discussing the ecology of values transmission, with the high-risk neighborhood as a "case study."

Microsystems

Microsystems are the immediate settings in which individuals develop. The shared experiences that occur in each setting provide a record of the microsystem and offer some clues to its future. Microsystems evolve and develop much as do individuals themselves from forces generated both within and without. The quality of a microsystem depends on its ability to sustain and enhance development, and to provide a context that is emotionally validating and developmentally challenging. This in turn depends on its capacity to operate in what Vygotsky (1986) called "the zone of proximal development," which is the distance between what the child can accomplish alone (the level of actual development) and what the child can do when helped (the level of potential development).

Children can handle (and need) more than infants. Adolescents can handle (and need) more than children. The social richness of an individual's life is measured by the availability of enduring, reciprocal, multifaceted relationships that emphasize playing, working, and loving. And the measurement is made over time, because microsystems, like individuals, change over time. Risk on the other hand, lies in patterns of abuse, neglect, resource deficiency, and stress that insult the child and thwart development (Garbarino, Guttmann, & Seeley, 1986).

Mesosystems

Mesosystems are relationships between microsystems in which the individual experiences reality. These links themselves form a system. The richness of a mesosystem is measured in the number and quality of its connections. One example is the case of a young child's day-care group and his or her home. Do staff visit the child at home? Do the child's parents know his or her friends at day care? Do parents of children at the center know each other? A second example concerns the hospital and the home for a chronically ill child. What role do the parents play in the hospital regime? Do the same health care professionals who see the child in the hospital visit the home? Is the child the only one to participate in both? If he or she is the only "linkage," the mesosystem is weak and that weakness may place the child at risk.

Exosystems

Exosystems are settings that have a bearing on the development of children, but in which those children do not play a direct role. For most children, key exosystems include their parents' workplace (for most children, since they are not participants there) and centers of power such as school boards, church councils, and planning commissions that make decisions affecting their day-to-day life. The concept of an exosystem illustrates the projective nature of the ecological perspective, for the same setting that is an exosystem for a child may be a microsystem for the parent, and vice versa. One form of intervention may aim at transforming exosystems into microsystems for children, such as by initiating greater participation in important institutions for isolated, disenfranchised, and powerless clients (e.g., by getting parents to visit the family day-care home or by creating on-site day care at the workplace).

In exosystem terms, both risk and opportunity come about in two ways. The first is when the parents or other significant adults in a child's life are treated in a way that impoverishes (risk) or enhances (opportunity) their behavior in the microsystems they share with children. Examples include elements of the parents' working experience that impoverish or enhance family life such as unemployment, low pay, long or inflexible hours, traveling, or stress, on the one hand, in contrast to an adequate income, flexible scheduling, an understanding employer, or subsidies for child care, on the other (Bronfenbrenner & Crouter, 1983).

The second way risk and opportunity flow from the exosystem lies in the orientation and content of decisions made in those settings that affect the day-to-day experience of children and their families. For example, when the state legislature suspends funding for early intervention programs, it jeopardizes development. When public officials expand prenatal health services or initiate specialized day care in high-risk communities, they increase developmental opportunities (and may reduce infant mortality or morbidity).

One of the most useful aspects of the ecological approach is its ability to highlight situations in which the actions of people with whom the individual has no direct contact significantly affect development. The following example illustrates the relationship between social policy and individual child development: Because of a leveraged corporate takeover, a board of directors decides to shift operations from one plant to another. Hundreds of families with young children are forced to move to new locations. Others are left unemployed. Local services are underfunded in a period of escalating demand. Parents who lose their jobs also lose their health insurance. Alcoholism, child abuse, and domestic violence increase. This is reflected in problems at school and in the community as some students act out in destructive ways what they have seen and experienced at home. This leads to a more combative and fearful atmosphere that makes internalization of positive values more difficult, particularly for children "on the edge," whose own home situation is not strong. This classic illustration of an exosystem effect highlights that such events may establish much of the agenda for day-to-day intervention on behalf of children at risk.

At this point, it is worth emphasizing that the ecological perspective forces consideration of influences on values transmission beyond the narrow confines of individual personality and family dynamics. In the ecological approach, both are "causes" of the child's developmental patterns and "reflections" of broader sociocultural forces. Mark Twain's well-known proverb warns, "If the only tool you have is a hammer, you tend to treat every problem as if it were a nail." Inflexible loyalty to a specific focus (e.g., the parents) is often a stumbling block to effective intervention. However, the obverse must also be considered: "If you define every problem as a nail, the only tool you will seek is a hammer." Viewing children at risk only in terms of organismic and interpersonal dynamics precludes an understanding of many other avenues of influence that might be open to investigators, or that might be topics of study for scientists.

Macrosystems

Meso- and exosystems are set within the broad ideological, demographic, and institutional patterns of a particular culture or subculture. These are the macrosystems that serve as master blueprints for the ecology of human development. These blueprints reflect a people's shared assumptions about how things should be done, as well as the institutions that represent those assumptions. Macrosystems are ideology incarnate, and societal blueprints can be contrasted based on their fundamental institutional expressions, such as a "collective versus individual orientation." Religion provides a classic example of the macrosystem concept because it involves both a definition of the world and a set of institutions reflecting that definition—both a theology and a set of roles, rules, buildings, and programs.

Macrosystem refers to the general organization of the world as it is and as it might be. Historical change demonstrates that the "might be" is quite real, and occurs through either evolution (many individual actions guided by a common reality) or revolution (dramatic change introduced by a small cadre of decision makers). The Iranian revolution of 1978–1979, for example, overturned a modernizing society and embodied a changed institutional and ideological landscape that shaped the most basic experiences of childhood. Current efforts to modernize in China include a massive shift from "collective reward" to "private initiative" as the dominating economic force. More directly relevant still is the "one child policy" that has altered the demography of the family and appears to be altering the social fabric at each level of the human ecology (Schell, 1982).

An ecological perspective has much to contribute to the process of formulating, evaluating, and understanding values transmission. It provides a social map for navigating through the complexities of programming. It helps to identify the relationships (potential and actual) among programs; for example, how some programs are complementary whereas others may be competitive. It is an aid in visualizing the full range of alternative conceptualizations of problems affecting children as well as multiple strategies for intervention. It provides a checklist for thinking about what is happening, and what to do about it when faced with developmental problems and social pathologies that afflict children, families, and communities. It does this by asking investigators always to consider the micro-, meso-, exo-, and macrosystem dimensions of developmental phenomena. It constantly suggests the possibility that context is shaping causal relationships. It always says, "it depends," and stimulates an attempt to find out "on what."

VALUES ACQUISITION IN COMMUNITIES AT RISK

In using the ecological approach to examine how at-risk communities affect values transmission to children, we will start with the concept of social toxicity. Then, to understand how some children in these communities grow up with sound values and become functional, we will draw on the findings of those who have studied resiliency in children despite harsh and difficult environments. This understanding will provide a basis for determining how to help parents and others plant sound values in the children of negative and dysfunctional communities.

The Concept of Social Toxicity

Researchers have sought to explore and validate the concept of "social toxicity" as a characteristic of high-risk environments, with identifying the environmental correlates of child maltreatment and community violence being an important context for this line of investigation (Garbarino, 1976; Garbarino, 1995; Garbarino & Crouter, 1978). In his book *Raising Children in a Socially Toxic Environment,* Garbarino (1995) describes social toxicity as "a parallel to the environmental movement's analysis regarding physical toxicity as a threat to human well-being and survival" (p. 4). Most of the physical toxicity results from harmful chemical substances in the water, air, soil and even home environments, which affect health for children and adults (e.g., leaded paint and air pollutants). The concept of social toxicity is less well understood, but Garbarino contends that for children, "the social context in which they grow up has become poisonous to their development" (p. 4). He identifies "violence, poverty . . . , disruption of relationships, nastiness, despair, depression, paranoia and alienation" as the elements of "social toxicity" and as the "social equivalents" to lead and air pollution (pp. 4–5).

The concept of social toxicity can serve as a useful basis for empirically screening neighborhoods to identify high- and low-risk areas. The foundation for this approach is the link between low income and a significantly elevated risk of child maltreatment and other forms of violence (Garbarino, 1987; National Center on Child Abuse and Neglect [NCCAN], 1981; Pelton, 1978, 1981, 1994). From this flows a twofold conception of "risk" as it applies to neighborhoods and families (Garbarino & Crouter, 1978). The first refers to areas with a high absolute rate of violence (based on cases per unit of population). In this sense, concentrations of socioeconomically distressed families are most likely to be at high risk for violence—most notably child maltreatment. For example, in one city (Omaha, Nebraska), socioeconomic status accounted for about 40% of the variation across neighborhoods in reported rates of child maltreatment.

The magnitude of this correlation may reflect a social policy effect. It seems reasonable to hypothesize that in a society in which low income is not correlated with access to basic human services (e.g., maternal-infant healthcare), this correlation would be smaller. In a society totally devoid of policies to ameliorate the impact of family-level differences in social class, it might be even larger.

This hypothesis merits empirical exploration, but is consistent with the observation that socioeconomic status is a more potent predictor of child development in the United States than in some European societies (Bronfenbrenner, 1979). This is evident in low infant mortality rates in some poor European countries (e.g., Ireland and Spain) rates that are lower than in the United States as a whole, and much lower than among poor communities in this country (Miller, 1987). This point emphasizes that "social support" is a concept operating at the macrosocial level, not just at the neighborhood level (cf. Thomson, 1992).

A second meaning of high risk is of greatest relevance here, however. High risk can also refer to an area with a higher rate of child maltreatment than would be predicted knowing its socioeconomic character. Thus, two areas with similar socioeconomic profiles may have very different rates of child maltreatment. In this sense, one is "high risk" whereas the other is "low risk," although both may have higher rates of child maltreatment than other, more affluent areas.

The Human Significance of "Community Risk"

What do low- and high-risk social environments look like? A study of contrasting neighborhoods in Omaha, Nebraska, selected to illustrate this phenomenon provided support for this hypothesis: Relative to the low-risk area, and even though it was socioeconomically equivalent, the high-risk neighborhood was found to represent a socially impoverished human ecology (Garbarino & Sherman, 1980). It was less well socially integrated, had less positive neighboring, and represented more stressful day-to-day interactions for families—overall, a more socially toxic environment.

Other studies have reaffirmed the general outlines of this analysis while refining the meaning of social toxicity and its relation to values transmission. There has been a movement away from a simple concept of "social support" and toward a more complex phenomenon of social integration, particularly as reflected in density of networks resulting from employment, neighboring, and organizational participation (cf. Deccio, Horner, & Wilson, 1994: a study in Spokane, Washington; Bouchard, 1987: a study of Montreal neighborhoods; Sattin & Miller, 1971: a study of two neighborhoods in a Texas city; Garbarino & Kostelny, 1992: a study of Chicago neighborhoods).

Escalation of Social Toxicity

The rapid escalation of social toxicity in many inner-city neighborhoods underlies the "crisis in values" so often cited in popular accounts. Up until the 1960s, the social organization of many inner-city black neighborhoods was enhanced by the presence of working- and middle-class families. A vertical integration of different income groups existed as lower, working, and middle-class professional black families lived in the same neighborhoods (Wilson, 1987). By the 1980s, however, most of the middle- and working-class population had moved away, leaving behind an underclass with few mainstream role models to help maintain the traditional values of education, work, and family stability. This is evident in data from Cleveland (Coulton & Padey, 1992) showing that the likelihood of poor families living in neighborhoods that are predominantly poor increased from 23% in 1960 to 60% in 1990.

Likewise, there was a breakdown in social control by members of these neighborhoods. For example, Dubow and Emmons (1981) suggest that for informal social control to be effective, a neighborhood must have a consensus on values or norms, be able to monitor behavior, and be willing to intervene if necessary, when that behavior is not acceptable. In such neighborhoods, such a consensus on values, as well as an ability to monitor behavior is often lacking.

Effect of High-Risk Communities on Values Transmission

Internalization of values was probably much simpler when all outside influences were more or less consistent—when the messages about right and wrong, obligations to others, relationships, respect, work, and loyalty were relatively similar, whether they came from one's family, school, church or other community or societal institutions. But today, few societies enjoy such a simple situation and children are likely to encounter strikingly different messages from the different sources that affect them. How do parents and others guide them in building a positive value system under these circumstances?

This is a difficult challenge in almost any community today, but it is extraordinarily difficult when the community itself is dysfunctional. How can parents transmit positive values when they live in community environments that are chronically violent? These include some large public housing developments and socially deteriorated, low-income neighborhoods in cities across the nation.

In Chicago, over 100,000 children live in public housing projects, where the rate of "serious assault" has increased 400% since the mid-1970s. An analysis of Chicago's police data (Reardon, 1988) revealed that the officially reported rate of violent crime victimization for residents in the housing projects was 50% higher than for the city as a whole (34 per 1,000 vs. 23 per 1,000). This means that children in public housing projects are twice as likely to be exposed than are other children (since the overall 23 per 1,000 victimization rate includes the housing projects, which inflates the overall figure substantially). No one who is familiar with these data doubts that the reported rate in the housing projects is a substantial underestimate (due to the intimidation of reporters and witnesses, anomie and demoralization of citizens in these neighborhoods, and a general estrangement between citizens and police).

Many children who live in such settings have seen violence and even murder firsthand. Sometimes a loved family member is the victim. A child's realization that no one, not even his or her parents, can protect the child from such violence is profoundly disturbing. Such a reality undermines the fundamental contract between parents and children under which parents provide safety—a contract taken for granted in middle-class settings.

In addition to exposure to crime, children living in these areas are more likely to be a victim of child abuse and neglect, another violation of this fundamental contract. We have found that for census tracts having high crime rates, child maltreatment rates were up to four times higher than the city average (Garbarino & Kostelny, 1992). These incidents of domestic violence interact with the incidents of community violence. Some of the incidents outside the homes are in fact related to domestic conflicts; children and parents are exposed to violence in other families indirectly (as part of their life experience as neighbors and friends).

Children in conditions of developmental risk need "teaching" relationships with adults to help them process their experiences in a way that prevents developmental harm. Developmentalists have come to recognize that it is the dynamic relationship between the child's competence alone and the child's competence in the company of a guiding teacher that leads to forward movement. Children who experience child maltreatment are generally denied that processing within the family. Indeed, they receive just the opposite of what they need, particularly in conditions of social risk derived from the social environment outside the home. This is one reason the problem of value transmission in the context of high stress/low support social environments deserves the highest priority as a matter of social policy; these are the children who can least tolerate inadequate value transmission.

The critical function of mediation and processing seems particularly important for moral development both as an interpersonal issue within families and as a social issue in communities. At issue is not whether adults and peers serve as moral "teachers" for the child: Children will learn from what they see and hear. Rather, the issue is whether adults and peers function as positive and deliberate teachers: Are they aware that they are teaching moral lessons through what they do and say, and make a commitment to make the lessons prosocial?

When all this happens in the context of a nurturant affective system such as a warm family, the result is ever-advancing moral development of a principled ethic of caring (Gilligan, 1982). What is more, even if the parents create a rigid, noninteractive "authoritarian" family context (and thus block moral development), the larger community may compensate: "The child of authoritarian parents may function in a larger more democratic society whose varied patterns provide the requisite experiences for conceptualizing an egalitarian model of distributive justice" (Fields, 1987, p. 5).

If school teachers, neighbors, and other adult representatives of the community are unable or disinclined to model higher-order moral reasoning, then the process of moral truncation that is natural to situations of family and community violence will proceed unimpeded. This may well be happening in many urban school systems in which teachers are demoralized, parents incapacitated, and students apathetic. The result is to permit the natural socialization of the depleted community to proceed, with its consequences in intergenerational aggression, neighborhood deterioration, and family malfunction. Without compensatory values transmission in the community, the result is likely to be impaired social and moral development, particularly among boys, who are more vulnerable to this consequence of living at risk as they are to most other risks (Werner, 1990).

Effects of Social Toxicity

Families may adapt in dysfunctional ways when forced to cope with highly stressful situations such as the chronic danger and social toxicity of many low-income neighborhoods or the unstable and alienated neighborhoods that reflect community disruption even in the absence of poverty. The psychopathological dimensions of such adaptation are now widely recognized, most notably posttraumatic stress disorder (PTSD) in the case of traumatic environments. The social dimensions are equally worthy of attention, however.

Families may cope with highly stressful conditions by adopting a worldview or persona that may be dysfunctional in any "normal" situations in which they are expected to participate (e.g., in school and in other settings of the larger community). For example, aggressive behavior may in the short run appear to be adaptive behavior in the abnormal situation of chronic crisis in which they live. However, such aggressive behavior may be maladaptive to school success, as it stimulates rejection at school.

What is more, some adaptations to chronic threat and social toxicity (such as emotional withdrawal) may be socially adaptive in the short run, but become a danger to the next generation, when the individual becomes a parent. This phenomenon has been observed in studies of families of Holocaust survivors (Danieli, 1988). The family's ability to be a good neighbor and to make use of social support (let alone to serve as a source of social support to others) may be one of the casualties of this developmental process.

Even without this intergenerational process, however, the links between threat and stress on the one hand, and social support on the other may operate directly on families. Their adaptations to socially impoverished and threatening environments may produce child-rearing strategies that impede normal development. For example, the parent who prohibits the child from playing outside for fear of shooting incidents may be denying the child a chance to engage in social and athletic play, as an undesirable side effect of protecting the child from assault.

Similarly, the fear felt by parents of children in high crime environments may be manifest as a restrictive and punitive style of discipline (including physical assault) in an effort to protect the child from falling under the influence of negative forces in the neighborhood (e.g., gangs). This adaptive strategy (which may be socially supported in the neighborhood) can significantly impede efforts to prevent child maltreatment (which seek to foster a more open, less punitive child-rearing style).

What is more, punitive child rearing is likely to heighten the child's aggression with one consequence being difficulty in succeeding in social contexts that provide alternatives to the culture of the highly stressed and socially impoverished neighborhood environment. In addition, it can lead to endorsing and accepting violence as the modus operandi for social control (which in turn rationalizes the "culture of aggression").

Holding the child back from negative forces through punitive restrictiveness is generally much less successful as a strategy than promoting positive alternatives to the negative subculture feared by the parent (Scheinfeld, 1983). As Flekkoy (1996) puts it, "The richer the variety of role-taking opportunities a child is exposed to, the better his/her possibilities are for moral learning" (p. 5). This finding parallels more generic conceptions of social influence that emphasize the need to communicate empowerment as a resource in coping.

Coping with High-Risk Environments and the Study of Resiliency

To understand how parents and children cope with such depressing realities, it may be helpful to examine more closely findings from the study of resiliency. This field represents a relatively new direction in which the focus moves from analyzing the reasons for deficits and pathology to analyzing the reasons for success in high-risk and even pathological environments. According to Benard (1991), who has reviewed literature in this area, researchers have found that although the failure rate is significantly higher, most children who grow up in negative family and community environments still succeed despite their surroundings. This is true in families coping with alcoholism, mental illness, and poverty.

If a child from a dysfunctional and violence-prone neighborhood grows up to become a healthy, competent adult, that child has somehow internalized positive values. In analyzing how some children grow up as competent adults despite negative surroundings and considerable adversity, researchers have identified three crucial factors: (a) a warm and affectionate relationship with an adult who cares for and supports the child; (b) an environment that includes high expectations for the child and faith in the child's ability; and (c) opportunities for the child to participate in the life and work going on around him or her (Benard, 1991).

These three factors apply to the family, school, and community. Caring and nurturing can come from one parent, a relative, a teacher, close friend, and/or someone else in the community. An alcoholic parent will not necessarily destroy a child's chances to develop positive values if the other parent is able to care for and nurture the child.

High expectations involve believing in the child, and conveying that belief through encouragement, standards, rewards, rules, and discipline. High expectations communicate to the child a belief that he or she has the ability to meet these expectations. Moral development comes from discussing and working out moral issues within the family. This gives children a sense of validity as worthwhile human beings and an optimism that moral difficulties can usually be worked out (Benard, 1991). Flekkoy (1996) says, "One of the clearest determinants of moral stage advance in children is the disposition of parents to allow or encourage dialogue on value issues."

Participation means giving the child a role, and responsibilities both of which convey a sense of importance. In the family, this means doing chores, caring for siblings, even working part time to help support the family. In school, the same things apply; children do better when they have opportunities to participate actively in their classes and in planning and carrying out various activities important to the life of the school. And the same is true at the community level. Jobs, apprenticeships, sports, clubs, community services all provide responsibilities and opportunities for participation. As Richardson says, "The family or community that learns to direct the energy, general good will and potential of these young adolescents into community or community improvement projects may find that they benefit the community as well as the individual" (Richardson et al., 1989; cited in Benard, 1991).

Resiliency in children is associated with certain attributes that Benard classifies under four headings: social competence, problem-solving skills, autonomy (ability to exert some control over one's life and environment), and a sense of purpose and future. Turner, Norman, and Zunz (1993), who have reviewed resiliency research more recently, produced an expanded list, including empathy, humor, self-efficacy, sense of direction, and adaptive distancing. Some of these traits may be genetically acquired, but others develop as a result of environmental supports.

In either case, these traits are closely associated with positive values. Empathy, compassion, the ability to believe in oneself, to see one's self as separate from pathology in one's family, to see oneself as able to solve problems, to set and accomplish goals— these are the results of strong and positive values.

Studying child development from this perspective helps in identifying ways to develop new approaches. Rather than trying to fix pathologies after they have developed, or determining when to remove children from pathological situations resiliency theory includes two options—ways to decrease risk factors and ways to strengthen protective factors. Instead of placing a child in foster care, an alternate approach might be finding another adult able to provide some care after school, helping the child to get into a club, and working out with parents and teachers ways to raise expectations for the child.

Karol Kumpfer (1993; cited in Turner et al., 1993) has proposed a framework for viewing this by defining the factors that influence a child's development as follows: The risk factors described in the context of social toxicity occur in the child's external environment—family, school, or community. Protective factors (a caring adult, high expectations, opportunity for participation, etc.) also occur in the child's environment, and mitigate the effects of risk factors. Resiliency is strength occurring in the individual. Vulnerability is weakness that also occurs in the individual. The individual's success in adapting positively is a result of the interaction of these four factors, not simply "a trait or characteristic within the individual" (Turner et al., 1993).

Children develop strong moral values when another person helps them analyze morality on a higher level than their own in response to situations they encounter. According to Thompson (1996), children internalize knowledge and beliefs through an "apprenticeship in thinking" under the guidance of a skilled mentor (a parent, an older sibling, a teacher, etc.). This apprenticeship typically occurs through joint participation in normal and natural activities—working, cooking, fishing, farming, caring for smaller children or animals, or participating in religious observances. As always, parents and children in high-risk communities encounter a special difficulty in this regard because of the relative scarcity of skilled mentors and the often limited opportunity for activities that permit this type of growth.

Religious beliefs and education, whether formal or informal, have played an important role in developing positive values, even in the face of atrocity. Religious faith helped some children who survived Nazi concentration camps to be able to love and feel compassion despite what they had experienced (Benard, 1991). These children likely benefited from earlier experience with strong religious institutions—something not always available to inner-city children.

Helping children to develop strong value systems in negative surroundings means identifying and strengthening protective factors in families, schools, and the community, as well as minimizing obvious risk factors. But while this represents something of a new paradigm, it has not yet been operationalized in detail; its advocates are still working to define what it means in practice. A number of demonstration programs have been established, but few have been rigorously evaluated with longitudinal research according to Turner et al. (1993). Nevertheless, the field of resiliency, with its message of faith and hope may show at least as much promise as the traditional focus on remediation of pathology. But even though the field of resiliency may help mitigate the effects of negative surroundings, it will not eliminate all the problems unless ways can be found to strengthen the community itself. For it is the community, regardless of how it is defined, that is the primary ecological unit in which the family must function.

INTERVENING IN COMMUNITIES

This last section begins with a review of two competing philosophies of helping, and then explores their implications for organizing help at the community level. We will look at the special difficulties and challenges confronted by those who work in violent communities and then will discuss various strategies that have been attempted to improve communities themselves, with a special note about the role of schools. We will look at the role of gangs and end with a brief discussion of the significance of community according to income level.

Levine and Levine (1970) have described two fundamentally different approaches to human problems that have shaped social policies in this country during the past century. The individual approach entails a remedial focus on changing or "helping" a maladapted individual to fill his or her expected role in society. The environmental or community approach attempts to alter negative aspects within the community that impede normal development and functioning of individuals.

According to Levine and Levine (1970), these two methods are based on opposite assumptions: The community or "situational" model "assumes a person who is basically 'good' but who has been exposed to poor conditions, therefore has not developed to his fullest potential. Improving his situation (making adjustments to his environment) will result in far reaching improvement in his psychological state" (p. 8). The Levines call the opposite model the "intra-psychic" mode, which assumes "goodness" of the environment . . . (that) a person is in difficulty, not because of his situation, but because of his inner weaknesses and failings . . . what has to be changed is not the circumstance, but the person (p. 8).

These two assumptions have alternately waxed and waned in popularity depending on politics and national mood, according to the Levines. The situational model formed the basis for the Settlement House movement during the 1880s and 1890s. This was a time of profound change in urban areas resulting from industrialization which attracted waves of immigrants from Europe and from rural areas in the U.S. to the cities. The intrapsychic model became popular during the 1920s and 1930s under the influence of Sigmund Freud, whose theory and analysis virtually ignored community and environmental factors beyond the child's earliest interaction with its parents. But the situational model became popular again in the 1960s during the civil rights movement and it constituted the theoretical basis for many of the War on Poverty programs.

Lofquist (1983) developed a matrix to classify different kinds of services according to whether they were remedial or preventive, and whether they focused on the individual or the community environment. Lofquist says a community needs a balance between all four approaches, but that the individual remedial approach has now become by far the predominant model in the United States.

According to the U.S. Advisory Board on Child Abuse and Neglect (1990), the individual remedial approach does not work in dysfunctional communities where "CPS agencies have become overwhelmed by families with serious problems; too many children need help and there are not enough resources to provide it" (p. 45).

We suggest that this imbalance in distressed communities is no accident. In healthy communities, most children grow up and acquire positive values as a result of naturally occurring forces and protective factors in the community (i.e., as in the proverbial "It takes a whole village to raise a child"). Even though the child may live in a dysfunctional home, he or she may be taken care of by a relative, a neighbor, or the parent of a friend— at least enough for the child to acquire positive values.

However, when the community itself becomes dysfunctional, these processes become blocked. Fear and distrust replace neighborliness and caring, formal and informal organizations shrivel and may disappear altogether. Children in such communities have fewer nurturers, mentors, and monitors, and their development suffers accordingly. Not only do our human services agencies lack the resources to do what healthy communities do for free, but by the time the problems come to light in individuals, the cost of remediation is likely to be far higher than it would have cost to offer normal preventive supports that children and their families take for granted in healthy communities.

How Do We Support the Child Care Takers in Violent Communities?

In the preceding situations, it is futile to concentrate only on trying to patch up the results of family dysfunction, because environmental factors causing the problem will undermine such efforts. It is essential to address the environment itself. But how? Workers who attempt to help in such communities and the people who live in them face formidable challenges. For example:

- In many areas, parents are afraid to attend night meetings at school. How can a neighborhood-based program to transmit prosocial values succeed if families are intimidated?

- Although most children engage in mock gun play, teachers report that they can distinguish between fantasy play and reenactment of violent events in the community. If an actual shooting occurs in the community, they observe that children's play takes on a more realistic quality, reenacting the witnessed events. But teachers don't know how to respond. How does this affect the classroom dynamics of teaching values about violence? How does it affect the role of the school vis-à-vis the neighborhood?

- One of the social service staff who conducts home visits with parents of Head Start children described how she had to take cover from the playground to avoid being hit by random bullets from two rival gang factions. ("I was caught in the cross fire.") She witnessed the shooting of one young man before the gunfire stopped. When it stopped, she ran back to the children's center and reported the event to a coworker, who listened sympathetically. The social worker commented, "Then it was over." The next day, the same social worker had to resume her responsibilities. There was no intervention. How can a neighborhood function as a support system for prosocial values when key players are traumatized?

Professionals who deal with these children of violence are often at a loss in responding to them. For example, in six training sessions involving Head Start staff from four major Chicago public housing complexes—Cabrini Green, Rockwell Gardens, Henry Horner Homes, and Robert Taylor Homes—the majority of the 60 staff participating expressed their feelings of inadequacy related to being unable to help their students deal with the violence they encounter in their daily lives. Many of these staff are "indigenous" to the communities they serve.

Successful values transmission programs must address the issues of powerlessness, traumatization, and immobilizing fear that impede effective family life and social development for a significant and growing proportion of children in Chicago and other areas with underclass populations. An essential part of this is understanding the needs of professionals who work in these environments.

These professionals themselves often feel powerless, traumatized, and afraid. How do they make sense of their "values missions" in neighborhoods so violent they fear for their personal safety? How are they to bring messages of family safety? Do they fall silent when confronted with harsh, even violent child rearing?

Halpern (1990) has identified such "domains of silence" as a significant impediment to the delivery of effective family services, most especially among paraprofessionals recruited from high-risk populations. This impediment is both significant and serious. A case study amplifies this point: After visiting a nationally recognized family support/prevention program in a major urban public housing project, Garbarino concluded that the interaction between program and social environment resembled what he had observed in Cambodian refugee camps in eastern Thailand (cf. Garbarino, Kostelny, & Dubrow, 1991).

In particular, he noted that the professionals in the family support program faced a difficult psychological and political challenge that derived from the realities of power in both settings. In both the public housing project and the refugee camp, all "outsiders" leave at the end of the business day. After dark, the setting is controlled by gangs (in the Cambodian situation they are more clearly political gangs, but are gangs nonetheless).

In the public housing project, the gangs have been known to set curfews for residents as a demonstration of their power. Thus, any decisions made or action taken during the day must be reconciled with the realities of who is in charge at night. People are afraid to come out of their apartments or to contest the power of the gangs. This is hardly a desirable environment in which to promote a prosocial values transmission program.

All of this highlights an important dilemma. Over time, negative neighborhoods stimulate and reinforce negative individual behavior by newcomers—new residents or children growing up. Thus, eventually negative individual behavior and attitudes become the cause and effect of negative neighborhoods. Attempting to change neighborhoods without changing individuals may be foolhardy. Instead, efforts must be designed and implemented that restructure the social and physical environment of the neighborhood in ways that induce and reinforce changed individual behavior. Such efforts are necessary to create a climate in which more conventional educational and therapeutic innovations can take root.

Strengthening Communities

Halpern (1995), in describing the evolution of public policy toward low-income communities states that by 1964 there was evidence that we could not end inner-city poverty with human services alone. The roots of the problem, he says, lay in the lack of jobs, lack of investment, eroding tax base, and racial discrimination. Much of our neighborhood-based initiative to help communities has burdened those with the fewest resources with the task of solving some of society's biggest problems—problems which they did not create.

A major factor affecting community vitality is employment. When the Settlement Houses started 100 years ago, most people had jobs although many earned very little. Today, jobs have moved away from many inner-city communities altogether, and according to Halpern, the unemployment rate for black males with limited education went from 19% to 50% from 1969 to 1987. High unemployment means many people lack a role and a purpose, and this depletes the number of functional role models for youth, as well as the purposeful economic activity and networking that develop in connection with jobs. The existence of jobs constitutes the basis for one of the three protective factors, participation in the community, not only for children but for adults too.

Although no model has emerged to successfully transform a dysfunctional community, Halpern believes the Community Development Corporations that started up during the 1960s have had a positive effect, although on a limited scale. These community institutions have organized economic activity in housing, healthcare, retailing, and other areas. They provide management experience, services, positive role models and hope for their communities. Their scale, however, has been insufficient to address the whole problem; Halpern notes that while they created dozens of jobs, thousands were needed.

Family Resource Centers are a more recent innovation to offer human services that build community without being bound to individual remedial categorical services. This means acting much as Settlement Houses did 100 years ago, by forming clubs and conducting community activities that benefit and involve people with each other, creating and allowing the formation of friendships and networks. But these and other positive attempts have been more ameliorative than transforming in their effects, according to Halpern.

Although Halpern does not discuss it, it is worth mentioning law enforcement when considering the most violence-prone communities. New York City reduced gun murders by 40% in one year when police adopted a policy of frequent questioning and frisking in connection with minor offenses that had previously been ignored. The result has been a sharp drop in the number of people carrying guns (which are illegal in New York) presumably leading to an overall drop of 30% in the murder rate and a substantial deescalation of the kind of random violence described earlier. (However, this action also generated complaints from civil liberties groups, which claimed that minorities were more likely to be stopped than whites; Krauss, 1995, p. 29.)

Community policing has evolved in New York, Philadelphia, and other cities with apparently positive results. Although it is not our purpose to discuss police tactics in detail here, it is important to recognize that basic safety is a prerequisite if economic development, family resource centers, and other community efforts are to be effective.

Outside resources and support are important for rebuilding community, but regeneration cannot be done from the outside. To build strong values in a community's children, it is vital to provide opportunities not only for them to participate meaningfully in the affairs of the community but for their parents to do so as well. It will be hard for children to develop positive values regarding the future, or to believe in their own ability to influence events if most of the adults they know have little influence in the institutions that affect their community. Services that always place residents in the role of recipients, usually on the basis of some deficit, may work against the goal of strengthening the community even though they may be very helpful to some individuals.

To strengthen community, residents must take on significant and important roles and responsibilities. This is one of the strengths of Head Start, because that program requires that parents become involved as volunteers in the classroom, as program employees, and as policy makers on governing committee. Bringing community people together to focus on the needs of their children gives people a participating role and provides ample opportunity for them to develop friendships and networks.

Community Development Corporations provide the same kind of involvement for community people, and many Family Resource Centers do as well. In fact, each of these institutions can provide the same protective factors for adults—nurturing, high expectations, and opportunities for participation—that children need to become successful. Providing these supports for adults makes it easier for them to meet this need in their children.

By establishing networks that reduce isolation, these institutions allow people to support each other and to develop their own social skills and leadership capabilities. These social skills and capabilities become very real community assets, contributing to a community's human and social capital, which in turn contribute to its capacity for economic development (Putnam, 1993). One of the tragedies of dysfunctional communities is the lack of opportunity for both children and parents to develop the social skills that people in middle-class communities take for granted.

Just as it is for working with individuals, prevention is a necessary strategy for working with communities. Waiting until a community deteriorates so far that it loses most of its institutions makes it extremely difficult to repair, just as it is difficult to rehabilitate a long-term alcoholic, drug user, or someone who has been unemployed for a long time. It is much easier to address community problems early, before they advance too far, or to prevent them from happening at all. In the case of communities, this is obvious because deterioration often causes community businesses, organizations and its most capable people to leave. It is much harder to revive a community with very little structure and few human resources.

Assessment and Planning

The Family Life Development Center at Cornell University is working to develop a community assessment process to help communities identify trends that may need to be addressed before it is too late, as well as ways to improve the community's ability to raise its children effectively. The process includes four steps: statistical assessment, identification of strengths and needs, setting of goals, and developing plans to accomplish them.

The Kids Count project, funded by the Annie Casey Foundation, has developed indicators of child well-being at the county and even neighborhood level. These can help local communities assess their effectiveness in raising children, and to identify the direction of movement—whether their community is becoming more or less successful over time. The Center for the Study of Social Policy in Washington is developing materials to help communities move toward measuring community and agency outcomes in terms of child well-being. Two especially relevant papers are "The Case for Shifting to Results-Based Accountability" (Schorr, 1995) and "Finding the Data: A Start-up List of Outcome Measures with Annotations" (Center for the Study of Social Policy, 1995).

Just as in working with people, it is important to identify and build on strengths as well as to identify problems when working with communities. Run-down communities may tend not to see their own strengths, but every church, school, legitimate business, or other organization is a community asset, and a community member who has developed a useful skill (whether employed or not) is an asset as well. McKnight and Kretzmann (1990) have developed a workbook for mapping community capacity.

Encouraging Community Participation

Participation and the ethos that supports it are a major component of social support interventions. What is known about the factors that enhance and sustain participation in neighborhoods and their social institutions?

Wandersman and his colleagues (Wandersman, Florin, Friedmann, & Meier, 1987; Wandersman, Jakubs, & Glamartino, 1981) have conducted research to identify the factors that enhance participation in neighborhood organizations, particularly "block organizations." This research is highly relevant because any effort to stimulate social support through neighborhood organization must accommodate to these factors.

A community development project conducted by Chavis and Wandersman (1990) found that participation in block organizations is related to being "rooted" in place demographically: older, married, homeowner, female, long-term resident. This confirms the observations that Collins and Pancoast (1976) made concerning "natural helping networks." It is primarily older women (whose children are grown) with a long history in the neighborhood who serve as "central figures" and "natural neighbors."

Beyond these demographic factors, Wandersman and his colleagues have identified some "psychological variables" that predict participation. These include a sense of civic duty and political efficacy, perception that problems exist that are within the realm of local control, a stronger than average sense of community, and a high level of self-esteem. Once again, there is a congruence between these findings and what Collins and Pancoast observed: Demographic position alone is insufficient; an individual must have attributes that translate opportunity into actual participation.

These findings are important in considering the role of neighborhood social support values transmission. Such programs must seek out self-confident, public-spirited older married women who are long-term residents of the neighborhood. In high-risk neighborhoods, these women are often already carrying a heavy load of family responsibility caring for their grandchildren, and sometimes providing a home and financial support for adult children. In some areas, these women may be overwhelmed with their responsibilities rather than "free from drain" as are the usual candidates for leadership roles in social support networks identified by Collins and Pancost.

As ever, workers face a Catch-22 situation. The neighborhoods most in need of preventive intervention are those in which the attributes cited by Wandersman are in shortest supply. They are by no means absent, but any effort must begin with the recognition that special efforts and investment will be required to identify existing resources for participation and to enhance these resources.

Margaret Slinski, of Massachusetts Cooperative Extension, has developed an approach called the Master Teacher Program, which identifies, trains, and builds networks among informal leaders trusted by residents in low-income communities. This allows them to reinforce each other in their unofficial roles as "pillars" of their neighborhood (Slinski, 1990). This program is now being replicated in other parts of the country.

The Central Role of the Schools

Since children spend so much of their waking hours at school, they will absorb values there whether or not the school attempts to control the process or define the values. The transmitters of values will include teachers and other school personnel and other children.

Many inner-city schools are well known for reflecting the conditions—including the pathology—of their community. Teachers often feel in danger, demoralized and wary of children; they are usually overworked and may not be able to provide the protective factors that many children need.

Yet James Comer (1980) has demonstrated that it is possible to transform demoralized schools into vital, responsive, and effective community institutions exerting a powerful positive influence on children. Comer has demonstrated in several deteriorated communities that participation can be a powerful transformer. He has successfully involved teachers, parents and students in identifying issues and developing plans to respond to them. Caring, high expectations and opportunities for participation—the qualities identified as elements of success by resiliency researchers—were evident in Comer's work as well.

The school, perhaps more than any other institution, has the potential to become the "Center of the Community." Except, perhaps, in "company towns," where everyone works for the same employer, the school usually affects the lives of more families with children than any other institution. (Often it even determines what time people get up in the morning.) Since it provides a common experience for virtually all parents, the school can be a uniting, empowering force, or it can be a destructive force that discourages student potential as well as participation and involvement of families.

In many towns, schools not only educate the children but its sporting events often provide the chief community entertainment as well. These functions provide ample opportunity for recognized participation in the life of the community, at least for those children involved in sports.

The Community Lifelines Project at Cornell University, which worked with both urban and rural schools in Chemung County, New York, found indications that student performance and behavior improved when their parents became involved in school or community activities (Ray, 1994). Seeing one's parents move from a bystander to a participatory role in which they influenced events, may improve a child's sense of his or her own importance and ability to influence future outcomes. Certainly it made their parents more effective role models.

Many schools have moved toward becoming community centers, by allowing their facilities to be used for other activities after hours. After-school programs for children can fill a very important community need, and the school may be the only facility large enough or suitable for the task.

Cause and Effect of Gangs

Whether schools assume their role as center for other community activities, or simply assume their traditional role, students will interact with their peers at school and outside school. If a school plays a positive role in the community and engages all its students effectively, it can actually reduce alcohol and drug use in the community (Benard, 1991, p. 13). In many inner-city communities, however, gangs also strongly influence value formation.

Richard Arthur (1992) has written an informative book on gangs and schools based on his 35 years as an educator in California inner cities. Arthur points out that gangs perform two functions: to serve as the retail arm for a vast and growing underground drug distribution system and to satisfy young people's normal needs. He comments that while some gang leaders and members may have pathological characteristics, the majority are the same type of children who would join the Boy Scouts or 4-H Clubs if those organizations were accessible. They join to have fun, to find excitement, to make friends, to belong to something, to gain some autonomy from adults, to feel good about themselves, and to be safe.

Because gangs are such strong groups, they are fertile ground for Thompson's "apprenticeship in thinking" model described earlier in this chapter; but in this instance, the skilled mentor is hardly the wise parent or guide Thompson envisions. Most gangs actually instill many of the same values the school would like to convey, such as the importance of teamwork, discipline, and loyalty. Some gangs even teach their members to read when the school has failed them! But according to Arthur, gang values tend to move children into a state of alienation toward the community and society. They are "academies of crime" that require negative values toward the school and even the family. Although many kids drop out of gangs as they get older, the behavior and values instilled by gangs may create serious problems for them in school and beyond.

Gangs often represent an invasion by outside financial interests, and they constitute a symptom of very serious needs for youth participation in the community. Gangs proliferate, as Arthur points out, in communities where there is nothing else. Community youth activities, formal and informal, connecting youth with positive adults, finding more jobs—all can presumably help contain the growth of gangs in a community. Because of the strong link to drug distribution, gangs may function even if other youth opportunities are available, but where strong protective activities exist, the market for their drugs will be small, as will be the pool for their recruits.

Importance of Community

There appears to be an inverse relationship between social class and the relevance of neighborhood (Lewis, 1978). Poor families and individuals are more dependent on local resources than are affluent families. This has at least two important implications.

The first implication is that middle-class professionals and policy makers are likely to underestimate the importance of neighborhood factors because they themselves depend less on such factors in their personal lives. A survey in South Carolina (Melton, 1992) reported that middle-class families were particularly likely to indicate that when facing a problem with their child they would go directly to professional specialists rather than rely on the social network. Low-income families often do not have this option, and because they have far less mobility than professionals, they also have less freedom to choose their friends or other members of their support system. This implies the need for special training and sensitization for professionals (including on-site "walkarounds") to emphasize the salience of neighborhood geography in family life.

The second implication is that advocacy efforts will be needed to preserve and enhance not just "neighborhoods in general," but "neighborhoods for poor families" in particular. One facet of this intervention is financial. Part of the process of neighborhood decline derives from the draining of banks and other financially stabilizing influences (e.g., the net outflow of insurance premiums starves investment).

Some neighborhoods engender negative social momentum, which attracts antisocial and deteriorating individuals and families while discouraging and displacing prosocial and functional families (Rutter, Cox, Tupling, Berger, & Yule, 1975). Reversing such a downward spiral may require outside intervention—"neighborhood revitalization"—to create a process of positive social momentum that attracts functional families and improves the social environment for children.

The mechanics and logistics of such efforts require the coordination of economic investment, social services, political mobilization, and law enforcement: Jobs, housing, and safety are basics of community well-being. But efforts to promote community cooperation to produce community self-reliance are essential (Stokes, 1981). Communities cannot improve without participation of their residents. Special attention needs to be devoted to involving youth, to tap their energy and to provide them positive and meaningful opportunities to participate in their community.

CONCLUSION

This review of factors that affect neighboring highlights the need for special investments in high stress/low resource neighborhoods to reverse negative social momentum as a precondition for relying on neighborhood-based social support efforts to reduce risk factors for children. In well-functioning (i.e., high resource/low stress) environments, it should prove easier to turn the neighborhood's focus to dealing with values transmission if organizers can deal successfully with the issues of family autonomy and privacy. But these neighborhoods account for relatively little of the total problem, and therefore emphasis on them should bring only a marginal improvement overall.

Neighborhoods at risk due to a deterioration of economic and social supports bear a relationship to "acute disaster" situations, in which there is a dramatic destruction of the infrastructure of daily life. Actually, however, the neighborhoods most at risk for violence usually have experienced a chronic deterioration rather than an abrupt calamity.

As families deteriorate in the group most at risk for exposure to negative values transmission (e.g., become characterized by deeply rooted, often multigenerational problems of drug or alcohol abuse, poverty, illiteracy, and psychological trauma) the relevance of "easy" neighborhood-based approaches to social support may diminish while (paradoxically) the need for a powerful neighborhood-based approach increases (Halpern, 1991). This should both encourage further efforts at exploring the implementation of neighborhood-based initiatives and serve as a warning to recognize that superficial investments and commitments are unlikely to resolve the issues faced by very high-risk families in multiproblem neighborhoods.

The study of resiliency offers some hope for encouraging development of sound values in dysfunctional surroundings through the enhancement of protective factors and mitigation of risk factors, but specific programs have yet to be rigorously evaluated. In healthy neighborhoods, much of this may occur naturally for children in dysfunctional families, or with some outside help from agencies to individuals involved.

In dysfunctional neighborhoods, agencies typically lack the resources to cope with all those who need help. In such communities, it is necessary not only to mitigate negative neighborhood effects, but to address the very problems and conditions that make the environment dysfunctional. This will usually require outside resources, including funds, economic investment, and effective municipal services, including policing. It will also require effective schools, building of positive community networks, and opportunities for involvement and participation for youths and adults alike.

It is much easier to prevent a neighborhood from becoming dysfunctional than to revive it once it has reached such a condition. Consequently, some attention should be placed on evaluating the health of neighborhoods by assessing the well-being of their children on a regular basis. Communities showing indications of decline should get attention to help them to reverse it.

Internalization of strong values in high-risk neighborhoods requires enhancing resiliency as an antidote to the effects of social toxicity, but open, grassroots community development with outside support and investment is necessary to reduce the toxicity itself. And prevention to avoid reaching a high-risk condition, is just as important at the community level as it is with individuals.

REFERENCES

Arthur, R. (1992). *Gangs and schools.* Holmes Beach, FL: Learning.

Benard, B. (1991). *Fostering resiliency in kids: Protective factors in the family, school and community.* Portland, OR: Northwest Regional Educational Laboratory.

Bouchard, C. (1987). *Child maltreatment in Montreal.* Montreal, Canada: University of Quebec.

Bronfenbrenner, U. (1979). *The ecology of human development: Experiments by nature and design.* Cambridge, MA: Harvard University Press.

Bronfenbrenner, U. (1986). Ecology of the family as a contest for human development: Research perspectives. *Developmental Psychology, 22*(6), 723–742.

Bronfenbrenner, U., & Crouter, A. C. (1983). The evolution of environmental models in developmental research. In P. Mussen (Ed.), *Influences on human development.* Hinsdale, IL: Dryden Press.

Center for the Study of Social Policy. (1995). *Finding the data: A start-up list of outcome measures with annotations.* Washington, DC: Author.

Chavis, D., & Wandersman, A. (1990). Sense of community in the urban environment: A catalyst for participation and community development. *American Journal of Community Psychology, 18*(1), 55–81.

Collins, A., & Pancoast, D. (1976). *Natural helping networks.* Washington, DC: National Association of Social Workers.

Comer, J. (1980). *School power: Implications of an intervention project.* New York: Free Press.

Coulton, C., & Padey, S. (1992). Geographic concentration of poverty and risk to children in urban neighborhoods: The impact of poverty on children [Special issue]. *American Behavioral Scientist, 35*(3), 238–257.

Danieli, Y. (1988). The treatment and prevention of long-term effects and intergenerational transmission of victimization: A lesson from holocaust survivors and their children. In C. Figley (Ed.), *Trauma and its wake* (pp. 295–313). New York: Brunner/Mazel.

Deccio, G., Horner, W. C., & Wilson, D. (1994). High risk neighborhoods and high risk families: Replication research related to the human ecology of child maltreatment. *Journal of Social Service Research, 18*(3/4), 123–137.

Dubow, F., & Emmons, D. (1981). Reactions to crime: The political context: The community hypothesis. *Sage Criminal Justice System Annuals, 16,* 167–181.

Fields, R. (1987, October 25). *Terrorized into terrorist: Sequelae of PTSD in young victims.* Paper presented at the meeting of the Society for Traumatic Stress Studies, New York.

Flekkoy, M. (1996). *What is an adequate standard of living for social development?* Paper prepared for study group on Article 27 of the United Nations Convention on the Rights of the Child, University of South Carolina, Institute for Families in Society, Columbia, SC.

Forrester, J. (1969). *Urban dynamics.* Cambridge, MA: MIT Press.

Garbarino, J. (1976). A preliminary study of some ecological correlates of child abuse: The impact of socioeconomic stress on mothers. *Child Development, 47,* 178–185.

Garbarino, J. (1987). Family support and the prevention of child maltreatment. In S. Kagan, R. Powell, B. Weissbourd, & E. Zigler (Eds.), *America's family support programs* (pp. 187–195). New Haven, CT: Yale University Press.

Garbarino, J. (1995). *Raising children in a socially toxic environment.* San Francisco: Jossey-Bass.

Garbarino, J., & Associates. (1992). *Children and families in the social environment* (2nd ed.). Hawthorne, NY: Aldine de Gruyer.

Garbarino, J., & Crouter, A. C. (1978). Defining the community context of parent-child relations. *Child Development, 49,* 604–616.

Garbarino, J., Gaboury, M. T., Long, F., Grandjean, P., & Asp, E. (1982). Who owns the children: An ecological perspective on public policy affecting children. *Child and Youth Services Review, 5*(1/2), 41–61.

Garbarino, J., Guttman, E., & Seeley, J. (1986). *The psychologically battered child: Strategies for identification, assessment and intervention.* San Francisco: Jossey-Bass.

Garbarino, J., & Kostelny, K. (1992). Child maltreatment as a community problem. *Child Abuse and Neglect, 16*(4), 455–464.

Garbarino, J., Kostelny, K., & Dubrow, N. (1991). *No place to be a child: Growing up in a war zone.* Lexington, MA: Lexington Books.

Garbarino, J., & Sherman, D. (1980). High-risk neighborhoods and high-risk families: The human ecology of child maltreatment. *Child Development, 51,* 188–198.

Gilligan, C. (1982). *In a different voice.* Cambridge, MA: Harvard University Press.

Halpern, R. (1990). Poverty and early childhood parenting: Toward a framework for intervention. *American Journal of Orthopsychiatry 60*(1), 6–18.

Halpern, R. (1991). *Neighborhood-based initiative to address poverty: Lessons from experience.* Chicago: Erikson Institute.

Halpern, R. (1995). *Rebuilding the inner city: A history of neighborhood initiatives to address poverty in the United States.* New York: Columbia University Press.

Hardin, G. (1966). *Biology: Its principles and implications.* San Francisco: Freeman.

Krauss, C. (1995, July 30). Shootings fall as more guns stay at home: Rise in frisking deters carrying of illegal arms. *New York Times,* pp. 29, 32.

Kumpfer, K. (1993). *Resiliency and AOD use prevention in high risk youth.* Unpublished manuscript.

Levine, M. L., & Levine, A. (1970). *A social history of helping services: Clinic, court, school and community.* New York: Appleton-Century-Crofts.

Lewis, M. (1978). Nearest neighbor analysis of epidemiological and community variables. *Psychological Bulletin, 85*(6), 1302–1308.

Lofquist, W. (1983). *Discovering the meaning of prevention: A practical approach to positive change.* Tucson, AZ: AYD.

Maccoby, E., Johnson, J., & Church, R. (1958). Community integration and the social control of juvenile delinquency. *Journal of Social Issues, 14,* 38–51.

McKnight, J., & Kretzmann, J. (1990). *Mapping community capacity.* Evanston, IL: Northwestern University, Center for Urban Affairs and Policy Research.

Melton, G. (1992). It's time for neighborhood research and action. *Child Abuse and Neglect, 16*(4), 290–305.

Miller, A. (1987). *Maternal health and infant survival: An analysis of medical and social services to pregnant women, newborns and their families in ten European countries.* Washington, DC: National Center for Clinical Infant Programs.

Moskovitz, S. (1983). *Love despite hate: Child survivors of the Holocaust and their adult lives.* New York: Schocken.

National Center on Child Abuse and Neglect. (1981). *The national incidence study of child abuse and neglect: Report of findings.* Washington, DC: Author.

Paquin, G. W., & Ford, J. (1996). A statewide study of neighbors' knowledge of and reactions to physical child abuse. *Journal of Sociology and Social Welfare, 23*(4), 147–155.

Pasamanick, B. (1987). Social biology and AIDS. *Division 37 Newsletter.* Washington, DC: American Psychological Association.

Pelton, L. (1978). The myth of classlessness in child abuse cases. *American Journal of Orthopsychiatry, 48,* 569–579.

Pelton, L. (1981). *The social context of child abuse and neglect.* New York: Human Sciences Press.

Pelton, L. (1994). The role of material factors in child abuse and neglect. In G. Melton & F. Barry (Eds.), *Protecting children from abuse and neglect: Foundation for a new national strategy* (pp. 131–181). New York: Guilford Press.

Putnam, R. (1993). What makes democracy work? *National Civic Review, 83,* 101–107.

Ray, M. (1994). *Community lifelines program evaluation report.* Ithaca, NY: Cornell University, Family Life Development Center.

Reardon, P. (1988, June 22). CHA violent crimes up 9% for year. *Chicago Tribune,* Sec 1, 1.

Richardson, J., Dwyer, K., McGuigan, K., Hansen, W., Dent, C., Johnson, C., Sussman, S., Brannon, B., & Flay, B. (1989). Substance use among 8th grade students who take care of themselves after school. *Pediatrics, 84*(3), 556–566.

Rosenbaum, J., Fishman, N., Brett, A., & Meaden, P. (1993). Can the Kerner Commission's housing strategy improve employment, education and social integration for low income blacks? *North Carolina Law Review, 71,* 1519–1556.

Rutter, M., Cox, A., Tupling, C., Berger, M., & Yule, W. (1975). Attainment and adjustment in two geographical areas. *British Journal of Psychiatry, 126,* 493–509.

Sattin, D., & Miller, J. (1971). The ecology of child abuse within military community. *American Journal of Orthopsychiatry, 41*(4), 675–678.

Scheinfeld, D. (1983). Family relationships and school achievement among boys of lower-income urban black families. *American Journal of Orthopsychiatry, 53*(1), 127–143.

Schell, J. (1982). *The fate of the earth.* New York: Knopf.

Schorr, L. (1988). *Within our reach: Breaking the cycle of disadvantage.* New York: Doubleday.

Schorr, L. (1995). *The case for shifting to results-based accountability.* Washington, DC: Center for the Study of Social Policy.

Slinski, M. D. (1990). *Building communities of support for families in poverty: Master teacher in family life program.* Amherst, MA: University of Massachusetts, Cooperative Extension.

Stokes, B. (1981). *Helping ourselves: Local solutions to global problems.* New York: Norton.

Thomson, R. (1992). Social support and the prevention of child maltreatment. In G. Melton & F. Barry (Eds.), *Protecting children from abuse and neglect: Foundation for a new national strategy.* New York: Guilford Press.

Thompson, R. (1996). *Spiritual development and an adequate standard of living.* Paper prepared for study group on Article 27 of the United Nations Convention on the Rights of the Child, University of South Carolina, Institute for Families in Society, Columbia, SC.

Turner, S., Norman, E., & Zunz, S. (1993). *From risk to resiliency, a paradigm shift: A literature review and annotated bibliography.* Unpublished manuscript, Fordham University Graduate School of Social Service, New York.

U.S. Advisory Board on Child Abuse and Neglect. (1990). *Child abuse and neglect: Critical first steps in response to a national emergency.* Washington, DC: U.S. Department of Health and Human Services, Administration for Children and Families.

Vygotsky, L. (1986). *Thought and language.* Cambridge, MA: MIT Press.

Wandersman, A., Florin, P., Friedman, R., & Meier, R. (1987). Who participates, who does not, and why? An analysis of voluntary neighborhood organizations in the United States and Israel. *Sociological Forum, 2,* 534–555.

Wandersman, A., Jakubs, J., & Glamartino, G. (1981). Participation in block organizations. *Journal of Community Action, 1,* 40–47.

Werner, E. (1990). Protective factors and individual resilience. In S. J. Meisels & J. P. Shonkoff (Eds.), *Handbook of early childhood intervention* (pp. 97–116). Cambridge, England: Cambridge University Press.

Wilson, E. (1978). *On human nature.* Cambridge, MA: Harvard University Press.

Wilson, W. J. (1987). *The truly disadvantaged: The inner city, the underclass and public policy.* Chicago: University of Chicago Press.

CHAPTER 13

Parenting and the Transmission and Internalization of Values: From Social-Cultural Perspectives to Within-Family Analyses

JACQUELINE J. GOODNOW

The focus of this chapter is on the usefulness of remembering that parenting and development always occur in a context larger than the family unit. That larger context may be a geographic space (e.g., a neighborhood or a region) or a social space (e.g., a network of friends or a national culture). In all cases, the argument runs, the values that emerge in any generation and the ways in which this emergence takes place will reflect the interweaving of people and contexts. Moreover, what we learn from considering the impact of these larger contexts can be taken back to analyses of what happens within families, enhancing our understanding even of dyadic interactions.

The chapter has two broad aims. The first is to provide an overview of perspectives emphasizing contexts beyond the family. That overview will necessarily be broad-brush in style. Particular attention will be given, however, to perspectives that offer alternatives to the emphasis on parental strategies that is usually found within developmental analyses, and that reexamine the concepts of "transmission" and "internalization." These terms are currently seen as open to question, especially if they suggest a static and unidirectional relationship between two groups of people: one conveying an established and unchanging set of values, the other involved only in understanding those values and accepting them as their own.

The second aim is to bring out the relevance of social-cultural perspectives for the analysis of interactions within the family. In the midst of current exhortations to consider the ecological or cultural contexts of parenting, it is easy to think of this advice as implying only the addition of something "extra": something to be placed on top of within-family analyses. That step may well need to be taken. In addition, however, a number of social-cultural perspectives imply that we review and expand the ways in which we look at interactions within the family. That less obvious step is the one I wish to emphasize and to turn into some specific suggestions for research directions.

The chapter begins with a background section that introduces social-cultural perspectives, outlining their points of overlap and difference and the reasons for grouping them under the term "social-cultural." The sections that follow concentrate in turn on proposals that stem from social-cultural perspectives. The first of these takes up the question: Where shall we look when we wish to study the emergence of values? What content areas shall we consider? The second considers proposals related to the nature of "internalization," with particular attention given to alternatives to its definition as the

333

conversion of external into internal controls. The third concentrates on proposals related to the nature of transmission. In essence, social-cultural perspectives frame questions about parental strategies in terms of the question, What conditions are children,
or newcomers to a group at any age, likely to encounter? More specifically, the emphasis falls on the likelihood and the consequences of encountering values that (a) are
tagged for their relative importance and their negotiability, (b) compete with one another, and (c) are expressed—often ambiguously—in ways ranging from the verbal statement of a principle to the involvement of the child or newcomer, without comment, in
everyday routines that other people also follow. The effects of parental strategies, or of
any other source of values, then stem from the extent to which they involve these general conditions. As in the previous two sections, the aim is again to lay out these proposals and then to indicate how they might be translated into within-family research.
The final section offers some summary remarks.

THE GENERAL NATURE OF SOCIAL-CULTURAL PERSPECTIVES

Developmental psychologists have often been reminded that development always takes
place in contexts larger than the family unit, and that parenting varies in its form and its
consequences from one social-cultural context to another. Those reminders have come
from within psychology (e.g., Bronfenbrenner, 1979) and from disciplines other than psychology (anthropology especially). The reminders have also been repeated over time. To
take research by John and Beatrice Whiting and their colleagues as an example, the span
is from 1953 (J. Whiting & Child, 1953), through the 1970s (e.g., B. Whiting & Whiting,
1975), and into the 1980s (e.g., B. Whiting & Edwards, 1988).

Nonetheless, most developmental analyses concentrate on dyadic interactions within
families, with little attention to larger contexts. The reasons are probably several in kind.
Analyses of the larger contexts may seem irrelevant because many of the studies use
samples drawn from groups other than one's own. They also often contain terms that, to
many developmentalists, are unfamiliar and seem unnecessarily complex. Many analyses
also stop with the statement that larger contexts are important, without noting how to
combine them with the within-family analyses. Some may even seem to imply that what
happens within families is unimportant. Above all, the sheer variety of labels for these
perspectives—"ecological," "cultural," "cross-cultural," "dialectic," "co-constructivist,"
"contextual"—is discouraging.

My goal throughout the chapter is to create some order within the variety, in ways that
encourage links to the kinds of analyses with which developmental psychologists are familiar. For that reason, I shall often cut across perspectives, rather than describe each of
them in any detail. For that reason also, I shall more often cut across disciplines than I
shall separate perspectives on a disciplinary basis (e.g., this one from anthropology, this
from sociology, this from psychology). At times, it will be important to note the discipline from which a proposal comes, but that will usually occur only when the theoretical
orientation of a discipline helps account for the nature of the proposal. The description is
necessarily minimal. For further descriptions, however, the reader might turn to a section
on social-cultural perspectives within a chapter on socialization processes (Bugental &
Goodnow, in press), to a handbook chapter on the cultural psychology of development
(Shweder et al., in press), or to any of the specific references that follow.

Why Label These Perspectives Social-Cultural?

Starting with the label may seem a strange beginning. It is, however, a way of bringing out several features to perspectives that emphasize social contexts. First of all, the term is a deliberate attempt to break away from the connotations often attached to the adjectives "cultural" or "cross-cultural." The term "sociocultural" (e.g., Higgins, Ruble, & Hartup, 1983; Hoffman, 1983) has the same aim; so also does the term "sociohistorical" (e.g., Cole, 1988). In all cases, the intent is to signal that the larger context does not always have to be an ethnic or national group. A class group at school, a friendship group, a support network, a work group, an audience of any kind—all of these may provide contexts that go beyond the family unit. The term social-cultural further implies that the relevant material may as readily come from the field of "social psychology" as from the field of "cultural psychology."

The term also signals a particular feature to the methods used by researchers interested in exploring the relevance of larger social contexts. These methods do not necessarily require turning to groups outside one's own national culture. Studies of national groups other than one's own are certainly desirable. They are often the most likely to present sharply different values and practices challenging assumptions about how values emerge, compelling investigators to examine what is often taken for granted as matters of fact or nature, and raising questions about the distinctions between one's own culture and others. A comparison across national cultures, however, is not a necessary step toward the analysis of social contexts and is one of the reasons for the rise of the term cultural psychology rather than cross-cultural psychology (e.g., Cole, 1990; Shweder, 1990).

More concretely, many researchers interested in development-in-context mix national comparisons with several other methods. Bronfenbrenner's research on the "ecology of development" ranges from comparisons of classrooms in Russia and the United States (e.g., Bronfenbrenner, 1970), to comparisons within the United States of values for children at different points in historical time (e.g., Bronfenbrenner, 1958), and analyses of the ways in which the values of several significant others combine to influence the development of individuals (e.g., Bronfenbrenner, 1993, 1996). A similar range of methods is to be found within activity-based analyses of development (e.g., Engestrom, 1993; Laboratory of Comparative Human Cognition, 1983; Scribner, 1984), approaches to development in terms of apprenticeship (e.g., Rogoff, 1990), and analyses of contexts in terms of everyday practices (e.g., Goodnow, 1996b; Lave, 1988; Miller & Goodnow, 1995; Shweder, Arnett Jensen, & Goldstein, 1995). In each case, comparisons across national groups are used as part of a repertoire, as one of several bases for the analysis of development within social contexts.

Implied also by the term social-cultural is the argument that the national origin of a group may be less important than some other features to the group. For example, the critical feature when it comes to the emergence of values may be the heterogeneity of the group: the extent to which an individual encounters a diversity of viewpoints rather than the solid wall of a single opinion. What may also matter more than national origin may be the ways in which groups and their members influence or define each other. People belong to a variety of groups or categories. They are classed as male or female, white or people of color, locally born or from a different region. These group memberships help define who they are, both for themselves and for others. At the same time, the members also help define the group. The members may change the criteria for entry. They may act to change the meaning of labels such as "liberal," "black," "queer," "wife," or "female."

They may also abandon a group in numbers that radically alter its composition or make it an empty shell. This aspect of groups is part of what prompts descriptions of cultures and people as "co-constitutive," as "making each other up," as "constructing one another," or as "mutually creating one another" (e.g., Briggs, 1992; Cole, 1985; Shweder, 1990; Valsiner, 1988). This kind of feature is easy to recognize within spontaneously formed groups (e.g., friendship groups). The same feature also occurs, however, in groups we may think of as having some independent, timeless, unchanging existence—churches, political parties, national groups. These groups help define their members. They are also defined and changed by their members. In all cases, the important feature to any group may then be not its surface type but the ways in which mutual influence occurs.

If the critical issue is the presence of distinctions among groups that go beyond the feature of national origin, why use the term cultural at all? Perhaps the term social is all that is needed. The reason for the additional term lies in the need for a particular kind of differentiation. Some groups—audiences at a concert or film, for instance—form and dissolve easily. They are nonetheless describable as social groups. In contrast, some groups have a history and an anticipated future. They are marked by a degree of consensus in the values they hold and the practices they follow. They invest effort in seeing that new members come to share the values and practices that make this group different from others, and they imply a particular identity for their members: Members come to be known and to see themselves, for example, as "a Kwoma" (Whiting, 1941), or "a female." This kind of group might best be termed cultural rather than social. In fact, that term might happily be used alone if it did not have the frequent connotation of referring only to a national origin. The addition of the term social acts essentially as a counterweight to that connotation, just as the addition of cultural to social is a reminder that transitory groups with little investment in continuity (in the "culturing" of particular kinds of people) are not the most useful groups to choose when studying values across generations.

Points of Difference

Up to this point, the features noted have been predominantly similarities among social-cultural perspectives. These perspectives, however, are not identical with one another, and it will be helpful to have some sense of where they differ. (Both the similarities and the differences affect the proposals offered for the nature of transmission and internalization).

Social-cultural perspectives vary along a number of dimensions. For proposals about values, however, the easiest route into a picture of differences is by way of the features of contexts that are emphasized. Differences along other dimensions—in the primary question, the metaphors for interaction, the routes emphasized for the emergence of values—may then surface as we proceed.

A long-standing approach emphasizes the physical ecology of a setting. To take one proposal, spatial skills come to be valued when people live in settings such as oceans or deserts (e.g., Goodwin, 1976; Lynch, 1960). To take another, differences between the sexes come to be prized when people settle in towns or villages and males and females come to live more separate lives (e.g., Berry, 1976). To take a third, the importance of children staying close to base and "not wandering" comes to be emphasized when the surrounding area is thick bush rather than open space with high visibility (Blurton-Jones, 1993). The specific proposals vary. The question emphasized in each case, however, has to do with the circumstances that promote a greater interest in some values than in others. The overall proposal is that value comes to be assigned to qualities that promote a child's survival and the economic well-being of the group.

Somewhat similar in style are proposals that emphasize the economic aspects of contexts. Obedience in a child is highly valued in settings where the child must fit in with a mother's regular involvement in agricultural work requiring a rhythm that cannot easily be interrupted by lengthy negotiations over why a child should do what he or she has been told to do (LeVine et al., 1994). Within Western industrialized societies, obedience and conformity are also valued when the conditions of a father's paid work allow for little autonomy and parents anticipate that their children will move into similar work conditions. The critical variable, several studies have demonstrated, is not the simple socioeconomic status of the father's work but the extent to which what he does is under his control, is self-directed (e.g., Kohn, 1969, 1996; Kohn & Schooler, 1982). Again, the primary question has to do with why some qualities are more highly valued than others. The general proposal is again one that emphasizes demands and rewards. Parents anticipate the child's economic future and promote the qualities they see as likely to be needed in stable or changing times.

Imagine, however, a perspective that, branching out from Bronfenbrenner's (e.g., 1979) broad view of the ecology of development emphasizes what may be called "social ecology." Now the concern is with variables such as the presence of like-minded people in one's environment. The presence of like-minded others in a school makes a difference to the extent to which students from an ethnic minority can sustain and act on the achievement values that their parents have encouraged them to hold (Steinberg, Darling, & Fletcher, 1996). The presence of "value consensus" between one's own parents and those of other parents in the neighborhood, when that value is in favor of high academic standards, makes a difference to the adolescent's orientation toward achievement (Steinberg et al., 1996, p. 458). The implied question has now shifted to a concern with the ways in which the values of parents and children can differ from one another. The implied process has also changed. Rather than being a process only of demand, it has come to include the extent to which the same values are to be found in the several sectors that exist within any setting. Implied also is a concept of values as needing to be maintained by supportive others. Values are not simply established once and for all by a particular social environment. They may instead need to be maintained, withering if support does not continue to be provided. Moreover, the conditions that influence the initial establishment may well not be the same as those that influence the maintenance.

None of the approaches mentioned so far, however, seems to be making direct use of the many descriptions of contexts or cultures as made up of "meanings" or "practices." Analyses in such terms are prominent within anthropology and sociology and, increasingly, within psychology. What kinds of perspectives are these and how do they link with those already mentioned?

To compress a great deal of discussion and to make this introduction as concrete as possible, I start with an approach known as the analysis of "social representations." The term is one of a family with several labels: cultural models (e.g., D'Andrade & Strauss, 1992; Holland & Quinn, 1987), consensus models (e.g., Romney, Wells, & Batchelder, 1986), folk theories (e.g., Reid & Valsiner, 1986). In essence, these several terms refer to ideas that are shared, to various degrees, by members of a group—hence the adjectives *social* or *cultural*—and to the conditions that give rise to various degrees of sharing. The disciplinary home for the particular approach known as the study of social representations is in social psychology. The basic theory comes from Moscovici (e.g., 1981). Duveen and Lloyd (1990) offer a set of extensions to developmental questions. Mugny and Carugati (1989) provide the study used here as an anchor-point. Their study examined the ideas that parents held about the nature of intelligence (in effect, the intellectual qualities they saw as possessing value). Definitions of intelligence, Mugny and Carugati point out, are of several kinds. They may take the form of an emphasis on practical and social adaptiveness, or on "cybernetic" skills (essentially skill with problems of the academic kind that schools present). Before their children's exposure to the school system, parents in Italy and Switzerland favor the first kind of definition. Once their children are in school, however, they come to favor the second. The shift, Mugny and Carugati state, brings out first of all that societies contain more than one definition of any quality. Several are to be found, even if one prevails within particular groups or across groups. The shift also brings out the functions that are served by coming to hold the values emphasized by the dominant members or the experts in a group. Coming to share their values or definitions—their representations—helps make a new situation more comfortable. It also makes for easier communication with others, in the sense that one comes to take the same position that others do and to use terms with the same meanings that others give to it. The establishment and maintenance of values, then, needs to be thought of as involving shifts in order to become part of a like-minded group and the potentially active selection of some values and interpretations from a larger available set.

That example helps introduce some of the themes that will recur in this chapter: themes of multiplicity, differential status, competition between one valued position and another, shifts in the positions taken, and the need to ask about what sustains a value. In the words of Strauss (1992, p. 1), it may once have been "conventional wisdom to think of cultures as integrated, stable sets of meanings and practices unproblematically reproduced through socialized actors. Now, anthropologists are beginning to stress conflict, contradiction, ambiguity, and change in cultural understandings—the way cultural understandings are 'contested' and 'negotiated' in current jargon." Anthropologists are not alone in this shift.

To round out this general introduction, I turn to an approach to contexts in terms of cultural practices. Briefly, practice approaches place less emphasis on what people understand or on their representations of the social world and more on what people do. To use one turn of phrase, the emphasis is less on "gender schemas" and more on the everyday ways of "doing gender" (West & Zimmerman, 1987, p. 125).

The term practice has come to be used in several ways. Its most usual meaning, however, especially within anthropology, refers to activities marked by several features. They have an everyday, routine quality to them. They are widely shared (this is one of the features that invites the adjective cultural). They are invested with meaning or significance and may readily come to be seen as part of a natural or moral order (at the least, to challenge a practice or to abandon it would not be taken lightly by oneself or by others in the group). They provide the routes by which people become members of their group. Children increasingly participate in and come to follow the practices regarded as appropriate for their age, sex, or status, developing in the process a sense of who they are and what their relationships are to others. Miller and Goodnow (1995) provide an expansion on this summary list; they also note the frequency with which analyses of ways of talking or of storytelling are framed as studies of cultural practice. The main theoretical impetus has come from Bourdieu (e.g., 1979, 1990). Ortner (1985) provides an anthropological overview. Lave (1988, 1991) has offered several major extensions to the analysis of cognitive development. The chapters in Goodnow, Miller, and Kessel (1995) introduce a further set of studies relevant to social and cognitive development; the following study is described in one of these chapters.

The study is by an anthropologist, Barbara Miller (1995). Her focus is on practices related to hair and dress among adolescents who are living in the United States and whose background is Indian (Hindu). Particular ways of wearing one's hair, and of dress, she points out, are strongly favored by parents in this group, along with attendance at temple and dating or marriage within the Hindu community. It is the everyday practices of hair and dress, however, that are often chosen by the adolescents in this group as ways of signaling a degree of difference from their parents. It is also the departures from everyday practices that cause their parents considerable anguish (the fathers in particular find extremely disturbing their daughters' abandoning the practice of long hair confined to a braid). The everyday practices then become the vehicles by which researchers may begin to understand the meanings that parents and adolescents attach to particular ways of behaving, and what some of the routes are by which they convey their values to one another.

With practice approaches, the questions at the forefront again have to do not with how some values come to be selected for emphasis but how they are established, maintained, varied, and negotiated. With practice approaches also, the cognitive or representational aspects of values may be seen as taking a particular form. The emphasis shifts from meanings or representations in the form of "propositions, rules, schematic programs or beliefs" (Rosaldo, 1984, p. 140) that have a high degree of internal order, stem from active mental work by a contructively minded individual, and specify how to behave in particular situations. The emphasis falls instead on looser sets of "associative chains and images" and on "public life—social facts . . . collective stories . . . ritual practices" as providing "the template for all human action, growth and understanding" (Rosaldo, 1984, p. 140). In Lave's (1991) phrasing of a similar emphasis, understanding is more often "situated" than it is general. It also arises less from mental abstraction than from involvement in a "community of practice"; that is, in activities that are already engaged in by members of a group that the newcomer now begins to join.

The only further introductory comment to be made has probably been anticipated by the reader. This has to do with the presence of some degree of tension among various social-cultural perspectives. As Cole (1995) points out, there is still work to be done toward differentiating among approaches that describe contexts in terms of activities, activity systems, and practices. The terms are sometimes used interchangeably even though they should be set apart from one another. In addition, there is a need to bring together perspectives that describe contexts and development in terms of shared activities or practices and perspectives that emphasize shared meanings and representations. That need has been highlighted by both Lave (1993) and by Strauss (1992), the one starting from a practice perspective, the other from an emphasis on internal "cultural models." The form of that rapprochement is as yet far from clear. In some of Bourdieu's (1979) arguments, the practices themselves emerge as all that matters. They are seen as having their own momentum, and as often unrelated to the ideas expressed by the practitioners. (It is possible, for example, to shift toward egalitarian schemas with regard to gender but to leave unexamined and unchanged one's everyday ways of marking a status difference between males and females.) In other practice approaches, the possibility is added that practices matter because they may also provide the potential basis for abstracting some general value (e.g., Goodnow, 1996b; Shweder et al., 1995).

At this point, however, it will be sufficient to note that multiplicity and tension exist and that these features form part of the background from which specific proposals about values emerge. Social-cultural perspectives display in themselves the qualities that most researchers using these perspectives would see as significant for the emergence of values in all social settings: multiplicity, some degree of ambiguity, and some degree of tension and competition among positions.

WHERE ARE VALUES TO BE FOUND?

In the previous section, I provided a general description of social-cultural perspectives on the emergence of values. In the process, some of the specific suggestions that social-cultural perspectives offer for the study of values began to surface. The sections that follow move to a more explicit statement of those and other suggestions. The first such statement has to do with the content areas pointed to as prime sites for the study of values.

Values within Matters of "Fact," "Nature," or "Necessity"

Social-cultural perspectives highlight first of all that what we often regard as an essential or natural step in development is not necessarily so. Anthropological studies of infancy and early development offer prime examples. Gusii mothers seldom gaze into the eyes of their infants. In fact, children are discouraged from looking adults "in the eye." Far from being a mark of honesty and directness, such forms of gaze are regarded as indicating a lack of respect. Most current theories of attachment or bonding would lead one to expect that Gusii infants should have difficulty forming secure attachment to their mothers. In fact, however, secure attachment seems to be readily established (LeVine, 1990). Disapproved also in a number of cultures may be the Western practice of a young child sleeping in a bed or in a space of its own. That "essential" step toward the development of independence may be regarded by people in other cultures as cruel, as unnatural, and as exposing the young child to unwarranted risk (Shweder et al., 1995). Even "the facts" of development may not have the value-neutral base that is often assumed. The young child's development of a sleeping rhythm that reduces the intervals between waking and feeding is often regarded in the West as primarily a sign of neurological maturation. The same changes, however, do not occur at the same pace in societies where infants have easy access to the breast and where the rhythm of a parent's day does not lead to a high value being placed on the earliest possible achievement of these longer intervals between periods of wakefulness (Super, 1981).

The *relevance for within-family analyses* lies in the proposal that the prime sites for the analysis of values may be precisely those content areas where values have become invisible, where the recognition of "value" rather than "fact" or "nature" emerges only when we are faced with groups that do not follow the same practices that we do and whose children, to our surprise, are nonetheless in viable shape. As Shweder et al. (1995) point out, it is difficult to regard the Japanese as totally damaged by their practice of allowing children to share beds or sleeping quarters with their parents. Nonetheless, both everyday thinking and formal psychology within the United States take it for granted that this practice is wrong or damaging. In similar fashion, it is widely assumed within

Anglo societies that children need to be assigned household tasks, becoming otherwise "spoiled." There are, however, many cultural groups where this kind of contribution to the family is not expected, without the expected consequence of children who have no concern for others in the family (Goodnow, 1996b). The interesting research question then takes the form: What gives rise to the conviction that some forms of parenting represent a natural or a moral order? The useful research procedure may be one of choosing precisely these areas of invisible values—these areas where divergence from what we take for granted creates a sense of surprise and shock—as the areas in which to explore the nature of transmission or internalization. These may well turn out to be the areas containing values that we hold most dearly.

Values within Ways of Acting, Thinking, and Feeling

It is easy to think of values in terms only of ways of acting, with a further restriction to actions of a clearly moral kind. On that basis, occasions of transgression come to be favored sites for analysis, with the mark of internalization taken to be the extent to which a person resists the temptation to depart from moral behavior when presented with attractive alternatives. A broader view of values, underlined by social-cultural perspectives, is that values are present whenever people judge some ways of acting, thinking, or feeling to be more desirable, more worthwhile, or more important than others.

The expansion to ways of feeling is exemplified especially well by Briggs's analyses of the ways in which Inuit children are led, through adults' repeated teasing until the child learns not to respond, both not to display anger and apparently not to experience anger (e.g., Briggs, 1992). Ways of thinking provide a second expansion. I give them particular emphasis because when we seek to explore values, the area of cognitive development does not always spring readily to mind. Cognition is often assumed to be separate from the world of values, to be concerned only with the emergence of skills, understanding, or expertise. That assumption has been questioned with particular sharpness by the anthropologist D'Andrade, who comments that studies of cognition are strange in the way they treat all skills, all tasks, and all errors as equally important. All cultural groups, he points out, regard some skills, tasks, and errors as more significant than others; they also put more effort into teaching the skills regarded as important and judge more harshly errors or shortcomings in these areas (D'Andrade, 1984). All groups, it has been added, display "cognitive values" (Goodnow, 1990). They regard some ways of thinking or problem-solving as intrinsically better than others, labeling some as "elegant" and setting others aside as "pedestrian," even though both may solve the problem. Judgments of taste or "good form," to take a comment from Bourdieu's (1979) analysis of "distinction," are as abundant in academic matters as they are in matters of dress. The term "privilege" extends that concept. Some ways of thinking and speaking, the term implies, are awarded a status that is often unearned. The "voice of science," for example, is often privileged by teachers, even when it is inappropriate to a narrative or a problem (Wertsch, 1991). In contrast, the use of personal narratives is often set aside as not being "real data" (Cazden, 1993). In related fashion, teachers often privilege particular ways of storytelling, to the point of actively "dismantling" (Michaels, 1991) the family style that a child has brought to school.

What is the *relevance* of such proposals for analyses of parenting in relation to the emergence of values? The most obvious extension lies in the recommendation that we look within families for the promotion of particular ways of feeling, thinking, learning, or storytelling. Dunn (e.g., 1988) has drawn attention to the ways in which parents of 2- and 3-year-olds talk about feelings, both labeling and evaluating them. For the promotion of particular forms of learning, a prime example is the elevation of mathematics to a particular status: either as the most important area of achievement for all students (e.g., Stevenson & Lee, 1990) or as more relevant, appropriate, or natural for boys than for girls (e.g., Eccles & Jacobs, 1986). Ways of storytelling are also emerging as prime sites for exploring the emergence of values. It is now clear that parents encourage some forms of storytelling, setting others aside as uninteresting (e.g., Miller & Sperry, 1988) or as too "fanciful," sometimes to the point of labeling as the telling of "lies" the stories that schoolteachers regard as "imaginative" (Heath, 1983). It is then within these everyday and early exchanges that children begin to learn the relative values placed on what they produce.

PROPOSALS FOR THE NATURE OF INTERNALIZATION

In the previous two sections, I outlined a number of general arguments from social-cultural perspectives, and then chose a particular set of proposals to examine more closely: proposals related to the question of where to look when choosing content areas for the analysis of values and their development.

The present section selects a further issue for closer examination: the nature of internalization. For this much-used concept, social-cultural perspectives offer two broad proposals. The first is that investigators should look to the past, asking what happened to the once-popular definition of internalization as the conversion of external into internal controls. The second is to treat the concept, at least as a starting point, as a matter of similarities and differences across generations. That framing then prompts researchers to ask about various kinds of similarity and difference, to treat both similarity and difference as potentially positive, and to consider each as having several possible bases.

Internalization: More Than the Conversion of External into Internal Controls?

The process known as internalization has attracted interest for some time. Lawrence and Valsiner (1993) trace much of its history within psychology, with particular attention to its emergence in psychoanalytic theory. Wentworth (1980) provides an historical description of changing interest within the field of sociology. Part of the basis for interest in both fields was a concern with issues of control, in particular with the transfer of control by external sources to control from within the individual.

To take anthropology and sociology as examples, one of the attractions to the notion of internalization was the possibility of answering the question: If people are basically "antisocial"—pursuing self-interest and ready to react with aggression when others frustrate their pursuits—how is society ever possible? How can people avoid either a supervigilant police state or the chaos of warring individuals? The problem is solved by thinking of individuals as taking into themselves the standards of their society and becoming their own "police." Interest turns then to the ways in which these internal controls are established. To take an example from anthropology, interest turns to testing the Freudian proposal that the construction of particular forms of personality structure (in particular, the construction of a relaxed or harsh superego) reflects the individual's experience of control or deprivation in the course of such child-rearing practices as weaning or toilet-training (e.g., J. Whiting & Child,1953).

This way of defining internalization, however, soon began to be noted as containing several gaps and difficulties. First, the content area appears narrow. Individuals surely take over from others more than policing procedures. Categories, customs, scripts, images: All of these are surely part of what is absorbed. Second, the alternatives seem too black and white. There are surely gradations over and beyond internalizing or not internalizing. Third, there is little attention to a more cognitive aspect of viewpoints: the level of awareness the individual has about their source. That is the quality underlined within psychological analyses of the extent to which individuals perceive ideas as having been generated by themselves or by others, perceptions related to the degree of overt pressure applied (e.g., Hoffman, 1983). It is also the quality underlined by social-cultural questions about the extent to which people ever ask questions about a value position: ever reflect on it or wonder if there might be alternatives (e.g., Watson-Gegeo, 1992).

Fourth, there is little room for a contribution from the individual. Moreover, to the extent that the individual matters, it is primarly by way of an adversarial relationship, an opposition between the interests of the individual and of the social group. That assumption is weakened, however, when the view of human nature ceases to be so negative. Suppose, for example, that people are primed at birth for positive social interactions with others; they are ready to pay attention to social cues, ready to attach themselves to others, and equipped with devices—from gurgles to smiles—that promote their being positive participants in interactions with others rather than hedonistic warriors determined to battle only for themselves. For psychologists, that view of nature was encouraged by the rise of ethological approaches to development (e.g., Bowlby, 1969). Even without any direct input from ethology, however, the social sciences in general reflected a move toward a more positive view of individuals and a less adversarial view of interactions between parents and children or individuals and society (Wentworth, 1980). The door then became open for other ways of regarding relationships between the individual and society or between new and established members of a group. Those ways encompassed codependence, mutual definition, or mutual change. Each such possibility then became one further step away from regarding internalization only as a way of keeping naturally unruly individuals under internal control.

Internalization Framed as Similarity across Generations

Are there alternatives to regarding internalization as the conversion of external into internal controls? One possibility consists of stepping back and asking in more open fashion: Why is an outcome such as internalization seen as needed? What is hoped for? If we ask that question with parents in mind, it is clear that all parents wish to see their children hold some values with some degree of commitment. These values should not be dropped at the first barrier or countersuggestion. Nor should they require constant external support and encouragement. Far less clear, however, are the circumstances that lead parents to believe that they need to encourage commitment. Does this view reflect a particular definition of virtue, a sense that children are naturally susceptible to temptation, or the sense that the world is full of attractive alternatives to the path that should be followed? Unclear also are the circumstances that lead parents to regard as reasonable or as optimal some particular accompaniments or bases to commitment—fear, respect for custom, an unquestioning assumption of the rightness of certain ways of acting, thinking, and feeling, or some enlightened understanding of the principles involved.

A second possibility consists of splitting apart two aspects to the concept of internalization: the notion of a particular quality to what develops (e.g., the presence of internal direction or commitment) and the notion of a particular source (e.g., the absorption of external points of view). Researchers may then be regarded as starting primarily from one of these aspects rather than the other.

Starting from an emphasis on commitment are analyses that ask how some values come to be regarded as beyond question (e.g., Shweder & Much, 1986; Watson-Gegeo, 1992). These values come to be seen as so much a part of a moral or a natural order that no reflection occurs. In effect, departures from the standard view or the standard practice become "unthinkable." Starting from a similar concern are the analyses of degrees of commitment offered by D'Andrade (1992) and Strauss (1992). Their concern is with the degrees of "directive force" that may come to be attached to particular values. For example, all people may come to believe that "everyone should help the poor" or that "everyone can be whatever they want to be, if they try hard enough." They may hold these ideas, however, at the level of a cliche. Alternately, they may hold them with a level of commitment that means these notions will guide action when a choice or a demand arises, or—at a still higher level—will initiate action in line with the idea they hold. The critical research issues then have to do with differentiating among levels of commitment and determining the conditions that may give rise to different levels. Strauss (1992) proposes that the third level occurs only when values are linked to a concept of self. D'Andrade (1992) emphasizes the accumulation of affect, in connectionist fashion, in the course of the episodes in which values have been encountered.

Starting instead from an emphasis on external sources are several analyses that ask: How do similarities and differences across generations come about? How is it, for example, that a home language can disappear from one generation to another (e.g., Kulick, 1992)? Do student activists have activist parents (e.g., Block, 1972)? How does change of any kind come to occur? This way of framing the issue of internalization gives rise to several research recommendations, each a departure from the emphasis on change within the individual that is more often to be found within developmental analyses. In summary form, the recommendations are these:

- *Specify the particular forms that similarity or difference across generations may take.* It is possible that two generations may be alike in the values that they hold but differ in their levels of commitment. One generation may be deeply committed to a particular religion. The next may simply observe its forms for convenience, turning up at the social occasions of marriages, funerals, or traditional gift-giving. A related possibility is that the two generations may hold the same general principle, with equal levels of commitment, but differ in the specific ways by which commitment is expressed. That possibility is suggested by Block's (1972) finding that the parents of student activists had not themselves been politically active. The two generations shared, however, the conviction that once a viewpoint came to be held, one should act on it.

- *Regard both similarity and difference as potentially positive.* The recommendation is to set aside any simple equation of similarity with success or of difference with failure of transmission. Instead of that simple equation, anthropology and sociology both contain the widespread view that society benefits from there being across generations both similarity and difference, both continuity and novelty, both "reproduction" and "production."

- *Allow for several bases to similarity.* It is temptingly easy to attribute similarity across generations to the efforts of parents. Similarity might stem, however, from the two generations sharing the same social environment, from both having been exposed to similar demands and possibilities. Within social-cultural perspectives, this possibility has led to designs where this confounding can be avoided such as by considering the children of immigrant parents (e.g., Cashmore & Goodnow, 1985) or by comparing parents and children within the same national group but at times of marked social change (e.g., Sloutsky, 1995).

- *Allow for several bases to differences.* These bases may be looked for both within the individual or within the circumstances that individuals encounter. Some possible shifts in the circumstances encountered have already been noted in commenting on designs that untangle within-family effects from the effects of both generations being in essentially similar social contexts. Thus the focus here will now turn to factors within the individual.

Among these, the emphasis is sometimes on cognitive factors. Differences across generations should always be expected, it has been argued, because of the inevitable transformation that constructive minds make to the events they encounter (Lawrence & Valsiner, 1993). Social patterns may set some limits to those transformations (some may be dubbed too "imaginative" or simply "wrong"). These patterns may also facilitate transformation. An ambiguous set of values in the social world makes personal transformation and variation among individuals all the more likely (D'Andrade, 1992). The notion that any position is absorbed unchanged and stays unchanged, however, should be abandoned.

More often, the emphasis within social-cultural perspectives falls on aspects of motivation rather than on the cognitive inevitability of construction and transformation. A proposal from Tajfel (1981), a social psychologist, includes two scenarios, both starting from the argument that belonging to a less privileged group may carry with it a potential threat to the image of self. (The threat lies in the possibility that a negative social identity may spill over into a negative personal identity.) In the face of such a threat, one scenario takes the form of attempting to leave the original group and join the more privileged group: to "pass" as an honorary male, as "young," as virtually a "local." The other scenario consists of challenging the value system that assigns one to a lesser place, pointing out, for example, that "women hold up half the sky," that "black is beautiful," that age is a state of mind, that the Irish brought civilization to Europe, or that the Chinese were literate at a time when most of the Western world was living in caves. These challenges are oriented toward changing others rather than changing only oneself. They may, as Tajfel points out, often be accompanied by group action and public statement. In that case, they then become available as a visible part of the heterogeneous set of positions from which individuals may draw in resisting the pressure to pass or to change oneself to fit the dominant values.

Translations into Within-Family Research

Several extensions have already been implied in breaking down the recommendations that are part of cross-generation comparisons. One addition to these consists of recognizing that periods of difference or similarity between the positions of parents and children are not likely to be unchanging. In fact, a period of difference may well be followed by one of similarity if parents are monitoring for signs of a gap between generations and feel that the gap is one that calls for action, either in the form of attempts to change where their children stand or to review and alter their own positions (Collins & Luebker, 1995).

A second kind of addition consists of looking more closely at the question: What are parents trying to achieve in particular content areas or at particular times? When do they aim or settle for similarity in the form of public observance of the family's customs? When do they aim instead at the understanding and acceptance of a principle, unhappy with simple observance? When do they actively seek a difference between generations or feel pleased when one occurs? Parents, for example, may well be pleased rather than distressed when their children turn out to be either more successful or less success-oriented than the parents themselves (Goodnow, 1992, 1994). Both of those questions point to the need for a fresh look at occasions framed in terms of compliance as a parent's goal. Parents, it has been pointed out, may be less interested in compliance than developmental analyses often imply. Within the United States and Australia, mothers emerge as often encouraging the child's learning to negotiate and to say no in acceptable ways (e.g., Kuczynski & Kochanska, 1990; Leonard, 1993). Once this kind of position is taken, the phenomena of interest come to be the particular areas in which negotiation or divergence in values are more versus less acceptable, and the particular ways in which differences are accepted, negotiated, or encouraged.

THE NATURE OF TRANSMISSION

The previous sections have taken up two sets of proposals that emerge from social-cultural perspectives: One set deals with the content areas investigators may select to study the emergence and maintenance of values; the other deals with ways to conceptualize and explore the concept of internalization.

Some of the proposals related to internalization began to raise suggestions as to how particular states of affairs might come about: how, for example, various levels of commitment might arise or various kinds of similarity or difference between generations come to pass. Proposals of this kind are the particular concern of the present section.

To be noted at the start is a particular point of difference from most developmental approaches to questions about the conditions that influence the emergence and the maintenance of values. Both developmental and social-cultural perspectives are concerned with conditions influencing the likelihood that new members of a group will come to display the values that the established members hold or wish to see upheld. In general, however, social-cultural perspectives currently give less attention to specific strategies than to the general conditions that new members are likely to encounter.

A concern with specific strategies is not absent within social-cultural perspectives. An example is an analysis of occupational socialization, where new workers are steered by the old hands toward the company of reliable coworkers who can be trusted to pass on the established values (Levine & Moreland, 1992). The stronger concern, however, is with the general qualities of experience that exposure to a particular strategy creates. For the specific strategy just cited, the general condition created is one in which the newcomer is temporarily cut off from diversity in the viewpoints encountered. The old hands control the ways in which the job is represented, together with the newcomers' access to other viewpoints or practices. The net effect is one of restricted awareness of diversity, a condition that might be created by several specific strategies.

What are the general conditions that children or newcomers to a group are likely to encounter and that influence the emergence and maintenance of values? Children or newcomers are seen as likely to find that (a) values are expressed in a number of ways, often ambiguously, (b) social contexts usually contain more than one position for values, often in a competitive relationship with one another, and (c) indications of what is valued are usually accompanied by signs of varying degrees of importance, leeway, and negotiability. For each of these conditions, the aim is again to outline the proposals and to indicate how they may be turned into research issues directly tied to parent-child interactions in relation to the emergence of values.

Values Are Expressed in Varied, Often Ambiguous, Ways

Social-cultural perspectives recognize, as developmental analyses also do, that values may be expressed or conveyed in numerous ways. They give particular emphasis, however, to three ways of expressing values and to a quality—ambiguity or indirectness—that may apply to any of them.

Of the three forms of expression, the first has to do with *arrangements of space*. The seperateness of sleeping spaces within a house, for example, signals ideas about the status of various family members, the importance given to the privacy of the couple, and the vulnerability of various family members—the vulnerability of young children to fear when alone or the vulnerability of young girls to the possibility of incest or the reputation of being unchaperoned (Shweder et al., 1995). The second has to do with *forms of talk*. Watson-Gegeo (1992) provides a strong example pointing to the use of a particular form of talk to mark the significance of a topic. Among the Kwara'ae (Solomon Islands), the elders use a particular form of oratory when they are about to raise a topic of importance with those who are younger, with the intention of changing the young people's behaviors or viewpoints. Occasions when this kind of talk is used are known as occasions of "shaping the mind," and young children—even though they are seldom the direct target of this form of talk—quickly come to recognize it and to imitate it for what they regard as important pronouncements.

The third form of expression is by way of *cultural practices*. In the background description of social-cultural perspectives, I listed a set of qualities that give rise to some particular actions being regarded as cultural practices. These are actions that have a routine, repeated aspect to them, that are observed by many or most members of a group, that provide the routes by which people become members of the group, that are invested with meaning and affect, and that come to be seen as reflecting a natural or moral order. Such qualities are often possessed, for example, by everyday divisions of labor in the household, or by the actions and statements commonly used when people greet one another, make requests, or receive gifts. The same qualities are also often present within the ways in which people tell stories about themselves, about others, or about the past. They learn to avoid the public discussion of "private" topics, forms of self-presentation that may seem self-serving, or endings that depart from such conventions as "they lived happily ever after." These several qualities are as well often present in the forms of address normally used between people in various relationships (e.g., first names are not for strangers) or in the ways in which one acts toward members of the opposite sex—from opening doors to feeling obliged to fill in silences or avoid interruptions. As those last examples suggest, practices are not static. When they change, however, it is often with a sense, on the part of many, of strangeness and—regardless of whether the move is happily or unhappily received—of a departure from what once seemed part of a natural social order.

Regardless of the particular mode that is used for the expression of values, however, social-cultural perspectives underline *the frequent presence of ambiguity.* The analysis is especially clear in relation to the verbal statement of values. Here, the expression of values is often indirect, rather than direct. In many cultures, values are expressed by reference to proverbs or legends. The impact, D'Andrade (1992) has suggested, lies in the implication that here is some timeless, hallowed truth, to be treated with respect and acceptance, rather than with frivolity, skepticism, or argument. It is not simply that the indirect form makes it difficult to know exactly what the meaning might be. The archaic, elliptical form in itself, it is argued, deflects reflection or questioning.

Elliptical forms of talk may also have other consequences. One type has already been noted. Elliptical talk creates ambiguity and that in turn faciliates personal interpretations and shifts across generations (D'Andrade, 1992). A further type of consequence is that people may come to see value in particular forms of talk or silence. Value may reside, for example, in saying less rather than spelling everything out. Among the Wolof, Irvine (1978) reports, the higher one's status, the less one says. "Talk is cheap," one might say, and lesser beings do it for you. In related fashion, Dumont (1972) reports the Inuit as valuing silence rather than talk, while Nagashima (1973) draws attention to the value that Japanese place on elliptical statements, regarding as relatively crude—especially among people who know one another—statements that are explicit.

Translations into Within-Family Analyses

The main translations are twofold:

1. *Examine the uses that family members make of various modes of expression, and their consequences.* Storytelling practices provide a prime example. In Miller and Sperry's (1988) African American sample, parents often recounted their everyday experiences in ways that presented themselves in an interesting and feisty light. Their children, Miller and Sperry noted, moved toward telling stories that cast them along similar character lines. The impact, it is argued, is not only on the kinds of stories that people tell about themselves. The stories are part of a "construction of self," built up by way of the accounts of everyday events that are offered and endorsed among family members (Miller, Potts, Fung, Hogstra, & Mintz, 1990). The analysis of transmission and internalization would now benefit from similar dissections of nonverbal practices such as arrangements of household space or the distinctions drawn between what is worn in public or in the privacy of the home.

2. *Examine the uses and consequences of ambiguity and explicit statement.* Ambiguity deserves particular comment given the tendency within developmental analyses of values to emphasize the uses and virtues of explicit statements of principle. Parents do make ambiguous statements. They use proverbs that are not easy to interpret and that may support opposing principles. They may say both "the race is to the swift" and "slow and steady wins the race." They say "Were you born in a tent?" when a child leaves a door unclosed. They say, "What's the magic word?" or "I didn't hear you" when they want the child to say "please" or "thank-you." Even more ambiguously, they say "She is the cat's mother," when what they want is for the child not to refer to the mother—when the mother is present—as "she" (Becker & Goodnow, 1992).

Documenting the frequency of indirect statements is a first step. In Becker's (1990) counts of mothers' statements to preschool children, indirect statements of what was wanted accounted for over 80% of the statements made to children. A second step lies in asking, When are ambiguous forms used and what consequences do they have? One possibility is that ambiguous forms are most often used at particular points of learning and are linked to the question, Whose job is it to understand? Becker and Goodnow (1992) suggest that mothers move into indirect modes only after a period of direct statements. It is only after they have said, "Say please," many times that they move into "What's the magic word?" What is being conveyed, Becker and Goodnow (1992) propose, is that it is now the child's task to translate the mother's message. Whether the child takes up that meaning is an open question.

A further possibility is that ambiguous statements are simply the norm. Explicit statements are then what need to be explained. They may be offered only when clear signs of misunderstanding occur (e.g., when transgressions occur that might be attributed to a child's not knowing what is expected, and when the child's behavior is perceived as likely to change if the rule or the principle is made explicit). Whatever their source, however, clear and explicit statements of what is expected are known to have one particular effect on the links between parents' values and children's values. To take an example from Cashmore and Goodnow (1985), children are far more accurate in estimating their parents' interest in the child being "neat" than in the child's being "curious" or "concerned for others." Children may not agree with their parents' position on the importance of neatness. When parents are explicit, however, children at least know what that position is, rather than happily taking over or rejecting a value that the parent does not in fact hold.

Multiplicity and Contest

One of the major moves within analyses of the nature of culture consists of the recognition that the term does not imply a single, neatly organized set of rules or values. I have already noted Strauss's (1992, p. 1) description of that change as being a shift from seeing cultures as "integrated, stable sets of meanings" to recognizing the presence of "conflict, contradiction, ambiguity, and change." Bruner (1986, p. 90) offers a further description of the change:

> It takes the form of a move away from the strict structuralism that held that culture was a set of interconnected rules from which people derive particular behaviors to fit particular situations, to the idea of culture as implicit and only semiconnected knowledge of the world from which, through negotiation, people arrive at satisfactory ways of acting in given contexts. The anthropologist Clifford Geertz likens the process of acting in a culture to that of interpreting an ambiguous text.

The ambiguity in this case, many would add, stems from the fact that cultures do not contain single positions, single principles. Instead, they contain many positions, with these often in some degree of tension or competition with one another. Examples are forms of religion and ways of speaking.

Most Western countries contain more than one religion, as well as the possibility of being unaffiliated. There is also usually some degree of tension or contest among several religions. One religion tends to prevail—to be the state religion, the religion of the majority, or the religion to which the elite belong. Moreover, one religion is usually presented to children as superior to others (a presentation sometimes accompanied by reasons but more often presented as a simple matter of fact). Religions are also often presented to people as an aspect of identity (e.g., "you are a Catholic"; "this family has always been Protestant"; "you will always be Jewish"; "how could you even consider becoming . . . ?"). What may then occur is not simple coexistence but the active derogation of one set of values by people who adhere to another, accompanied at times by active attempts at weakening or wiping out the alternatives.

The same double quality applies to ways of speaking. In most countries, there are both several ways of speaking and the attachment of greater or lesser value to each variant. Regional accents in most English-speaking countries, for example, may be seen as possessing a certain charm (in itself a judgment of differential value). Accents indicative of class, however, are seldom regarded in this light and are likely to meet with active attempts at replacement.

Do multiplicity and contest matter? One consequence proposed is an increase in the likelihood of change across generations. The presence of more than one position provides something to switch to when circumstances change: The alternative does not have to be constructed de novo (D'Andrade, 1992). Another is a possible increase in the likelihood that people will reflect on the values or beliefs that they hold. In Piagetian-style, they may be encouraged by diversity to ask how these different positions have arisen and how they might be reconciled. In Berger's (1977) terms, being "urbane" springs from being "urban": from being exposed to many variations in viewpoints and compelled to come to some kinds of terms with them. That type of effect, however, seems to be contingent on some particular circumstances. History makes it clear that groups may live side-by-side for considerable periods but still retain the conviction that the "others" have nothing of value to offer, nothing that warrants thought or inspection of one's own viewpoint. There perhaps needs to be first, as Habermas (1979) suggests, the sense of a common project, the completion of which is being impeded by a difference in viewpoints and a difficulty in communication. Only then do people work at understanding each other's words or values.

A third implication has stronger overtones of affect. When there are competing views, it is argued, what is likely to occur is the emergence of a particular emotional stance toward what is constructed as "the other." For example, Bakhtin analyzes people's attitudes toward the past, in terms of the ways that one literary text is related to previous texts. All new texts have a history: They are part of a series of past images, narratives, "voices." One of the critical questions to ask about any new text then takes the form: What is its relation to that past? Does it continue in the same genre in an unreflective or respectful fashion? Does it deliberately seek to make a break? Is the break made in a spirit of playful novelty, or is it accompanied by scorn, a deliberate parody of the past, or a deliberate violation of what is not supposed to be said—taking up topics that are not supposed to be written about, using settings that are not supposed to be proper places in which to work out a theme, using words that are not supposed to be uttered in print? On this kind of basis, Bakhtin singles out writers such as Rabelais as exemplifying a shift in texts that takes a changed stance toward the past and a changed use of the past, breaking its mold. Writers such as Joyce break even its sentence structure rather than simply modifying it (e.g., Bakhtin, 1965/1968).

Bakhtin's type of argument does not need to be confined to literary texts. The essence of the Chinese Cultural Revolution lay in its promotion of a deliberately disrespectful, scornful, and physically destructive stance toward the past in a culture that previously had advocated at least official veneration. "Never trust anyone over 30" advocates a much milder form of the same stance, but the message is similar. "The old" and "the new" are in contest with one another, and the strategy to adopt—for those interested in promoting the new—is to discount the old by encouraging a stance of suspicion toward it.

Occasions of Homogeneity

The proposals just considered all have to do with the presence of multiplicity and contest. What happens when there is little diversity in the values presented?

Within social-cultural perspectives, interest in that state of affairs takes two forms. One is interest in what happens when the same value or message comes in from several different sources. Watson-Gegeo (1992) uses the term "multilayered" to describe such situations. The example she provides is the experience of Kwara'ae children in the Solomon Islands. Parents, relatives, teachers, the irrelevance of the curriculum taken over from New Zealand schools: All combine to say "school has little to offer you." Under such circumstances, Watson-Gegeo points out, a value is highly likely to be accepted without reflection or opposition.

The second form of interest looks more at consensus within a group of one's peers, rather than at sources of different kinds. The studies by social psychologists Frijda and Mesquita (1994) are examples. These studies are more experimental than those to be found within most of anthropology: The extent of consensus may be deliberately varied. In style, however, the consequences are similar to those argued for by Watson-Gegeo (1992). When most of the others in one's group are seen to hold a common viewpoint, the chances are increased that the individual will assume that this is the only view possible and that others will hold the same view as oneself. Likely to increase also is the probability that an issue will come to have the features of what Mesquita and Frijda (1992, p. 184) label as "focal events." In their terms, some issues represent "socially defined and shared concerns" (p. 184). Most people in the group agree not only in the sense that they hold the same value but also in the sense that *they show the same kind and level of affect toward its being endorsed or ignored.* Under such circumstances, the individual is especially likely to organize perceptions and actions around this value, to monitor for situations in which the value might apply, and to be alert for occasions in which this value is respected by oneself or by others. In the language of social cognition, the value or the concern will become "highly available" or "accessible" (Mesquita & Frijda, 1992, p. 184).

Translations into Analyses of Parenting

What do these proposals from social-cultural perspectives suggest for the analysis of parenting and the transmission of values within the family? Among the possibilities are these, framed again in terms of possible research directions:

* *Look for the presence of competing messages among members of a family, or within one parent.* Australian parents, for example, hold two positions with regard to

money and children's household jobs. One is that "money and jobs should be quite separate." The other is that "if children are receiving money, they should do some work in return." For a small minority (about 10% of the sample), these two positions are incompatible. The seperateness of money means that it should never enter into any transactions about household jobs. For the majority, however, the two positions appear simply to coexist, possibly serving different functions or being aimed at different goals (Goodnow & Warton, 1992a; Warton & Goodnow, 1995).

• *Note the parent's position in relation to those of other parents in the social group.* Parents may be close to the norm of their group or on the margins; they may be close to the mode or be the outliers in any distribution. There is some evidence that a parent's position in relation to other parents makes a difference in the extent to which children are judged by others to be well adjusted (Deal, Halvorson, & Wampler, 1989). The closer parents are to the norm of the group, the better-adjusted the child is judged to be. That kind of data, however, is only a starting point. Now investigators need to know about (a) the extent to which children's perception of similarity deflects any questioning of the positions that their parents and other adults take, (b) the extent to which children are aware of where their parents stand in relation to other parents, and (c) the circumstances that lead children to regard their parents as different from others in pleasing or embarrassing ways. Data about these questions are in scarce supply.

• *Ask about the strategies parents use to cope with group values that differ from their own.* It is extremely unlikely that children will grow up in a world that contains only one set of values. Moreover, those "other values" may run counter to those that parents wish to see their children hold and have some attractiveness to their children. The alternatives may, for example, hold out the promise of an easier life or a more favorable reputation among one's peers. They may also present to children an image of themselves and of the family that is not the image that parents are promoting. Few parents wish their children to be told, for example, that they and their families are weird, unimportant, or "going nowhere." The struggle for parents is then not simply with a child's frailties or susceptibilities, but with these qualities in relation to a world that may support or undermine a parent's efforts to establish particular values.

How do parents respond to such risks? Two possible strategies may be distinguished: "cocooning" and "prearming." In the former, parents keep children at a distance from "bad" influences for as long as possible. They shield their children when they can, hoping that by the time encounters with negative others occur, the family's own values or the child's self-esteem will be so well established that little undermining will occur. Slights, putdowns, or the lure of another way of life will have little effect. In the latter strategy, parents may teach their children specific defensive tactics ("stand up for yourself," "ignore what they say, keep your dignity," "give as good as you get," etc.). They may also encourage children to regard the offending others as of no great account ("they're just ignorant [jealous, rednecks, honkies, thoughtless, badly brought up]" etc.). The circumstances that prompt particular parental tactics seem unclear. One report, however, suggests that parents' actions are influenced by their judgments about the likelihood of negative encounters. African American parents who live in mixed neighborhoods are more likely to raise the topic of racial differences with their children than are parents who live in neighborhoods that are less mixed (Thornton, Chatters, Taylor, & Allen, 1990).

Differential Importance, Leeway, and Negotiability

This is the third and last feature to encountered conditions that is emphasized by social-cultural perspectives. (The previous two have been the presence of values expressed in a variety of ways, with ambiguity a possible feature of every mode, and the presence of multiplicity and contest among sets of values). Again, proposals that are in general relevant for analyzing the emergence of values will be discussed first, and then suggestions will be offered for translating these proposals into within-family research.

Social-cultural perspectives contain several reminders that indications of what is expected or valued come with signs of relative importance. This suggestion is made especially clear by D'Andrade (1984). Most analyses of cognitive performance, he points out, proceed as if all problems were of equal importance. That might be true in the laboratory. In everyday life, however, some skills are more highly valued than others. To be regarded as a competent or acceptable member of a unit, some particular skills will be essential to acquire, whereas others will be labeled trivial. Part of becoming a competent or acceptable member of a unit, then, consists of developing the essential qualities, and letting the others be treated as options, as areas of "acceptable ignorance" or "acceptable incompetence"(Goodnow, 1996a).

The concept of moratoria (e.g., Erikson, 1959) also points to the presence of leeway, this time in the form of leeway with regard to time. At various points in our lives, Erikson proposes, we are allowed time to explore alternative values or to delay taking up expected positions. Adolescence, periods after a war or other traumas, times just before the last transition to "settling down": The specific time periods and the specific grounds for tolerating delay may vary from one social group to another. What is negotiable then is not the ultimate adoption of particular values but the time frame within which that adoption will take place.

A third proposal comes from an analysis of modernity by the sociologist Peter Berger (1977). In what particular areas, and under what particular circumstances, Berger asked, are people encouraged to make their own decisions, to "do their own thing"? For adults, he proposed, an emphasis on doing one's own thing increases at times when the possibilities for personal choice are in fact diminishing. Moreover, the areas where creative decision making is encouraged are in fact limited to areas (e.g., home decorating, personal adornment) where doing one's own thing is not likely to interfere with the functioning of modern society. In effect, the illusion of choice is maintained but not its reality.

These proposals may seem remote from parenting. Specifically concerned with parenting, however, is a proposal from a sociologist (Rodman, 1963), whose initial interest was in locating the sources of differences in achievement by children from various socio-economic groups. Rodman's proposal is summarized by the term "value-stretch." Parents may start out with the hope that their children will enter a profession with high social status such as law or medicine. As time goes on, that value may stretch to cover "any decent job," "finishing high school," or "just staying out of trouble." Stretch, Rodman proposed, is a feature of all parental values. Where parents differ, however, is in the degrees of stretch they can tolerate and in the content areas where stretch is more likely to occur. In the area of schooling, Rodman described middle-class parents as moving more quickly to corrective action (their values exhibited less stretch) than did parents in a less advantaged group. The content areas where parents in the latter group display the lesser degree of stretch are not brought out in Rodman's study, but it is easy to imagine that they exist. Differences in stretch seem likely to be content-specific rather than general, and the challenge now is to determine the areas and the circumstances under which they occur.

Extensions to the Analysis of Parenting and Children's Values

How can proposals of this kind be applied to analyses of parenting in relation to the emergence of values? Research on parenting, these proposals suggest, might well:

- *Check for areas and occasions of leeway.* Valsiner (1984) describes parents' interactions with toddlers as organized around actions that are encouraged, actions that are discouraged, and actions that are tolerated. The band of tolerance in his study appeared related to the extent to which a mother's primary goal had already been reached. For example, once a young child had taken in a fair degree of food from the mother's being in control of the spoon, the child's insistence on self-feeding could be more readily tolerated than at the start of a meal. Nucci (e.g., 1995) and Smetana (e.g., 1988, 1995) report a similar phenomenon for a later age range. In Anglo societies, they note, children are often encouraged to make their own decisions in some areas. These areas of personal decision, it is proposed, are those in which the child's making the decision neither breaks a moral rule nor constitutes a threat to the parent's possession or appearance of authority. In Berger's (1977) language, the sense of choice and control, and the value of having a choice, are fostered, but limits to choice are also present.

   Nucci's (1995) results suggest that choice needs to be considered as often containing an implicit time limit. American parents may start by saying that a decision is "up to" the child. They begin to structure the decision for the child, however, if no decision is made within a period of time that the parent sees as sufficient. After this time has elapsed, the child's choice—what to wear, for example—is made less open, with mothers proposing specific alternatives and promoting specific choices. The interesting research phenomena then become the ocasions when negotiation concentrates not on whether something will be done but on when this might occur. At the moment, little is known about the situations that especially invite negotiations over "when" or about the nature of those negotiations. In some negotiations about work, for example, the preferred strategy seems to be an initial proposal that the work can be indefinitely deferred: The room is clean enough, the grass is not that high, and so forth. Many preschoolers are aware that "later" is more acceptable than "no" (Leonard, 1993). And adolescents regard as objectionable requests or directives that do not respect their right to get around to tasks "in their own good time"(Goodnow & Warton, 1992b).

- *Ask whether areas of negotiability are defined differentially by parents and children.* This is the essence of Smetana's interest in whether adolescents and parents agree on areas of personal decision making where the adolescent may set the rules (e.g., Smetana, 1988, 1995). Areas that involve potential harm to others attract no disagreement. The disagreements begin with items that might be classed as "legitimately areas of parental authority" or as "areas of personal decision making" (e.g., use of the phone, modes of dress, hours of sleep over the weekend, visits to relatives with the family). In these "grey" areas, the two generations differ, with adolescents—not unexpectedly—seeing the grey areas as more a matter for them to decide.

- *Look for signals of negotiability, used by either parents or children.* At the moment, the only data appear to deal with parents' signals of varying degrees of negotiability. American parents use phrases such as "that's up to you" or "you choose." Australian mothers use the phrase "not on" to mark a position as not negotiable (Goodnow & Warton, 1991). Whether a parent will pay a child for a job may be negotiable. Whether a child may pay a sibling to do the original child's job, however, is not negotiable. That is "not on." (The North American equivalent may be "no way.") At this point, it is not clear how children or adolescents indicate that their rejection of a parent's decision is nonnegotiable, but parents undoubtedly learn to recognize the signals used.

- *Ask about connections among values.* Australian mothers—when their children object that "this isn't all my stuff"—are much given to saying "Yes, you have a point, but" (Bowes, 1994). In effect, they simultaneously endorse one value ("it is reasonable to object to putting away stuff that you have not used") *and* give that value a subordinate position in relation to another (e.g., the mother's need or the family's need for the table to be cleared, or the mother's authority) (Bowes, 1994). The phenomena of most interest then become the ways in which children learn that values form hierarchies and come to understand the circumstances under which one principle or value may be set aside in favor of another.

Links among valued positions are also indicated by some of Smetana's (1988) results. Smetana reports that a difference in vewpoints between parents and adolescents is less likely to escalate into a conflict when the adolescent presents objections that follow a sophisticated, adult-style argument. It is as if, when the children meet one of their parents' goals (present a good case), it diminishes the sting of their not meeting another (do what I wish you to do, or become what I wish you to be). There appear to be little data available on the ways in which parents may substitute a child's acceptance of one parental value for the nonacceptance of another, or on the ways in which children perceive the possibilities of trade-offs. Research in those directions, however, is feasible. It would also be a step forward in the analysis both of the degree of flexibility that may accompany parents' values and of the ways in which children understand that flexibility.

CONCLUSION

This chapter began with a double aim. One was to outline what social-cultural perspectives offer regarding the emergence of values. The other was to indicate in relatively specific fashion how proposals from these perspectives—often developed to account for the nature and consequences of various links between individuals and society, or to demonstrate the importance of contexts other than the family—may be translated into research on within-family interactions and their consequences for the values that children develop.

That double aim has called for taking several steps: providing a background picture of social-cultural perspectives, asking about the content areas that are likely to be prime sites for studying the emergence of values, considering some of the main meanings given to internalization, and—as a way of specifying what "transmission" or parental actions may involve—exploring proposals about signs of leeway or negotiability, the presence of multiplicity and contest among values, and the ways in which values may be expressed ranging from the use of proverbs or stories to the everyday routine practices of a household.

These several steps, it is hoped, will have established order within the current confusing array of social-cultural perspectives available to developmental psychologists. The same steps, it is also hoped, will have made it clear that social-cultural perspectives do not present some arcane field that is irrelevant to those who wish, for conceptual or practical reasons, to concentrate on within-family analyses. On the contrary, here is a body of theory and research that both overlaps with and extends within-family analyses, offering not the criticisms of their concepts and research procedures that developmentalists might expect to find but instead opportunities for profit.

REFERENCES

Bakhtin, M. (1968). *Rabelais and his world* (Helene Iswolsky, Trans.) Cambridge, MA: MIT Press. (Original work published 1965)

Becker, J. (1988). The strength of parents' indirect techniques for teaching preschoolers' pragmatic skills. *First Language, 8,* 173–182.

Becker, J., & Goodnow, J. J. (1992). "What's the magic word?" "Were you born in a tent?" The challenge of accounting for parents' use of indirect speech with children. *Newsletter of Laboratory for Comparative Human Cognition, 50,* 517–522.

Berger, P. L. (1977). *Facing up to modernity: Excursions in society, politics and religion.* New York: Basic Books.

Berry, J. W. (1976). *Human ecology and cognitive style: Comparative studies in cultural and psychological adaptation.* New York: Wiley.

Block, J. (1972). Generational continuity and discontinuity in the understanding of societal rejection. *Journal of Personality and Social Psychology, 22,* 333–345.

Blurton-Jones, N. (1993). The lives of hunter-gatherer children: Effects of parental behavior and parental reproductive strategy. In M. E. Pereira & L. A. Fairbanks (Eds.), *Juvenile primates: Life history, development, and behavior* (pp. 309–326). New York: Oxford University Press.

Bourdieu, P. (1977). *Outline of a theory of practice.* Cambridge, England: Cambridge University Press.

Bourdieu, P. (1979). *Distinction: A social critique of the judgment of taste.* London: Routledge & Kegan Paul.

Bourdieu, P. (1990). *A logic of practice.* Stanford, CA: Stanford University Press.

Bowes, J. M. (1994, June). *Mother-child negotiations about household tasks: Perceived legitimacy of request justifications.* Paper presented at the workshop of the International Society for the Study of Behavioral Development, Beijing.

Bowlby, J. (1969). *Attachment and loss: Vol. 1. Attachment.* New York: Basic Books.

Briggs, J. (1992). Mazes of meaning: How a child and a culture create each other. In W. A. Corsaro & P. J. Miller (Eds.), *Interpretive approaches to children's socialization* (pp. 25–50). San Francisco: Jossey-Bass.

Bronfenbrenner, U. (1958). Socialization and class through time and space. In E. E. Maccoby & L. Petrullo (Eds.), *Readings in social psychology* (3rd ed., pp. 400–424). New York: Holt.

Bronfenbrenner, U. (1970). Reaction to social pressure from adults versus peers among Soviet day school and boarding school pupils in the perspective of an American sample. *Journal of Personality and Social Psychology, 15,* 179–189.

Bronfenbrenner, U. (1979). *The ecology of human development.* Cambridge, MA: Harvard University Press.

Bronfenbrenner, U. (1993). The ecology of cognitive development: Research models and fugitive findings. In R. H. Wozniak & K. Fischer (Eds.), *Development in context* (pp. 3–44). Hillsdale, NJ: Erlbaum.

Bronfenbrenner, U. (1996). Developmental ecology through space and time: A future perspective. In P. Moen, G. H. Elder, Jr., & K. Luscher (Eds.), *Examining lives in context* (pp. 619–648). Washington, DC: American Psychological Association.

Bruner, J. S. (1986). *Actual minds, possible worlds.* Cambridge, MA: Harvard University Press.

Bugental, D. B., & Goodnow, J. J. (in press). Socialization processes. In W. Damon (Ed.), *Handbook of child psychology* (5th ed.). New York: Wiley.

Cashmore, J., & Goodnow, J. J. (1985). Agreement between generations: A two-process model. *Child Development, 56,* 493–501.

Cazden, C. (1993). Vygotsky, Hymes and Bakhtin: From word to utterance and voice. In E. Forman, N. Minick, & C. A. Stone (Eds.), *Contexts for learning* (pp. 197–212). New York: Oxford University Press.

Chaiklin, S., & Lave, J. (Eds.). (1993). *Understanding practice.* Cambridge, England: Cambridge University Press.

Cole, M. (1985). The zone of proximal development: Where culture and cognition create each other. In J. V. Wertsch (Ed.), *Culture, communication, and cognition* (pp. 146–161). Cambridge, England: Cambridge University Press.

Cole, M. (1988). Cross-cultural research in the socio-historical tradition. *Human Development, 31,* 137–152.

Cole, M. (1990). Cultural psychology: A once and future discipline? In J. Berman (Ed.), *Nebraska Symposium on Motivation* (Vol. 37, pp. 279–336). Lincoln: University of Nebraska Press.

Cole, M. (1995). The supra-individual envelope of development: Activity and practice, situation and context. In J. J. Goodnow, P. J. Miller, & F. Kessel (Eds.), *Cultural practices as contexts for development* (pp. 105–118). San Francisco: Jossey-Bass.

Collins, W. A., & Luebker, C. (1995). Parent and adolescent expectancies: Individual and relational significance. In J. Smetana (Ed.), *Beliefs about parenting: Origins and developmental implications* (pp. 65–80). San Francisco: Jossey-Bass.

D'Andrade, R. G. (1984). Cultural meaning systems. In R. A. Shweder & R. A. LeVine (Eds.), *Culture theory: Essays on mind, self, and emotion* (pp. 88–119). Cambridge, England: Cambridge University Press.

D'Andrade, R. G. (1992). Schemas and motivations. In R. G. D'Andrade & C. Strauss (Eds.), *Human motives and cultural models* (pp. 23–44). Cambridge, England: Cambridge University Press.

D'Andrade, R. G., & Strauss, C. (Eds.). (1992). *Human motives and cultural models.* Cambridge, England: Cambridge University Press.

Deal, J. E., Halvorson, C. F., & Wampler, K. S. (1989). Parental agreement on child-rearing orientations: Relations to parental, marital, family, and child characteristics. *Child Development, 60,* 1025–1034.

Dumont, R. V. (1972). Learning English and how to be silent: Studies in Sioux and Cherokee classrooms. In C. B. Cazden, V. P. John, & D. Hymes (Eds.), *Functions of language in the classroom* (pp. 344–369). New York: Teachers' College Press.

Dunn, J. (1988). *The beginnings of social understanding.* Cambridge, MA: Harvard University Press.

Dunn, J., & Brown, J. (1991). Becoming American or English? Talking about the social world in England and the United States. In M. Bornstein (Ed.), *Cultural approaches to parenting* (pp. 155–172). Hillsdale, NJ: Erlbaum.

Duveen, G., & Lloyd, B. (1990). *Social representations and the development of knowledge.* Cambridge, England: Cambridge University Press.

Eccles, J., & Jacobs, J. E. (1986). Social forces shape math attitudes and performance. *Signs: Journal of Women in Culture and Society, 11,* 367–380.

Engestrom, Y. (1993). Developmental studies of work as a testbench of activity theory: The case of primary care medical practice. In S. Chaiklin & J. Lave (Eds.), *Understanding practice.* New York: Cambridge University Press.

Erikson, E. (1959). *Identity and the life cycle.* New York: Norton.

Frijda, N. H., & Mesquita, B. (1994). The social roles and functions of emotions. In S. Kitayama & H. R. Markus (Eds.), *Emotion and culture* (pp. 51–88). Washington, DC: American Psychological Association.

Goodnow, J. J. (1990). The socialization of cognition: What's involved? In J. Stigler, R. A. Shweder, & G. Herdt (Eds.), *Cultural psychology: Essays on comparative human development* (pp. 259–286). Cambridge, England: Cambridge University Press.

Goodnow, J. J. (1992). Parents' ideas, children's ideas: The bases of congruence and divergence. In I. E. Sigel, A. V. McGillicuddy-DeLisi, & J. J. Goodnow (Eds.), *Parental belief systems* (2nd ed., pp. 293–318). Hillsdale, NJ: Erlbaum.

Goodnow, J. J. (1994). Acceptable disagreement across generations. In J. Smetana (Ed.), *Beliefs about parenting: Origins and developmental implications* (pp. 51–64). San Francisco: Jossey-Bass.

Goodnow, J. J. (1996a). Acceptable ignorance, negotiable disagreement: Alternative views of learning. In D. R. Olson & N. Torrance (Eds.), *Handbook of education and human development* (pp. 345–368). Oxford, England: Blackwell.

Goodnow, J. J. (1996b). From household practices to parents' ideas about work and interpersonal relationships. In S. Harkness & C. Super (Eds.), *Parents' cultural belief systems* (pp. 313–344). New York: Guilford Press.

Goodnow, J. J., Miller, P. J., & Kessel, F. (Eds.). (1995). *Cultural practices as contexts for development.* San Francisco: Jossey-Bass.

Goodnow, J. J., & Warton, P. (1991). The social basis of social cognition: Interactions about work and lessons about relationships. *Merrill-Palmer Quarterly, 37,* 27–58.

Goodnow, J. J., & Warton, P. M. (1992a). Contexts and cognitions: Taking a pluralist view. In P. Light & G. Butterworth (Eds.), *Context and cognition* (pp. 85–112). Oxford, England: Oxford University Press.

Goodnow, J. J., & Warton, P. M. (1992b). Understanding responsibility: Adolescents' concepts of delegation and follow-through within the family. *Social Development, 1,* 89–106.

Goodwin, T. (1976). *East is a big wind: Navigation and logic on Pulawat atoll.* Cambridge, MA: Harvard University Press.

Grusec, J. E., & Goodnow, J. J. (1994). The impact of parental discipline methods on the child's internalization of values: A reconceptualization of current points of view. *Developmental Psychology, 30,* 4–19.

Habermas, J. (1979). *Communication and the evolution of society.* London: Heinemann.

Heath, S. B. (1983). *Ways with words: Language, life and work in communities and classrooms.* Cambridge, England: Cambridge University Press.

Higgins, E. T., Ruble, D., & Hartup, W. (Eds.). (1983). *Social cognition and social development.* New York: Cambridge University Press.

Hoffman, M. L. (1983). Affective and cognitive processes in moral internalization. In E. T. Higgins, D. Ruble, & W. Hartup (Eds.), *Social cognition and social development* (pp. 263–274). New York: Cambridge University Press.

Holland, D., & Quinn, N. (Eds.). (1987). *Cultural models in language and thought.* Cambridge, England: Cambridge University Press.

Irvine, J. (1978). Wolof "magical thinking": Culture and conservation revisited. *Journal of Cross-Cultural Psychology, 9,* 300–311.

Kohn, M. L. (1969). *Class and conformity: A study in values.* Homewood, IL: Dorsey Press.

Kohn, M. L. (1996). Social structure and personality through time and space. In P. Moen, H. H. Elder, Jr., & K. Luscher (Eds.), *Examining lives in context* (pp. 141–168). New York: Guilford Press.

Kohn, M. L., & Schooler, C. (1982). Job conditions and personality: A longitudinal study of their reciprocal effects. *American Journal of Sociology, 87,* 1257–1286.

Kuczynski, L., & Kochanska, G. (1990). Development of children's noncompliance strategies from toddlerhood to age 5. *Developmental Psychology, 26,* 398–408.

Kulick, D. (1992). *Language shift and cultural reproduction: Socialization, self and syncretism in a Papua New Guinea village.* New York: Cambridge University Press.

Laboratory of Comparative Human Cognition. (1983). Culture and cognitive development. In W. Kessen (Ed.), *Handbook of child psychology* (4th ed.) (Vol. 1, pp. 295–356). New York: Wiley.

Lave, J. (1988). *Cognition in practice.* New York: Cambridge University Press.

Lave, J. (1991). Situating learning in communities of practice. In L. S. Resnick, J. M. Levine, & S. D. Teasley (Eds.), *Perspectives on socially shared cognition* (pp. 63–84). Washington, DC: American Psychological Association.

Lave, J. (1993). The practice of learning: In S. Chaiklin & J. Lave (Eds.), *Understanding practice: Perspectives on activity and context.* New York: Cambridge University Press.

Lave, J., & Wenger, E. (1991). *Situated learning: Legitimate peripheral participation.* New York: Cambridge University Press.

Lawrence, J., & Valsiner, J. (1993). Conceptual roots of internalization: From transmission to transformation. *Human Development, 36,* 150–168.

Leonard, R. (1993). Mother-child disputes as arenas for fostering negotiation skills. *Early Development and Parenting, 2,* 157–167.

Levine, J. M., & Moreland, R. L. (1991). Culture and socialization in work groups. In L. B. Resnick, J. M. Levine, & S. D. Teasley (Eds.), *Perspectives on socially shared cognition* (pp. 257–182). Washington, DC: American Psychological Association.

LeVine, R. A. (1990). Infant environments in psychoanalysis: A cross-cultural view. In J. Stigler, R. A. Shweder, & G. Herdt (Eds.), *Cultural psychology: Essays on comparative human development* (pp. 454–476). New York: Cambridge University Press.

LeVine, R. A., Dixon, S., LeVine, S., Richman, A., Leiderman, P. H., Keefer, C. H., & Brazelton, T. B. (1994). *Child care and culture: Lessons from Africa.* Cambridge, England: Cambridge University Press.

Lynch, K. (1960). *The image of the city.* Cambridge, MA: MIT Press.

Mesquita, B., & Frijda, N. F. (1992). Cultural variations in emotions: A review. *Psychological Bulletin, 112,* 179–204.

Michaels, S. (1991). The dismantling of narrative. In A. McCabe & C. Petersen (Eds.), *Developing narrative structure* (pp. 303–354). Hillsdale, NJ: Erlbaum.

Miller, B. D. (1995). Precepts and practices: Researching identity formation among Indian Hindu adolescents in the United States. In J. J. Goodnow, P. J. Miller, & F. Kessel (Eds.), *Cultural practices as contexts for development* (pp. 71–86). San Francisco: Jossey-Bass.

Miller, P. J., & Goodnow, J. J. (1995). Cultural practices: Towards an integration of culture and development. In J. J. Goodnow, P. J. Miller, & F. Kessel (Eds.), *Cultural practices as contexts for development* (pp. 5–16). San Francisco: Jossey-Bass.

Miller, P. J., Potts, R., Fung, H., Hoogstra, L., & Mintz, J. (1990). Narrative practices and the construction of self in childhood. *American Ethnologist, 17,* 292–311.

Miller, P. J., & Sperry, L. L. (1988). Early talk about the past: The origins of conversational stories of personal experience. *Journal of Child Language, 15,* 293–315.

Moscovici, S. (1981). On social representations. In J. P. Forgas (Ed.), *Social cognition: Perspectives on everyday understanding* (pp. 181–210). London: Academic Press.

Mugny, G., & Carugati, F. (1989). *Social representations of intelligence.* Cambridge, England: Cambridge University Press.

Nagashima, N. (1973). A reversed world, or is it? In R. Horton & R. Faber (Eds.), *Modes of thinking in Western and non-Western societies.* London: Faber & Faber.

Nucci, L. (1995). Mothers' beliefs regarding the personal domain of children. In J. Smetana (Ed.), *Beliefs about parenting: Origins and developmental implications* (pp. 81–98). San Francisco: Jossey-Bass.

Nucci, L., & Weber, E. K. (1995). Social interactions in the home and the development of young children's conceptions of the personal. *Child Development, 66,* 1438–1452.

Nunes, T. (1995). Cultural practices and the conception of individual differences. In J. J. Goodnow, P. J. Miller, & F. Kessel (Eds.), *Cultural practices as contexts for development* (pp. 91–104). San Francisco: Jossey-Bass.

Ortner, S. (1985). Theory in anthropology since the Sixties. *Society for Comparative Study of Society and History, 26,* 126–166.

Reid, B. V., & Valsiner, J. (1986). Consistency, praise, and love: Folk theories of American parents. *Ethos, 14,* 1–15.

Rodman, H. (1963). The lower-class value stretch. *Social Forces, 42,* 205–215.

Rogoff, B. (1990). *Apprenticeship in thinking.* Oxford, England: Oxford University Press.

Romney, A. K., Weller, S. C., & Batchelder, W. H. (1986). Culture as consensus: A theory of culture and informant accuracy. *American Anthropologist, 88,* 313–332.

Rosaldo, M. (1984). Toward an anthropology of self and feeling. In R. Shweder & R. LeVine (Eds.), *Culture theory: Essays on mind, self, and emotion* (pp. 137–157). Cambridge, England: Cambridge University Press.

Scribner, S. (1984). Studying working intelligence. In B. Rogoff & J. Lave (Eds.), *Everyday cognition: Its development in social context* (pp. 9–40). Cambridge, MA: Harvard University Press.

Shweder, R. A. (1990). Cultural psychology: What is it? In J. Stigler, R. A. Shweder, & G. Herdt (Eds.), *Cultural psychology: Essays on comparative human development* (pp. 1–43). Cambridge, England: Cambridge University Press.

Shweder, R. A., Arnett Jensen, L., & Goldstein, W. M. (1995). Who sleeps by whom revisited: A method for extracting the moral goods implicit in practice. In J. J. Goodnow, P. J. Miller, & F. Kessel (Eds.), *Cultural practices as contexts for development* (pp. 21–40). San Francisco: Jossey-Bass.

Shweder, R. A., Goodnow, J. J., Hatano, G., LeVine, R. A., Miller, P. J., & Markus, H. R. (in press). The cultural psychology of development. In W. Damon (Ed.), *Handbook of child psychology* (5th ed.). New York: Wiley.

Shweder, R. A., & Much, N. C. (1986). Determinations of meaning: Discourse and moral socialization. In W. Kurtines & J. Gewirtz (Eds.), *Moral development through social interaction.* New York: Wiley.

Sloutsky, V. (1995, March). *Family congruence in a rapidly changing society as a measure of cultural continuity.* Paper presented at the biennial meeting of the Society for Research in Child Development, Indianapolis, IN.

Smetana, J. G. (1989). Adolescents' and parents' conceptions of parental authority. *Child Development, 59,* 321–335.

Smetana, J. G. (1994). Parenting styles and beliefs about parental authority. In J. G. Smetana (Ed.), *Beliefs about parenting: Origins and developmental implications* (pp. 21–36). San Francisco: Jossey-Bass.

Steinberg, L., Darling, N. E., & Fletcher, A. C. (1996). Authoritative parenting and adolescent adjustment: An ecological journey. In P. Moen, G. H. Elder, Jr., & K. Luscher (Eds.), *Examining lives in context* (pp. 423–466). New York: Guilford Press.

Stevenson, H., & Lee, S. Y. (1990). Contexts of achievement. *Monographs of the Society for Research in Child Development, 55*(1/2, Serial No. 221).

Strauss, C. (1992). Models and motives. In R. G. D'Andrade & C. Strauss (Eds.), *Human motives and cultural models* (pp. 1–20). New York: Cambridge University Press.

Super, C. M. (1981). Behavioral development in infancy. In R. H. Munroe, R. L. Munroe, & B. B. Whiting (Eds.), *Handbook of cross-cultural human development* (pp. 181–270). New York: Garland.

Tajfel, J. (1981). *Human groups and social categories: Studies in social psychology.* Cambridge, England: Cambridge University Press.

Thornton, M. C., Chatters, L. M., Taylor, R. J., & Allen, W. R. (1990). Sociodemographic and environmental correlates of racial socialization by Black parents. *Child Development, 61,* 401–409.

Valsiner, J. (1984). Construction of the zone proximal development in adult-child joint action: The socialization of meals. In B. Rogoff & J. Wertsch (Eds.), *Children's learning in the zone of proximal development* (pp. 65–76). San Francisco: Jossey-Bass.

Valsiner, J. (1988). Ontogeny of co-construction of culture within socially organized environmental settings. In J. Valsiner (Ed.), *Child development within culturally structured environments* (Vol. 2, pp. 283–297). Norwood, NJ: ABLEX.

Warton, P. M., & Goodnow, J. J. (1995). For love or money: Parents' views of money in relation to children's household jobs. *International Journal of Behavioral Development, 8,* 235–350.

Watson-Gegeo, K. A. (1992). Thick explanation in the ethnographic study of child socialization: A longitudinal study of the problem of schooling for Kwara'ae (Solomon Islands) children. In W. A. Corsaro & P. J. Miller (Eds.), *Interpretive approaches to children's socialization* (pp. 51–66). San Francisco: Jossey-Bass.

Wentworth, W. M. (1980). *Context and understanding: An inquiry into socialization theory.* New York: Elsevier.

Wertsch, J. (1991). *Voices of the mind.* Cambridge, England: Cambridge University Press.

West, C., & Zimmerman, D. H. (1987). Doing gender. *Gender and Society, 1,* 125–151.

Whiting, B. B., & Edwards, C. P. (1988). *Children of different worlds: The formation of social behavior.* Cambridge, MA: Harvard University Press.

Whiting, B. B., & Whiting, J. W. M. (1975). *Children of six cultures.* Cambridge, MA: Harvard University Press.

Whiting, J. W. M. (1941). *Becoming a Kwoma.* New Haven, CT: Yale University Press.

Whiting, J. W. M., & Child, I. L. (1953). *Child training and personality: A cross-cultural study.* New Haven, CT: Yale University Press.

CHAPTER 14

The Coherence of Individual Development: An Evolutionary Perspective on Children's Internalization of Parental Values

KEVIN MACDONALD

The thesis of this chapter is that evolutionary theory can make a major contribution to conceptualizing children's internalization of values; the subject matter is broadly divided into four sections. The first section develops an evolutionary framework in which internalization is a facet of high-investment parenting and is expected to covary with a number of other life history variables, including age of puberty, developmental plasticity, and intelligence. This section stresses the tendency for intercorrelations among a large number of variables related to internalization and other aspects of parental investment—what I term the coherence of development.

The second section discusses adolescent sexual behavior as an example of developmental coherence, stressing its interrelationships with other variables associated with internalization and parental investment. I argue that external cultural supports for adaptive behavior are of less importance for high-investment families than for families that are, for genetic and/or environmental reasons, less inclined toward high-investment parenting. This is because relatively low-investment parents are less able to rely on an internalized motivational system to keep children's behavior "on an adaptive track." Children from relatively low-investment families are less likely to accept cultural choices valued by adults. As a result, external cultural supports for culturally adaptive behavior are of critical importance for children and families toward the low-investment end of the parental investment distribution.

The third section contrasts two theoretical approaches to life history theory. One approach suggests that variation in parental investment patterns and internalization results from "alternate strategies" in which different levels of parental investment are evolved responses to variation in resource availability. The other approach suggests that variation in life history strategies is influenced primarily by genetic variation in viable reproductive strategies. I argue on theoretical and empirical grounds that the latter interpretation provides the most parsimonious fit with the available evidence.

Finally, the fourth section discusses some specific mechanisms related to internalization. Internalization is here conceptualized as resulting from a generalized motivational system that makes children receptive to parental influence independent of specific content. Following a brief discussion of temperament influences, attention is focused on warmth as a central motivational component of the internalization of parental values. Warmth is viewed here as an evolved reward system that motivates family members to

362

bond together by making close relationships pleasurable to their participants. Parent-child warmth therefore channels children's social learning because children are motivated to attend to adult values and seek parental approval.

At the outset, however, it is useful to provide a few definitions and general ideas. Evolutionists accept as a fundamental postulate that the process of natural selection over the course of evolutionary time has shaped every aspect of the human mind. Humans, like other species, evolved a set of adaptations that functioned to solve particular problems occurring in the environment of evolutionary adaptedness (EEA). (The EEA is the environment in which humans evolved. The EEA presented the set of problems whose solutions constitute the set of human adaptations.) Thus, for example, Bowlby (1974) proposed that a recurrent problem of our evolutionary past was that human infants were helpless in the face of danger from predators. This problem was solved by the evolution of the human attachment system as a mechanism that reliably results in infants staying close to their mothers.

The general principle that natural selection sculpted the human mind, by itself, explains little about the structure of the human mind and even less about development. Basic evolutionary logic, however, requires that at least some evolved systems be domain-specific (Cosmides & Tooby, 1987). Domain-specific mechanisms have two important characteristics: They evolved to solve a specific recurrent problem in the human EEA; and the mechanisms are content-specific in that they take in only a delimited set of stimuli and, via a decision rule, produce only a limited set of outcomes that solve a highly discrete adaptive problem (Buss, 1995). Domain-specific psychological adaptations evolved in specific environments and responded to the recurrent properties of that environment. For example, Bowlby (1973, 1974) proposed that infants have natural likes and dislikes, such as a natural liking for contact comfort and a natural dislike for being in strange situations in the absence of an attachment figure. These natural likes and dislikes are adaptive responses to recurrent features of the EEA.

Within this perspective, then, domain-specific mechanisms are construed as species-typical universals that evolved to solve recurrent adaptive problems posed by recurrent features of the environment. However, there is every reason to suppose that domain-general mechanisms are also an important feature of human adaptation. Domain-general mechanisms did not evolve to solve a specific recurrent problem in the human EEA, but rather can be utilized to solve a wide range of nonrecurrent problems. Moreover, domain-general devices are able to take in a wide range of stimuli and produce a wide range of responses to solve these nonrecurrent problems.

An important example of a domain-general mechanism central to research on children's internalization of values is social learning. From an adaptationist perspective, social learning is an important adaptation because it facilitates the attainment of evolutionary goals (e.g., acquiring economic resources, obtaining mates) by allowing individuals to profit from others' experience and knowledge. These evolutionary goals may themselves involve domain-specific mechanisms such as evolved mechanisms underlying sexual attraction or status seeking. However, the nature of these domain-general mechanisms is to be able to attain evolutionary goals in a very flexible manner. For example, parents who learn the proper use of a tool useful in farming can transmit this information to children, thereby saving the children a prolonged process of discovery and trial-and-error learning, and ultimately facilitating the evolutionary goal of obtaining food. Learning mechanisms are thus able to solve nonrecurrent problems presented by an ever-changing and incredibly complex human environment. Within this perspective, social learning evolved because it permitted organisms to adapt successfully to relatively variable, non-recurrent, and unpredictable aspects of the environment (Boyd & Richerson, 1985; Pulliam & Dunford, 1980).

Boyd and Richerson (1985, 1988) show that in general social learning is evolutionarily favored where the problems to be solved are not recurrent features of the EEA and where there are high costs to individual learning. By observing the consequences experienced by others, social learners can avoid the costs of individual trial-and-error learning. In the case of humans, social learning is therefore likely to be most important for issues with high potential costs for children. Such issues include career choices, religious affiliation, and behaviors, such as sexual behavior, driving habits, or drug use, that are dangerous or could prevent the attainment of long-term goals favored by parents. In the following sections, I will argue that parent-child warmth functions to channel children's social learning within the family. Moreover, it does so in a manner that leads children to make cultural choices about potentially costly behavior that are more in line with adult values. Although this chapter concentrates on the influence of warmth on social learning, an evolutionary perspective on social learning is also compatible with supposing that evolution has shaped children's preferences for other features of models such as dominance, high social status, and similarity (MacDonald, 1988).

INTERNALIZATION AND THE COHERENCE OF INDIVIDUAL DEVELOPMENT

Traditional developmental research as well as some evolutionary perspectives (e.g., Tooby & Cosmides, 1992) tend to compartmentalize humans into discrete domain-specific and/or domain-general systems. Within this perspective, discrete systems have different functions, and there would be no reason to suppose a general coordination among developmental systems. This is because there is no overarching goal of development—no overarching problem that required a coherent developmental response. Instead, there is a large set of unrelated problems that pulled for a set of specialized, unrelated systems.

This does not appear to be the whole story, however, and in the following I will argue that there is also evidence for a substantial coherence of individual development that can ultimately be linked with life history theory. Life history theory attempts to understand variation in the reproductive strategies adopted by different life forms. Life history theory implies developmental coherence because a reproductive strategy involves a coordinated response to the organism's environment resulting from the need to optimally partition mating and parenting effort. The fundamental dimension of reproductive strategies may be construed as ranging from a high-parental-investment/low-mating-effort strategy to a low-parental-investment/high-mating-effort strategy (e.g., Wilson, 1975).

A particular life history strategy of parenting results in a coordinated suite of traits at all stages of the life span. This is because a reproductive strategy involves a response to a central external ecological contingency that selects for optimum levels of partitioning mating effort (i.e., the effort expended in attracting mates) and parenting effort (i.e., effort expended in rearing offspring). Variables such as mortality rates, longevity, pair bonding, age of first reproduction, period of preadult dependency, and levels of paternal and maternal investment evolve as a coordinated response to the environment.

Thus, for example, species adapted to environments where there is a relatively stable, predictable resource base tend to have a suite of traits allowing them to produce highly competitive offspring. Such species would be likely to have traits such as pair bonding between parents, high-investment parenting (including paternal provisioning of the young), low fertility, and delayed maturation of the young.

From the perspective of life history theory, mechanisms of internalization are a central aspect of a coherent pattern of development involving high-investment parenting. I will first review data showing the coherence of development and then review data showing that internalization is a facet of a coherent pattern of development.

Data Showing the Coherence of Development

The coherence notion of development is based on the proposal that the parent-child relationship is a coevolving system with only limited independence of systems. Ultimately, this occurs because of the unifying force of parental investment as a critical focus of natural selection. The result is that there is a great deal of overlap among the variables central to parental investment. For example, increasing brain size is associated with increasing intelligence and increasing levels of parental care across a wide range of species (Lovejoy, 1981; Rushton, 1995; Schultz, 1960). The expectation is that among humans variation in parental investment will co-occur with variation in intelligence as well as with mechanisms such as parental warmth that play a critical motivational role in high-investment parent-child relationships.

Moreover, there is the general expectation that the high-investment end of the parental investment continuum will be characterized by greater developmental plasticity, at least during the period of preadult dependence on parents. This follows because developmental plasticity is a necessary condition for the effectiveness of important aspects of the environments provided by parents. Plasticity is a two-edged sword because it opens up the organism to environmental influences that may be detrimental to individual development (Lerner, 1984; MacDonald, 1985). As a result, one expects to find associations among brain size, mental ability, learning ability, flexibility of response, and developmental plasticity. And one expects to find associations among these variables and the elaboration of costly parenting practices, delayed sexual maturation, and a prolonged juvenile period in which social learning is of great importance. This is indeed the general evolutionary thrust among the mammals, and in particular, among humans (Bonner, 1980; Eisenberg, 1981; Gould, 1977; Jerison, 1973; Johanson & Edey, 1981; Lerner, 1984; Lovejoy, 1981).

Support for these associations is also indicated by findings showing higher levels of parent-child play and generally better developmental outcomes in parent-rearing societies compared with sibling-rearing societies (MacDonald, 1993). Play, parental investment, and plasticity are intimately connected. If there were no plasticity, there would be no reason to engage in play. The decline in play during adulthood is an important prediction of this perspective. Similarly, if there were no plasticity, other aspects of parental involvement, such as the high levels of verbal communication apparent in high-investment parent-child relationships, would be ineffective and therefore result in costs to parents with no corresponding benefits to children.

These associations imply that greater mental ability is a critical coevolutionary concomitant of plasticity (including social learning) because it minimizes the risk of maladaptive environmental influences while allowing beneficial effects (MacDonald, 1991). Parents with greater mental ability are better able to respond flexibly to adaptive demands. They are more likely to model behavior that is an adaptive response to non-recurrent, non-EEA environments than are individuals with less mental ability. And, at least partly because of the warmth of their relationship with their children, the children are more motivated to attend to them as models and more likely to conform to parental values.

The data reviewed by Belsky, Steinberg, and Draper (1991) are highly compatible with this perspective. They especially note the large intercorrelations among spousal harmony, parent-child relationship quality, children's interpersonal style, timing of puberty, sexual behavior, and level of parental investment. As indicated earlier, behaviors related to parental investment and reproduction are central to life history theory.

The coherence of individual development also appears to involve measures of general intelligence (*g* factor). The IQ is the single most powerful measure of individual differences psychologists have developed and is related to variation in a very wide range of human activities. While IQ tests are mainly used as a measure of individual differences, it is also relevant to note that, compared with, say, chimpanzees, even humans with a low IQ are able to solve a wide array of problems that were not recurrent problems in the human EEA. The average human level of *g* therefore may be conceptualized as resulting from a set of species-typical, domain-general mechanism(s) underlying the specifically human advantage in mental ability compared with other species.

Like social learning, human intelligence may be viewed as set of domain-general systems that function to achieve evolutionary goals. Research on IQ indicates correlations with socioeconomic status (e.g., Scarr & Weinberg, 1978). If one assumes that social status is an evolved human motive disposition (e.g., Barkow, 1989; Buss, 1994), the implication is that individuals higher on *g* are better able to use their domain-general cognitive abilities to achieve an evolved motive disposition (social status) in an environment far removed from the human EEA. For example, individuals with high *g* in the contemporary world would score well on standardized tests used to select applicants to prestigious graduate schools. They would be able to solve a wide array of problems presented in the curriculum of these schools and would excel their colleagues after graduation, with the result that they would achieve higher social status, make more money, and be a more desirable mate (i.e., achieve evolutionary goals). Their higher intelligence implies that their mental ability is not narrowly restricted to the ability to solve highly discrete problems presented by recurrent situations in the human EEA. Rather, their high level of general intelligence would allow them to master the intricacies of many fields requiring a high level of general intelligence. An individual with a high *g* would, all things being equal, be more likely to succeed not only, say, in the legal profession but also in medicine, business, academia, or government.

Within this perspective, natural selection for intelligence as a domain-general attribute would be favored because it enabled humans to attain evolutionary goals. Moreover, variation in IQ is linked to the different patterns of development reviewed by Belsky et al. (1991; see reviews in Herrnstein & Murray, 1994; Rushton, 1988, 1995; Wilson & Herrnstein, 1985). Besides variables directly related to mental testing, such as school performance, these results indicate associations among IQ, proneness to illegitimacy, child abuse, low birth weight, sexual behavior, divorce (unstable pair bonding), rates of physical maturation, parent-child relationships, poverty, welfare dependency, and crime.

The data may therefore be interpreted as indicating that there is a very important central core of covarying systems (many of them presumably domain-specific) that includes at least one highly domain-general ability—the *g* factor of IQ tests. While the

associations among the various systems are not robust enough to preclude a semiinde-
pendent role for discrete evolved systems such as the human affectional system, the substantial coherence of individual development strongly suggests the importance of
life-history theory in conceptualizing human development. As indicated, life history
approaches to human development focus fundamentally on variation in reproductive
strategies (e.g., Belsky et al., 1991; Chisholm, 1993; MacDonald, 1994; Miller, 1994b;
Rushton, 1988, 1995), and within such perspectives parental investment is the critical
variable.

Environmental and Genetic Aspects of Parental Investment

Within this perspective, a critical aspect of high levels of parental investment is the provision of optimal environments for children. If we accept the proposition that there was
natural selection for high-investment parenting among humans (e.g., Fisher, 1992; Flinn
& Low, 1986; Lancaster & Lancaster, 1987; Lovejoy, 1981; MacDonald 1988), then it is
reasonable to suppose that one result of this process is that high-investment parents provide certain types of high-quality environments for their children and that these environments contribute to the child's development. Parental investment involves the provision of
certain environments, and parents incur a considerable cost in providing these environments: Parental investment includes developing a strong affective relationship with the
child, providing relatively high levels of verbal stimulation and parent-child play,
and active parental involvement in monitoring virtually every aspect of the child's life
(e.g., children's progress in school, children's peer relationships) (Belsky et al., 1991;
MacDonald, 1988, 1992, 1993). From a theoretical perspective, the best evidence that
the environments provided by high-investment parents must have benefits is the clear
evidence that they are costly to provide. Theoretically, it is difficult to conceive a costly
behavior remaining in a population without some compensating benefits. For example, if
children do not benefit from paternal investment, it is difficult to conceptualize why either
males or females would seek such investment. Under these circumstances, males would
be better off competing with other males for access to additional females (i.e., increasing their mating effort) than to invest in the offspring of one female (i.e., maintaining
high levels of parenting effort). Indeed, minimal parenting effort by males is a common
pattern in nature, especially among mammals (e.g., Kleiman, 1977, 1981).

While the foregoing argues for the importance of children's environments, it is not inconsistent with evidence that high-investment parenting is itself genetically influenced.
There is evidence for reasonably high heritability of all the behaviors related to parental
investment. Thus measures of parents' and children's perceptions of parental control
and especially parental warmth are genetically influenced (Rowe, 1994). Parental stimulation and involvement (including measures of parental warmth and control) as measured by the Home Observation for Measurement of the Environment (HOME) and the
Family Environment Scale (FES) also have a strong genetic component (Plomin, 1994).
These measures of parental investment covary to a considerable degree with high IQ
which is itself substantially heritable (Plomin, 1994). Interestingly, research with the
HOME also supports the coherence of development: There is substantial covariation
among the HOME subscales of emotional and verbal responsivity, provision of play materials, maternal involvement, and opportunities for variety of stimulation (Bradley &
Caldwell, 1984). Parents who provide verbal stimulation and monitor their children
closely also tend to have close emotional relationships with them.

The behavioral genetic evidence may be interpreted as indicating that parents and their children are a coevolving system in which passive genotype-environment correlations are of great importance. (Passive genotype-environment correlations are correlations between children's genotypes and the environments provided to children. For example, there may be correlations between children's genotypes and the environments provided by their biological parents. Intelligent parents have children with a high genetic potential for intelligence and they also provide optimal environments for the expression of their children's intelligence.) Children would be expected to differentially benefit from the environments provided by high-investment parents depending on their genotype. Thus far the evidence does indeed indicate that, in early childhood at least, passive genotype-environment correlations are more important contributors to the correlations between measures of IQ and the HOME and FES measures of the environment than are active or reactive genotype-environment correlations (Plomin, 1994). (Active genotype-environment correlations occur because the child seeks out environmental niches consistent with his/her genotype; reactive genotype-environment correlations occur because children's genotypes influence the way others respond to them.) The evidence does not show that the environments parents provide are of no importance.

Internalization and the Coherence of Development

On the basis of the foregoing, it is expected that the literature on internalization of parental values will have the following characteristics: Variation in the internalization of parental values will be difficult to disentangle from the influences of genetic variation as well as from a large number of other environmental correlates related to adaptive functioning, including socioeconomic status, parents' and children's intelligence, parental disciplinary styles, parental warmth, parental monitoring of children's behavior, and encouragement of adaptive behavior. Within this conceptualization, children's internalization of values is viewed as a concomitant of high-investment parenting. Internalization of values is proposed as a critical aspect of high investment parenting that effectively limits the potential costs of the open-ended, domain-general, and highly flexible systems associated in a coevolutionary complex with high-investment parenting.

There is substantial evidence that the internalization of parental values is deeply embedded within the context of high-investment parenting. The coherence notion is compatible with Lewis's (1981) suggestion that parenting typologies show a large overlap among different measures of parenting making it difficult to ascertain which aspects of parenting produce which developmental outcomes. Measures of warmth and control are difficult to separate in practice. Measures of parental control may actually tap lack of parent-child conflict (which is influenced by parent-child warmth) or the ability of the children of authoritative parents to change the rules by rational discussion. Such a view is highly compatible with the patterning of differences in parenting styles. For example, lower socioeconomic status (SES) parenting is associated with rigidity, power-assertive styles of discipline, lower warmth and affection, and less verbal interaction and less use of complex language in interaction with children (Maccoby, 1980). Given data indicating strong associations among IQ, social class, and occupation in the contemporary world, the general findings strongly support the coherence of development. Moreover, these data indicate that external methods of controlling children (high on power assertion, low on warmth) are more characteristic of the low-investment complex than the high investment complex.

Moreover, Darling and Steinberg (1993) note that global parenting styles are associated with different parenting practices in different domains. For example, authoritative parenting involves a disparate set of parenting practices that would constitute competent parenting in a correspondingly wide range of specific domains. The coherence of parenting styles occurs therefore despite the occurrence of different behaviors in different situations. Presumably many of these situation-specific behaviors are the result of domain-general mechanisms responding adaptively to variable, nonrecurrent and unpredictable aspects of the environment. More intelligent people are better able to respond to such environments adaptively and flexibly. The literature on internalization of values indicates that authoritative parents (whose children are relatively likely to internalize parental values) are more flexible in their response patterns, while authoritarian parents respond with punitiveness regardless of situation (Grusec & Goodnow, 1994).

The coherence of individual development can be seen by focusing on studies that include a sufficiently wide range of variables. In their pioneering study of children's internalization of values within an evolutionary framework, Stayton, Hogan, and Ainsworth (1971) found strong correlations among measures of parental acceptance of child, parental sensitivity and responsiveness to the child, children's compliance and internalized control of behavior, and child's IQ. Clarke-Stewart (1973) and Lytton (1980) also found that parent-child warmth is associated with children's cognitive competence.

Steinberg, Lamborn, Dornbusch, & Darling (1992) utilized several variables including authoritative parenting (consisting of independent factors of acceptance/involvement, behavioral supervision and strictness, and autonomy-granting), parental involvement in schooling, and parental encouragement to succeed academically in an effort to predict academic outcomes. Academic outcomes were measured by a *school performance* variable (grade point average, time spent on homework, educational expectations, and academic self-conceptions) and a *school engagement* variable (classroom engagement, school orientation, bonding to teachers, and school misconduct). The correlation between the composite dependent measures was .39 ($p < .001$). Moreover, parental authoritativeness was correlated with parental school involvement ($r = .46$; $p < .001$) and with parental academic encouragement ($r = .33$; $p < .001$), and the latter variables were also intercorrelated ($r = .39$; $p < .001$). All these variables were positively associated with the dependent measures of academic outcomes, including the *school engagement* variable which presumably reflects the internalization of parental values related to education. Similarly, Steinberg, Elmen, & Mounts (1989) found a high level of intercorrelation among grade point average and measures of adolescent perceptions of parental acceptance, psychological autonomy, and adolescent perceptions of their own psychosocial maturity, self-reliance, work orientation, and identity (self-esteem).

This does not imply that the independence among the measures is trivial. In the Steinberg et al. (1992) study, there was a pattern showing a substantial number of significant correlations for the dependent variables with parental involvement and parental encouragement within each level of parental authoritativeness. The average of these correlations was .066, but correlations ranging from .21 to .28 were found among the top three of the four categories of authoritativeness and school performance over two years. The data also reveal a substantial coherence to individual development. And because of the nature of IQ tests, academic performance and all the parenting variables are inevitably linked with IQ, whose heritability is responsibly estimated to be in the range of .4 to .8.

The work of Applegate and his colleagues also supports the fundamental coherence of parenting and child development while casting doubt on the relationship between parenting and either social class or intelligence. Applegate, Burke, Burleson, Delia, and Kline (1985) distinguished between two types of parents. One type engaged in relatively elaborated verbal coding that described highly individuated motivations, intentions, and feelings of the individual actors. The other type engaged in restricted coding associated with socially stereotyped role definitions. The former group also used relatively differentiated, abstract, and complex verbal messages in their disciplinary encounters with children, and they appeared to be more nurturant and aware of children's feelings in their descriptions of comforting behavior. Although Applegate et al. (1985) did not find a link between these different styles of parenting and verbal intelligence, they did find an association among these styles, mother's education, and social class (see also Bernstein, 1974) which are well-known to be associated with differences in intelligence (Scarr & Weinberg, 1978).

In a later study, however, Applegate, Burleson, and Delia (1992), found strong linkages between measures of abstractness of communication and nurturance in both parents and children but no linkages with social class, thus failing to replicate their earlier results. Applegate et al.'s (1985; Applegate et al., 1992) results support the general coherence of the coevolving parent-child system, but the tenuous links with social class and intelligence require replication, especially since a great many studies have indicated associations between lower social class and authoritarian parenting styles characterized by rigidity, power-assertive styles of discipline, lower warmth and affection, and less verbal interaction and less use of complex language in interaction with their children (Maccoby, 1980), as well as data indicating strong associations among IQ, social class, and occupation (Herrnstein, 1973).

Finally, internalization of values as an aspect of the coherence of development is apparent in the ethnographic literature and psychometric data on the Ashkenazi Jews (see MacDonald, 1994, for a summary). There is historical evidence that Jews have been relatively quick to adopt a low-fertility/high-investment strategy if such a strategy leads to upward social mobility. Evolutionary perspectives on the demographic transition have emphasized the importance of fertility control and high-investment parenting in achieving upward mobility in response to the altered conditions following industrialization (e.g., Borgerhoff Mulder, 1991). Jews entered the demographic transition considerably earlier than gentiles in the same society (e.g., Goldstein, 1981; Knode, 1974). This shift to a higher-investment style of child rearing was accompanied by theoretically expected demographic markers of high-investment parenting, including low rates of infant and adult mortality compared with gentiles even after controlling for SES, as well as lower levels of illegitimacy, premarital conception, and divorce rates (Cohen, 1986; Goldstein, 1981; Guttentag & Secord, 1983).

There is also evidence that Ashkenazi Jews as a group have a very high average IQ. The average full-scale IQ is approximately 117, with large differences between performance and verbal IQ compatible with an average verbal IQ of 125 and a performance IQ in the average range. There is good historical evidence for eugenic pressures as a result of marriage practices that produced a large overlap among intelligence, resource acquisition, and reproductive success in traditional Ashkenazi Jewish society. However, in addition to this greater genetic potential for intelligence, Jewish parents provide very high levels of verbal stimulation to their children. There is a preoccupation with elaborate verbalization, much of it directed at children, and this type of verbal stimulation has also been observed in contemporary Ashkenazi Jewish populations (Blau, 1969; Herz & Rosen, 1982; Zborowski & Herzog, 1952).

Further, there is a very strong emphasis on developing an intensely affectionate mother-child relationship in early childhood. Mothers have an "unremitting solicitude" (Zborowski & Herzog, 1952, p. 193; see also Blau, 1969) regarding their children. They engage in "boundless suffering and sacrifice. Parents 'kill themselves' for the sake of their children" (p. 294). The children were "reminded constantly of all their parents have done and suffered in their behalf."

As will be elaborated in the final section, the result is an intense motivation to please parents. "All the sacrifice, all the suffering, all the solicitude pile up into a monument to parental love, the dimensions of which define the vastness of filial indebtedness" (Zborowski & Herzog, 1952, p. 297). Children are treated with a great deal of indulgence and permissiveness and elaborate methods of inductive reasoning are used to modify children's behavior (Blau, 1969). There is also powerful internalized motivation to conform to extremely high parental expectations. Jewish children are expected to provide their parents with *naches* (i.e., desired rewards) in the form of achievement, financial success, and grandchildren, and the failure to provide them causes guilt. "Of course, there can never be enough *naches,* and their failure to provide 'enough' inevitably results in guilt" (Herz & Rosen 1982, p. 380). Blau (1969, pp. 60, 61) mentions "the profound fear of the guilt that denial of [the mother] would engender. . . . It was the discomfort—anxiety and guilt—that parental disapproval induced rather than fear of coercion that led Jewish children at a relatively tender age to internalize those norms of behavior which are of paramount importance to Jews."

ADOLESCENT SEXUAL BEHAVIOR: THE IMPORTANCE OF INTERNALIZATION OF PARENTAL VALUES AND INTERACTIONS WITH CULTURAL SHIFTS

Internalization of values as an aspect of the coherence of development is also apparent in the literature on adolescent sexual behavior. Sexual behavior is particularly interesting here because reproductive behavior is central to an evolutionary approach and it raises issues of children's compliance with parental interests. In evolutionary perspective, sexual behavior is a very costly behavior for females because of the possibility of pregnancy. In the parenting literature (e.g., Miller & Moore, 1990), it is assumed that children's physical maturation outpaces their cognitive and emotional maturation. Adolescents are relatively prone to risk-taking behavior (including behavior related to low-investment sexual relationships) accompanied by cognitive distortions of invulnerability and infallibility (Arnett, 1995). This results in adolescents being prone to making maladaptive reproductive decisions. This gap between adolescents' physical maturation and their ability to make adaptive choices results in parental attempts to control adolescent sexual behavior. In the same way that due to their cognitive immaturity, very young children benefit from adult guidance and control, adolescent tendencies toward risk taking and cognitive distortions suggest that adolescents continue to benefit from parental influence. And parents, because of their greater mental ability and experience, are better able than children to make adaptive cultural choices for their children.

External Controls as the Norm for Adolescent Sexual Behavior

Parental attempts to control the sexual behavior of their relatives, particularly their daughters, occur in many societies (Flinn & Low, 1986). Often the methods used involve coercion, an externalized form of motivation. Marriage arrangements are typically agreements between men involving exchanges of women. Adolescents (or even infants and unborn children) are often betrothed to men in exchange for reciprocal access to females controlled by the men. In addition, many societies practice seclusion or claustration of young women prior to marriage to assure that the women's reproductive assets are not squandered on an inappropriate relationship (Dickemann, 1981). Flinn (1988) finds that Caribbean villagers controlled their daughters' sexual behavior between the ages of 11 and 20 by physical violence and verbal threats directed at the daughter or suitor, restricting the daughter's movements, surveillance, and economic sanctions. Successful "guarding" behavior was related to the daughter's eventual marriage with a more prosperous male (who, as expected within an evolutionary framework [Buss, 1994] tend to prefer chaste females) and to more stable marriages among these daughters.

The cross-cultural data then suggest that heavy-handed, extrinsic methods of control are commonly used to control daughters' sexual behavior, while there is little evidence for the importance of internalization of values as an important mechanism. Because of the widespread nature of these practices and because of the critical adaptive importance of controlling daughters' reproductive assets, it is reasonable to suppose that externalized mechanisms of control were a recurrent practice during human evolution.

The Importance of Internalization in Contemporary Western Societies

There is evidence from the contemporary United States and other Westernized countries suggesting that authoritative parenting, parental warmth, and the internalization of values are related to adolescent girls' sexual behavior. Contemporary individualistic Western societies place a relatively strong emphasis on personal freedom and there has been a corresponding decrease in parents' ability to exert extrinsic controls on their children as they approach adulthood. At a broader level, the relative lack of control over children's sexual behavior typical of contemporary societies is likely to be a departure from practices prevalent in the EEA. In this radically different context, internalized mechanisms of control assume much greater importance. A basic feature of the present framework is that parent-child warmth is an internalized motivational system that serves to motivate adaptive behavior in non-EEA environments.

Data on children's sexual attitudes and behavior from contemporary Western societies are highly compatible with supposing that internalization of parental values is of considerable importance. These data also show that sexual behavior is a component of a coherent pattern of individual development. Jessor and Jessor's (1977) problem-behavior theory posits a general association among behaviors and attitudes. Consistent associations have been found among high valuation of independence, low valuation and expectations of academic achievement, social alienation, more tolerant attitude toward deviance, lesser religiosity, fewer parental controls, less compatibility between expectations of friends and parents, and greater influence of friends relative to parents. Adolescents with this intercorrelated constellation of behaviors do more poorly at school and are more likely to have problem behaviors, including earlier age of first sexual intercourse and greater likelihood of alcohol or drug use. They also have lower educational and occupational outcomes in later life.

This implies that sexual experience is regulated by a covarying "network of personality, social, and behavioral factors. . . . The pervasiveness of these variables across the different systems of problem behavior theory suggests that there is a general psychosocial patterning of proneness to, or readiness for, transition rather than proneness being confined to only one or two variables or to one or another system or only to those variables that are specifically sex related" (Jessor, Costa, Jessor, & Donovan, 1983, p. 623; see also Tubman, Windle, & Windle, 1996). As Belsky et al. (1991, p. 660) note in commenting on this program of research, "In a society that no longer labels nonmarital sexual activity as 'deviant,' one must ask why this behavior covaries with such censured behaviors as delinquency and substance abuse." Notice particularly the lack of consistency between parent and child expectations and greater peer influence in the early-prone group—a clear indication that these children have not internalized parental values. Moreover, it is apparent from other research (e.g., Murstein & Holden, 1979) that another aspect of this covarying constellation is affective closeness to parents.

Interaction between Parental Investment and Cultural Supports for High-Investment Parenting

A prediction of the coherence perspective is that cultural supports for children's behavior will be most important at the low-investment end of the parental investment distribution. This is because the children of high-investment parents are internally motivated to accept parental values and to attend to parents as models of appropriate behavior. Moreover, independent of parental influences, they are likely to be more prone to adopt a high-investment pattern of behavior because of their genetic proclivities. Children on the low-investment end of the distribution, on the other hand, are expected to be relatively little motivated to accept adult values (low internalization). And, independent of internalizing parental influences, children on the low-investment end are expected to be more prone to cultural choices involving immediate gratification and low-investment sexual relationships, as well as more prone to choosing cultural influences, including peers, disapproved by adults.

Cultural supports for high-investment parenting act as external forces of social control to maximize high-investment parenting among all segments of the population, even those who are relatively disinclined for genetic and/or environmental reasons to engage in such practices. One may view cultural supports for high-investment parenting as a form of external social control that is formally analogous to externalizing methods of parental discipline.

In the contemporary world, systems of parental socialization of children must compete with other influences. Especially important are the peer world, the media, and other influences emanating from the wider culture whose values often conflict with parental views on appropriate sexual behavior. There are also secular trends in external influences, especially in the media and the wider culture, that impact the parent-child system. In some historical eras, there has been more congruence between the wider culture and parental values than at others. As a result, it is reasonable to suppose that children's internalization of parental values occurs more easily at some historical periods than at others.

The historical data on marriage in Western societies indicate that traditionally there have been very low levels of divorce and illegitimacy, even during periods of relative economic hardship (MacDonald, 1995a). The prototypical response to environmental adversity has been to delay reproduction and there has been a consistently low level of illegitimacy during periods of economic decline as well as periods of economic prosperity. Moreover, there is excellent evidence that this pattern was maintained by powerful social controls embedded in the religious and legal framework of Western societies. For example, during the medieval period, the Church successfully opposed divorce, concubinage, and illegitimate birth for all classes of society, including the wealthy. And in later periods, women and lower- and middle-status males were important interest groups that maintained these cultural supports for high-investment parenting.

Since approximately 1965, however, there has been a massive cultural shift away from these traditional patterns toward a dramatically increasing prevalence of a low-investment reproductive style in the United States and other Western societies. The interesting point from the present perspective is that there has been a powerful interaction between this cultural shift and individual tendencies toward high-investment parenting.

Since 1970, the rate of single parenting has increased from 1 in 10 families to 1 in 3 families (Norton & Miller, 1992), and there have been dramatic increases in teenage sexual activity and teenage childbearing without marriage (Furstenberg, 1991). There is excellent evidence for an association among teenage single parenting, poverty, lack of education, and poor developmental outcomes for children (e.g., Dornbusch & Gray, 1988; Furstenberg & Brooks-Gunn, 1989; McLanahan & Booth, 1989).

All the negative trends related to the family show very large increases that developed in the mid-1960s (Herrnstein & Murray, 1994, pp. 168–190), including increases in trends toward lower levels of marriage, "cataclysmic" increases in divorce rates (p. 172), and rates of illegitimacy. In the case of divorce and illegitimacy rates, the data indicate an enormous shift upward during the 1960s from previously existing trends, with the trend lines established during that period continuing into the present. The 1960s decade was a watershed period in American social and cultural history.

Whatever the cause of these secular trends, Herrnstein and Murray (1994) show that these changes in social functioning have not fallen evenly across the continuum of parental investment. Only 2% of the white women in Herrnstein and Murray's top category of cognitive ability (IQ minimum of 125) and 4% of the white women in the second category of cognitive ability (IQ between 110 and 125) gave birth to illegitimate children, while the corresponding rates for the bottom two categories of cognitive ability are 17% (IQ between 75 and 90) and 32% (IQ below 75) respectively. Thus the cultural shift in which the traditional social controls characteristic of historical Western societies have been severely attenuated has had little effect on individuals predisposed toward high-investment parenting, whereas it has resulted in a massive alteration of behavior among individuals not so inclined.

There is evidence that an important contributor to this cultural shift in reproductive behavior is low paternal investment in children. Marriage, far more than mother's IQ, is the most important variable in predicting poverty among children and its correlative negative developmental outcomes (Herrnstein & Murray, 1994, p. 138). Moreover, the adolescent girls who are most likely to become pregnant are least under the control or influence of adults, especially fathers. Herrnstein & Murray (1994) found that father-absence at age 14 was a strong predictor that the woman's first birth would be illegitimate. Given the general association between precocious adolescent sexual behavior and deviant behaviors, it is relevant that Dornbusch et al. (1985) found that single parenting is associated with lower levels of parental control of adolescents and higher levels of deviant behavior by adolescents.

These results imply that culturally transmitted information has a major role in child development, but that the effects of cultural transmission interact with individual tendencies toward parental investment, which are in turn influenced by individual differences in life history strategy.

The data reviewed in this section indicate the importance of considering complex processes of social control and their interaction with individual differences in life history strategies in attempting to understand historical processes that influence child development. At a theoretical level, social controls on reproductive behavior may be viewed as influenced by evolved motivational systems and conflicts of interest over the construction of culture. Nevertheless these social controls are underdetermined with respect to evolutionary theory, human nature/nurture (i.e., the characteristics of humans), or external ecological variables (MacDonald, 1995a). And while understanding the origins of important cultural shifts, such as those occurring during the 1960s, takes one a long way from developmental psychology, the conclusion must be that child development occurs in a highly embedded, socially constructed cultural context.

THEORETICAL PERSPECTIVES ON THE COHERENCE OF INDIVIDUAL DEVELOPMENT

The data previously reviewed indicate a substantial coherence to individual development. Internalization is a critical component of a coherent pattern of high-investment parenting, and I will describe two different approaches to conceptualizing variation in parental investment in the contemporary world, an approach in which variation in parental investment results from environmental cues interacting with universal human psychological mechanisms and an approach in which variation in parental investment patterns results primarily from heritable variation.

Belsky et al. (1991; see also Chisholm, 1993) argue that the differing patterns of coherent development reflect a universal psychological mechanism that results in different reproductive strategies as a response to the presence or absence of environmental stress and high or low resource availability. They propose an "alternate strategy" perspective in which a low-investment reproductive strategy results as an adaptive response to environmental stress. Low resource availability leads to spousal disharmony and insensitive, unresponsive parenting styles. This in turn leads to insecure attachment and an opportunistic interpersonal style among children. Children adopting this strategy enter puberty at an earlier age and they are sexually precocious compared with children in a resource-abundant environment. As adults, they are prone to unstable pair bonds.

While Belsky et al. (1991) argue for this alternate strategy perspective, they also note that additive genetic variation (i.e., heritability) may influence these patterns. Moffitt, Caspi, Belsky, and Silva (1992), while replicating the findings of an association between childhood stress and pubertal timing, suggest that a genetic model provides a more parsimonious fit for the data. Supporting a genetic interpretation, pubertal timing was associated with mother's age of menarche, and there was no support for the idea that early puberty was mediated by childhood behavior problems. On the other hand, Graber, Brooks-Gunn, and Warren (1995) found that depressive affect (but not internalizing or externalizing behavior) added to the variance explained by mother's age of menarche. However, the influence of depressive affect was greatly attenuated by the addition of breast development or weight to the model. In any case, neither of these studies can test between a heritability model and a contextual model of pubertal timing: Mother's age of menarche is a fairly crude index of genetic influences on daughter's age of menarche.

In the following, I will argue for a theory that emphasizes the importance of heritable variation for understanding patterns of high- and low-investment reproductive strategies. There is evidence that variables related to reproductive strategies are heritable. Pubertal timing is substantially heritable (Fischbein, 1977a, 1977b; Tanner, 1990), and there are moderate heritabilities for age of first sexual intercourse (Martin, Eaves, & Eysenck, 1977), warmth/nurturance and impulsivity/extraversion as personality traits (i.e., Factors I and II of the Five-Factor Model; Digman, 1990), parental warmth toward children (Rowe, 1994), parenting styles (Plomin, McClearn, Pedersen, Nesselroade, & Bergeman, 1989), and likelihood of divorce (Rowe, 1994). Also, the reproductive strategy perspective developed here includes intelligence as a critical, highly heritable variable.

Conceptualizing Human Reproductive Strategies: Adversity Selection and r/K Reproductive Strategies

The basic assumption of the alternate strategy perspective is that the presence of either short-term or long-term environmental stressors would have the general effect of promoting a low-investment reproductive style. There are reasons to question this assumption. Theoretically, high-investment parenting is associated with adaptation to ecologically adverse or highly competitive environments where high levels of parental investment are critical to rearing successful offspring (Diamond, 1986; Kleiman, 1977, 1981; Miller, 1994a; Southwood, 1981; Wilson, 1975). This makes intuitive sense because in ecologically adverse or highly competitive situations, male provisioning of food or other resources might tip the balance in favor of their offspring compared with the offspring of males who do not provision their young. Several theorists have proposed that the adverse environment created by the Ice Age had an important role in shaping the intelligence and high-investment reproductive behavior of northern populations (Lenz, 1931; Lynn, 1987; MacDonald, 1994; Miller, 1994a, 1994b; Rushton, 1988, 1995). Within this framework, natural selection resulted in a uniform tendency toward high-investment parenting as a result of long-term resource scarcity: Males who did not provision their young left few descendants. This is quite different from the alternate strategy perspective. Moreover, contrary to the alternate strategy perspective, long-term selection in resource-scarce environments is likely to lead to high-investment parenting, not low-investment parenting.

In addition to adverse environments, highly competitive environments may also lead to high-investment parenting. Here the theoretical focus has been on the r/K continuum of reproductive strategies by which r-selected species evolve in response to highly unstable environments where there is little predictability of resource availability. These species adopt a low-investment/high-fertility reproductive strategy to take advantage of temporary situations where there are abundant resources and little competition. The low investment of relatively r-selected species is not a response to a temporary lack of resources, but rather a response to a highly unpredictable resource environment in which there is selection for very rapid reproduction with little parental effort during the relatively short-lived periods of resource abundance.

On the other hand, K-selected species evolve in response to a highly stable, predictable resource environment. These species adopt a high-investment/low fertility strategy to compete with conspecifics (i.e., members of the same species) and with other species (Southwood, 1981). While r-selected species respond to temporary periods of resource abundance with a low-investment reproductive style, K-selected species adapt to a highly predictable resource environment in which parents must forgo additional matings to invest their time and energy in producing highly competitive offspring.

Within the r/K framework, then, low-investment parenting is not a response to resource scarcity, but rather a response to unpredictable short-term resource abundance. Moreover, while r-selected species tend to overshoot their resource base, adversity-selected and K-selected species remain within the carrying capacity of the environment. The expected response, therefore, of a K-selected or adversity-selected species to resource scarcity would be to delay reproduction until reproduction was viable, but not to respond to adversity with low-investment reproduction (see also Miller, 1994a). The expectation would be that cues to environmental adversity would result in a delay of maturation and reproductive viability, rather than an acceleration as predicted by the theory of Belsky et al.

Both competition and environmental adversity tend to result in animals having fewer and more widely spaced offspring, prolonged parental care, longer life span, and lower mortality rates at all stages of the life span. Conversely low-investment parenting is associated with environments rich in resources and with little competition. In the natural world, resource-rich, competition-free environments are typically ephemeral because a stable resource-rich environment will ultimately lead to intense competition and K-selection.

Genetic Variation and Environmental Influences on Human Reproductive Strategies

In the following section, I will argue that the available evidence is most compatible with supposing that selection for competitive ability (K-selection) and/or an adversity-selected pattern of parental investment is a universal feature of human evolution. Within this perspective, individual differences in parental investment patterns result largely from heritable variation remaining in the population because natural selection did not remove all the genetic variation related to parental investment. This perspective implies that genetic variation continues to underlie a range of more or less viable strategies within contemporary populations, as is also the case with personality variation (MacDonald, 1995b) and intelligence. (There may also be continuing natural selection in favor of high- or low-investment parenting in present-day societies.) And, in addition to within-group genetic variation, there may also be between-group differences resulting from different selection pressures affecting groups that evolved in somewhat different ancestral environments (e.g., northern versus southern populations).

First, there is a consistent pattern indicating that stressors of all kinds uniformly result in a lowered tempo of maturation, including age of menarche, but this pattern is superimposed on a pattern of heritable variation for all measures related to physical growth and development (Tanner, 1990). Some of the more interesting data gathered by Tanner (unless otherwise referenced) include the following:

- Malnutrition (e.g., in times of war) or disease slows down physical maturation. Psychosocial stressors (e.g., abusive family relationships, sadistic teachers) have similar effects on physical maturation. Nutritional deficits or deficits due to disease also slow the developmental tempo. Consistent with these findings, Flinn and colleagues (Flinn & England, 1995; Flinn, Quinlan, Decker, Turner, & England, 1996) show that stressful life events, including family quarreling, living with nonrelatives, residence change, divorce, and death of a family member, are associated with infectious diseases and other health problems.

- When controlled for environmental variables, rates of physical maturation reflect ancestral environments rather than current environments (see also Rushton, 1995). This finding emphasizes the importance of heritable variation in physical maturation.

- In Britain, upper SES children continue to mature more rapidly than lower SES children. Additional children of manual workers show more of a growth decrement compared with their older siblings than children of nonmanual workers. These findings are compatible with the proposal that the greater nutritional and psychological stresses occurring in the lower classes delay maturation.

- Social class differences in growth rates have been obliterated in Sweden and Norway, a result that Tanner suggests is due to the success of social welfare programs in those countries.

- There is a pronounced secular trend (beginning at least 150 years ago in England) of lowered age of menarche associated with better nutrition coincident with modernization. It is unlikely that these changes are the result of increasing stress in the modern world, since this rise is associated with increases in the birth weights of babies (e.g., Gruenwald, Funakawa, Mitani, Nishimura, & Takeuchi, 1967) and increases in brain size (e.g., Miller & Corsellis, 1977), and increases in height (Tanner, 1990). More likely, the changes are the result of better nutrition consequent to higher living standards. Real standards of living have approximately doubled between the 1930s and the 1980s (Coleman & Salt, 1992). Flinn and England (1995) summarize data indicating that chronic stress is associated with immune deficiency, inhibited growth, and delayed sexual maturity.

- The stress of high levels of physical exercise, as among dancers and athletes, is known to delay the onset of puberty (Calabrese et al., 1983; Warren et al., 1991; Warren, Brooks-Gunn, Hamilton, Hamilton, & Warren, 1986).

- Zajonc's (1976; see also Zajonc, Markus, & Markus, 1979) confluence model indicates that intelligence declines as a function of birth order and less spacing between births.

These findings suggest that the coherence of individual development implicated in the review of Belsky et al. (1991) derives mainly from heritable variation. Psychosocial and physical stressors actually appear to work in a manner contrary to the theory of Belsky et al. These stressors uniformly delay physical growth and development and result in less robust developmental outcomes as expected on the hypothesis that humans are a relatively K-selected and/or adversity-selected species. On the basis of the data provided by Tanner and others, stressful conditions actually appear to result in delayed maturation, not earlier maturation.

Also supporting the present perspective are historical examples where populations have responded to environmental adversity by delaying reproduction and/or continuing a high-investment style of reproduction. The Great Depression and the depression of the 1890s were associated with later marriage, delays in having children, and markedly lower levels of fertility. On the other hand, the prosperity during and after World War II resulted in a decline in age of marriage and earlier childbearing (Coleman, 1990; Moss, 1964). This pattern is typical of Western societies over historical time (Hajnal, 1965, 1983; Laslett, 1983; MacFarlane, 1980, 1986; Wall, 1983; Wrigley & Schofield, 1981). The prime mechanism for the regulation of population in preindustrial Western Europe centered around a flexible age of marriage, preconjugal chastity, and variance in the percentage of females marrying. In times of resource scarcity, the age at marriage, especially for males, increased, while in economically expansive times, the age of marriage was lowered. At the end of the 17th century, approximately 23% of individuals of both sexes remained unmarried between ages 40 and 44, but as a result of altered economic opportunities, this percentage dropped at the beginning of the 18th century to 9%, and there was a corresponding decline in age of marriage (Wrigley & Schofield, 1983). The illegitimacy rate throughout the pre-modern period was usually far less than 3% until after 1750 (Laslett, 1977), and there was no tendency for the rate to increase during times of resource scarcity.

Elder's (1974) data on children experiencing the Great Depression during adolescence are particularly interesting. Consonant with the general tenor of the theory of Belsky et al. (1991; see also Conger et al., 1992), economic hardship and status loss during the Depression resulted in strained interpersonal relationships and emotional distance from the parents. The deprived group from middle-class backgrounds tended to marry earlier (i.e., before age 20) than the nondeprived group. (There was no effect of deprivation on age of marriage among working-class women. These women tended to marry relatively early in any case.) Deprived women from middle-class backgrounds who married relatively young tended to have emotionally distant relationships with parents (especially the father), and they were characterized by earlier dating and heterosexual experience.

Nevertheless, women with deprived backgrounds had no more children and actually gave birth to their first child 8 months *later* on average than nondeprived women. Their marriages were no less stable than those of the nondeprived group, and their husbands had higher levels of education, income, and social status than those of the nondeprived women. Both women and men from deprived backgrounds were more highly committed to family life and parenthood and to secure interpersonal relationships than nondeprived subjects.

It would appear then that the relatively precocious dating and sexual activity found among the deprived women was not in the service of low-investment reproductive relationships, but rather in the service of attaining economic stability and a high-investment reproductive style characterized by high levels of commitment to family and to rearing children. The general picture one gets is that economic insecurity and status loss resulted in a highly conservative strategy for both sexes combined with an intense desire for upward social mobility: *"Signs of family change among the offspring of deprived families are consistently in a conservative direction, toward traditional values and relationships"* (Elder, 1974, p. 286; italics in text). In addition to data indicating a strong orientation toward family concerns, parental responsibility, and domesticity, deprived males valued economic security and were highly risk-averse in their economic decisions.

Deprived individuals were more likely to be upwardly mobile in later life than were nondeprived individuals. Interestingly, there was a stronger relationship between the physical attractiveness of the woman and status of husband among the deprived women, suggesting that these women were particularly interested in upward social mobility and were better able to capitalize on their reproductive assets to do so. In addition, boys from families who lost most from the depression scored higher on desiring status and power in social relationships, and in later life boys from deprived, formerly middle-class families achieved somewhat higher social status than the middle-class nondeprived group.

The suggestion is that the long-term effect of economic deprivation in this Caucasian sample was to intensify the motivation for upward social mobility and responsible, high-investment parenting. These general findings and the fact that these results were strongest in those with a middle-class background are highly compatible with the present perspective. If one supposes that, compared with the lower-class group, the middle-class group was more prone to developing a high-investment style of parenting for genetic reasons, then their response to economic adversity is understandable: When confronted with economic hardship and status loss, they did not switch to a low-investment reproductive strategy (as proposed by the alternate strategy idea), but increased their striving for upward social mobility and increased their involvement in family and children.

Elder's data therefore do not support the proposal that poverty or downward social mobility causes low-investment parenting, and especially so in formerly middle-class samples. In addition, the Depression resulted in markedly lower fertility and a dramatically lower rate of marriage in general (Statistical Abstract of the United States [SAUS], 1992, Table 127). This finding is consistent with the historic patterns of marriage in Western societies: Economic hardship results in postponing marriage rather than adopting a low-investment reproductive style. It is also noteworthy that this trend toward delaying marriage was not accompanied by a rise in the rate of illegitimacy (a marker of low-investment parenting) (Herrnstein & Murray, 1994, p. 178). Rather, the revolution in illegitimacy began in the 1960s, at a time when levels of poverty were at a historic low (Ross, Danziger, & Smolensky, 1987).

Similarly, the rate of divorce actually decreased in the early 1930s and only began its long-term steep rise in the affluent 1960s (*SAUS,* 1992, Table 127). Divorce may be viewed as an index of unstable pair bonding, which is often associated with single-parenting and higher levels of poverty among children. (There was also a temporary peak in divorce rate in the period immediately after World War II, during a period of relative prosperity compared with the years of the Great Depression. However, this temporary rise presumably resulted from ill-advised marriages occurring under wartime conditions.)

One might argue that it is not poverty experienced during adolescence that causes low-investment parenting, but rather poverty occurring during the period when affectional relationships are established within the family. Children, such as Elder's subjects, who were exposed to poverty during adolescence may have established close personal relationships (secure attachments) during early childhood. These secure attachments then predisposed them to pair bonding and high-investment parenting as adults. As a result, these individuals readily adopted a high-investment style of parenting when they achieved reproductive maturity.

The problem with such a perspective is that it would predict that children born during the late 1920s and early 1930s would be prone to low-investment parenting because they had been reared during an era of economic dislocation that resulted in distant, acrimonious parent-child relationships during early childhood. However, as indicated, the revolutionary increases in the trends toward illegitimacy and divorce began only in the mid-1960s when childbearing in this cohort was largely finished. The revolution in illegitimacy occurred primarily to cohorts born after 1950, during a period of economic prosperity that lasted (as indexed by lowering rates of poverty) until 1970.

Finally, the argument that poverty causes illegitimacy fails to consider the powerful status of IQ as a predictor of illegitimacy for white women living below the poverty level (Herrnstein & Murray, 1994, p. 188). Rather than finding that low-investment parenting is a uniform response to poverty, low-investment parenting therefore appears to be strongly influenced by the highly heritable trait of intelligence, which is the centerpiece of a high-investment parenting strategy. IQ also predicts scores on the HOME instrument independent of SES, and IQ predicts poverty and welfare dependency independent of parental SES. Again, the suggestion is that variation in parental investment co-occurs with relative resource scarcity, but there is no reason to suppose that the latter causes the former.

The most promising life history perspective on development attributes the coherence of individual development to heritable variation in parental investment patterns as modified by environmental influences. Chief among the environmental influences are psychosocial and nutritional stressors that have the uniform effect of delaying and/or stunting physical, intellectual, and reproductive development. From this perspective, there has been a trend toward the coevolution of parents and children. On the high-investment end of the distribution, children are more prone to internalizing parental values and internalization serves as a potent mechanism of cultural transmission. There is more warmth in parent-child relationships and higher levels of verbal stimulation of children in these high-investment families. There are also relatively powerful tendencies toward stable pair bonding, sexual restraint, and high intelligence.

SPECIFIC MECHANISMS: WARMTH AS A MOTIVATIONAL SYSTEM UNDERLYING CHILDREN'S INTERNALIZATION OF VALUES

Research on internalization has focused on two types of mechanisms: One involves the temperament/personality trait of inhibitory control, and the other involves another personality system—warmth. While I will concentrate on the latter mechanism, the temperament trait of inhibitory control is also important. Kochanska, Murray, Jacques, Koenig, and Vandegeest (1996) have shown that this temperament trait is related to children's internalization as indicated by maternal reports of children's daily behavior and by their greater compliance with mother's and experimenter's rules in situations where they believed they were unsupervised. Inhibitory control appears to involve mechanisms in the prefrontal cortex underlying focusing attention, planning orderly sequences of behavior, inhibiting immediate but inappropriate response tendencies, delaying gratification, persevering in tasks that take a great deal of effort, and planning for the future (Luria, 1980; Mesulam, 1986; Rothbart, Derryberry, & Posner, 1994; Tucker & Derryberry, 1992). This system, whose adaptive functions are perhaps obvious, has been linked to the Conscientiousness dimension of the Five-Factor Model (FFM) of personality (MacDonald, 1995b).

There is every reason to suppose, however, that parent-child socialization contingencies involving parent-child warmth are also important for internalization. Evolutionary accounts of children's compliance and internalization of values have emphasized these processes as natural consequences of children's relationships of attachment and affection with their parents (Stayton et al., 1971). The human affectional system (warmth) may be viewed as a system that evolved to underlie intimate family relationships (including spousal relationships and parent-child relationships). The proposed function of this system is to facilitate parental, including paternal, investment in children (Fisher, 1992; MacDonald, 1988, 1992). And, as emphasized in this chapter, warmth also functions as a mechanism for the transmission of cultural values from parents to children (MacDonald, 1988, 1992). As expected in the view that there is considerable coherence to development, Eysenck's psychoticism superfactor of personality theory includes items related to warmth and affection as well as items related to conscientiousness (see Eysenck & Eysenck, 1976). This indicates that the two personality/temperament systems emphasized here as underlying children's internalization of values share common variance.

An Evolutionary Perspective on the Human Affectional System

The human affectional system is of central importance here because of its proposed role as underlying children's internalization of values. As with other evolved appetitive motivational systems (Wilson, 1975), the human affectional system may be conceptualized as a reward system (see Hatfield & Rapson, 1994; Kohl & Francoeur, 1995; Liebowitz, 1983). The stimuli that activate this system act as natural eliciting cues for pleasurable affective response, just as the stimulus of sugar water naturally leads to pleasure in an infant. The stimuli that activate the human affectional system are thus "natural clues" in Bowlby's (1974) sense. Intimate relationships are therefore naturally pleasurable to the participants and are actively sought after. Their termination is met with disappointment and grief, while there is eager anticipation of reunion with a loved one.

At a basic level, warmth is one of several personality systems understood as normative, species-typical adaptations that functioned to produce adaptive behavior in the human EEA. Within this perspective, individual differences in attraction to the rewards of intimacy and affection are viewed as a personality dimension—Factor II of the FFM. Digman (1990) notes that such a dimension has been consistently found in factor analytic studies of personality performed over the past 50 years. He characterizes the dimension as involving "the more humane aspects of humanity—characteristics such as altruism, nurturance, caring, and emotional support at the one end of the dimension, and hostility, indifference to others, self-centeredness, spitefulness, and jealousy at the other" (pp. 422, 424). (See also descriptions of reward dependence, Sigvardsson, Bohman, & Cloninger, 1987; psychoticism [reversed], Eysenck & Eysenck, 1976; and agreeableness, John, 1990.) In addition, the well-studied circumplex model of interpersonal descriptors results in a dimension of Nurturance/Love (Kiesler, 1983; Trapnell & Wiggins, 1990; Wiggins, Trapnell, & Philipps, 1988). Here this dimension of personality is proposed to underlie adaptive relationships of intimacy and other long-term relationships, especially family relationships. These relationships involve reciprocity between spouses and transfer of resources to children (e.g., maternal and paternal investment in children).

The reward-system idea implies that the affectional system is above all a motivational system. Moreover, it is a system based predominantly on positive, appetitive motivation. The child who is high on the affectional system finds the stimuli characteristic of intimate, affectionate relationships to be highly rewarding. Such a child eagerly seeks out relationships, including peer relationships of friendship, in which this stimulation is available. Because the other person in such a relationship also finds this stimulation rewarding, the relationship is characterized by reciprocal positive affective exchanges. Friends are "intimate associates" and their relationships are characterized by reciprocity, commitment, cooperation, and reciprocated prosocial support, intimacy, and affection (Hartup, 1989).

Warmth and Children's Internalization of Values

A continuing relationship of warmth and affection between parents and children is expected to result in the acceptance of adult values by the child, identifying with the parent, and a generally higher level of compliance—"the time-honored concept of warmth and identification" (Maccoby & Martin, 1983, p. 72). The finding that warmth of the model facilitates imitation and identification has long been noted by social learning theorists (Bandura, 1969; Mischel, 1976). From the present theoretical perspective, this is expected because the behavior of the child is part of a relationship characterized by reciprocated positive interactions. Moreover, the parent's evaluation of the child's behavior is an aspect of this reciprocated positive interchange. Children in a warm parent-child relationship are expected to be positively motivated to seek the approval of their parents and to identify with their parents.

However, parents would be expected to respond negatively to children's failure to live up to parental values and standards of appropriate behavior. It would therefore be a dissonant element in a continued relationship based on reciprocated positive interaction. For a child who had developed a powerful relationship with the parent based on warmth and affection, children's behavior that contravenes parental standards of appropriate behavior is expected to result in guilt and anxiety. Thus the affective motivational component of internalization includes both negative emotions aroused at the threat of parental disapproval of child's behavior as well as the positive emotion of warmth that results in attraction to and identification with parents. As with other evolved motivational systems underlying personality, both positive emotions and negative emotions are associated with the same system (MacDonald, 1995b). For example, the behavioral avoidance system responds with fear and anxiety to perceived threats and dangers, but there is intense relief upon the attainment of safety.

In conformity with these expectations, there is good evidence that parental warmth is associated with internalization of parental values (Grusec & Goodnow, 1994). Parental warmth is also associated with the development of conscience and an internalized moral orientation (Brody & Shaffer, 1982; Hoffman, 1970; Londerville & Main, 1981; Zahn-Waxler, Radke-Yarrow, & King, 1979). These findings are consistent with supposing that parental warmth plays a motivational role in children's internalization of values. The motivating power of parental affection is also implicit in the finding that love-withdrawal can serve as a mechanism of discipline (Hoffman, 1970): Children are highly motivated to avoid behaving in a manner that results in love-withdrawal.

Nevertheless, while the power of love-withdrawal results from the motivational properties of the human affectional system, there remains considerable doubt about the extent to which love-withdrawal produces internalization (Brody & Shaffer, 1982). In conceptualizing this phenomenon, it should be noted that most parent-child disciplinary encounters have elements of power assertion, love-withdrawal, and induction.

Moreover, parents commonly use different disciplinary methods in response to different situations (e.g., Brody & Shaffer, 1982; Grusec & Goodnow, 1994; Hoffman, 1994). The entire context of an inductive disciplinary encounter carries an inevitable implication that the parent disapproves of the child's behavior. Minimally, it is a note of dissonance, if not love-withdrawal, in an otherwise affectively positive parent-child relationship. Induction, as Hoffman (1983) notes, involves criticism of the child's behavior but in a way that does not threaten the overall relationship between parent and child. It is therefore reasonable to suppose that inductions tap into the same motivational system as love-withdrawal. However, they do so at a lower level that produces low-level guilt in the child and motivation to restore the temporary departure from the generally positive tone of the parent-child relationship. The finding that parents who use inductive techniques also tend to have a warm parent-child relationship (Hoffman, 1970) is highly compatible with this interpretation.

Within the present perspective, it is expected that more severe forms of love-withdrawal (such as threats of a complete disruption of the parent-child relationship) would lead to intense anxiety in the child. Hoffman (1970, p. 285) states that love-withdrawal involves relatively prolonged episodes that pose "the threat of abandonment or separation." The parent-child relationship characterized by this type of disciplinary encounter would be ambivalent at best and not properly described as warm and affectionate.

Warmth is intimately involved in the effects of power-assertive styles of discipline as well. Fairly high levels of parental control and even power-assertive styles of discipline are more effective with children if the control is accompanied by parental warmth (Brody & Shaffer, 1982; Grusec & Goodnow, 1994; Hoffman, 1970). Within the present perspective, power-assertive discipline combined with warmth has this effect because children in warm parent-child relationships are more motivated to maintain the relationship even when this involves costs to them. Similarly, parents in warm parent-child relationships are expected to be more motivated to maintain close relationships with their children. They are therefore more likely to avoid negative confrontations with their children and more likely to avoid highly detailed, explicit requirements in the expectation that in the long run children will be motivated to comply with parental requirements if the affective quality of the relationship is maintained (Goodnow, 1992; Higgins, 1981, 1989).

It is thus not surprising that measures of warmth and control are difficult to separate in practice (Lewis, 1981). Warm parents are more likely in general to use inductive reasoning successfully, at least partly because of the motivating role of parental warmth, and children are more (internally) motivated to comply with instances of power assertion by warm parents. Warm parents may well criticize children's noncompliant behavior and often expect children to conform to high parental standards. But the dissonances resulting from the strictures related to these issues occur within a context in which the overall positive affective tone of the relationship is not in jeopardy.

A Hierarchical Perspective on Warmth as a Motivational System

The perspective developed here is compatible with a hierarchical system of motivation (see Emmons, 1989) in which many of the highest level human goals, such as affection and love, are profoundly shaped by our ontogenetic and phylogenetic history (MacDonald, 1991, 1995b). In this view, evolution does not act by programming for a host of motivational (reward) systems geared for specific environmental contingencies. Rather, the affectional system motivates behavior partly by facilitating the transmission of parental values and culture. As a result, a child may be motivated to refrain from drug use and getting pregnant, and work diligently in school (behaviors with high potential costs or benefits) to preserve a relationship based on reciprocated affection.

The human affectional system may therefore be viewed as a mechanism that can influence children's behavior in wide-ranging situations that evolution could never have foreseen. Warmth as an adaptation therefore fits well into the fundamental logic of the interaction between domain-specific (warmth) and domain-general adaptations described earlier: Warmth is a domain-specific system in the sense that it results in a well-defined emotional response to particular types of stimulation typical of warm parent-child relationships. However, children in warm, affectionate parent-child relationships are more likely to profit from adults' greater cognitive competence, greater experience, and lower impulsivity in the pursuit of long term goals. These goals need not be goals derived from our evolutionary past, but may include goals such as avoiding drug use, that are unique to contemporary society.

Warmth and Attachment Security

Finally, contrary to recent theorizing, I propose that it is the affectional system, not security of attachment that underlies internalization. The analysis in terms of warmth as an evolved motivational system is consistent with supposing that warmth and security of attachment are two independent systems with different motivating emotions. In previous work (MacDonald, 1992), I have given several reasons to distinguish warmth from security of attachment, although there is often a large overlap between warm parent-child relationships and secure attachment, at least in samples from Western societies. Particularly relevant is the finding that despite the virtual absence of sex differences in attachment classification, there are theoretically expected robust sex differences in warmth as a personality dimension (Trapnell & Wiggins, 1990). Girls are also more prone to engage in intimate, confiding relationships than boys throughout development (Berndt, 1986; Buhrmester & Furman, 1987; Douvan & Adelson, 1966; Hunter & Youniss, 1982). Females also tend generally to place greater emphasis on love and personal intimacy in sexual relationships (Buss & Schmitt, 1993; Douvan & Adelson, 1966; Haas, 1979; Hinde, 1984; Kenrick & Trost, 1989; Lewis, Casto, Aquilino, & McGuffin, 1978; Miller & Simon, 1980; Normal & Harris, 1981; Peplau, Rubin, & Hill, 1977). Females are more empathic and desire higher intimacy in relationships (Lang-Takoc & Osterweil, 1992), and both sexes perceive friendships with women as closer, richer, more intimate, more empathic, and more therapeutic (Aukett, Ritchie, & Mill, 1988; Buhrke & Fuqua, 1987; Reis, Senchak, & Solomon, 1985; Wright & Scanlon, 1991). Because of its central role in underlying parental investment, nurturance of children, and mate selection, it is expected that there will be mean differences in the affectional system such that females are more attracted to close, intimate relationships of love and affection. Such relationships are particularly important to females because they serve as a cue to male investment in children.

Also relevant is Ainsworth's (1967) Ugandan study indicating that secure attachment can occur in the absence of parent-child warmth. These results are corroborated by other studies indicating minimal parent-child and husband-wife warmth in African and African-derived samples in the presence of a robust attachment system (see also

Ainsworth, 1977; Draper, 1989; Field, 1993; LeVine & LeVine, 1966, 1988). These considerations suggest that one could test whether security of attachment in the absence of warmth facilitates children's internalization of values. One could do so by studying the correlates of security of attachment in samples, such as Ainsworth's Ugandan sample, where security of attachment is not confounded by the presence of parent-child warmth.

Within Bowlby's theory, the attachment system is conceptualized as a system designed by natural selection to keep infants and very young children close to adults. Its basic emotions are fear and anxiety in the absence of caregivers and a feeling of safety or "felt security" in the presence of caregivers who are responsive to evolved infant desires for proximity maintenance. These desires for proximity are triggered especially in unfamiliar surroundings or in the presence of strangers. As a result of experiences with caregivers, children build up generalized internal working models of expectations regarding relationships. These models, while having a certain degree of inertia, may be revised by later experiences with relationships.

Such a conceptualization of attachment implies that there is a great deal of domain-generality to attachment as an adaptation. Within current attachment theory (e.g., Bretherton, 1991), internal working models of relationships differ little if at all from other schemas. These models may be constantly updated and, like social learning, allow the organism to successfully adapt to relatively variable, nonrecurrent, and unpredictable aspects of the environment. While such a perspective is certainly theoretically conceivable, the implication is that the central construct of a system that is proposed to be fundamental to perhaps the most basic task facing humans—regulating relationships central to reproduction and parental investment—does not presuppose the evolution of any specialized cognitive or affective mechanisms. Moreover, it is at least paradoxical that while all other life history variables related to parental investment show heritability, within standard attachment theory the tendency to form close, intimate relationships is conceptualized as a function of developing cognitive schemas that differ solely as a function of the relationships the child is exposed to.

The contrary view is that the cognitive and affective foundations of close relationships involve highly specialized, domain-specific systems. Central to this perspective is that a critical component of the affectional system is a specialized reward system in which such relationships are experienced as pleasurable. Rather than suppose that children develop generalized, but highly flexible expectations of relationships, the domain-specific view is compatible with *compartmentalized* relationships in which the affectional system is preferentially directed at family members and other intimate associates, while relationships with others—especially outgroup members—may be exploitative.

The difficulty for attachment theorists within the Bowlby tradition is to specify how and why a system designed to provide security in the face of threat would come to underlie intimate relationships of love and affection and be strongly associated with high-investment parenting and children's internalization of values. The attachment system is present in many animal species that do not form pair bonds or have paternal investment in offspring. It is a system whose central emotions are fear and the feeling of safety, emotions that are quite separate from love and affection. Minimally, there is a need to suppose that a system designed for proximity maintenance was transformed at some point in human evolution into a system designed to underlie parental investment and close family relationships. Yet the evidence from Ainsworth's Uganda study as well as the other material mentioned earlier indicates that these systems remain conceptually and empirically separable. Such a transformation could have occurred in some human groups, but all the evidence indicates that if so, it was accompanied by a new motivational system centered around warmth and affection with emotions quite different from fear and felt security. Therefore, one must assume a qualitative shift from previously existing systems designed for proximity maintenance.

Fundamentally, what is required is a theory of why and how some relationships are pleasurable to begin with, so that children's expectations of relationships may include, at least as one alternative, positive affective involvement with another person—what we term love. There is no reason to suppose that such a system is present in many animals with well-developed attachment systems, and positing an evolved reward system underlying close relationships is consistent with considerable evidence from personality research and neurobiology.

CONCLUSION

The main message of the foregoing is the coherence of individual development. An evolutionary perspective is certainly compatible with the general idea that specific, highly dedicated systems will evolve as a response to highly specific adaptive problems. Here I have discussed the human affectional system as a highly dedicated system that functions to make family relationships rewarding and, ultimately, to produce high-quality children. I also noted that adolescents are relatively prone to impulsivity and risk-taking behavior (including behavior related to low-investment sexual relationships). Within an evolutionary approach to personality systems, these traits may be conceptualized as domain-specific elements of behavioral approach systems (Factor I of the Five-Factor Model). These traits are also psychometrically and neurophysiologically linked with aggression, dominance, and attraction to reward, including attraction to sexual behavior (MacDonald, 1995b).

It is of interest that these traits, including the promiscuous sexual activity loading on the Disinhibition subscale of Sensation Seeking (Zuckerman, 1979), and aggression (Wilson & Daly, 1985) peak in late adolescence and young adulthood, followed by a gradual decline during adulthood. This "young male syndrome" is highly compatible with evolutionary thinking: Sex-differentiated systems are expected to be strongest at the time of sexual maturation and maximum divergence of reproductive strategies. Because mating is theorized to be relatively problematic for males, it is during young adulthood, when males are attempting to establish themselves in the wider group and accumulate resources necessary for mating, that the male tendencies toward sensation seeking, risk taking and aggression are expected to be at their peak.

From the present perspective, it is during this period when the internalization of parental values may be of critical importance as a force that counteracts these adolescent tendencies toward risk taking, impulsivity, and low-investment sexual relationships. Again, the parent-child system is a coevolving system. Like personality systems within an individual that pull in different directions and result in intrapsychic conflict (MacDonald, 1995b), there may be conflicts within the coevolving parent-child system that function to moderate and channel the children's evolved tendencies in an adaptive manner. While there are excellent reasons to suppose that adolescent risk taking is a highly adaptive general tendency, it is also reasonable to suppose that an important aspect of high-investment parenting involves moderating and channeling these adolescent tendencies in an adaptive manner.

However, while domain-specific systems are of undoubted importance in conceptualizing human development, there is also a fundamental coherence to development centered around intelligence as a powerful domain-general human faculty. The big picture is that there is a large and socially important coherence to individual development. On the whole, smarter people are better parents and they are prone to providing affectionate, supportive, and stimulating environments for children. They are also better role models, and their children are more likely to attend to them and be concerned with parental approval of their behavior. The children of these high-investment parents are also better able to benefit from all this parental solicitude.

From an evolutionary perspective, this large coherence of individual development makes excellent adaptive sense. Parental investment looms as a critically important activity that has a unifying force on development because it is intimately related to reproductive success in ancestral environments. All things being equal, individuals who invest highly in children must be able to incorporate themselves in viable family relationships, and they must be able to inhibit attraction to short-term gains (e.g., low-investment sexual relationships) in favor of long-term benefits. Correspondingly, their children must be programmed to benefit from the added attention and the better advice their parents are able to provide.

Ultimately, there must be a reproductive payoff for whatever levels of parental investment are viable. In ancestral environments, individuals who failed to invest sufficiently in children must have been outcompeted in at least some times and places by those who did. But there remains considerable variation in parental investment in the contemporary world. And it has presumably always been the case that individuals who invested too much in their children were outcompeted by those who concentrated instead on finding additional low-investment mating opportunities. And while individual differences in parental investment represent the vestiges of viable adaptive strategies in ancestral environments, it is, as always, an open question what levels of parental investment will be successful in the contemporary world or the future.

REFERENCES

Ainsworth, M. D. S. (1967). *Infancy in Uganda*. Baltimore: Johns Hopkins University Press.

Ainsworth, M. D. S. (1977). Infant development and mother-infant interaction among the Ganda and American families. In P. H. Leiderman, S. R. Tulkin, & A. Rosenfeld (Eds.), *Culture and infancy* (pp. 119–149). New York: Academic Press.

Ainsworth, M. D. S., Blehar, M. C., Waters, E., & Wall, S. (1978). *Patterns of attachment*. Hillsdale, NJ: Erlbaum.

Applegate, J. L., Burke, J. A., Burleson, B. R., Delia, J. G., & Kline, S. L. (1985). Reflection-enhancing parental communication. In I. E. Sigel (Ed.), *Parental belief systems: The psychological consequences for children* (pp. 107–142). Hillsdale, NJ: Erlbaum.

Applegate, J. L., Burleson, B. R., & Delia, J. G. (1992). Reflection-enhancing parenting as an antecedent to children's social-cognitive and communicative development. In I. E. Sigel, A. McGillicuddy-DeLisi, & J. J. Goodnow (Eds.), *Parental belief systems* (pp. 3–39). Hillsdale, NJ: Erlbaum.

Arnett, J. (1995). The young and the reckless: Adolescent reckless behavior. *Current Directions in Psychological Research, 4,* 67–71.

Aukett, R., Ritchie, J., & Mill, J. K. (1988). Gender differences in friendship patterns. *Sex Roles, 19*, 57–67.

Bandura, A. (1969). Social learning theory of identificatory processes. In D. A. Goslin (Ed.), *Handbook of socialization theory and research* (pp. 213–261). New York: Rand McNally.

Barkow, J. (1989). *Darwin, sex, and status: Biological perspectives on mind and culture.* Toronto, Ontario, Canada: University of Toronto Press.

Belsky, J., Steinberg, L., & Draper, P. (1991). Childhood experience, interpersonal development, and reproductive strategy: An evolutionary theory of socialization. *Child Development, 62*, 647–670.

Berndt, T. J. (1986). Children's comments about their friendships. In M. Perlmutter (Ed.), *Minnesota Symposia in Child Development: Vol. 18. Cognitive perspectives on children's social and behavioral development* (pp. 189–212). Hillsdale, NJ: Erlbaum.

Bernstein, B. (1974). *Class, codes, and control: Vol. 1. Theoretical studies towards a sociology of language* (Rev. ed.). New York: Schocken.

Blau, Z. S. (1969). In defense of the Jewish mother. In P. I. Rose (Ed.), *The ghetto and beyond: Essays on Jewish life in America* (pp. 57–68). New York: Random House.

Bonner, J. T. (1980). *The evolution of culture among animals.* Princeton, NJ: Princeton University Press.

Borgerhoff Mulder, M. (1991). Human behavioural ecology. In J. R. Krebs & N. B. Davies (Eds.), *Behavioural ecology: An evolutionary approach* (3rd ed., pp. 69–98). London: Blackwell.

Bowlby, J. (1973). *Attachment and loss: Vol. 2. Separation, anxiety and anger.* London: Hogarth Press.

Bowlby, J. (1974). *Attachment and loss: Vol. 1. Attachment.* London: Hogarth Press.

Boyd, R., & Richerson, P. J. (1985). *Culture and the evolutionary process.* Chicago: University of Chicago Press.

Boyd, R., & Richerson, P. J. (1988). An evolutionary model of social learning: The effects of spatial and temporal variation. In T. R. Zentall & B. G. Galef (Eds.), *Social learning: Psychological and biological perspectives* (pp. 29–48). Hillsdale, NJ: Erlbaum.

Bradley, R. H., & Caldwell, B. (1984). Children: A study of the relationship between home environment and cognitive development during the first 5 years. In A. W. Gottfried (Ed.), *Home environment and early cognitive development: Longitudinal research* (pp. 5–56). Orlando, FL: Academic Press.

Bretherton, I. (1991). Pouring new wine into old bottles: The social self as internal working model. In M. Gunnar & L. A. Sroufe (Eds.), *Minnesota Symposia on Child Development: Vol. 23. Self processes in development* (pp. 1–41). Hillsdale, NJ: Erlbaum.

Brody, G. H., & Shaffer, D. R. (1982). Contributions of parents and peers to children's moral socialization. *Developmental Review, 2*, 31–75.

Buhrke, R. A., & Fuqua, R. R. (1987). Sex differences in same- and cross-sex supportive relationships. *Sex Roles, 17*, 339–352.

Buhrmester, D., & Furman, W. (1987). The development of companionship and intimacy. *Child Development, 58*, 1101–1113.

Buss, D. M. (1989). Sex differences in human mate preferences: Evolutionary hypotheses tested in 37 cultures. *Behavioral and Brain Sciences, 12*, 1–49.

Buss, D. M. (1991). Evolutionary personality psychology. *Annual Review of Psychology, 42*, 459–491.

Buss, D. M. (1994). *The evolution of desire.* New York: Basic Books.

Buss, D. M. (1995). Evolutionary psychology: A new paradigm for psychological science. *Psychological Inquiry, 6*, 1–30.

Buss, D. M., & Schmitt, D. P. (1993). Sexual strategies theory: An evolutionary perspective on human mating. *Psychological Review, 100,* 204–232.

Calabrese, L. H., Kirkendall, D. T., Floyd, M., Rapoport, S., Williams, G. W., Weiker, G. F., & Bergfeld, J. A. (1983). Menstrual abnormalities, nutritional patterns, and body composition in female classical ballet dancers. *Physician and Sports Medicine, 11,* 86–98.

Chisholm, J. S. (1993). Death, hope, and sex. *Current Anthropology, 34,* 1–24.

Clarke-Stewart, A. K. (1973). Interactions between mothers and their young children: Characteristics and consequences. *Monographs for the Society for Research in Child Development, 38*(6/7, Serial No. 153).

Cohen, S. M. (1986). Vitality and resilience in the American Jewish family. In S. M. Cohen & P. E. Hyman (Eds.), *The Jewish family: Myths and reality* (pp. 221–229). New York: Holmes & Meier.

Coleman, D. A. (1990). The demography of social class. In N. Mascie-Taylor (Ed.), *Biosocial aspects of social class* (pp. 59–116). Oxford, England: Oxford University Press.

Coleman, O., & Salt, J. (1992). *The British population.* Oxford, England: Oxford University Press.

Conger, R. D., Conger, K. J., Elder, G. H., Lorenz, F. O., Simons, R. L., & Whitbeck, L. B. (1992). A family process model of economic hardship and adjustment of early adolescent boys. *Child Development, 63,* 526–541.

Cosmides, L., & Tooby, J. (1987). From evolution to behavior: Evolutionary psychology as the missing link. In *The latest on the best: Essays on evolution and optimality* (pp. 277–306). Cambridge, MA: MIT Press.

Darling, N., & Steinberg, L. (1993). Parenting style as context: An integrative model. *Psychological Bulletin, 113,* 487–496.

Diamond, J. (1986). Biology of birds of paradise and bowerbirds. *Annual Review of Ecology and Systematics, 17,* 17–37.

Dickemann, M. (1981). Paternal confidence and dowry competition: A biocultural analysis of purdah. In R. D. Alexander & D. W. Tinkle (Eds.), *Natural selection and social behavior: Recent trends and a new theory* (pp. 417–438). New York: Chiron Press.

Digman, J. M. (1990). Personality structure: Emergence of the five-factor model. In M. R. Rosenzweig & L. W. Porter (Eds.), *Annual Review of Psychology, 41,* 417–440.

Dornbusch, S. M., Carlsmith, J. M., Bushwall, S. J., Ritter, P. L., Leiderman, H., Hastorf, A. H., & Gross, R. T. (1985). Single parents, extended households, and the control of adolescents. *Child Development, 56,* 326–341.

Dornbusch, S. M., & Gray, K. D. (1988). Single parent families. In S. M. Dornbusch & M. Strober (Eds.), *Feminism, children, and the new families* (pp. 274–296). New York: Guilford Press.

Douvan, E. A., & Adelson, J. (1966). *The adolescent experience.* New York: Wiley.

Draper, P. (1989). African marriage systems: Perspectives from evolutionary biology. *Ethology and Sociobiology, 10,* 145–169.

Eibl-Eibesfeldt, I. (1989). *Human ethology.* New York: Aldine de Gruyter.

Eisenberg, J. F. (1981). *The mammalian radiations.* Chicago: University of Chicago Press.

Elder, G. (1974). *Children of the great depression.* Chicago: University of Chicago Press.

Emmons, R. A. (1989). The personal striving approach to personality. In L. A. Pervin (Ed.), *Goal concepts in personality and social psychology* (pp. 87–126). Hillsdale, NJ: Erlbaum.

Eysenck, H. J., & Eysenck, S. B. G. (1976). *Psychoticism as a dimension of personality.* New York: Crane, Russak.

Field, T. (1993). Persistence of play and feeding interaction differences in three Miami cultures. In K. MacDonald (Ed.), *Parent-child play: Descriptions and implications* (pp. 331–347). Albany: State University of New York Press.

Fischbein, S. (1977a). Onset of puberty in MZ and DZ twins. *Acta Geneticae Medicae et Gemellologiae, 26,* 151–158.

Fischbein, S. (1977b). Intrapair similarity in physical growth of monozygotic and dizygotic twins. *Annals of Human Biology, 4,* 417–430.

Fisher, H. (1992). *The anatomy of love.* New York: Norton.

Flinn, M. V. (1988). Parent-offspring interactions in a Caribbean village: Daughter guarding. In L. Betzig, M. Borgerhoff-Mulder, & P. Turke (Eds.), *Human reproductive behavior: A Darwinian perspective* (pp. 189–200). Cambridge, England: Cambridge University Press.

Flinn, M. V., & England, B. G. (1995). Childhood stress and family environment. *Current Anthropology, 36,* 854–866.

Flinn, M. V., & Low, B. S. (1986). Resource distribution, social competition, and mating patterns in human societies. In D. I. Rubenstein & R. W. Wrangham (Eds.), *Ecological aspects of social evolution: Birds and mammals* (pp. 217–243). Princeton, NJ: Princeton University Press.

Flinn, M. V., Quinlan, R. J., Decker, S. A., Turner, M. T., & England, B. G. (1996). Male-female differences in effects of parental absence on glucocorticoid stress response. *Human Nature, 7,* 125–162.

Freeman, W. J. (1995). *Societies of brains.* Hillsdale, NJ: Erlbaum.

Furstenberg, F. F. (1991). As the pendulum swings: Teenage childbearing and social concern. *Family Relations, 40,* 127–138.

Furstenberg, F. F., & Brooks-Gunn, J. (1989). Teenaged pregnancy and childbearing. *American Psychologist, 44,* 313–320.

Galef, B. J. (1987). Social influences on the identification of toxic foods by Norway rats. *Animal Learning and Behavior, 15,* 327–332.

Gallistel, C. R. (1990). *The organization of learning.* Cambridge, MA: MIT Press.

Gallistel, C. R., Brown, A. L., Carey, S., Gelman, R., & Kail, F. C. (1991). Lessons from animal learning for the study of cognitive development. In S. Carey & R. Gelman (Eds.), *The epigenesis of mind: Essays on biology and cognition* (pp. 3–36). Hillsdale, NJ: Erlbaum.

Gangestad, S. W., & Simpson, J. A. (1990). Toward an evolutionary history of female sociosexual variation. *Journal of Personality, 58,* 69–96.

Garcia, J., Ervin, F. R., & Koelling, K. J. (1966). Learning with a prolonged delay of reinforcement. *Psychonomic Science, 5,* 121–122.

Garcia, J., & Koelling, K. J. (1966). Relation of cue to consequence in avoidance learning. *Psychonomic Science, 4,* 123–124.

Goldstein, S. (1981). Jewish fertility in contemporary America. In P. Ritterband (Ed.), *Modern Jewish fertility* (pp. 160–208). Leiden, The Netherlands: E. J. Brill.

Goodnow, J. J. (1992). Parents' ideas, children's ideas: Correspondence and divergence. In I. E. Sigel, A. McGillicuddy-DeLisi, & J. J. Goodnow (Eds.), *Parental belief systems* (pp. 293–317). Hillsdale, NJ: Erlbaum.

Gould, S. J. (1977). *Ontogeny and phylogeny.* Cambridge, MA: Harvard University Press.

Graber, J. A., Brooks-Gunn, J., & Warren, M. P. (1995). The antecedents of menarcheal age: Heredity, family environment, and stressful life events. *Child Development, 66,* 346–359.

Gruenwald, P., Funakawa, H., Mitani, S., Nishimura, T., & Takeuchi, S. (1967, May 13). Influence of environmental factors on foetal growth in man. *Lancet, 1*(7498), 1026–1028.

Grusec, J., & Goodnow, J. (1994). Impact of parental discipline methods on child's internalization of values: A reconceptualization of current points of view. *Developmental Psychology, 30,* 4–19.

Gutmann, D. L. (1977). The cross-cultural perspective: Notes toward a comparative psychology of aging. In J. E. Birren & K. W. Shaie (Eds.), *Handbook of the psychology of aging* (pp. 302–326). New York: Van Nostrand-Reinhold.

Guttentag, M., & Secord, P. F. (1983). *Too many women: The sex ratio question.* Beverly Hills, CA: Sage.

Haas, A. (1979). *Teenage sexuality: A survey of teenage sexual behavior.* New York: Macmillan.

Hajnal, J. (1965). European marriage patterns in perspective. In D. V. Glass & D. E. C. Eversley (Eds.), *Population in history* (pp. 101–143). Hawthorne, NY: Aldine.

Hajnal, J. (1983). Two kinds of pre-industrial household formation systems. In R. Wall, J. Robin, & P. Laslett (Eds.), *Family forms in historic Europe* (pp. 65–104). Cambridge, England: Cambridge University Press.

Hartup, W. W. (1989). Behavioral manifestations of children's friendships. In T. J. Berndt & G. Ladd (Eds.), *Peer relationships in child development* (pp. 46–70). New York: Wiley.

Hatfield, E., & Rapson, R. L. (1994). *Love, sex, and intimacy.* San Francisco: HarperCollins.

Herrnstein, R. J. (1973). *IQ in the meritocracy.* Boston: Little, Brown.

Herrnstein, R. J., & Murray, C. (1994). *The bell curve: Intelligence and class structure in American life.* New York: Free Press.

Herz, F. M., & Rosen, E. J. (1982). Jewish families. In M. McGoldrick, J. K. Pearce, & J. Giordano (Eds.), *Ethnicity and family therapy* (pp. 364–392). New York: Guilford Press.

Higgins, E. T. (1981). The "communication game": Implications for social cognition and persuasion. In E. T. Higgins, C. P. Herman, & M. P. Zanna (Eds.), *Social cognition: Vol. 1. The Ontario Symposium* (pp. 343–392). Hillsdale, NJ: Erlbaum.

Higgins, E. T. (1989). Continuities and discontinuities in self-regulatory and self-evaluative processes: A developmental theory relating self and affect. *Journal of Personality, 57,* 407–444.

Hinde, R. (1984). Why do the sexes behave differently in close relationships. *Journal of Social and Personal Relationships, 1,* 471–501.

Hoffman, M. L. (1970). Moral development. In P. H. Mussen (Ed.), *Carmichael's manual of child psychology* (Vol. 2, pp. 261–360). New York: Wiley.

Hoffman, M. L. (1983). Affective and cognitive processes in moral internalization: An information processing approach. In E. T. Higgins & D. Ruble (Eds.), *Social cognition and social development: A socio-cultural perspective* (pp. 236–274). Cambridge, England: Cambridge University Press.

Hoffman, M. L. (1994). Discipline and internalization. *Developmental Psychology, 30,* 26–28.

Hucyk, M. H. (1990). Gender differences in aging. In J. E. Birren & K. W. Shaie (Eds.), *Handbook of the psychology of aging* (3rd ed., pp. 124–132). New York: Academic Press.

Hunter, F. T., & Youniss, J. (1982). Changes in functions of three relations in adolescence. *Developmental Psychology, 18,* 806–811.

Jerison, H. J. (1973). *The evolution of the brain and intelligence.* New York: Academic Press.

Jessor, R., Costa, F., Jessor, L., & Donovan, J. E. (1983). Time of first intercourse: A prospective study. *Journal of Personality and Social Psychology, 44,* 608–626.

Jessor, R., & Jessor, S. L. (1977). *Problem behavior and psychosocial development.* New York: Academic Press.

Johanson, D. C., & Edey, M. A. (1981). *Lucy: The beginnings of humankind.* New York: Simon & Schuster.

John, O. P. (1990). The "big five" factor taxonomy: Dimensions of personality in the natural language and in questionnaires. In L. A. Pervin (Ed.), *Handbook of personality* (pp. 66–100). New York: Guilford Press.

Kenrick, D. T., & Trost, M. (1989). A reproductive exchange model of heterosexual relationships: Putting proximate economics in ultimate perspective. In C. Hendrick (Ed.), *Close relationships* (pp. 92–118). Newbury Park, CA: Sage.

Kiesler, D. J. (1983). The 1982 interpersonal circle: A taxonomy for complementarity in human transactions. *Psychological Review, 90,* 185–214.

Kleiman, D. G. (1977). Monogamy in mammals. *Quarterly Review of Biology, 52,* 39–69.

Kleiman, D. G. (1981). Correlations among life history characteristics of mammalian species exhibiting two extreme forms of monogamy. In R. D. Alexander & D. W. Tinkle (Eds.), *Natural selection and social behavior* (pp. 332–344). New York: Chiron Press.

Knode, J. (1974). *The decline in fertility in Germany, 1871–1979.* Princeton, NJ: Princeton University Press.

Kochanska, G. (1993). Toward a synthesis of parental socialization and child temperament in early development of conscience. *Child Development, 64,* 325–347.

Kochanska, G., Murray, K., Jacques, T. Y., Koenig, A. L., & Vandegeest, K. A. (1996). Inhibitory control in young children and its role in emerging internalization. *Child Development, 67,* 490–507.

Kohl, J. V., & Francoeur, R. T. (1995). *The scent of eros: Mysteries of odor in human sexuality.* New York: Continuum.

Lancaster, J. B., & Lancaster, C. S. (1987). The watershed: Change in parental-investment and family-formation in the course of human evolution. In J. B. Lancaster, J. Altman, A. S. Rossi, & L. R. Sherrod (Eds.), *Parenting across the life span: Biosocial dimensions* (pp. 187–205). New York: Aldine de Gruyter.

Lang-Takoc, E., & Osterweil, Z. (1992). Separateness and connectedness: Differences between the genders. *Sex Roles, 27,* 277–289.

Laslett, P. (1977). *Family life and illicit love in earlier generations.* Cambridge, England: Cambridge University Press.

Laslett, P. (1983). Family and household as work group and kin group: Areas of traditional Europe compared. In R. Wall, J. Robin, & P. Laslett (Eds.), *Family forms in historic Europe* (pp. 513–563). Cambridge, England: Cambridge University Press.

Lenz, F. (1931). The inheritance of intellectual gifts (E. Paul & C. Paul, Trans.). In E. Baur, E. Fischer, & F. Lenz (Eds.), *Human heredity* (pp. 565–699). New York: Macmillan.

Lerner, R. (1984). *On human plasticity.* New York: Cambridge University Press.

LeVine, R. A., & LeVine, S. E. (1966). *Nyansongo: A Gusii community in Kenya.* New York: Wiley.

LeVine, R. A., & LeVine, S. E. (1988). Parental strategies among the Gusii of Kenya. In R. A. LeVine, P. M. Miller, & M. M. West (Eds.), *Parental behavior in diverse societies* (pp. 27–35). San Francisco: Jossey-Bass.

Lewis, C. C. (1981). The effects of parental firm control: A reinterpretation of the findings. *Psychological Bulletin, 90,* 547–563.

Lewis, R. A., Casto, R., Aquilino, W., & McGuffin, N. (1978). Developmental transitions in male sexuality. *The Counseling Psychologist, 7,* 15–19.

Liebowitz, M. (1983). *The chemistry of love.* Boston: Little, Brown.

Londerville, S., & Main, M. (1981). Security of attachment, compliance and maternal training methods in the second year of life. *Developmental Psychology, 17,* 289–299.

Lovejoy, O. (1981). The origin of man. *Science, 211,* 341–350.

Luria, A. R. (1980). *The higher cortical functions in man.* New York: Basic Books.

Lynn, R. (1987). The intelligence of the Mongoloids: A psychometric, evolutionary and neurological theory. *Personality and Individual Differences, 8,* 813–844.

Lytton, H. (1980). *Parent-child interaction: The socialization process observed in twin and singleton families.* New York: Plenum Press.

Maccoby, E. (1980). *Social development.* San Diego, CA: Harcourt Brace Jovanovich.

Maccoby, E., & Martin, J. (1983). Socialization in the context of the family. In E. M. Hetherington (Eds.), *Handbook of child psychology: Vol. 4. Socialization, personality, and social development* (pp. 1–102). New York: Wiley.

MacDonald, K. B. (1985). Early experience, relative plasticity and social development. *Developmental Review, 5,* 99–121.

MacDonald, K. B. (1988). *Social and personality development: An evolutionary synthesis.* New York: Plenum Press.

MacDonald, K. B. (1989). The plasticity of human social organization and behavior: Contextual variables and proximate mechanisms. *Ethology and Sociobiology, 10,* 145–169.

MacDonald, K. B. (1991). A perspective on Darwinian psychology: Domain-general mechanisms, plasticity, and individual differences. *Ethology and Sociobiology, 12,* 449–480.

MacDonald, K. B. (1992). Warmth as a developmental construct: An evolutionary analysis. *Child Development, 63,* 753–773.

MacDonald, K. B. (1993). Parent-child play: An evolutionary analysis. In K. MacDonald (Ed.), *Parent-child play: Descriptions and implications* (pp. 113–143). Albany: State University of New York Press.

MacDonald, K. B. (1994). *A people that shall dwell alone: Judaism as a group evolutionary strategy.* Westport, CT: Praeger.

MacDonald, K. B. (1995a). The establishment and maintenance of socially imposed monogamy in western Europe. *Politics and the Life Sciences, 14,* 3–23.

MacDonald, K. B. (1995b). Evolution, the five factor model, and levels of personality. *Journal of Personality, 63,* 525–567.

MacFarlane, A. (1980). Illegitimacy and illegitimates in English history. In P. Laslett, K. Ooseterveen, & R. M. Smith (Eds.), *Bastardy and its comparative history* (pp. 71–85). London: Edward Arnold.

MacFarlane, A. (1986). *Marriage and love in England: Modes of reproduction 1300–1840.* London: Basil Blackwell.

Main, M., & Cassidy, J. (1988). Categories of response to reunion with the parent at age six: Predictable from infant attachment classifications and stable over a one month period. *Developmental Psychology, 24,* 415–426.

Martin, N. G., Eaves, L. J., & Eysenck, H. J. (1977). Genetical, environmental, and personality factors influencing the age of first sexual intercourse in twins. *Journal of Biosocial Science, 9,* 91–97.

McLanahan, S., & Booth, K. (1989). Mother-only families: Problems, prospects, and politics. *Journal of Marriage and the Family, 51,* 557–580.

Mesulam, M. M. (1986). Frontal cortex and behavior. *Annals of Neurology, 19,* 320–325.

Miller, A. K., & Corsellis, J. A. N. (1977). Evidence for a secular increase in human brain weight during the past century. *Annals of Human Biology, 4,* 253–257.

Miller, B. C., McCoy, J. K., Olson, T. D., & Wallace, C. M. (1986). Parental discipline and control attempts in relation to adolescent sexual attitudes and behavior. *Journal of Marriage and the Family, 48,* 503–512.

Miller, B. C., & Moore, K. A. (1990). Adolescent sexual behavior, pregnancy, and parenting: Research through the 1980s. *Journal of Marriage and the Family, 52,* 1025–1044.

Miller, E. M. (1994a). Optimal adjustment of mating effort to environmental conditions: A critique of Chisholm's application of life history theory, with comments on race differences in male paternal investment strategies. *Mankind Quarterly, 34,* 297–316.

Miller, E. M. (1994b). Paternal provisioning versus mate seeking in human populations. *Personality and Individual Differences, 17,* 227–255.

Miller, P. Y., & Simon, W. (1980). The development of sexuality in adolescence. In J. Adelson (Ed.), *Handbook of adolescent psychology* (pp. 383–487). New York: Wiley.

Mischel, W. (1976). *Introduction to personality* (2nd ed.). New York: Holt, Rinehart and Winston.

Moffitt, T. E., Caspi, A., Belsky, J., & Silva, P. A. (1992). Childhood experience and the onset of menarche: A test of a sociobiological model. *Child Development, 63,* 47–58.

Moss, J. J. (1964). Teenage marriage: Cross-national trends and sociological factors in the decision of when to marry. *Acta Sociologica, 8,* 98–117.

Murstein, B. I., & Holden, C. C. (1979). Sexual behavior and correlates among college students. *Adolescence, 14,* 625–639.

Newcomb, M. D., Huba, G. J., & Bentler, P. M. (1986). Determinants of sexual and dating behaviors among adolescents. *Journal of Personality and Social Psychology, 50,* 428–438.

Normal, J., & Harris, M. (1981). *The private life of the American teenager.* New York: Rawson, Wade.

Norton, A. J., & Miller, L. F. (1992). *Marriage, divorce, and remarriage in the 1990's* (Gov. Doc: C3.186: P-23/180). Washington, DC: U.S. Department of Commerce, Economics and Statistics Administration.

Peplau, L. A., Rubin, Z., & Hill, C. T. (1977). Sexual intimacy in dating relationships. *Journal of Social Issues, 33,* 86–109.

Plomin, R. (1994). *Genetics and experience: The interplay between nature and nurture.* Thousand Oaks, CA: Sage.

Plomin, R., & Fulker, D. (1987). Behavioral genetics and development in early adolescence. In R. Lerner & T. Foch (Eds.), *Biosocial interactions in early adolescence* (pp. 63–94). Hillsdale, NJ: Erlbaum.

Plomin, R., McClearn, G. E., Pedersen, N. L., Nesselroade, J. R., & Bergeman, C. S. (1989). Genetic influence on adults' ratings of their current family environment. *Journal of Marriage and the Family, 51,* 791–803.

Pulliam, H. R., & Dunford, C. (1980). *Programmed to learn: An essay on the evolution of culture.* New York: Columbia University Press.

Reis, H. T., Senchak, M., & Solomon, B. (1985). Sex differences in the intimacy of social interaction: Further examination of potential explanations. *Journal of Personality and Social Psychology, 48,* 1204–1217.

Ritterband, P. (1981). Introduction. In P. Ritterband (Ed.), *Modern Jewish fertility.* Leiden, The Netherlands: E. J. Brill.

Ross, C., Danziger, S., & Smolensky, E. (1987). The level and trend of poverty in the United States, 1939–1979. *Demography, 24,* 587–600.

Rothbart, M. K., Derryberry, D., & Posner, M. I. (1994). A psychobiological approach to the development of temperament. In J. E. Bates & T. D. Wachs (Eds.), *Temperament: Individual differences at the interface of biology and behavior* (pp. 83–116). Washington, DC: American Psychological Association.

Rowe, D. C. (1994). *The limits of family influence: Genes, experience, and behavior.* New York: Guilford Press.

Rushton, J. P. (1988). Race differences in intelligence: A review and evolutionary analysis. *Personality and Individual Differences, 9,* 1009–1024.

Rushton, J. P. (1995). *Race, evolution, and behavior.* New Brunswick, NJ: Transaction Books.

Scarr, S., & Weinberg, R. A. (1978). The influence of "family background" on intellectual attainment. *American Sociological Review, 43,* 674–692.

Schultz, A. H. (1960). Age changes in primates and their modification in man. In J. M. Tanner (Ed.), *Human growth* (pp. 1–20). Oxford, England: Pergamon Press.

Sigvardsson, S., Bohman, M., & Cloninger, C. R. (1987). Structure and stability of childhood personality: Prediction of later social adjustment. *Journal of Child Psychology and Psychiatry, 28,* 929–946.

Southwood, T. R. E. (1981). Bionomic strategies and population parameters. In R. M. May (Ed.), *Theoretical ecology: Principles and applications* (pp. 30–52). Sunderland, MA: Sinauer Associates.

Statistical Abstract of the United States. (112th ed.). (1992). Washington, DC: U.S. Department of Commerce, Bureau of Census. (Gov. Doc: C3.134/112)

Stayton, D. J., Hogan, R., & Ainsworth, M. D. S. (1971). Infant obedience and paternal behavior: The origins of socialization reconsidered. *Child Development, 42,* 1057–1069.

Steinberg, L., Elmen, J. D., & Mounts, N. S. (1989). Authoritative parenting, psychosocial maturity, and academic success among adolescents. *Child Development, 60,* 1424–1436.

Steinberg, L., Lamborn, S. D., Dornbusch, S. M., & Darling, N. (1992). Impact of parenting practices on adolescent achievement: Authoritative parenting, school involvement, and encouragement to succeed. *Child Development, 63,* 1266–1281.

Symons, D. (1979). *The evolution of human sexuality.* New York: Oxford University Press.

Tanner, J. M. (1990). *Foetus into man: Physical growth from conception to maturity.* Cambridge, MA: Harvard University Press.

Thorndike, E. L. (1898). Animal intelligence. An experimental study of the associative process in animals. *Psychological Monographs 2*(8).

Tooby, J., & Cosmides, L. (1992). The psychological foundations of culture. In G. Barkow, L. Cosmides, & J. Tooby (Eds.), *The adapted mind: Evolutionary psychology and the generation of culture* (pp. 3–136). New York: Oxford University Press.

Trapnell, P. D., & Wiggins, J. S. (1990). Extension of the Interpersonal Adjective Scales to include the Big Five dimensions of personality. *Journal of Personality and Social Psychology, 59,* 781–890.

Trivers, R. (1972). Parental investment and sexual selection. In B. Campbell (Ed.), *Sexual selection and the descent of man* (pp. 136–179). New York: Aldine de Gruyter.

Tubman, J. G., Windle, M., & Windle, R. C. (1996). The onset and cross-temporal patterning of sexual intercourse in middle adolescence: Prospective relations with behavioral and emotional problems. *Child Development, 67,* 327–343.

Tucker, D. M., & Derryberry, D. (1992). Motivated attention: Anxiety and the frontal executive functions. *Neuropsychiatry, Neuropsychology, and Behavioral Neurology, 5,* 233–252.

Turner, B. (1981). Sex-related differences in aging. In B. B. Wolman & G. Stricker (Eds.), *Handbook of developmental psychology* (pp. 493–512). Englewood Cliffs, NJ: Prentice-Hall.

Wall, R. (1983). The household: Demographic and economic changes in England, 1650–1970. In R. Wall, J. Robin, & P. Laslett (Eds.), *Family forms in historic Europe* (pp. 493–512). London: Cambridge University Press.

Warren, M. P., Brooks-Gunn, J., Fox, R., Lancelot, C., Newman, D., & Hamilton, W. G. (1991). Lack of bone accretion and amenorrhea in young dancers: Evidence for a relative osteopenia in weight bearing bones. *Journal of Clinical Endocrinology and Metabolism, 72,* 847–853.

Warren, M. P., Brooks-Gunn, J., Hamilton, L. H., Hamilton, W. G., & Warren, L. F. (1986). Scoliosis and fractures in young ballet dancers: Relationships to delayed menarcheal age and secondary amenorrhea. *New England Journal of Medicine, 314,* 1348–1353.

Wierson, M., Long, P. J., & Forehand, R. L. (1993). Toward a new understanding of early menarche: The role of environmental stress in pubertal timing. *Adolescence, 28,* 913–924.

Wiggins, J. S., & Broughton, R. (1985). The interpersonal circle: A structural model for the integration of personality research. *Perspectives in Personality, 1,* 1–47.

Wiggins, J. S., Trapnell, P., & Phillips, N. (1988). Psychometric and geometric characteristics of the Revised Interpersonal Adjective Scales (IAS-R). *Multivariate Behavioral Research, 23,* 517–530.

Wilson, D. S. (1994). Adaptive genetic variation and human evolutionary psychology. *Ethology and Sociobiology, 15,* 219–235.

Wilson, E. O. (1975). *Sociobiology: The new synthesis.* Cambridge, MA: Harvard University Press.

Wilson, J. Q., & Herrnstein, R. J. (1985). *Crime and human nature.* New York: Simon & Schuster.

Wilson, M. A., & Daly, M. (1985). Competitiveness, risk taking, and violence: The young male syndrome. *Ethology and Sociobiology, 6,* 59–73.

Wright, P. H., & Scanlon, M. B. (1991). Gender role orientation and friendship: Some attenuation, but gender differences abound. *Sex Roles, 24,* 551–566.

Wrigley, E. A., & Schofield, R. (1981). *The population history of England, 1541–1871.* Cambridge, MA: Harvard University Press.

Zahn-Waxler, C., Radke-Yarrow, M., & King, R. A. (1979). Child rearing and children's prosocial initiations toward victims of distress. *Child Development, 50,* 319–330.

Zajonc, R. B. (1976). Family configuration and intelligence. *Science, 192,* 227–236.

Zajonc, R. B., Marcus, H., & Marcus, G. B. (1979). The birth order puzzle. *Journal of Personality and Social Psychology, 37,* 1325–1341.

Zborowski, M., & Herzog, E. (1952). *Life is with people: The Jewish little-town of Eastern Europe.* New York: International Universities Press.

Zuckerman, M. (1979). *Sensation seeking: Beyond the optimal level of arousal.* Hillsdale, NJ: Erlbaum.

Future Directions for a Theory of Parental Socialization

LEON KUCZYNSKI and JOAN E. GRUSEC

The chapters in this book have offered varied approaches to understanding how children acquire values and what the role of parents is in that process. Certainly there are differences between positions presented in basic assumptions about mechanisms underlying socialization processes. More impressive, however, are the diverse emphases and interests displayed by different authors. For some, the challenge of addressing issues concerning parenting strategies and children's internalization of values was less straightforward than for others. The focus of attachment theory, for example, has never been explicitly on the acquisition of values, and so the relevant data and theoretical bases have been less well worked out. Similarly, evolutionary theory has a limited history with respect to parenting strategies and values internalization. Cognitive developmental theory historically has made a point of deemphasizing the role of parents as has the ecological perspective. In all these cases, then, our contributors were forced to stretch beyond the usual stance of their theoretical positions. But this stretch has been invaluable for opening up a range of possibilities for constructing a comprehensive theory of socialization. How do the approaches fit together? How would a theory of socialization look that was based on what has been presented in this book?

THEMES

In this concluding chapter, we have chosen to identify a number of themes that such a comprehensive approach might address. Where appropriate, we have also taken a position on an issue identified in the theme or have suggested what might be relevant to that issue in a theory about the role of parenting strategies in children's internalization of values. The themes identified represent a sampling of possibilities, but seem of particular interest. They are:

- How central is the parent in the task of socialization?
- How central is the child in the task of socialization?
- What are the outcomes of socialization?
- How do similarities and differences develop in the values held by children and their parents?
- What parenting strategies should we be studying?

HOW CENTRAL IS THE PARENT IN THE
TASK OF SOCIALIZATION?

Harris (1995) has argued that groups external to the family have more influence in the socialization process than do parents. Others have suggested that children make their own environments and that parent rearing activities have little impact on child development unless they are outside the normal range of such activities (e.g., Scarr, 1992; Scarr & McCartney, 1983). In the Introduction, we noted Bugental and Goodnow's (in press) observation that a positive feature of contemporary research on socialization is its acknowledgment that there are many sources of impact on children in addition to that of the parent. Yet we have urged contributors to this book to focus on the much-studied role of the parent and they have done so. By focusing so narrowly, however, it is possible that we have forced them to contemplate a position that may be untenable: that parents have an influence in the socialization of values greater than that of the children's genes, or the children's peers, or the larger societal context.

Parents have serious competition in their role as socializing agents. Not least among these are children themselves who, as Kuczynski, Marshall, and Schell have argued, have a substantial impact on their own socialization. Garbarino, Barry, and Kostelny have documented the nearly impossible task parents have in high-risk neighborhoods where supports for parenting efforts are virtually nonexistent and where negative influences are exaggerated in an environment of fear and lawlessness that most of us cannot even imagine. But even in low-risk neighborhoods, children are subject to a wide range of less than benign influences. The global community in which we live ensures this. Television, for example, is a constant source of antisocial values that is easily available to almost any child regardless of socioeconomic status. These antisocial values arise not only in the context of fictitious portrayals but also of reports of the divergence of viewpoints that exists in the real world. The Internet is beginning to pose a whole new set of problems with respect to children's exposure to undesirable influence. Increasing use of substitute child care also increases the risk of exposure to divergent values. This is especially likely when dual-earner parents cannot afford good quality care in a political environment that does not support their needs and those of their children. Schools and the educational system are also significant contributors to child socialization as are daily and extended contacts with peers who may not always be the source of prosocial values. Added to these external influences is the growth in number of single-parent households, many of which operate under conditions of poverty and high stress, which take their toll on adequate parenting.

Given the potential diversity of systems of influence and the increasing emphasis on the ecological context in the promotion of values, why is the parent worthy of selective attention? We argue that it is the parent who potentially is in the best position for effectively setting the conditions for the acquisition of prosocial values. First of all, although there is much opportunity to undermine and deflect parental influence, socialization is a biosocial system set up to favor the parent's primary influence on the child. Discussions about parenting invariably equate parental influence with environmental influence. However, MacDonald's chapter reminds us that there are biological underpinnings to the environmental influence provided by parents. The fact of parenting and parent-child relationships is not arbitrary but has evolved as part of an adaptive strategy in human evolution. Moreover, MacDonald elaborates on the emergence of phenomena such as close parent-child relationships, high-investment parenting, and children's receptivity to parental influence as central to an evolutionary perspective on value transmission. Thus, on evolutionary grounds, one might suspect the parent-child system has emerged with a biologically determined bias favoring parental influence.

Parental influence can also be highlighted for cultural reasons. Despite the acknowledged serious competition that parents have in their roles as socializing agents, and despite unrealistic popular beliefs about the vast power of parents to shape children, our society still designates principal authority for child rearing to the parent. Ultimately, parents (correctly or incorrectly) are held responsible for the behavior of their children. Parents have legislated rights and responsibilities in the domain of child rearing that provide significant assistance for their control over the child. They are formally supported by societal regulations in virtually all their attempts, successful or not, to determine what are the best experiences for their children. Thus society is reluctant to intervene except in the most extreme cases, where it appears blatantly obvious that the child's interests are not being well served. Of all of society's agents of socialization, then, parents have been given the most formal authority and control. The context is set to ensure that parents have the first opportunity to influence their children. Parents are the most significant part of children's initial environments, at least in Western society.

Parental influence is also unique because of the potentially privileged position parents enjoy in the relationship context of socialization. One fact that has become evident in the work reviewed in this book is the singular importance of relationships in the development of children's values (e.g., Bretherton, Golby, & Cho; Collins, Gleason, & Sesma; Kochanska & Thompson; Kuczynski & Hildebrandt). Relationships can provide either a motivational resource or a motivational liability for the acceptance of values and for the preparation of children for life in society. It is parents who are the primary participants, along with their children, in these relationships. Certainly teachers and day-care workers, for example, can also develop relationships with children, and when parenting is maladaptive, these relationships can frequently make a significant difference in child outcomes. Television sets and computers, on the other hand, do not develop close personal relationships with those who use them. From the moment of birth and for many years thereafter, parents feed, warm, comfort, protect, nurture, and play with their children, activities that form the basis for a strong parent-child tie. The immense quantity and often intense quality of these interactions ensures that children cannot be as indifferent in their relationships with parents as they can be in their other relationships. The special quality of children's relationships with parents is also pointed out by Collins et al. when they contrast relationships with parents and peers. The former, unlike the latter, are closed-field, confined and constrained by unalterable kinship and legal definitions. Moreover, unlike the latter, they entail extensive routinized interactional scripts that resist autonomous behavior in favor of internalization of parental values.

A final reason for arguing that parents have preeminence in the socialization process is that they have more opportunity for monitoring and understanding their children's behavior than anyone else. Patterson underlines the singular importance of lack of knowledge of the child's actions and whereabouts in producing antisocial children, and Grusec, Rudy, and Martini argue that knowledge of a child's thoughts and feelings facilitates the socialization process. It is parents who, through long and sustained exposure to their children, are in the best position to know them intimately, to know how they perceive their world, and to correct those perceptions when necessary.

It is essential to understand how forces beyond the family have an effect on children. What such understanding should not lead to, however, is a deemphasis on the singular importance of the parent in children's acquisition of values. Instead, it should point to steps that must be taken to use the larger context as an aid in the process of socialization. Parents (be they single or in pairs) are the most important feature of the socialization equation because they have been given primary power by evolution and by society to socialize, because they are preeminent in their potential to form significant relationships with their children including what may be the basic one of protection (as attachment theory suggests), and because, through long and sustained association, they know their children better than anyone else.

HOW CENTRAL IS THE CHILD IN THE TASK OF SOCIALIZATION?

The question of the importance or extent of the child's contribution to socialization should no longer be asked in this way because it evokes an old polemic between parent effects versus child effects to which most researchers no longer subscribe. It has been a long time since developmental researchers have thought of the child as a lump of clay awaiting the molding hand of a socialization agent. One can find an evolution during the past several decades of the idea that the child's contribution is as inherent in the process of socialization as the parent's contribution. Moreover, an important theme that colors developmental compared with sociological perspectives on socialization is that the source of the child's active contribution is rooted in biology. This emphasis is so ingrained in developmental perspectives on parenting that it is often taken for granted.

One can see this biological theme in the writings of the earliest exponents of the children's active dealings with the environment. For example, Piaget suggested that the active construction of knowledge was inherent in the child's activity as a biological entity. Rheingold (1969) argued that infants are biologically prepared to engage in social interactions and to exert influence on their parents. Bell (1968) described the contributions of congenital differences in temperament in shaping parents' child-rearing behaviors.

Similar references to biological sources for children's participation in their socialization continue in the present book. The idea that it is in the "nature" of children to actively construct messages from the environment is implicit in treatments by Smetana and by Valsiner, Branco, and Dantas. Grolnick, Deci, and Ryan begin their exposition of self-determination theory with a discussion of needs for autonomy, competence, and relatedness as biologically based impulses that underlie children's stance as active agents. Two chapters describing the relationship context of socialization also start with an assumption that children's participation in relationships, whether construed as attachment (Bretherton et al.) or as intimacy (MacDonald), has evolutionary origins. Kochanska and Thompson describe the influence of congenital temperamental characteristics on the efficacy of different parental child-rearing strategies.

Acknowledgment of the biological nature of the child's activity in socialization does not mean that researchers must study genes or gene-environment interactions as suggested by behavior geneticists (Plomin, 1994; Rowe, 1994; Scarr, 1992). Once the child begins responding to the parent (environment) and "learns," there is also, henceforth, an environmentally influenced/biological child whose socialized characteristics now carry on bidirectional transactions with the environment. The idea of bidirectionality enables socialization researchers to assume a biological child without necessarily directly studying the biology of the child. Once the authors in this book stated their starting assumptions about the nature of the child and how children's activity is inherent in all their interactions with parents, biology received little direct attention. Bidirectionality is what links children and all their biological propensities with their environment.

Treatments of Bidirectionality

Having said that bidirectionality is a "given" in current theory and research, it can also be said that treatments vary considerably in the meaning of bidirectionality to which they subscribe and in the extent to which conceptions of the parent's behavior accommodate bidirectional assumptions. Thus, the idea of bidirectionality underlying Valsiner et al.'s chapter and the idea of bidirectionality underlying Patterson's chapter are markedly different. Patterson's social interactional perspective is an external behavioral bidirectionality where parent and child in interaction sequentially elicit and exchange coercive behaviors and the child's agency is displayed in his or her behavioral initiations. In Valsiner et al.'s co-constructionist perspective, bidirectionality occurs on an internal cognitive plane where ideas rather than behaviors are mutually formed during interaction and the child's active "filiating" is manifested in the personal interpretations that the child constructs from parental communications. Smetana and Kuczynski et al. think of bidirectionality as a process of adaptation to changing contexts presented by the other's behaviors. Still others think of bidirectionality as a property of the parent-child relationship where interactions are colored by the distinctive, interdependent relationship context of their lives together. The relationship context is one that makes possible such bidirectional family dynamics as mutual conflict, mutual responsiveness, and tensions between interconnectedness and autonomy (Collins et al.).

That there are such diverse interpretations of the meaning of bidirectionality is a sign of the concept's maturity but also an indication that socialization researchers are beginning to form different conceptual camps. It may be useful to enter into a new phase of theory and research where the conceptualization of bidirectionality moves to the foreground. An important goal would be a consideration both of internal cognitive activities of parents and children and the external social interactions in which they engage. Several contributors already have incorporated both cognition and behavior into their accounts of parent-child interchange, and the chapter by Kuczynski et al. proposes a way in which such a process might proceed.

WHAT ARE THE OUTCOMES OF SOCIALIZATION?

There is substantial consensus among the contributors regarding the outcomes of the socialization process. Three general categories can be distinguished: (a) regulatory and motivational outcomes—the development of appropriate and adaptive processes for self-regulation, (b) content outcomes—the development of repertoires of specific ideas and values that are appropriate to the culture and adaptive for individual functioning, (c) collateral outcomes—indirect and often unintentional outcomes of the socialization process. Each will be discussed in turn.

Self-Regulation

Some kind of mechanism for behavioral conformity, cooperation, and acceptance of regulation by others is generally viewed as a desirable outcome of the socialization process. One reason is that behavioral compliance is considered to be a prerequisite to other attainments such as conscience (Kochanska & Thompson), achievement in school, and the formation of positive relationships (Patterson). It is also possible, however, to view appropriate forms of conformity regulation as important values in their own right. Patterson is unequivocal in asserting that compliance is the foundation of socialization and cooperative living in society and in equating children's compliance with competence.

From the first years of life, children are socialized to live in families, peer groups, schools, and a multitude of other social contexts. To do so, they must develop an orientation to society that is receptive to standards and regulation by others whether those others be family members or institutional authority figures. Viewed in this way, some form of receptivity to influence by others, including appropriate submission to authority figures, can be considered a fundamental value in itself. What distinguishes deviant from nondeviant socialized behavior in contemporary Western culture is not conformity to particular ideas so much as the willingness to cooperate or go along on a behavioral level. The separation of behavioral conformity from value conformity makes it possible to consider children who display such a willingness to go along, or to participate cooperatively in relationships, as instances of successful socialization even when their specific ideas and values differ markedly from those of their parents.

There is consensus among the contributors to this handbook that the quality of regulation is important. Several have moved beyond traditional dichotomies of external control and internal control in conceptualizing various qualities of regulatory processes in children. Kochanska and Thompson distinguish between a coercive kind of regulation that they call situational compliance and a voluntary, willing form of cooperation they call committed compliance. Kuczynski and Hildebrandt describe three categories of regulatory processes. To the familiar categories of external and internal control, they add coregulation, a category that involves consideration of the special features of conformity and resistance in relationships. Thus accommodation and negotiation are described as aspects of coregulated interactions in close social relationships that serve to balance individual needs for autonomy and mutual needs for cooperation and connectedness. Similar themes of interacting in relationships are described by Collins et al. and Grolnick et al. The most differentiated system of regulatory mechanisms comes from Grolnick et al. They distinguish four categories that lie on a continuum of internalized regulation. External regulation corresponds to control by external pressures and consequences, introjected regulation is perceived as maintained by internal forms of coercion, and identification is regulation by self-imposed goals. Only in integrated regulation is the motivation for behavior perceived as fully autonomous and goals as fully self-accepted.

Specific Values

In addition to regulatory mechanisms, children acquire the content of a culture's values. This consists of the specific ideas, values, and beliefs that they adopt during socialization. The content of internalization traditionally has been emphasized more in other disciplines such as sociology, anthropology, and philosophy. In psychological approaches to socialization, there has been little attempt to distinguish among values that a child might hold or among the specialized child-rearing experiences that might underlie different values. However, a number of contributors to this volume have argued that content matters in outcomes of socialization.

Considering the content of the values that parents pass on to children quickly makes untenable conceptions of socialization as a transmission of ideas from one generation to another. Several contributors (Goodnow; Kuczynski et al.; Valsiner et al.) note the changeable and historic nature of the values that parents may wish to pass on to their children. Values undergo transformation as they are assimilated and organized in novel ways by the child (Valsiner et al.). The values held by parents also undergo changes throughout the parents' lives and throughout the child's life as society changes and as new perspectives challenge received beliefs (Kuczynski et al.; Valsiner et al.). Parents also may wish to prepare their children for future experiences that are different from their own and may sometimes be more concerned with facilitating the intergenerational transformation of values than with their transmission (Goodnow).

The whole idea of value transmission as a desirable outcome is made problematic in the chapter on value transmission in the high-risk neighborhood (Garbarino et al.). Here one must consider the predicament of children who are at risk for receiving values that are antisocial and maladaptive in terms of society at large but that may be present within the family and supported by the immediate, dysfunctional community context. Thus the desirable outcome that Garbarino et al. envision is hardly the prototype of transmission within the family. Instead, the outcome they contemplate involves intervening within family transmission by importing adaptive values into the neighborhood and, in worst cases, into the family.

The idea of value socialization outcomes that emerges here is quite different from earlier views that considered values to be stable and unchanging once they were transmitted in early childhood socialization. An implication for the conceptualization of outcomes is that a degree of adaptability to change and periodic reexamination of values in response to new realities and alternative perspectives must be a feature of the value system of the well-functioning individual. Thus Kuczynski et al.'s idea of a "working model of internalization" was proposed to capture the idea of a value system that serves to guide behavior for a time but is periodically transformed in the history of the individual. It might be useful to consider internalization not as a static outcome or product of socialization but as an outcome that is continually in process.

Another point of agreement is that the content of a person's repertoire of specific values must also be considered with some degree of specificity. Grolnick et al. consider the content of socialized values in addition to the regulatory mechanisms that maintain them. They distinguish two general categories of values or aspirations, extrinsic and intrinsic. Extrinsic values include aspirations for financial success, physical attractiveness, and social recognition. Intrinsic values include aspirations for personal growth, meaningful relationships, social responsibility, and physical health. These outcomes are related to different parental antecedents and are also differentially associated with happiness and well-being. The need to consider children's outcomes in terms of specific contents of values is also the basic assumption of social domain theory. Smetana argues that children's social knowledge and behavior is inherently contextualized and not organized in a generalized value system or conscience.

This research on situational specificity in child-rearing environments opens the door to a contextual view of children's competence. Implicit in contextual definitions of competence is the idea that the child's motives, knowledge, and patterns of regulation should be appropriate to the context of the behavior. Goodnow makes the general point that parents are not only concerned that their children hold the right values but also that they hold them for the right reasons. Smetana suggests that competent children behave and react in a domain-appropriate manner. Kuczynski and Hildebrandt also suggest that a sensitivity to situation-specific standards for conformity is a mark of children's competence.

Collateral Effects

The third class of outcomes has to do with unintended or collateral effects of socialization. In directly training values or standards of regulation, the parent may unintentionally foster other positive and negative outcomes as an indirect consequence.

A concern with collateral effects was a major theme for Collins et al. They suggest that the quality of parent-child exchanges and shared decision making during values socialization makes an independent contribution to the development of competencies such as role-taking skills, advanced ego development, and identity exploration. Parenting behaviors that encourage both independent decision-making and connectedness with family members are considered to promote mature levels of these behaviors. In contrast, inadvertent fostering of antisocial values, drug use, lower levels of maturity, and competence is the result of both coercive and neglectful styles of discipline. Collins et al. also suggest that overly strict or coercive parental practices may encourage adolescents to form maladaptive peer relationships and to withdraw from family relationships, thereby prematurely severing the continuity of parental influence. The idea that how parents handle power struggles with their children may have repercussions for the quality of their attachment or affiliative relationships is echoed by other contributors (Bretherton et al.; Grusec et al.; Kuczynski et al.; Patterson).

Collateral effects of parental socialization may also be found in children's development of social strategies for interacting with others. Kuczynski and Hildebrandt suggest that how parents deal with children's noncompliance is important not only because of its direct influence in maintaining parents' capacity to control children's behavior but also because it has consequence for other child-rearing functions such as teaching skills of conflict resolution and promoting children's sense of efficacy in the parent-child relationship. In a similar vein, Smetana suggests that parental use of reasoning and explanation may be important not only because it aids the parental goal of accurate transmission of ideas but also because, by helping children to understand the parent's position, it opens the door to further discussion and persuasive initiations by the child.

Patterson's social interactional perspective suggests that collateral damage from poor parental practices may evolve over time in an escalating vicious circle of causal transactions between parent and child. For example, poor child management skills are problematic not only because they do not promote compliance but because they train children in coercive ways of social interaction that lead to many other problems such as rejection by parents and peers, poor self-esteem, poor academic performance, and association with deviant peer groups. Finally, Grolnick et al. suggest that parental child-rearing strategies may have unintended negative and positive outcomes for the values that children develop. They report that children who have cold, controlling, or uninvolved mothers may develop an unhealthy orientation toward extrinsic values such as material acquisition and financial success. In contrast, children whose mothers are high on autonomy support, nurturance, and involvement tend to develop more healthy intrinsic aspirations for personal growth, close relationships, and community involvement.

HOW DO SIMILARITIES AND DIFFERENCES DEVELOP IN THE VALUES HELD BY CHILDREN AND THEIR PARENTS?

Both Kuczynski et al. and Valsiner et al. argue that the important question for socialization theory is to show how differences, as well as similarities, arise between parent and child. The point that children alter the material they receive from their environment is surely incontestable. The issue is what determines the extent to which they alter it. This is the old question of whether values are transmitted from one generation to another or whether they are constructed. On the one hand is the Freudian position that children take over the values of parents in a wholesale manner as part of the identification process. On the other is the position of cognitive developmental theory that children contribute substantially to the formulation of a moral system, responding to input by modifying it to fit with their own existing structures as well as changing structures when the input can no longer be assimilated. In Chapter 1, one resolution of the issue is noted in terms of selection. Thus Bandura (1986) argues that children are exposed to many conflicting values and that they are therefore forced to choose among them, with their choice determined by variables such as the degree of similarity between themselves and the source of a particular value, expectations about what behaviors are likely to be reinforced, and feelings of self-efficacy in the domain of the value.

Although not all contributors have specifically addressed the issue of transmission versus construction, it is evident that no one today would endorse the classic notion of transmission. On the other hand, both Goodnow and Grusec et al. argue in their chapters that construction is not always the norm and that in certain cases transmission may be the more apt metaphor for what happens as parents attempt to influence the values of their children. It seems that the basic question of construction versus transmission must be reworded.

We suggest, along with Goodnow, Kuczynski et al., and Valsiner et al. that a new question for developmentalists be one of asking about conditions that determine how closely children match values to those of their parents. When are they likely to accept parental values in their totality, and when are they likely to add considerable input of their own? This is what Goodnow refers to as gradations between internalizing and not internalizing parental values. One way to think of the issue is in terms of a continuum from total transmission to total construction. A first point to be noted is that neither end point of this continuum can be a reality. Beginning with transmission, there are several reasons for this impossibility that have been emphasized by various contributors. Even when children are highly motivated to act in accord with parental wishes because of the nature of their relationship, their perceptions of parental input are affected or colored by many variables such as their cognitive capacity, mood state, temperament, goals, domain appropriateness of the parent's message, and attributional style. No matter how skilled the efforts of the parent to make a message clear and acceptable, the child's interpretation of that message is going to vary somewhat from that intended and hoped for by the parent. Second, no parental message occurs in a vacuum and there is no way of avoiding input from other sources that will temper the impact of the parental message. In Smetana's chapter, she notes that an important aspect of how children develop prescriptive moral judgments is from their experiences as victims and observers of transgressions. This first-hand knowledge cannot help but affect the child's adoption of a parental value, particularly if the value is discrepant from what the child has learned on the basis of other experiences. There is a third reason why wholesale transmission is not possible, developed particularly by Kuczynski et al. and Valsiner et al., which is that parents' values are also being constructed or modified as they interact with their child. To the extent, then, that the value never remains exactly the same over time, it becomes impossible to identify what it is that is actually being conveyed. Closely related is Goodnow's suggestion that parents do not always want to pass on their own values, and they may be pleased when their children turn out differently from them—more successful, for example, or less success-oriented than themselves.

Just as it is impossible to conceive a case of pure transmission, so too it is impossible to conceive a case of pure construction. Parent input has to be part of the material employed in construction. Even if the ultimate product is diametrically opposed to that of the parent (because the child is angry or oppositional) diametric opposition is a response or reaction to parental input. What conditions, then, might be likely to lead to greater similarity between the values a parent attempts to pass on to a child and the values subsequently held by that child; what are the conditions that determine placement along a continuum of similarity/dissimilarity? We offer the following proposal. Values may be less prone to construction when the parent cares deeply about them (see Goodnow & Grusec et al.). Here there will be little room for negotiation, toleration of a different position, or a changing of position on the part of the parent. In contrast, when the value is not so important, the parent may be very willing to allow leeway and construction. Smetana in her chapter adds to this notion of bottom line by noting that parents may be reluctant to allow their children to construct knowledge in certain areas such as harm to self, presumably an area about which they feel quite strongly. She adds a new dimension when she suggests there are conditions under which it is less trying to inform children about expectations (e.g., with respect to table manners) than to wait for them to construct the knowledge through observation of regularities in behavior or differences in expectations across different contexts. Finally, an analysis of values acquisition that is informed by a social domain approach tells us that similarity between generations is more likely in the case of moral, prudential, and social conventional issues than in the case of personal concerns. Research indicates that while adolescents are influenced by the values of their peers, this influence extends primarily to less serious, or nonmoral issues (Devereux, 1970). In serious or moral issues, parental influence remains dominant. Presumably, heterogeneity of values is more likely in the personal domain where parents are less likely to intervene. It is here that the child is exposed to the greater variety of existing viewpoints and is therefore in a position to make more selections as well as observe regularities in behavior or differences in expectations across different contexts.

WHAT PARENTING STRATEGIES SHOULD WE BE STUDYING?

The number of parenting strategies that have been traditionally of interest to researchers interested in children's internalization of values is remarkably limited, considering the wide range of things that parents probably do to and for their children. Strategies can be divided into two categories. The first includes proactive strategies such as modeling of appropriate behavior, structuring the environment (Holden, 1983, talks of mothers who minimize conflict in the grocery store by avoiding aisles that contain objects attractive to their children), compliance with children's wishes (a technique that sets the conditions for reciprocal compliance from the child), and warmth (a style that makes the child anxious to please the parent). The second category concerns responses to deviation, conflict, and disagreement and focuses on reasoning and power assertion, as well as stylistic variables such as degree and quality of control exerted by the parent over the child's activities (with a moderate degree of noncoercive control generally advocated) as well as the extent to which the parent is willing to listen to and accommodate to the child's desires. Another parenting strategy that has been of concern to researchers (see the chapters by Grolnick et al.; Patterson) is monitoring. Monitoring refers primarily to the knowledge the parent has of the child's activities but is also implicated in the ability of the parent to notice and correctly identify a deviant behavior. It has elements both of proactive activity as well as reaction to a child's misdeeds.

Elaborations of Traditional Strategies

These strategies have been elaborated by many of the contributors to this book. Kuczynski and Hildebrandt describe extensive developments that have occurred in our knowledge of the role of accommodation to the child's wishes, or negotiation, in successful child socialization. Smetana underscores the important interaction between the content of a value and the form of strategy: Reasoning, for example, is effective only if coordinated with the domain of the act under consideration. For Grolnick et al., autonomy-supporting strategies include involvement with children (spending time with them and knowing about their daily life), the provision of clear guidelines for behavior, and constraints on behavior that are supportive, not controlling. Included in discussions of the latter is the avoidance of close surveillance, locution (tone of voice and use of language) and acknowledgment that the child might not want to conform to limits. MacDonald comments on the degree to which various strategies such as control, warmth, and monitoring are interrelated, an argument that leads one to look for some underlying dimension. Conditions that lead to parental investment is MacDonald's suggestion.

Features of Elaborations

One feature of these and other expansions is that parenting strategies are increasingly being characterized in a way that is compatible with a bidirectional view of socialization. In the early history of parenting research, strategies were conceived in a unidirectional fashion as having a source completely within the parent (e.g., a static propensity to punish or to be warm regardless of the child's characteristics or behavior). In contrast, discussions of parenting strategies are now more likely to presuppose an active, powerful child operating in a bidirectional causal context with the parent. The beginnings of this trend can be found in some of the later statements of the research traditions considered in Chapter 1. Grusec and Goodnow's (1994) model of disciplinary interventions presupposes a child who is active in processing parental messages and has motivational requirements independent of those of the parent. Effective discipline is that which is tailored to the child's needs for accurate perception and voluntary acceptance of the parent's messages. Similarly, Maccoby and Martin (1983) have conceptualized effective parenting as responsivity to children's requests and demands. An awareness of the child's activity and the bidirectional context also pervades many of the new treatments of parental strategies in the present work.

A second cross-cutting characteristic of the treatments in the present volume is a sensitivity to the larger context of parent-child interaction. Earlier treatments of parenting strategies seldom ventured beyond the context of immediate exchanges that might occur in parent-child interaction. In contrast, the larger contexts of culture (Goodnow; Grusec et al.), social change (Kuczynski et al.), the high-risk neighborhood (Garbarino et al.), contextual stress (Patterson), and multiple relationships in which adolescents are involved (Collins et al.) are often the focus in this book. An important dimension of parenting in current thinking concerns how parents manage the ecological context so that they reinforce their own socialization efforts or ensure that the context does not undermine their goals and influences. Thus, again in accord with a bidirectional perspective, parents are conceived as resisting or acting on the macrocontext rather than being its passive victim.

Expanded Strategies

Having noted these features of current approaches, we turn now to specific discussion of an expanded list of parenting strategies emerging from the preceding chapters. We begin with additions to the list of proactive strategies. Shared discourse is one raised by several contributors (e.g., Goodnow; Kochanska & Thompson; Smetana) who focus on the fact that parents talk to their children and that in doing so they provide information about implicit values and acceptable and unacceptable behavior. Parents also provide information intended to stimulate the child to think reflectively about values, a notion that fits with Grolnick et al.'s idea that values are more likely to be enhanced when children are encouraged to solve their own problems rather than experience external intervention. These observations point to an area worthy of inquiry—the differentiated tendency of parents to engage children apparently spontaneously in discussions of values. This discussion of values can emerge in different contexts, in some of which parental intention might not be so obvious. Storytelling, for example, is a domain in which activity is less specifically addressed to values per se, be it in the guise of myths, fictitious stories, or the recalling of family memories and adventures.

Goodnow stresses the importance of everyday routines as sources of information about values. Another parenting strategy needing study, then, would be one in which parents deliberately attempt to devise everyday routines that impart a particular set of values. A parent who wished to instill a principle of helping others less fortunate than the self, for example, might make volunteer work a formal part of family life, or enroll the child in a group where such volunteer work was a part of the group's function. A parent who wished to promote the idea that family interaction is important might structure the environment so that at dinnertime all members of the family were expected to be present for an extended period not interrupted by other demands. In both cases, words, reasoning, and control would not be necessary—habits would develop simply as a function of repetition or routine. One might attempt to assess, then, what family routines are considered important and what value they might serve, and relate them to internalization of values.

As already noted, one of the messages in this book is that there is heterogeneity of values in the world that surround the child (Garbarino et al.; Goodnow; Kuczynski et al.). Goodnow directs us to a way in which parents might attempt to deal with this heterogeneity by either cocooning or prearming the child. In the first approach, the child is kept away from conflicting values as much and as long as possible in the hope that values will become well enough entrenched that they are safe from opposing input. In the second effort, parents anticipate alternate value systems and provide, in advance, rationales and advice for why they are wrong. Again, it would not be difficult to assess the degree to which parents strive to protect their children from negative influences (e.g., monitoring of television watching, careful selection of friends) and the degree to which they provide arguments about why certain values, attitudes, and behavior are wrong (e.g., watching television with the child and discussing its content) and relate these strategies to value internalization.

A final arena for proactive intervention in great need of study is how parents manage the relationship context of their interactions with their children. The experiences that take place in the relationship context temper the receptivity of the interacting partners to each other's influence. And, to the extent that the individuals wish to maintain a good relationship, the relationship context also may place constraints on the strategies that the partners use in their interactions with each other. Thus strategies such as bilateral negotiation and communication, reasoning, and parental flexibility may be important not so much for their direct effects on children's value acquisition as for their role in maintaining a positive relationship (which then mediates the effects of other parental strategies). If the relationship context does indeed play a central mediating role in the value transmission process, then research is needed to explore more direct strategies (play, conversation, quality time) that parents employ to build, maintain, and repair their relationships with their children. Considering its potential importance in socialization, there is a surprisingly small literature on the creation of relationships beyond the infancy period.

The next set of additions is to ways of disciplining the child—reactive as opposed to proactive interventions. One idea that emerges repeatedly is the importance of appropriate flexibility. Traditionally, consistency and firm control have been the strategies of choice, and changing demands seen as signs of weakness, although Baumrind left room for some degree of responsiveness to the child's desires. Kuczynski and Hildebrandt, however, have pointed out just how frequently parents negotiate with their children and they underline the importance of that negotiation in the development of autonomy. Bretherton et al. describe flexibility as a technique that indicates the parent's willingness to respond sensitively to the needs of the child in a discipline situation, with the assumption that reassurance given to the child who is experiencing negative emotions may assist that child in the task of self-regulation. For Goodnow, flexibility comes in terms of bottom lines or "value-stretch" and the fact that children have a sense of choice and control but that limits to choice are clearly present. Some things are simply "not on." In the social domain perspective described by Smetana, one determinant of what is not on has to do with the domain under consideration. Presumably, negotiation in the areas of morality, prudence, and social convention is not on. The personal domain provides the major arena for negotiation and the encouragement of feelings of control and autonomy. Flexibility is good, then, so long as it is appropriate. Even in the personal domain, parents' bottom lines may differ. But the variable for study is the extent to which parents are willing to share control with their children in areas in which such sharing is seen as cooperative interaction rather than caving in or unreasonable rigidity.

Flexibility also emerges in the area of specific conditions that require the modification of parenting strategies to promote a desired value. A given strategy may work when a child is in a positive mood but not when he or she is in a negative mood. It may be necessary to respond to unacceptable behavior in different ways, depending on why it was exhibited in the first place: A child who misbehaves because he or she is tired or bored may need a different form of intervention than one who is distracted or angry. Here, then, flexibility is defined in terms of tailoring discipline to current conditions (even when the same act is under consideration). The task for socialization researchers is to measure appropriate flexibility (defined conceptually) not only with respect to values but with respect to current conditions and to relate this flexibility to socialization outcomes.

A discussion of flexible responding as a function of the child's mood state sets the stage for consideration of another reactive parenting strategy, which emerges from the concepts of attachment theory. This strategy involves acknowledgment and legitimization of children's feelings. Bretherton et al. and Grolnick et al. both propose this addition when they talk about the importance of acknowledging and responding to the child's feelings, even when the child has deviated. Bretherton et al. describe the mother who, rather than tell her child that there is no need to cry because nothing is wrong, sets out to discover the cause even if it does not seem reasonable to her. Grolnick et al., discussing the role of autonomy support in the promotion of internalization of values, identify one important parenting variable as acknowledgment or validation of the thoughts and feelings of the child. Thus individuals who were asked to engage in a boring task and whose feelings of boredom were acknowledged spent more free time on the task and reported more positive feelings than those whose feelings were not acknowledged. This is empirical evidence that responding to the negative feelings of individuals who do not want to engage in a particular activity may facilitate such engagement.

We propose that the role for attachment in value internalization may lie not in its function in the relationship between parent and child, as many researchers have suggested, but rather in the fact that parents who legitimize their children's negative feelings help their children to cope with the stress involved in discipline and conflict situations. By identifying the emotions, acknowledging their acceptability, and possibly by suggesting ways of controlling them, parents promote or assist the task of self-regulation. Grolnick et al. suggest that secure attachment facilitates exploration and mastery-oriented behavior and that intrinsically motivated activity is therefore more likely to occur if individuals have the security of distal relational support. Kochanska and Thompson have suggested that toddlers who are securely attached to their parents will have more harmonious relationships with them, will be receptive to parental values, and will be uncomfortable when violating parental standards. Our alternative proposal is that securely attached toddlers have been taught to cope with stress and, thereby, to deal with the challenge of regulating their own problematic behavior.

A final reactive parenting strategy raised here has to do with consistency. Usually, when consistency is discussed, it is in the context of consistency in the demands made on a child, either from the same parent or from both parents. Another form of consistency emerges, however, in Grusec et al.'s description of mothers who have a low control schema. Bugental, Mantyla, and Lewis (1989) report that these mothers often send conflicting messages, with facial expression, vocal quality, and content inconsistent in what they convey. In their analysis, such conflicting messages are confusing to the child and lead to continued difficult behavior. The observation highlights another strategy worthy of study, and that is the extent to which parents send clear messages to their children, with words, actions, and emotional accompaniments in harmony.

We end this section with some observations on monitoring. This is an important variable for Patterson, who finds that parents of aggressive boys tend to be less aware of the activities and whereabouts of their children. Grolnick et al. describe the extent to which a parent puts effort into child rearing, spends time with the child, and knows about the child's daily life as conditions that comprise involvement and that are contributors to successful self-determination. Grusec et al. suggest that parents' knowledge about their children's thoughts and feelings is an important feature of successful socialization. In a more molecular vein, Grusec et al. cite the work of Bugental (1992) who reports that parents who have low self-efficacy are less able to cognitively process events in their environment, including those surrounding the behavior of a difficult child. All these observations appear to converge on the suggestion that concepts of monitoring might be extended to include general knowledge of and awareness of what is going on in the child's external environment as well as what the child is thinking and feeling. Presumably, parents who monitor their children's behavior in the sense of being aware of what is happening to the child (did someone say something to provoke the child into some misdeed, did the child try to comply but was prevented in some way from doing so, did the child appear to misunderstand what someone had said) are better equipped to provide input necessary for successful internalization of values.

CONCLUSION

The time is right for a major step forward in understanding how children come to acquire the values of society. Such an understanding must include an emphasis on bidirectional processes operating between the parent and the child within the family, transactions between the family and the social and cultural context, and the parent as central in managing the complex task of socialization. It must also address the several outcomes of socialization including self-regulation, the learning of specific beliefs and values, and incidental by-products such as skills for handling conflict. A question of singular importance is the description of conditions that promote not only similarity but dissimilarity between parent and child in the values they espouse. Finally, a comprehensive theory of socialization must deal with a set of parenting strategies considerably expanded from that currently investigated.

The world is presently filled with politicians, commentators, parents, and others who express serious and legitimate concern over loss of "family values," violence, and lack of caring and respect for others. We hope this book has provided some new ideas for directions in which researchers might look for ways to address these genuine and serious problems.

REFERENCES

Bandura, A. (1986). *Social foundations of thought and action: A social cognitive theory.* Englewood Cliffs, NJ: Prentice-Hall.

Bell, R. Q. (1968). A reinterpretation of the direction of effects in studies of socialization. *Psychological Review, 75,* 81–95.

Bugental, D. B. (1992). Affective and cognitive processes within threat-oriented family systems. In I. E. Sigel, A. McGillicuddy-DeLisi, & J. J. Goodnow (Eds.), *Parental belief systems: Psychological consequences for children* (2nd ed., pp. 219–248). Hillsdale, NJ: Erlbaum.

Bugental, D. B., & Goodnow, J. J. (in press). Socialization processes. In W. Damon (Ed.), *Handbook of child psychology* (5th ed.). New York: Wiley.

Bugental, D. B., Mantyla, S. M., & Lewis, J. (1989). Parental attributions as moderators of affective communication to children at risk for physical abuse. In D. Cicchetti & V. Carlson (Eds.), *Current research and theoretical advances in child maltreatment* (pp. 254–279). New York: Cambridge University Press.

Devereux, E. C. (1970). The role of peer-group experience in moral development. In J. P. Hill (Ed.), *Minnesota Symposia on Child Psychology* (Vol. 4, pp. 94–140). Minneapolis: University of Minnesota Press.

Grusec, J. E., & Goodnow, J. J. (1994). The impact of parental discipline methods on the child's internalization of values: A reconceptualization of current points of view. *Developmental Psychology, 30,* 4–19.

Harris, J. R. (1995). Where is the child's environment? A group socialization theory of development. *Psychological Review, 102,* 458–489.

Holden, G. (1983). Avoiding conflict: Mothers as tacticians in the supermarket. *Child Development, 54,* 233–240.

Maccoby, E. E., & Martin, J. A. (1983). Socialization in the context of the family: Parent-child interaction. In E. M. Hetherington (Ed.), *Handbook of child psychology* (4th ed.) (Vol. 4, pp. 1–102). New York: Wiley.

Plomin, R. (1994). *Genetics and experience: The interplay between nature and nurture.* Thousand Oaks, CA: Sage.

Rheingold, H. L. (1969). The social and socializing infant. In D. A. Goslin (Ed.), *Handbook of socialization theory and research* (pp. 779–790). Chicago: Rand McNally.

Rowe, D. (1994). *The limits of family influence: Genes, experience, and behavior.* New York: Guilford Press.

Scarr, S. (1992). Developmental theories for the 1990s: Development and individual differences. *Child Development, 63,* 1–19.

Scarr, S., & McCartney, K. (1983). How people make their own environments: A theory of genotype → environment effects. *Child Development, 54,* 424–435.

Author Index

Aber, J. L., 110
Aboud, F. E., 87
Adam, E., 264
Adams, G. R., 31, 78, 81, 206
Adelson, E., 37, 106
Adelson, J., 80, 385
Ageton, S. S., 206
Ahadi, S. A., 61, 62
Ainsworth, M. D. S., 4, 17, 63, 64, 107, 108, 109,
    110, 111, 138, 234, 238, 246, 264, 369, 382,
    385, 386, 388
Aksan, N., 65, 66, 74, 183, 184, 207, 234, 238,
    280
Alafat, K. A., 145
Alessandri, S. M., 82
Allen, J. P., 85
Allen, W. R., 353
Almquist-Parks, L., 213
Alpern, L., 112
Alpert, R., 55, 63
Alvarez, A., 284
Alwin, D., 28, 30, 231, 247
Amabile, T. M., 145
Amato, P., 80, 86
Ambert, A. M., 25, 40, 41
Amish, P. L., 266
Andrews, D. W., 89, 212, 213
Anthony, E. J., 45
Apostoleris, N. A., 155, 156
Applegate, J. L., 10, 370
Aquilino, W., 385
Archer, S. L., 81
Arend, R., 17, 133, 238, 239
Arnett, J. L., 335, 340, 347, 371
Aronfreed, J., 7, 55, 227, 229, 244
Arsenio, W. F., 172, 173, 174, 185
Arthur, R., 327
Asendorpf, J. B., 62
Ashbourne, D. T., 261
Asp, E., 311
Asquith, P., 39, 166, 175, 176, 184, 269
Atkinson, J. W., 294
Atkinson, L., 266
Aukett, R., 385

Austin, E. W., 42
Avery, R. R., 148
Azar, S. T., 266
Azuma, H., 268, 272, 275

Baaske, K. T., 245
Bachman, J. G., 206
Baden, A. D., 261
Baer, D. M., 215
Bakhtin, M., 285, 351
Baldwin, A., 12
Baldwin, A. L., 150, 151
Baldwin, D. A., 57
Baldwin, D. V., 205
Baldwin, J. M., 286
Baldwin, M. J., 262
Bandura, A., 18, 19, 35, 78, 84, 87, 215, 263, 273,
    276, 294, 383, 407
Bank, L., 91, 194, 196, 198, 199, 204, 206, 212
Baranowski, M. D., 39
Barclay, M. S., 26
Barker, R. G., 195
Barkley, R. A., 196
Barkow, J., 366
Barnes, H., 86
Barraclough, R., 244
Barrett, K. C., 57
Bartkowski, J. P., 302
Barton, M. L., 110
Bartz, K. W., 273
Batchelder, W. H., 337
Bates, J. E., 112, 208, 217
Bauer, W. D., 261
Baumeister, R. F., 30
Baumrind, D., ix, 9, 13, 14, 45, 84, 86, 87, 88,
    115, 150, 152, 162, 163, 177, 181, 182, 227,
    231, 240, 241, 273
Beardsall, L., 67
Becker, J., 242, 349
Becker, J. B., 82
Becker, W. C., 12, 150
Behar, L. B., 113
Bell, K. L., 85
Bell, R. Q., 19, 24, 35, 69, 155, 163, 402

415

Subject Index